# HAND IN HAND

## Essentials of Communication and Orientation and Mobility for Your Students Who Are Deaf-Blind

### Volume I: Units 1, 2, and 3

Kathleen Mary Huebner
Jeanne Glidden Prickett
Therese Rafalowski Welch
Elga Joffee, Editors

**AFB**

**PRESS**

NEW YORK

Printed in the United States of America

Library of Congress Cataloging-in-Publication Data

Hand in hand : essentials of communication and orientation and
    mobility for your students who are deaf-blind / Kathleen Mary
    Huebner ... [et al.] editors.
        p.    cm.
    Includes bibliographical references and index.
    ISBN 0-89128-937-2 (set : pbk.)
    1. Blind-deaf children--Study and teaching.   2. Blind-deaf
children--Orientation and mobility.   3. Blind-deaf children--Means
of communication.   4. Teachers of the blind-deaf--Training of.
I. Huebner, Kathleen Mary.
HV1597.2.H34   1995
371.91'1--dc20                                          95-8272
                                                           CIP

This publication was funded through Cooperative Agreement #H086A00005 from the U.S. Department of Education, Office of Special Education and Rehabilitative Services. The opinions or policies expressed herein do not necessarily reflect those of the U.S. Department of Education, and no official endorsement should be inferred. ■

# TABLE OF CONTENTS

## UNIT 1: KEY CONCEPTS

# UNIT 2: COMMUNICATION

*I*n this country, students who are deaf-blind frequently receive services from teachers who are doing their best to meet these students' needs but who have not been formally trained in working with them. This means that the specific needs of both students and teachers are often not fulfilled. The book that you have just opened and its companion materials are the result of more than four years of intensive efforts to help remedy this situation.

*Hand in Hand: Essentials of Communication and Orientation and Mobility for Your Students Who Are Deaf-Blind* is the outcome of the American Foundation for the Blind (AFB) Deaf-Blind Project, a federally funded effort designed to provide teachers who work with students who are deaf-blind with information and resources. The project was significant for many reasons, but primarily for its scope. In every way, it was a nationwide endeavor to help teachers deliver effective educational services to deaf-blind youngsters.

What was significant about the Deaf-Blind Project? First, it reflected a recognition on the part of the federal government of the realities that teachers face when there are few personnel preparation programs available to offer them instructional strategies helpful in work with deaf-blind youngsters. Second, its length and the amount of the funds awarded demonstrated a strong commitment on the part of the U.S. Department of Education, Office of Special Education and Rehabilitative Services, to the delivery of special services to students with disabilities. Third, it included in various ways the major national service organizations concerned with the field of deaf-blindness and ensured their participation through the establishment of a national consortium. Fourth, it encompassed every part of the country through a national field test of the materials conducted as part of the project. The project's scope was also evident from the large number of authors—more than 30—considered experts who contributed to the final publication and from the even larger number of subject experts who reviewed the materials prior

prior to their field test. Finally, the materials themselves focused on two key areas of instruction, communication and orientation and mobility, to give teachers and other service providers integrated, comprehensive information to help them do their jobs well.

Over the years, AFB has devoted its resources to countless noteworthy efforts that have made important contributions to the field and to the lives of people who are blind and visually impaired. Even among those efforts, the Deaf-Blind Project was a standout and a milestone for those of us at AFB. By assembling the array of information you will find in the *Hand in Hand* materials and disseminating it nationwide, we hope to enhance the success of teachers and others working in the field and to improve the lives of their students.

Carl R. Augusto
*President*
*American Foundation for the Blind*

*H*and in Hand: Essentials of Communication and Orientation and Mobility for Your Students Who Are Deaf-Blind was developed through the American Foundation for the Blind (AFB) Deaf-Blind Project, a 4½-year effort funded by the U.S. Department of Education, Office of Special Education Programs, Branch for Severe Disabilities. The project's mandate was to develop self-study and in-service training materials for teachers in the area of deaf-blindness, with a focus on communication and orientation and mobility (O&M). This focus was felt to be vital for teachers because these are the two areas most influenced by the presence of combined hearing and vision losses in individuals. The project was initiated in the fall of 1990 and concluded in the spring of 1995.

## BACKGROUND

A national consortium of representatives from significant organizations in the field of deaf-blindness assisted project staff members in developing materials, starting with learner objectives that are based on knowledge and skills that consortium members believed are crucial for teachers working with students who are deaf-blind, from birth through age 21. Throughout the project, consortium representatives met and offered guidance, recommendations, and assistance in many major project activities. (The names of consortium members and their affiliations appear in a separate listing after this Introduction.)

More than 30 authors contributed to the draft curriculum written to address the learner objectives, which was reviewed by a group of experts in the field of deaf-blindness. In 1993, a field evaluation of the resulting materials was conducted by 110 teachers and related service providers in 46 states across the nation and by an additional group of experts, including the consortium members. Field reviewers included teachers trained in the education of individuals who have multiple disabilities, hearing impairments, or visual impairments; regular educators; O&M instructors; and speech therapists, as well as occupational and physical therapists. This extensive development and review process, resulting in many modifications to the original materials, has served to make the *Hand in Hand* materials in their published form broad in scope and representative of contemporary thought regarding the education of infants, toddlers, children, and youths who are deaf-blind.

## PURPOSES

The *Hand in Hand* materials have two major purposes: self-study and in-service training. The primary audience for whom they were written, especially for self-study use, is teachers with training and certification in the education of students who are deaf or hard-of-hearing, blind or visually impaired, or severely or multiply disabled. The materials are designed to provide

- basic knowledge and skills regarding how deaf-blindness affects and interacts with a child's ability to learn strategies for instruction and interaction with deaf-blind students
- strategies for instruction and interaction with deaf-blind students
- ways to assist other individuals who work and interact with deaf-blind students, such as families or related service providers
- detailed information on the development of communication and O&M skills and how these skills are taught to deaf-blind students
- discussion of important concepts that are vital for working with deaf-blind students, such as the transdisciplinary educational team and the ecological model of assessment and program implementation
- lists of resources and ways to obtain them for ongoing information gathering and skill development.

The focus on teachers as the primary audience for the *Hand in Hand* materials reflects the recognition of the field and of the Office of Special Education Programs of the U.S. Department of Education that information and resources are needed by teachers of students who are deaf-blind to work effectively with their students. The project was established to meet the need of teachers around the nation who often have little or no formal training in working with deaf-blind students. These service providers also may not have ready access to teacher-training opportunities in the area of deaf-blindness. For this reason, the *Hand in Hand* materials were designed for possible use for self-study or in-service training when no other formal training is available. These materials will also benefit individuals other than teachers trained in special education—including family members, teachers in regular school settings, paraprofessionals (teaching assistants, tutors, aides), related service providers, personnel in rehabilitation, and others who interact with students who are deaf-blind in the community—either directly, by using them for self-study, or indirectly, by learning from others who have used them.

## GUIDING PRINCIPLES

The *Hand in Hand* materials are intended to be primary learning tools. They are based on an underlying philosophy and set of assumptions that served as the guiding principles for the AFB Deaf-Blind Project and for all the *Hand in Hand* components. The guiding principles are listed here; they are the basic premises from which the content in the *Hand in Hand* materials was developed and reflect practices that have been found to be effective in working with students who are deaf-blind.

- All individuals who are deaf-blind can learn, communicate, and move with purpose. Independence and interdependence are key goals for all people, including those who are deaf-blind. The materials of the AFB Deaf-Blind Project are intended to help teachers maximize students' development of communication and orientation and mobility skills.
- The materials are self-instructional and focus on the unique learning needs of students who are deaf-blind, including those with multiple disabilities and progressive conditions. To emphasize the individuality of each student, they avoid the use of a developmental or comparative approach.

- The materials are intended for the use of teachers working with children who are deaf-blind and from diverse ethnic, cultural, national, and socioeconomic backgrounds. They reflect practices that are appropriate for teachers and deaf-blind children regardless of background.

- Families play the key role in educating their children who are deaf-blind. Therefore, it is important for teachers and other service providers to encourage them to participate fully in educational planning and implementation, especially if they have little experience in doing so.

- A student's educational team is composed of all the individuals who are involved in educating the student, including the student.

- Assessment is a vital, ongoing activity of the educational team. The ecological model of assessment and program implementation, which stresses the importance of functional assessment, natural settings, and long-range goals, is emphasized in these materials. It is also stressed that all interventions need to be monitored for their effectiveness.

- Like all people, students who are deaf-blind need and are entitled to participate fully in their homes, communities, schools, and workplaces and to be treated with dignity and respect. These materials have been designed to help teachers support the development of students' skills in programs that fulfill this goal and provide the services students need to live and work as independently as possible as adults.

## PROJECT MATERIALS

There are four major components of the *Hand in Hand* materials, beginning with *Hand in Hand: Essentials of Communication and Orientation and Mobility for Your Students Who Are Deaf-Blind*. Designed primarily as a self-study guide, this book is divided into three units—Key Concepts, Communication, and Orientation and Mobility—which, in turn, are further divided into 20 self-contained modules. The modules present essential information about deaf-blindness, how deaf-blindness affects learning, and how students who are deaf-blind can develop critical communication and O&M skills. All the material is designed to address the learner objectives based on the knowledge and skills that project staff and consortium members believed to be crucial for teachers who work with students who are deaf-blind.

The modules are designed for individual, self-paced study. They have been laid out for ease of use, with certain elements highlighted for the convenience of those who use them. The following features of each module will help readers make optimal use of the extensive material contained in the modules:

- *Key Concepts*: Summarize the major points of knowledge in each module. Readers can use the key concepts to preview the information contained in the module and, after reading the material, to check that they have absorbed the important concepts.

- *Help at a Glance*: Provides tips and summarizes valuable information for immediate use. Teachers can share these sections with families, teaching assistants, and other service providers so their interactions with students who are deaf-blind will be more effective, too.

- *Theory into Practice*: Presents applications of knowledge and concepts, usually as they relate to instructional activities. These tips are also useful to share with families, teaching assistants, and other service providers who work with students who are deaf-blind.

- *Other Sidebars*: Feature illuminating commentary and other supplementary information to highlight or complement material presented in the text, contributed by experts in the field.

- *Self-Study Questions and Answers*: Allow readers to check their understanding of the information and concepts in the modules. After answering the questions, readers can check their responses against those provided at the end of each unit. The rationales given for each answer indicate the most important concepts addressed in that module.

In addition to the three units, this self-study guide includes in its second volume four appendixes containing medical and related information, descriptions of assessment instruments and forms, and an overview of federal programs for deaf-blind students; a glossary; and a substantial resources section that lists sources of information and services, basic reading, equipment and materials, distributors and manufacturers, and university training programs. There is also an index covering the three units. Thus, every effort has been made to compile comprehensive information and to ensure that it can be found easily.

This two-volume manual can be used alone or in conjunction with the other components of the project, which include the following:

**Hand in Hand: It Can Be Done!** is a videotape with accompanying discussion guide that provides an introduction to working with deaf-blind students and lends visual support for many of the concepts discussed in this guide. Starring many people who are deaf-blind, along with their families and teachers, this one-hour videotape can be used not only as an introduction to deaf-blind people and the field of deaf-blindness, but also as a self-contained overview or a reinforcer of the information in the self-study guide. The discussion guide provides thought-provoking questions to use in self-study or in-service training situations.

**Hand in Hand: Selected Reprints and Annotated Bibliography on Working with Students Who Are Deaf-Blind** is a collection of important supplementary articles on specific topics, together with a listing and description of additional basic resources on deaf-blindness, blindness, deafness, and severe disabilities. The reprinted articles may be read on their own or as a supplement to specific topics in the self-study guide. The Annotated Bibliography, which covers both print and audiovisual materials and where to obtain them, serves as a supplementary reading and viewing list for the self-study guide or as a stand-alone reference guide to the field of deaf-blindness.

**Hand in Hand: Essentials of Communication and Orientation and Mobility for Your Students Who Are Deaf-Blind—A**

**Trainer's Manual** is a complete guide to in-service training using the *Hand in Hand* materials. It includes a suggested structure and specific training activities for training sessions based on each major topic of the self-study guide and directs the trainer to the appropriate resources in each of the *Hand in Hand* components. In addition, the manual includes special training considerations in working in the field of deaf-blindness and general tips for trainers.

Each of these components is useful in its own right in providing different types of information and assistance to those who work with students who are deaf-blind. Together, the components present a complete constellation of information for service providers who need to know how to work effectively with deaf-blind students.

## LEARNER OBJECTIVES

In every instance, the work the teacher is doing with students who are deaf-blind, their needs, and their learning characteristics will determine the information he or she needs to be more effective. For example, teachers or other personnel who are new to working with deaf-blind students and are using these materials as a basis for understanding their students' needs will find the fundamental concepts about deaf-blindness in Unit 1 most useful to study first.

To begin a self-study program, the reader can examine the learner objectives designed for the project to determine which are of greatest interest and relevance, based on his or her teaching situation, the particular students in his or her program, and those students' needs. A review of the table of contents will also indicate specific topics that will meet the needs of the individual reader. The learner objectives are as follows:

### Part 1: Key Concepts

1. The learner will understand essential information about distance sensory impairments and how these impairments can affect students who are deaf-blind.
2. The learner will understand educational service needs and educational service provision for students who are deaf-blind,

including the importance of a team approach.

3. The learner will understand the vital interrelationship of communication and movement for students who are deaf-blind.

4. The learner will understand the importance of an ecological approach in the education of students who are deaf-blind.

## Part 2: Communication

1. The learner will understand the basic nature of communication and how individuals develop the ability to communicate.

2. The learner will understand how communication development can be affected by deaf-blindness.

3. The learner will have knowledge of communication modes, systems, and devices for use with students who are deaf-blind, including how to select and design these modes, systems, and devices appropriately.

4. The learner will understand important concepts in assessing communication skills of students who are deaf-blind.

5. The learner will understand basic instructional strategies to help students who are deaf-blind develop concepts and communication skills, including specific strategies for working with infants and toddlers.

6. The learner will understand the importance of assisting students who are deaf-blind to develop lifelong communication skills for full community participation.

## Part 3: Orientation and Mobility

1. The learner will understand the importance of orientation and mobility in the lives of students who are deaf-blind.

2. The learner will understand how students' knowledge of body concepts and the environment can be affected by deaf-blindness.

3. The learner will understand the importance of teaching students who are deaf-blind to become aware of their surroundings and move or be guided purposefully and safely.

4. The learner will understand foundations of motor and move-

ment development and how they can be affected by deaf-blindness.

5. The learner will understand basic information about orientation and mobility instruction and how orientation and mobility is taught to students who are deaf-blind, including those with multiple disabilities.

6. The learner will know basic instructional strategies and activities that encourage infants and toddlers who are deaf-blind to develop environmental awareness, purposeful movement, and basic mobility skills.

7. The learner will know appropriate strategies for embedding opportunities to practice and use orientation and mobility skills in the daily activities of students who are deaf-blind.

8. The learner will understand the importance of assisting students who are deaf-blind to develop lifelong orientation and mobility skills for full community participation.

To help readers address the learner objectives effectively, an Advance Organizer has been compiled. In this organizational tool, which follows this Introduction, a great deal of information has been strategically arranged for readers in the form of a grid that shows where to find the information to fulfill each learner objective. The Advance Organizer identifies the modules, videotape sections, reprints, and annotated bibliography categories that relate to each objective and lists them all conveniently in one place.

## USE OF THE MATERIALS

The *Hand in Hand* materials are not intended to tell teachers everything they need to know about deaf-blindness or everything that children who are deaf-blind must learn. They are intended to provide guidance about how to work comfortably and effectively with deaf-blind students and how to help students make gains in achievement and develop critical skills. In doing so, they are also intended to help teachers derive success and personal satisfaction. They will help readers work on goals that they and a child's team have selected, using specially adapted techniques that often include communication modes, systems, or devices and movement strategies that are different from those they would use with children who see and hear. Overall, they are intended to provide the basics for successful interaction with students.

It should be noted that because these materials are designed for self-study, there are some things they cannot do. For example, although they present essential concepts *about* such skills as sign language and cane travel, they cannot teach a reader to be a signer or a teacher of cane travel. Instead, the materials can guide teachers in adapting and modifying their current teaching strategies to work with students who are deaf-blind so they can plan and implement effective instruction with more confidence.

As self-study students, readers can proceed at their own comfortable pace to read the modules and, if they are doing so, to augment their reading with the *Hand in Hand* video and reprints and annotated bibliography. Some readers may prefer to study in short intervals, to be able to reflect on a concentrated amount of information before continuing with new material. Others may use the materials for longer periods of time, but less often. In addition to the resources suggested throughout *Hand in Hand*, using resources available locally, for example in nearby school districts or service centers, will supplement and reinforce the information being learned.

In the end, the most important outcome of using the *Hand in Hand* materials should be the application of new and helpful information to teaching situations with students who are deaf-blind. Teachers and other personnel will find here the information they need to become more comfortable with their students and the instructional strategies they are using and, ultimately, to enhance their students' skills and ability to lead independent lives. By providing educators with resources so they may feel more confident about their work with deaf-blind students and their contribution to their students' lives, the materials produced by the AFB Deaf-Blind Project are intended to help meet the needs of teachers and students alike. ∎

| LEARNER OBJECTIVE | WHERE THE INFORMATION IS COVERED |
|---|---|
| **PART 1: KEY CONCEPTS** | |
| 1. The learner will understand essential information about distance sensory impairments and how these impairments can affect students who are deaf-blind. | **Primary:** Modules 1, 2, 3, 4, 15<br>**Supplementary:** This objective is addressed explicitly or implicitly in all modules and Appendixes A and B.<br>**Video:** *Hand in Hand: It Can Be Done!* Section 1, "Learn from Your Students." (All sections illustrate this learner objective, but Section 1 provides an overview.)<br>**Reprints:**<br>"The CHARGE Association: Implications for Teachers," by T. W. Jones and M. T. Dunne.<br>"A Classroom Environment Checklist for Students with Dual Sensory Impairments," by C. H. Rikhye, C. R. Gothelf, and M. W. Appell.<br>"Services for Children and Youths Who Are Deaf-Blind: An Overview," by A. M. Zambone and K. M. Huebner.<br>**Annotated Bibliography Categories:**<br>*Primary:* Deaf-blindness, education.<br>*Supplementary:* Blindness and low vision, communication, deafness and hearing impairments, disabilities (moderate, multiple, and severe disabilities), families, medical information, motor development, orientation and mobility, transition. |
| 2. The learner will understand educational service needs and educational service provision for students who are deaf-blind, including the importance of a team approach. | **Primary:** Modules 1, 2, 5<br>**Supplementary:** Modules 4, 13, 14, 15, 16, 17, 18, 20<br>**Video:** *Hand in Hand: It Can Be Done!* Section 1, "Learn from Your Students"; Section 4, "It Can Be Done!"<br>**Reprints:**<br>"A Local Team Approach," by J. M. Everson.<br>"Perspectives of Parents Whose Children Have Dual Sensory Impairments," by M. F. Giangreco, C. J. Cloninger, P. H. Mueller, S. Yuan, and S. Ashworth.<br>"A Classroom Environment Checklist for Students with Dual Sensory Impairments," by C. H. Rikhye, C. R. Gothelf, and M. W. Appell.<br>"Strategies for Educating Learners with Severe Disabilities in Their Local Home Schools and Communities," by J. S. Thousand and R. A. Villa. |

| LEARNER OBJECTIVE | WHERE THE INFORMATION IS COVERED |
|---|---|
| | **Annotated Bibliography Categories:**<br>*Primary:* Deaf-blindness, education, families<br>*Supplementary:* None. |
| 3. The learner will understand the vital interrelationship of communication and movement for students who are deaf-blind. | **Primary:** Modules 1, 2, 3<br>**Supplementary:** Modules 4, 7, 16, 18, 19, 20<br>**Video:** *Hand in Hand: It Can Be Done!* Section 1, "Learn from Your Students"; Section 3, "No Turning Back."<br>**Reprints:**<br>"Providing O&M Services to Children and Youth with Severe Multiple Disabilities," by B. R. Bailey and D. N. Head.<br>"Orientation and Mobility for Students with Severe Visual and Multiple Impairments: A New Perspective," by E. Joffee and C. H. Rikhye.<br>"Early Intervention for Infants with Deaf-Blindness," by M. G. Michael and P. V. Paul.<br>**Annotated Bibliography Categories:**<br>*Primary:* Deaf-blindness, communication, motor development, orientation and mobility, early intervention.<br>*Supplementary:* Cognitive development, education. |
| 4. The learner will understand the importance of an ecological approach in the education of students who are deaf-blind. | **Primary:** Modules 5, 11, 18<br>**Supplementary:** Modules 1, 2, 12, 13, 14<br>**Video:** *Hand in Hand: It Can Be Done!* Section 1, "Learn from Your Students"; Section 4, "It Can Be Done!"<br>**Reprints:**<br>"Developing Vision Use within Functional Daily Activities for Students with Visual and Multiple Disabilities," by J. Downing and B. Bailey.<br>"A Classroom Environment Checklist for Students with Dual Sensory Impairments," by C. H. Rikhye, C. R. Gothelf, and M. W. Appell.<br>"Strategies for Educating Learners with Severe Disabilities in Their Local Home Schools and Communities," by J. S. Thousand and R. A. Villa.<br>**Annotated Bibliography Categories:**<br>*Primary:* Deaf-blindness, education.<br>*Supplementary:* Assessment, communication, early intervention, families, motor development, orientation and mobility. |

| LEARNER OBJECTIVE | WHERE THE INFORMATION IS COVERED |
|---|---|
| **PART 2: COMMUNICATION**<br><br>1. The learner will understand the basic nature of communication and how individuals develop the ability to communicate. | **Primary:** Modules 6, 7<br>**Supplementary:** Modules 2, 3, 8<br>**Video:** *Hand in Hand: It Can Be Done!* Section 1, "Learn from Your Students"; Section 2, "Every Child Is a Communicator."<br>**Reprints:**<br>"Preverbal Communication of Blind Infants and Their Mothers," by C. Rowland.<br>"Prelanguage Communication of Students Who Are Deaf-Blind and Have Other Severe Impairments," by N. E. Tedder, K. Warden, and A. Sikka.<br>**Annotated Bibliography Categories:**<br>*Primary:* Deaf-blindness, communication.<br>*Supplementary:* Cognitive development, education, early intervention, families. |
| 2. The learner will understand how communication development can be affected by deaf-blindness. | **Primary:** Modules 1, 2, 3, 7<br>**Supplementary:** Modules 6, 8, 9, 10, 11, 12, 13, 14<br>**Video:** *Hand in Hand: It Can Be Done!* Section 1, "Learn from Your Students"; Section 2, "Every Child Is a Communicator."<br>**Reprints:**<br>"Tactile Iconicity: Signs Rated for Use with Deaf-Blind Children," by P. L. Griffith, J. H. Robinson, and J. H. Panagos.<br>"The CHARGE Association: Implications for Teachers," by T. W. Jones and M. T. Dunne.<br>"Preverbal Communication of Blind Infants and Their Mothers," by C. Rowland.<br>"Prelanguage Communication of Students Who Are Deaf-Blind and Have Other Severe Impairments," by N. E. Tedder, K. Warden, and A. Sikka.<br>**Annotated Bibliography Categories:**<br>*Primary:* Deaf-blindness, cognitive development, deafness and hearing impairments.<br>*Supplementary:* Education, families, medical information. |

| LEARNER OBJECTIVE | WHERE THE INFORMATION IS COVERED |
|---|---|
| 3. The learner will have knowledge of communication modes, systems, and devices for use with students who are deaf-blind, including how to select and design these modes, systems, and devices appropriately. | **Primary:** Modules 8, 9, 10, 12<br>**Supplementary:** Modules 1, 3, 7, 20<br>**Video:** *Hand in Hand: It Can Be Done!* Section 1, "Learn from Your Students"; Section 2, "Every Child Is a Communicator."<br>**Reprints:**<br>"Tactile Iconicity: Signs Rated for Use with Deaf-Blind Children," by P. L. Griffith, J. H. Robinson, and J. H. Panagos.<br>"Clarifying the Role of Classroom Interpreters," by P. L. Hayes.<br>"Interpreting for Deaf-Blind Students: Factors to Consider," by K. Petronio.<br>"Analytic Study of the Tadoma Method: Effects of Hand Position on Segmental Speech Perception," by C. Reed, N. I. Durlach, L. D. Braida, and M. C. Schultz.<br>**Annotated Bibliography Categories:**<br>*Primary:* Deaf-blindness, communication (augmentative communication, braille, interpreting, sign language).<br>*Supplementary:* Blindness and low vision, deafness and hearing impairments, disabilities (moderate, multiple, and severe disabilities), education. |
| 4. The learner will understand important concepts in assessing communication skills of students who are deaf-blind. | **Primary:** Modules 11, 12<br>**Supplementary:** Modules 8, 9, 10<br>**Video:** *Hand in Hand: It Can Be Done!* Section 1, "Learn from Your Students"; Section 2, "Every Child Is a Communicator"; Section 4, "It Can Be Done!"<br>**Reprints:**<br>"Developmental Scales Versus Observational Measures for Deaf-Blind Children," by M. H. Diebold, W. S. Curtis, and R. F. DuBose.<br>"Functional Vision Screening for Severely Handicapped Children," by B. Langley and R. F. DuBose.<br>**Annotated Bibliography Categories:**<br>*Primary:* Assessment.<br>*Supplementary:* Education, blindness and low vision, deafness and hearing impairments, disabilities, early intervention, medical information. |

| LEARNER OBJECTIVE | WHERE THE INFORMATION IS COVERED |
|---|---|
| 5.  The learner will understand basic instructional strategies to help students who are deaf-blind develop concepts and communication skills, including specific strategies for working with infants and toddlers. | **Primary:** Modules 1, 7, 13<br>**Supplementary:** Modules 2, 3, 14<br>**Video:** *Hand in Hand: It Can Be Done!* Section 1, "Learn from Your Students"; Section 2, "Every Child Is a Communicator"; Section 3, "No Turning Back"; Section 4, "It Can Be Done!"<br>**Reprints:**<br>"Developing Vision Use within Functional Daily Activities for Students with Visual and Multiple Disabilities," by J. Downing and B. Bailey.<br>"Instructional Strategies for Learners with Dual Sensory Impairments in Integrated Settings," by J. Downing and J. Eichinger.<br>"Teaching Students Who Are Deaf-Blind and Cognitively Disabled to Effectively Communicate Choices During Mealtime," by C. R. Gothelf, D. B. Crimmins, C. A. Mercer, and P. A. Finocchiaro.<br>"Concepts and Issues Related to Choice-Making and Autonomy among Persons with Severe Disabilities," by D. Guess, H. A. Benson, and E. Siegel-Causey.<br>"An Approach to Teaching Self-Dressing to a Child with Dual Sensory Impairment," by J. L. McKelvey, L. A. Sisson, V. B. Van Hasselt, and M. Hersen.<br>"Early Intervention for Infants with Deaf-Blindness," by M. G. Michael and P. V. Paul.<br>"A Classroom Environment Checklist for Students with Dual Sensory Impairments," by C. H. Rikhye, C. R. Gothelf, and M. W. Appell.<br>**Annotated Bibliography Categories:**<br>*Primary:* Deaf-blindness, communication, early intervention, education, families.<br>*Supplementary:* Blindness and low vision, cognitive development, deafness and hearing impairments. |

| LEARNER OBJECTIVE | WHERE THE INFORMATION IS COVERED |
|---|---|
| 6. The learner will understand the importance of assisting students who are deaf-blind to develop life-long communication skills for full community participation. | **Primary:** Modules 13, 14<br>**Supplementary:** Modules 8, 9, 10, 11, 12 prepare the reader to use Modules 13 and 14.<br>**Video:** *Hand in Hand: It Can Be Done!* Section 1, "Learn from Your Students"; Section 2, "Every Child Is a Communicator."<br>**Reprints:**<br>"Supported Employment for Persons with Deaf-Blindness and Mental Retardation," by S. L. Griffin and J. Lowry.<br>"The Usher's Syndrome Adolescent: Programming Implications for School Administrators, Teachers, and Residential Advisors," by W. Hicks and D. E. Hicks.<br>"The Impact of Retinitis Pigmentosa on Young Adults: Psychological, Educational, Vocational, and Social Considerations," by L. A. Nemshick, M. Vernon, and F. Ludman.<br>"Maximizing the Independence of Deaf-Blind Teenagers," by J. J. Venn and F. Wadler.<br>**Annotated Bibliography Categories:**<br>*Primary:* Transition, deaf-blindness, education.<br>*Supplementary:* Blindness and low vision, deafness and hearing impairments, communication. |
| **PART 3: ORIENTATION AND MOBILITY**<br><br>1. The learner will understand the importance of orientation and mobility in the lives of students who are deaf-blind. | **Primary:** Modules 1, 4<br>**Supplementary:** Modules 7, 15, 16, 17, 19, 20<br>**Video:** *Hand in Hand: It Can Be Done!* Section 1, "Learn from Your Students"; Section 3, "No Turning Back."<br>**Reprints:**<br>"Providing O&M Services to Children and Youth with Severe Multiple Disabilities," by B. R. Bailey and D. N. Head.<br>"Orientation and Mobility for Students with Severe Visual and Multiple Impairments: A New Perspective," by E. Joffee and C. H. Rikhye.<br>**Annotated Bibliography Categories:**<br>*Primary:* Deaf-blindness, orientation and mobility.<br>*Supplementary:* Disabilities (moderate, multiple, and severe disabilities), motor development. |

| LEARNER OBJECTIVE | WHERE THE INFORMATION IS COVERED |
|---|---|
| 2. The learner will understand how students' knowledge of body concepts and the environment can be affected by deaf-blindness. | **Primary:** Modules 2, 15<br>**Supplementary:** Modules 7, 16<br>**Video:** *Hand in Hand: It Can Be Done!* Section 1, "Learn from Your Students."<br>**Reprints:**<br>"Providing O&M Services to Children and Youth with Severe Multiple Disabilities," by B. R. Bailey and D. N. Head.<br>"Orientation and Mobility for Students with Severe Visual and Multiple Impairments: A New Perspective," by E. Joffee and C. H. Rikhye.<br>**Annotated Bibliography Categories:**<br>*Primary:* Deaf-blindness, education, motor development, orientation and mobility.<br>*Supplementary:* Disabilities (moderate, multiple, and severe disabilities). |
| 3. The learner will understand the importance of teaching students who are deaf-blind to become aware of their surroundings and to move or be guided purposefully and safely. | **Primary:** Module 4<br>**Supplementary:** Modules 15, 17, 18, 19<br>**Video:** *Hand in Hand: It Can Be Done!* Section 1, "Learn from Your Students"; Section 3, "No Turning Back."<br>**Reprints:**<br>"Providing O&M Services to Children and Youth with Severe Multiple Disabilities," by B. R. Bailey and D. N. Head.<br>"Orientation and Mobility for Students with Severe Visual and Multiple Impairments: A New Perspective," by E. Joffee and C. H. Rikhye.<br>**Annotated Bibliography Categories:**<br>*Primary:* Deaf-blindness, motor development, orientation and mobility.<br>*Supplementary:* Disabilities (moderate, multiple, and severe disabilities), education. |

| LEARNER OBJECTIVE | WHERE THE INFORMATION IS COVERED |
|---|---|
| 4. The learner will understand foundations of motor and movement development and how they can be affected by deaf-blindness. | **Primary:** Module 15<br>**Supplementary:** Module 16<br>**Video:** *Hand in Hand: It Can Be Done!* Section 1, "Learn from Your Students"; Section 3, "No Turning Back."<br>**Reprints:** None.<br>**Annotated Bibliography Categories:**<br>*Primary:* Deaf-blindness, early intervention, motor development.<br>*Supplementary:* Disabilities (moderate, multiple, and severe disabilities), orientation and mobility. |
| 5. The learner will understand basic information about orientation and mobility (O&M) instruction and how O&M is taught to students who are deaf-blind, including those with multiple disabilities. | **Primary:** Modules 17, 18<br>**Supplementary:** Modules 16, 19<br>**Video:** *Hand in Hand: It Can Be Done!* Section 1, "Learn from Your Students"; Section 3, "No Turning Back"; Section 4, "It Can Be Done!"<br>**Reprints:**<br>"Providing O&M Services to Children and Youth with Severe Multiple Disabilities," by B. R. Bailey and D. N. Head.<br>"Orientation and Mobility for Students with Severe Visual and Multiple Impairments: A New Perspective," by E. Joffee and C. H. Rikhye.<br>"Modifications of the Long Cane for Use by a Multiply Impaired Child," by K. A. Morse.<br>**Annotated Bibliography Categories:**<br>*Primary:* Deaf-blindness, education, motor development , orientation and mobility.<br>*Supplementary:* Disabilities (moderate, multiple, and severe disabilities). |
| 6. The learner will know basic instructional strategies and activities that encourage infants and toddlers who are deaf-blind to develop environmental awareness, purposeful movement, and basic mobility skills. | **Primary:** Module 16<br>**Supplementary:** Modules 2, 15<br>**Video:** *Hand in Hand: It Can Be Done!* Section 1, "Learn from Your Students"; Section 3, "No Turning Back"; Section 4, "It Can Be Done!"<br>**Reprints:**<br>"Early Intervention for Infants with Deaf-Blindness," by M. G. Michael and P. V. Paul. |

| LEARNER OBJECTIVE | WHERE THE INFORMATION IS COVERED |
|---|---|
| | **Annotated Bibliography Categories:** <br> *Primary:* Deaf-blindness, early intervention, education, families, motor development, orientation and mobility. <br> *Supplementary:* Disabilities (moderate, multiple, and severe disabilities). |
| 7. The learner will know appropriate strategies for embedding opportunities to practice and use orientation and mobility skills in the daily activities of students who are deaf-blind. | **Primary:** Module 18 <br> **Supplementary:** Modules 16, 19, 20 <br> **Video:** *Hand in Hand: It Can Be Done!* Section 1, "Learn from Your Students"; Section 3, "No Turning Back." <br> **Reprints:** <br> "Providing O&M Services to Children and Youth with Severe Multiple Disabilities," by B. R. Bailey and D. N. Head. <br> "Orientation and Mobility for Students with Severe Visual and Multiple Impairments: A New Perspective," by E. Joffee and C. H. Rikhye. <br> **Annotated Bibliography Categories:** <br> *Primary:* Deaf-blindness, education, early intervention, families, motor development, orientation and mobility. <br> *Supplementary:* Disabilities (moderate, multiple, and severe disabilities). |
| 8. The learner will understand the importance of assisting students who are deaf-blind to develop lifelong orientation and mobility skills for full community participation. | **Primary:** Module 20 <br> **Supplementary:** Modules 4, 19 <br> **Video:** *Hand in Hand: It Can Be Done!* Section 1, "Learn from Your Students"; Section 3, "No Turning Back"; Section 4, "It Can Be Done!" <br> **Reprints:** <br> "Providing O&M Services to Children and Youth with Severe Multiple Disabilities," by B. R. Bailey and D. N. Head. <br> "Orientation and Mobility for Students with Severe Visual and Multiple Impairments: A New Perspective," by E. Joffee and C. H. Rikhye. <br> **Annotated Bibliography Categories:** <br> *Primary:* Transition, deaf-blindness, orientation and mobility. <br> *Supplementary:* Blindness and low vision; disabilities (moderate, multiple, and severe disabilities). |

*T*he publication of *Hand in Hand: Essentials of Communication and Orientation and Mobility for Your Students Who Are Deaf-Blind* and the other components of the *Hand in Hand* materials produced by the American Foundation for the Blind (AFB) Deaf-Blind Project would not have been possible without the significant contributions of literally hundreds of people. This 4½-year project involved the efforts of professionals from the fields of deaf-blindness, blindness, deafness, severe disabilities, adult education and rehabilitation, orientation and mobility, physical therapy and other related fields, publishing, and video production, as well as the participation of many children and adults who are deaf-blind and their families, teachers, program administrators, and other service providers. It is not possible to list all the participants here, but the contributions of each one are valued.

Some individuals need to be recognized for their outstanding contributions to the *Hand in Hand* materials. First and foremost, Natalie Hilzen, the project editor, executive editor at AFB Press, consistently shared her expertise with patience and skill and masterfully brought the jigsaw puzzle together. Members of the AFB Deaf-Blind Project's National Consortium contributed to the development of the learner objectives and guiding principles that served as the foundation for the project and were always responsive to our questions and requests for help, indeed, frequently initiating offers of assistance. These materials bear their influence. The members of the National Consortium are listed separately after these acknowledgments. We sincerely thank them.

Charles W. Freeman, of the Office of Special Education and Rehabilitative Services, U.S. Department of Education, was the project's federal program officer. He provided consistent and constructive guidance throughout the project and was always there for us. We are indebted to him not only for his leadership in regard to the project, but for his years of inspiring commitment to the provision of services for children and youths who are deaf-blind. Also,

Juanita Bowe, who served as the project's federal grants officer, was always supportive and candid with us and provided us with needed counsel.

The large number of contributing authors to *Hand in Hand: Essentials of Communication and Orientation and Mobility for Your Students Who Are Deaf-Blind* added breadth and scope to these materials. Their names are listed separately after these acknowledgments. Thanks to these experts in the field of education of individuals who are deaf-blind, the readers of *Hand in Hand* have at their fingertips a wealth of experience and knowledge. In addition to those who contributed written work to *Hand in Hand*, the following experts who specialized in a wide range of content areas reviewed the materials and shared their expertise with the project staff:

Kay Adamson, Seattle Public Schools, Seattle, WA; Brent R. Bailey, Madison Metropolitan School District, Madison, WI; Sandra Ruth Boris-Berkowitz, Perkins School for the Blind, Watertown, MA; Wendy L. Buckley, Perkins School for the Blind; Linda J. Burkhart, Center for Technology in Education, Baltimore; Kathee M. Christensen, San Diego State University, San Diego, CA; Joseph Cioffi, New York City; Linda Collins, Perkins School for the Blind; Michael Collins, Perkins School for the Blind; Pamela J. Cress, University of Kansas, Parsons; Susan M. DeCaluwe, Perkins School for the Blind; Jane M. Everson, Helen Keller National Center for Deaf-Blind Youths and Adults, Sands Point, NY.; Diane L. Fazzi, California State University, Los Angeles; H. D. Bud Fredericks, TRACES, Monmouth, OR; Toni Gartner, Whittier Union High School District, Whittier, CA; Lori Goetz, San Francisco State University, San Francisco; Melissa Hanson, Portland Public Schools, Portland, OR; Kathryn Wolff Heller, Georgia State University, Atlanta; Nancy Holahan, St.-Luke's–Roosevelt Hospital Center, New York City; Judy Davidhizer

Holmes, Milwaukee Public Schools, Milwaukee, WI; Nancy Johnson-Dorn, Oregon Department of Education, Salem; Thomas W. Jones, Gallaudet University, Washington, DC; M. Beth Langley, Pinellas County Schools, Largo, FL; Barbara B. Mason, Perkins School for the Blind; Barbara A. B. McLetchie, Boston College, Chestnut Hill, MA; Thomas R. Miller, Perkins School for the Blind; Pat Mirenda, University of Nebraska–Lincoln; Lydia Barden Peterson, St. Paul Public Schools, St. Paul, MN; Rona L. Pogrund, Austin, TX; John W. Reiman, DB-LINK, Monmouth, OR; Marianne Riggio, Perkins School for the Blind; Catherine Hall Rikhye, New York City Board of Education; Pamela Ryan, Perkins School for the Blind; Maria Schauer, Queens Center for Multiply Handicapped Children; Little Neck, NY; Brenda L. Shepard, Aurora Public Schools, Aurora, CO; Rosanne K. Silberman, Hunter College, New York City; Bookoladeniya Sirisena, New York City Board of Education; W. Robert Smith, Holliston, MA; Robert J. Smithdas, Helen Keller National Center for Deaf-Blind Youths and Adults; Janet D. Steveley, Helen Keller National Center for Deaf-Blind Youths and Adults; and Elizabeth Yi, Helen Keller National Center for Deaf-Blind Youths and Adults.

Many organizations and individuals graciously consented to participate in the video and photographic shoots that were part of this project, and we wish to thank them all. For the filming of the *Hand in Hand* video, Washington State Services for Children with Deaf-Blindness, located in Seattle, and the Deaf-Blind Program of the Perkins School for the Blind in Watertown, MA, allowed us access to their programs and staff and introduced us to the families and children to whom they provide services. The Technical Assistance Center, Northwestern Regional Office of the Helen Keller National Center for Deaf-Blind Youths and Adults in Seattle was equally cooperative and helpful, as was Metamorphosis of the Greater Puget Sound Area. In addition, we are indebted to Brent R. Bailey for his advice and suggestions prior to filming. The Blind Children's Learning Center in Santa Ana, CA, the Helen Keller National Center for Deaf-Blind Youths and Adults in Sands Point, NY, and P. S. 396 in Brooklyn, NY, also generously permitted us to photograph their programs, staff, and students. Our appreciation is extended to everyone who assisted and cooperated with us during these shoots, such as Allison Burrows, Bea Fogle, and Richard Kelleher of the Helen Keller National Center in Sands Point and JoAnn Enos at the Helen Keller National Center in Seattle; Jerry Purdy of Metamorphosis; Lois Greene, Janet Healey, Fran Schuster, and John Stevenson of P. S. 396; Carol Crook, Martha Majors, and Barbara Mason of Perkins School for the Blind; Melvin Eisenbach of Education Vision Services, New York City Public Schools; Kay Adamson, Sharon Bolton, Marcia Fankhauser, Sandy Honeycutt, and Bob Huven of Washington State Services for Children with Deaf-Blindness; and, especially, the children, adults, and families who were willing to share their experiences and lives.

The field-test versions of the self-study manual, annotated bibliography, and video developed during the project were evaluated in 46 states by 110 teachers and related service providers. In addition to reviewing the materials, these field reviewers were asked to apply them, to complete questionnaires, and to offer comments and suggestions. Their feedback had a profound impact on the published version of the materials. The following individuals were field reviewers for the project:

Cathy Adams, Parkersburg, WV; Annette Allen, Mitchell, SD; Linda Alsop, Logan, UT; Jan F. Aster, Richmond, VA; Ellie Atkinson, Boise, ID; Pat Baker, Washington Crossing, PA; Maggie Barnett, North Little Rock, AR; Evelyn Beasley, Texarkana, TX; Tammy Belt, White Sulphur Springs, WV; Lynnda Biek, Lacey, WA; Ellen Boyd, Carson City, NV; Fred Breininger, Salem, OR; Jeff Brennan, Davenport, IA; Phyllis Brodsky, Tucson, AZ; Billi L. Bromer, Augusta, GA; Viktoria A. Brown, Lexington, MA; Melinda Buhl, New York City; Kathy Mack Burton, San Diego, CA; Dael Cohen, Philadelphia; Sarah Cooper, Kirkland, WA; Virginia Cutler, Long Valley, NJ; Joan Davies, San Diego, CA; Karlin Davis, Jacksonville, FL; Rosetta Davis, Newton, GA; Susan Dell, East Providence, RI; Stephanie Doeren-Rasmussen, Salt Lake City, UT; Judith Dokus, Tewksbury, MA; Krista Eaton, Reston, VA; Janice Etsinger, Salt Lake City, UT; Renee Farrell, Louisville, KY; Barbara Ferguson, Ellsworth, ME; James C. Fili, Batavia, NY; Lorna Gallimore, Lawrenceville, GA; Stephanie A. D. Garber, Staunton, VA; D. Jay Gense, Salem, OR; Jill Gierach, Jefferson, WI; Deborah Gouch, Gravette, AR; Karla J. Gray, Green Forest, AR; Patrika L. Griego, Albuquerque, NM; Bobbye Gurley, Conway, AR; Alice M. Hall, Des Moines, IA; Eric D. Hallingstad, Rice Lake, WI; Corrine Haynie, Orem, UT; Marge Heron, Columbus, OH; Janus Hinson, Gladstone, MT; Viola Hoelting, Green Cove Springs, FL; Dana Jacobson, Kirkland, WA; Michelle Jaeger, Dickinson, ND; Terry Johnston, Carson City, NV; Cindy Jones, Wichita, KS; Kathryn J. Jones, Mobile, AL; Lydia Jones-Nunn, Capitol Heights, MD; Ted Karanson, Lacey, WA; Susan Kephart, Romney, WV; Carol Anne Kruse, Glenwood, IA; Jodi L. Kurey, Rome, NY; Barbara H. Larsen, Indianapolis, IN; Laurel Leigh, Jersey City, NJ; Bonnie Lenz, Vinton, IA; Carol Lohse, Salem, OR; Sarah Majerick, Coralville, IA; Victoria Maley, El Cajon, CA; Katrina Marchant, American Fork, UT; William H. McGeachy, Baltimore; Bill McIver, Anchorage, AK, Colleen McMullen-Bailey, Columbus, OH; Mary Rose Meholter, Jersey City, NJ; Tammy Miller, Orem, UT; Eileen Milner, Jackson, MS; Katherine Morgan, Granby, CT; Rose Morin, Upper Frenchville, ME; Mary T. Morse, Suncook, NH; Kathy Mott, Warner Robins, GA; Karen Moullet, Bozeman, MT; Carolyn T. Nakata, Bremerton, WA; Debra Nelson, Morgantown, GA; Kathleen M. Newman, Ashland, NE; Paul H. Olsen, Grand Forks, ND; Elizabeth Owens, Salem, OR; Vickie Parker, Cedar Rapids, IA; Anna Persons, Silver Spring, MD; Thomas Puleo, Batavia, NY; Kristen G. Rapsher, Philadelphia; Sharon Reid, Council Bluffs, IA; Marilyn Reighard, Albuquerque, NM; Kathy R. Rivers, Columbia, SC; Doris A. Roberts, Sante Fe, NM; June Russell, Cedartown, GA; Mary Schilling, Ottumwa, IA; Jean Schipke, Richmond, VA; Elaine Sofinski, Richmond, VA; Wanda Spatzer, Winchester, VA; Cinthia Sprouse, Goldsboro, NC; Sharon Stelzer, Watertown, MA; Jean Beary Stolle, Vancouver, WA; Wendy Stoltman-Findlay, Lafayette, CO; Andrea Story, Anchorage, AK; Elizabeth Succar, Miami, FL; Bill Sullivan, Watertown, MA; Rosanne M. Swiercz, Waterville, MI; Peggy Miller Tarver, Austin, TX; Debra Barbieri Taylor, Cleveland, MS; Nancy Trenbeth, Seattle, WA; Toni Trujillo, Las Cruces, NM; Mary Beth Tuck, Chesterfield, VA; Steven P. Ware, Stone Mountain, GA; Barbara Wiggins, Des Moines, IA; Carol Wild, Indianapolis, IN; Becky Wilson, Hattiesburg, MS; Laurie L. Young, Sturgis, SD; and Elizabeth Young-Dove, Newark, OH.

We are also grateful to the coordinators of deaf-blind programs across the country that are funded under Section 307.11 of the Individuals with Disabilities Education Act for their perspectives, support, and assistance in locating field reviewers. We look forward to their cooperation in the dissemination and training efforts to apply the *Hand in Hand* materials. In addition, special thanks are due to the focus group who reviewed a post-field-review version of the *Hand in Hand* video and provided production recommendations:

Carole R. Gothelf and Daniel B. Crimmins, Jewish Guild for the Blind, New York City; Harvey H. Mar, St. Luke's–Roosevelt Hospital Center, New York City; Joseph J. McNulty, Helen Keller National Center for Deaf-Blind Youths and Adults, Sands Point, NY; and Rosanne K. Silberman and her graduate students, Hunter College, New York City.

This project could not have been initiated or completed without the support of the administration and staff of AFB. In 1990, when the project was an idea and nothing more, William F. Gallagher, then president and executive director of AFB, encouraged AFB's submission of the proposal for the federal cooperative agreement and continued to support AFB's involvement in the project. Carl R. Augusto, current president of AFB, enthusiastically embraced the project and indeed made it the focus of AFB's 1994 Annual Report.

Susan J. Spungin, vice president of National Programs and Initiatives at AFB, was a steadfast supporter of and contributor to the project, as was Mary Ellen Mulholland, former director of AFB Press and one of the executive producers of the *Hand in Hand* video. The AFB support staff, who patiently inputted information, monitored databases, and served as administrative assistants, were Frank Kamolvathin, Sara Hernandez, Nora Ricciardi, and Hooman Bakhtiar. Carol Wallace, secretary of AFB Press, provided essential support as well. We would also like to thank Peter Cipkowski, who was project editor in the early years; Traci Barnes of the secretarial staff of the Pennsylvania College of Optometry; and Ellen Bilofsky, who recently served as an effective copy editor and assistant to Natalie Hilzen. Wendy Almeleh, copy editor; Marcia Kovarsky and John Lucas, proofreaders; and John Mead, word processor, played vital roles in bringing the project materials to press.

All the deaf-blind children and adults who contributed to this project were essential, not only to the project, but to the depth and authenticity of the resulting materials. Some provided written materials; some participated in the video; and numerous others taught us, the consortium members, and the contributing authors many things

about being deaf-blind. We sincerely thank them and hope that the *Hand in Hand* books and video will enhance others' teaching and working with individuals who are deaf-blind.

Finally, we wish to thank our families for their patience, understanding, and continued support.

Kathleen Mary Huebner

Jeanne Glidden Prickett

Therese Rafalowski Welch

Elga Joffee

**Kathleen Mary Huebner,** Ph.D., Director of the AFB Deaf-Blind Project, is the Chairperson of the Division of Graduate Studies in Visual Impairment and Director of Education and Rehabilitation Programs of the Institute for the Visually Impaired at the Pennsylvania College of Optometry in Philadelphia. Previously, she was Director of the National Program Associates Department and National Consultant in Education at the American Foundation for the Blind and directed the Graduate Teacher Training Program at the State University of New York at Geneseo. A former instructor of individuals with visual impairments and an orientation and mobility specialist, Dr. Huebner has co-authored and edited several books and written numerous articles on services for individuals who are visually impaired. She has given numerous presentations and consulted at schools, teacher training programs, and government agencies nationwide and abroad on topics related to blindness and multiple impairments.

**Jeanne Glidden Prickett,** Ed.D., is the Coordinator of Materials Development for the AFB Deaf-Blind Project. She was previously Assistant Professor and Coordinator of the Program in Visual Impairments at the Johns Hopkins University Division of Education in Baltimore, as well as Technical Assistance Consultant to the Maryland Deaf-Blind Project. Dr. Prickett was also the Coordinator of the National Information Center on Deaf-Blindness at Gallaudet University in Washington, DC. A former supervisor of special education services and teacher of children who are visually impaired, hearing impaired, and deaf-blind, she has published articles and given numerous presentations on the education of children and youths who are deaf-blind.

**Therese Rafalowski Welch,** M.Ed., the Coordinator of Consortium Activities for the AFB Deaf-Blind Project, is the former Director of Washington State Services for Children with Deaf-Blindness and a former teacher of children who are deaf-blind. She has given numerous presentations and provided in-service training at program sites throughout the United States and abroad on issues related to the education of children who are deaf-blind. Her publications include a guide on early intervention for families of children who are blind or visually impaired and articles on services for children who are deaf-blind and their families.

**Elga Joffee,** M.Ed., M.P.S., is National Program Associate at the American Foundation for the Blind (AFB) and Chairperson of AFB's National ADA (Americans with Disabilities Act) Initiative. A certified orientation and mobility specialist, she is the producer of *We Can Do It Together,* a videotape and companion curriculum for teaching orientation and mobility to students with severe visual and multiple impairments, used systemwide in New York City public schools. She has written and presented widely on orientation and mobility, the Americans with Disabilities Act, and other issues in the field of visual impairment. ■

**Brent R. Bailey,** Ph.D., is a vision/orientation and mobility teacher in the Vision Department, Madison Metro Public School District in Madison, Wisconsin.

**Vic Baldwin,** Ed.D., is Director of Teaching Research at Western Oregon State College in Monmouth, Oregon.

**Sharon Bolton,** M.Ed., is a special education teacher in the White River School District in Buckley, Washington.

**Deborah Chen,** Ph.D., is Associate Professor in the Department of Special Education, California State University in Northridge.

**Chigee Jan Cloninger,** Ph.D., is Director of the Vermont State Program for Students with Dual Sensory Impairments; Coordinator of the State of Vermont Interdisciplinary Team for Intensive Special Education; and Research Associate Professor at the University Affiliated Program of Vermont, Center for Developmental Disabilities, University of Vermont in Burlington.

**Anne L. Corn,** Ed.D., is Professor of Special Education in the Department of Special Education, Peabody College, Vanderbilt University in Nashville, Tennessee.

**Daniel B. Crimmins,** Ph.D., is Director of Psychology at the Westchester Institute for Human Development in Valhalla, New York; and Associate Director of the Developmental Disabilities Program, Graduate School of Health Sciences and Assistant Professor, Department of Psychiatry and Human Behavior, New York Medical College in Valhalla.

**Carol Crook,** M.Ed., is Communication Specialist/Teacher in the Deaf-Blind Program, Perkins School for the Blind in Watertown, Massachusetts.

**June E. Downing,** Ph.D., is Director of the Teacher Training Program in Severe and Multiple Disability, University of Arizona in Tucson.

**Joyce Ford** is President of the National Family Association for Deaf-Blind and lives in Boise, Idaho.

Barbara Franklin, Ph.D., is Coordinator of the Deaf/Hard of Hearing Program, Department of Special Education, San Francisco State University in San Francisco, California.

Charles W. Freeman, M.Ed., is Education Program Specialist with the U.S. Department of Education, Office of Special Education Programs, in Washington, DC.

Kathleen Gee, Ph.D., is Assistant Professor, Department of Special Education, University of Kansas, Lawrence.

D. Jay Gense, Ed.S., is Deaf-Blind/Orientation and Mobility Specialist, Mid-Oregon Regional Services in Salem.

Marilyn Gense, M.A., is Education Program Supervisor and Orientation and Mobility Specialist, Oregon School for the Blind, Salem.

Lori Goetz, Ph.D., is Director of the California Research Institute and Professor in the Department of Special Education, San Francisco State University, in San Francisco, California.

Carole R. Gothelf, Ed.D., is Director of Education at the Jewish Guild for the Blind, New York, New York.

Margaret M. Groce, M.S., is Supervisor of Travel Training, District 75, New York City Board of Education, New York, New York.

Arline B. Isaacson, M.S., is Teacher-Travel Training Specialist in the Travel Training Program, Division of Special Education, New York City Board of Education in Brooklyn, New York.

Steven B. Johnson, M.S., is Assistant Director, Special Education Division, and Administrator, Management and Coordination, Deaf-Blind Services, California Department of Education in Sacramento.

Nancy Johnson-Dorn, M.Ed., is Education Specialist in the Office of Special Education, Oregon Department of Education in Salem.

Thomas James Langham, M.Ed., is Coordinator of Services in Augusta and surrounding areas for Mobility Services, Inc., in Augusta, Georgia.

Angela Linam, M.S., is Research Associate, Callier Center for Communication Disorders, University of Texas at Dallas.

Dennis Lolli, C.A.G.S., is Orientation and Mobility Low Vision Consultant for Perkins Outreach Services and Hilton/Perkins International Program, Perkins School for the Blind in Watertown, Massachusetts.

Harvey H. Mar, Ph.D., is Psychology Coordinator and Assistant Professor of Clinical Psychology in Pediatrics, Developmental Disabilities Center, St. Luke's–Roosevelt Hospital Center in New York, New York.

Colleen D. McNerney, Ph.D., is Coordinator, National Forum on Education about Sustainable Development, Washington, DC.

David Miller, M.A., is Orientation and Mobility Specialist in the Deaf-Blind Program, Lighthouse for the Blind in Seattle, Washington.

Steve Perreault, M.Ed., is Education Consultant, Hilton/Perkins International Program, Perkins School for the Blind in Watertown, Massachusetts.

Rona L. Pogrund, Ph.D., is a private consultant in visual impairment in Austin, Texas.

Sandra Rosen, Ph.D., is Associate Professor and Coordinator of programs in orientation and mobility, rehabilitation teaching, and physical disabilities, Department of Special Education, San Francisco State University in San Francisco, California.

Charity Rowland, Ph.D., is Faculty Research Associate at Washington State University at Vancouver in Portland, Oregon.

Dona Sauerburger, M.Ed., is Orientation and Mobility Specialist at Volunteers for the Visually Handicapped in Silver Spring, Maryland.

Philip D. Schweigert, M.Ed., is Research Supervisor at Washington State University at Vancouver in Portland, Oregon.

**Ellin Siegel-Causey,** Ph.D, is Assistant Professor in the Department of Special Education and Communication Disorders and Director of the Severe Disabilities Training Program, University of Nebraska in Lincoln.

**Robert J. Smithdas,** M.A., is Assistant Director of the Community Education Department, Helen Keller National Center for Deaf-Blind Youths and Adults in Sands Point, New York.

**Robert D. Stillman,** Ph.D., is Associate Dean of the School of Human Development and Program Head, Communication Disorders Program, Callier Center for Communication Disorders, University of Texas at Dallas.

**Kathleen Stremel,** M.A., is Senior Researcher in the Department of Special Education, University of Southern Mississippi in Hattiesburg.

**Samuel J. Supalla,** Ph.D., is Director, Sign Language/Deaf Studies, Department of Special Education and Rehabilitation, College of Education, University of Arizona in Tucson.

**Christy Williams,** M.S., is Project Coordinator, Callier Center for Communication Disorders, University of Texas at Dallas.

**Sara B. Woolf,** M.A., is Project Coordinator at New York Medical College and Westchester Institute for Human Development in Valhalla, New York.

**Diane P. Wormsley,** Ph.D., is Education Manager, Overbrook School for the Blind in Philadelphia, Pennsylvania, and at the time of writing was Director, National Initiative on Literacy of the American Foundation for the Blind in Atlanta, Georgia.

**George J. Zimmerman,** Ph.D., is Associate Professor and Coordinator of the Vision Studies Program, Department of Instruction and Learning, University of Pittsburgh in Pittsburgh, Pennsylvania. ■

**Lou Johnson Alonso,** M.A., is Professor in the Department of Counseling, Educational Psychology, and Special Education and Coordinator of the Program for Blind, Deaf-Blind, and Orientation and Mobility Teacher Education at Michigan State University in East Lansing.

**Kevin D. Arnold,** Ph.D., is a psychologist in private practice in Columbus, Ohio, and on the clinical faculty of the University of Dayton School of Education. Previously he was the Director of the Great Lakes Area Regional Center for Deaf-Blind Education at Ohio State University in Columbus.

**Vic Baldwin,** Ed.D., is Director of Teaching Research at Western Oregon State College in Monmouth, Oregon.

**Chigee Jan Cloninger,** Ph.D., is Director of the Vermont State Program for Students with Dual Sensory Impairments; Coordinator of the State of Vermont Interdisciplinary Team for Intensive Special Education; and Research Associate Professor at the University Affiliated Program of Vermont, Center for Developmental Disabilities, University of Vermont, Burlington.

**Michael T. Collins,** M.Ed., is Director of the Hilton/Perkins Program and previously Supervisor of the Deaf-Blind Program of the Perkins School for the Blind in Watertown, Massachusetts.

**Joyce Ford,** parent representative on the National Consortium, is President of the National Family Association for Deaf-Blind and lives in Boise, Idaho.

**H. D. Bud Fredericks,** Ed.D., is Research Professor at Teaching Research, TRACES Project (Teaching Research Assistance to Children and Youth Experiencing Sensory Impairments), Western Oregon State College in Monmouth, Oregon.

**Charles W. Freeman,** M.Ed., is Education Program Specialist with the U.S. Department of Education, Office of Special Education Programs, in Washington, DC.

**Lori Goetz,** Ph.D., is Director of the California Research Institute and Professor at San Francisco State University, Department of Special Education, in San Francisco, California.

**Steven B. Johnson,** M.S., is Assistant Director, Special Education Division, and Administrator, Management and Coordination, Deaf-Blind Services, California Department of Education in Sacramento.

**Thomas W. Jones,** Ph.D., is Professor of Education at Gallaudet University in Washington, DC.

**Roderick J. Macdonald,** M.A., is Management Analyst with the U.S. Department of Labor, Office of Information Resources Management, in Washington, DC, and Past President of the American Association of the Deaf-Blind in Silver Spring, Maryland.

**Joseph J. McNulty,** M.A., is Director of the Helen Keller National Center for Deaf-Blind Youths and Adults in Sands Point, NY.

**Rosanne K. Silberman,** Ed.D., is Professor in the Department of Special Education and Coordinator of the Teacher Preparation Program in Visual Impairment and Severe Disabilities Including Deaf-Blindness at Hunter College of the City University of New York in New York City.

**Susan J. Spungin,** Ed.D., is Vice President, National Programs and Initiatives, of the American Foundation for the Blind in New York City.

**Louis M. Tutt,** M.Ed., is President of the Maryland School for the Blind in Baltimore and Outgoing President of the Council of the Schools for the Blind. ■

# UNIT 1
## KEY CONCEPTS

# The Deaf-Blind Child and You

*THERESE RAFALOWSKI WELCH*

*KATHLEEN MARY HUEBNER*

- *Observe what works for the student*

- *Adopt a holistic approach*

- *Wait for the student to respond*

- *Make use of all the senses*

- *Be consistent*

- *Encourage the student to move and explore*

- *Provide a safe, organized environment*

- *Allow extra time*

- *Educate the class about deaf-blindness*

*H*ave you recently been told that you will soon be working with a student who is deaf-blind? Or have you been working with a deaf-blind student for the first time—or perhaps for some time now—and found that you need information and strategies to help you do your job effectively? If so, you've come to the right place—this book was written with you in mind. To get you started, this module gives you a preview of the themes and material that you will find in the modules that follow, which have been carefully assembled to help you work with deaf-blind students successfully.

## AN OVERVIEW

All across the country, people who are deaf-blind are going to school, working, spending time with their friends, and participating in family and community life. Although "deaf-blind" is a term that seems to imply a complete absence of hearing and sight, people known as deaf-blind are actually very diverse—many have useful vision or hearing, some have additional disabilities, and others are totally deaf and totally blind. Nevertheless, they all share the need for sound educational programs from infancy through young adulthood to reach their goal of living as independently as possible in the community. Your role in providing these programs is vital. Yes, it is a challenging role, but it is one that provides you with the opportunity to be creative, to learn new things and to enjoy doing so, and to make an important contribution to someone else's life. *Hand in Hand: Essentials of Communication and Orientation and Mobility for Your Students Who Are Deaf-Blind* was designed to help you meet this challenge. It introduces you to the essential concepts of how to work effectively with students who have both impaired vision and hearing.

If you have never worked with a student who is deaf-blind, you may be wondering how to communicate with deaf-blind students, how deaf-blind people get around safely on their own, and a great number of other things. Some questions that are frequently asked by teachers and other staff members when they first meet deaf-blind children are touched on in this module. As you work through the modules that follow and the other components of the *Hand in Hand* materials, you will find more in-depth responses and information related to these and other questions. But, to begin, it is important to know that teaching deaf-blind children is about motivating them to become involved with other people and a world they may not see or hear. It's about helping them gain the confidence to become as independent as possible. It's about brainstorming with them, their families, and other professionals to individualize and appropriately tailor their educational programs. And, finally, it's about finding new ways to convey information that is usually presented visually or aurally.

## BASIC PRINCIPLES

Few generalizations can be made about deaf-blindness because "deaf-blind" refers to combined hearing and vision losses, and there are as many possible combinations of hearing and visual impairments as there are individuals who are deaf-blind. However, here are a number of key principles that are useful to follow:

- There is no single profile of a deaf-blind student.
- Most deaf-blind students have and make use of some hearing and vision.
- Deaf-blind students can participate in almost any activity.
- Deaf-blind students communicate in a variety of ways.
- Many deaf-blind students can get around their communities independently.
- Deaf-blind students can be included in every teaching environment.
- Educational teams are essential for the design and delivery of educational programs for deaf-blind students.
- The families of deaf-blind students are key players on the educational team.

Because the characteristics and abilities of deaf-blind children vary so widely, it is important to view these children holistically and to use an ecological approach when working with them. The ecological approach, in which all aspects of a student's skills and needs are examined in all areas of his or her life, can be the foundation of educational planning and programming for a child who is deaf-blind, and it is emphasized throughout this book (see Modules 5, 11, and 14, for example).

Another approach that is both helpful to teachers and others who work with deaf-blind children and critical to addressing the needs and abilities of these children is the team approach. Since the instructional needs; visual, auditory, and tactile skills; learning styles; and physical capabilities of deaf-blind students differ enormously, no one person can or should be expected to address all these factors adequately when planning and implementing an instructional program. Even someone who is a specialist in deaf-blindness may have had experience only with students of a particular age. Therefore, drawing on the knowledge and expertise of the families of students, colleagues and peers, specialists, therapists, administrators, assistants, and medical personnel is key to designing the most effective, appropriate program for your deaf-blind student.

## COMMUNICATION: HOW TO BEGIN

The first question that usually occurs to people about a student who is deaf-blind is "How do I communicate with this student?" Related questions are "How should I approach the student?" "How will I make my presence known to the student?" and "How will the student know it's me?"

There is no one answer to these questions. Find out what works by trying different approaches and letting the child who is deaf-blind guide you to the ways that he or she communicates or learns best. Different students not only prefer different approaches, but may respond more effectively to particular ones. Remember that although deaf-blind students may wish to interact with you, they do not have the same kind of information about your presence that you have about theirs. Also keep in mind that they may not always welcome interaction. Therefore, proceed slowly and sensitively. Give a student the choice to accept or reject an interchange, so the student has and feels that he or she has a sense of control over the situation, and do not force interaction every time you approach the student.

In general, however, you can make the first move and present opportunities for communication. Here's how:

- To get the student's attention, approach him or her gently and identify yourself. You may want to develop a cue that identifies you. For example, a double tap on the elbow can alert a deaf-blind student to your presence. Use the cue and wait. Be sure to use that cue consistently.

- Let the student know you are available for and interested in interaction by bringing your hand up lightly beneath the student's hand, so the back of your hand touches the student's palm. Or, lightly touch the student's upper arm or shoulder to indicate your presence. Wait briefly until you think that the student is ready to interact with you.

- You will know if the student is ready to communicate by observing his or her movement toward you or watching for changes in body language or activity level, such as the student's becoming quiet.

- Do not grab the student's wrist. Being grabbed or held is confining for a person who uses his or her hands to communicate.

People who are deaf-blind communicate in a variety of ways (see Basic Methods of Communication in this module). Fingerspelling, or forming letters into the hand, may be the type of communication you most readily associate with persons who are deafblind because it is the method that Helen Keller and her teacher Anne Sullivan Macy used most. However, numerous other means of communication are used by and with deaf-blind people, including speech, body language, braille, tactile sign language, augmentative communication systems, amplification systems, and combinations of these methods (see Module 3 and Unit 2, especially Modules 8–10, for more on these and other communication methods). Not only do deafblind people have a wide range of communication choices, but most deaf-blind people use several methods of communicating. Some methods will be easier for you to master than are others. While you are still learning some methods, you may want to use an interpreter, so the student can continue to understand you and to develop his or her communication skills (Module 9 provides information on how to find and work with an interpreter).

Overall, it is essential to help the deaf-blind student develop as many communication skills as possible and learn all appropriate communication methods. In fact, the development of these skills needs to be your highest priority. Along with the student and members of his or her educational team, you can devise a communication system that is effective even for a student with severe disabilities, and subsequent modules, especially 3 and 6–12, present information and strategies to help you do so. Communication is the basis for learning all other skills. Along with movement, it is a critical building block in a child's development. If a child cannot obtain and convey information, explore the environment, and interact with others, his or her growth and potential

# BASIC METHODS OF COMMUNICATION

People who are deaf-blind use many methods to communicate. Here are some basic ones that are important for you to know:

● **Touch cues:** communication prompts that are made on a child's body, such as a light touch on the lips for eating. Touch cues encourage the child to anticipate the next activity and to begin to respond appropriately.

● **Object cues:** communication prompts that are made with objects that touch the child's body or are presented visibly to the child. For example, a washcloth touched to the face can indicate the activity of washing the face. An object cue encourages the child to anticipate an activity and can be the precursor for using objects as symbols.

● **Gestures:** mutually understood natural movements or signals, such as pointing or waving good-bye, that are used to communicate specific ideas consistently. Gestures can be used to prepare a child for the use of signs as symbols.

● **Vocalizations:** sounds made with the voice that can be used to get attention, make wants and needs known, and communicate specific things to others. Vocalizations may precede speech.

● **Tangible symbols:** items, such as objects (either partial or whole), pictures, or textured materials, that can be used to represent a concept or activity. Their use does not require the cognitive ability that formal language does, and they can be readily manipulated to convey an idea.

● **Sign language:** a formal language that uses hand and arm movements, natural gestures, body and facial movements, and expressions symbolically.

● **Tactile sign language:** sign language that is used with touch. Both the person signing and the receiver may use touch, or the receiver alone may use touch and then sign back visibly or speak.

● **Fingerspelling:** hand shapes that symbolize alphabet letters that can be read visibly or through touch.

● **Spoken language:** the use of speech to articulate concepts.

● **Braille:** written language that is embossed, so it can be read by touch.

● **Large print:** writing that is made large for persons who are visually impaired, so they can read more easily.

● **Print-on-palm:** "writing" on a person's palm with the index finger.

For more information on these and other methods of communication, see Module 3 and Unit 2. ■

will be dramatically restricted. The development of communication and mobility skills makes possible and enhances opportunities for participation in family and peer relationships, work and school tasks, and leisure and community activities—in short, everything one does in life.

## MOBILITY: CRITICAL STEPS

The distance senses of vision and hearing are usually people's primary means of getting information. Because their vision and hearing are impaired, children who are deaf-blind need to reach out to their environment to discover what is beyond them. When information from the distance senses is distorted or absent, children need to learn adapted mobility techniques, as well as alternative communication methods (see Module 4 and Unit 3 for information on mobility techniques). Therefore, children have to be given opportunities to learn about and explore their environments as safely, confidently, and independently as possible.

But, to begin, how do you make sure that your student moves about safely? A primary method is to learn the sighted guide technique (this method and other orientation and mobility [O&M] techniques are described in detail in Modules 17 and 18), which can be introduced easily and quickly both to school staff members and to other students. Outlined in Sighted Guide Basics in this module, the technique follows these steps:

- Start out by touching the arm, shoulder, or hand of the person you are guiding to let him or her know you are there.
- Identify yourself and discuss where you are going and how you will get there.
- As a sighted guide, you are always in front. The person you are guiding grasps your arm firmly above the elbow with his or her four fingers to the inside and the thumb to the outside.

Grasping your arm gives the person you are guiding information about the pace and terrain to follow. As you move along as a guide, you need to indicate changes or obstacles, such as curbs or stairs, primarily by pausing. When guiding someone up or down stairs, stop before the first step to let the person being guided line up with the step and grasp the railing. Then proceed up or down the stairs in front of the person you are guiding. At the end of a flight of stairs, take one step forward and stop, so the person you are guiding can take the last step.

## SIGHTED GUIDE BASICS

The following technique is a way to help deaf-blind students move about safely:

• Always identify yourself when you approach the student.

• Always stay in the forward position—in front of the student you are guiding.

• The student should hold your arm, just above your elbow (unless the student is small and cannot reach that high, in which case, the student should hold your wrist or hand).

• Be a half step in front and to the side of the student while walking.

• Bring the student to a seat, describe it (a desk chair or a picnic bench, for example), and either have the student locate it or place the student's hand on it.

• Before you leave the student, always inform him or her and be sure the student has contact with a stable physical object in the environment, such as a wall, water fountain, tree, or parking meter.

When guiding someone up or down stairs, follow these basic principles:

• Stop at the beginning of a flight of stairs (up or down).

• On stairs, the student should be on the side of the stairway railing and use the railing.

• Always be one step ahead of the student while going up or down stairs.

• Take one step forward and stop at the end of the flight of stairs (up or down). ■

Other simple protective techniques like trailing, in which a person maintains some contact with a wall or other surface, usually by running the back of the hand along it lightly, can add to a student's safety while traveling or moving about. Students who are deaf-blind travel at various levels of independence, and after their needs for training are assessed, they generally should receive instruction in O&M by a qualified instructor who has been especially trained in this field (for more information, see Module 4, especially How to Find an O&M Instructor, and Unit 3). But there are many O&M skills that you will be able to teach your students, and it is vital that you encourage them to explore the environment while they are feeling safe. Through movement, children obtain knowledge and find opportunities for communication, interaction, and learning, all of which promote their overall development and help them build skills. But for deaf-blind children, who need to reach out and interact with the environment to obtain sensory information they may not be able to receive clearly through vision and hearing, mobility is critical. Therefore, helping a deaf-blind student to learn and grow means providing stimulation, motivation, and opportunities for movement. Ways in which you can organize the classroom and environment so the student is safe, receives clear information, and is motivated to move—and so you can do your job with the student more effectively—are outlined later in this module and Module 19.

# WHAT YOU NEED TO KNOW

When you work with a deaf-blind student, various sources of information and assistance are available. To begin, however, you need to get as much information about the student as you can.

## QUESTIONS TO ASK

The student, his or her family, former instructors, other school staff, classmates, medical personnel, and other members of the educational team can provide information that may be invaluable to you. Try to get the answers to the following questions in as detailed a form as possible, especially if the student does not use formal language or has additional impairments that may affect his or her communication or mobility.

- How does the student communicate, and how do others communicate with the student?

- How does the student move about, and how do others facilitate his or her movement?

- How does the student receive information and interact with the environment best? Does the student have and use residual hearing and/or vision? Does he or she use touch and tactile information?

- What assistive devices or adaptations does the student need?

    Does the student use eyeglasses or hearing aids or both?

    Does the student use other devices, such as a closed-circuit television (CCTV) or glare shade, to enhance vision or hearing?

    Does the student use a mobility device, such as a cane, an adapted cane, or a wheelchair?

Does the student require other equipment for additional needs? If so, what type of equipment?

- Where should others stand so the student can see or hear them?

- Which people, activities, or materials does the student seem to like or to resist, and what seems to motivate the student to interact?

- Does the student have special medical needs?

    Does the student require medication, and if so, how does the medication affect him or her?

    Are the student's vision and hearing stable, or are they likely to deteriorate?

    Does the student have restrictions on food or activities?

    Does the student engage in behavior or have a condition that is a warning sign of situations to which the staff should be alert?

    Are there special emergency procedures for the student that the staff should know?

- Have long-range goals been established for the student?

    What are the student's or his or her family's priorities?

    What have previous Individualized Family Service Plans (IFSPs), Individualized Education Programs (IEPs), Individualized Transition Plans (ITPs), and Individualized Written Rehabilitation Programs (IWRPs) contained? (Since an IWRP is basically a contract between a visually impaired person and the state rehabilitation agency serving people who are blind or visually impaired that outlines the services needed to achieve the person's job goals, this last item does not relate to younger students.)

The answers to these questions will help you plan how to meet the student's educational needs. After you have met the student, observe him or her during activities that require vision, hearing, or touch. Do not rely solely on medical records or the results of formal tests because the student may not respond well to formal procedures in unfamiliar environments. Continue to gather information about the student as you come to know him or her and as you continue to work with his or her family and the educational team. You will find that you learn most about a student through direct experience with him or her.

## OTHER SOURCES OF INFORMATION AND ASSISTANCE

In addition to members of the educational team, a number of resources can be contacted for help when working with a deaf-blind student. For example, Where to Get Help in this module describes the state and multistate deaf-blind projects that can be called, as well as DB-LINK. Other organizations that can provide help are listed in the Resources section.

It may also be helpful for you to talk with others who have had experience with children who are deaf-blind to gain tips and to "brainstorm" ways of making your instruction more successful. Here are a few ways you may be able to find such persons:

- The director or coordinator of the deaf-blind project in your state may be able to put you in contact with educational specialists or other instructors who work with deaf-blind children or adults, as well as with experienced parents and caregivers.

## HELP at a GLANCE

### WHERE TO GET HELP

The federal government funds state and multistate programs that address the needs of students who are deaf-blind. These programs are called deaf-blind projects, or sometimes 307.11 programs (because they are funded under Section 307.11 of the Individuals with Disabilities Education Act) (see Appendix D for more information), and they can provide you with information about state and local services, programs, and training opportunities. You can get the name of the director and the address and telephone number of a specific project by calling DB-LINK, the National Information Clearinghouse on Children Who Are Deaf-Blind, at (800) 438-9376 or (800) 854-7013 (TTY/TDD [Teletype for the Deaf/Telecommunications—or Telephone—Device for the Deaf]).

DB-LINK is a consortium of organizations that are leaders in the field of deaf-blindness and includes the American Association of the Deaf-Blind (AADB), American Foundation for the Blind (AFB), Helen Keller National Center for Deaf-Blind Youths and Adults (HKNC), Perkins School for the Blind, and Teaching Research of Western Oregon State College. Its information specialists, who have access to extensive databases of resources, can give you reference information and answer questions on the education of students who are deaf-blind (see Resources for more information). ∎

- The state department of education may have a formal mentor program, especially in conjunction with state colleges and universities. (This department is also a source of information on services and personnel that may be helpful.)

- The national and, often, the state and regional conferences of the Association for Persons with Severe Handicaps (TASH) and the Association for Education and Rehabilitation of the Blind and Visually Impaired (AER) have sessions on deaf-blindness that are attended primarily by instructors. The national conferences of the American Association of the Deaf-Blind (AADB) have numerous informational sessions that are attended by deaf-blind persons, interpreters, and others (see Resources for how to contact these organizations).

- Interactive electronic information and communication systems allow you to link up with other educators and programs. SpecialNet, which covers the full range of special education topics, can be contacted through its administrator, GTE Educational Services Network, at (800) 927-3000. It has a bulletin board—*deafblind*—for information in the field of deaf-blindness on which you can make known your desire to communicate with other educators. Professionals have also used e-mail and Internet to correspond with others in the field.

Some states have formally organized delivery systems, called instructional materials centers (IMCs), instructional resource centers, clearinghouses, or depositories, that provide consultation and specialized materials in special education. Some IMCs conduct in-service training sessions, workshops, and weekends with experts to inform teachers and families about various aspects of deaf-blindness. Contact information for state departments of education and IMCs can be found in the *Directory of Services for Blind and Visually Impaired Persons in the United States and Canada* (1993).

IMCs have many different types of materials for direct use by students, as well as materials to help teachers. Student-oriented materials include braille, large print, audiotape materials, communication boards, amplification devices, and CCTVs. Teacher-oriented materials include curricula, training videos, assessment devices, teaching aids, instructional programs and kits, and reference materials.

Organizations for parents and families can be very helpful and provide useful information for all individuals involved in the life and education of students who are deaf-blind. The National Family Association for Deaf-Blind (NFADB) is a national organization for families of individuals who are deaf-blind, and it, along with a number of other organizations, is listed in the Resources Section.

# IN THE CLASSROOM

When you first begin to work with a deaf-blind student, you may find that many of your concerns relate to personal interaction and the student's physical safety. Accompanying these concerns are probably numerous questions about effective instructional strategies. Module 5 and other subsequent modules contain much useful information on how to teach deaf-blind children and help them develop communication and mobility skills. However, you may find the following guidelines of help in dealing with the immediate issues of how to interact personally and organize the environment to maximize a child's safety and potential to learn.

## INTERPERSONAL INTERACTION

When you work with a student, try to think "deaf-blind." If you could not see and hear well, what would help you understand the world and the environment around you? The critical identifying features of an item may not be only visual or auditory. Instead, texture, size, and scent may be essential elements. Determine the features that the student can use to understand or identify something and help him or her focus on these features for learning. Once your consciousness of this principle is heightened, try to adapt your activities with the student accordingly.

As you focus on establishing a relationship of trust and rapport with the student, it will be important to observe what is important to him or her. In doing so, you will probably find that the sense of touch assumes great importance.

Touch may be *the* essential means for a child to receive and convey information if the child's two major distance senses of vision and hearing are impaired. Therefore, in working with students who are deaf-blind, teachers need to appreciate the importance of touch for the students and to try to overcome any feelings of discomfort they may have with its use. Here are a few suggestions:

- "Think" deaf-blind and supplement visual and auditory information with touch. For example, because a student may not see a smile of approval or hear a compliment for a job well done, add a pat on the back or arm.

- Guide the student's hands as he or she touches you. If you have designated a tangible cue, such as a distinctive piece of jewelry that you always wear or your long hair, as a means of identifying yourself to the student, help the student quickly and easily make contact with the cue. As you and the student become more familiar with one another, you may guide the student's hands to touch your face.

- Help the student learn appropriate ways to touch people. Again, guide the student's hands to use light pressure and not to touch body parts indiscriminately. Gently move the student's hands away and prohibit him or her from touching you in an inappropriate way.

- Teach the student's classmates the appropriate ways to touch and receive touch from their peer who is deaf-blind.

In addition to becoming comfortable with using the sense of touch, basic to working regularly with a deaf-blind student is to make certain that the student becomes familiar and comfortable with you. Some additional strategies you can use to help a deaf-blind student recognize you quickly and consistently are these:

- Routinely wear the same perfume, cologne, or after-shave lotion.

- Consistently touch the student on the same place on the student's body and in the same way. For example, gently stroke the student's right forearm three times or gently grasp the student's shoulder and gently squeeze. These are touch cues (see Modules 7 and 8 for further information).

- Use a physical or distinctive feature, such as a beard, eyeglasses, or long hair, that remains constant to identify yourself to your student. Be sure you are the only one on the educational team who uses the selected feature.

- Routinely wear a distinctive ring, watch, bracelet, or other jewelry that the student can feel as you contact him or her.

- Use a tangible symbol (for example, a cane for O&M or sandpaper for woodworking) that the student identifies with you because of what you teach him or her.

- Create a "name sign" for yourself that is understood by you and the student as being representative of you. Teach the sign to the student and use it consistently (for more on name signs, see Module 9).

- If the student can hear you, say hello and identify yourself.

- If the student can see you, get the student's attention and identify yourself.

Other tips for working with students who are deaf-blind are listed in Working with Deaf-Blind Students in the Classroom and Community in this module.

Another important aspect of interaction with a deaf-blind student is how the student and his or her classmates interact. Fostering relationships among a student who is deaf-blind and other students is

# Working with Deaf-Blind Students in the Classroom and Community

**Lori Goetz and Kathleen Gee**

Dear Teacher:

Remember that my disability is in information gathering. Take just as much time to plan how I will receive information about routines, activities, and tasks as you do to decide what I should do in the activities.

- *Wait!* Allow extra time for me to make a response, answer a question, or reciprocate a greeting. It takes me longer to receive and make use of incoming information.

- *Interact with me*, not with my interpreter or my augmentative communication system. It is easy to overlook my presence and talk to my support system instead of me.

- *Alert me* through consistent and respectful cues, like touching me gently on the shoulder, that you are going to communicate with me.

- *Get as close to me as is necessary*, depending on my communication system and interaction styles. Touch cues, signing or spelling into my hands or palms, and talking closely into my better ear are examples of how it is fine not to follow conventional expectations about personal space.

- *Enhance the context for learning and interacting*. I need to know what is going on around me—things *you* are continuously seeing and hearing.

- *Consider my immediate visual and auditory environment*. Seating me where there is a glare or near a heater that makes a persistent background buzz will make it harder for me to use my residual sight and hearing. Consult with my hearing and vision specialists. ■

important for the student, for the other children, and for the harmonious operation of your class. Children who have not before been acquainted with someone who is deaf-blind may have many concerns and questions, and teaching them about deaf-blindness can do much to promote understanding that can lead to cooperation and friendship. General information about deaf-blindness and activities that are tailored to their age range can help classmates of students who are deaf-blind gain insights into what it means to be deaf-blind. Here are a few suggestions:

▲ *Encouraging class-room interaction helps deaf-blind students develop their skills and promotes a positive learning environment.*

• Try simulation experiences during which the students perform ordinary classroom activities using blindfolds or simulator lenses and earplugs.

• Invite speakers to address the class: service providers for individuals who are deaf-blind, adults or young adults who are deaf-blind, or family members of the student who is deaf-blind. To find speakers, ask the state deaf-blind project for assistance. (Call DB-LINK (800) 438-9376 or (800) 854-7013 TTY/TDD [Teletype for the Deaf/Telecommunications—or Telephone—Device for the Deaf] to get the name, address, and phone number of the director of the state project.)

• Have the student who is deaf-blind address the class if he or she is able to. Be sure to have the student demonstrate any special equipment or materials he or she uses.

• View and discuss the *Hand in Hand* video and other videos on deaf-blindness.

• Have students study the life of Helen Keller. Numerous books and some films about her and her teacher, Anne Sullivan Macy, are available.

• Get information from the Helen Keller National Center— (516) 944-8900 voice and TTY/TDD—about the current occupations and accomplishments of individuals who are deaf-blind and about possible activities for the annual Deaf-Blind Awareness Week that is celebrated in late June.

- Tell the students that they can talk with you or some other designated staff person whenever they have questions about deaf-blindness.

- Get answers to specific questions about deaf-blindness by contacting DB-LINK.

In addition, promoting communication among classmates is important, and suggestions for fostering communication in your class can be found in Modules 3 and 13. By providing a positive interpersonal and learning environment, you will smooth the way for your deaf-blind student to become integrated into the life of your class and help all the students to develop social, communication, and cognitive skills.

## EFFICIENTLY ORGANIZED SPACE

Organizing the classroom or work space in a simple way can help make learning easier for the deaf-blind student and ensure that he or she can become oriented more quickly and can move about with safety. Some of the accommodations you can make will also be beneficial to the entire class. These accommodations primarily involve creating well-defined work areas; paying attention to levels of lighting and illumination; making effective use of color and contrast; and designating easy-to-reach, consistent areas for storing materials (for details on how to organize a classroom, see Module 19).

In general, try to arrange the classroom furniture, equipment, and materials simply and in a manner that creates straight paths of travel. Designate storage areas for students' clothing, books, and other equipment in places that are easily accessible and clearly marked. Adaptations will have to be individualized for the deaf-blind student. Here are some simple changes that can be made:

- Install rheostat switches to control lighting in work areas.
- Use shades or blinds on windows to control light and glare.
- Place large-print or braille or other tactile identification symbols on desks and storage areas, including clothing cubicles and shelves for equipment, that the deaf-blind student may use.
- Place a high-intensity lamp with an adjustable arm in the student's work area or desk.
- Increase the working area of the deaf-blind student's desk to

accommodate the lamp, supplementary and adapted equipment, and other materials.

- Use carpeting or other flooring material to define a work space tactilely, as well as to improve the quality of sound.
- Place distinctive room-identification markers on the doorjambs of various rooms.
- Place a shadow box around the edges of a computer monitor to reduce glare.
- Use acoustical panels to absorb extraneous noise.
- Install an amplification system.

Before you make adaptations to the classroom for the student who is deaf-blind, you need to know the student and his or her auditory and visual, as well as physical, needs. Observe the student in the classroom and as he or she moves about the school and on the grounds. Watch for the student's reactions or lack of reactions to changes in lighting; noise levels; and terrain, including texture and level. Observe the student performing tasks to see if these or similar tasks are performed differently under different environmental conditions, such as the presence of fluorescent, rather than incandescent, lighting. Also, make use of the educational team. Ask various specialists for recommendations for tailoring the classroom and school to the student's needs. When considering the school, you need to follow several basic principles to facilitate the creation of an accessible environment for the student who is deaf-blind:

▲ Well-organized classrooms in which aisles are free of clutter promote safe movement for all students, including those who are deaf-blind.

- Provide adequate amounts of lighting in the hallways, stairwells, cafeteria, auditorium, and classrooms.
- Eliminate glare and deep shadows cast by lighting fixtures.
- Provide figure-to-ground contrast that highlights important elements in the school, such as doorways, handrails, and control buttons in elevators.
- Highlight the outer edges of objects, such as telephone call boxes, water fountains, bulletin boards and display cases, and fire extinguishers, to help make these objects visible.

- Provide clear aisle space in hallways, the cafeteria, the auditorium, and classrooms that is kept free of clutter.

- Use carpeting to absorb environmental noise.

- Place acoustic panels in areas where high noise levels may be a problem.

- Reduce motor noise from air-conditioning and heating units and from lighting sources.

As you plan how to lay out and enhance the physical environment, it is critical that you also plan emergency procedures to allow for any special needs of the student who is deaf-blind. Classmates, along with all members of the educational team, should be fully aware of and comfortable with these procedures. Once you have worked out what to do in an emergency, you may find that you are more confident and relaxed about the possibility of unanticipated events.

## EMERGENCY PROCEDURES

It is vital to establish procedures for evacuation in the case of fires, tornados, earthquakes, and similar emergencies, depending on where you live, that are tailored to the needs of the deaf-blind student and to practice them with your students and classroom assistants, so that everyone can respond safely and efficiently. The following are some guidelines:

- Since the student may not see or hear an alarm, he or she must be individually alerted using the most appropriate communication method.

- One person should be responsible for assisting the student, and a back-up person should be designated in case that person is absent. If the student has additional medical needs and equipment, it may be necessary for two adults to be assigned to help him or her.

- Be sure that all emergency procedures are designed to allow the student the extra time he or she may need to move—even with a sighted guide or assistant. It is advisable that school staff members and classmates all become familiar with the sighted guide technique.

- If you plan to use classmates to assist the student who is deaf-blind, select them carefully and train them well. You may want to have an adult monitor them each time they practice the emergency procedures. Also, check with the school's administrators to make sure that the school's policy permits the use of peer guides in emergencies.

- The universal symbol for an emergency that an adult who is deaf-blind usually responds to is the tactile symbol "X," "drawn" on his or her back by the person who is alerting him or her. The deaf-blind person knows that the "X" means there is an emergency and so follows the directions of the other individual to move to safety, without asking questions or getting immediate information, which would cost time. Once the symbol is drawn, the individual who has alerted the deaf-blind person moves out quickly with the person. Teach all staff members and students the symbol, whether or not the student seems to comprehend it immediately when it is first introduced.

- Practice using emergency procedures frequently, especially when they are first instituted.

- Modify the procedures as needed for various school and community activities.

- If a student can use a tactile (vibrating) alarm device, include instruction and practice in using it.

- Although the student who is deaf-blind may seem independent, in an emergency, he or she may respond differently than you expect. Therefore, be sure that the student is supported in an emergency, regardless of his or her skills.

# THE HEART OF INSTRUCTION

Several general principles that will be explored in the modules that follow can help you work effectively with any student who is deaf-blind:

- Develop a secure, positive, and reinforcing relationship.
- Provide a safe, organized, and responsive environment.
- Provide extensive, reinforcing experiences in many settings and situations.
- Establish and use effective communication systems.
- Motivate the student to move, and encourage purposeful movement.

- Promote the use of existing hearing and vision.

- Maximize the use of touch and all other senses.

- Use and encourage the student to use a multisensory approach.

- Teach in natural situations and settings.

- Be consistent.

- Promote independence by providing opportunities to make choices.

- Use a team approach to the student's education.

- Allow ample time for the student to receive and process information.

- Have high expectations for the student.

Many additional strategies are presented throughout the *Hand in Hand* materials. Take your time in working through the modules, so you can identify the strategies that are most applicable to a particular student. Although your immediate focus may be the student in school and the school years, it is important to keep in mind the broader picture of the student as a member of a family, a circle of friends, and the community. As you plan a child's educational program, keep in mind that your contribution to laying down a sound foundation can help the child find a way to a satisfying, independent life. The materials now in front of you offer one way to begin.

# REFERENCES

*Directory of services for blind and visually impaired persons in the United States and Canada* (24th ed.) (1993). New York: American Foundation for the Blind.

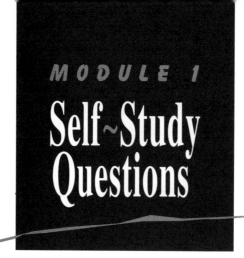

**MODULE 1**

# Self~Study Questions

1.  Which of the following is *not* a basic principle that applies to students who are deaf-blind?
    a.  Most deaf-blind students have some hearing and vision.
    b.  Communication systems will vary among deaf-blind students.
    c.  Independent mobility for deaf-blind students is limited to indoor travel.
    d.  Families are key members of education teams serving students who are deaf-blind.

2.  Which is *not* a suggested strategy for helping a deaf-blind student identify you?
    a.  Wear a different ring each day, but always on the same finger, and have the student feel it when you approach.
    b.  Use a physical feature that remains constant to identify yourself.
    c.  Wear the same perfume, cologne, or after-shave lotion.
    d.  Teach and use a name sign.

3.  Which of the following would *not* be recommended as a strategy to improve the classroom environment for elementary school students who are deaf-blind?
    a.  Install rheostat switches to control lighting.
    b.  Utilize high-intensity desk lamps with adjustable arms in students' work areas.
    c.  Install amplification systems in classrooms.
    d.  Decrease the work area of students' desks.

*Answers to self-study questions for this module appear at the end of Unit 1.*

# Deaf-Blindness: Implications for Learning

JEANNE GLIDDEN PRICKETT

THERESE RAFALOWSKI WELCH

- *Understand the effects of deaf-blindness*

- *Use sensory cues other than vision and hearing*

- *Be alert for signs of vision and hearing loss*

- *Provide additional explanations*

- *Focus on direct experience and repetition*

- *Teach formally what children often learn incidentally*

*I*n people who are deaf-blind, the two major channels for receiving information—hearing and vision—are not functioning or are impaired. This limitation on the ability to receive information can have far-reaching effects, including an influence on the child's general development. It challenges deaf-blind individuals, their families, and their teachers to find alternative means and strategies for exchanging information. Deaf-blindness can also have an impact on the development of motor skills and the ability to move about freely and with purpose and challenges the individual to develop systems and skills for moving from place to place safely. The combined effects of a vision and a hearing loss make deaf-blindness a unique disability. In this module, the effects of deaf-blindness on general development, communication, orientation, and mobility will be explored.

# IMPACT OF DEAF-BLINDNESS

Because degrees of vision and hearing loss vary greatly from individual to individual, the effects of deaf-blindness vary greatly as well. In general, however, the loss of both vision and hearing affects certain aspects of the development of individuals that need to and can be addressed in effective educational programs. From limiting a child's access to sensory input to influencing his or her emotional growth, deaf-blindness can often be seen to present the child with particular challenges.

## ACCESS TO SENSORY INFORMATION

Sensory experiences make children aware of the environment and are the basis on which they build knowledge about the environment, themselves, and other people with whom they come into contact. Each sense provides access to distinct and useful information, but the depth and breadth of the information acquired through each sense are not equal. This notion can best be illustrated by dividing the senses into two categories—near senses and distance senses—as is often done in the literature on deaf-blindness.

Taste, touch, and smell are classified as near senses. To acquire information through a near sense, an item must be immediately and physically present. For example, to taste a cookie, one must have it in one's mouth.

Touch is not as physically constricted as taste because most people can extend their limbs to reach something and feel items that come into contact with their bodies. But items just inches beyond one's body or reach are nevertheless "out of touch."

Smell stretches the notion of nearness in that scents that are well beyond an arm's length can often be detected. Still, the sensory information that can be gained from smell is limited compared to the information that can be acquired from the distance senses of vision and hearing.

Vision and hearing are the primary channels through which most people collect information. These senses have decided advantages over the near senses: No sensory channel other than vision can take in so much information all at once; one cannot always feel an entire object at the same time, but one can see all of it in one look. And some information obtained through sight cannot be obtained through the other senses, for example, in the case of things that are too distant, like clouds, or too dangerous, like fire. Hearing also has unique qualities, for it is the only sense that can literally "bend around corners" and attend to several kinds of input at the same time; for example, someone can listen to someone talking, while being aware that the radio is on in the next room and the baby is crying upstairs (Freeman, 1985, p. 8). Children who are deaf-blind and cannot receive complete information from the distance senses may develop incomplete or distorted concepts of the world around them and therefore need opportunities to obtain additional information in alternate ways.

## COMMUNICATION AND MOVEMENT

Communication and movement are among the essential building blocks of development, and they are inextricably linked. When infants see objects or hear sounds, they are stimulated to interact with their environment—that is, to communicate and to move and explore. When their ability to see and hear is impaired and they cannot easily perceive such stimulation, their motivation is diminished, they may not communicate and move as frequently, and they may not strongly develop the skills involved in communicating and moving.

Emerging movement and communication skills are linked in several ways. First, communication involves some form of movement—from blinking an eye to nodding the head to changes in body positions or facial expressions to moving the lips for speech. Second, through early movement skills, infants gain experience in using actions to influence other people and objects in their environment, which is a form of communication. Third, through movement, young children also have opportunities to associate daily experiences with symbols, words, and concepts—a fundamental aspect of communicating with others. Fourth, emerging communication skills motivate and encourage infants to explore and help them develop the strength, confidence, and skills they need for moving in and learning about their world.

Infants learn that their early facial or body movements, such as smiling at a family member, raising their arms to be picked up, reaching for a toy, or pulling back from an unpleasant sensation, are ways to control what is happening around them. As others respond to their movements or movement helps them achieve their desired aims, infants feel encouraged to continue to move about and communicate.

As children's communication skills increase, others can convey information about people, places, and things that are farther away, as well as more abstract ideas and feelings, and the children can communicate more complicated ideas and feelings to others. This expanded communication can motivate children to learn skills for moving about in new and increasingly complex environments. Experience in more complex environments, in turn, presents greater opportunities for developing more sophisticated communication skills. As their communication and mobility skills increase, children can have more chances to interact with their families and other children at home and at school and eventually in the general life of their communities. Because communication and mobility skills are essential for the development and overall well-being of children, the modules that follow emphasize the ways in which individual children can learn and practice them.

## LEARNING

### Incidental Learning

When you enter a room where a party is under way, you can gain a great deal of information through vision quickly and with little effort. Even a quick scan of the room will give you information about how many people are there, how they are dressed, whether you know them, who is talking to whom, and so on. A closer look at the guests' facial expressions will give you an indication of their moods. Then, you can view the furnishings, food, and size and arrangements of the room.

If there is a window in the room, you can probably tell what the weather is like and perhaps how well nearby traffic is moving. If a television is playing, you may catch a glimpse of an event occurring halfway around the world.

As you step into the room, you can also obtain much information through hearing. You may be able to hear some conversations, and the tones of the voices will tell you about the various speakers' moods. You also may be able to detect familiar voices and know that friends are nearby. If the window is open, you may hear the wind blowing, a plane passing, or street traffic. If the television is on, you may hear the speech of a foreign leader delivered from a faraway city.

All this information is incidental and is available to people who are sighted and hearing almost effortlessly. Although incidental information may seem trivial, it guides the individual's interactions with the environment, increasing his or her knowledge and the experience base. An individual who is deaf-blind, however, does not have effortless access to such information—even with the assistance of an interpreter. Moreover, the details that this person can absorb through the remaining senses or that can be conveyed to him or her are not captured instantaneously. Instead, a person who is deaf-blind will need to be made aware of elements of the environment that are not readily accessible and to be formally taught many things that sighted and hearing people learn incidentally. The example of Claudio illustrates this point:

> *Claudio, aged 8, has physical disabilities in addition to being deaf-blind. One afternoon he was involved in his teacher's lesson on vegetables. The teacher was careful to use real vegetables and helped the students form the correct signs with their hands after they felt each vegetable. When Claudio held the potato, he smiled and signed "Rock." The teacher corrected him and signed "Potato." Claudio rejected the correction and signed "Wrong, rock." The teacher then signed "Not wrong— this really is a potato." Claudio persisted, convinced he was right and hurriedly signed "No, teacher wrong. Potato is hot. Potato is soft. Wrong. Wrong. Rock!"*

Clearly, Claudio was describing a potato as it would be served at mealtime, which probably was his only experience with potatoes. Therefore, for him the critical features that identified a potato were texture (soft and dense) and temperature (warm). Claudio logically concluded, on the basis of his personal sensory experiences, that the hard, cold, gritty object that his teacher handed him was not a potato. The critical features of the object more closely matched those that Claudio had come to associate with a rock.

The lesson was an unexpected learning experience—for the teacher. She understood that Claudio needed to be able to recognize a potato in all its forms and states. He would have to be taught where and how potatoes grew, where to shop for them, and different ways of cooking them. Claudio's sighted and hearing classmates could learn such information from casual observations in a garden or on family grocery shopping trips or by watching family members cook meals. Claudio would need to be actively involved in and receive appropriate communication about all these experiences to have a full understanding of a simple potato.

## Concept Development

Information that is gained through sensory experiences, including incidental information, provides the basis for concept development. The primary senses of vision and hearing greatly aid the development of the most elementary as well as the most abstract concepts.

Peggy Freeman, an expert on deaf-blindness and the mother of a young woman who is deaf-blind, discussed the impact of vision and hearing on the early development of the concepts of object permanence (knowing that things exist whether or not they are present) and cause and effect (what makes things happen):

*The baby drops his rattle, he watches it roll until it is out of sight under a chair, he watches Mummy retrieve it from under the chair and give it back to him; or she hides it under a cushion and he finds it.... The child with a visual impairment who does not see where an object has gone will not know where to find it again, or even know that he could. If he is also deaf, you cannot tell him what is happening either. When he throws a toy it has gone—forever. He does not know when we hand it back to him that it is the same one that he threw away.... Secondly, it is by* seeing *that a child realizes his hands can be used to achieve what he desires.... It is when he sees the relationship between a piece of string and the toy to which it is attached that he will understand its role in getting him the toy. (Freeman, 1985, pp. 25, 26)*

Teachers and parents or other caregivers of children who are deaf-blind need to find alternative strategies for teaching these and other basic concepts. The strategies may vary from child to child, so it is important to observe carefully how a child best receives information and respond to his or her learning strengths. As you interact with a child who is deaf-blind consider

- supporting and enhancing the use of any residual vision and hearing (pay attention to color, contrast, size, distance, loudness, pitch, and so forth)

- providing other sensory and multisensory cues (scent, texture, vibration, temperature, and the like)

- repeating activities many times

- encouraging exploration

- ensuring appropriate communication for activities and experiences.

Communication and language skills are critical to understanding more abstract concepts, such as those related to movement, position, time and distance, and speed and motion. For students who are deaf-blind to learn such concepts, teachers and caregivers must build on their concrete experiences and previous learning, provide the language to label new concepts, and help them to generalize what they learn and to use new information accurately.

## Mental Imagery

Individuals who are deaf-blind are further challenged as they attempt to construct mental images of simple objects. Natalie, for example, has myopia and a constricted visual field and can see only a small section of a car—not the whole car. To create a total visual image of a car, she must piece together the various parts. If Natalie were to examine the car tactilely, she would still have to "assemble" the parts in her mind.

A possible teaching strategy would be to use a small model of a car. It is important to note, however, that Natalie may not grasp the relationship between a real object and a model unless she has reached the cognitive level of symbolic thought. If Natalie is not yet able to understand the relationship between a model car and a real car, her teachers can use other means to help her develop an image of a car. For example, for Natalie to get a sense of the size of a real car, they can have her lightly touch the exterior of a car as she walks its perimeter, starting and stopping at a clearly identifiable point. They can also determine which features (such as the type of door and the number and position of seats, and the inside space) may be essential for someone who is deaf-blind to distinguish a car from other vehicles, such as buses, vans, or trucks, and help Natalie explore and identify them.

Just as Natalie sees small parts of large objects, she encounters a parallel situation with her hearing. When someone speaks to her, even in close proximity, she hears only parts of the words. The consonant sounds that allow the listener to distinguish between similarly constructed words, such as *man* and *pan* or *tin* and *did*, are inaudible to her. A total communication approach that emphasizes both speech and sign language is vital for providing Natalie and children with similar vision and hearing losses with complete information (see the next module for more information on total communication).

## EMOTIONAL DEVELOPMENT

### Bonding and Attachment Behaviors

Sensory impairments can have a profound influence on a child's emotional and social as well as cognitive development. In early infancy they can interfere with the interactive dialogue between the child and his or her parents: The infant is often unable to perceive and respond to the parents' voices or facial expressions, and it may not be possible for them to establish eye contact. This interference can disrupt a basic developmental foundation for communication and relationships. Barraga (1992, p. 33) noted that the interplay between the infant and his or her parents "provides a basis for establishing trust and security, and may supply the framework from which the infant organizes responses into a 'cognitive map' of self in relation to someone else and knowledge that there is a larger environment."

For infants who are deaf-blind, physical contact, such as touching, patting, and stroking, is especially important. Van Dijk (1989) encouraged parents to make touching and handling as meaningful as possible to their infants. He argued that deaf-blind people may engage in stereotypical behaviors, such as clinging, clutching them-selves, and other self-stimulating behaviors, in an attempt to seek security because their nurturing needs had not been met in infancy.

## Sense of Self and Body Image

As was already noted, early relationships affect an infant's sense of self, or self-concept. When combined vision and hearing losses limit early interactions, the establishment of a sense of self is a formidable task, since, as Warren (1984, p. 206) stated, "the blind child... does not have the visual experience of the relationship of his body parts or of the similarity of the parts and whole of his or her body to those of other people." Children who are deaf-blind may have difficulty form-ing the concept of where they end and someone else begins or what their bodies and beings truly encompass. As McInnes and Treffry (1982) noted, many do not develop the perception that their extrem-ities are parts of them. It can take effort for these children to develop this body awareness and sense of self, which hearing and sighted children seem to develop automatically.

The following example illustrates the difficulties that some chil-dren who are deaf-blind may have with body image:

*While waiting for the school buses to arrive, a teacher decided to play a version of hide-and-seek with a group of students, aged 7 to 11, who were deaf-blind. The teacher explained that she would hide somewhere in the classroom. From her hiding place, she watched the students look for her in the most unlike-ly places. They opened books and desk drawers, checked inside shoe boxes, ran their hands along the shelves of the bookcases, and tried to find her in places in which even their own smaller bodies could not possibly fit. The teacher was surprised that these bright students—who were at their grade level for many academic skills—had distorted concepts of the size of people in relation to other objects.*

As a result of her discovery, the teacher began to use hiding and obstacle-course games, art and measuring activities, and any sponta-neous opportunity to teach the students to become more aware of their bodies. She also recognized the importance of physical educa-tion and exercise in the students' programs, as well as activities that are designed to teach body image and environmental awareness (see Ideas for Enhancing Awareness of Body Image in this module).

## Motivation

From early infancy, visual and auditory stimuli provide children with motivation to interact with the environment. Infants smile when they see their parents' faces, pull themselves to standing when they see favorite toys, and localize their parents' voices and crawl to find them. Visual and auditory stimuli make the world an enticing place to infants, who are motivated to explore and interact in their environments because of this beguiling stimulation. Children who are deaf-blind, however, have severely limited access to these powerful stimuli; therefore, caregivers and teachers need to provide other means to interest them in engaging in interactions with other people and their environment. In addition to physical contact with other people, enticing stimuli for these children may include objects that vibrate, move, smell, and have textures, but it is important to use those that an individual child prefers.

THEORY into PRACTICE

## IDEAS FOR ENHANCING AWARENESS OF BODY IMAGE

Because children who are deaf-blind may need help to develop a clear sense of their bodies and the environment as a result of limited sensory input, activities that promote their awareness in these areas are particularly valuable. Here are some examples:

● During play and exercise periods with young children, include games, such as "Simon Says" and "Take a Giant Step," or interactive songs, such as "Head, Shoulder, Knees, and Toes," using the children's individualized communication systems.

● Carry out a regularly planned program of mat activities that require the children to crawl, roll, do push-ups and sit-ups, stretch, bend, and turn, using the children's individualized communication systems.

● Teach the children to be responsible for putting on, taking off, and storing their outer garments.

● Provide the children with opportunities to explore further the concept of body image by asking them to find parts of the teacher's body, such as the head, hair, shoulders, and extremities, using their individualized communication systems.

● Teach the children to use common communication gestures, including waving, pointing, and nodding yes or no, using their individualized communication systems. ■

## Perception of Safety

One's perception of safety is closely tied to one's motivation and willingness to interact with one's environment. The failure to interact with the surrounding environment will greatly influence a child's formation of basic concepts, establishment of relationships with others, knowledge of the surrounding world, and development of physical dexterity. Basic behavioral principles state that if experiences and interactions have been positive, they are likely to be repeated (Kazden, 1980). Positive experiences may further motivate a person to seek new experiences. However, if the individual does not feel safe, he or she will probably avoid certain situations.

Children who are deaf-blind may not always feel safe, and their daily routines can condition them to withdraw from the world because they are more vulnerable to potential danger. Dual sensory impairments often prevent access to the simplest cues for self-protection—a quick glimpse of a ball in flight or a low-hanging branch or the whine of a speeding bicycle. Deaf-blind individuals do not have the temporal margin of safety—those few seconds of advance warning—afforded by vision and hearing, so they cannot quickly move out of harm's way.

Many parents and teachers who work with students who are deaf-blind become overprotective because of their concerns for the children's safety in such situations as traffic, bodily attacks, and fires. Even with the best intentions, it is possible to stifle a child's curiosity, to patronize him or her, and to eliminate natural possibilities for learning and self-development. The modules in Unit 3 that emphasize orientation and mobility (O&M) skills offer numerous strategies for enhancing the safety of children who are deaf-blind, encouraging their involvement at home and in the community, and promoting their independence.

## Learned Helplessness

Parents and teachers may not only overprotect children who are deaf-blind, they may "overdo" things for children. This tendency can result in children developing what is called learned helplessness, the feeling that their lives do not make a difference and that they have no control over the environment. In a sense, they are "taught" to become unnecessarily dependent on their caregivers (Seligman, 1975; van Dijk, 1989).

People who are deaf-blind may fall into a pattern of learned helplessness because their access to visual and auditory information is severely limited, and they may be unaware that their actions can and do affect their environment. Thus, they may find it easier to let others intervene, resolve problems, and make decisions, and sometimes come to expect others to do so.

Teachers can unintentionally foster learned helplessness in their students, as the following example illustrates:

> *Rita is deaf-blind and attends a preschool class. Teachers, teaching assistants, and fellow classmates bring her anything she needs for classroom activities, including snacks and lunch. As she completes an activity, materials vanish from her desk. Rita cannot see or hear these comings or goings and is often not told what is taking place. She has no idea where things come from or what will appear next. What should Rita think when hands cross her desk all day long, making things appear or disappear? It is difficult to imagine that she feels any control over her environment. Rather, she has learned to expect that everything will be done for her.*

To foster Rita's independence, her teachers would have to let her know what activities are being planned and encourage her to participate in every step of the process: planning activities, gathering supplies, preparing snacks, and returning supplies. Her parents would need to encourage her independence at home as well. Rita could be given the assistance she needs while she is helped to become more interactive and involved in her daily activities and opportunities to exercise choices, so she could have some control over her environment.

## Isolation

Deaf-blindness may be the most isolating disability, given that society's chief forms of communication rely on visual and auditory devices, such as printed language, television, radio, telephones, and computers, and that purposeful independent movement is strongly related to the ability to see. As a result, people who are deaf-blind frequently may not participate fully in social activities.

Even simple social contact requires much effort for deaf-blind individuals, especially for those who do not have strong communication and mobility skills. Imagine, for example, a deaf-blind woman in a social gathering that includes many hearing and sighted people. Unless others have introduced themselves to her or she is told who is attending the event, she may not be aware of the kind and size of a room or who is in the room with her. Without the assistance of an interpreter who knows sign language or basic assistance in orienting herself to her surroundings, she will not be able to interact easily with the other guests. Even with a skilled tactile sign interpreter, it would be difficult for her to participate in group conversations because the pace is brisk, many people are speaking at once, and information conveyed by facial and body language may be difficult to discern. Social cues, signaling that it is time to circulate from group to group, may be difficult to interpret, and even if they are understood, mobility in an unfamiliar crowded room may present a formidable challenge. If food is served, the woman may need clear information about where it is and may have to stop conversing (communicating tactilely) to use her hands to eat the food. Without effective communication and mobility skills and accommodations by the group, it is likely that a person who is deaf-blind would feel isolated in this kind of social situation.

In the modules that follow, numerous strategies to help people who are deaf-blind counteract potential isolation are explored: effective ways to communicate, environmental adaptations that foster full participation, efficient means of movement, and a variety of means to support independence. Teachers can play a key role in helping deaf-blind students and students who are hearing and sighted interact as true peers. (For a sense of the importance of this role, see Growing Up with Deaf-Blindness.)

▲ *By helping her student have direct physical contact with an object, this teacher is contributing to the child's concept development and ability to form mental images.*

# CRITICAL FACTORS

The effects of deaf-blindness on the individual and his or her development are influenced by a number of factors. Four key factors in particular contribute to the impact of deaf-blindness on an individual child:

- age at onset of vision and hearing loss
- degree and type of vision and hearing loss

- stability of each sensory loss
- educational intervention.

The first three factors are physical, and the last factor is environmental. Understanding them will help families, teachers, and other service providers to design more effective instructional programs for children who are deaf-blind. (For more information about the causes of deaf-blindness, see Appendix A.)

# Growing Up with Deaf-Blindness
Robert J. Smithdas

When I was 4½ years old, I was stricken with cerebrospinal meningitis and became totally blind and lost nearly all my hearing. I could not hear my own voice, and only loud sounds, such as hammering or thunder, penetrated my silence. But within four years, what little hearing that remained disappeared overnight, leaving me totally deaf.

I was fortunate while growing up that my parents and other members of my family did not inhibit my curiosity and initiative. Within reason, I was permitted to explore my environment and experiment with new objects, such as tools, and was included in as many family activities as possible. I was equally fortunate that most of my teachers at the Western Pennsylvania School for the Blind, which I eventually attended, were also flexible. They restricted me only when there was a possibility of danger or inappropriate action.

During my first year in school, I was given private instruction in reading and writing braille. Later, I learned the manual alphabet and print-on-palm to communicate with my family. All my school assignments were given to and completed by me in braille.

I did not participate in the classroom, however, because the speech I had developed before I lost my hearing began to blur and become unintelligible. Some of my classmates learned to communicate with me via fingerspelling, but I was excluded from their play activities. This situation might have led to an intense sense of isolation if I had not been fond of reading and doing hobbies.

At 16, I was sent to the Perkins School for the Blind, where I learned the Tadoma method of lipreading by vibration and received intensive speech therapy. The skills I have learned (speech, fingerspelling, basic sign language, print-on-palm, braille, and Tadoma) and keeping mentally and physically active have helped me overcome the isolation imposed by deafness and blindness. But most important, I know I am accepted as a human being who is part of society and the lives of others. ■

## AGE OF ONSET

The earlier in life a disability develops, the more significant the effects are for learning, and this is especially so regarding disabilities of vision and hearing. Reduced access to precise information from interactions with people and objects may affect the development of basic concepts during critical developmental periods. The development of motor skills and cognitive skills is affected most by early losses of vision and hearing. As a result, the formulation of concepts and mobility skills requires more time and repetition in the face of these sensory losses. Early intervention provides a child who is deaf-blind with ways to get information that is vital for concept development. Early support for parents gives them tools to help their infants and toddlers who are deaf-blind develop. (For more information on infancy and toddlerhood, see Modules 7 and 16.)

The loss of vision and hearing in adulthood can present difficulties, but concept development and mobility are less likely to be affected because most basic concepts have been learned and new information can be obtained by adapting the mode for receiving it. Adjustments in mobility and daily routines can be learned, building on previously learned information and concepts.

## DEGREE, TYPE, AND STABILITY OF EACH LOSS

Even a small amount of residual vision or hearing can be helpful for gaining information and learning new concepts and skills. Most people who are called deaf-blind have either some useful hearing or some useful vision; few lose all their hearing and vision. In either case, they have access to some of the same environmental information as do other people. All information that can be obtained and used supports the development of concepts and greater independence in decision making for daily activities.

Some disorders, diseases, and other conditions that contribute to deaf-blindness are progressive. For example, the hearing loss from Usher syndrome is usually stable, but the vision loss from retinitis pigmentosa (RP) is progressive. Neurological disorders may be stable or progressive, and some or all the resulting disabilities may increase quickly or gradually over time. Information-processing abilities may change or become more limited; in addition, tactile perception and processing may decrease.

When progressive losses occur for whatever reason, people who are deaf-blind may need to adjust how they obtain and use environmental information. They can adapt independent travel techniques, find new ways to perform tasks, and learn new ways to communicate.

Progressive losses may be confusing or upsetting to individuals who do not know what to expect. Instruction in new skills as they are needed, for example, in using braille or a cane or a hearing aid, can help a student with a progressive loss prepare for life with reduced sight or hearing through a knowledge of new strategies for obtaining auditory and visual information and for performing daily tasks.

Older students with progressive vision and hearing losses may find it helpful to discuss the emotional issues with a counselor who is sensitive to the life changes that must be made, such as dealing with the inability to listen to the radio, watch television, or read. Counselors can also help students deal with the perceptions of and interactions with peers. For example, a student with Usher syndrome among classmates who are deaf may be reluctant to use a long cane or begin to use large print or braille to read because these obvious symbols of vision loss can set the student apart from other students who use vision for virtually all communication. Few teenagers, including students who have Usher syndrome, want to be different from peers, and they may resist the adaptations they need to travel and read.

Children who do not have strong communication skills may have a more difficult time understanding and managing the adjustments they must make to progressive losses of vision or hearing. Teachers who are aware of the medical factors in students' lives can be alert to behavior that signals decreasing vision or hearing (see Signs of Vision Loss and Signs of Hearing Loss in this module and Appendix A for information on various causes of deaf-blindness, including progressive forms).

Students with limited communication skills may not be able to express what is bothering them. Therefore, it is important to watch for changes in behavior that may signal frustration, confusion, or a different level of functioning that is due to decreasing sensory information. Ongoing observation and documentation of behavior, as well as periodic formal assessments, allow teachers to detect rapidly any changes in students' vision or hearing and to help students adjust to these changes.

## SIGNS OF VISION LOSS

- Bumps into objects.

- Moves hesitantly or walks close to the wall.

- Gropes for objects or touches them in an uncertain way.

- Squints or tilts the head to see.

- Requests additional or different kinds of lighting.

- Holds books or other visual material close to the face.

- Drops objects or knocks them over.

- Shows difficulty in making out faces or the numbers that designate rooms or floors.

- Looks ungroomed or sloppy, with stains on clothing or uncombed hair.

- Acts confused or disoriented, for example, walks into the wrong room by mistake. ■

If a student, especially one with limited communication skills, seems to be experiencing additional losses of vision or hearing, what can a teacher do to help?

- Work constantly with the student's family members to learn which behaviors they are noticing at home and how they interact with the child.

- Increase physical closeness while teaching; use more one-to-one individualization, particularly for learning new skills; and encourage more "hands-on" work, especially if the child has been using residual vision for many tasks.

- Demonstrate more activities and be sure that the student has access to tactile information (in addition to visual or auditory information) for the activity or object being presented.

- Review the environment to see what adaptations may be needed, including increased lighting on the child's communication board or desk and the reduction of noise.

- Adapt materials or activities to include (1) more tactile information (for example, by outlining picture figures on a communication board with puffy paint), (2) increased visual information (for instance, by photocopying enlargements of

## *SIGNS OF HEARING LOSS*

- Gives no response when spoken to.

- Often gives irrelevant or incorrect responses to questions.

- Seems unable to follow spoken directions to carry out an activity.

- Often says "huh?" or "what?" and requires repetition.

- Seems unaware that others are talking and interrupts conversations.

- Seems to have a behavioral problem or is irritable.

- Expresses confusion or uncertainty when unable to understand.

- Holds head in an abnormal position to listen "better"; seems unable to locate the source of a sound.

- Watches a speaker's face intently.

- Seems inattentive, but pays more attention to visual things.

- Speaks more loudly or softly than expected for a situation. Has an unusual vocal tone or resonance or patterns of speaking.

- Uses gestures to get attention and objects more than would be expected.

- Seems to have language problems (structure, syntax, vocabulary).

- Seems to withdraw from interactions in groups.

- Has frequent colds, earaches or ear infections, and allergies.

- Breathes through the mouth more than through the nose.

- Complains or shows signs of ear pain, fullness in the ear, dizziness, or balance problems.■

pictures or print materials), and (3) increased auditory information (such as by moving closer to the student or putting a room-size carpet remnant on the floor to reduce noise).

- Introduce new activities or changes in routines or classroom arrangements carefully. Give the student time to adjust to the new routines and introduce them as many times as is necessary.

- Give the student more time to perform newly adapted tasks.

- Provide the student with more tactile feedback and frequent assurance that you are nearby, with a pat on the shoulder, for example. For a child whose sensory information is diminishing over time, this kind of reassurance is comforting and can help reestablish environmental predictability that once came primarily with visual or auditory information.

Any student whose loss of vision or hearing (or both) is progressive needs help in confirming that many aspects of the world are the same as they were, but access to them is changing. The student needs to know that the teacher is still present and ready to interact with and assist him or her, although with more tactile than visual and auditory features. Observing the student's behavior and adapting tasks as necessary are the best tools for helping the student adjust to the progressive visual and auditory changes he or she is experiencing.

## EDUCATIONAL INTERVENTION

The amount and type of educational intervention a child who is deaf-blind has had will influence the overall effects of his or her combined vision and hearing losses. If adequate assistance and information are provided for parents of an infant or toddler who is deaf-blind, the child's understanding of the immediate environment and relationships with people in it can be enhanced, and the child can participate more fully. If consistent, ongoing, and appropriate instruction is provided, the child can learn skills for independent communication, movement, and overall daily living.

# FORMS OF DEAF-BLINDNESS

Teachers can work with students more effectively when they are familiar with the major forms of deaf-blindness and the implications of these forms for children's educational needs. In the descriptions that follow, the interplay among the age of onset, the degree of sensory loss, and the stability of each loss can be seen.

## EARLY DEAF-BLINDNESS

People tend to think of early onset when they hear the term "deaf-blind." This is the most obvious form, since it is the most extreme, although it is not the most frequent. People with early deaf-blindness

- have both visual and hearing losses at birth or by age 2
- have severe to profound losses of both vision and hearing

- lack access to much environmental information, except within arm's reach.

The most well-known person with early deaf-blindness is Helen Keller, who had an infection with a high fever at around 18 months that left her without useful vision and hearing. Although Keller had been learning the ordinary things that infants and toddlers learn before age 18 months, her access to her environment changed dramatically after she became deaf-blind. She no longer learned new concepts by observing and listening to people, events, and things around her. Several years later, it took many hours at the water pump with her new teacher Anne Sullivan before Keller remembered the word that she had just begun to learn to say before her illness, "wa-wa" for water. With intense individualized instruction, she developed many skills for independent living.

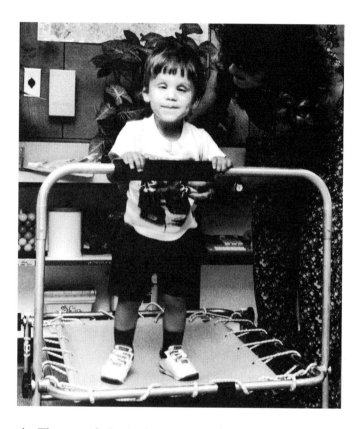

▲ *The use of physical closeness and one-to-one individualization is a particularly effective strategy, especially when teaching new skills.*

Clearly, there are many implications for the development and learning of a child with this form of deaf-blindness. However, the major overall implication is that the observation and imitation of actions and language (both spoken and signed) probably will not occur naturally because visual and auditory inputs are inaccessible, which may limit learning and cause delays in the development of skills. Some techniques that parents and teachers can use to facilitate development are these:

- Parents and teachers can interact with the child using movement, physical closeness, and touch to promote the development of communication. (Even tactile sign language may be used early.)

- One-to-one interaction (typical for parents with young children) promotes the development of relationships with significant people and can easily be expanded to include siblings, extended family members, and neighbors.

- Information from smell and taste can supplement information from touch and movement.
- Parents and teachers can introduce concepts with hands-on demonstrations and repetition.

## EARLY, LESS SEVERE HEARING AND VISUAL IMPAIRMENTS

Most people who are identified as deaf-blind have some useful residual vision, residual hearing, or both. People in this category

- have the combined partial impairments from birth or early childhood
- have mild to moderate losses of both senses
- usually receive incomplete or indistinct visual and auditory information (blurry, vague, muffled)
- can learn to interpret even minimal visual and auditory information meaningfully with training and assistive devices
- can use this information for developing language, communication, mobility, and conceptual skills
- are likely to have gaps in concept development because of the reduced information available to them
- can benefit from multisensory input to fill in the gaps in concept development.

Parents and teachers often assume that if vision losses are corrected with eyeglasses and hearing losses are amplified with hearing aids, children should not be regarded as deaf-blind. Some children use residual vision with eyeglasses and hearing with hearing aids well, but some do not. Many factors can interfere with the children's information gathering, including background noise, such as traffic noise from a major street or an air-conditioning system, and variable lighting, as when natural lighting from windows is dimmed on a cloudy day.

Parents and teachers can and should continually monitor and interact with students with partial vision and hearing to ensure that they are getting the information they need to learn concepts accurately. They can use the following simple techniques to do so:

- To check the child's perceptions of what is occurring in the environment and his or her general concept development, ask the child: "What just happened here? What did you see [or hear]?"

- To check the child's comprehension of a message, have the child retell what you described or demonstrate something you have just shown and explained.

- Repeat and rephrase what you have previously explained for more clarity.

- Provide multisensory information with each new experience or concept; adapt information for touch, movement (together or by imitation), smell, or taste if appropriate.

Children with partial vision and hearing can often participate in a variety of activities using their residual vision and hearing. With some structured training and much repetition, they can learn to interpret information more easily and automatically.

## EARLY HEARING DISABILITY WITH LATER VISION LOSS

Some children have been deaf or have had significant hearing impairments from birth or early childhood and use vision for most information gathering and learning. A number of them may have significant vision losses later in life and become deaf-blind. A child who is deaf or hard-of-hearing and later loses vision

- has the hearing impairment at birth or by age 2
- has a mild to profound hearing loss that may contribute to delayed language and speech development
- has subsequent delays in learning reading and writing skills, as well as delays in developing related academic skills because of delays in language development
- can generally master daily living activities through visual imitation without major difficulty.

Significant educational implications are related to the last two items on the list. Parents and teachers can adapt daily living activities, like dressing and eating, with visual imitation. More formal adaptation may be required to teach communication effectively (see the following module for more information).

The leading cause of this form of deaf-blindness is Usher syndrome, which affects from 3 percent to 10 percent of all people who have hearing impairments (Duncan, Prickett, Vernon, Finkelstein & Hollingsworth, 1988). The vision loss that accompanies Usher syndrome can become especially significant during the teenage years and adulthood (see Usher Syndrome for more information). Other causes of this form of deaf-blindness include early deafness, followed later by detached retinas; Refsum's syndrome; Friedreich's ataxia (which also results in a motor disability and progressive dam-

**T H E O R Y into P R A C T I C E**

## USHER SYNDROME

Usher syndrome involves both a genetic hearing loss and a genetic vision loss that is due to retinitis pigmentosa (RP). Although the hearing loss is usually obvious from birth or early childhood, the vision loss is often more gradual (Duncan, Prickett, Vernon, Finkelstein & Hollingsworth, 1988; Stiefel, 1991).

Two visual problems that children with Usher syndrome develop early are night blindness and the loss of peripheral vision. Central vision is affected later, and because children with Usher syndrome may have sharp acuity for reading print and for daily living activities, the diagnosis of Usher syndrome may not be made until adolescence or adulthood.

Two types of Usher syndrome are prevalent—Type I and Type II. In Type I, severe to profound hearing loss is present at birth, but vision loss does not become obvious until adolescence, and by middle age, most individuals have lost much of their vision. In Type II, mild to moderate or even more significant hearing loss is usually present at birth, but the vision loss is more gradual than in Type I, and some people never become totally blind.

Because only peripheral vision is lost in childhood, and Usher syndrome is usually not diagnosed in childhood, children may experience difficult social and emotional circumstances as a result of misunderstandings. For example, they may be labeled clumsy because they bump into or stumble over objects or be considered inattentive or stuck-up because they cannot detect people or objects from the side.

In addition, children with Usher syndrome are often edu-cated with other children who are deaf and hard-of-hearing and grow up participating in recreational activities in the deaf culture. Therefore, when their vision losses become severe in young adulthood, they may be unable to participate in these activities or to use sign language or speechreading and hence may feel isolated from the close-knit, supportive deaf community. Furthermore, their communication with their families can become limited, and family members often become overprotective. Therefore, counseling is important especially for deaf teenagers with RP to help them cope with the gradual and anticipated changes in their vision; to deal with possible comments and teasing from peers and others; and to make decisions about a number of issues, including driving and letting others know what visual adaptations they need. ■

age to the central nervous system); and early deafness with later trauma or loss of vision from an accident or medication (see Appendix A for specific conditions mentioned in this module that cause deaf-blindness).

Most people with significant early hearing losses have learned many basic concepts and skills using visual information and experiences, and many also use American Sign Language (ASL). As their visual impairments progress, they are likely to need to learn new ways to get written and signed information, including the use of tactile sign language or fingerspelling for communication directly with other people and reading in large print or braille (see Modules 3 and 8–10 for more information).

## EARLY VISUAL DISABILITY WITH LATER HEARING LOSS

An individual who has been blind or visually impaired from birth may acquire a hearing loss later and become deaf-blind. Some causes of this form of deaf-blindness include

- damage to the ears from accidents or infections
- the use of medicines, such as mycin drugs, that can damage hearing
- syndromes like Leber's amaurosis (in which the hearing loss, if there is one, may occur in childhood).

Children with this form of deaf-blindness

- have mild to significant visual impairment or are blind at birth or by age 2
- have access to auditory information, especially language, and their parents tend to rely on spoken language, movement, and tactile information to support their concept and mobility development
- learn to read and write using braille or regular or large print, depending on the degree of vision loss and the amount of remaining useful vision, with spoken language as the basis for reading
- probably will not need an adapted reading method (braille or large print) if the visual impairment is mild and stable because a later hearing loss will not affect already developed reading skills

- can learn academic subjects normally in elementary and secondary school if their hearing loss does not occur until adulthood and they have no additional disabilities

- have already learned to perform daily living activities (such as selecting clothing, brushing teeth, or crossing streets safely) that would typically be learned through visual imitation using adaptations and demonstrations involving movement and tactile information combined with auditory information, including spoken descriptions

- will need to learn new ways to obtain auditory information, for example, by reading news in braille, rather than listening to television or radio, or by having a person read mail with fingerspelling.

## LATER SENSORY LOSSES

People who lose both vision and hearing either as young adults or later in life also may be considered deaf-blind. Those whose sensory losses occur when they are young adults

- have already mastered essential movement and communication skills using vision and hearing

- can learn new adaptive life skills for movement and communication based on previously learned concepts and skills

- may have additional disabilities resulting from the same diseases or conditions that caused their visual and hearing losses, such as accidents, brain tumors, stroke, or spinal meningitis

- may find counseling helpful for psychological-emotional issues that are sometimes associated with the sudden or gradual loss of vision and hearing that interferes with long-established ways of communicating and performing daily routines

- may need to relearn academic or job skills without visual and auditory information or may need to train for different types of work entirely.

The ease with which individuals relearn concepts and skills for daily life varies greatly. Traumatic brain injury, for example, can cause neurological and processing difficulties that affect a person's ability to use auditory and visual information meaningfully. Strategies for getting information and completing activities can be adapted, though, to include more information from touch, as well as taste, smell, and movement. Special training and assistance are often available through state rehabilitation agencies that serve adults with disabilities or through the Helen Keller National Center for Deaf-Blind Youths and Adults (see the Resources section for more information).

## DEAF-BLINDNESS AND ADDITIONAL DISABILITIES

Many children who are deaf-blind have additional disabilities, including motor and cognitive disabilities, usually for the same reasons they are deaf-blind. Additional disabilities may entail further learning challenges for children and instructional challenges for their families and teachers. In general, such multiple disabilities further remove the child from easy access to and understanding of the environment. Not only may the child have limited access to sensory information, but he or she may have difficulty processing interactions with people and objects and attaching meaning to these interactions. The profile of early deaf-blindness (including partial vision and hearing) applies to these students as well, and additional factors are considered here.

Some common reasons for deaf-blindness with multiple disabilities are rubella (German measles), cytomegalovirus inclusion disease (CMV), and prematurity (see Appendix A). Intervention that begins early and is consistent promotes concept development. Children who are deaf-blind and have multiple disabilities benefit from interactions with family members, other relatives, and neighbors in their communities. With these interactions, the children can learn important communication and movement skills to become more independent.

### Motor Disabilities

Some children who are deaf-blind have significant motor disabilities, such as from cerebral palsy. It may be more difficult for them to get information from the environment because they do not move easily to explore and interact with people and objects in the environment and their motor disabilities may limit their ability to grasp and manipulate objects to get tactile information. Restricted movement, in addition to the lack of access to visual and auditory information, can dramatically delay concept building, communication, and the development of life skills. Children who are deaf-blind and have motor disabilities must have access to all the elements of their environments to understand what is happening around them, just as do all other children. "Purposeful movement is communication with the environment... [and] the development of movement is inseparably linked to communication skills" (Langley & Thomas, 1991, p. 2). Parents and teachers therefore need to adapt environments and routines at home and at school so these students have access to information (Dunn, 1991). Some practical solutions are these:

- Keep the learning environment safe and uncluttered, to promote movement.

- Show children how to explore and encourage them to do so by moving with them to and through an activity.

- Set up instructional and play activities on low tables or the floor and ensure that children who move with wheelchairs, walkers, and other equipment can do so safely and easily in all areas.

- Help students position themselves at each activity area, so they can perform activities comfortably. Consult the physical therapist and the occupational therapist on the educational team to learn the best ways to do so.

- Encourage children to move very close to objects, people, and areas, so they can interact with and gain useful information from them.

## Cognitive Disabilities

Cognitive disabilities also can challenge children who are deaf-blind and those who interact with them. Impairments of cognitive functioning hinder the way the brain processes information and responds to it. When a child lacks access to information from the environment, making sense of the available information is even more difficult. Some of the common causes of deaf-blindness, like those mentioned in the introduction to this section (rubella, CMV, and prematurity) can cause cognitive disabilities (Batshaw & Perret, 1986). Children who are deaf-blind and have impaired cognitive abilities

- may not always process the auditory and visual information they receive quickly or meaningfully, even with guidance.

- can have difficulty with learning "strategies" or tools because they do not always relate previous experiences to the present and do not respond from their previous exposure to and interpretation of similar information (McCormick, 1984, p. 179).

- may have difficulty learning abstract concepts, but can learn concrete and immediate concepts with repeated experience and interaction. Examples of concrete experiences include daily routines, such as getting ready for school, going to swim with family members at a local pool on a scheduled basis, and mealtime or bedtime routines.

- can benefit from functional curricular activities that develop essential life skills like dressing and feeding themselves, performing basic hygiene tasks, and understanding basic safety concepts (see Teaching Functional Activities).

- can benefit from community-based activities and instruction that occurs in natural settings, such as pools, playgrounds, and stores.

- need multisensory information from touch, movement, smell, and taste for every activity to supplement any visual or auditory information that may be accessible.

Functional and community-based activities that begin early and occur frequently are the most advantageous for children who are deaf-blind and have cognitive disabilities.

## Neurological Disorders

Some forms of deaf-blindness are accompanied or caused by neurological disorders. Neurological disorders that affect the central nervous system (the brain and spinal cord, primarily) can affect the processing of information and can cause additional deterioration of vision, hearing, and cognitive and motor function (Batshaw & Perret, 1986).

In some cases, the reasons for neurological disorders are unknown. In other cases, identified genetic or congenital disorders bring about neurological problems. For example, prematurity may be accompanied by neurological problems, depending on the newborn's gestational age at birth and complications with oxygen in an incubator. Premature infants who were born early in gestation may not have had adequate time for their neurological systems to develop completely.

Head injury (traumatic brain injury) from an accident or another trauma may also cause disorders that include visual and hearing losses. A child with a head injury or similar neurological disorder (for example, childhood stroke, a rare occurrence) learns differently

HELP *at a* GLANCE

## TEACHING FUNCTIONAL ACTIVITIES

When a task or activity is strictly functional, it means that it must be done either by the student or for the student if the student cannot accomplish it. Examples of functional tasks and activities include these:

- Brushing teeth and hair, bathing, dressing, and eating.
- Functional communication skills, such as getting another person's attention appropriately, requesting something, or making a need known.
- Functional academic skills, including reading and writing one's name and address or knowing how much change one should get when one pays for an item.
- Leisure activities.

Teaching functional skills involves

- *Modeling—showing the student how to perform an activity.* For students with little vision and hearing, use full touch guidance and move with them using hand-over-hand guidance. For students with some vision or hearing or both, use close visual demonstration (with touch as a supporting sense) to clarify specific movements or concepts.

  As you model, "explain" what you are doing and why, using the student's most effective communication mode (speech, signing, indicating a picture from the student's vocabulary board, gesturing, and so on).

- *Practicing—after initial instruction, reinforcing the new activities by doing them over and over with the student until the activity patterns and communication about them become spontaneous.* For some students, only parts of activities will become spontaneous. Let the students do those parts independently and assist with the rest.

- *Incorporating situations and routines that require the skills.* Design the instructional day so the most vital functional routines, natural and anticipated, are included. Students are more likely to perform functional activities successfully if the activities are routine, predictable, and meaningful on a daily basis. ■

from a child with more "traditional" forms of deaf-blindness. Children who are deaf-blind and have neurological impairments

- may have various degrees of vision, hearing, cognitive, and motor impairments
- may process and interpret visual and auditory information with minor errors or with more significant distortions
- may have organic forms of deaf-blindness resulting from impairment in the eyes and ears or may have brain damage such that even with intact eye and ear function, the brain does

not use any of the visual or auditory information it receives (sometimes called "cortical deaf-blindness")

- may have sensory integration problems, or difficulty sorting and processing information from the senses when several forms of information are received at the same time (Morris, 1991)

- may resist touch or any kind of tactile stimulation (called "tactile defensiveness")

- can benefit from the slow and repeated introduction of movement and tactile information and touch cuing, combined with any auditory and visual cues they can use

- can benefit from the structured, individualized, multisensory instructional programs that are described throughout these materials.

Sensory integration problems occur when a child's brain receives much more sensory stimulation than it can process at one time. The amount of information that causes a sensory overload differs for each child with sensory integration problems, however. Therefore, parents and teachers may need to monitor a child's response to unusual or new sensory information and reduce some of the information the child receives for a time until the child can manage it, as the example of Nicky illustrates:

> *Nicky participated with the entire school in assemblies, but his teachers noted that during assemblies he would become rigid in his wheelchair and breathe heavily, as if hyperventilating— behavior that he did not exhibit anywhere else in school. A visiting teacher who worked with Nicky suggested that all the visual and auditory information in the large crowd of children might be difficult for Nicky to process with his remaining vision and hearing. After staff members turned his hearing aid to a lower volume for the next assembly, Nicky did not become rigid or breathe heavily during the assembly.*

Nicky's deaf-blindness and motor disability resulted from a head injury with neurological damage, and his difficulties with the noise and visual activity in assemblies were probably due to sensory integration problems. Reducing one of the sensory factors, the volume of sound, allowed Nicky to participate more effectively in this group situation.

## SPECIAL HEALTH CARE NEEDS

Chronic, significant medical problems may occur with some forms of deaf-blindness. Children who have special health care needs because of their medical problems are sometimes referred to as "medically fragile" and may

- use respirator equipment for breathing
- be limited in their movement as a result of the equipment they need for health conditions, such as a respirator with a long tube attached directly to their chests
- be fed with gastrointestinal tubes
- have motor disabilities
- need frequent medical attention from a qualified medical service provider, such as a nurse
- have repeated absences from school for health care
- miss out on some family interactions because of hospitalizations
- benefit from being in ordinary instructional settings with appropriate medical supports
- benefit from as much community interaction and experience as is possible
- benefit from having experiences "brought to them" (such as visits from neighborhood children), so they do not miss opportunities for interaction.

Children who are medically fragile often need special support for participation. When you work with them, their participation depends on your understanding and accommodating these special needs. Here are some things you can do:

- Learn everything you can about a student's medical needs and consider how the child's medical and educational needs can be linked, so both are met.
- Find out how the family handles everyday activities at home and visit the family to get ideas.
- Check with the child's physician to learn about health and safety considerations. Include the physician on the child's educational planning team.
- Be sure that everyone who works with the student under-

stands emergency procedures. You can request an in-service session on monitoring the student for an emergency condition and how to know when the student needs medical help.

- To ensure that instructional routines and schedules accommodate the student's medical needs, you may have to alter activities to allow time to move the student and any equipment he or she uses, change the classroom setup to allow room for extra equipment, and schedule more rest periods for the student or for the entire class.

- Develop strategies for including the student in field trips, assemblies, and other out-of-class activities that all students attend. You may need to request one or more volunteers or a temporary aide, who can help with other students during these events, so you and the regular aide who is assigned to the student can concentrate on helping the student participate.

- As the teacher, it is important for you to monitor the student's participation in all class activities to ensure that the student has access to all the instructional opportunities that the other students have.

# SUGGESTIONS FOR LEARNING

Given the variation in the effects and forms of deaf-blindness, the most effective way to understand the implications of being deaf-blind for an individual student is to get to know the student. By observing students in various environments and situations and while performing daily living, recreational, academic and/or job-related tasks, you will learn what information is important to them and how they gather information. Observe them explore, manipulate, respond to, and learn about new clothing, toys, household items, tools, foods, low- and high-tech communication systems, new classrooms, recreational facilities, and other environments in their communities. Observe them communicate their wants, likes, and dislikes through body language, facial expressions, and language systems. Keep in mind that you need to give them sufficient time to respond to information provided through the senses. These students may need considerably more time than you might expect because they need to explore objects and environments, using their sense of touch and other senses to gather information slowly and systematically, and relate the new experiences to those of the past.

Children who are deaf-blind usually do not have the advantage of effortless learning and access to information. And they may not have access to visual and auditory information, or the visual and auditory information they receive may be limited, distorted, or incomplete. Therefore, they need to

- be taught many of the things that others learn incidentally
- be provided with direct experience, information, and repetition, so they can learn to predict situations and develop concepts
- be given opportunities to apply what they have learned to new and varied situations and environments
- complement visual and auditory information with information from the other senses
- maximize the use of tactile information
- be instructed in how to examine things systematically
- be motivated to explore and get involved with other people and things in the environment
- feel secure, so they can reach out and engage people and things and realize some control over their environments.

For students who are deaf-blind to get the most information possible from experiences and to compensate for the loss of the distance senses, it is essential that teachers help their students fully develop their communication and O&M skills. The modules that follow provide suggestions for ways in which these skills can be promoted and instruction can be delivered effectively.

# REFERENCES

Barraga, N. C. (1992). *Visual handicaps and learning* (3rd ed.). Austin, TX: PRO-ED.

Batshaw, M. L., & Perret, Y. M. (1986). *Children with handicaps: A medical primer*. Baltimore: Paul H. Brookes.

Duncan, E., Prickett, H. T., Vernon, M., Finkelstein, D., & Hollingsworth, T. (1988). *Usher's syndrome: What it is, how to cope and how to help*. Springfield, IL: Charles C Thomas.

Dunn, W. (1991). The sensorimotor systems: A framework for assessment and intervention. In F. P. Orelove & D. Sobsey (Eds.), *Educating children with multiple disabilities* (pp. 33–78). Baltimore: Paul H. Brookes.

Freeman, P. (1985). *The deaf/blind baby: A programme of care*. London: William Heinemann Medical Books.

Kazden, A. E. (1980). *Behavior modification in applied settings*. Homewood, IL: Dorsey Press.

Langley, M. B., & Thomas, C. (1991). Introduction to the neurodevelopmental approach. In M. B. Langley & L. J. Lombardino (Eds.), *Neurodevelopmental strategies for managing communication disorders in children with severe motor dysfunction* (pp. 1–28). Austin, TX: Pro-Ed.

McCormick, L. (1984). Intervention planning. In L. McCormick & R. L. Schiefelbusch (Eds.), *Early language intervention* (pp. 157–200). Columbus, OH: Charles E. Merrill.

McInnes, J. M., & Treffry, J. A. (1982). *Deaf-blind infants and children: A developmental guide*. Toronto: University of Toronto Press.

Morris, S. E. (1991). Facilitation of learning. In M. B. Langley & L. J. Lombardino (Eds.), *Neurodevelopmental strategies for managing communication disorders in children with severe motor dysfunction* (pp. 251–296). Austin, TX: PRO-ED.

Seligman, M. E. (1975). *Helplessness: On depression, death, and development*. San Francisco: W. H. Freeman.

Stiefel, D. H. (1991). *The "madness" of Usher's: Coping with vision and hearing loss*. Corpus Christi, TX: Business of Living Publications.

van Dijk, J. (1989). *The Sint-Michielgestel approach to diagnosis and education of multisensory impaired persons*. Paper presented at Warwick, England.

Warren, D. (1984). *Blindness and early childhood development* (2nd ed.). New York: American Foundation for the Blind.

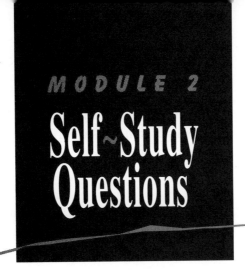

# Self~Study Questions

1. The incidental learning of students who are deaf-blind is limited primarily because the students
   a. are not motivated to learn.
   b. receive reduced information from the distance senses.
   c. have developed learned helplessness.

2. The use of models may not be effective with students who are deaf-blind because
   a. they are based on visual information.
   b. the students are not yet able to think symbolically.
   c. both a and b.

3. Van Dijk, a leader in the field of deaf-blindness, contended that the stereotypical behaviors exhibited by some individuals who are deaf-blind may be due to
   a. the lack of early bonding and attachment with parents.
   b. overstimulation.
   c. health problems.

4. Knowing specific facts about the origins of a student's deaf-blindness can help service providers
   a. decide on adult living preferences during transition years.
   b. decide how much mobility training an individual should receive.
   c. determine how much information a student may be getting and how concepts are learned.

5. Students who are deaf-blind as a result of combined losses of hearing and vision that are progressive
   a. must constantly adjust how they obtain and use information.
   b. will be able to continue to use their original methods of communication.
   c. may need extensive genetic counseling to assist them with treatment options.

6. A child who has been blind since birth and loses hearing at age 10
   a. is likely to need instruction in braille, so he or she will be able to continue participating in class and to keep up with written classwork.
   b. will need an evaluation for O&M training and may need to learn many new mobility techniques.
   c. has learned basic concepts through hearing spoken language and may be able to continue reading in the format he or she was used to, but is likely to need to learn new ways of getting information from classroom discussions.

7. Children who have combined significant vision and hearing losses from birth
   a. readily gain basic environmental information through informal interactions with caregivers in the course of everyday activities.
   b. usually need carefully structured one-to-one interaction with caregivers on a routine basis.
   c. usually benefit from sign language input that relies on vision at close range ("near" or "close" vision).

8. Additional disabilities that children who are deaf-blind may have can affect learning by
   a. preventing them from moving freely within their environments to explore and interact.
   b. preventing them from sharing with siblings.
   c. affecting their processing and understanding of information because of sensory integration problems.
   d. all the above.

*Answers to self-study questions for this module appear at the end of Unit 1.*

# Deaf-Blindness and Communication

## JEANNE GLIDDEN PRICKETT

### CONTRIBUTORS

**STEVE PERREAULT**
*Teaching Methods to Expand Communication*

**ROBERT D. STILLMAN**
**ANGELA LINAM**
**CHRISTY WILLIAMS**
*Use of Routines*

- *Interact frequently and consistently*

- *Use multisensory information*

- *Use tactile and close-range signing as appropriate*

- *Focus on individualized interaction*

- *Stress structure, repetition, and routines*

- *Encourage direct communication among classmates*

Deaf-blindness greatly reduces the amount and kind of information an individual gets from others and from the environment. That information is the key to the development of all basic concepts and subsequent learning. The development of communication skills can be especially affected, since people typically rely on a combination of vision and hearing to learn how to communicate.

The loss of one distance sense, sight or hearing, changes the nature of communication somewhat, but not as dramatically as deaf-blindness does. The impact of blindness, deafness, and deaf-blindness on communication and language development is explored in this module, as are ways to foster communication skills in children who are deaf-blind.

# EFFECTS OF VISUAL IMPAIRMENTS

Children who are born with significant visual impairments can hear spoken language and learn it naturally, although they may never fully comprehend certain concepts. For example, the relative sizes of large buildings may not be clear because the visual information to support the concept is inaccessible. Jack, a college student who was completely blind before his first birthday, said that he thought that he might understand the concept of "skyscraper" better by climbing all the steps to the top because knowing how much time it took to do so might give him a sense of the physical distance.

Children with visual impairments lack access to other nonlinguistic forms of communication. For instance, they may be unable to use eye contact to initiate and end conversations or to understand turn-taking. They may also not be able to interpret body language visually to help them understand a speaker's mood and meaning, since typical communication distances may be out of their useful visual ranges.

Although much of the information that people get from communication is nonverbal, or nonlinguistic, spoken language nevertheless gives a visually impaired person adequate information for daily living. A person who is visually impaired can participate in daily activities on an equal footing with those who are sighted, especially when spoken language is a central feature of the interaction, as in a classroom. With some adaptations and special training, an individual who has significant vision loss can lead an independent life in the community.

# IMPACT OF HEARING LOSS

Children who are born with significant hearing losses or who lose hearing early do not have easy access to spoken language and information for daily living. Typically, parents and other caregivers interact frequently with infants and toddlers by commenting on people, events, and objects in the environment. Infants and toddlers begin to attach meaning to those comments, making associations between spoken language and the people, activities, and items that are described. (For additional information on communication development, see Modules 6 and 7.)

The early development of concepts in deaf children is based on a primarily visual interaction with caregivers, and the children learn many concrete visual concepts. Abstract concepts, however, are more difficult to learn without accessible language to explain them. Thus, children who are deaf easily learn what to do with utensils and clothing, but may have more difficulty with ideas like "sick" and "pain."

The child who is deaf from birth and has ordinary cognitive abilities can observe his or her environment and learn many basic concepts, such as how to put on clothes, just by watching family members. The child's hearing loss may go undetected until late toddlerhood or even the preschool years because he or she performs daily activities so well, as the case of Brenda illustrates.

> The mother of Brenda, a child who has been deaf since birth, said, "She did so many things like my other children that it never occurred to me that she couldn't hear. She sat up when the others did and she fed and dressed herself. Brenda has always been alert and has always watched what her brother and sister do. I never guessed she didn't hear us too well until I noticed she wasn't talking. She was 2½ then. Her sister and brother both talked by the time they were that age."

An activity like toilet training, however, is more abstract and difficult to learn. Ordinarily, parents stress the importance of the activity, compare the toddler to "big" brothers and sisters, and encourage the child's efforts with praise. For example, early interaction may include the terms *wet diapers* and *dry diapers* during changing. Without this spoken interaction, the child who is deaf may have difficulty grasping the concepts needed for toilet training.

By the time children are about 3 years old, parents expect to hear them using language regularly. If children have not used spoken language to express themselves, parents become concerned and seek help, as Brenda's mother did. Then a hearing loss may be identified. Occasionally, a hearing loss may not actually be detected until a child enters some kind of program or school, since teachers and children often interact using spoken language, and a child who does not respond as expected stands out.

The child who is deaf or hard-of-hearing from birth or soon after birth relies on visual information to learn basic concepts, supplemented by any residual auditory information that is accessible. Deaf children whose language development relies on visual information can use sign language or speechreading (lipreading) with residual hearing (if any) to learn basic and advanced abstract concepts, since both sign language and speechreading have visual features and yield visual information (see Module 9 for more information on these modes of communication). However, sign language may be partly or completely inaccessible in its visual form to a child who has significant vision loss.

# IMPLICATIONS OF DEAF-BLINDNESS

In the absence of sensory impairments, hearing and vision facilitate the natural flow of interaction between parents and caregivers and their infants or young children. This flow encompasses certain elements vital for communication development, such as

- eye contact, which helps establish and maintain communication
- body language, which helps convey meaning
- reciprocal interaction and turn-taking, which help the child learn prompts and anticipation (see Module 6)
- inflection and tone of voice, which also help convey meaning.

As adults point out people, objects, and events in the environment and explain or name them with many repetitions, children soon learn the names of people, objects, and events; how things work; natural consequences; and virtually every important concept about their immediate environments. They also learn to communicate using the same methods that their caregivers do.

Deaf-blindness of any type or degree significantly alters the natural flow of interaction and information-gathering for the infant or young child, with many results that were already outlined in Module 2. Communication development in particular can be affected and delayed. It is therefore essential to make sure that the child who is deaf-blind has opportunities to explore, interact, and gather information through adaptations that best suit his or her learning style, for example, by using touch to support remaining vision and hearing, or by using touch as the primary sense for learning. Because a child's communication abilities and skills are basic factors in his or her classroom participation as well as overall growth and development, it is particularly important for deaf-blind students to have their unique communication and learning needs addressed so they can be full participants in instructional settings.

The first issue to be addressed is how the deaf-blind child will get vital information for communication development. The sense of touch is a logical choice since it provides the most information of the three near senses. Nevertheless, touch is less efficient than either vision or hearing for information gathering (Freeman, 1985; Warren, 1984), and it is necessary to supplement the use of touch with any remaining hearing or vision the child has and to use movement experiences, taste, and smell as well to help the child obtain information and develop communication skills.

The communication methods and systems used with some deaf-blind students may be based on spoken or signed language. Many students will not use language at all, but instead will use touch or object cues or a number of other methods and modes explained in Modules 8–10.

For most children who are deaf-blind, communication development is supplemented with tactile information, and many families begin to use sign language in addition to spoken language (or instead of it) early. If sign language is used, some important factors need to be taken into account.

There has been little research on how children who are deaf-blind perceive sign language tactilely (Griffith, Robinson, & Panagos, 1983). How the brain processes sign language information may be different when it is done through touch rather than sight. Still, with repeated experiences, children who are deaf-blind can learn to identify the visual features of signs through touch or their remaining vision; doing so requires repeated pairing of tactile experiences with objects or people and the corresponding signs in a tactile or close-vision form. The implications for parents and educators are important. Tactile or close-range sign language can be an effective mode of communication for students who are deaf-blind, including those who have been deaf-blind from birth.

Some American Sign Language (ASL) signs appear to have high levels of "tactile iconicity" (Griffith et al., 1983); that is, these signs are easier to recognize through touch than are other ASL signs with more complex features. For example, the sign for "telephone" appears to have a high degree of tactile iconicity: It is made in a stabile location at the side of the head, which keeps it close to the body with no movement in space, and its handshape and location are tactilely representative of a telephone handset. Here are some important considerations for teachers:

- If a child uses sign language (or any communication system) that has been greatly individualized and modified, he or she can communicate easily only with others who know that system.

- The development of early communication with tactile signs may need to focus on vocabulary concepts that are signed with minimal movement and maximum body contact, such as "apple" or "home."

- As a child's communication skills increase, concepts with more complex signed features (for example, multiple movements away from the body and changing handshapes) can be introduced.

- Parents and service providers who have sign language skills can promote interaction and communication development that is multisensory (uses remaining vision and hearing as well as touch) (see Where to Learn to Sign). They should work together as team members to be sure they use signs consistently for children who have the ability to develop formal language skills. It is critical to remember that a child who is deaf-blind and is capable of using spoken or signed language but does not have language input will not learn language, despite his or her potential, because he or she has no other way to experience and acquire language.

*H E L P*
*at a*
*GLANCE*

## WHERE TO LEARN TO SIGN

You may need to learn to sign if you want to help students whom you think can benefit from sign language. Here are some sources of sign language instruction:

• Adult education classes in the community.

• Local colleges or universities with programs in education of students who are deaf or in interpreter training.

• Local churches or synagogues that offer interpreter services for people who are deaf.

• Local libraries.

• Recreational groups like the YMCA or YWCA.

• Local schools or programs for deaf students that may provide sign language instruction for families and friends of their students.

• Interpreters or interpreter referral agencies.

• People who are deaf.

• Videotapes and books (see the various titles listed in *Hand in Hand: Selected Reprints and Annotated Bibliography on Working with Students Who Are Deaf-Blind* [Huebner, Prickett, Welch, & Joffee, 1995], one of the companion volumes to this book, and in the Resources section).

These sources of sign language instruction are geared to signing with people who are deaf, not deaf-blind, but simple adaptations involving touch can be used with signs (for additional information, see Module 9). You do not have to find a sign language class that is specific to deaf-blindness.

Also, it is easier to learn to sign with a teacher who provides three-dimensional demonstrations, observes your progress, and corrects you. Line drawings or photographs in books, videotaped materials, and computer programs can show you the movements you need to learn, but they are two-dimensional media. ■

Children who are deaf and have visual impairments may have problems discriminating the visual details of sign language. Thus, a visually impaired sign language user may

• benefit from close interactions of approximately one to five feet, where he or she can identify the details of signs because the other person's arms are physically close enough to be seen adequately.

• miss parts of closely viewed signs because the signs may be made outside his or her useful field of vision. The person who is using sign language at close range may need to make the sizes of the signs much smaller than usual to accommodate the other person's smaller visual field.

- need sign interaction that is slower than usual if his or her visual impairment impedes visual tracking (visual following) of the signer's hands. Fast-moving, forceful signs may need to be modified.

- benefit from touching the other person's hands to add tactile information to the reduced visual information. For example, a child can be encouraged to cup the back of the wrist of a person who signs to him or her (tracking), so the child can follow the signs with his or her own hand, providing a point of reference, and can learn to recognize the finer features of sign language. Once the child has actually learned to understand the concepts that are being signed, he or she may no longer need to track.

# INFLUENCE OF ADDITIONAL DISABILITIES

Disabilities in addition to vision and hearing losses can further limit a child's ability to explore the environment and gather and process information. The previous module outlined the implications of these limitations for children who are deaf-blind; the sections that follow provide additional information and suggestions for dealing with them.

## COGNITIVE IMPAIRMENT

When cognitive impairments are present, a child's perception of and ability to process information may be restricted or distorted, with a variety of consequences for his or her ability to communicate. Teachers need to know the following factors about cognitive impairments and how these factors interact with deaf-blindness to affect communication skills:

- Cognitive ability and the development of communication skills are correlated (Lindfors, 1987; McCormick, 1984; Reichle & Keogh, 1985).

- Some cognitive skills may facilitate the acquisition of communication skills (Reichle & Keogh, 1985, p. 30). For exam-

ple, if Jesse understands that an action of his can cause something to occur or bring a response from someone (the abstract concept of causal relationships), he understands that he can control his environment and make choices through interactions with others.

- Significant cognitive impairment can alter or diminish the brain's ability to process and make judgments about the meaning of information and to respond, especially in relation to abstract concepts.

- For a child with a cognitive impairment, repeated experiences can be beneficial for getting information, processing it by comparing it to information from previous experiences, and responding according to how he or she comprehends the information.

- Cognitive abilities can be developed with tactile information, as well as with information from residual vision and hearing. The process may be slower and require more exposure for each new concept when a child is deaf-blind and has a cognitive impairment than it might be if the child did not have a cogni-

▲ *Through the use of tactile and close-range forms, signing can be adapted to meet the communication needs of students with various degrees of vision.*

tive challenge. Nevertheless, solid conceptual development can occur when a child who is deaf-blind and has a cognitive impairment has consistent and frequent interaction with family members and service providers, as Samantha's story illustrates:

*Samantha, age 10, has significant losses of vision and hearing and moderate cognitive impairment. She is considered legally blind and is in the mild-to-moderate range of hearing loss even with hearing aids. Her early language development was delayed because of limited interaction with her parents. Samantha recently came to live with a foster mother, who talks and signs to her often about everyday activities at home and at school, and the staff at her school program now does the same. Samantha has just started to put simple three- and four-word phrases together using both signs and speech. She is able to communicate her preferences, comment on daily events, and request things she wants to happen in the future. Samantha has developed a language base that will help her communicate with others.*

For children like Samantha who are deaf-blind and have cognitive impairments, not only is information less accessible than it is for their classmates with unimpaired hearing and sight, but the process of attaching meaning to the information that is accessible is more difficult. Thus, structured, consistent interaction with them is crucial for developing solid concepts and effective communication skills.

## NEUROLOGICAL DISABILITIES

Students with neurological disabilities can have difficulty processing concrete, familiar visual and auditory information and making associations. They often do not respond as expected because of faulty interpretation of the information they have received. They may not understand what they see and hear even though they do not have actual vision or hearing losses because their brain-processing mechanisms may fail to detect or register basic visual and auditory information, interpret it for meaning, and create responses. When the processing of information does occur, it is often distorted or slower than for children without such impairments, or it may be inconsistently appropriate.

Children whose deaf-blindness is caused by conditions that also result in neurological damage, including traumatic brain injury, can have problems processing sensory information, as was described in the previous module. Even with multisensory information derived from touch, smell, taste, and movement, they may fail to attach appropriate meaning consistently to events, objects, and people because their sensory integration, or "the organization of sensory input for use" (Ayres, 1979, p. 184) may be faulty. An overload of several kinds of sensory information may be overwhelming to a child who is deaf-blind and has a neurological disability and a sensory integration problem. Some ways to help such a child make effective use of all the sensory information that is accessible to him or her are these:

- Be aware of all the possible responses the child exhibits. Even the slightest movements or behaviors may be attempts to respond (Langley, 1991). Reinforce these movements and behaviors as if they were responses, when appropriate.

- Videotape interactions and analyze them to identify patterns in the child's responses to sensory stimulation and interaction.

- When you believe that the child has "residual competence that must be teased out and rechanneled" (Langley, 1991, p. 239), you can more readily expect responses to interactions.

- Watch for such signs as fatigue, overload of sensory information, "dampened states of alertness" (Langley, 1991, p. 239), or other overt physical signs that activities need to be changed and that close interaction should be temporarily suspended.

- Build trust. Show the child that you are willing to wait a long time for him or her to respond (Langley, 1991). Gently repeat an action to draw a response.

- Give as much sensory stimulation—visual, auditory, tactile, and motor—as the child appears to be able to accept while interacting. Withdraw all but one of these stimuli if the child seems to accept interaction with that stimulus more than he or she does with the others.

- Remember that it is vital to try to interact as frequently as possible, despite indications that the child may be experiencing sensory overload. Reduce the sensory input for a short time, but maintain some contact with the child or come back frequently enough that the child knows you are still available.

Consistency and well-planned, structured interactions in both school and family situations can provide the necessary support for communication development. They can also support the child's development of a more balanced sensory integration mechanism, gradually and through time, which can, in turn, enhance the child's ability to accommodate interaction with others and the environment.

## PHYSICAL DISABILITIES

Children who are deaf-blind may have physical disabilities also. They may use wheelchairs for mobility, need frequent changes in positioning, and require assistance for eating, dressing, and other basic self-care tasks. These students not only lack distant access to environmental information for communication development, they often do not move easily around their environments to get close enough to explore and interact. When they do have the opportunity to be within arm's reach of an object or person, some children with physical disabilities may lack muscle control or have other physical factors that interfere with manipulating objects effectively to get tactile information about them. A child with physical disabilities can be helped by family members and teachers in the following ways:

- Bring the child close to people and activities consistently, or bring the activities and people close to ensure that opportunities for close interaction occur.

- Allow even more time for tactile exploration than other deaf-blind children would require.

- Develop strategies to help people who interact with the child to accommodate his or her physical limitations; for example, physically assist the child to hold on to objects long enough to obtain information he or she needs.

- Arrange home and classroom areas so that the child can be part of all activities.

## OTHER FACTORS

Additional factors beyond a child's sensory or motor impairments influence the development of concepts and communication. Many children who are deaf-blind have significant medical needs resulting from the same causes as their deaf-blindness. Frequent hospitalizations relating to these needs can interrupt family and school life. In hospitals, few nurses or physicians have the time or skills to interact with deaf-blind children, and worried parents may not interact with their children the same way in a hospital as at home. A deaf-blind child's energies may be exhausted in responding to the reason for hospitalization, such as surgery. Daily home and school routines are disrupted for a time.

School vacations can also interrupt consistent interaction and concept development because parents and teachers may not be able to explain these interruptions to children who are deaf-blind and whose language and concept development are minimal. Furthermore, often both parents work, and other caregivers frequently do not have fluent communication skills for children with special needs. Thus, children who already have significant delays in the development of concepts and communication can fall further behind their peers. If the need for constant and consistent interaction is not accommodated, they lose ground that could be difficult to regain.

For situations like school vacations and hospitalizations, establishing and maintaining a framework for interaction may be the most practical solution. If the members of a child's educational team know when such events will occur and the duration of each event, they can develop a set of basic communication routines to be used in these situations. For example, the team members can

- develop a list of important events for interaction that must occur daily, and briefly outline routines for such events as mealtime, naptime, and bedtime
- post simple procedures (or develop a small flip-chart for rapid use) for hospital staff or other caretakers (such as day care providers) to follow, so there is some consistency with what would be communicated at home
- include touch and object cues and information about them
- show the hospital staff and others how to communicate.

Adults' responses can also influence children's attempts to interact. If adults fail to respond consistently to deaf-blind children who try to communicate, the children do not get the reinforcement they need. When their attempts to communicate are ignored, the children may stop trying.

Families and service providers can overlook or misinterpret genuine attempts of children who are deaf-blind to communicate because those interactions are not always what they expect. Just as consistent and constant input are important, consistent and constant responses to deaf-blind children's output are vital. If families and service providers understand how deaf-blindness affects communication, they may look for ways to accommodate, enhance, and encourage that communication. Overall, families and teachers need to work together to identify the communication needs of deaf-blind children and determine the most appropriate ways to meet them. Unit 2 explores in detail issues and strategies relating to helping children build communication skills. The remainder of this module offers suggestions and insights on how to begin to foster communication development for children who are deaf-blind.

# FOSTERING THE DEVELOPMENT OF COMMUNICATION

Consistency and satisfactory amounts and kinds of sensory and informational input are the most vital factors in ensuring communication development. Jon's story illustrates what may happen without consistent and adequate interaction for a deaf-blind child and how one team worked to develop consistency among his communication partners.

> *Jon's teacher and parents requested help from a specialist in deaf-blindness because they were concerned that 5-year-old Jon was not using language expressively. Jon's deaf-blindness resulted from prematurity, and his parents and teacher were concerned that other effects of prematurity were impeding his development.*
>
> *The specialist observed Jon in school and at home to see what skills he had developed. She found that he demonstrated good independent travel skills both in school and at home despite severe vision and hearing losses and that he often "made up" his own routes to go to familiar places like the gym and the cafeteria. He had not had much formal orientation and mobility (O&M) training, so it was clear he had devised these routes on his own. The specialist thought that Jon's travel skills showed he had formed some solid concepts about his world and reflected satisfactory cognitive ability. The*

*reports from the teacher and Jon's parents were accurate, though. Jon did not seem to respond much to tactilely signed interaction and did not use signs to request favorite foods or activities.*

*A teacher assistant worked with Jon all day, especially when the classroom teacher worked with the other children. It seemed like an ideal situation. Yet, the gap between Jon's apparent ability and his expressive use of language puzzled the specialist. After several days of observing and working with Jon, his teacher, his parents, and the teacher assistant, the specialist noted that Jon's reported vocabulary for receiving information included only 35 signs. Jon's teacher, parents, and teacher assistant had documented Jon's use of these signs and were confident he understood and responded to all 35 concepts. But Jon had never expressed anything with signs spontaneously. The specialist determined that two important factors had contributed to Jon's lack of communication: None of the people who interacted with him knew more than 75 signs, and none communicated often with him, especially by signing. All the adults were startled. It had never occurred to them that Jon needed to interact with them far more frequently and that they needed to know more signs to help him develop concepts. The specialist and Jon's parents, teacher, and teacher assistant began to work immediately on developing new strategies to ensure that Jon got the input he needed, often and consistently.*

Children who are deaf-blind, like Jon, may not have teachers and teaching assistants who are fluent in sign language (tactile or visual). Also, if such children are placed in settings in which staff members change frequently, it may be difficult to maintain consistency of interaction. Repetition of daily routines is crucial for deaf-blind children to develop basic concepts and communication. In some cases, the failure to interact consistently may mean that the child does not use language or another appropriate communication system. Families and educators need to provide multisensory information that may include signed or spoken language during daily routines. Some children who are deaf-blind may never use language effectively because of cognitive impairments, neurological damage, or other factors described previously. They may need other communication modes, systems, or devices, including tangible symbols and picture booklets. (These and many more special augmentative or alternative communication systems and devices can be developed, and they are described in Modules 8–12.) Nevertheless, consistent and appropriate interaction is the important common factor for communication development. This and a number of specific techniques and methodologies outlined in the following sections can be used to foster communication skills.

## CONSISTENCY OF INTERACTION

The human brain is like a computer in many ways. Computer programs do not run well if the command information is not entered completely and accurately. Computer input does not happen automatically: People must enter the information. Like computer processing, if human language input is consistent, appropriate, and adequate, the "output" or response will be satisfactory, too. Like all children, children who are deaf-blind need full input to respond. If they do not receive full and accurate information about concepts related to their environments, they will be less able to respond to the environments or make decisions about how to participate in them.

Children typically get a great deal of "input" as infants and toddlers during interactions with family members, neighbors, and others in their communities. Such interactions are characterized by repetition; experiences with objects, people, and events that are accompanied by others' comments or descriptions of them; concept development that is based on the application of what the children have previously learned; and spoken language, which is the mediating factor between children and their environments. Children who are deaf-blind can miss much basic information about their surroundings that the natural repetition of daily interactions with people and the environment supply. Therefore, concepts must be built in different ways, and the input must be given often and in the same way each time by each person who interacts with the children. For example, her teacher uses a touch on LaToya's shoulder to indicate that she can sit down and places LaToya's hand on a chair to indicate where LaToya can sit. LaToya's parents use *exactly* the same pair of cues to help LaToya seat herself for meals, and the driver cues LaToya the same way when he shows her the seat on the school bus. In art class, a classmate gives LaToya the same cues. This consistency and the use of touch for the communication cue allow LaToya to participate in ordinary activities with a better understanding of what she is doing and why.

## TOTAL COMMUNICATION

In many contemporary instructional programs, service providers who work with children who are deaf use "total communication"; few programs have solely a manual (sign language only) or an oral (speaking, speechreading, and use of residual hearing) focus. A total communication approach ensures that all available information will be used for interaction because it is based on the principle that many methods of communication should be used with a child to ensure the reinforcement of information and the development of effective communication techniques. The goal is to help the child master as many communication skills as possible to ensure that he or she has maximum access to information.

Total communication programs for children who are deaf or hard-of-hearing emphasize

- sign language, usually in a form based on the order of spoken words (see Module 9 for additional information on sign language)
- the use of any remaining hearing (auditory training) for both spoken and environmental sounds
- the development of speech skills
- the development of speechreading skills
- printed words (written forms of language)
- pictures and objects to clarify concepts.

The total communication approach integrates all these communication efforts when any new concept is developed. Since the approach uses both hearing and vision and most children who are deaf-blind have some residual hearing and vision, these components are also helpful for the children's development of language and communication skills. For deaf-blind students, it may also be necessary to adapt visual factors, for example, to enlarge pictures or written words, and to use tactile information, for instance, to touch new objects or to use braille.

## COACTIVE MOVEMENT

"Coactive movement" is a term that is often used to refer to a comprehensive instructional method developed by van Dijk that uses movement to establish interaction and, ultimately, a communication system for an individual who is deaf-blind. A crucial feature of the method is that movement and communication are integrally related, and skill development is to incorporate both in an integrated manner. The method was designed initially to meet a recognized need with students who were deaf-blind as a result of rubella, to help teachers assist students to make connections with and interact more effectively within their environments (van Dijk, 1991). It is not delivered for a specific time period daily or weekly but is meant to be part of all interactions with deaf-blind students to promote responsiveness for several levels of skill development in all sensory areas (Writer, 1987).

The most well-known component of the comprehensive set of components listed by van Dijk is coactive movement, which is sometimes defined as "hand over hand" instruction (Freeman, 1984). In hand-over-hand instruction, the teacher's hands touch and guide the student's hands (or feet) in a movement or sequence of actions.

For a student who is functioning at early levels of interaction, full body movement with touch contact may be suggested in this methodology. As a child shows progress in making environmental connections, the full contact may be reduced to partial contact, and finally to prompts. An important factor in delivering instruction using van Dijk's concepts is consistency of interaction, regardless of the specific level of the interaction.

The goal of coactive movement, and of all the component techniques of van Dijk's method, is to move the child who is minimally interactive to being very interactive with the environment. The earliest steps involve establishing reciprocity (that is, mutual, complementary, shared interactions) by following the child's lead and working with the most concrete of concepts, such as establishing a pattern for pushing a swing, stopping it, and starting the movement again, or bringing a spoonful of food to the child's mouth, letting the child eat the food, dipping the spoon to get more food, and repeating the action. Reciprocity is established through initially imitating the child's actions and promoting the development of an understanding of cause-and-effect concepts based on the immediacy of interaction and consequences.

Very close interaction, especially physical proximity and imitation of a child's movements, is vital initially in this instructional scheme, which consists of distinct stages and techniques for progression. Eventually, the child can move from immediate and concrete levels of interaction with people and the environment to increasingly abstract and symbolic levels with more physical distance from the teacher, so that increased independence can be established through skill development.

# ADAPTATIONS FOR COMMUNICATION

Obstacles to communication affect not only people who are deaf-blind, but all the people who want or need to interact with them. Adaptations for communication can be made to meet the special communication needs and challenges of deaf-blind people and should be shared by all the communicators. Children who are deaf-blind especially need to have support for adaptations from all those who interact with them so they can learn concepts and communication skills.

## INDIVIDUALIZED INTERACTION

Helen Keller had advanced cognitive abilities, yet she needed close one-to-one interaction for her potential to develop fully. Until she received consistent, structured, one-to-one assistance, her environment was largely inaccessible to her because of her sensory losses. Helen Keller's accomplishments, supported by the one-to-one instruction provided by her teacher, Anne Sullivan Macy, show how essential individualized interaction is. Individualized, or one-to-one, interaction is often the first and most important adaptation that families and service providers need to make to communicate with children who are deaf-blind. Individualized interaction is based on communicating by touch or close vision; its importance to a child who is deaf-blind cannot be overemphasized.

Many children who are deaf-blind do not have the advantage of working with specific individuals who link them to information all the time, as Macy did for Keller. Few, including those who have residual vision and hearing, can learn all the basic daily living concepts they need in group settings without assistance because they will receive incomplete information about events and the environment around them. Without individualized support in such circumstances, full participation is difficult and competitive participation almost impossible. Group instruction can be successful, however, if individual assistance is provided to facilitate children's participation in groups, as is discussed later in this module.

For deaf-blind children who have advanced abilities and skills, individualized assistance in the classroom can mean having an interpreter, a teacher assistant, or someone else who facilitates communication and helps convey classroom concepts. In the case of infants and toddlers, individualized assistance means frequent, close individual contact with family members and home intervention specialists who facilitate the development of effective and consistent communication. The goal of individualized interaction in any setting is for the person who is deaf-blind to have access to all the information that is important for participation and learning.

Using touch may not be comfortable or easy for some people in communication situations. For example, in some cultural groups, touching others is considered improper, yet for the deaf-blind child, touch may be the only way to get information and develop communication skills. Therefore, it is important to share information with families about the significance of touch for children who are deaf-blind.

Families and service providers may need to consider strategies to feel comfortable using touch for everyday interactions. Families can begin using touch with deaf-blind babies in daily routines more often than would be expected with other babies. For example, when parents hold their baby who is deaf-blind, they can guide the baby's hands to their faces often until the baby learns to keep contact between his or her hand and the parents' faces, so the baby has access to their facial vibrations. For an infant with residual hearing, the vibrations supplement any sounds he or she may hear; for a child with no useful hearing, the vibrations still give an indication of a parent's interaction. Comfortable physical contact helps when formal touch interaction, such as the use of touch cues or tactile signs, is established. Families can look at their daily routines and find activities and interactions for which the greater use of touch would be appropriate. Some possibilities include these:

- When a toddler who is deaf-blind is being fed, the person feeding can lightly touch the child's cheek with a few fingers and then give touch cues for the child to open his or her mouth by gently tapping the child's lips as the other hand with the spoon comes close to the lips.

- When family members are sitting on a sofa, keeping some form of physical contact with the deaf-blind child will increase the child's awareness of others in the environment, as well as establish the concept of ongoing contact through touch.

## PARTICIPATION IN GROUPS

Children who are deaf-blind participate best when one person in a group facilitates communication among the members. That person may be a teacher, an interpreter, a peer, a teacher assistant, or any other person who is skilled in facilitating communication and the exchange of information. Children who are deaf-blind or have partial sight and hearing cannot participate fully if they have little or no access to the information exchanged by other participants in a group.

When a deaf-blind child participates in group activities, the structure of the group's interactions needs to be modified. Although these modifications may at first diminish spontaneity in the group, with practice, the pace of interactions will become more comfortable and natural and every member will have a chance to communicate and otherwise participate. The following are some tips for modifying a group's interactions:

- Have each participant identify himself or herself before the activity starts, especially if the group is new. These introductions help the deaf-blind child who has some residual vision to identify other group members and to orient himself or herself to their positions in the room. They also help an interpreter-assistant to supply information to the child that the other classmates would get simply by looking, and allow the child to get to know the other children's names. Repeated exposure to other children's name signs (see Module 9 for information on name signs) or fingerspelled names will give the child a sense of being a member of the group and help the child recognize that another child is a member of the group when that child initiates interaction by communicating his or her name.
- Slow down the interaction, so the deaf-blind child and the interpreter or communication facilitator have time to find and

adjust to a new speaker. You can do so by requiring each group member to raise his or her hand and be recognized before he or she begins to speak and by gesturing, tapping the hand of the child, pointing in the direction of the participant who wants to speak next, or even calling out the person's name (depending on the level of the child's hearing and vision loss).

- Remind the other children in the group to speak slowly and clearly, so the interpreter-assistant can convey the information accurately. Find gentle ways to remind them if they speak more quickly as they interact.

- Have the children identify themselves by name each time before they begin to speak, for the same reasons that they did so when they introduced themselves at the beginning of the activity.

- If the person speaking is referring to visual information, such as on an overhead projector or chalkboard, give the deaf-blind child a chance to move closer to see the information better or explain in detail what is being presented. If an interpreter-assistant is conveying the information, allow time for him or her to convey the information from the visual source to the child.

- For movies and videotapes, be sure that the child who has some remaining vision can see the interpreter-assistant or the screen, depending on how the child obtains information. To do so, you may have to arrange for a light in the darkened room.

## USE OF ROUTINES

For many children who are deaf-blind, their experiences or the feedback they receive on how behaviors affect others are neither structured nor consistent. This disorganization may be the result of combined sensory impairments and possible motor and cognitive impairments that limit their abilities to acquire information and to monitor the effects of their actions, as well as the fact that their experiences may be dictated by simple convenience and the needs of many of the people around them. Teachers especially can help children develop positive relationships with adults by introducing consistency and responsiveness into daily activities.

Routines are a way of consistently drawing students' interest to the environment and to others. Students are encouraged to interact because the components and sequence of routines are familiar and can be anticipated, which makes interactions less threatening and more interesting and pleasurable.

Teachers need to rely on timing and pacing to maintain the flow of routine interactions. By choosing the best point to act and setting an optimal pace for doing so, they can communicate with students and understand their communications better. By focusing on students' interests, they may discover ways to facilitate the development of skills and students' active involvement in interactions.

Communication thrives in conditions in which people are motivated to interact with reciprocity. The establishment of an enabling social environment may go a long way to promote communication.

## COMMUNITY INVOLVEMENT

Helping people in local communities become aware of the unique communication modes and needs of deaf-blind individuals helps foster these individuals' communication skills. When many people know how to communicate with persons who are deaf-blind, deaf-blind students benefit through greater access to information and increased opportunities to participate in social activities and everyday life. Family members, service providers, and people who are deaf-blind can work cooperatively to develop educational strategies that are appropriate in their own areas. Teachers and other school staff who participate in these efforts can help by determining the nature of these interactions, where and with whom they take place, and what local people need to know. Public awareness activities can include such actions as visiting community businesses and showing workers how to interact effectively and distributing information about sign language instruction that is available locally to interested parties. Deaf-blind individuals themselves might even offer instruction in communication that includes basic sign language at a nearby church or synagogue or school.

Community education should emphasize both awareness and support for members of the community who are deaf-blind. Some of the adaptations that are necessary for deaf-blind people to participate in their own communities can be costly. Well-qualified interpreters must be paid each time they are engaged; thus, their services are clearly more expensive than is building a ramp for wheelchair users that can be used for years. Building community support for services is important, and members of educational teams and students—for example, as part of a class project—can be involved. With increasing community awareness, greater access to transportation, and more skills for communicating, people who are deaf-blind can expect to participate more fully in their communities.

# TEACHING METHODS TO EXPAND COMMUNICATION

Teachers can use a number of methods to enhance the use of communication and the development of interactions at school and in the com-

**H E L P**
*at a*
**G L A N C E**

## FOSTERING COMMUNICATION AMONG STUDENTS

Often, efforts to teach communication skills focus almost exclusively on the student who is deaf-blind. However, since it truly takes two to communicate, classmates and others who will be the communication partners of the deaf-blind student also need to learn these skills. You can foster communication between the student and others by

● Encouraging direct communication between the student who is deaf-blind and his or her classmates. Interpreters are essential for instructing deaf-blind students, but during more informal interactions, direct communication with classmates is desirable. Interpreters can help maximize opportunities for such communication.

● Emphasizing (especially at first) interaction between the deaf-blind student and his or her classmates, rather than perfect communication techniques, such as for signing or using an electronic communication board. The classmates' techniques will improve as they have more opportunities and become more motivated to communicate.

● Ensuring that the deaf-blind student has a means to communicate with others in all situations. For example, if the student uses mainly sign language, he or she needs to know other ways to convey information to and receive it from people who do not understand sign language. Similarly, if the student uses an electronic device, he or she should have a "low-tech," portable alternative for when a power source or adequate space is not available. ■

munity by children who are deaf-blind. (Additional information on fostering communication both in the classroom and in the community can be found in Module 13. See also Fostering Communication among Students.)

## PREPARATION: ESTABLISHING ANTICIPATION

The use of object, gesture, or touch cues, including signs (see Module 8), allows a child who is deaf-blind to anticipate an activity, express a reaction to its occurrence, and become ready to participate in it. A child can come to dislike a preferred activity if he or she is not ready for it or is unaware that it will take place soon, as the following example of Tim illustrates:

> *Tim is totally blind and has a moderate hearing loss. He suddenly finds himself in a cold locker-room, with a person who indicates that he must take off his clothes. He becomes confused and resistant, struggling with his aide for an entire hour until it is time for lunch. The next time the activity is scheduled, his teacher brings him to a calendar box, where he finds his bathing suit in one section. He smiles and signs "swim." By the time he arrives at the local YMCA, he is laughing and teasing his aide. The lifeguard at the pool offers to teach him how to dive.*

## CHOICES

Everyone likes an activity one day but may not like it the next, depending on his or her mood, physical well-being, or other factors. Structuring settings so the child can make choices allows the child to communicate his or her preferences and to exercise control over his or her environment. Successful control over the environment stimulates the student to communicate more and to exercise still more control, as in the case of Carol:

> *Carol, who is 8 years old, indicates choices through a communication board attached to her wheelchair. She has made several friends at the local museum of science and enjoys playing with the computers in the museum's activity room. One day her friends were upset because she cried and refused to participate with them. Later, it was learned that she did not sleep*

▲ *Devices like communication boards that show a wide range of choices enable students to communicate their preferences and feel a sense of control.*

*well the night before. Her communication board was expanded to include symbols for looking at a book in the school library and for taking a nap. She still asks to go the museum, but occasionally chooses a quiet activity.*

## ENVIRONMENT

For children who have visual and hearing impairments of various degrees, environmental conditions, such as the amount of lighting and noise, can have an impact on the enjoyment of an activity or interaction and the amount of communication they understand and express, as the example of Joe shows:

*Joe is 15 and has Usher syndrome. He is a member of his school's track team and often goes to a restaurant with his teammates after practice. Sometimes his teammates choose a table in a dark corner, where he is unable to see them well or read the menu. Even though his teammates have learned some sign language, Joe feels distant and isolated in this situation. He finally discussed this problem with his teacher, who encouraged him to tell his teammates what he needs in these situations and to ask them to sit at a well-lit table, so he can participate in their conversations.*

## SAFETY

If a child feels unsafe or insecure in an environment, then he or she may come to dislike even a highly anticipated activity. Safety factors encompass travel conditions, adequate O&M instruction and skills, and familiarity with the person who acts as a guide. Mary's experience is an example:

*Mary, a teenager with both hearing and vision loss, enjoys walking to the library with a school friend who is her sighted guide. After a snowstorm one day, the roads were icy, but Mary did not know it until she and her friend began to walk to the library. Her friend failed to avoid icy patches, and they both fell frequently. By the time they arrived at the library, Mary was irritable and did not feel like looking at books or magazines. If Mary or her friend had thought to check out the weather conditions, they could have considered a number of options: choosing a different mode of transportation—getting a ride to the library or taking a bus if buses were available; walking a route that might have been better cleared or might have avoided icy patches; wearing footwear better suited to snowy weather conditions; or rescheduling the library visit.*

## FAMILIARITY

All people, including children who are deaf-blind, are more likely to communicate with people in environments that are familiar, as Eric discovered:

*Eric has been learning the names of various fruits and vegetables. He enjoys cooking and is learning to go to a grocery store to purchase food to make lunch. Since he has limited vision and no hearing, his first trip to the store was confusing because of the different lights, smells, and vibrations. He could not remember the signs for any of the items he wanted to purchase, and his teacher had to help him locate items. After weekly trips to the store, he was able to identify more items visually, and with practice and instruction, he came to remember the signs for these items.*

## DIRECT COMMUNICATION

Often, when teachers, interpreters, or parents introduce children who are deaf-blind to new environments, they provide primary communication, relaying the children's choices and desires. However, if the long-term goal is for a child to establish relationships in a community, members of the educational team must consider how to teach the child to communicate directly. The child may initially communicate through eye contact (if he or she has some vision), a vocalization, a smile, or another form of greeting (if he or she is blind). As the child's communication abilities develop, the child can learn to use augmentative aids, such as object or picture cards, to request desired items or services, as was the case with Pascal:

*Every Saturday afternoon, Pascal and his mother go to his favorite restaurant, where he signs his choices and his mother interprets so he can order food. When his favorite cousin, who knows little sign language, invited Pascal to go to McDonald's, Pascal's mother wondered if her son was dependent on her for the activity. She talked with Pascal's teacher, and together they developed a picture menu. Gradually, Pascal learned how to place his own order by communicating directly with the counter clerks through pointing to pictures of the items he wanted. He was then able to go to the restaurant with anyone.*

Information is the powerful tool that people need to make decisions and carry on daily life activities. Deaf-blindness can reduce a person's access to this information. Teachers, family members, and service providers who understand these communication and information needs can accommodate, adapt, and encourage interaction with children who are deaf-blind and can help these children explore and gain experiences in their homes, schools, and communities. Families and service providers can structure intervention so it is constant and consistent. They can ensure that the design and implementation of programs minimize the effects of deaf-blindness on communication and learning by providing the deaf-blind child with maximum opportunities to interact, build communication skills, and receive full information from the environment.

# REFERENCES

Ayres, A. J. (1979). *Sensory integration and the child.* Los Angeles: Western Psychological Services.

Freeman, P. (1985). *The deaf/blind baby: A programme of care.* London: William Heinemann Medical Books.

Griffith, P. L., Robinson, J. H., & Panagos, J. H. (1983). Tactile iconicity: Signs rated for use with deaf-blind children. *Journal of the Association for Persons with Severe Handicaps, 8,* 26–38.

Huebner, K. M., Prickett, J. G., Welch, T. R., & Joffee, E. (Eds.). (1995). *Hand in hand: Selected reprints and annotated bibliography on working with students who are deaf-blind*. New York: AFB Press.

Langley, M. B. (1991). Assessment: A multidimensional process. In M. B. Langley & L. J. Lombardino (Eds.), *Neurodevelopmental strategies for managing communication disorders in children with severe motor dysfunction* (pp. 199–250). Austin, TX: PRO-ED.

Lindfors, J. W. (1987). *Children's language and learning* (2nd ed.). Englewood Cliffs, NJ: Prentice-Hall.

McCormick, L. (1984). Perspectives on categorization and intervention. In L. McCormick & R. L. Schiefelbusch (Eds.), *Early language intervention* (pp. 89–116). Columbus, OH: Charles E. Merrill.

Reichle, J., & Keogh, W. J. (1985). Communication intervention: A selective review of what, when, and how to teach. In S. F. Warren & A. K. Rogers-Warren (Eds.), *Teaching functional language* (pp. 25–59). Baltimore: University Park Press.

van Dijk, J. (1991). *Persons handicapped by rubella: Victors and victims—A follow-up study*. Amsterdam: Swets & Zeitlinger Publishers.

Warren, D. (1984). *Blindness and early childhood development* (2nd ed.). New York: American Foundation for the Blind.

Writer, J. (1987). A movement-based approach to the education of students who are sensory impaired/multihandicapped. In L. Goetz, D. Guess, & K. Stremel-Campbell (Eds.), *Innovative program design for individuals with dual sensory impairments*. Baltimore: Paul H. Brookes.

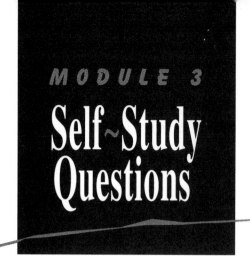

# MODULE 3
# Self~Study Questions

1. The most important effect of a hearing loss for communication development is
   a. the child's lack of access to spoken language and to the natural repetition of comments about the environment, objects, events, and people that ordinarily promote the development of concepts and communication skills.
   b. the child's limited ability to make observations that promote incidental learning for such daily living activities as dressing and feeding himself or herself.
   c. the lack of access to substantial tactile interactions with others in the environment.

2. Input can be considered consistent or appropriate when
   a. a child's interactions with others are reduced and cause further delays in concept and language development, for example, during hospitalizations.
   b. explanations are provided of scheduled routines and activities during a day at school and home in combined modes of tactile sign language, speech, and a tangible communication system.
   c. input from parents and service providers is minimal because these individuals do not interact often or do not use a communication system that is appropriate for the student (including signs) each time they interact.

3. Choose the statement that is *not* correct about sign language that is used by people who are deaf, including many who are deaf-blind:
   a. It can be read tactilely.
   b. It has too many visual features to be read effectively by tactile processes.
   c. It may be processed differently when it is read tactilely instead of visually.

4. Which of the following is *not* a strategy to use to facilitate the interaction of deaf-blind individuals in group situations?
   a. Slow down the interaction.
   b. Quicken the interaction so there are no lag times.
   c. Speak slowly and clearly.
   d. Have each participant identify himself or herself before the activity begins.

*Answers to self-study questions for this module appear at the end of Unit 1.*

*KEY CONCEPTS*

# Purposeful Movement

MARGARET M. GROCE

ARLINE B. ISAACSON

- *Recognize the importance of movement*

- *Introduce purposeful movement early*

- *Take advantage of natural opportunities for movement*

- *Teach self-protection skills*

- *Consistently encourage the student to move and explore*

- *Help the student learn to make choices*

- *Include the family in movement instruction*

Purposeful movement—self-directed movement to fulfill one's needs—plays a fundamental role in the lives of all people. By moving purposefully, we can hug people we love or express other emotions through gestures and changes in body position, reach or bend for objects that we want to hold, remove ourselves from people and objects that are undesirable or dangerous, engage in recreational activities, or simply go from place to place as we carry out daily tasks. Most children acquire movement skills as a natural part of their growth and maturation. Self-initiated movement is related to a variety of developmental achievements in early childhood and provides the foundation for the development of many types of cognitive, emotional, social, communication, and life skills (see, for example, Barraga, 1992; Pogrund, Fazzi, & Lampert, 1992).

Sensory information plays an important role in the emergence of movement skills. It motivates infants to move, guides their movements, and verifies their interactions with the environment and thus acts as a stimulus for the development of motor activity.

Because deaf-blind children have fewer ways to gain access to sensory stimulation and information, learning to move about the environment at will may not always come naturally to them. Therefore, they may need instruction in concepts related to the self and the environment, in addition to instruction in specific travel skills and techniques. Children typically have numerous opportunities to learn movement skills during their daily routines at home, in school, and in the community. By taking advantage of these natural opportunities, families and teachers can encourage the development of movement skills by deaf-blind children that are integral to the achievement of purposeful movement and that contribute to the children's independence.

# TEACHING PURPOSEFUL MOVEMENT

## THE IMPORTANCE OF PURPOSEFUL MOVEMENT SKILLS

Traditionally, the focus of educational programs has been on teaching academic subjects, "preacademic" subjects (reading readiness, for example), or life skills (such as personal hygiene), whereas teaching students to go to the locations where these skills are performed has been of secondary importance or has not been addressed at all. But students who do not develop purposeful movement skills may be unable to go anywhere or do anything without assistance, and thus their ability to develop and express their independence is limited. Families, teachers, and other service providers need to be aware of how movement skills benefit students throughout their lives and to recognize that they are in the best position to give students the opportunities to learn and use these skills in their daily lives by structuring specific activities to encourage movement and independence. It is essential to expand educational programs to include instruction in the purposeful movement skills needed to carry out daily activities. Teaching students to travel independently or with guidance increases their awareness of their surroundings and confidence in themselves, as well as their mobility skills. Taking students to specific locations is not the same as teaching them to move about, however. Rather than building skills, leading students from place to place teaches them to be passive and to wait to be moved and does not give them a chance to satisfy their curiosity to explore.

As previous modules have discussed, students with sensory impairments can have significant difficulties developing concepts that their peers commonly understand. For students who are deaf-blind, motor activities are the primary and essential vehicle for gathering the information about environmental objects and events that is necessary to form concepts and to learn about the larger world. An instructional program that includes movement provides natural opportunities for them to do so. Learning to move with purpose also helps students gain confidence in their abilities to enter and make use of various environments and, consequently, to learn other skills that are necessary for carrying out daily activities in these environments.

Helping a student learn purposeful movement can do much to dispel assumptions that children with severe disabilities are dependent, assumptions that are often based on observing students who have not been encouraged to move and explore. When students have to rely on others to lead them because they do not know how to move about on their own, they may become withdrawn and dependent and lose confidence in their ability to handle new situations. This situation in turn confirms others' beliefs about their dependence. Instruction in purposeful movement, embedded in educational programs, breaks this cycle of dependence, fosters independence, and promotes a "can-do" perspective (see Tips for Teaching Purposeful Movement Skills in this module).

## TIPS FOR TEACHING PURPOSEFUL MOVEMENT SKILLS

- Start early to encourage movement (see Modules 15–18).

- Stress functional skills (see Module 2).

- Encourage independence.

- Make use of the child's useful vision and/or hearing and preferred communication systems (see Modules 8–12).

- Use an interpreter if you need one (see Modules 3, 9, and 18).

- Learn sign language or tactile sign language, depending on the level of the child's visual impairment (see Modules 3, 9, and 12).

- Ensure that the initial routes that a student learns are straight, simple, and uncluttered; that the student uses all possible sensory information to determine where he or she is in the environment; that instruction is consistent and repetitive; and that the student is motivated to learn and develops self-confidence by being encouraged to use purposeful movement skills.

- Identify the persons in school who can help develop purposeful movement programs.

- Obtain the services of a qualified orientation and mobility (O&M) instructor.

- Include students and their families as part of the transdisciplinary educational team. ■

## COMPONENTS OF PURPOSEFUL MOVEMENT

The goal of purposeful movement is to be able to travel in whatever mode possible for a desired outcome. To do so, students need to learn and use a number of specific skills. In this module, movement skills have been divided into the following five interrelated components, all of which are necessary if purposeful movement is to be a reality:

- *Awareness of surroundings*: knowing that a world of people, places, and things exists and understanding their nature and one's physical relationship to them.

- *Initiating and sustaining movement*: knowing that one needs to start to move to reach a desired location and to continue to move until the destination is reached.

- *Recognizing a destination*: recognizing and identifying the objective of movement—the destination—when it is reached and responding accordingly.

- *Protecting oneself from danger*: recognizing obstacles or other dangers in the path and dealing with them safely.

- *Decision making*: choosing when and how to move about (Do I want to or need to go? Shall I go now or later? Do I want to go to a friend's house or stay home? Shall I take a bus or a taxi or walk?).

## MICHAEL'S STORY

The following case of Michael illustrates each component of purposeful movement.

*Michael, aged 7, was deaf-blind and had multiple disabilities. He attended an urban public school with many available resources. In school, Michael traveled with a classroom aide, who led the way when movement was required. Michael's teacher knew that programs existed to help students learn travel skills and remembered hearing about a program called mobility instruction, but she did not know much about it. Although the teacher thought that Michael could do more on his own, she was at a loss as to how to plan a movement-instruction program or to structure Michael's day at school to help him learn how to travel independently.*

*The teacher learned that the school system employed orientation and mobility (O&M) instructors to teach travel skills and techniques to students with visual impairments [see How to Find an O&M Instructor in this module for more information]. She contacted an O&M instructor to assess Michael's travel needs and to discuss how to implement a mobility program for him. The transdisciplinary educational team developed an instructional program that addressed all the skills inherent in purposeful movement. It was decided that having Michael follow specific routes would be an effective strategy for teaching travel skills. The O&M instructor taught Michael mobility techniques, and the communication specialist developed a system of communication cues that all members of the educational team could use with Michael as he moved from activity to activity.*

Here is how Michael was introduced to the five components of purposeful movement as he followed his first simple, straight, and uncluttered route, moving from the door of his classroom to his desk.

## HOW TO FIND AN O&M INSTRUCTOR

Teachers who wish to consult with an orientation and mobility (O&M) instructor can begin by contacting their local school district or state education department in addition to administrators in their school. There are several strategies that school districts may use to find an O&M instructor to join their staff or to provide part-time consultation services for a student who is deaf-blind. Some school districts make special arrangements to provide home-based O&M instruction when an O&M instructor is not available to provide services during regular school hours. In areas where there is a shortage of qualified O&M instructors, it may be necessary to be creative and resourceful in reaching beyond a school district's immediate community.

• Contact the Association for Education and Rehabilitation of the Blind and Visually Impaired (AER) at (703) 548-1884 (see Resources for more information). AER maintains a database of certified O&M instructors and can provide referrals to instructors. It also has a monthly newsletter, *Job Exchange,* that lists job vacancies.

• Contact a local organization that provides services to persons who are blind or visually impaired. It may be possible to contract with the organization to obtain the consultation services of the organization's O&M instructor. (O&M instructors who provide rehabilitation services may, however, be experienced in adult services and require in-service training for teaching school-aged students.)

• Contact a local state or private school for blind students. Such schools may provide the services of an O&M instructor for specialized in-service training programs. In addition, the school's O&M instructor may agree to provide home-based services to students after school or on weekends.

Additional sources of information concerning O&M instructors are university training programs in O&M and related areas and national organizations serving blind and visually impaired people, their families, and the professionals who work with them. Lists of training programs and national organizations are in the Resources section of this book. ■

## Becoming Aware of Surroundings

*While Michael learned the route from his classroom door to his desk, he developed a working awareness of his surroundings. As part of this experience, he was given the opportunity to explore the area he was negotiating to increase his knowledge and awareness of it. Michael learned about the objects and landmarks that were located along his route by touching them each time he passed them on the route. He also began to realize the distance he traveled between the door and his desk and started to acquire basic information for figuring out the size of his classroom and the placement of objects within it. Thus, he built his awareness of where he was, where he wanted to go, and how he was going to get there.*

An awareness of surroundings also includes being conscious of the people, places, and things that surround us. We are more willing to move and are more confident in our movement if we have some basic information, such as "What or who is near me?" "Where do I get what I want or need?" "Is it safe around me?" These concepts are important for all students, including those who appear to have few language skills.

## Initiating and Sustaining Movement

*As Michael worked on learning to travel from the door of his classroom to his desk, he learned another important component of purposeful movement: initiating and sustaining movement. Michael learned that to go from the door to the desk, he had to start to move and to keep moving until he reached his destination.*

People move about constantly. However, their movements would serve no purpose if they could not be initiated at will, directed toward achieving desired ends, and sustained until desired objectives were reached.

Students who are deaf-blind need to be taught that there are good reasons for moving and that they will not reach their goals unless they initiate movement and keep moving until they find what they are looking for. This principle is also true for students who have physical disabilities and may not move freely because of physical constraints, but must initiate and sustain movement to go from place to place.

Frequently, the lack of opportunities to initiate and sustain movement has limited students' understanding of why they move or why movement is necessary and beneficial. Often, decisions about when and where to move are made by other people, and objects or activities are brought to the students. Therefore, an essential objective for anyone who works with deaf-blind students is to provide the stimulation and opportunities for students to initiate and sustain movement related to daily activities. These opportunities will help them understand that moving is a way to fulfill their needs.

Teaching older students who have not had opportunities to initiate activities may be a challenging task. These students may have learned to be dependent and may not appreciate the advantages of initiating actions on their own.

However, time, patience, and efforts by teachers and family members will be worthwhile, since purposeful movement becomes increasingly important as students mature and have more frequent and independent interactions with the larger community. Classroom teachers and parents, with the assistance of communication specialists, can establish and use individualized communication cues (see Modules 6–14, especially 8–12) to help students recognize the reason for initiating movement. The use of favorite objects or activities helps students learn that initiating and sustaining movement are necessary to obtain what they want.

## Recognizing a Destination

Moving with purpose means reaching a place one wants to or has to be. Without this goal, there may be no reason to move.

In an instructional program for teaching purposeful movement, techniques are devised to enable students to recognize their destinations and to know where to stop. In some instances, the communication specialist creates object cues—everyday objects from daily activities that are presented to a child as cues for these activities—to help students identify destinations. For example, a floppy disk for a computer can be mounted on the door to the school's computer room to help children identify the room. In other cases, students learn to recognize natural features of their environments as cues that they have located their destinations; for example, a student may use the smell of food cooking and the feel of a tile floor to recognize the doorway to a kitchen (see Modules 8 and 17 for more information on object cues and on cues and landmarks in the environment).

## Protecting Oneself from Danger

The ability to deal safely with obstacles or other dangers along a route is probably the most important component of purposeful movement. Learning to be cautious, to recognize danger, to request assistance when it is needed, and to acquire techniques to deal with obstacles that may be encountered during travel increases students' awareness of themselves and their environment. A review of

Michael's movement-instruction program shows how self-protection skills were included in his lessons.

▲ *By helping students learn specific routes and techniques for independent travel, orientation and mobility instructors also help them learn purposeful movement.*

*Michael had not yet developed an awareness of danger because he had never encountered it. He was monitored closely by his family at home and traveled with the classroom aide in school. His instructional program in purposeful movement planned for the placement of obstacles and small dangers in the path along his route. At various times during his lessons, a cardboard box was placed in his path and a small object, such as a stuffed animal, was placed on his chair, requiring him to check his seat before he sat down. When Michael was unable to move around the cardboard box by himself, he was taught how to ask for help, so he could continue moving to reach the destination. The objective was for Michael to learn that problems and obstacles are a natural part of the environment and to gain techniques for self-protection.*

Teachers and families may find it helpful to structure or limit the environments in which movement takes place for students who are just learning the meaning of self-protection and the skills necessary to ensure it. Later, they can expand the range of environments for independent movement as the students learn safety rules, skills, and techniques.

Often, caregivers remove all the obstacles and small dangers from paths of travel or automatically guide students to different routes that are free and clear of hazards. As a result, students are protected not only from danger, but from learning what danger and obstacles are and how to respond to them. In encountering problems along their everyday travel routes, students have natural opportunities to learn and practice the necessary skills for moving through their environments safely (see Modules 17–19 for specific strategies for doing so).

## Decision Making

Decision making is the ability to recognize that more than one option is available and to choose the one that is most beneficial. Any place one goes involves making decisions: What do I want? Where do I get it? How will I get there? Do I really want to go, or would I rather stay in this place? Sometimes, the choices are difficult and the decisions are not automatic. Then one looks at the options, selects one, and accepts the consequences.

Frequently, this natural process is left out of the daily routines of students who are deaf-blind because others decide for them out of various motivations—expediency or habit or the desire to protect them and to try to make life easier. The lack of opportunity for decision making is usually reflected in students' behaviors. Some students may sit and do nothing until adults around them directly intervene and engage them in activities, whereas others may act out in an attempt to gain attention. When students learn to move purposefully, they have to make choices and learn to deal appropriately with the consequences. For example, they may choose to move immediately, rather than later when they are hungry and need to go from their classroom to the school cafeteria. The choice to go later or not at all may mean that the student will arrive at the cafeteria after lunch has stopped being served or stay hungry. Although learning to make choices and understanding the consequences are some of the skills necessary for purposeful movement, students sometimes have problems making choices because they do not grasp the possibilities that are available or do not know what is expected in a given circumstance. Therefore, it is important for a teacher to observe a student carefully to determine when he or she does not know what is expected and to respond appropriately. Often, when students are familiar with routines and indicate that they anticipate what is to follow, it can be assumed that they know what to expect and can make choices.

> *While focusing on this component of choice and decision making, the teacher allowed Michael to stand alone and gave him time to decide to initiate movement by himself. After Michael stood in the spot for a few minutes, he sat down on the floor. He had made a choice. The teacher and classroom aide were unsure if Michael knew what he was doing and was enjoying a "game" or if he was confused. When Michael did not initiate an action in a reasonable time, the teacher prompted him to get up and continue his movement.*

Deliberate waiting is part of active instruction with students who are deaf-blind. It provides students with the time and opportunity to absorb and use information at their own speed and according to their own learning styles. Service providers, families, and others who interact with a student who is deaf-blind can use this time to observe—to read the student's body language and intervene if frustration or confusion or the need for more information becomes evident.

## THE ROLE OF TEACHERS AND FAMILY MEMBERS

Teachers have an essential role to play in requesting and helping to implement mobility instruction programs for students who are deaf-blind if the students are not traveling purposefully or at their maximum levels of independence. Informal assessments are an important part of this process (see Modules 17 and 18), as is learning how to work with the educational team to teach mobility skills.

Teachers know that a student's motivation is an essential factor if instruction is to be successful. When teaching skills related to purposeful movement, they may initially use an external form of motivation, such as a preferred or desired object or activity. However, as a student becomes more experienced with movement and more independent, motivational factors become more intrinsic and self-imposed, as in Michael's case:

> *The first time Michael reached his desk on his own and sat down, he grinned. Everyone involved was motivated to press on.*

Teachers are also in a pivotal position to observe firsthand the importance of setting realistic goals and objectives for students and integrating family members and other school personnel into programs to teach purposeful movement. Goals that are not consistent with students' skills, needs, preferences, and interests generally will not foster purposeful travel because the students will not be motivated to achieve them.

The support and involvement of families are essential if mobility is to become an embedded life skill. In addition, families and teachers have an important role to play in introducing young children with sensory impairments to the community. Exposing young children to the natural demands and routines of family and community life encourages the development of travel skills, communication skills, appropriate behavior, and cooperation. As the opportunities for students to have natural interactions with people, objects, and events are increased, the foundation is laid for them to develop skills for independent purposeful movement in their communities.

# NATURAL SETTINGS FOR MOVEMENT

## HOME

The home is the first, most familiar environment that students experience. It is a relatively small space occupied by people who are intimately involved with each other. Adjustments in the placement of furniture and objects can be made easily to ensure clear, uncluttered, safe paths that facilitate the development of purposeful movement skills (see Modules 15–19 for more information).

The home is a natural place for students who are deaf-blind to learn to use purposeful movement skills. Students can be encouraged to be active in their homes and to develop safe and independent movement within them.

Purposeful movement skills also enable students to participate in the variety of activities involved in daily routines, such as helping to set the table, wash dishes, or get the mail. Each task a student learns increases his or her autonomy at home. Participating in household chores also improves a student's relationships with siblings and relieves other family members from having to perform the chores.

As they acquire purposeful movement skills at home, students also can learn to be independent. When they have the skills to move about their home environments to attend to their basic needs safely, their families can begin to plan structured situations that allow the students to be more independent in activities at home that will move them toward independence as adults. Students who have purposeful movement skills to manage daily living tasks may have increased options for living outside their homes as they make the transition to adulthood (see Modules 14 and 20). Knowing this makes planning for the future an ongoing activity that is easier both for the individual who is deaf-blind and for the family as the person matures.

## SCHOOL

Students have many opportunities to practice all the components of purposeful movement throughout the school day. While traveling to school from home and moving through the school building during the course of the day, a student encounters peers and participates in activities in rooms other than the primary classroom. When a student moves through the school independently and purposefully, he or she increases knowledge and awareness of the surroundings in general and gains confidence to handle various aspects of the environment (elevators, stairs, lines, crowds, and obstacles) safely.

As students who are deaf-blind become increasingly mobile in school, they become more visible to and have greater opportunities to interact with the other students and the staff. This natural interaction allows everyone to see their abilities and to perceive them as active learners and partners in all school activities.

## COMMUNITY

Purposeful movement skills give students who are deaf-blind greater access to experiences in their communities. The benefits include personal autonomy; increased awareness of persons, places, and objects in the community at large; and the possible evolution of more "user-friendly" services in the community for persons with disabilities (see Modules 3, 13, and 19). Beyond the school and home, there are streets, sidewalks, public transportation, stores, restaurants, and many people who are unfamiliar to students who are deaf-blind. Exploration and involvement increase the students' awareness and environmental knowledge and opportunities to participate in recreational activities, such as going to the park or eating in neighborhood restaurants.

The Americans with Disabilities Act of 1990 requires that community facilities be made accessible to people with disabilities. Its regulations include specifications for the design of barrier-free buildings and transportation, as well as requirements for places that accommodate the public to provide aids and services to make their programs and services accessible. The intent of this legislation is to enable individuals who are disabled to exercise their right to negotiate and use community resources. Purposeful movement skills enable students who are deaf-blind to take advantage of these changes.

It may be that not all students who are deaf-blind will learn to move independently through their communities. Still, they can all learn to move purposefully using travel skills that meet their individual needs. Students' abilities to use guided assistance effectively in new or complex environments ensure that they will have opportunities to interact in their communities.

As the students gain self-confidence and autonomy by participating in their communities, their interactions with peers, workers, and others in the community are expanded and enhanced. In turn, people in the community learn much when given opportunities to interact with students who are deaf-blind. The more such opportunities individuals have, the more responsive they will be to students' needs as consumers and community members.

## WORKPLACE

Transition programs help students with disabilities leave their school environments and enter the world of work. Students' abilities to travel to and from jobs and to move purposefully and independently through their workplaces are major issues for planning such transitions (for more information, see Modules 14 and 20).

Students who have had opportunities to learn and practice the skills associated with the components of purposeful movement throughout childhood and adolescence are likely to find it easier to get to or about the workplace during the transition years. Purposeful movement and communication skills also enable them to establish relationships and to interact with employers and co-workers. When deaf-blind students can interact and participate actively in this way, their employers and co-workers tend to think of them as being like themselves: workers with jobs to do. When students have purposeful movement skills, their job skills and interests, rather than movement in the workplace, can be the major focus of vocational planning and training.

## LEISURE SETTINGS

Since adult living arrangements and social activities are important parts of students' lives, skills related to purposeful movement are also critical in these areas. Having the skills to communicate the desire to move, to initiate action, and to travel with purposeful movement enables students to participate in a wide range of social activities. Accompanying friends to events and visiting their homes are also enhanced when movement through social and recreational settings in the community is possible.

# LONG-RANGE BENEFITS

## ENSURING PERSONAL SAFETY

Fear or anxiety that is generated by not knowing where one is or what is ahead certainly impedes movement. For students who are deaf-blind, the unknown can be as near as the space surrounding them that is beyond arms' reach. However, their ability to perform movement skills expands the space and hence enlarges their world. By learning to move through natural environments, students can come to recognize objects that are specific to daily living settings (safety belts in vehicles, toilets in bathrooms, and refrigerators in kitchens, for example) and those that are found in various environments (stairs and doors). With this knowledge, they can generalize information and develop concepts about the natural environments that, in turn, help them protect themselves.

As students learn when it is safe to move, when not to venture out, and when to request assistance, they usually are more willing to enter unfamiliar settings. Family members also become more confident and comfortable in accepting the students' increased freedom of movement when the students demonstrate their understanding of safety principles.

## ENHANCING AUTONOMY AND INDEPENDENCE

The level of independence that students attain is affected by the nature and degrees of their disabilities, their individual skills and interests, and the opportunities available to them. The population of students who are deaf-blind is diverse, and not all students will achieve the same degree of independence. Nevertheless, all can develop some independence and assume some control over their own activities. The goal of instruction in purposeful movement is for students to conceive of themselves as separate individuals who are able to initiate movement. For example, with three children who are hungry, the first child may cry to get attention, remaining dependent on an adult to respond, interpret the act, and satisfy the need; the second child may take an object, such as a spoon or a bowl, and give it to the adult, performing a more autonomous act with appropriate interaction (the act of communication is independent because it is initiated by the child, even though the child is still dependent on the adult to respond to the request); and the third child may move independently into the kitchen and take food from the refrigerator, requiring no intervention from another person.

Many students achieve independent movement only within protected environments. Other students may learn to travel independently in their communities, using public transportation. But every student can gain the satisfaction of independent action from purposeful movement.

Knowing how to move purposefully encourages the development of autonomy as a student realizes that he or she can have control over and influence the world through his or her actions. Increased autonomy leads to a greater sense of independence and affects how the student who is deaf-blind perceives other people and how he or she is perceived by others.

## BUILDING SELF-CONFIDENCE

Having a good self-image and a sense of self-esteem is necessary to develop the confidence to meet new challenges, and being able to complete tasks independently increases students' self-esteem and self-confidence. These personal attributes influence students' interactions with their environments throughout their lives.

Teaching purposeful movement to young children provides the foundation for developing more confident behavior as they grow older. As they mature and their patterns of behavior are set, it becomes more difficult for them to change these patterns. Introducing purposeful movement to young children by allowing them to initiate an activity and to perform it "independently" encourages them to believe in their own abilities and to develop self-confidence and self-esteem, as the following case of Juanita illustrates:

*The mobility instructor developed a purposeful movement program to teach Juanita, who is 15 years old and deaf-blind, to move around the school by herself. Juanita first learned to go*

▲ *Encouraging children to move can contribute to their self-confidence as well as their ability to travel safely and obtain information about the environment.*

*to the main office from her classroom to deliver the attendance sheet. She performed this task each day using a route that involved going up and down a few steps that she had never used alone. There was much to learn, and it was some time before Juanita was able to deliver the attendance sheet by herself. However, she did learn and became the monitor for her class.*

*A visitor who saw Juanita at the start of her instruction thought she would never be able to walk through the building alone. When he later saw Juanita go to the office independently, he remarked that he did not think she was the same person. He described Juanita as someone who has "confidence in herself and walks with an air of independence." This was not so dramatic a change to her teachers who worked with her every day, but to the visitor, the difference was great.*

Purposeful movement instruction encourages such gains for a student who is deaf-blind.

## EXPANDING OPTIONS FOR INDEPENDENT LIVING

Students will benefit greatly from their abilities to move independently about their environments in performing the various tasks of daily living for themselves. For example, the student who has the skills necessary for taking care of personal hygiene may still be dependent on another person unless he or she is able to locate the bathroom alone.

In addition to these task-related gains, there may be personal life-long benefits for students. Eliminating students' dependence on others, when possible, promotes a sense of comfort and well-being. Having the skills necessary to ensure safety makes life easier and more comfortable. The ability to go someplace when one wants to encourages the development of self-confidence and self-esteem. Being independent, self-confident, and autonomous promotes students' full participation as productive adult members of the community.

Another important facet of students' lives that can be affected by purposeful movement skills is the settings in which they will ultimately live as adults. Purposeful movement skills that are acquired throughout childhood and adolescence enhance independence for carrying out daily living tasks, including shopping, working, and using public transportation. Students who have traveled in their communities have firsthand knowledge of community resources. This knowledge can help them make informed decisions about selecting from various housing options when the time comes for them to do so.

# MOBILITY PROGRAMS

Mobility programs teach students to move purposefully and safely at home, at school, at work, and in the community. Embedding instruction for purposeful movement in the educational programs of students who are deaf-blind is fundamental to the students' ultimate ability to participate in daily life.

In Unit 3, you will learn about the motor development of students who are deaf-blind and about how transdisciplinary educational teams go about including mobility education, in the form of O&M instruction, in students' educational programs. By helping students develop the ability to move about as safely and independently as possible, teachers and other members of the educational team can help them expand the horizons of their activities and lives.

# REFERENCES

Barraga, N. C. (1992). *Visual handicaps and learning* (3rd ed.). Austin, TX: PRO-ED.

Pogrund, R. L., Fazzi, D. L., & Lampert, J. S. (Eds.). (1992). *Early focus: Working with young blind and visually impaired children and their families.* New York: American Foundation for the Blind.

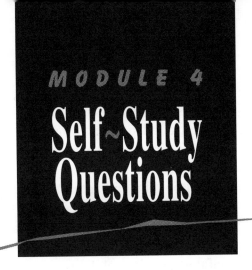

**M O D U L E  4**

# Self~Study Questions

1. Learning to move purposefully helps students
   a. develop independence in all environments.
   b. overcome physical limitations.
   c. gain confidence in their ability to move and learn various environments.
   d. take greater risks in outside environments.

2. Students who are deaf-blind need to know that
   a. they can move purposefully and independently.
   b. they have the right to move, rather than be led.
   c. they must learn special skills to move about safely.
   d. all the above.

3. Being aware of their surroundings requires students to identify
   a. the objects and persons in the environment.
   b. all the hazards and obstacles that could be in the way.
   c. all the people who are near.
   d. the distance between objects in the environment.

4. The home is a natural environment for teaching students to move with purpose because it
   a. is a relatively small space occupied by people who are involved with the student.
   b. provides opportunities for students to become responsible for managing their daily routines.
   c. provides opportunities for students and their families to develop confidence in purposeful movement skills.
   d. all the above.

5. After a student has had the opportunity to learn and practice purposeful movement in familiar environments,
   a. learning to move independently in the workplace becomes a major issue.
   b. the student will not require instruction to move about the workplace and community.
   c. the student can be an active learner and partner in school and the community.
   d. none of the above.

**6.** For a person who is deaf-blind, choosing a living situation
   a. is dependent on the ability to move independently through the community.
   b. is influenced by the individual's degree of personal independence and mobility.
   c. has nothing to do with movement skills.
   d. is taken care of by the family without the individual's direct participation.

**7.** A long-range benefit for students who can move safely and with confidence is
   a. their complete independence in performing basic life skills.
   b. their families' increased confidence in their abilities.
   c. their complete independence from adults.

*Answers to self-study questions for this module appear at the end of Unit 1.*

# Effective Service Delivery

*THERESE RAFALOWSKI WELCH*

## CONTRIBUTORS

**CHIGEE JAN CLONINGER**
*Educational Teams*

- *Appreciate the importance of assessment*

- *Build a program around a student's strengths and needs*

- *Recognize the family's essential role*

- *Make use of team efforts*

- *Take advantage of all available resources*

**B**ecause of the combined effects of vision and hearing loss, deaf-blindness is a unique disability, bringing with it unique learning needs for the individual child. Effective teaching of deaf-blind children means meeting these unique needs to the maximum extent possible.

Previous modules have outlined various aspects of deaf-blindness, particularly the importance of providing deaf-blind children with as many skills and options for communication and orientation and mobility (O&M) as possible; the units that follow provide in-depth information on these aspects, as well as instructional strategies for helping deaf-blind children develop these essential skills. This module explores concepts and strategies that are fundamental to teaching deaf-blind children effectively. Primary among these ideas are adopting a holistic approach based on the assessment of the individual student's abilities and needs; working as part of a team; involving the student's family and using input provided from family members; and making use of all available resources.

# ASSESSMENT

Assessment is at the heart of planning an educational program for a child. How can anyone know what a child needs to learn if it has not been determined what the child already knows and already can do? Often, students who are deaf-blind have many more capabilities than may be apparent. This may be true especially if a student has not

- had ongoing instruction or intervention that has mediated for the lack or limitations of vision and hearing
- been taught how to use remaining vision or hearing
- had instruction in effective means of communicating with others
- been encouraged or instructed in how to move purposefully and efficiently
- had the benefit of having learned to seek information.

Assessment can be described as the gathering of information to help guide decisions about a student's needs. Its purpose is to facilitate planning of the educational program, services, and interventions from which the student can benefit the most. Module 11 presents an

in-depth discussion of the numerous principles and procedures involved in assessment (see also Assessment Tips for Teachers in this module). A key point in the assessment of students who are deaf-blind is that it is essential to apply an ecological approach, in which the individual child is viewed as a whole and his or her everyday environments are carefully considered (for detailed information on this approach, see Modules 13 and 14).

Teachers who use assessment as the basis of their educational planning will find that the input of other professionals and of the child's family is critical. The benefits of being part of a transdisciplinary educational team cannot be overestimated in working with deaf-blind students.

▲ *Setting goals and teaching skills relevant to a student's daily life and environments are essential to meeting the student's educational needs.*

# EDUCATIONAL TEAMS

Teamwork is a key concept for teachers of deaf-blind students. It is unrealistic to expect one person to have all the answers for teaching a student who is deaf-blind, even when that person is considered an

# Assessment Tips for Teachers

June E. Downing

Assessment should be viewed not as an end product of instruction or intervention, but as an ongoing information-gathering process in specific contexts that are meaningful for a student. The information that is obtained should alert the teacher to the most effective way to teach, the optimal learning environment for the student, and the learning activities that reflect the student's needs and motivation. Here are some guidelines for conducting assessments:

• Information obtained in interviews with the student and those closest to him or her (family members and friends) should guide the assessment. Such information will help determine which activities are important for the student to learn, which skills are needed to perform the activities and in which environments, which motivating factors are necessary for optimal learning, which activities should be avoided, and the most effective way of teaching.

• Assessment is always contextually bound, since the student's environments and the important activities in them demand different types and levels of participation.

• There are no absolute levels of performance. Rather, the need for a certain level of performance depends on the expectations of the physical and social environment and the student's desire to meet them. Therefore, the strengths and limitations of both the student and the environment must be assessed.

• To gain a clear picture of a student's strengths and limitations, it is necessary to gather as much information about the student in as many different activities and situations as possible.

• All members of the educational team should collaborate to collect the necessary information. Thus, it is necessary for the team to appraise honestly when, where, and how each member can contribute best.

• The assessment should help the educational team decide when the student can learn a particular skill and when the skill must be adapted to his or her sensory or physical disabilities.

• To shorten his or her part of the assessment process, the teacher can incorporate an information-gathering process into lesson plans and data collection procedures.

• The identification of the natural cues of an activity and environment is part of an assessment and will help the teacher determine how best to direct the student's attention to the cues. If these cues are not identified, the teacher tends to teach the student how to respond to a prompt from him or her, rather than to natural environmental situations.

• Clinical and out-of-context assessments (ophthalmological, intellectual, physical, or auditory) provide only a small part of the picture. How the motivated student responds in familiar activities and environments with the support of trusted others can present a much broader picture of the student's strengths and limitations. ■

expert on deaf-blindness. Instead, a team approach with a strong home-school partnership is essential. The best educational programs are developed when a group of individuals who are invested in a student's success—the student, family members, instructors, classmates, various specialists, and other service providers—share their knowledge and skills (Thousand & Villa, 1992).

Often, the team does not capitalize on its potential power because the team is a team in name only, individuals who are key to the student's education are only minimally involved, and the plans may foster a compartmentalized approach. It is in the best interests of all who are invested in the student's education to try to build a truly collaborative team and to deliver services in an integrated manner.

Ideally, each student who is deaf-blind should have a strong, effective team to develop and deliver an educational program. That ideal, however, may not yet be a reality in some schools. If it is not, the teacher may have to assume nearly the full responsibility for carrying out a student's educational program and to use an informal process (telephone calls, outside consultations, and the like) to receive and compile information from other service providers and specialists. In such circumstances, checking with one's supervisor, building principal, or special education director about obtaining some in-service training on collaborative teaming can be helpful. Whatever the situation, it is vital to have a strong partnership with the student's family and to build the educational program on the foundation of the family's priorities.

## PRINCIPLES OF TEAM COLLABORATION

Depending on the child's needs, team members should include parents and other family members, special education teachers, O&M instructors, physical therapists, communication specialists, occupational therapists, providers of related services, teacher assistants, transitional specialists, rehabilitation counselors, independent living personnel, community-based service providers, administrators (see Shared Efforts in this module), staff of residential programs, university trainers, community members, and the student's classmates. Although the general responsibilities of all team members are to design, implement, and evaluate a student's Individualized Education Program (IEP), the specific responsibilities of team members are unique to each student. Common team activities include conducting

# Shared Efforts

Steven B. Johnson

It is critical for teachers and other educational team members to remember that they and their administrators are on the same team. We are a partnership working for students. As part of the team, it is essential to call on the knowledge, expertise, and resources of the other members. Here are suggestions for working effectively in team efforts with administrators:

• Members of the team need to hear about what is working. They may not have the daily feedback of seeing students progress. Teachers and other staff do. Please let others know about this feedback.

• When working with students, it is important to look at what has been tried before, what has worked, and what has not been so successful. Review the Individualized Education Program (IEP) and identify the services that are to be provided. Remind others who are responsible for services of the commitments that have been made.

• Teachers and others on the team should be encouraged to be confident in their skills and abilities. And when they do not have an answer,

they should be encouraged to let their administrators know. The next stage, the next idea, the next technique can be explored together.

• Notes and records are essential, and sharing them with administrators and other team members is essential, too. Shared information also means talking with others who see the child in different settings, letting them know what you are doing, and asking them what they are doing and what they see.

• Plans for the student's future should not be a surprise for anyone. Discuss them with team members, and try to have administrators be the facilitators to help.

• Plans, discussions, and strategic management make a difference. Knowledge of the laws and regulations that govern programs and define the rights and protections for students and families is invaluable, as is a knowledge of district services.

• It also helps to remember that teachers are teachers because they care about children and their families and that other team members are in education for the same reason. ■

assessments for program planning, developing lesson plans, preparing materials, monitoring and evaluating the student's progress in attaining goals and objectives, providing support to the student and to each other, adapting the curriculum, scheduling activities, sharing expertise, synthesizing information, and completing paperwork.

The skilled professionals on the team must be encouraged to share their expertise with each other and to work in collaboration.

Collaboration fosters an atmosphere of focused programming that enables the team members to tackle both the day-to-day and larger (or long-term) educational challenges of the student.

From the design of the student's program to implementation and evaluation, teamwork is essential. The foundations of an effective team lie in its shared framework and pursuit of unified goals. In an effective team effort, the identification, provision, and evaluation of individual educational services is based on the following factors:

- *The identification of the student's needs based on the student's current performance.* The development of the student's educational program needs to be founded on an assessment that is child specific and also needs to reflect learning outcomes valued by the family (including the student), the student's preferences and learning styles, and a broad curriculum.

- *The content of the student's program—the skills a student learns—which has been selected as a result of the team's assessment of the student's needs.* Learning should be functional and relevant to the student and age appropriate. The skills to be acquired should promote the student's independence and interdependence.

- *The provision of all general supports necessary to help the student attain the identified goals according to the student's identified needs.* The student's needs, not the setting or placement, ought to dictate the adaptations or accommodations that are made. The five areas in which supports may be required are (1) personal needs (feeding, dressing, tending to personal hygiene and medical needs), (2) physical needs (managing special equipment, making environmental modifications), (3) sensory needs (accommodating for visual and hearing impairments, for example), (4) staff and peer education about the student (informing others how to communicate with the student and what certain sounds or behaviors mean), and (5) provision of access and opportunities (arranging a vocational setting, enrolling a student in extracurricular activities) (Giangreco, Cloninger, & Iverson, 1992).

- *The determination of the educational services needed to implement the educational program.* This determination is made on the basis of the student's identified goals, objectives, and general supports.

- *The evaluation of the outcomes and goals of the program.* The team needs to design the evaluation to acquire information about all aspects of the educational program and to answer the basic question: "Is this student's life better as a result of the program?" Changes in the program are based on the outcomes. The following are basic questions to consider in an evaluation: Has learning occurred? How has learning occurred? What has been effective or ineffective? Is the evaluation of learning easy to do and ongoing, and does it involve all team members, including the student? Is the way in which the team accomplishes its tasks and works together also being evaluated? Has the program expanded opportunities for integration?

Team collaboration is more effective when it is governed by the following principles:

- The student who is deaf-blind is the most important member of the team.
- Families are essential to individualizing education.
- Teamwork is an ongoing cooperative and problem-solving process.
- Team members have high expectations that an IEP will strengthen the quality of the student's life.
- The use of consistent interactions in natural contexts is generally the most effective teaching strategy.

The team needs to be alert to barriers that interfere with its effective functioning. One such barrier is its size. Thus, when many individuals are working with a student, the team members may choose to organize themselves into a core team of individuals who have daily responsibility for the student (such as one of the child's parents, the general education teacher, the special education teacher, and the teacher assistant) and an extended team that includes members of the core team plus those who interact less frequently with the student, such as the O&M instructor, physical therapist, teacher of students with visual impairments (itinerant personnel), principal, and school nurse (Giangreco, Cloninger, & Iverson, 1989, 1992). Subteams may be formed at any point to focus on a specific need or challenge (Skrtic, 1991). Other configurations may enable teams to function with a reasonable number of members—usually five to seven.

Various models of team functioning exist, such as interdisciplinary and multidisciplinary models (see, for example, Perske & Smith, 1977), all of which involve the efforts of a variety of specialists who collaborate to varying degrees. In the trandsdisciplinary model, referred to throughout this book, one or a few people are primarily responsible for direct contact with the child, and the deliberate pooling and exchange of information, knowledge, and skills from all team members is ongoing (Hutchinson, 1974; Fazzi, Pogrund, & Zambone, 1992).

## CHARACTERISTICS OF EFFECTIVE TEAMS

The following are seven basic characteristics of an effective team (Giangreco, 1989):

1.  The team members (including the family) have unique skills and experience in instructional and managerial practices that serve specific functions. For example, they may function as trainers of trainers, adapters of O&M equipment, lesson designers, evaluators of communication skills, or teachers. The various members explain, model, and provide feedback about specialized techniques in ways that enable all the members to understand the information at their own levels of need.

2.  The team develops coordinated programs and pursues unified goals and educational supports for the student. All the team members, including the O&M instructor and the communication specialist, decide what learning outcomes in communication and O&M are desirable for a student and how they may be learned in all settings, from the homeroom to the physical education class to the language arts class. These specialists are not solely responsible for carrying out instruction in all settings or even in one setting—all team members are responsible for instruction.

3.  The team engages in problem-solving and collaborative activities to reach shared goals. Strategies that facilitate collaboration include engaging in regular interactions, following meeting agendas, sharing leadership, using good interpersonal and group skills, and using creative problem-solving strategies for resolving conflicts and making decisions. Team members face problems as challenges to be met and believe

that their shared expertise and problem-solving skills are sufficient for designing and carrying out a student's IEP. Most teams benefit from continuing instruction and practice in effective team strategies because the various traditional professional preparation programs do not prepare professionals to work intensively on teams.

4. The team shares and allocates resources to help the student attain his or her goals. Again, all team members contribute expertise, materials, and time to design and carry out instruction, monitoring, and evaluation. At any given time, each person is both an expert-consultant and a recipient-consultee; no one member has sole authority.

5. The team members decide how they will operate to accomplish tasks and maintain working relationships. They need to decide many issues, including these:

   - how often to meet
   - where to meet
   - which members should be on core and extended teams
   - how meetings are to be run
   - how leadership roles are to be distributed and rotated
   - how all members can participate in the meetings
   - how agendas should be set
   - how minutes are to be kept
   - how absent or late members will be updated
   - how communication among the members is to be maintained
   - how successes can be shared and celebrated
   - how members should be held accountable for responsibilities.

6. The team members regularly monitor and evaluate not only the student's program, but the work of the team and support each other to improve their skills in various areas, including communication, O&M, and team collaboration. They also define a process for the ongoing instruction, monitoring, and evaluation of teacher assistants.

7. The team judges its successes or failures by the group's achievement of the unified set of goals, rather than by the

performance of individual members. Because all members have contributed to the design, implementation, and evaluation of a student's program, all are responsible for the progress and setbacks that occur. When a problem arises, the entire team deals with it by identifying the parameters of and specifically stating the problem, brainstorming ideas to solve the problem, and designing a concrete plan of action to resolve the problem.

A crucial focus for any team is to ensure ongoing communication among all team members and with others, such as the district special education coordinator, the principal, and the state coordinator of deaf-blind services. Integrated assessment, initial and ongoing planning, monitoring, evaluating, and training depend on communication, which occurs primarily in the team meetings. In these meetings, the team members identify formal and informal systems of communication (minutes, report writing, updating absent members, shared decision making) and have the opportunity to practice and maintain communication skills, including giving and receiving information and feedback, problem solving, resolving conflicts, and evaluation.

Administrators and school personnel who support a team approach to education need to establish the expectation that teachers will collaborate. They must also give the team time to meet—before or after school or by hiring a full-time contracted substitute to rotate among classes or by assigning specialists, nurses, counselors, teacher assistants, and administrators to cover classes when their own teams are not meeting.

The team meetings should focus on the tasks at hand and how the tasks are being accomplished. During the meetings, the members need to look carefully at their group and individual operations and performance, both successes and mistakes; apply new skills to the situations; and set goals for change. Discussions of how the team is functioning as a cooperative unit prevent breakdowns in communication, misunderstandings, and members' sense of isolation and increase the members' interdependence.

Paperwork—and lots of it—is an inevitable part of teaching. A team can minimize the paperwork, yet maintain essential records of activities, by formulating a policy that everyone must contribute, and by deciding which types of written communication are required.

Some paperwork is mandatory, so the decisions involve whose turn it is to do it, when and by what method (written or audio- or videotape) it will be done, how it will be distributed, and how it will be stored, keeping in mind the tenet of shared contribution and responsibility. The team should establish a simple format for recording the minutes of its meetings, so the minutes can be taken by any member whose turn it is to be the recorder and can be easily reproduced and distributed.

# WORKING WITH FAMILIES

The student's family, including parents, siblings, and extended family members, as well as others who play a primary role in the student's life, such as caregivers, are vital members of the educational team. As the team plans and implements the educational plan, the family members' concerns, observations, and priorities need to be considered the core of the plan. The family members know the student best. Thus, they are an essential resource and source of information, and the partnership between them and professionals who work with a child can be the cornerstone of educational efforts.

## BASIC PRINCIPLES

In working with a child's family, the other members of the educational team need to keep the following principles in mind:

- Talk with parents as peers. Avoid the use of jargon and "legalese."

- Make every effort to get information from the family for a student's program, recognizing that the family members are the child's primary teachers.

- Let the family members know that their involvement is important and valued, not that you are simply obliged to ask them to participate.

- Be positive, patient, and respectful. Negative experiences with professionals may color the family members' initial responses to you. It may take time to win their trust.

- Take a broad view of "participation" and provide the family members with options. They may want to attend meetings, talk with you over the phone, meet with an individual team member, or respond to questions and concerns in writing.

- Keep families informed about the program and give them access to information on resources.

- Respect the family's culture, including its distinctive beliefs, values, and traditions.

- Communicate with the family members in their preferred language and use an interpreter if necessary.

- Link the parents with other parents of deaf-blind children.

- Provide data when decisions need to be made. Distinguish your opinions from actual facts.

- Respect the family's choices, privacy, and right to disagree with you.

- Set convenient meeting times and places to accommodate the schedules of working parents and parents of young children. Consider the parents' child care and transportation needs.

- Do not give up. Do not assume that family members will never participate just because they have not responded to invitations. It is impossible to understand fully a family's circumstances at a particular time. Be sensitive to the stresses that family members may be undergoing.

Teachers' efforts to help students develop skills can be powerfully reinforced by family members. Whether in the area of communication, O&M, daily living skills, cognitive development, or social skills, early interactions at home with family can support a child's development. It is important to help families find strategies that enhance their children's progress and to support their involvement as members of the educational team (see Helping Families Communicate: A Parent's View in this module).

## FOSTERING CONTACT AMONG FAMILIES

It can be helpful for families of students who are deaf-blind (especially parents) to be in contact with each other. With such contact, they can provide moral support to one another; share their experiences and information on specific issues of family care, resources, and developments in the field; and advocate for developing and improving services to individuals who are deaf-blind and their families. How contact is established, either formally or informally, will depend on the families' needs and preferences at a particular time, as well as the options that are available. Teachers and other members of the educational team can help parents gain access to the most appropriate options. Here are a few suggestions:

## One-to-One Contacts

Personal contacts may be preferred by parents who are not "joiners" or by those whose first language is not English. One-to-one contacts can be especially helpful for parents whose children have rare disor-

# Helping Families Communicate: A Parent's View

Joyce Ford

Families need ongoing help to improve their and their children's communication skills at home. Such help leads to a strong partnership between them and service providers in which the partners complement each other's efforts and maximize the student's opportunities to participate in a variety of environments.

Family members may believe that the home environment should mirror the educational environment. However, meaningful communication can best be fostered if they and other members of the educational team consider the uniqueness of the home environment and find ways to include the student in the family's daily routines, special occasions, and visits with relatives and friends.

Here are some points to keep in mind in helping the family build communication skills:

• Family members benefit when they receive information that applies to everyday occurrences. Some of the many questions that they may ask include these: How do family members introduce themselves when they enter a room with the child? What means can they use to convey information about an activity that is going to occur? How can they incorporate choices for the child?

• Language is only one aspect of communication, regardless of a person's age, environment, or abilities. Gestures, posture, touch, and objects are also important for communicating, as are fragrance, temperature, and taste.

• Simulating the experience of being deaf-blind may make it easier for family members to recognize opportunities for communica-

*(continued)*

ders or special needs. To help parents establish such contacts, you may find the following strategies useful:

- Introduce interested families to other families you know.

- Ask organized groups of parents, other teachers, or staff at the state or multistate deaf-blind project if they know of parents who would be willing to talk with interested families.

- Encourage parents to attend workshops and conferences where they may meet other parents.

## Parent or Family Groups

Ideally, your area would have a group specifically for parents or families of individuals who are deaf-blind. If no such group exists,

## Helping Families Communicate
### Continued

tion. When family members perceive information the way the deaf-blind child does, they may develop a new approach to adaptations and accommodations. All family members, including siblings, can participate in simulation activities, which can be repeated when the student progressess to a new level of independence.

- Recognize ways to increase siblings' ability to communicate and the value of their opinions. Start by asking, What interests do the children have in common? Which activities will encourage interaction and be enjoyable for them all? Because the home environment offers a wide range of opportunities to communicate, interactions do not have to be staged; rather, the children's relationships should develop naturally, in the context of everyday life, and without pressure.

- The concept of shared pleasure is basic to all sound relationships. It can be fostered if the immediate family teaches the student's grandparents, aunts and uncles, and cousins to communicate with the student and to engage in activities that they all enjoy.

- As family members acquire greater confidence and skill in their ability to communicate and encourage the student to interact with others in the community, the student may have many more opportunities to build meaningful communication, both receptively and expressively; to learn to communicate in a variety of ways; to make choices; and to engage in mutually enjoyable activities, from buying a cookie at a bakery to participating in games with nondisabled children, and hence to become more independent. ∎

parents may find it helpful to join groups that address more general disability-related concerns. They may also be interested in forming their own group or a deaf-blind subgroup of a larger organization. To help parents join or form a group, you can contact the following resources:

- the state or multistate deaf-blind project, for information on existing groups in your area or on starting a group (see Module 1 for more information)

- the National Family Association for Deaf-Blind, (800) 255-0411, and the Hilton/Perkins Program, (617) 972-7220, for information on and support in starting a group on leadership-development opportunities

- the National Information Center for Children and Youth with Disabilities, (800) 695-0285, for a State Resource Sheet that lists parents' groups by state and information on developing groups. (Additional information on the organizations mentioned in this list is in the Resources section.)

You may also find the following hints to be helpful:

- Encourage families to subscribe to local and national newsletters on deaf-blindness, which often have columns devoted to questions from families, including families who are interested in corresponding with other families (see Resources).

- Be mindful of confidentiality issues when linking families. Carefully negotiate ways to share essential information without violating individuals' rights to privacy and agencies' policies on confidentiality.

- Consider all family members, not only parents; siblings, grandparents, and other relatives may want the support that personal or group contacts provide.

# USE OF AVAILABLE RESOURCES

The job of working successfully with students who are deaf-blind—and deriving satisfaction from that success—can be facilitated when teachers make use of any and all resources available to them. Module 1 provided information on a variety of sources of information and assistance, and others—for example, the American Printing House for the Blind (APH), which is discussed here—exist as well.

## AMERICAN PRINTING HOUSE

APH is a national organization that produces literature and manufactures educational aids for students who are blind or visually impaired. It publishes braille books, music, and magazines; large-type textbooks, Talking Books and magazines; microcomputer software; and electronic books. It also has a reference-catalog service and maintains an educational research and development program that concentrates on educational procedures and methods and the development of educational aids.

Since 1879, through a federal act "To Promote the Education of the Blind," APH has received an annual appropriation from Congress to provide textbooks and educational aids for all students attending primary- and secondary-level schools or special educational institutions. States can get materials and equipment from APH without cost up to the amount of their federal quota allocations.

The APH quota program is administered by a designated state agency, generally the state instructional materials center (IMC), department of education, or residential school. You can find out the designated agency in your state by calling APH at (502) 895-2405 or (800) 223-1839. (For more on IMCs, see Module 1; for more on APH, see the Resources section.)

During January of each year, the designated state agency conducts a registration of students who are blind or visually impaired in the state to establish the state's proportional credit allotment with APH. Teachers of students who are visually impaired and their supervisors generally complete the registration forms and submit purchase requests for materials available through the APH quota program. Other teachers may complete the registration forms as well, along with a special education supervisor.

The allotment to the states is based on the number of students in the state. It is distributed to students in a state who apply for funds, but it should be noted that the allotment is modest, averaging around $100 per student. APH publishes a free catalog of its educational materials and updates that are available on request.

## INSTRUCTIONAL MATERIALS

As Module 1 indicated, IMCs provide many different types of materials for direct use by students, as well as materials to help teachers. They receive and process requests, arrange for shipment, and keep an inventory so materials can be recirculated. Materials are generally lent to teachers or students for certain periods, such as the academic year; however, some are lent for long-term use, and others, including interactive large-print workbooks for students, are not expected to be returned. IMCs can provide a wealth of information. Furthermore, they perform additional roles that may vary from state to state. Some administer the APH quota program, some determine the in-service training needs of teachers and develop and administer in-service training programs, some serve all disability areas and others are specific to low-prevalence populations, and still others serve the needs of single-disability areas.

Other sources of assistance can be found through the state deaf-blind projects described in Module 1 (see also The Annual Census in this module). In addition, a number of professionals who specialize in vision or hearing can be consulted.

## VISION AND HEARING PROFESSIONALS

Consulting with specialists knowledgeable about vision and hearing can provide valuable information and insights about a particular child. When educational staff meet with these specialists, it is helpful to be prepared with any questions posed by educational team members. Accompanying a student to evaluation sessions and checkups is a valuable opportunity to learn more about the student and provide specialists with useful information on the student's progress and performance in school. Figures 5-1 and 5-2 at the end of this module are assessment forms that can be used to gather information from vision and hearing specialists. The following professionals evaluate and treat people with visual impairments and work with them in education and rehabilitation:

- *Ophthalmologist*: a physician who specializes in diseases of the eye. An ophthalmologist is licensed to perform surgery and to prescribe medications and corrective contact lenses and eyeglasses.
- *Optometrist*: a licensed, nonmedical practitioner who is trained and specializes in the measurement of refractive

# The Annual Census
## Vic Baldwin

The U.S. Department of Education conducts an annual census of all children with deaf-blindness in the United States. Each year the directors of every state or multistate deaf-blind project are required to collect information on their state's or region's children who are deaf-blind and to fill out a census data form. Teaching Research in Monmouth, Oregon (see the Resources section for more information), assists the department in collecting and reporting these national data.

The following information is reported on the census data form for each child: identification code (the child's name is not reported), sex, birthdate, major cause of deaf-blindness, degree of vision loss, degree of hearing loss, other disabilities, the category under which the state or region reports the child for Part B or Chapter 1 of Title I, whether the child receives services under Part H of the Individuals with Disabilities Education Act, and the settings in which the child receives services. These data provide a national profile of the population of children who are deaf-blind.

This information is reported to Congress and is used to determine funding for the U.S. Department of Education's Services for Children with Deaf-Blindness Program, which includes all the state and multistate deaf-blind projects and other projects serving children and youths who are deaf-blind, and can directly affect the funding received by individual state or multistate deaf-blind projects. The number of children reported is also an important factor in awarding grants to projects.

The census is important to teachers because having a student on a state's census for children with deaf-blindness is the key to the receipt of services from the state or multistate deaf-blind project by the student and his or her family and his or her teachers, instructors, and service providers. These services include training, consultation, provision of instructional and informational materials and resources, and educational program support. Therefore, teachers who have students with vision and hearing impairments should contact their state or multistate deaf-blind project to make sure that the students are included in the census. For information on whom to contact, phone DB-LINK, the National Information Clearinghouse on Children Who Are Deaf-Blind at (800) 438-9376 or (800) 854-7013 (TTY/TDD). Data collection procedures may vary from state to state. ■

errors and eye-muscle disturbances. An optometrist may prescribe corrective contact lenses and eyeglasses.

- *Optician*: a technician who prepares contact lenses and eyeglasses according to prescription. An optician is trained to fit eyeglasses and to adjust frames.

- *Orthoptist*: a technician who makes and fits ocular prostheses (artificial eyes).

- *Teacher of visually impaired students*: a certified teacher in special education of children with visual impairments who is also usually certified in elementary or secondary education.

- *Low vision specialist*: a rehabilitation teacher, an O&M specialist, or another professional who has been trained and specializes in the assessment and development of residual vision.

- *O&M specialist*: a professional who has been trained and specializes in the delivery of O&M services to children or adults who are visually impaired. An O&M specialist is sometimes referred to as an O&M instructor, O&M therapist, or peripatologist.

The following professionals evaluate and treat people with hearing impairments and work with them in education and rehabilitation:

- *Otolaryngologist*: a physician who specializes in the treatment of diseases affecting the auditory system, the nose, and the throat. An otolaryngologist is licensed to perform surgery and to write prescriptions for medications.

- *Audiologist*: a trained service provider who is certified to specialize in the identification and measurement of hearing loss, as well as the rehabilitation process. An audiologist usually has a graduate degree and may be certified by the American Speech-Language-Hearing Association (see Resources).

- *Speech-language pathologist or communication specialist*: a certified specialist who is trained to help people with communication problems achieve their maximum communication potential, which may involve compensatory techniques and equipment. This specialist has a graduate degree and may also have a certificate of clinical competence in speech-language pathology from the American Speech-Language-Hearing Association.

- *Hearing aid dealer*: a representative of a company that manufactures or distributes hearing aids or other amplification devices, who works closely with an audiologist to provide requested equipment and habilitative aids.

- *Teacher of students who are hearing impaired*: a certified special education teacher who has graduate training in the techniques and methods of educating children with hearing impairments. This teacher may also be certified in elementary or secondary education.

- *Interpreter*: a person who interprets spoken language into sign language for an individual or group of people who have hearing impairments and interprets sign language for those unfamiliar with it.

The roles and activities of the specialists described here are referred to throughout this book. The Resources section lists numerous organizations that are sources of information on these professionals and their activities and on how to contact them.

# GUIDELINES FOR TEACHING

In the modules that follow, specific instructional strategies and teaching techniques related to communication and O&M are presented in greater detail. But it may also be helpful to keep in mind general guidelines that can enhance the effectiveness of instruction, regardless of the age of the students or the nature of the teaching environment. Because of their importance, many of these points are reinforced throughout this book. In addition to using a team approach and working with the student's family as part of the educational team, which were discussed earlier, these guidelines are as follows.

## Develop Secure and Positive Relationships

We all are more likely to step beyond our usual limits with the help of people we trust. Take the time and make an effort to build good rapport with students. Be aware of factors that can affect the quality of interactions, such as a student's likes and dislikes, attention span, general health, and level of tolerance for a particular activity or environment, as well as your temperament and level of comfort, and make adjustments to them when necessary. Touch and physical reinforcement (a pat on the back or a hug, for example) are important because the student may not be able to see your smile of approval or hear your praise.

## Promote a Sense of Self and Body Awareness

Develop a specific sign, signal, or symbol that designates each student and you. Be sure to use these name signs or cues (see Module 9) to identify yourself each time you approach or initiate communication with a student. Encourage students to use their name signs or symbols to identify themselves and their belongings.

Foster students' development of a sense of self and body awareness by helping them use their bodies as points of reference. For example, to teach positional and directional concepts, have students start with the physical activities of moving their bodies "in," "on," and "under" before you use objects. When teaching a young child, you may find it helpful to stand behind the student when you are demonstrating a sequence of steps for a particular activity to allow the student to feel the correct body positions and movements involved in the activity. Use recreational opportunities, such as swimming and exercise, to teach body awareness.

▲ *Using physical contact to help build rapport can contribute to a positive teaching relationship.*

## Provide a Safe, Organized, and Responsive Environment

Students should feel secure not only with you, but in all their learning environments. Examine your classroom, keeping the safety of individuals who cannot see or hear in mind, and make the necessary adaptations, so that passageways and exits are clear and wires and extension cords are taped to the floor. The vision and hearing specialists are important resources in this regard.

Although a safe, organized environment is important, it is necessary to guard against overprotection. Students who are overprotected may not learn how to protect themselves, anticipate danger, and avoid potentially dangerous situations. A classroom can provide opportunities to learn lessons about safety in a carefully supervised environment.

Proper positioning can also help students feel more secure. For example, make sure the students' backs and feet are supported in a sitting position and that their work surfaces are stable. Vision helps an individual maintain balance and correct his or her physical position. Since the students may not have the advantage of using visual information, they may "lock" into stiffened postures, holding the desk top or seat to prevent themselves from toppling when they are not in secure positions. If you want their hands free to work, be sure they are comfortably and securely positioned.

A well-organized teaching environment will make it easier for your students to move independently and to find needed materials. If a student cannot visually scan an area, searching "somewhere out there" can be frustrating. Have a designated place for all materials and make sure the materials are consistently returned to that location. If desks or storage cabinets have been moved, be sure to let the students know.

All students need to believe that what they do can make a difference. Therefore, it is important to select activities that provide feedback for students and that generate consequences the students will recognize. Choose engaging toys and recreational materials that spin, flash, buzz, or feel good to touch. Acknowledge the students' attempts to communicate—even if it is not possible to respond to a specific request. Students who are ignored may avoid communicating or may communicate in unproductive ways. Unit 2 will help you develop these communication goals.

## Provide Extensive Experience

Because of their reduced access to incidental information, students who are deaf-blind need to be taught formally many things that their classmates learn informally. Use real objects (clothing and food) and natural contexts to teach specific skills of dressing, making purchases, and eating, especially in the beginning, because many students will not understand models until they have had many experiences with the real objects. In addition, make note of the people, places, and things the students enjoy and understand most; they can be used as powerful reinforcers for activities.

Orientation and repetition are also essential. Keep in mind the words of a mother of a young woman who is deaf-blind: "As far as possible, do let your deaf-blind child know what is going on around him. It will not be meaningful to him the first time, perhaps not the twentieth time, but only if he has the experience can things possibly ultimately be remembered, recognized and understood. Only by knowing 'what is there' will he want to know 'what it is', 'what it is for' etc., and 'what else is there'" (Freeman, 1985, p. 92).

## Promote the Use of Hearing and Vision and of Other Sensory Information

Most students who are deaf-blind have some residual hearing and vision. Use information from both formal and informal assessments to determine how much vision and hearing remain. Seek the assistance of vision and hearing specialists to develop strategies to incorporate the development of visual and auditory skills in the students' programs. These specialists can also recommend adaptations to the environment, materials, and teaching strategies that will optimize a student's use of vision and hearing.

Keep in mind that a student's ability to use hearing or vision may seem inconsistent from day to day or even from task to task. A number of factors can affect how well a student is able to make use of residual hearing or vision, including the student's general health; use of medications; and a variety of environmental factors, such as lighting and background noise.

Tactile and olfactory stimuli can provide important information, especially when visual and auditory input are limited. Help the students become aware of the tactile features and scents that can aid in the identification of objects and places. For students who do not have reading skills in print or braille, use tactile or visual markers, such as different fabrics and objects, to label their desks and lockers. Your consistent use of a particular cologne will make it easier for the students to recognize when you are near.

Beware of sensory overload. When the amount, duration, or combination of sensory input exceeds a level that a student can process, the student may withdraw or turn away from the source of stimulation, fuss, cry, or even experience extreme changes in muscle tone. Careful observation is your best guide to how much simultaneous sensory input (such as the combination of vibration, sound, and light produced by a toy) a student can tolerate, as well as what types of sensory stimuli provide the most usable information. Adapt the amounts and types of sensory stimuli you use for instruction to identify which combinations work best.

## Provide Anticipatory Information

Always let students know that you are near before you handle or move them. Without being able to see or hear your approach, the students may become startled by your sudden grasp or attempt to move them. A gentle pat on the arm will alert a student to your presence. This advice is especially important for deaf-blind children who also have neurological disabilities; it may take a considerable amount of time to refocus their attention and body position after they are startled. Because problems of sensory integration (the ability to receive and process sensory information and respond appropriately) are often associated with neurological disabilities, students who have difficulty with sensory integration may also need additional time to process information and sensory prompts. Therefore, it is helpful to seek the advice of the physical therapist on the educational team for the best ways to approach and handle these students.

Be sure to inform your students of the activities that they will be involved in each day. Students who are deaf-blind may miss the auditory and visual situational clues that could help them know what may take place. Having some information about the day's activities can increase their sense of security and comfort.

## Allow Extra Time

Because of the student's vision and hearing impairments, he or she may need extra time to receive, process, and respond to information. Tactile examination takes more time than does visual scanning, as does "piecing together" information from limited visual and auditory input. The presence of additional disabilities can also require additional processing and response time. Resist the urge to intervene quickly; you may interfere with the student's attempt to shape and execute a response. Also consider building extra time into your teaching schedule.

## Teach Functional Activities

When you select activities for inclusion in a student's program, it is important to consider the family's priorities, the practicality of an activity, the activity's usefulness in the future, the immediacy of the need, the frequency of use, and whether the activity builds on a student's strengths and interests. Teaching activities in their natural contexts can aid a student's recall; the environment can provide the cues and clues for the needed skills. Minimize the use of simulation experiences, and focus on functional activities in natural contexts, for example, making purchases in a real supermarket. It may be helpful, however, to role-play and practice communication skills for later use in community settings. Timing is also important. For instance, have a student practice putting on his or her coat when there is a reason to do so.

## Be Consistent

Establish a sense of order in a student's day by keeping the sequence of activities consistent. The predictability of events can foster the student's independence and security. This does not mean that you must keep a strictly rigid schedule. Just be sure to inform the student of any changes that may take place.

It is also important to use consistent teaching strategies. The discovery or trial-and-error method of learning can be frustrating for a student who is deaf-blind. Analyze an activity to determine the most effective teaching sequence for a student, and consistently follow that sequence until the student has learned the skill. Also remember to be consistent about the signs, signals, and symbols you use with a student, especially while he or she is learning to use new modes of communication.

## Provide Opportunities for Making Choices and Problem Solving

Keep in mind the issue of learned helplessness (see Module 2). Providing opportunities for making choices helps students gain control over their environments and focuses their attention. You can start with simple and obvious choices, such as selecting between a strongly preferred food and a strongly disliked food at mealtime.

Once a student has mastered a skill, help him or her build on the accomplishment by problem solving. Alter the materials used in a particular activity, and allow the student to find a solution to the problem presented. For example, if a student is able to dress herself, you might turn her jacket inside out or provide her with gym socks that are too small. Do not let the situation become frustrating, however. Provide help as needed, and always select a skill that has been already mastered for a problem-solving activity. Making choices and problem solving are natural opportunities for building communication and purposeful movement skills. Include them in your teaching plans.

# ADDITIONAL CONSIDERATIONS

## USE OF AN ECOLOGICAL APPROACH

A truly individualized program for a student who is deaf-blind may be best developed using an ecological approach. In an ecological approach, age-appropriate skills relevant to an individual's daily life are taught, using adaptations that are individualized for a student's disability (Rainforth, York, & Macdonald, 1992). In this approach, the educational team considers the student's environments, the activities performed in them, and the particular skills and adaptations that the student needs to participate in the activities. The findings of the team's ecological assessment help to fine-tune the program planning process, in which the family's input is vital to the establishment of priorities.

## INTEGRATION OF COMMUNICATION AND O&M

Communication and movement-mobility are essential components of nearly every activity in every environment, and throughout a student's day, there are continual, naturally occurring opportunities to build, refine, or expand these skills. Having a specified communication period or O&M period that is designated as *the* time when such skills are taught is artificial; it is not the natural way people learn to communicate and move. Rather, communication and mobility and the teaching of these skills should be integrated into every activity. For example, in class, students communicate with the teacher, teaching assistant, and classmates and move about the classroom to participate in various activities. They also move throughout the school to go to the cafeteria, gym, auditorium, bathroom, and art and music classrooms. They communicate in their preferred mode or modes (see Unit 2) en route, as well as when they participate in various classes and activities. As the students help prepare meals at home, they move about and communicate with other family members in the kitchen. When the telephone rings (and lights up), they communicate with the caller via the telephone or a Teletype for the Deaf/Telecommunications (or Telephone) Device for the Deaf (TTY/TDD). (For further information on TTY/TDD, see Module 10.) Students also take walks, participate in sports and other recreational activities, and communicate with others while doing so.

Consider the communication and O&M skills that are involved in eating lunch at school and the naturally occurring opportunities to build communication and travel skills. For example, one student may need to travel from the classroom to the cafeteria or lunchroom, carry a tray through a cafeteria line, find a table and seat, eat, clear and stack the empty tray at the kitchen entrance, and then return to the classroom. Throughout this routine, the student has several opportunities to communicate: He or she notes that it is time for lunch, greets other students and cafeteria workers, asks what is on the menu and selects food, and communicates with classmates. For a student with a severe physical disability, lunchtime may involve traveling in a wheelchair to the cafeteria, raising his or her arms to allow another student to position a lunch tray on the wheelchair tray, pointing to various pictures of food to indicate his or her meal choices, and feeding himself or herself the foods that he or she can hold and asking for help with other foods by turning toward the person seated to the right. When the student is finished eating, another student pushes the wheelchair to the kitchen entrance, where the tray is deposited, and the student travels back to the classroom.

Once the educational team establishes instructional priorities, its members can analyze a student's environments and activities to determine their communication and mobility demands. Instruction is done as a natural part of activities, building on a student's current skills. Instructional supports or adaptations may be provided on the basis of a student's sensory, physical, and cognitive needs.

As you and other members of the educational team begin to develop goals, plans, and instructional strategies, consider the following questions:

- Is the method of communication appropriate? Can the student perform the required movements? Is some sort of physical support or adaptation needed? Is there a more efficient way of performing the task?

- Is learning the skill a priority for the student and/or his or her family?

- Will learning a particular skill increase the student's self-esteem? Will it enhance others' views of the student's competence?

- Will learning the skill expand the quality of the student's interactions with others, including family members, friends, classmates, and people in the community? Will it broaden his or her opportunities for interaction?

- Will learning the skill make the student less dependent on others or on the use of only specialized materials and equipment?

- Will learning the skill give the student more control over his or her interactions and environments and offer more opportunities for making choices?

138

- Is the skill useful in a variety of the student's environments?

- Can the student use the skill throughout his or her life?

## ACADEMICALLY ABLE CHILDREN

Although academically able students who are deaf-blind have cognitive abilities that are generally the basis for academic success, they may lack environmental information and experiences and, as a result, may need help in developing various concepts and skills. Because of their lack of exposure to information that other students gain incidentally, students who are deaf-blind and academically able need adaptations and enrichment that will support solid cognitive development and allow them access to the experiences that others with unimpaired access to sensory input have naturally.

It can be difficult to determine if a child who is deaf-blind has above-average cognitive ability because delays in language development can interfere with accurate assessments. Still, families and teachers can observe how a child interacts with the world to get an idea of his or her ability. They can look for the child's

- understanding of how things work, even without formal language. For example, a child who can take things apart and put them back together quickly and with minimal or no demonstration is likely to have good internal logic and reasoning that are characteristic of advanced ability.

- interest in exploring everything in the environment—a strong natural curiosity. A child who seeks opportunities to interact with people and objects in the environment is usually motivated by a strong desire to understand and communicate.

- effective use of space and good O&M skills, regardless of the amount of O&M training. A child who can go anywhere he or she chooses, using several routes and shortcuts (especially routes that have never been formally taught and that the child has "invented" from compiled experiences with other routes to the same place), demonstrates an innate organizational ability that also suggests superior intellect.

- rapid learning of sign language or other language-based communication (see Module 9) and ability to use a signed concept appropriately after only minimal exposure.

If you have a student who seems to have superior cognitive ability, it is important for you to work with the family and others to provide maximum exposure and experiences that will help the student to develop that ability. Students can be easily frustrated if their programs do not allow them to meet their potential. Here are some guidelines:

- Provide consistent exposure and many experiences that will develop concepts for daily living and be a base for academic work, and be sure that the child has maximum language input (spoken or signed or both, as appropriate) to explain each experience.

- Start with functional academics and then proceed to more abstract academic work as the child's development becomes more solid. Even for gifted students who are deaf-blind, learning is most effective if it revolves around familiar places, people, and objects.

- A student who is deaf-blind and has superior cognitive ability needs instruction from a skilled communicator. A teacher with a beginning 200-sign vocabulary, for example, will not provide the strong language model necessary for the child to learn language effectively.

- Once the student has learned a concept, go on to new experiences. Periodically monitor previously learned skills, but avoid repetition. Move the student through goals and objectives as quickly as possible.

- Provide as much one-to-one instruction and interaction as possible, especially during the early childhood years. When a child's communication abilities and concept development are well established, the child will find it much easier to perform activities independently.

## DISRUPTIVE BEHAVIORS

When a student's behavior is disruptive, it is important to stay calm and prevent the student as gently as possible from injuring himself or herself or others. Later, step back and carefully analyze the situation to try to determine why a particular behavior occurred. Here are some tips for doing so:

- Look for what may trigger the behavior: particular persons, places, activities, or materials. Determine if there is a pattern to when the behavior occurs: particular times of the day, when unfamiliar tasks are introduced, and so forth. Tools, such as the *Motivation Assessment Scale* by Durand and Crimmins (1992), are excellent resources for the careful and systematic collection of this and other essential information.

- Be aware that your behavior and your response to the disruptive behavior may reinforce it. Again, carefully analyze what you do when disruptive behaviors occur.

- Establish a positive teaching environment, liberally reinforcing the behavior you want to foster.

- Try to determine what the student is communicating through the behavior: frustration, fear, boredom, and so forth. Develop a communication system that will help the student learn more acceptable ways to express himself or herself. Be sure that whoever works with the student is familiar with and consistently uses the student's communication system and provides clear and essential information for all activities.

- The disruptive behavior of a student who has limited communication skills may be related to a situation that is not readily apparent and cannot be easily conveyed, such as changes at home or the start of an illness. This is another reason to have ongoing contact with the student's family or other caregivers. Be sure to keep up to date with information about the student's health and use of medications.

- A sudden change in a student's behavior should also alert you to the possibility of a change in the student's hearing and/or vision. Carefully observe the student, and refer him or her to appropriate professionals, if necessary.

- In dealing with disruptive behavior, focus on prevention. By providing a predictable, positive, and nurturing environment and by using clear communication, you can head off numerous problems.

## STUDENTS WHOSE REACTIONS ARE TACTILELY DEFENSIVE

A tactilely defensive reaction from a student may be a sign of over-stimulation, so carefully pace the introduction of materials with which the student will interact. Furthermore, it is advisable to seek the assistance of a physical therapist and/or occupational therapist to help you with strategies to desensitize the student. Here are additional points to keep in mind:

- The student may tolerate some tactile stimulation and then suddenly react adversely. Therefore, it is important to be aware of a student's threshold for overstimulation.

- The degree of tactile defensiveness exhibited by a student may vary from day to day and may be exacerbated if he or she is fearful, sick, or experiencing stress.

- The student may react defensively only to certain materials or textures. Thus, it is necessary to observe the student to identify which materials cause a reaction and then make needed adaptations to them or to the student's program. For example, if a student resists touching metal items, substitute plastic ones.

- Students who are tactilely defensive seem to tolerate a firm touch more easily than a light touch.

- The student may tolerate touch from a familiar person, but not from new or less familiar individuals. Consider initially limiting the number of individuals who work with the student.

- Never force a student to touch something. Rather, gradually introduce new materials in a relaxed and nonthreatening way.

- It may be helpful to pair new items with familiar, tolerated items in routine activities.

## THE SCHOOL ENVIRONMENT

Effective service delivery can be enhanced when school staff, classmates, and all ancillary personnel (such as bus drivers) who have contact with the student who is deaf-blind receive specific and practical information about how to interact best with the student. Facilitating interaction between the student and others contributes to a positive environment for everyone involved, as well as to the development of the student's social, communication, and mobility skills (see Modules 1, 3, and 13 for details). This information should include:

- *how the student communicates:* the system and modes the student uses.

- *how to communicate with the student:* how to greet the student, convey information and converse, and use any special materials or equipment and interpreters.

- *general parameters of the student's hearing and vision:* the optimum viewing conditions for the student, including the best positions, distance, colors, size, layout arrangements, and lighting, and the optimum conditions for hearing, including position, distance, volume, pitch, and degree of ambient noise. Remember that hearing and vision can fluctuate because of illness, fatigue, medications, and other factors.

- *how the student travels:* how to guide or assist the student when help is needed or to encourage the student to travel independently.

- *health and safety concerns:* specific conditions to be noted (such as the possibility of seizures); procedures for emergencies, including evacuating the building and soliciting help; and any restrictions on foods or activities.

Providing in-service training about deaf-blindness to school staff can also enhance the learning environment for all students and staff. Here are a few suggestions for topics:

- the effects of combined vision and hearing losses on learning
- the heterogeneity of the deaf-blind population
- how individuals who are deaf-blind communicate
- how individuals who are deaf-blind can travel independently in various environments.

Some complementary activities include the following:

- presentations by guest speakers, such as staff of the state deaf-blind project, deaf-blind adults, other service providers for individuals who are deaf-blind, and parents or other family members of the students

- simulation experiences: simple tasks performed using blindfolds or simulator lenses and earplugs

- viewing and discussing relevant videotapes: the *Hand in Hand* videotape or others listed in Resources.

Be sure to inform the staff members that they can contact DB-LINK, the National Information Clearinghouse on Children Who Are

Deaf-Blind, at (800) 438-9376 or (800) 854-7013 (TTY/TDD) for further information on deaf-blindness and related topics.

By enlisting the participation of many skilled and interested people, by obtaining the support of resources that may be available, and by paying attention to the deaf-blind child as an individual, teachers who work with students who are deaf-blind can promote the skills that the students need in school and in the community. Units 2 and 3 offer in-depth information on ways to promote these skills.

# REFERENCES

Durand, V. M., & Crimmins, D. B. (1992). *Motivation assessment scale*. Topeka, KS: Monaco & Associates.

Fazzi, D. L., Pogrund, R. L., & Zambone, A. M. (1992). Team focus: National trends, services, and advocacy in programs for young blind and visually impaired children. In R. L. Pogrund, D. L. Fazzi, & J. S. Lampert (Eds.), *Early focus: Working with young blind and visually impaired children and their families*. New York: American Foundation for the Blind.

Freeman, P. (1985). *The deaf/blind baby: A programme of care*. London: William Heinemann Medical Books.

Giangreco, M. F. (1989). Making related service decisions for students with severe handicaps in public schools: Roles, criteria, and authority (Doctoral dissertation, Syracuse University, Syracuse, NY). *Dissertation Abstracts International 50(6A)*, No. 89-19.516.

Giangreco, M. F., Cloninger, C. J., & Iverson, V. S. (1989). *C.O.A.C.H.: Cayuga-Onondaga assessment for children with handicaps* (Version 5.0). Stillwater: Oklahoma State University.

Giangreco, M. F., Cloninger, C. J., & Iverson, V. S. (1992). *Choosing options and accommodations for children (COACH)*. Baltimore: Paul H. Brookes.

Hutchinson, D. A. (1974). A Model for transdisciplinary staff development. In *A nationally organized collaborative program for the provision of comprehensive services to atypical infants and their families* (Technical Report No. 8). New York: United Cerebral Palsy Association.

Perske, R., & Smith, J. (1977). Interdisciplinary and transdisciplinary teamwork. Seattle, WA: AAE-SPH Review.

Rainforth, B., York, J., & Macdonald, C. (1992). *Collaborative teams for students with severe disabilities: Integrating theory and educational services*. Baltimore: Paul H. Brookes.

Skrtic, T. M. (1991). Students with special education needs: Artifacts of the traditional curriculum. In M. Ainscow (Ed.), *Effective schools for all*. London: David Fulton.

Thousand, J., & Villa, R. (1992). Collaborative teams: A powerful tool in school restructuring. In R. Villa, J. Thousand, W. Stainback, & S. Stainback (Eds.), *Restructuring for caring and effective education: An administrative handbook for creating heterogeneous schools*. Baltimore: Paul H. Brookes.

**FIGURE 5-1:**
**Educationally Oriented Vision Report**

Date _____ Completed by _____

Student's name _____ Date of birth _____

1. What is the cause of the visual impairment? _____

2. Is any special treatment required?  ☐ Yes  ☐ No
   If so, what is the general nature of the treatment? _____
   _____

3. Is the visual impairment likely to  ☐ get worse  ☐ get better or  ☐ stay the same?

4. Should the staff be alert to any particular symptoms (such as eye rubbing, etc.) that would
   signal the need for professional attention?  ☐ Yes  ☐ No
   If so, please describe. _____
   _____

5. What, if any, restrictions should be placed on this individual's activities?_____
   _____

6. Should this individual wear eyeglasses or contact lenses?  ☐ Yes  ☐ No
   If so, under what circumstances? _____

7. Was an accurate visual acuity measure able to be determined?  ☐ Yes  ☐ No
   If so, what was it? _____
   _____

8. If a visual acuity was not able to be determined, please describe what this individual sees.
   _____
   _____

*(continued)*

**FIGURE 5-1:**
**Continued**

9. Is this individual's focusing ability and eye muscle balance adequate?

   ☐ Yes   ☐ No   ☐ Not able to determine

   If not, how is it inadequate? _____

   _____

10. Were you able to determine the field of vision?   ☐ Yes   ☐ No

    If so, were there areas of no vision in the field?   ☐ Yes   ☐ No

    Where? _____

11. Was this individual able to follow a moving object visually?   ☐ Yes   ☐ No

    Were there directions in which s/he could not track a moving object?   ☐ Yes   ☐ No

    If not, what directions? _____

    _____

12. Will this individual work better with   ☐ large or   ☐ small objects and pictures?

    At what distances? _____

13. What print size _____ and paper contrast _____ is optimal for reading for this individual?

14. What lighting conditions would be optimal for this individual's visual functioning?

    _____

15. Will night travel or activities in low lighting cause a problem for this individual? ☐ Yes ☐ No

    If so, what are the problems? _____

16. What are your specific recommendations concerning this individual's use of vision in learning

    situations? _____

    _____

17. When should this individual be examined again? _____

*SOURCE: Adapted from M. Efron & B. R. DuBoff,* A Vision Guide for Teachers of Deaf-Blind Children, *Raleigh: North Carolina Department of Public Instruction, 1975.*

**FIGURE 5-2:**
**Educationally Oriented Hearing Report**

Date _____ Completed by _____

Student's name _____ Date of birth _____

1. What is the cause of the hearing impairment? _____

2. Is any special treatment required?  ☐ Yes  ☐ No

   If so, what is the general nature of the treatment? _____

   _____

3. Is the hearing impairment likely to  ☐ get worse  ☐ get better or  ☐ stay the same?

4. Should the staff be alert to any particular symptoms (such as draining ear, etc.) that would

   signal the need for professional attention?  ☐ Yes  ☐ No

   If so, please describe. _____

   _____

5. What, if any, restrictions should be placed on this individual's activities? _____

   _____

6. Should this individual wear a hearing aid(s)?  ☐ Yes  ☐ No

   If so, under what circumstances? _____

7. Was an accurate hearing measure able to be determined?  ☐ Yes  ☐ No

   If so, what was it? _____

   _____

8. If a hearing acuity measure was not able to be determined, please describe what this individual hears.

   _____

   _____

*(continued)*

**FIGURE 5-2:**
**Continued**

9. Was this individual able to locate sound sources? ☐ Yes ☐ No

   If so, please explain. _____

   _____

10. Do you have specific suggestions regarding an auditory training program for this individual?

   _____

   _____

11. What acoustic conditions would be optimal for this individual's hearing?

   _____

   _____

12. What effect could this individual's hearing have on speech discrimination?

   _____

   _____

13. Is telephone usage possible for this individual? ☐ Yes ☐ No

   Are any adaptations necessary? ☐ Yes ☐ No

   Please explain. _____

14. What are your specific recommendations concerning this individual's use of hearing in learning

   situations? _____

   _____

15. Do you recommend any environmental adaptations in the home or school? ☐ Yes ☐ No

   Please identify. _____

   _____

16. When should this individual be examined again? _____

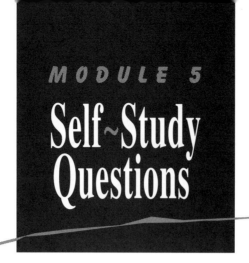

1.  Which of the following are general responsibilities shared by all educational team members of students who are deaf-blind?
    a.  Designing IEPs.
    b.  Implementing IEPs.
    c.  Evaluating IEPs.
    d.  None of the above.
    e.  All the above.

2.  Which of the following is *not* an area in which supports are needed to help students who are deaf-blind attain their goals?
    a.  Physical needs.
    b.  Personal needs.
    c.  Structural modifications.
    d.  Sensory needs.
    e.  Staff and peer education.

3.  Which of the following are basic principles to apply to working with families as team members?
    a.  Be positive, patient, and respectful.
    b.  Interact with parents as peers.
    c.  Respect the family's culture, beliefs, values, and traditions.
    d.  a and c.
    e.  All the above.

4.  When you select activities for inclusion in a student's program, which of the following are important considerations?
    a.  The student's known abilities, the family's written communications, and long-term vocational goals.
    b.  The student's anticipated abilities, the family's written communications, and the immediacy of the need.
    c.  The family's priorities, the activity's usefulness, and the student's long-term needs.
    d.  The family's priorities, the activity's usefulness in the present and future, and the frequency of use.

5. For students who are deaf-blind, their daily schedules should
   a. be varied and changed daily.
   b. be as consistent as possible, with changes kept to a minimum.
   c. allow the students to select their favorite activities and be built around these choices.

6. The best way to tell whether a student may have difficulty tolerating multisensory input is to
   a. observe the student carefully.
   b. check the student's medical records.
   c. consult the physical therapist.

7. A student is most likely to be successful at a problem-solving activity if
   a. it is related to a daily living skill.
   b. it is built on a skill he or she can do well.
   c. it is recreational.


*Answers to self-study questions for this module appear in the section that follows.*

# MODULE 1

**1. (c):** Individuals who are deaf-blind have the capability to achieve independent mobility. Specific instruction in orientation and mobility by family, mobility instructors, and other teachers and support staff can provide the learning experiences needed for the development of the environmental and spatial concepts and specific travel skills needed for safe and independent travel skills in all environments.

**2. (a):** The method used for identification should be used consistently and should be unique to the person. Wearing the same unique ring and presenting your hand to the student when you approach would provide the student with immediate and consistent information.

**3. (d):** Lighting and acoustics should be controlled as much as possible to maximize any vision or hearing that deaf-blind students may have. It is often necessary to increase the work area of a deaf-blind student's desk to accommodate supplementary and adapted equipment.

# MODULE 2

**1. (b):** Because of limited access to visual and auditory information, students who are deaf-blind may not be able to learn through routine observations. Thus, they have to learn formally what their hearing and sighted peers learn informally (through ongoing visual and auditory information). The lack of visual and auditory stimulation can also affect their motivation to interact with the environment.

**2. (c):** Often, models emphasize visual features instead of tactile information, weight, scent, true size, and other nonvisual features. Most important, students are frequently given models before they have reached the level of symbolic thought and can understand the correspondence between a model and the object it represents.

**3. (a):** Van Dijk stated that self-stimulatory behaviors, such as clinging and self-clutching, are attempts to seek security by people who have not developed attachments with caregivers. If a student exhibits stereotypical behavior, it is important to analyze carefully all possible causes, including overstimulation or understimulation; other sources of anxiety, such as the environment and caretakers; and health problems.

**4. (c):** Knowing specific facts about a student's deaf-blindness can support others' understanding about what the student may be expected to gain from visual and auditory information. This kind of understanding supports overall program planning and instruction. Adult living preferences and needs for O&M training may be affected by specific factors of an individual's deaf-blindness, but many more factors need to be considered when planning a student's program.

**5. (a):** Genetic counseling may be important to older students who have progressive forms of deaf-blindness, but genetic counseling alone is not necessarily helpful in planning treatment options. Obtaining information is vital for daily living and decision making, so changes in the senses that reduce information gathering will compel a student to make frequent adjustments to perform daily activities and routines. Learning new communication methods for reading and writing is often necessary.

**6. (c):** Children who have visual impairments early in life depend on hearing to get their basic information, and their skills with spoken language and written forms are generally well established by age 10. Therefore, braille instruction may or may not be needed, depending on the nature and extent of the vision loss that occurred early. These children's O&M skills are also likely to be well established, but additional strategies may need to be taught for traveling safely without the auditory information that was previously accessible to them.

**7. (b):** Children who have combined significant vision and hearing losses from birth do not readily gain environmental information, but can learn most effectively with carefully structured interactions that provide much individualized and close contact. Sign language input using close vision may be important for some of these children, but it is not necessarily appropriate for all of them. One-to-one interaction will help families and service providers begin to observe and evaluate children's needs, skills, and preferences and to provide the children with environmental information they need to learn.

**8. (d):** All these factors are potential problems for children who are deaf-blind and have additional disabilities. Depending on their nature and extent, additional disabilities can prevent access to the environment and to others, including siblings, that would support learning. Family interactions and exploration within the environment are vital activities of early childhood that support concept development. Children who are deaf-blind already lack access to important information because of vision and hearing losses that prevent them from gaining information from family members and their environments. Additional disabilities further compound their difficulties and may prevent them from interpreting the information that the brain can process, which also delays concept development.

## MODULE 3

**1. (a):** A hearing loss affects communication at the most basic level of language development: hearing others speak. Typically, children learn to communicate first by listening to parents, family members, and others comment on the environment and describe the world. Then, they begin to imitate others according to their own previous experiences with specific objects and concepts. Daily living activities can be seen and imitated without full spoken explanations. Tactile aspects of interactions are not impeded by a hearing loss and are likely to be less necessary if a child can see.

**2. (b):** Input is consistent and appropriate when all appropriate forms of communication are provided before an activity, to give the child who is deaf-blind much information about the routine to follow. The failure to recognize that a student is attempting to communicate and not responding to that communication with adequate knowledge and skills to meet the child's interaction needs will result in inconsistency for the student that can eventually affect his or her overall communication development. Hospitalizations and school vacations may be facts of life for students who are deaf-blind, but can also cause gaps in input and affect the development of communication skills.

**3. (b):** Sign language, which uses visual features, such as specific arm movements, can still be read with touch, although the information may be processed differently by the brain than the same information received through vision. Tactile sign language can be an effective communication mode for children who are deaf-blind and are capable of learning formal language concepts. If early concept development includes many signs that have high levels of tactile iconicity (are easily recognizable because they are stable in space and are characterized by strong tactile resemblance to what they represent), overall development may be better supported. Then, concepts with signs that are more abstract in the tactile mode may be introduced.

**4. (b):** Interactions should be slowed down so that both the child who is deaf-blind and the interpreter or communication facilitator have time to find and adjust to new speakers. Speakers should identify themselves before the activity begins and state their names before speaking so the interpreter can identify the presenter of ideas, thoughts, and questions. It is helpful to the deaf-blind person who has some hearing, as well as to interpreters, if individuals speak clearly and slowly.

## MODULE 4

**1. (c):** Purposeful movement enhances students' ability to gather information and develop concepts that are useful in all environments. Knowledge of one's ability to move around in an environment contributes to the development of self-confidence, which, in turn, allows for openness to additional learning in new situations.

**2. (d):** Often, students who are habitually taken from one place to another by adults become so dependent on the adults that they do not realize they can move purposefully and independently. In addition to realizing that they are able to move from one place to another, they need to recognize that they have the right to move about their environment as safely and independently as possible and have to learn skills to do so.

**3. (a):** Awareness implies the students' ability to identify the objects and people in their environments that allow them to know where they are in a particular space. Students gain awareness of their surroundings by learning to identify and use information about people, places, and things. This information can be generalized and used to increase their awareness in unfamiliar settings.

**4. (d):** The home is usually the most protective and familiar environment for a child and gives the child the security to learn to move without fear. The home also provides natural opportunities for motivating the student to become more responsible for daily routines, most of which originate or take place there. As a student learns to take care of his or her personal needs, other family members can have more time to address other activities.

**5. (c):** When a student learns and becomes comfortable with the components of purposeful movement in familiar environments, he or she develops confidence and skills for moving about in new settings. The student also has more freedom to interact with others as an equal participant in the regular activities of the school, home, community, and workplace.

**6. (b):** As his or her level of independence increases, the student has more options in living situations from which they can choose. With increased personal independence, there is less need for a full-time caregiver and greater access to community resources and public transportation. The individual can play an active role in choosing the best situation for himself or herself.

**7. (b):** When a student moves confidently and in a safe manner, his or her family becomes comfortable allowing even more freedom of movement. This mutually reinforcing belief in the student's abilities contributes to the continued growth of the student's confidence.

## MODULE 5

**1. (e):** All the above. Although each team member has unique responsibilities for students who are deaf-blind based on his or her specific relationship to the students and their knowledge and skills, all the members are responsible for designing, implementing, and evaluating students' IEPs.

**2. (c):** Structural modifications. Supports are needed to ensure access to materials and environments for students who are deaf-blind. Environmental modifications that would improve the acoustical quality of sound in a room by adding carpeting or that would reduce glare from windows might be made. However, structural modifications, such as adding ramps or widening doorways, would be made only for deaf-blind students with physical disabilities.

**3. (e):** All the above. It is important to interact with parents as equals. Mutual respect, sensitivity, and a positive approach are all important principles to apply to working with families.

**4. (d):** The factors that are important to consider when you select activities for inclusion in a student's program are the family's priorities, which do not need to be written; the practicality of an activity; the usefulness of the activity in the future, as well as in the present; the immediacy of the need; the frequency of the use; and whether the activity builds on the student's strengths and interests.

**5. (b):** A consistent schedule contributes to predictability and can help make the student feel more secure. Since changes in a schedule are inevitable, however, try to make the student aware of a change before it occurs, when possible.

**6. (a):** The student's medical records and the educational team's physical therapist may provide useful information, especially if the student has a known neurological disability, but observation is still the best way to determine the types or combinations of sensory input that are most appropriate for the student.

**7. (b):** A problem-solving activity can be frustrating for a student if he or she is not familiar with or proficient in the original task.

# UNIT 2
## COMMUNICATION

# Basic Concepts of Communication

DANIEL B. CRIMMINS

CAROLE R. GOTHELF

CHARITY ROWLAND

ROBERT D. STILLMAN

ANGELA LINAM

CHRISTY WILLIAMS

- *Use your observational skills constantly*

- *Respond to all attempts to communicate*

- *Build opportunities to communicate in all activities*

- *Try to understand the communicative intent of behavior*

*C*ommunication is interaction, the means by which people of all cultures socialize with each other, instruct their children, and share information. Other species communicate, too, but people use far more formal systems for communication than do animals, insects, fish, plants, or birds.

There are two important elements in any interaction between two people: receptive communication and expressive communication. Expressive communication is what one person tries to convey to another by gesturing, speaking, writing, or signing. It involves selecting words, signs, or concepts to get a message across to another person and using specific body language or vocal inflections that add to the meaning of the message. Receptive communication is what a listener or reader receives from a speaker, signer, or writer and understands. To communicate satisfactorily, both people who are interacting need to have similar skills and styles of receptive and expressive communication.

Why is it important to know the basics of communication and how communication develops? People who work with deaf-blind children, who frequently need special assistance to learn communication skills, in general need a fundamental understanding of communication and how it develops. If you have already studied these concepts, this module will be a refresher for you, but it may also give you some new ideas that you can relate to your students who are deaf-blind. In addition to this essential knowledge, information about adaptations you can make to assist your students effectively as they develop communication skills that will be useful in their everyday lives and activities is presented in this unit. Methods and basic concepts of communicating are the focus, as are how to make individual adaptations for students and how to encourage the development of communication skills. Concepts relating to orientation and mobility (O&M) and the development of O&M skills are examined in the unit that follows, but the information presented in the two units is intended to be used together by teachers and others who work with deaf-blind students because communication and O&M instruction need to be integrated and because skills in these areas are so essential to students' growth and development.

Since communication is the basis for all other skills and for interaction between student and teacher and student and all others, its fundamental concepts are the first point of focus in this module, which begins to look at the development of language. Language in its major forms—spoken, signed, and written—is the most widely used form of communication, and its use is a formal and abstract way of interacting. More about language will be offered later in this module. But first, the earlier stages of communication are outlined, since many of your students are likely to have communication skills at these levels.

# FUNDAMENTAL CONCEPTS

## PREINTENTIONAL–INTENTIONAL COMMUNICATION

You communicated information to your parents as soon as you were born and perhaps even before birth. Your parents were able to tell when you were comfortable or hungry by the sounds and expressions you made. They interpreted your behavior as if you were trying to tell them something. At this early stage of development, you were communicating preintentionally. That is, you were not intentionally producing the behaviors and did not know how your parents would react. Later, you learned to communicate intentionally: You learned that you could whine when you wanted attention, hold your arms above your head when you wanted to be picked up, and push away something you did not want.

Individuals who communicate preintentionally are not aware that they affect the way other people react. Individuals who communicate intentionally understand that they can affect the behaviors of other people by communicating. They understand the power of their own behaviors—especially if they live in a responsive environment.

Preintentional behaviors can still serve as powerful clues to the needs and desires of your students. If your students do not use intentional behaviors to communicate, respond consistently to their preintentional behaviors. By doing so, you will show them that a relationship exists between what they do and what you do. When your students vocalize and smile, make a point of paying attention; they can learn to smile and vocalize intentionally to gain your attention. Intentionality is an essential concept in communication, and it is discussed again later in this module.

# PRESYMBOLIC–SYMBOLIC COMMUNICATION

## Presymbolic Communication

The earliest forms of communication that young children use are presymbolic (also called preverbal or prelinguistic) because they do not involve symbols. In presymbolic communication there is a direct, often physical relationship between the person who is communicating and the messages that are being sent. For instance, presymbolic vocalizations, such as crying, fussing, and cooing, indicate the physical state of a child and are direct reflections of how the child feels. Although they are not intentional initially, they communicate something about the current experience or state of the child and can become more expressive and intentional. The following are examples of preintentional and intentional communication using presymbolic behaviors:

*Presymbolic Behaviors–Preintentional Communication*
- general body movement (for instance, stiffening the body)
- arm, leg, and hand movements
- facial expressions (such as grimacing).

*Presymbolic Behaviors–Intentional Communication*
- approaching and avoiding people or objects
- touching things
- pushing things away
- extending objects
- smiling, pointing, kissing, and hugging.

## Symbolic Communication

Symbolic communication is a less direct, but much more flexible and powerful way to communicate. Without symbols you are limited to communicating about the here and now—about things that are physically present and about topics that are in the present. You can communicate only about current bodily states or about something that you can touch, look at, or point to. Communication through symbols opens up a potentially limitless scope of topics—both present and absent—occurring in the past, present, or future.

A symbol is something that stands for or means something else (the referent). The most common forms of symbolic communication are spoken and written language—that is, systems that use abstract symbols. They are abstract because there is no clear physical relationship between spoken or written symbols and their referents. The symbols are arbitrary sequences of sounds or letters that a particular culture has agreed will have a specific meaning. Other abstract symbolic systems include sign language and fingerspelling (covered in depth in Module 9).

Some symbols are concrete because they are physically similar to their referents. For instance, when you play charades, you use gestures that resemble the shape and movement of what you are trying to communicate; these gestures function as concrete symbols. Some sounds also function as concrete symbols, as when you make a kissing sound to tell a child, "I want a kiss." Pictures have an obvious visual similarity to their referents. Three-dimensional objects may also function as concrete symbols; for example, a cup may symbolize a drink or a handlebar grip may symbolize a bicycle.

When considering communication systems for students who are deaf-blind, it is essential to determine whether the students currently communicate symbolically or presymbolically. (Module 12 contains additional information on how to select communication systems.) Often, it is tempting to use a symbolic communication system, but if a student does not have good presymbolic communication skills, it may be more appropriate to improve the student's presymbolic skills before you introduce symbols by responding appropriately and consistently to the student's behaviors as though they had communicative intent. If you introduce symbols, you must also decide whether your student can deal best with concrete or abstract ones.

To determine if a student is ready for symbolic communication, it is important to observe him or her carefully. Some behaviors you can observe that suggest a student could use symbols (either concrete or abstract) are:

- In play situations or other interactions, the student will use objects to represent other things. For example, the student will use pots and pans or a spoon and a bowl to act out cooking or will use a concrete symbol like a cup to indicate a desire for a drink.

- In play situations or other interactions, the student will imitate the movement of a favorite or preferred activity, like rocking, to indicate the desire to play on a rocking horse, or stepping, to indicate the desire to exercise on a step climber.

- In interactions, the student will use conventional gestures that people typically use, like pointing or waving appropriately (Wetherby & Prizant, 1992).

- In interactions, the student will guide an adult to an activity or item that is desired, like a swing or a water fountain.

Children with limited mobility may not be able to guide you to a desired item or activity and may not be able to make conventional gestures in ways you expect. Therefore, you may have to use some creative observational techniques. You can watch more carefully or set up situations that will help you determine if the children can interact using symbols. For example, if a student vocalizes in the same way each day at snack time, you can offer choices, like raisins or crackers, and see which causes the most positive response from the child. Later, you can build a communication device that uses raisins that are glued in one spot as a symbol and a cracker that is glued to another place (Rowland & Schweigert, 1990). These concrete symbols represent the snacks, and as you work with the child

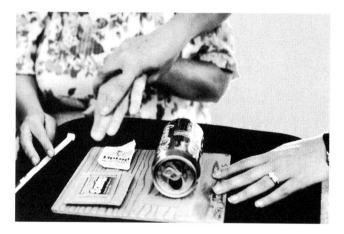

▲ *Concrete symbols attached to portable boards or other displays can be used as communication devices with which students can learn to indicate preferences and choices.*

to choose between them, you can encourage a consistent response from the child each time—reaching, pointing, or gazing toward the preferred choice. With a child who has limited or no vision, you can read facial expression or body language when you guide his or her hand to touch each choice. In this way, students can work toward developing spontaneous requests for specific treats by indicating the selected symbols.

It is not always obvious what a child is trying to convey with body language, facial expressions, or other responses. You can observe, interpret what you think the child may be trying to communicate, and change your interpretation if it seems to be inaccurate on the basis of the child's next response. In Modules 8–12, you will read more about systems, modes, and devices for communication, how to select them, and the use of concrete or abstract symbols to communicate with a student and help him or her increase other communication skills.

## RECEPTIVE–EXPRESSIVE COMMUNICATION

Most forms of communication may be used for both expressive and receptive communication. This distinction may be confusing, since a single interaction usually involves both expressive and receptive communication. Expressive communication is the way your student conveys information to you or other people. Receptive communication is the way you or your student receives information from others.

People generally convey and receive information in the same way, often through a combination of spoken and written language. It is important to realize, however, that many people who are deaf-blind may receive information differently from the way they convey it. People who can hear speech, perhaps with the help of hearing aids, may not speak. They may use sign language, pictures, or gestures to communicate. Others who are totally deaf may be able to see and understand sign language. However, they may have physical impairments that prevent them from producing sign language themselves and so may point to pictures or printed words to communicate. In most cases, you will use more than one system to communicate with a person who is deaf-blind, and that person may use more than one system to communicate with you. These expressive and receptive modes of communication will not necessarily be the same.

# FACTORS IN THE DEVELOPMENT OF COMMUNICATION

The early development of communication is influenced by many factors, among them the quality and characteristics of the interaction of the communication partners. It is helpful to examine caregiver-infant interactions to understand the behaviors and concepts that are

▲ *A concrete symbol, pictures, and printed words can all be used to convey a particular concept and provide a student with more than one communication system.*

the basis of effective communication development (more information on these early interactions is provided in the following module).

Communication develops in a sequence, from preintentional to intentional, that generally leads to the acquisition of language. Some children who are deaf-blind may remain at the earlier levels of intentionality. Information related to the various levels may help teachers and others determine which methods to use to enhance the communication skills of students at various levels.

## PREINTENTIONAL ACTIONS

Certain concepts, such as responsiveness, attention getting, reciprocity, repetition and consistency, predictability and anticipation, and receptive and expressive roles, are important in understanding how infants move through the levels of preintentional actions. Initially, infants' behaviors (such as smiling, grimacing, vocalizing, crying, and moving arms and legs randomly) are not directed communications, but reactions to pleasant and unpleasant sensations. They are unintentional, yet caregivers respond as if they were intentional. These behaviors help caregivers evaluate their infants' likes and dislikes and keep infants active and engaged.

Caregivers attract and maintain their infants' attention by playing such games as "peek-a-boo" or "I'm gonna get you"; moving their faces, toys, or other objects closer, then away from the infants; or responding to the infants' actions (for instance, gently shaking the arm or leg that an infant has just moved). These games establish a pattern of reciprocity in which the caregiver and infant alternate their actions so that sometimes one or the other leads and sometimes they act together. At first, the caregiver fits her or his actions with or between the infant's movements, vocalizations, and facial expressions. The infant may show pleasure with a smile or laugh, so the caregiver continues.

The repetition and consistency not only of these games, but of the sequence of events, activities, and experiences within daily routines

**166**

(for example, the order in which clothes are put on after baths, which always are given after lunch) and the people, objects, and actions that define these daily routines, increase the infant's sense of order and stability in what may initially seem to be an unpredictable world.

The predictability of and the infant's growing familiarity with events allow the infant to begin to anticipate what is about to happen by recognizing that certain behaviors or situations or adults predict the occurrence of other familiar events. Anticipation indicates that the infant has begun to comprehend the regularities or rules that govern events, especially interaction with others. It is a natural outcome of caregiver-infant games, in which actions are in a consistent order and there is a cycle of actions and pauses and a relationship between one partner's action and the other's response.

Caregiver-infant games are thus an introduction to the patterns, procedures, and uses of communication. The interactive structure of the games and reversible roles of both partners as senders and receivers of communication follow the pattern of verbal (symbolic) conversation. During these interactions, infants acquire initial communication skills.

## INTENTIONAL ACTIONS

Soon, infants purposefully use actions to achieve goals. The transition is gradual. They learn through repeated experiences that particular actions that are performed in certain contexts produce reliable effects. The anticipation of these effects encourages them to experiment with the effects of other behaviors.

Although intentional actions often resemble communicative actions, at this stage, infants do not use them specifically for this purpose. Their focus on the outcomes, not on their partners, suggests that they still do not fully recognize their partners' roles in achieving goals. These actions have an impersonal quality that sometimes makes the recipient feel more like a tool than a communication partner. Such actions as repeatedly touching the caregiver's lips to get him or her to make noises, looking at an object so it will be activated, and pushing a spoon away to avoid a disliked food appear mechanical because expression and goal are interlocked.

Because infants now begin to anticipate their caregivers' responses, they are likely to perform some anticipatory actions during pauses (if they have been bouncing on someone's lap, they may try to bounce; if they have been clapping, they may try to clap). Caregivers respond to these actions as though their babies are communicating a desire to repeat previous actions or a recognition of what is about to happen, whereas the infants are only carrying out actions in the hope that they will continue.

Because they can anticipate events, infants can now indicate their preferences or dislikes for activities before they occur (for example, clinging to their mothers before naptime) or plan to bring about or avoid certain events. These abilities to choose among actions give them great control in interactions. Therefore, caregivers should selectively provide opportunities for their infants to choose among appropriate options.

## *INTENTIONAL COMMUNICATION*

### Purposeful Actions or Vocalizations

Eventually, children purposefully use actions or vocalizations to communicate with other people. The key word is *communicate*, because both unintentional and intentional actions may affect another person and thus function as communications. Communication is intentional when children recognize that others serve as intermediaries in achieving goals and when they select forms of communication that have the desired effects on the recipients. For example, if a child wants a toy that is out of reach and the caretaker is in the room, the child may reach toward the toy while alternately looking at the caretaker and the toy. If the action does not work, the child may reach more demonstratively while vocalizing or gesturing.

To perform such apparently simple sequences of actions, children must acquire some sophisticated skills. First, they must recognize that adults can obtain objects that are out of reach. Second, they must consider what actions or behaviors their caretakers will probably understand. Third, they must gain and maintain their caretakers' attention while indicating what their caretakers should do. Thus, they must be able to keep in mind both their goals and how to influence other people so their goals can be achieved.

### Reference

Intentional communication requires the ability to use actions to *refer* to something, not just to achieve something. In the foregoing example, the child's reaching is an intentional effort to indicate the desired object to his or her caretaker. Reaching, pointing, and other such gestures are among the first "referential acts" that children perform. Once children understand that actions and vocalizations can represent something, rather than simply cause something, they have reached the level at which it is possible for them to acquire language.

## EMERGENCE OF FIRST WORDS

A number of stages may be involved as children begin to use words to communicate with others.

### Convention

During early stages, mutually understood signals (for example, the taking of the caregiver's hands to initiate a routine in which the caregiver and child pretend to be dancing) are replaced by conventional actions and gestures (such as moving in a dancing motion). Later, these actions and gestures are combined with and then replaced by first words (in this case, *dance*). The routine nature of the interaction establishes a predictable sequence of steps that a caregiver typically "marks" with words that the child can imitate and begin to use. The nonthreatening and pleasant environment created by these interactions encourages the child to explore the effects of his or her first words and to assess the effectiveness of this communication.

### Scope

Although first words are often used primarily to regulate actions (for example, to ask to begin a favorite game), the nature of caregiver-infant interactions encourages the emergence of other communicative intentions. Since caregivers and infants fulfill a variety of roles in their interactions and engage in a great variety of games in different situations, children soon use words for many different purposes (to comment, to direct attention, and to obtain information).

### Comprehension

Children who are beginning to communicate intentionally and to use communication in reference to things that are not present are also beginning to understand the communications of others. In fact, they must recognize, understand, and imitate the communications of others to progress toward the acquisition of conventional forms of communication.

## Context

Children may first understand a word (such as *shoe*) only when its referent (the actual shoe) is present or in conjunction with a familiar routine (for example, a child and his or her caregiver playfully look together for a missing shoe when the word *shoe* is mentioned at the appropriate time during dressing). Later, they may understand words in places or at times different from where and when they initially learned or usually used them (for instance, a child begins to know that the word *bed* represents any one of the beds in the house, but not that it represents every bed). Finally, they understand a word when it is used in many situations and by different people.

In the early development of communication, meaning is also clearer to a child when it is paired with a descriptive gesture. For example, a child will understand the word *throw* better when the caregiver makes the motion of throwing a ball while saying the word, even if there is no ball in the room.

Because of visual and hearing impairments, children who are deaf-blind may miss some of the signals their caregivers are providing during infancy and toddlerhood for everyday interactions. The vital information and skills that are learned through sight and hearing do not come easily to these children. Still, caregivers touch infants who are deaf-blind and move them; hold them; and perform basic routines with them, such as bathing, changing, and feeding, with some regularity. Caregivers can devise interaction routines in relation to these natural activities that are systematic, occur at specific times each day, and have specific cues. With these structured routines, deaf-blind children will learn to anticipate and develop reciprocal interactions than can lead to the development of more sophisticated communication skills. The module that follows provides information that you can share with families about adapting their early interactions to promote the development of communication for infants and toddlers who are deaf-blind.

# COMMUNICATIVE PURPOSES OF BEHAVIOR

Even with structured routines and other adaptations that caregivers can make, some children who are deaf-blind do not develop strong communication skills. Because of sensory isolation, multiple disabilities, or a number of other factors, these children may experience significant delays in acquiring formal language (both receptive and expressive) and use a wide range of behaviors other than language to interact, such as pointing to a desired object, pushing away an unwanted one, leading a caregiver to another room, vocalizing when in physical distress, or gaining attention by hitting.

Communication is vital for all individuals, including people who are deaf-blind and do not use spoken or signed language, so over time students may devise their own ways of gaining attention and interacting that teachers, service providers, and family members do not recognize as attempts to communicate. It is important for teachers, service providers, and family members who are working together to determine if behaviors seem to be attempts to communicate (intentional), particularly behaviors regarded as negative or as "acting out" by others. If such behaviors do seem to represent a student's strong desire to communicate, members of the student's educational team can plan instruction that includes the development of skills that accommodate the child's abilities and needs and promote understandable communication with those around the child.

Any behavior can serve a significant communicative function (Carr, 1977; Donnellan, Mirenda, Mesaros, & Fassbender, 1984; Durand, 1986). Therefore, it is important for all who are involved in the education of a deaf-blind child to examine the child's communicative behavior and behavioral patterns with various people in different settings to obtain the desired outcomes.

The remainder of this module discusses how the examination of behaviors is central to planning the education of students who are deaf-blind and whose acquisition of formal communication skills is delayed. Such evaluations can lead to responsive instruction in communication that can help students learn how to say what they want to say.

## COMMUNICATIVE INTENT

Not all behaviors are necessarily communicative. As was discussed earlier, the development of communication progresses through preintentional to intentional stages (see also Rowland & Stremel-Campbell, 1987). Since these behaviors always evolve in social situations, to understand the communicative meaning of a behavior, one must evaluate it in the social context of how it affects others. For example, if a behavior always obtains a desired response, it serves as an effective form of communication, but if it is sometimes ignored or misunderstood, a child is likely to use another, sometimes less productive, behavior to get the response.

The behavior of Shannelle, who was born with significant visual and hearing impairments, is an example. As she grows up, her ability to communicate using language is likely to be significantly delayed, partly because she will have had less access to many routine interactions that sighted and hearing children experience and thus she may not have learned many of the conventional (and sometimes subtle) ways to influence others socially. If Shannelle wants someone's attention, she is unlikely to call out his or her name or raise her hand, since she has not heard or seen others do so. Rather, she may approach the person, tap his or her hand, or cry or fall to the floor to get attention. In other words, she will use whatever behavior she has found results in the attention, comfort, or help (reinforcement) she wants or needs (rewards).

Everything that students with delayed communication skills do, both seemingly productive and unproductive, positive and negative, should be considered a potential form of communication. Some students display behaviors, such as tantrums or self-injury, for which there is no obvious reinforcing consequence and that do not diminish in response to various forms of intervention. Nevertheless, it ought to be assumed that the students are reinforced in some way for these behaviors.

## FUNCTIONAL ANALYSIS

Educators and other team members can examine and assess students' behaviors for potential communication functions and then design instruction to support the development of positive, productive communication skills (Siegel-Causey & Downing, 1987). One systematic approach to the assessment and treatment of behavior is functional communication training (Durand, 1990). The specific type of behavior that is considered in this approach is usually nonconventional presymbolic behavior that is disruptive or harmful and whose communicative intent is not easily understood. In this approach, a functional analysis is conducted to determine whether a behavior reflects communication intent. If it does, an alternative, appropriate, recognizable, and less disruptive way of achieving the same outcome is systematically taught. The case of Rashan illustrates this analysis.

*Rashan, aged 15, has significant hearing and visual impair-
ments, is identified as having a severe cognitive disability, and
engages in injurious behavior. Until he was 12, he used no
meaningful signs, refused to cooperate with instruction, and
frequently dropped to the floor. Rashan hit his head with his
fist and threw objects several hundred times a day. A year
before he began functional communication training, a tangi-
ble-cue communication system for a number of classroom
activities was established for him and goals were developed
for functional, age-appropriate activities. In addition, environmental factors that contributed to his self-injurious behavior
were minimized, and demands were negotiated with him on an
as-needed basis. Despite these efforts, his behaviors continued.*

The behavioral assessment focuses on how a behavior may be
functional, in other words, why the behavior "makes sense" to the
individual. It requires information about the behavior itself, as well as
about a number of other physical and environmental factors, including the student's general well-being, sensory capacity, and sleep
cycle; the layout of the environment; the number of people in the
environment; the types of activities the individual is being asked to
do; and the range of social interactions in which the individual
engages. This analysis should result in hypotheses about why problem
behaviors persist and the identification of more appropriate responses
that may be developed to replace them. A functional analysis consists
of nine steps, which are listed in Steps in a Functional Analysis.

In Step 1, the behavior is defined in *observable* and *measurable*
terms. Thus, rather than a student's being labeled as angry, the specific behaviors that are determined to be problems, such as hitting,
yelling, stomping feet, or throwing objects, should be identified and
then described in detail, so a person who never met the student can
visualize them. For Rashan, the functional analysis documented his
hitting his head and throwing objects several times a day.

In Step 2, the reinforcing consequence for the behavior is determined by using an evaluation tool like the Motivation Assessment
Scale (MAS) (Durand & Crimmins, 1992). With a tool like the MAS,
the functional significance of behaviors for gaining attention, escape,
tangible and sensory consequences, and multiple consequences can
be identified. Each question describes a different situation in which
problem behaviors are frequently encountered. It is helpful to estab-

## STEPS IN A FUNCTIONAL ANALYSIS

A functional analysis can help you determine whether a child's behavior reflects communicative intent. The following are the nine steps in this process:

**Step 1:** Define the individual's behavior.

**Step 2:** Evaluate what motivates the behavior.

**Step 3:** Observe when the behavior occurs.

**Step 4:** Assess the individual's preferences.

**Step 5:** Select a mode of communication.

**Step 6:** Implement strategies to minimize the occurrence of the behavior.

**Step 7:** Structure frequent opportunities for communication.

**Step 8:** Develop a plan for generalization and maintenance.

**Step 9:** Assess the outcomes. ■

---

lish the pattern of responses if one or more of the following classes of stimulus events are associated with a behavior:

- *Attention:* Behaviors may be used to gain the attention of others under specific circumstances, for example, when two people are talking.

- *Escape:* Behaviors may be used to make demands or to end unpleasant situations or difficult tasks, as if the person were saying, "Leave me alone" or "I can't do this without help."

- *Tangible consequences:* Behaviors may be used to obtain specific tangible rewards, such as food, music, or the opportunity to jump on a trampoline.

- *Sensory consequences:* Behaviors, such as flicking the hands between the eyes and sources of light, may be used to provide sensory feedback that is reinforcing—that feels good or is stimulating.

- *Multiple outcomes:* Behaviors may be used and maintained for more than one reason. In such cases, the behavior and setting in which it occurs need to be redefined more precisely to determine the circumstances under which the behavior may be more clearly seen to have a single function. For example, a more detailed examination may confirm that although a girl gazes at and flicks her fingers for sensory feedback in some situations, she also does so when she is faced with increased demands to participate in an activity; thus, she may be using the behavior to avoid participating in demanding situations, as did Rashan.

*Both of Rashan's self-injurious behaviors were rated as being associated with tangible events; that is, they seemed to be a means of getting something he preferred. Observation in his classroom and follow-up questions of his mother and teacher revealed that Rashan often seemed to engage in self-injurious behavior to obtain food or music. His pushing and throwing were found to be related to wanting attention and specific items and to escaping demanding situations.*

In Step 3, how often the behavior occurs and the situations in which it is most likely and least likely to occur are examined. Most teachers are familiar with a number of methods for doing so. One method is to keep a log or diary of incidents of the behavior. A more formal and systematic method is to record every occurrence of a behavior, its time and location, the events that preceded it, and the events that followed it (an antecedent-behavior-consequence [ABC] analysis). This method yields a rich body of information, but requires a great deal of time to record and to analyze.

A method that is not so demanding of the teacher's time is to record information on a "scatter plot"—a grid in which the days of the week are marked along a horizontal line and the times of the day are marked along a vertical line (Touchette, MacDonald, & Langer, 1985). Incidents are recorded for specific periods (such as every half hour or an instructional period) on the day they occur, and the same response is recorded whether the behavior occurred one time or 20 times.

There are several reasons for using this approach:

1. If the behavior is dangerous or otherwise socially unacceptable, one occurrence is too many.

2. The teacher can spend the greatest amount of time on direct instruction, rather than on record keeping.

3. This approach provides a quick visual analysis of the behavior. For example, if a behavior consistently occurs in the late morning, it may be considered whether the student is hungry

at that time. If the behavior occurs more often on some days than on others, the schedule of activities for those days, the physical setting of the different activities (Is the room too hot or cold or too cluttered?), the tasks (Are they too difficult or repetitious?), or the interactional styles used in these activities (Are requests clearly presented to the student? Does the student have an appropriate means of making his or her desires known?) can be examined. In each case an attempt would be made to determine the ways in which the student's behavior is functional for a particular setting.

*Rashan's behaviors were observed at half-hour intervals using a scatter plot. Observations revealed that Rashan's self-injurious behaviors occurred in approximately 70 percent of these intervals each day (his pushing and throwing occurred in approximately 30 percent of the intervals). The behaviors were rarely seen during mealtimes. Rashan's self-injurious behavior was still a concern because it posed a continuing risk to him. However, his pushing and throwing were not considered an immediate priority because they could be minimized by controlling his access to items.*

Because some behaviors occur infrequently (less than once a week), it is difficult to determine the circumstances that immediately influence them. In these cases, the checklist developed by Gardner, Cole, Davidson, and Karan (1986) is useful. It assesses the events of the previous day, such as whether the person became ill, slept fitfully, or experienced a particular disappointment.

In Step 4, the individual's style of communication and preferred activities (see Modules 11 and 12 for descriptions of various data-gathering formats) are assessed. For example, staff and family members are asked questions about how the student makes his or her needs known, what types of information the student spontaneously communicates, who the student enjoys spending time with, and what the student's most and least preferred activities are. The specific objective is to examine the relationship between behaviors that seem to be problems to others and communication skills and the degree to which the student is interested in communicating.

*Although efforts were made to revise Rashan's educational program to emphasize age-related and community-referenced skills, including communication, the review of his Individualized Education Program (IEP) indicated that the activities did not reflect all his individual needs and preferences. The only activities that were consistently described as being pleasurable to Rashan were eating or listening to loud music, and Rashan had relatively few opportunities during the day to engage in them. Most of his instructional day was spent in activities that he did not enjoy. Therefore, Rashan's IEP and instructional program were redesigned to reflect the activities he preferred and that would motivate him.*

Instructional design can be adapted to accommodate a student's preferences and behaviors. For behaviors that are motivated by a desire to avoid or escape unpleasant situations, consider

- making the task more pleasant
- making the task shorter in duration
- dropping the task if it is not a crucial activity for present instructional needs
- retaining the task and teaching the student to ask for "help" if it is difficult, to indicate "I don't understand" for a new task, or to request "break, please" for a long task.

For behaviors that are motivated by tangible outcomes, consider

- offering the student opportunities to request desired items spontaneously on a regular basis and granting such requests
- incorporating rewards (toys, food, or choices of activities) into the instructional routine.

To maximize sensory consequences that the student enjoys, consider

- finding ways to use pleasant sensory stimulation to reward the student for completing other tasks
- encouraging the student to communicate his or her desire for an activity that provides enjoyable sensory stimulation, as in the case of Jesse.

*Jesse is multiply disabled with a severe visual impairment and a hearing impairment. When he gazes out the window, especially on bright days, he often waves his fingers in front of his eyes. Therefore, he was taught to request a set of translucent, colored paddles by signing "look" as a way of choosing an activity, communicating his choice, and getting the sensory stimulation he enjoyed.*

Similarly, since the assessment indicated that Rashan's behavior was associated with his apparent desire to eat and to listen to music, it was thought that he would benefit from being able to make frequent requests for these activities. This goal was consistent with a previously established goal of teaching Rashan to select foods at mealtime.

In Step 5, a mode of communication is selected for the individual. It should be kept in mind that students who are deaf-blind can use various methods of communication—speech, American Sign Language, gestures, picture cues, object cues, and a range of augmentative systems, depending on their needs (Mustonen, Locke, Reichle, Solbrack, & Lindgren, 1991; see also Modules 8 and 9) and that one with which the student is likely to have rapid success should be used. For a student with no speech and poor fine motor control, for example, consider an augmentative system in which the response mode is to press a switch or a tangible symbol system with easily manipulated objects. Allow adequate time for the student to learn, but if a mode seems ineffective fairly soon, modify or change it.

With regard to Step 6, strategies that can be used to minimize the occurrence of behaviors like hitting, scratching, and throwing objects include the following:

- changing staffing schedules
- changing activities
- changing settings
- postponing or dropping goals
- distracting the student
- interrupting the behavior.

Many service providers object to making accommodations "just" to give students "what they want." However, there is nothing wrong in giving students what they want if they communicate their preferences in appropriate ways, since an objective of communication is to make one's wants and needs known, so they may be met. The following describes modifications that were made in Rashan's schedule:

*Rashan was given the opportunity to request music as soon as he arrived at school. Furthermore, after his mother was consulted, instruction was postponed in several areas in which Rashan was not successful. For instance, Rashan frequently hit himself during the prolonged time in the bathroom for toilet training. Since he was making little progress in toilet training, this goal was not thought to be immediately critical. Greater attention was given to the types of demands placed on him.*

With regard to Step 7, communication skills are learned best when individuals have frequent, systematic opportunities during the day to request and reject items and activities, to offer information, and to try to structure frequent opportunities for communication. Since communication is the primary goal, a range of responses are acceptable in these interactions, among them the following:

- Help a student request attention by communicating your proximity, prompting an appropriate communication response, and then paying attention to the student.

- Structure opportunities for a student to communicate his or her desire to take a break from or stop an activity. During an activity, offer the student the opportunity to choose to keep working (for example, to fill another saltshaker) or to take a break (for instance, to get a drink of water and then return to work) as often as the situation dictates—every two minutes, every 10 minutes, or whatever interval is appropriate.

- Support a student's desire for sensory reinforcers by providing frequent opportunities for the student to communicate his or her request for the pleasurable experience and designating an appropriate location for the student to engage in such activities.

- Help students with tangibly motivated behaviors to choose among preferred items or activities that have been identified as appropriate (choice-making time is instructional time). Rashan, for example, was offered the choice between "music" and "eat" approximately every half hour during the day. This interval was selected because there were some half-hour intervals in which he was free of his self-injurious behavior.

After students learn these communicative skills, Step 8 involves the development of a plan to generalize and maintain the skills, so the student can use them spontaneously in different situations. Prompts must be faded out so that the communicative response is more likely to occur than the behavior of concern, and efforts should be made to expand the student's interactions with others to include more communicative responses with a broader range of people.

*Although Rashan was given a choice between food and music, it did not mean that he ate and listened to music all day long. Demands were gradually introduced into his instruction to expand his communication and other skills. For example, after Rashan spontaneously signed "eat," his teacher began to present another choice of cookie or bread, with the request to select one or the other. In addition, after signing "cookie," Rashan was asked to open the package; throw away the wrapper; and, after eating a few bites, sign "more" to get more.*

In assessing the effectiveness of functional communication training in Step 9, it is determined whether there has been a significant decrease in the occurrence of the target problem behavior and an accompanying increase in the use of appropriate communication skills. Evidence that the student can generalize skills in many settings over time, with new responses, and with new people is also examined. In addition, attempts should be made to extend interactions so that soliciting attention leads to reciprocal social exchanges, requests for breaks lead to negotiations about what work will be done next, and choosing an item leads to another set of choices. In this way, the means by which the student can participate in activities that he or she prefers are extended. The goal is for the student to recognize that he or she has control over the environment through appropriate communication. The assessment of Rashan's training found improvements within three years.

*Rashan's self-injurious behavior decreased from 70 percent to 20 percent of the half-hour intervals. Within these intervals, his teachers and his mother regularly reported that he was not hitting himself as hard, and the physical evidence indicated that his self-injury had greatly diminished (he no longer had welts on his face). In addition, Rashan was using over 12 signs and responding to more than 20. He was communicating more to control his environment, and the environment was more appropriately responsive to him.*

Understanding basic concepts of communication, especially those factors that foster the development of communication, can help you to analyze a student's behavior and help the student find more appropriate means of establishing a responsive relationship with the environment. Once such a positive relationship is established, the goal is to expand further the communication options that are available to the student. The modules that follow explore these options.

# REFERENCES

Carr, E. G. (1977). The motivation of self-injurious behavior: A review of some hypotheses. *Psychological Bulletin, 84*, 800–816.

Donnellan, A. M., Mirenda, P. L., Mesaros, R. A., & Fassbender, L. L. (1984). Analyzing the communicative functions of aberrant behavior. *Journal of the Association for Persons with Severe Handicaps, 9*, 201–212.

Durand, V. M. (1986). Self-injurious behavior as intentional communication. In K. D. Gadow (Ed.), *Advances in learning and behavioral difficulties* (Vol. 5, pp. 141–155). Greenwich, CT: JAI Press.

Durand, V. M. (1990). *Functional communication training: A treatment program for severe behavior problems.* New York: Guilford Press.

Durand, V. M., & Crimmins, D. B. (1992). *The Motivation Assessment Scale: Administration manual.* Topeka, KS: Monaco & Associates.

Gardner, W. I., Cole, C. L., Davidson, D. P., & Karan, O. C. (1986). Reducing aggression in individuals with developmental disabilities: An expanded stimulus control assessment and intervention model. *Education and Training of the Mentally Retarded, 21*, 3–12.

Mustonen, T., Locke, P., Reichle, J., Solbrack, M., & Lindgren, A. (1991). An overview of augmentative and alternative communication systems. In J. Reichle, J. York, & J. Sigafoos (Eds.), *Implementing augmentative and alternative communication: Strategies for learners with severe disabilities.* Baltimore: Paul H. Brookes.

Rowland, C., & Schweigert, P. (1990). *Tangible symbol systems.* Tucson: Communication Skill Builders.

Rowland, C., & Stremel-Campbell, K. (1987). Share and share alike: Conventional gestures to emergent language for learners with sensory impairments. In L. Goetz, D. Guess, & K. Stremel-Campbell (Eds.), *Innovative program design for individuals with dual sensory impairments* (pp. 49–75). Baltimore: Paul H. Brookes.

Siegel-Causey, E., & Downing, J. (1987). Nonsymbolic communication development: Theoretical concepts and educational strategies. In L. Goetz, D. Guess,

& K. Stremel-Campbell, K. (Eds.), *Innovative program design for individuals with dual sensory impairments* (pp. 15–48). Baltimore: Paul H. Brookes.

Touchette, P. E., MacDonald, R. F., & Langer, S. N. (1985). A scatter plot for identifying stimulus control of problem behavior. *Journal of Applied Behavior Analysis, 18,* 343–351.

Wetherby, A. M., & Prizant, B. M. (1992). Profiling young children's communicative competence. In S. F. Warren & J. Reichle (Eds.), *Causes and effects in communication and language intervention* (Vol. 1, pp. 217–253). Baltimore: Paul H. Brookes.

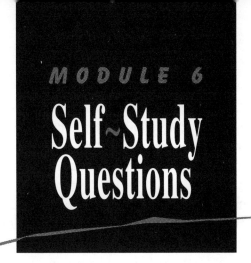

# MODULE 6
# Self~Study Questions

1. You point to a picture of the dining room table and sign "lunchtime" to your student. This is an example of communication that is
   a. receptive, expressive, and symbolic.
   b. expressive and nonsymbolic.
   c. receptive and nonsymbolic.

2. Something that is used to stand for something else but that has no clear physical similarity to it is called
   a. a concrete symbol.
   b. a symbol.
   c. an abstract symbol.

3. Which of the following statements is false?
   a. Communication begins at birth, although early communication behaviors are preintentional.
   b. You should not respond to preintentional communication because it may encourage aberrant behavioral patterns.
   c. Someone who uses intentional communication realizes that she or he can control the behavior of another person.

4. The central concept of a functional communication training approach, that behavior serves a communicative function, is best supported when
   a. a successful intervention is developed after the student's responses to antecedents and consequences are assessed.
   b. an intervention that teaches the student a communicative response that serves the same function as the behavior is successful.
   c. an intervention that targets the suppression of excess behavior is successful.

5. What information is essential to determining the communicative function of a behavior, that is, what the student is attempting to communicate by behaving in this way?
   a. Structured interviews of instructional staff and those who know the student best to document their impressions about the influence of the variables that they think maintain the student's problem behavior.
   b. Behavior rating scales used to assess adaptive behavior and information from antecedent-behavior-consequence charts (ABC analysis), and incident logs.
   c. A functional analysis to determine the situations in which the behavior is likely to occur; an assessment of the relative influence of social attention, tangible gain, escape and sensory consequences on the student's behavior; and an evaluation of the student's preferences.

6. Luke is 9 years old. He has frequent tantrums that sometimes result in injury to himself. He prefers to be by himself. When he wants something, he points to it. The assessment suggests that he is likely to get upset when he is working on an activity that is difficult for him. Given this situation, which of the following intervention strategies should be implemented?
   a. Involve Luke with other children during free time, so he has the opportunity to develop more age-appropriate social communication skills.
   b. As soon as Luke begins to have a tantrum, remove the activity. When the tantrum is over, direct him, with full physical prompts, to restart the activity. Instruct him to sign "more work" and introduce the activity again.
   c. Offer him the opportunity to choose the activity on which he wants to work. Teach him to communicate that he needs help by pointing to a picture of a teacher helping a student.

7. Justine is 18 years old. Her parents have reported that when she is not involved in an activity, she sits and rocks back and forth. Justine uses a voice output communication device to make her needs known. She successfully performs many domestic and personal care activities. The assessment suggests that she is most likely to rock when she has been unoccupied for at least 10 minutes. Given this situation, which of the following intervention strategies would be best?
   a. The school social worker should arrange for the family to obtain a home health care worker whose primary job will be one-to-one involvement with Justine.
   b. Encourage the family to purchase an exercise bike. Teach Justine to request the activity with her communicator. Provide Justine with a schedule of chores to complete when she arrives home and allow her to determine the order in which she will complete them or to choose ones she wants to complete.
   c. Encourage the family to purchase a rocking chair in which Justine can sit and rock all the time.

*Answers to self-study questions for this module appear at the end of Unit 2.*

# The Beginnings of Communication: Early Childhood

*DEBORAH CHEN*

*CONTRIBUTORS*

**SHARON BOLTON**
*Movement-based Activities*
*Practical Tips on Play*

- *Encourage emotional attachment to promote communication*

- *Create responsive and interactive environments*

- *Recognize different tolerance levels for stimulation*

- *Develop predictable caregiving and play routines*

- *Introduce new concepts and objects through familiar ones*

Although the capacity to communicate is inborn, the skills that infants need to communicate are acquired with the assistance of other people. Therefore, the primary goal of early intervention with infants who are deaf-blind is to encourage the growth of their bonds with their parents and other caregivers because attachment and bonding can promote the development of essential communication skills.

Providers of early intervention services frequently meet the families of deaf-blind infants soon after family members have first learned of the children's disabilities and are feeling frightened or overwhelmed by the information. Many caregivers are depressed and do not know how to reach out to the infants; some infants may not be responding to their caregivers' loving overtures. When they do not receive the desired responses, many caregivers may become discouraged and stop interacting with the infants. As a result, in some cases, both infants and caregivers feel dissatisfied and rebuffed.

This module presents information to help service providers work with the families and other caregivers of infants and young children and includes strategies to meet the unique communication needs of infants who are deaf-blind. It also discusses how caregivers, other family members, and others can create responsive and interactive environments for infants that promote the development of communication. Strategies for teaching young children who are deaf-blind to be oriented to their environments and to use communication skills for movement are explored in Modules 16 and 18. The use of these strategies to help young deaf-blind children begin to develop communication and movement skills early is essential for meeting their educational needs and encouraging their overall growth and development.

# RESPONSIVE EARLY ENVIRONMENTS

To an infant, there is a significant difference between a responsive environment and one that is merely stimulating. A responsive environment is interactive and adjusts expectations according to the infant's needs, preferences, and reactions. Creating a responsive environment requires an understanding of (1) attachment behaviors (bonding), (2) an infant's sensitivity to specific sensory stimulation, and (3) an infant's temperament.

## ATTACHMENT BEHAVIORS

During the first year, infants develop behaviors that enhance their emotional attachments to their primary caregivers. They smile, cry, make eye contact, and begin to differentiate people from objects in their environments. Eventually, they try to maintain contact with their primary caregivers through specific attachment behaviors, such as vocalizing, clinging, and smiling.

Bonding is a crucial step in an infant's development. If an infant does not form a secure bond with his or her caregiver, the ability to form relationships with others may be affected. Infants who are deaf-blind may have difficulty developing attachment behaviors, especially since their medical needs and hospitalizations may interrupt the bonding processes. Depending on the severity of their sensory impairments, such infants may not respond to eye contact, smiles, familiar faces, or voices. If they do not know when their caregivers are present or absent, they may have no sense of separation from others. Moreover, their caregivers may often be afraid or depressed and may not know how to interact with them. Therefore, it is important to be sensitive to the concerns of parents and other caregivers when suggesting strategies to promote bonding, such as those about to be described.

### Strategies

Ask the caregivers to identify the infant's reactions to familiar and unfamiliar people. Encourage them to answer the questions presented in the Infant Profile in Figure 7-1 at the end of this module.

To develop emotional bonds, an infant who is deaf-blind needs contact with caregivers that is consistent and predictable. Discuss the following suggestions for holding, touching, comforting, attending, engaging, and responding with the caregivers, and encourage them to adapt and apply the suggestions to their own situations.

- When possible, *hold* the infant in a secure and comfortable position for caregiving routines, such as bottle feeding, and identify other routines in which holding is possible.
- *Touch* the infant during play and other interactions. Identify the types of touching that the baby enjoys, such as patting, stroking, kissing, tickling, cuddling, and bouncing.
- Respond quickly to *comfort* an infant who is crying, fussy, or frightened. Identify ways to calm the baby, such as rocking,

providing opportunities for sucking, or gently patting the baby's chest.

- Give as much *attention* as possible to the infant by maintaining eye contact (at close range for infants who are visually impaired), smiling, talking, touching, and so on. Encourage the caregivers to identify how they pay attention to their infant.

- *Engage* the infant's attention by making faces, cooing or babbling, humming and singing, tickling, blowing on the baby's stomach, and so forth. (Encourage the infant to touch the caregiver's throat and feel vibrations of sound, especially when an infant has significant hearing loss.) Encourage the caregivers to identify how they engage the attention of their infant.

- *Respond* to the infant's behavior, such as by vocalizing when the baby makes a sound or shifting the baby's position when he or she begins to fidget. Observe the baby's body language and identify what gets the caregiver to respond.

## SENSITIVITY TO STIMULATION

An infant's first challenge is to achieve a balance between the waking, sleeping, and feeding cycles and to remain calm and relaxed in the midst of a stimulating environment (Greenspan & Greenspan, 1985). Some infants have extremely high or low thresholds of reaction to stimulation. An infant who has a high threshold and thus is not sensitive to stimulation may be calm and relaxed but uninterested in the environment, whereas an infant who has a low threshold and hence is extremely sensitive to stimulation may become overstimulated and stressed by normal sensations. Signs of stress include tensing or arching the body, pulling or turning away, crying and fussing, closing the eyes, hiccuping, and spitting up.

Infants who are deaf-blind tend to be extremely sensitive to certain types of sensory stimulation (such as excessive movement and abrupt handling) and not sensitive to others (such as a loud but distant sound). Their thresholds of reactions depend on their neurological makeup and degree of sensory impairment.

### Strategies

Ask the caregivers to identify the infant's preferences for different types of sensory stimulation. Learning these preferences will enable them to help the infant be calm and attentive. Also encourage the caregivers to discuss the questions presented in Figure 7-1.

If an infant has special physical needs, it is important to consult an occupational or physical therapist to identify optimal positioning and handling techniques. Discuss the following suggestions for touching, movement, position, vision, and hearing with the caregivers and consider the questions under each item in Figure 7-1.

**Touch**. Experiment with massage when the infant is awake; apply gentle strokes, beginning at the feet and working up to the face, the arms, and the hands. Observe the baby's reactions to being touched on different parts of the body, as well as to light touches and to firm strokes.

**Movement**. During playtime, observe the infant's reactions to lively movements: Hold the infant out in front of you and move him or her gently side to side or up and down. Also observe the baby's reactions to gentle rocking.

**Positions**. Try different positions to help the infant to be calm, alert, and interested in the environment. Observe his or her responses to being held in different positions—vertically, horizontally, and at a 45-degree angle. Observe the baby's reaction to lying on his or her back, stomach, or side; to lying prone over a bolster; and to sitting in an infant seat.

**Vision**. If the infant has some vision, observe his or her reactions to facial expressions, variously colored objects (including brightly colored, black-and-white, and shiny objects), colored lights, and other sources of light. (These observations will be helpful to the vision specialist.)

**Hearing**. If the infant has some hearing, experiment with different sounds and intonations. Observe the baby's reactions to sounds when his or her hearing aid is in place. (These observations will be helpful to the hearing specialist.)

## DIFFERENCES IN TEMPERAMENT

Everyone has seen infants who are calm and responsive and those who are fussy, slow to respond, and difficult to engage. These differences are due to variations in temperament.

In their research involving three groups of infants—those without disabilities, those with mental retardation, and those with congenital rubella syndrome—Thomas, Chess, and Birch (1970) identified nine qualities of temperament that influence an infant's response to the caregiving environment. These qualities are described in the following Strategies section. Specific combinations of these qualities characterize infants as easy, slow to warm, or difficult.

*Easy infants* have predictable eating, sleeping, and elimination patterns; adapt quickly to changes in routines; and have pleasant moods and mild reactions.

*Slow-to-warm infants* have low-to-moderate activity levels, vary in the regularity of their physical needs, slowly accept changes and initially withdraw from the new and unfamiliar, and have slightly unpleasant moods and mild reactions. These infants need gentle prompting to respond and sensitive introductions to changes in routines.

*Difficult infants* have irregular physical needs, slowly accept the new or unfamiliar, and have unpleasant moods and intense reactions. These difficult reactions and irregular patterns are a challenge to any caregiver. Infants with disabilities are more likely to have difficult temperaments than are infants without disabilities (Chess & Fernandez, 1976).

It is useful to remember that the temperaments of caregivers and service providers may affect the way they work with infants who are deaf-blind. An active, boisterous adult may frighten and overstimulate a placid, subdued baby, and an active, boisterous infant may challenge a quiet, placid caregiver. Caregivers may have to modify their natural styles to promote pleasurable interactions. The goal is to achieve a "good fit"—when a caregiver can adapt his or her interactions, expectations, and caregiving routines to match an infant's temperamental style. This match facilitates an affective bond or emotional attachment between the caregiver and the infant and contributes positively to the infant's development.

## Strategies

Discuss the concept of temperament with the caregivers and ask them to describe the infant's temperament on the basis of the nine qualities (Thomas et al., 1970) whose description follows.

**Activity Level, or Amount of Motor Activity**. Infants with high activity levels enjoy movement and dislike being still or contained. Infants with low activity levels cooperate with caregiving routines and prefer quiet play to roughhousing. Active toddlers require more interaction and greater supervision than do toddlers with low activity levels. Without vision and auditory stimulation to attract them, infants and toddlers who are deaf-blind may remain passive and may not initiate physical activity, but they may crave touch and vigorous movements and enjoy physical play.

**Rhythmicity, or Regularity of Physical Needs**. The eating, sleeping, and toileting needs of infants with regular rhythmicity are predictable, whereas infants with irregular rhythmicity or neurological impairments have difficulty establishing mealtime, bedtime, and toileting routines. In the face of infants' irregular routines, especially unpredictable sleeping patterns, caregivers may have to develop creative ways of getting the sleep or other forms of respite they need while providing safe, worry-free environments for their infants. However, consistent routines can help infants develop more predictable patterns. For example, an active day, followed by a calm, predictable bedtime routine, may help infants relax and go to sleep.

**Distractibility from Ongoing Activity**. Infants who are easily distracted are easily soothed when they cry, but those who are not distractible are not easily comforted. As was previously discussed, caregivers need to discover ways to comfort infants. Infants who are easily distracted may have difficulty paying attention to significant social stimuli because they are overstimulated by what they perceive as confusing multiple stimuli. They do not easily sort out important stimuli from less important ones and therefore cannot attend to and respond appropriately to the most important stimuli. These infants may benefit from calm and controlled environments that provide carefully structured sensory input and allow them to focus on just one sensory modality at a time.

**Approach or Withdrawal Response**. Infants who willingly taste new foods and play with unfamiliar toys have a positive approach response, whereas those who reject unfamiliar things have a withdrawal response. Unfamiliar things may be frightening to infants, especially if they cannot see or hear well; therefore, these infants need gentle introductions to new people, objects, and activities and may more readily accept something unfamiliar if it is linked to something familiar, for example, a new game when introduced through the use of a favorite toy. Furthermore, the painful and frightening medical interventions to which infants who are deaf-blind are often subjected may make them more wary of unfamiliar people and places.

**Adaptability to Changes in the Routine or Environment**. Adaptive infants accept changes in their routines, but those who are

▲ *Introducing young deaf-blind children to new objects carefully and gently encourages a positive response.*

not adaptive will not adapt to changes easily. Deaf-blind infants usually require support in adapting to changes in their routines and environments, especially because they may be unaware of visual or auditory cues that mark these changes. Familiar objects can provide information on changes in routine; for example, a spoon can be used to indicate mealtime.

**Attention Span and Persistence in an Activity**. Infants with long attention spans and persistence engage in activities for extended periods and are not easily distracted. Some infants who are deaf-blind show persistence in self-stimulating behaviors and need encouragement to interact and discover other ways of playing. Infants with short attention spans and persistence are easily distracted from activities and benefit from interactions and activities that are brief.

**Intensity of Reaction**. Infants with intense reactions will laugh, cry, or scream heartily in response to everyday and unusual situations, and their strong negative reactions may be disconcerting to their caregivers. Infants with mild reactions are subdued and fuss infrequently.

**Threshold of Responsiveness to Stimulation**. Infants with low thresholds of responsiveness are extremely sensitive to the mild stimulation of their senses. Infants who are deaf-blind may be sensitive to touch, movement, smells, or tastes. Depending on the severity of their vision and hearing losses, some infants may not react to visual or auditory stimulation. However, many deaf-blind infants have some functional vision or hearing; with appropriately fitted hearing aids or corrective lenses and training, they can learn to make sense of visual and auditory information.

**Quality of Mood or General Disposition**. Infants with a positive mood are pleasant and attract interaction because others want to interact with them, and cheerful infants who are deaf-blind benefit from increased and enjoyable social interaction. Infants with negative moods are fussy, demanding, and difficult to interact with, and fussy deaf-blind infants may not experience enjoyable social interactions. Although interacting with crying infants is not much fun and is hard work, caregivers need ways to comfort them. Deaf-blind infants who tend to be fussy may become less fussy when caregiving environments become more responsive to their needs.

## PROGRAM DEVELOPMENT

Gathering information about a child is essential to developing efforts to meet that child's needs. Figure 7-1 has been provided for this purpose. To plan a program, carefully review all information collected about an infant. Discuss the information with the infant's caregivers and other service providers. Be aware of the conditions that help make the infant most responsive and try to adapt your own interactions with the infant to suit his or her needs and preferences. A review of the strategies in this module may help you develop your program plans. In addition to the strategies already presented, movement-based activities and other suggestions offered in the remainder of this module may be helpful.

# MOVEMENT-BASED ACTIVITIES

Movement-based instruction helps a child who is deaf-blind and an adult develop a trusting, interactive relationship that can be the basis for the development of communication over time. Movement-based activities and instruction are associated with the work of Dr. Jan van Dijk, whose "coactive movement" approach to teaching deaf-blind students has been useful to teachers for several decades. The first two levels of van Dijk's multistep approach—resonance and coactive movement—are especially well suited to early intervention with infants and toddlers. (See Module 3 for more information on this approach.)

## RESONANCE

At the first level, resonance, you hold the child close to support the child's body and to give the child a strong sense of security. "Conversations," or interactions, involve turn-taking by you, the adult, and the child, with movement as the basic response, rather than spoken or signed words.

Use familiar movements, such as rocking and clapping, so the child can learn to accept your physical closeness and to move in unison with you. As the child gradually accommodates to this close body contact and movement, he or she can learn to use a signal to request that the movement should start again. By observing the child, you can detect cues that may help you identify the movements that are likely to be effective; for example, if the child rocks himself or herself, that movement may be reinforcing for him or her and hence may be useful for instruction.

To begin, place the child in your lap and initiate a movement, such as rocking, with the child. (Older students can be placed on the floor, a bench, or a bolster.) First, you move and then stop and wait for any response to indicate that the child wants to move more, such as a facial expression or the child's own movement. Allow enough time for a response; some students take longer to understand what is expected and may need many repetitions. If the child seems to resist the shared movement, stop it and try again later for short periods. Establishing the child's level of trust is vital, and it cannot be accomplished if the child is resisting. When you feel strongly that the child is consistently indicating a desire to move again with you, pair the movement with a sign or another signal to "start."

Movement games can be effective in bringing about reciprocal responses in infants and toddlers. Several that can be used to establish interactions follow.

### "Pat a Cake"

Pat a cake, pat a cake, baker's man!
Bake me a cake as fast as you can.
Roll it, pat it, and mark it with a B.
And put it in the oven for baby and me.

The movement used with "Pat a Cake" is clapping. Some children first participate in the movement by opening their hands when the movement starts. The specific signal is hitting or clapping their hands.

### "Row, Row, Row Your Boat"

Row, row, row your boat, gently down the stream.
Merrily, merrily, merrily, merrily, life is but a dream.

The movement used with "Row, Row, Row Your Boat" is rocking. While holding both the child's hands, rock back and forth together. When the movement stops, the child may signal to begin the movement by rocking, moving one hand back and forth, or leaning his or her head forward or backward.

### "Two Little Monkeys"

Two little monkeys jumping on the bed.
One fell off and bumped his head.
Mama called the doctor and the doctor said,
"No more monkeys jumping on the bed."

While the child sits on your lap, gently bounce him or her. The child can start the movement again by bouncing.

### "London Bridge"

London Bridge is falling down, falling down, falling down.
London Bridge is falling down, my fair lady.

While singing this song, sway with the child from side to side. After the song ends, the child may request the song again by leaning to one side or the other.

At the resonance level, introduce objects (referents) to let the child know what is going to happen. Examples of objects or referents include a bib for eating, a blanket for nap time, a toy for playtime, and keys to represent an outing to the store.

## COACTIVE MOVEMENT

In the next instructional level, coactive movement, a variety of sequences of movements are used. These sequences have different lengths and levels of difficulty and can be used in daily activities. First, move with the child to establish these sequences and then gradually distance yourself from the child. When the child becomes accomplished at the movement sequences that are no longer performed with close body contact between you and the child, he or she will be able to sit and repeat back an entire sequence through observation and imitation. Again, a fingerplay can be used, with the expectation that the child will observe (tactilely or visually) the sequence and repeat it back. Routine activities, such as washing hands and putting socks on the feet, can also be used at this level of movement-based activity.

# ENVIRONMENTS THAT PROMOTE COMMUNICATION

By participating in consistent and predictable exchanges, infants who are deaf-blind discover their capacity to influence their environments. Therefore, it is important for caregivers to react consistently to the infants' behaviors. That is, they need to interpret an infant's behavior as a signal to communicate and respond to the baby's signals consistently. Consistent responses help deaf-blind infants discover that they can make things happen, and predictable patterns encourage the development of their communication skills. If infants' behaviors are misread and caregivers' responses are inconsistent, communication skills will be slow to emerge (Goldberg, 1977).

If infants cannot hear the soothing voices or see the smiling faces of their caregivers, they may not respond to caregiving behaviors or show much interest in their surroundings. Hence, the caregivers of deaf-blind infants need to interpret the most subtle cues— changes in body posture, hand movements, and specific vocalizations. Gradually, these behaviors are given precise meanings and provide specific responses.

## THE HOME ENVIRONMENT

At home, caregivers can encourage the early development of communication skills in infants who are deaf-blind by (1) interpreting and responding to the infants' signals, (2) engaging the infants with sensory cues, (3) developing caregiving routines, (4) developing play routines, and (5) encouraging other caregivers who are involved in the infants' routines to use the same cues (see Tips for Communicating: A Summary).

### Interpretation and Response to Signals

The early communication signals of infants who are deaf-blind are often difficult to recognize or interpret, and some are subtle and unexpected. For example, infants who are totally blind and have moderate hearing losses may tilt their heads and become quiet as they try to listen. A caregiver may misinterpret this signal of attention as a kind of disinterest and ignore it. Infants who have visual and hearing impairments may appear passive and unresponsive to interaction, and some may withdraw from social interaction, especially when overstimulated or confused, and engage in self-stimulatory behaviors or fussing.

Careful observation of a deaf-blind infant will enable the caregivers to learn how to recognize, interpret, and respond to his or her

**HELP at a GLANCE**

## TIPS FOR COMMUNICATING: A SUMMARY

- Infants' behaviors are often subtle. Observe carefully, interpret, and respond.

- Use features of sensory cues that the infant can perceive.

- Develop predictable caregiving and play routines.

- Follow the infant's lead (interest, focus of attention, and level of communication).

- Imitate the infant's sounds or actions and add a little more.

- Create opportunities for turn-taking by pausing and prompting the infant's turn.

- Provide opportunities for making choices.

- Use tactile cues and object signals. ■

behavior. The following example presents a possible scenario that features a caregiver's interpretation and responses to the signals of an infant who is deaf-blind and has useful hearing.

> *The caregiver is holding the infant on her lap. The infant begins to squirm. The caregiver asks, "Do you want to bounce?" The caregiver bounces the infant on her lap and then pauses for a moment. The infant smiles and shakes his leg. The caregiver says, "You like that; let's bounce more." The caregiver again bounces the infant on her lap. The infant begins to fuss and pulls away. The caregiver says, "You want down? All done." The caregiver puts the infant on the floor. The infant says, "Da da." The caregiver responds, "Daddy's at work."*

The behaviors of infants have specific functions for communication. Even a newborn communicates an awareness of the change or absence of a desired stimulus, such as a mother's voice, by looking startled, blinking repeatedly, or tensing the body, for example. The behavior of an infant also indicates a desire for attention, often by visual fixation, alertness, smiling, frowning, eye widening, and reaching or moving the body toward the stimulus, or a protest of the presence of a disliked stimulus or the absence of a desired stimulus, by fussing, crying, or turning away. As was previously mentioned, infants may also engage in self-stimulatory behaviors.

**Strategies**. Ask the caregiver to identify and to respond to the subtle behavioral cues that are offered by the infant who is deaf-blind. If possible, videotape the caregiver interacting with the baby. After you review the videotape, discuss the caregiver's responses to the infant's signals. Encourage the caregiver to discuss the following questions:

- What situations motivate the infant to communicate? (Identify activities, objects, and people whom the infant likes.)
- How does the infant communicate? (Identify observed communication behaviors, including facial expressions, body tension, laughing, crying, screaming, body movements, postural orientation, sounds, gestures, and words.)
- What messages are conveyed by the infant's behaviors? (Identify what the infant is trying to communicate, such as a desire for attention, more food or a drink, or a specific activ-

ity or object; tiredness, boredom, or illness; or a dislike or enjoyment of something.)

- How does the caregiver respond to the infant's signals? (Evaluate the caregiver's action and the infant's reaction.)

## Use of Sensory Cues

Researchers have found that caregivers interact with infants in special ways to attract attention. Typical interactions involve speaking in a high-pitched voice; using repetition; using short, simple phrases and sentences; displaying exaggerated facial expressions and intonations; and touching, gesturing, and pausing to allow the infant to take a turn. These unique adaptations have been called "motherese" (Cooper & Aslin, 1990). Motherese promotes effective interpersonal communication and maintains an infant's attention through touch, intonation, gestures, and facial expressions; these nonverbal features of communication are more meaningful to infants than are words. Depending on an infant's temperament and disability, the consistent use of hearing aids and corrective lenses will provide the infant with a greater access to the auditory or visual features of motherese. Auditory cues include voice and intonation, sounds made by people or objects, and other sounds. Some totally blind children with mild hearing losses are startled and upset by unfamiliar sounds that are unpredictable, loud, or confusing.

The nonvisual aspects of motherese should be emphasized with infants who are deaf-blind. That is, caregivers should caress and handle the infants. Deaf-blind children will recognize primary caregivers by the way they are handled and by the familiar smells of the caregivers, such as those of shampoos and perfumes.

The use of consistent touch cues, or tactile signals made in contact with the infant's body, is essential. Touch cues tell the infant what to expect; for example, a caress on the infant's foot signals that a sock will be put on, and a touch on the baby's lips indicates that it is mealtime (for additional examples, see Touch Cues for Infants and Toddlers).

Object cues—objects associated with a particular activity—are also important. Like touch cues, they tell the infant what to expect; for instance, putting on a bib indicates that the baby will be fed. Cues help infants understand that sounds, sights, smells, tastes, textures, and movements are related to familiar people, objects, and activities (for additional examples, see the discussions of touch cues and object cues in Module 8).

**Strategies.** You can do the following to foster the use of motherese:

- Help caregivers identify how they use motherese with their infants.
- Help caregivers develop and use consistent touch cues and object cues with infants during caregiving and play routines.
- Help caregivers identify and use other cues with infants during caregiving and play routines.

### Development of Caregiving Routines

Everyday activities are natural opportunities for developing early communication and helping children who are deaf-blind feel secure (Freeman, 1985). Interactive routines that support communication between caregivers and infants can be simple and effective, as shown in the following example of the steps in a bathtime routine with a toddler who is deaf-blind (see also Touch Cues for Infants and Toddlers and information on touch cues, Module 8).

## Touch Cues for Infants and Toddlers
**Sharon Bolton**

A set of touch cues can be developed to meet the needs of a specific child. The same cues should be used to represent the same activities for the child in every environment. If touching the child's lip is the touch cue for time to eat, this cue should be used whenever the child eats—at home, in school, or in the community. Only by receiving consistent cues will the child be able to attach meaning to them. The following are examples of touch cues:

- *Time to:* Tap the back of the child's wrist to let him or her know that something is going to happen.
- *Up:* Before you lift the child, gently lift under his or her upper arms.

- *Diaper change:* Gently brush down the child's thigh.
- *Go to the bathroom:* Tap the front of the child's hips.
- *Eat:* Tap the child's mouth.
- *Sleep:* Place your hand by the side of the child's face.
- *Sit down:* Press down gently on the child's shoulder.
- *Play:* Touch the child's hand and bring a toy to the child's hand or the child's hand to the toy.
- *Finished, or all done:* Help the child push his or her materials away. ■

**Beginning.** The caregiver lets the child feel the running water and then says, "Bathtime" and signs "bath" on the child's chest. She next says, "Clothes off" and tugs on the child's diaper. The child handles the sponge and gets undressed.

**Middle.** While the child is playing in the bath, the caregiver says, "Wash your foot" and touches the child's foot. She then rubs the child's foot with a sponge.

**End.** The caregiver says, "Time to get out" and signs "finished." She helps the child out of the bath, lets the child feel the towel, and says and signs, "rub, rub."

**Strategies.** Encourage the caregiver to identify daily caregiving routines that can be used to promote natural and consistent communication with the deaf-blind infant. Use the following steps to analyze these routines:

- Identify a specific routine.
- List steps in the routine (the beginning, middle, and end of the activity).
- Identify cues that occur during each step of the routine. Include natural cues (what the caregiver does and says and objects, smells, or sounds that accompany the steps), as well as touch and object cues (touching the infant, providing an object for the infant to touch) that may help the infant understand what is about to happen.
- Identify the caregiver's communication (speech, signs, gestures, objects, touching) in each step of the routine.
- Identify how to encourage the infant's participation and communication behaviors during each step of the routine.

## Development of Play Routines

Repetitive play routines teach infants how to take turns and build anticipation of a predictable climax. (For a discussion of the importance of repetition and consistency and the relationship of these factors to the development of communication skills, see the previous module.) Many infants who are deaf-blind enjoy the stimulation of physical games that involve movement. Some caregivers and infants enjoy rough-and-tumble physical games, while others prefer less active interactions, such as blowing on an infant's stomach and waiting for a signal that indicates "more" or swinging the infant in a blanket. Games without objects, such as peekaboo and "I'm coming to get you," provide infants with early opportunities for turn-taking, for understanding what comes next, and for using actions to develop an understanding of words. For information on the development of turn-taking with infants and toddlers, see How to Establish Turn-taking.

## THEORY into PRACTICE

# HOW TO ESTABLISH TURN-TAKING

Usually, caregivers establish turn-taking with infants and toddlers by imitating their actions or sounds or by supplying responses on their behalf if the children are too young to talk or respond as expected. Infants soon cue in to the imitations and may deliberately make sounds or movements to see how their caregivers will respond.

As more formal communication is established, language is used in the interactions, and caregivers model the expected responses, rather than imitating the children's actions or sounds. For example, a father may say, "Look at that! There is a red truck! Where is the red truck? Do you see a red truck?" The expected response would be for the child to look in the correct direction, point at the truck, or say, "Over there." For an infant who has not yet learned to respond this way, the father may point and say, "Yes, there is the red

truck, over there!" and thus direct the child's attention to the truck and give a model response to the question. Both vision and hearing are typically used in these interchanges, and with adequate exposure, infants and toddlers can learn to respond as expected—first, by looking in the correct direction when asked and later, by gesturing and commenting appropriately.

Infants and toddlers who are deaf-blind need interaction that establishes turn-taking for communication, too. Each time the child makes a movement or sound, respond in a way that is meaningful to the child, and treat it as an attempt to interact, as in the following example:

• Place the child in a situation where movement is likely to occur, such as on a waterbed.

• When the child moves, respond by gently rocking the child on the waterbed.

• Stop your movement and wait until the child begins to move again. Respond immediately, then stop and wait again.

• Work to establish a "game" pattern with the child, so he or she moves intentionally to bring about your response; respond immediately each time and then wait.

• To establish more formal communication turn-taking, direct the child's attention to a joint activity that is a frequently occurring routine, such as changing a diaper or eating. Use the communication forms that are most appropriate for the child, for example, touch cues, object cues, signs, or speech; comment on the activity to the child and wait for a response. If the child does not respond within a reasonable time, give a little "help" with it and move to the next part of the activity, just as in the example of the father supplying the expected response about the red truck. ■

Playing a game that involves an object and a person is developmentally more advanced than is playing a game just with another person. However, since some deaf-blind infants are more interested in objects than in people, their caregivers can use objects to develop interactive games (for example, using a container to take turns putting objects in or taking objects out).

**Strategies.** Playful routines support the development of communication. You can help the caregiver create simple, mutually enjoyable interactive games with the infant by doing the following:

- Identifying actions or activities that elicit smiles and laughs (blowing on the baby's stomach; tickling; playing peekaboo; making exaggerated facial expressions, intonations, or funny noises; swinging; or bouncing).

- Helping the caregiver develop his or her own games by using the activities that the infant enjoys. It is important that these games are fun for the caregiver, too.

- Encouraging the caregiver to select a specific time for playing these games at least once a day.

- Helping the caregiver who feels inhibited or silly while playing games feel more comfortable doing so. Emphasize the importance of the game for the child's concept development.

## Consistent Use of Cues

Infants who are deaf-blind may understand the meaning of signs more easily if the signs are produced in flexible ways. Adaptations may include signing on the infant's body, helping the infant to make the sign, or placing the infant's hands on those of the signer (which is the receptive form used in true interactive tactile signing). Making the sign close to the object may engage the attention of an infant who is visually impaired and has residual vision.

**Strategies.** Infants who are deaf-blind are more likely to produce signs if they are introduced to signs, just as children who hear will produce spoken words they have heard (Chen, Friedman, & Calvello, 1990). Signs are most readily learned when they are

- *useful*; that is, there are frequent opportunities for their use (eat, up, down)

- *motivating*; that is, they relate to the child's interests or preferences (for food, activities, and people)

- *easy to make*; that is, they are symmetrical (more, bath) or touch part of the body (bath, mama)
- *easy to understand*; that is, they are iconic or look like what they represent (a drink, a comb).

## OTHER SETTINGS

Service providers need to help family members develop communication strategies that can be used in a variety of settings. Many infants and toddlers who are deaf-blind participate in activities in day care centers, special nurseries, and community playgroups, as well as during visits to the homes of relatives, friends, and neighbors. Thus, it is important to discuss the specific communication needs of these infants and toddlers with the people who staff such settings or whom the infants visit. For example, all caregivers need to know how to handle and supervise the use of special equipment, such as hearing aids, contact lenses, or prosthetic eyes. (See Appendix B.)

However, to promote the development of communication in deaf-blind infants and young children who interact in many different settings, primary caregivers, service providers, and secondary caregivers, such as the staff of day care settings, need to maintain open dialogues. Everyone involved with the infants and toddlers should strive to create similar responsive environments that include the use of predictable routines, consistent tactile cues, and simple language.

### Strategies

To help create responsive environments that will foster the development of communication, parents and other caregivers should be encouraged to do the following:

- Develop a list that explains how the infant initiates interaction and signals requests for his or her primary wants, significant people, familiar objects, favorite activities, and feelings and explain how the infant communicates at home.
- Develop a list of the caregiver's signals, cues, and signs for routine activities, familiar objects, people, and other frequently communicated concepts.
- Prepare the infant to go to a new setting. Use an object cue related to the destination (such as a particular toy to represent day care), and select and use a specific sign for each setting.

In assisting staff members in an early childhood setting to communicate with the infant who is deaf-blind, discuss the following strategies:

- To help the infant recognize and associate significant people with certain settings, develop name signs, signs used to identify particular individuals, and cues and use them consistently (for more information, see Name Signs: A Sense of Oneself in Module 9).

- To help the infant know that someone is nearby, use physical contact to greet the infant in ways that he or she can perceive.

- Develop predictable caregiving and play routines. (Encourage the staff members to watch for such behaviors as smiling and body movements that signal that the infant enjoys the routines.)

- Provide opportunities for choices of toys, foods, people, and activities.

- Match the infant's level of communication by imitating the infant's actions and adding a little more information.

- Use gestures. Before the infant is picked up, for example, the adult should say or sign "up" or gently pull the infant's arms above his or her head. The person should wait for the infant to lean forward, raise his or her arms, or somehow show anticipation to be picked up. A prompt for the infant should be provided if necessary.

- Use simple words, actions, and gestures to describe the infant's interest and focus of attention. (Demonstrate the signs used for key words. Encourage staff members to keep a list of the most frequently used words: names of significant people; favorite foods, toys, and activities; clothing; household objects; and everyday activities.)

- Encourage family members and other caregivers to help the infant develop a "picture" of the early childhood setting by helping the infant to recognize familiar people and familiar places.

# RESPONSIVE PRESCHOOL ENVIRONMENTS

At age 3, children with disabilities usually attend preschool programs, where they learn how to play together; follow simple rules;

develop friendships; and expand their language, social, and self-help skills. The primary goal of these programs is to promote developmental skills, especially through social interaction among children.

High-quality preschool programs usually include structured and unstructured activities; creative, cooperative, and imaginative play; self-help tasks, such as cleaning up; cooking; art; and opportunities for problem solving and developing language skills. These are important learning experiences for all children.

Children who are deaf-blind may attend a variety of preschool programs in the community: programs for typically developing preschoolers, such as Head Start or private preschools; programs for preschoolers who are visually impaired; programs for preschoolers who are deaf; or programs for children with a variety of disabilities. Whatever the setting, many preschoolers who are deaf-blind need specific encouragement to interact with other children and to support their participation in the preschool routine. This section presents strategies to achieve both goals.

## STRATEGIES

The unique communication and learning needs of deaf-blind children can be met in preschool settings by preparing the program staff, involving the parents, and encouraging social interactions among the children. The communication strategies discussed in the previous section also apply to preschool programs. The strategies to be selected will depend on the preschooler's degree of vision and hearing impairment, severity of other disabilities, and cognitive delays. However, the following general practices will support the participation of a child who is deaf-blind in a preschool routine.

### Selecting a Program

- Identify the philosophies of specific preschool programs, such as a focus on child-directed, play-oriented, or cognitively based activities, and choose the program that matches the child's interests and special needs. Some preschoolers who are deaf-blind do well in developmentally based, cognitively oriented programs, whereas others need the structure, systematic reinforcement, and functional curriculum of behavioral programs.

- Identify what the particular preschool program expects of children, for example, following directions, listening to a story, having a quiet time, playing outside, or washing their hands. In integrated settings, it is especially important to conduct an ecological inventory, that is, to list the activities of nondisabled children and the program's expectations in that context. This information will give you the basis for developing a functional and chronologically age-appropriate individualized instructional program for the preschooler who is deaf-blind.

- Identify the supports that the deaf-blind preschooler requires to participate in the selected preschool setting, such as help with personal needs and tasks, the adaptation of activities or materials, or more time to complete tasks. The child may need alternative communication methods, sighted guide assistance or other mobility techniques, or opportunities to touch and handle objects that are described during group activities.

- Evaluate the preschool environment from the child's perspective. For example, will the setting allow the preschooler who is totally blind and hard-of-hearing to develop and use his or her listening skills? Or is the room noisy and are the sounds confusing? For the child who is visually impaired and deaf, is there sufficient lighting for his or her visual needs?

- Identify the specific strengths and interests of the preschooler who is deaf-blind, for instance, enjoying active play, following routines, and signing, and use them to develop activities that encourage social interaction and promote other skills.

- Identify the particular supports that the preschooler who is deaf-blind will need to participate in the preschool routine, including a paraprofessional who will facilitate active involvement with other children and activities, an orientation and mobility (O&M) instructor, or a speech and language specialist.

- Provide the preschool staff with the consultation and training they need to support the preschooler's successful participation in the program.

## Planning the Program

- Organize the physical environment to encourage the child's movement, exploration, and involvement in activities.

- Develop daily routines, for example, outside play, morning circle songs, snack time, inside activities, and bathroom time. Also develop clear transitions between activities to provide a familiar structure for the preschooler and natural opportunities for communication.

- Orient the deaf-blind preschooler to the physical environment initially and whenever changes are made.

- Develop name signs for significant adults and children in the program (see Name Signs: A Sense of Oneself in Module 9). Some preschoolers who are deaf-blind recognize people by their personal characteristics, so you can incorporate these obvious traits (such as long hair, eyeglasses, or a particular wristwatch) into individuals' name signs for easy recognition.

- Use an object or tactile schedule of daily activities (see Tips for Using Calendar Boxes in Module 8) and, if appropriate, review it with the class during morning circle time.

- Identify and provide activities and toys that encourage children to interact with each other; for instance, playing with cars and blocks promotes more social interaction than does playing with puzzles or painting. Encourage opportunities for social interaction in small-group play involving the deaf-blind preschooler and one or two other children.

- Teach children how to interact with each other. For example, show sighted preschoolers how to use modified or tactile signs with a deaf-blind child, and show the preschooler who is deaf-blind how to touch the next child who is to take a turn in a game.

- Develop small-group activities according to the deaf-blind preschooler's interests and strengths. One such activity could be following the leader through an obstacle course.

- Have an adult provide nonintrusive help to facilitate the deaf-blind preschooler's participation in activities and interaction with other children, for example, by remaining near the child to model behavior for nondisabled classmates, prompting the preschooler who is deaf-blind to respond, and communicating what is happening.

- Because preschoolers who are deaf-blind may often need more time to complete tasks than do sighted children, identi-

fy when the child needs more time to complete a task independently and whether completing part of the task is sufficient for him or her to keep up with the other children.

- Develop a "buddy" system with sighted classmates, so they can learn sighted guide techniques through imitating adults to assist the child who is severely visually impaired with O&M.

- Adapt activities so the preschooler who is deaf-blind can understand them. For example, during story time, include objects that illustrate the story for the children to handle, and use sign language in telling the story.

- Model interaction and communication strategies for other preschoolers and adults. Teach the staff and children how to communicate appropriately with the preschooler who is deaf-blind through sign language, object or tactile cues, gestures, or pictures.

- Provide simple answers to the other children's questions about the preschooler who is deaf-blind. Preschoolers are naturally curious. They will ask, "Why doesn't Mary talk?" "Why do her eyes look funny?" Matter-of-fact explanations and simple discussions of individual differences will promote an accepting attitude.

▲ *Effective preschool programs organize the environment to meet children's needs for exploration and involvement.*

- Establish clear expectations for behavior and participation in activities, such as going down the slide (not sitting at the top), taking turns, and sharing toys. Like the majority of preschoolers, those who are deaf-blind require consistent and reasonable limits for acceptable behavior.

- Give positive feedback. Praise not only reinforces a child's behavior, but promotes self-esteem and a nurturing atmosphere.

- Provide opportunities for making choices (for example, between two inside activities, two fruits at snacktime, or two colors for painting) to enable the children to express their preferences, expand their communication skills, and develop a sense of control.

- Provide opportunities for solving problems in play with children, so the preschoolers can learn how to share, get along with each other, and take turns.

Responsive preschool environments have nurturing adults who provide instruction and materials that encourage children to explore and interact with each other. These essential characteristics offer children who are deaf-blind opportunities to develop skills while having fun and making friends.

## PRACTICAL TIPS ON PLAY

Deaf-blind children love to play as much as anyone; however, many toys and activities may be intimidating and confusing to a child with vision and hearing impairments. The discussion that follows offers some practical methods for approaching play that will make it enjoyable and rewarding.

### Use Hands-on Demonstrations

- Introduce the material to the child by allowing the child to touch it, feel it, smell it, and taste it. If the child is apprehensive about touching the material, bring the material to the child's hand.

- Demonstrate the activity for the child by placing your hands under the child's hands and having the child "ride" your hands while you demonstrate the activity; do as much as possible under the child's hands.

- When you introduce a new toy, show the child how to operate the toy and then allow him or her to do so alone.

## Teach Confirmation

- Because a child who is deaf-blind often cannot confirm either visually or auditorally if he or she has completed a task, show the child how to confirm the task tactilely. For example, when children place pegs in peg boards, have them try to push the pegs over sideways. If they cannot do so, it is confirmation that the pegs are in the holes.

- Teach confirmation in as many situations as possible. It helps the child retain information and gain a sense of accomplishment. Be prepared, however, to spend additional time doing so in each play activity.

## Select the Best Materials

- When you teach a new skill, choose the best example of materials that you can find. It is better to teach the skill with one good example than with many poor examples.

- Use real objects, when possible, because they provide more cues for the child to use in identification.

- If you want the child to classify materials, use a variety of fruits and clothes. The child will learn to identify them by color, smell, texture, and taste. The greater the variety of cues, the greater the child's ability to identify and confirm what the objects are.

## Integrate New and Familiar Materials

- Integrate a favorite toy when introducing new materials because it gives the child a sense of safety when confronting something unknown.

- If the child likes vibration, place a vibrator on a toy, so the child feels the vibration while playing with the new item.

- If the child has a favorite rattle or pacifier, place it on or in the new material that you want the child to explore.

## Choose a Defined Play Space

- When playing with a deaf-blind child, do so within a defined area, such as on a blanket.

- To define the space further, use a tray. Small work trays from the American Printing House for the Blind (see Resources) and small television trays made for children work well because they enable the child to search for lost toys and they provide closer access, so the child is more likely to play with the toys.

## Teach a Search Pattern

It is important to teach a child who is deaf-blind a search pattern to locate toys. The easiest method for most children to learn is the circular method, as follows:

- Have the child start with both hands together and search straight out from his or her body and then out to the sides and back in toward his or her body in a circular motion.

- Then have the child place his or her hands on your hands; with your hand, show the child how to use the circular search pattern to locate materials.

- It is best to start with large objects and then graduate to smaller objects. A large peg board with one peg placed in it can be used to teach the child a search pattern because the peg will not move when the child locates it.

## Determine When the Child Is Finished

Many children who are deaf-blind will pick up toys, hold them briefly, and then drop them. This is not a signal of rejection, but a form of exploration. To determine if a child is finished playing with a toy, give it back to the child and observe his or her reaction. If the child clenches his or her fists or pulls away, the child is finished with the toy. If the child starts to cry during play, stop the play session, comfort the child, and then give the child a toy that you know he or she enjoys.

## Choose Easy-to-Manipulate Toys

A child's success in learning to play with a toy and continuing to play with it independently fosters the child's sense of competence. Select toys that are easy to manipulate because it is easier to learn to play with them.

## Gain the Child's Visual Attention

To direct a child's visual attention to a toy, shine a light on the toy or place the toy on a light box or table that provides high visual contrast. Many children who have light perception also have shape perception and can learn to use small amounts of vision.

## Establish Routines

Present play activities in consistent routines. When activities are presented in a consistent order, the child knows what to expect, prepares for the coming activities, and may participate in the activities because he or she knows which activity is coming next and what he or she is expected to do.

Using the strategies presented in this module can do much to encourage the development of communication and positive social interaction for young deaf-blind children. The modules that follow elaborate on ways to encourage this development and also explore such issues as the wide variety of ways in which deaf-blind students communicate.

# REFERENCES

Chen, D., Friedman, C. T., & Calvello, G. (1990). *Learning together*. Louisville, KY: American Printing House for the Blind.

Chess, S., & Fernandez, P. (1976). Temperament and the rubella child. In Z. S. Jastrzembska, (Ed.), *The effects of blindness and other impairments on early development*. New York: American Foundation for the Blind.

Cooper, R. P., & Aslin, R. N. (1990) Preference for infant-directed speech in the first month after birth. *Child Development, 61*, 1584–1595.

Freeman, P. (1985). *The deaf/blind baby: A programme of care*. London: William Heinemann Medical Books.

Goldberg, S. (1977). Social competence in infancy: A model of parent-infant interaction. *Merrill-Palmer Quarterly, 23*, 163–177.

Greenspan, S., & Greenspan, N. T. (1985). *First feelings: Milestones in the emotional development of your baby and child*. New York: Viking Press.

Thomas, A., Chess, S., & Birch, H. G. (1970). The origin of personality. *Scientific American, 223*, 102–109.

**FIGURE 7-1:**
**Infant Profile**

Name _____

Date of Birth _____

Service Provider _____

Date _____

## BONDING

Who are the infant's favorite people? _____

_____

Why does the infant like them? _____

_____

How does the infant react to unfamiliar people? _____

_____

How does the infant establish contact with the caregivers? _____

_____

How do the caregivers establish contact with the infant? _____

_____

## STIMULATION

When does the infant seem calm and relaxed? _____

_____

When does the infant seem attentive? _____

_____

What seems to engage the infant's interest? _____

_____

When does the infant seem overstimulated or stressed? _____

_____

What signals of overstimulation does the infant give? _____

_____

*(continued)*

*FIGURE 7-1:*
**Continued**

## TOUCH

Does the infant seem to enjoy being stroked? _____

_____

Is there a change in the level of the infant's alertness, muscle tone, or facial expression when he or she is being touched? _____

_____

When is the infant attentive, fussy, or indifferent? _____

_____

## MOVEMENT

Does the infant become tense or relaxed while being moved? _____

_____

Does the infant snuggle or fall asleep during rocking? _____

_____

Does the infant prefer lively or gentle movements? _____

_____

## POSITIONS

In which positions is the infant attentive, fussy, or indifferent? _____

_____

Which positions does the infant seem to prefer? _____

_____

## VISION

If the infant wears corrective lenses, is there a difference in visual reactions when he or she wears them? _____

_____

What catches the infant's visual attention? _____

_____

Does the infant prefer to look at moving or stationary objects? _____

_____

When is the infant attentive, fussy, or indifferent? _____

_____

*(continued)*

**FIGURE 7-1:**
**Continued**

## HEARING

What attracts the infant's auditory attention? _____

_____

What are the signals the infant gives that he or she has heard a sound? _____

_____

Does the infant prefer a low-pitched or a high-pitched sound? _____

_____

When is the infant attentive, fussy, or indifferent? _____

_____

## TEMPERAMENT

Comment on the following:

Activity level, or amount of motor activity _____

_____

Rhythmicity, or regularity of physical needs _____

_____

Distractibility from ongoing activity _____

_____

Approach or withdrawal response _____

_____

Adaptability to changes in the routine or environment _____

_____

Attention span and persistence in an activity _____

_____

Intensity of reaction _____

_____

Threshold of responsiveness to stimulation _____

_____

Quality of mood or general disposition _____

_____

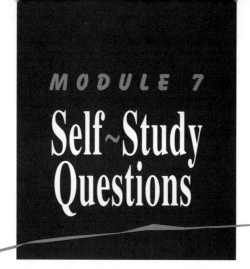

# MODULE 7
# Self~Study Questions

1.  Why are attachment behaviors important in infancy?
    a.  They help caregivers to provide a stimulating environment.
    b.  They attract attention and affection from caregivers.
    c.  They develop an infant's sense of self and recognition of caregivers.

2.  Is there a difference between the effects of a responsive and a stimulating environment on an infant's development?
    a.  A responsive environment has the same impact as does a stimulating environment on an infant's development.
    b.  A stimulating environment is more important for an infant's development than is a responsive environment.
    c.  A responsive environment is more important for an infant's development than is a stimulating environment.

3.  How does the caregiver achieve a "goodness of fit" with the infant?
    a.  By adapting caregiving routines to the infant's temperamental style.
    b.  By providing object cues to help the infant anticipate what will happen next.
    c.  By developing a consistent caregiving schedule.

4.  If a baby who is deaf-blind fusses and pulls away from you during multisensory activity, what should you do?
    a.  Increase sensory stimulation because the infant is not being stimulated enough.
    b.  Maintain your level of sensory stimulation because the infant needs to get used to stimulation.
    c.  Decrease sensory stimulation because the infant is being overstimulated.

5.  How can caregivers provide consistent and natural communication environments for infants who are deaf-blind?
    a.  By learning sign language and by prompting infants to make signs for their needs and wants.
    b.  By using tactile and object cues during caregiving routines.
    c.  By responding contingently to the infants' behaviors and developing turn-taking routines.

6. What is the purpose of motherese in caregiver-infant interactions?
   a. To encourage an infant's vocalizations and development of speech.
   b. To attract and engage an infant's attention.
   c. To provide appropriate language input.

7. Why are play routines helpful in caregiver-infant interactions?
   a. Because they are enjoyed by both the caregiver and the infant.
   b. Because they provide critical sensory stimulation for the infant who is deaf-blind.
   c. Because they provide opportunities for turn-taking, for understanding what comes next, and for developing an understanding of words.

8. Why is it important for staff members of programs to use name cues or signals when working with infants who are deaf-blind?
   a. So infants will learn significant people's names.
   b. So infants will recognize significant people.
   c. So infants will pay attention to significant people.

9. Why is it important to know the philosophy of a preschool program?
   a. To decide whether the program will be appropriate for a particular child's learning needs.
   b. To decide whether the program is well developed and organized.
   c. To determine whether the program may be restructured to meet the needs of a child who is deaf-blind.

10. Why should the individual interests and strengths of a preschooler who is deaf-blind be considered in planning a preschool program?
    a. To identify particular activities that will allow the child to succeed.
    b. To identify areas that do not require intervention.
    c. To have something positive to report to parents.

11. Why should an ecological inventory of a regular preschool program be conducted?
    a. To find out what the children are really learning.
    b. To find out what assistance or adaptations the preschooler who is deaf-blind will need in that setting.
    c. To find out whether the preschool will accept a child who is deaf-blind.

*Answers to self-study questions for this module appear at the end of Unit 2.*

# Communication Systems, Devices, and Modes

CHARITY ROWLAND

PHILIP D. SCHWEIGERT

JEANNE GLIDDEN PRICKETT

- *Use a total communication approach*

- *Develop communication systems based on students' specific needs*

- *Be consistent in the use of touch and object cues*

- *Provide students who use aided devices with alternate ways of getting attention*

- *Consider how sensory, motor, and cognitive abilities affect communication choices*

$C$ommon forms of communication—speaking, listening, reading, and writing—are used by some people who are deaf-blind. In addition, many alternate modes, devices, and systems are commonly used by deaf-blind individuals. A wide variety of adaptations for communication exist that can be made for an individual who is deaf-blind. Each mode, system, or device that is described in this module has distinct features, and its use or selection is based entirely on the individual's communication needs. The overall features of the communication modes, systems, and devices that are often used by deaf-blind people will be described in this module, along with the considerations involved in their selection.

# MULTIMODAL COMMUNICATION

The modes and devices described here may be used alone or in combination, but it should be pointed out that since deaf-blind individuals rarely use a single mode or device for communication, they are likely to be used in combination. Furthermore, these variations in communication may be used for a lifetime or may change, depending on the person's needs over his or her life. Figure 8-1 delineates the range of communication components that are available to a person who is deaf-blind.

Note that no single mode is more important than the others and that all the modes center on the individual's needs. A total communication approach supports the development of the available modes that a person may use for receptive or expressive communication, or for both. As a teacher, you may use sign language, speech, pictures, *and* tangible symbols, depending on the purpose of your communication and the concepts that the student currently knows. Often, deaf-blind individuals communicate most effectively with one mode for expressive communication and a different mode for receptive communication. (For additional information on expressive and receptive communication, see Module 6.) Therefore, it is vital that your students have both expressive and receptive means of communicating.

As an educational team plans a communication development program for a deaf-blind student, it is critical for the team members to know all the available modes and devices that could be effective

**FIGURE 8-1:**

**The Range of Communication Components**

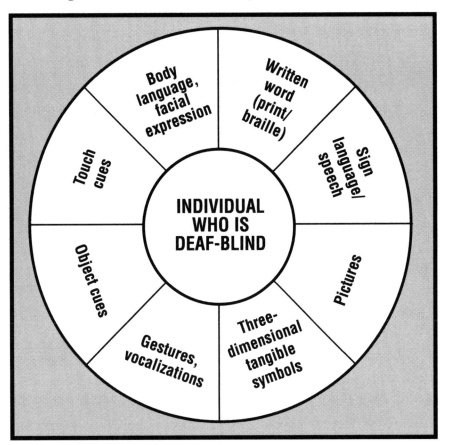

in meeting the student's communication needs. Also, it is important to know how these components can be designed into a comprehensive communication system for someone who is deaf-blind. The information in this module will give you a basis on which you can start your planning.

## AIDED AND UNAIDED COMMUNICATION

Communication can be categorized as *unaided* or *aided*. Unaided communication requires no props and nothing more than the communicator's abilities, and it includes

- vocalizations
- speech
- gestures
- sign language.

These forms are typically used for daily face-to-face communication. Unaided forms can be used expressively or receptively.

Aided forms of communication require something beyond one's own body, such as

- a paper and pencil to write in print or a slate and stylus to write in braille
- a sophisticated technological device that provides synthetic speech
- a set of pictures
- a collection of objects that are used as symbols.

This distinction is important because aided communication systems require extra efforts that unaided ones do not. Items for aided communication, for example, a computer or paper and pencil, must be available and maintained so they will work when needed. An aided device may include a "vocabulary" of words or concepts specifically for the user, and most devices allow for only a limited selection of concepts. Individuals who use aided communication devices or systems may therefore need alternate ways of getting others' attention if the aided devices are limited or not available. Joe's combination of communication strategies demonstrates how he used aided and unaided strategies to interact.

*Joe has an electronic voice-output device that allows him to gain attention and communicate about various items that are shown with pictures on the device. What happens when his mother forgets to recharge the battery overnight or when his younger brother runs over the device with his bike? First, Joe needs an unaided method of gaining attention, so he can indicate his needs. When he is in his motorized wheelchair, he can approach another person in his chair to gain attention. When he is out of the wheelchair and not mobile, he does not vocalize in any reliable fashion, but he has learned to bob his head up and down in a way that people seem to notice if they are in the same room with him. Joe is able to gain attention without his usual communication system, but he still needs a way to tell people exactly what he needs. For this purpose, he has a backup system of pictures, exactly like those that identify the words and concepts on his electronic device. When someone holds up a page of pictures, Joe is able to move his hand to touch the desired word or concept, just as he does on his high-tech system.*

# AUGMENTATIVE AND ALTERNATIVE COMMUNICATION

Some people who have significant obstacles for receptive and expressive communication, especially those with severe or multiple disabilities, need a means to offset the difficulties and support effective communication. The use of forms of aided communication will often accomplish this objective. Aiding communication with a device or designing an entire system with which a person can compensate and communicate is referred to as *augmentative* or *alternative communication* (AAC) (Beukelman & Mirenda, 1992). An AAC device (a specially designed item to enhance communication) or system (an individually developed communication approach that can incorporate several modes, techniques, and devices to enhance interaction) may use formal language (spoken or signed) or symbols that are different from what people typically use, such as pictures or objects, to convey concepts. A communication system typically reflects several important considerations:

- It can incorporate a variety of modes of communication, for example, both pictures and sign language, depending on the purposes of the communication.

- It is especially designed for one person, with a vocabulary that reflects the individual's needs and interests for communication with others.

- It may have a "display" on which the vocabulary is laid out, and the visual and physical features of the display will affect how the person can most effectively use the system to communicate (discussed later in this module).

- It may be high tech and use electronic devices.

- It may be low tech and use nonelectronic devices, such as a picture book combined with sign language and speech.

- Its design will allow the user to have ways to receive and deliver communications (receptive and expressive) that are appropriate for the person, for example, tangible symbols and signs for receptive communication and tangible symbols alone for expressive communication.

- Its design will give the user mechanisms for expressive communication that include appropriate input and output (for example, a microswitch that the user can touch to activate a synthesized voice signal to "help me").

**TABLE 8-1:**

**Major Considerations in Choosing an Alternative Communication System**

| CONSIDERATION | QUESTIONS ABOUT THE STUDENT AND THE PROPOSED SYSTEM |
|---|---|
| MOTOR DEMANDS | Does the student have the oral-motor or fine motor skills necessary to use this system? |
| ADAPTABILITY TO POSITIONS | Will the student be able to use this system in all positions (for those with significant motor disabilities)? |
| TACTILE FEATURES | Does the student primarily use touch to perceive items? Is this system tactilely discriminable? |
| INTENTIONALITY OF COMMUNICATION | Does the student communicate intentionally now? If not, then symbolic systems are not appropriate; look first at nonsymbolic systems. |
| SYMBOLIC DEMANDS | What kind of representation does this system use? Nonsymbolic or symbolic? If symbolic, is it concrete or abstract? Does the student understand this type of symbol, or can he or she easily be taught to do so? |
| MEMORY DEMANDS | Does this system require recognition or recall memory? Does the student need the low memory demands that an aided system offers? |
| PORTABILITY | Is the system easily portable, so the student can use it in any context? Can the student transport the system, or must someone else? |
| DURABILITY | Will the system withstand frequent use by the student? Can it be adapted to make it more durable? |
| MAINTENANCE DEMANDS | Does the system require frequent maintenance? Is someone available to provide this service, as needed? |
| COMPREHENSIVENESS | Does this system allow for all the student's current communication needs and those of the near future? Will the student be able to "say" what he or she needs and wants to say? |
| FLEXIBILITY | Can new vocabulary be easily added to the system? Is someone available to do so when necessary? |

*(continued)*

**TABLE 8-1:**
Continued

| CONSIDERATION | QUESTIONS ABOUT THE STUDENT AND THE PROPOSED SYSTEM |
|---|---|
| **DEMANDS ON PARTNERS** | Are potential communication partners likely to want to respond to the student's use of this system? Will they understand it? Can they be easily taught to understand it? Can strangers understand it? Will partners provide the necessary support for the student to use it (transport it, recharge it, and so on)? |
| **PERSONAL PREFERENCE** | Does the student want to use this system? If not, will the student want to do so once he or she learns how to use it? |

The next several sections describe the various types of standard and alternative communication techniques or augmentative devices and systems that you can use to enhance communication instruction. Modules 9 and 10 address language-based communication modes. In Module 12, you will learn more about how to use this information to select and design complete communication systems for your students.

Remember as you read this module that your students' needs and emerging skills must be assessed carefully when you choose and design communication options. A series of basic questions to explore is listed in Table 8-1. (More information on assessment can be found in Module 11.) Some students who are deaf-blind may have needs and a potential to expand their communication that goes beyond your current level of skills, and you may find that you need additional training so the students' skill development will not be defined by the level at which you are comfortable, but by the students' identified needs.

# SYSTEMS FOR RECEPTIVE COMMUNICATION

A number of alternative communication systems, modes, and devices exist that are useful for people who are deaf-blind and do not use speech or sign language. Some systems are used for either receptive or expressive communication. A number of factors need to be considered when designing and choosing a system for an individual student. This discussion covers factors related to the visual and motor skills of students, as well as environmental considerations and students' preferences.

## TACTILE CUES

As indicated in Module 6, many individuals with severe disabilities, including those who are deaf-blind, use different means to communicate expressively and receptively. In other words, a learner may need to receive information in a different mode than he or she uses to respond. For instance, if a student who is deaf-blind misses a significant amount of communication information through the auditory and visual modes, you may find it helpful to communicate with the student through touch.

Tactile sign language (signing with tactile contact) is one form of tactile communication, and it requires adequate tactile discrimination skills and the cognitive ability to associate an abstract signed linguistic symbol with a concept. The student, though, to communicate expressively, may sign in the air instead of into the communication partner's hands. (Language-based communication, including sign language, is discussed in the following module.) Many individuals who are deaf-blind need less abstract receptive-input cues that are strongly associated with specific contexts and that are presented through touch. Two types of tactile cues are described here: *touch cues* (specific signals that are executed on the student's body) and *object cues* (everyday objects that are presented to the student as cues and that may be touched on the body).

Anticipation—the expectation the child has of a specific response from the environment—is an important factor in communication. It is based on the child's learning over time that when "this" happens, "that" will follow (cause and effect, causal relationships). For example, when a child feels a spoon near her lips, she opens her mouth, expecting to be fed. Such anticipatory responses to meaningful cues show that she has some awareness of predictable relationships in her world. This awareness fosters further exploration for similar relationships, adds predictability to a child's world, and encourages the child to exert some control over the world through specific behavior, including communication. Tactile cues—touch cues, object cues, or some combination of the two—can be systematically and consistently provided to children who are deaf-blind to help them develop some anticipatory responses. In the following sections, some characteristics of touch and object cues are described, including what can be used and how they are used, and additional considerations for the development of cuing systems.

## TOUCH CUES

Touch cues help develop receptive communication skills and are used most often with individuals at early stages of the development of communication (preintentional and emerging intentional communication skills), described in Module 6. These tactile signals are made

- directly onto an individual's body
- specifically for an individual's receptive communication needs
- the same way each time by every person who uses them with that individual
- immediately preceding an action or activity
- to alert the individual that something will follow the cue
- to focus the individual's attention on the interaction or event that follows
- to help the individual begin to anticipate what will follow and begin to make associations of meaning between the cue and the event or action
- with the expectation of a response from the individual, perhaps not initially, but after repeated cuing over time.

A student's responses to consistent touch cues can give you information about his or her level of awareness regarding an interaction. As you use touch cues, you can carefully observe whether the student is beginning to respond as expected. At first, there may be no response. If the student appears to be responding to a cue consistently, you can infer some things about his or her ability to anticipate, memory from previous cuing, and cognitive processing. This information, in turn, may support the idea that the student is developing an anticipatory response—that the student can make and is making associations between the cue and the event that follows. When this occurs, you may see evidence that the student understands what has happened or is going to happen and is preparing for the forthcoming activity. You can observe whether he or she is trying to assist with the activity (by moving toward the appropriate area or lifting an arm to put a coat on, for example) once the cue has been given, which is also an indication of anticipation and the student's ability to associate a meaning with a cue.

## Purposes of Touch Cues

A few basic purposes are generally associated with touch cues. As you consider using touch cues with a student and begin to select cues to use, ask yourself, "What am I trying to convey to this child, and what, if any, response do I expect from the child?" For example, you may touch or tug at the child's waistband to indicate that you will change a diaper and expect the child to lift his hips slightly when you do so. You may offer a drink and cue the child by touching a cup to her lips, expecting her to turn her head away to refuse or open her mouth to accept. By using touch cues with children who are at early levels of receptive communication skills, you can provide

- information
- a directive
- feedback (either positive or negative).

Some examples of touch cues are included in Table 8-2. (Other examples can be found in Touch Cues for Infants and Toddlers in Module 7.) These examples may be appropriate for one student with whom you work, or several. You may wish to select different cues than the ones described here. Remember that the selection of cues is arbitrary, but that you should choose cues on the basis of some relationship to the event or action that follows, if possible. To provide feedback like "no" or "good!" a touch cue may be arbitrary, but for "eat," you can use the context of touch on the child's lips to support the associated meaning of opening the mouth to eat.

## Selection of Touch Cues

The exact form you select for the various touch cues you use with a student is not critical; you may make up your own. What is important is that

- the cues you select are different enough from one another that the child may easily discriminate among them
- the cues you select are associated with a coming activity or event as much as possible

**TABLE 8-2:**

**Examples of Practical Touch Cues and Possible Meanings**

| CUE | PURPOSE | | |
|---|---|---|---|
| | PROVIDE INFORMATION | PROVIDE DIRECTIVE | PROVIDE FEEDBACK |
| **TOUCH THE SHOULDER** | | Sit down | |
| **RUB THE BACK** | | | Good! |
| **TAP THE FOOT** | | Take your sock off | |
| **PRESS LIGHTLY ON THE FOREARM** | | | No, don't do that |
| **TOUCH THE CHEST LIGHTLY** | Time for a bath | | |
| **TUG THE DIAPER** | Time to change | | |

- the cues are used consistently—every time the appropriate conditions occur and in the same form each time and by all the people who interact with the child

- you present a specific cue and then wait to allow the child to process the cue and make an anticipatory response if the child can respond.

When you execute a cue that is *directive*, you expect the student to comply with a specific motor response, for example, sitting down if directed to sit. When using directives, it is important to make it clear that you expect a response. You therefore need to wait long enough for the student to respond and to show the student (through your posture or by maintaining physical contact with the student, for example) that you are waiting. If you are providing a cue for *negative feedback*, you also expect a specific motor response, such as the student's ceasing the unwanted behavior or correcting it, and you similarly have to convey this expectation of a response. With *positive feedback* cues, you may expect no particular response, or you may see an affective or emotional response, such as smiling or laughing.

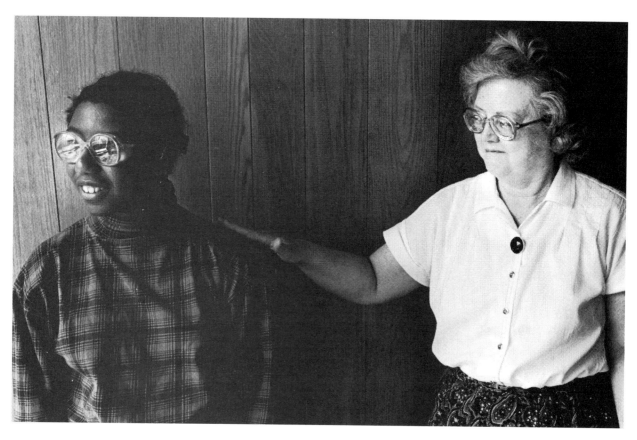

▲ *This teacher is using a touch cue to make her student aware of her presence.*

If no response is expected, you may move to the next step in the interaction more rapidly.

It is important to consider a student's motor abilities when you create touch cues. Often it is possible to incorporate a student's specific movement in the touch cue itself. For example, when you inform the student that you are about to do some leg exercises with him or her, you could move the student's leg as part of the touch cue (see Module 18 for a discussion of how touch cues are used for teaching orientation and mobility [O&M] skills). The anticipatory response you are shaping could be a repeat of that leg movement by the student. Be familiar with the student's repertoire of responses. When possible, incorporate a behavior already within the student's repertoire that the student could eventually use as a signal. For instance, if a child has some voluntary arm movement, the touch cue you might use before you pick the child up could be a gentle tap beneath the child's elbow. The child's anticipatory response to this might be moving or raising the arm, and the child may eventually initiate a request for "up" by raising his or her arm. Overall, the use of touch cues should reduce startling, help the student develop anticipatory responses, and provide the student with clearer information about your expectations.

## Shanon's Story

Shanon is 7 years old. In addition to vision and hearing impairments, she has severe cerebral palsy that greatly reduces her voluntary movements. As part of classroom instruction, the teacher and staff have implemented and posted a touch cue–object cue system.

**Touch cues for personal identification.** Some of the cues are used with several of Shanon's classmates as well. With three full-time staff members and several support personnel routinely in the classroom, it is important that all the potential communication partners have unique personal cues to identify themselves to the children. Shanon has a few favorite people, as was evident from her immediate and consistent smile each time one woman identified herself to Shanon by helping Shanon to touch her long hair.

**Touch cues for activities.** Part of Shanon's physical therapy involved assisting her to stretch her legs and arms. The staff called this activity fluffing, and Shanon particularly enjoyed it and considered it a game. The touch cue to announce the beginning of each game involved a brief light bounce of either her arms or legs. The generally expected response was a smile because Shanon liked this game. If Shanon frowned or gave a negative vocalization, the partner might wait or proceed more gently, thinking that Shanon might be a bit stiff or uncomfortable that day. Over time the staff members began to notice that in addition to smiling, Shanon would attempt to repeat the arm or leg movement when she was cued. Her responses appeared to be getting more specific. Now the anticipatory response that the partner expected was expanded to include one of these movements. Soon Shanon began to take much more control in this game. She came to expect that when she raised her arm, she would play the arm-fluffing game, and when she raised her leg, that she would play the leg-fluffing game. Eventually, a choice was offered through these touch cues. With a movement that was part of her limited response repertoire incorporated into the game, Shanon could develop clear expressive signals and was able to take control of the interaction.

Cuing procedures should be implemented in functional contexts throughout the student's day, as in the case of Shanon's therapy cues. By embedding them within the routines of daily activities, you are ensuring that the student will generalize his or her expectations to a variety of people and settings. You are also allowing the student to take advantage of other contextual cues that will assist him or her to develop anticipatory responses quickly.

Cuing procedures should be implemented consistently. Use the following steps to maximize the student's opportunities for interaction and for the development of anticipatory responses:

- Post a list of the specifics of the cuing strategy.
- Model the cues for all potential communication partners.
- Monitor the delivery of the cues.
- Identify and monitor the specific nature of the expected responses from the student.
- Collect data on these responses. The data can provide valuable feedback about the appropriateness of specific cues and foster the development of anticipatory responses and signals. This information will contribute to your efforts to empower the student with more readable and detectable signals with which he or she can further control the environment. (For more information on collecting data and other aspects of monitoring or assessing a student's responses, see Modules 11 and 12.)

Touch cues can be used in combination with other cues, such as objects, speech, and signs. Using speech or signs or both makes the interaction much more natural for both parties who are communicating.

## OBJECT CUES

Object cues are everyday objects from daily activities that are presented to the student as cues for these activities. As with touch cues, the three major functions of object cues are to provide information, direction, and positive or negative feedback. Also, the expected responses are likely to be anticipatory. The aim of the cuing procedures is to give the student enough concrete information to develop some expectation about events that will happen immediately. In so doing, you are allowing the student to ready himself or herself; form some accurate notion of what is to occur; and, through consistency and time, develop a means of responding to you. You are also helping the student to develop an expectation based on your consistency and predictability that will allow the student to realize and look for predictable relationships in his or her world of social interaction.

### Types of Object Cues

The selection of objects to use as cues should move from the concrete to the abstract. That is, objects initially chosen should be those that a child is most likely to associate with the activity—for example, a towel for a bath or a diaper for changing—or that are unique to that activity (or type of activity) and not used in numerous different activities.

In the beginning, the object selected should be the actual object that will be used for the activity. As the student begins to demonstrate anticipatory responses that would indicate some connection between the object and the activity or event it is related to (for example, independently traveling to the area that corresponds to the object), you may decide to use a different object that is also commonly associated with that activity or event (thus showing the student that more than one object may represent a particular activity). Or you may replace the object actually used in the activity, such as a particular ball for playing a game, with one identical to it but not used in the activity (thereby introducing the idea that the object represents, stands for, or symbolizes the activity).

**Partial or Associated Object Cues.** Partial representations of the object may be used in place of the whole object as the student continues to demonstrate an understanding of the relationship between object cues and the event. The student is now able to associate correctly a more abstract representation with the activity for which it stands. Partial object cues are generally smaller and more portable than the whole object and thus more versatile to use. For example, having used a cane to cue a child that it is time for a walk, you may eventually find that it is possible to use part of the cane, such as the handle or strap, to inform the child of the same thing. Or in the case of riding a tricycle, you may use a handle grip, rather than the entire tricycle. Associated objects are another type of object cue that are related to the activity but in a less direct or clear way. For example, lunchtime in the cafeteria could be represented by a spoon, which is an integral part of the activity, or a lunch ticket, which is needed to enter the cafeteria.

**Arbitrary Object Cues.** When no object is logically related to a specific activity, you may need to devise a symbol to represent that activity and to create the relationship between the activity and the artificial object cue. For example, if a student routinely goes to the school office, you may decide to fix a block to the office door, so when you hand the student a block as a cue, the relationship may be reinforced when the student feels a similar block on the door.

As with touch cues, object cues are more meaningful if the communication partners implement them consistently, expect a response, and have a clear notion of what the response should be. Once again, attention to the student's repertoire of responses is necessary. When possible, the selection of object cues should be guided by an awareness of the objects that are relevant to the student. Object cues are often used in combination with touch cues and with speech or signs or both.

## Use of Object Cues in Calendar Boxes

Object cues are often used in conjunction with calendar boxes (also known as "anticipation shelves" or sequential displays) during transitions between activities. When the student begins to anticipate specific events as he or she is given or shown certain objects, these objects may be placed in a central location not associated with a particular activity. The student may begin to associate the object with what it represents even though the object is out of its original physical context. At some point more than one object may be displayed in this area at the same time. Multiple items that are displayed on a shelf that is partitioned into individual sections or a calendar box will help the student distinguish one object from another. The sequential display of objects that symbolize various daily activities in the order of their occurrence to represent a schedule, or "calendar," may even enable the student to anticipate a coming preferred activity (see Tips for Using Calendar Boxes).

With multiple object cues, the student should be allowed, at least occasionally, to choose an activity that he or she would like to do next by selecting the corresponding object. The expressive use of the object will be encouraged if every time the student selects the object, he or she is required to show it to the communication partner. This requirement helps to establish the power of objects or symbols for communicating and exerts control over another person in the environment. Nicky's story illustrates how object cues helped one student become more interactive and independent.

*Nicky, age 5, has a severe bilateral hearing loss and is totally blind. A new classroom placement, with new classmates and teachers, left Nicky uncertain and therefore timid about exploring his new social and physical surroundings. The classroom is arranged so he can trail [see Module 17] walls to most activity areas within the room. Nicky's desk is located several steps from the wall. This desk area is a central area for the students in this room, so it was decided that the wall directly behind it would be the location for Nicky's object cues. It could also serve as a landmark for him.*

▲ *Object and picture cues like these placed in a series of containers create a calendar box that helps students form a mental sequence of events.*

*In most instances, objects identical to ones Nicky used in certain activities were selected as object cues. In one case, the staff had to make an artificial association when there was no obvious object to use. Since fabric covered the back of Nicky's chair in that area, another piece of the same fabric became the object cue for the activity.*

*Because of Nicky's unfamiliarity with this environment, the classroom staff thought they could not immediately expect Nicky to move independently to the corresponding area when he was given an object cue. However, they thought it appropriate to expect some affective response to the object cue as an indication of anticipation and recognition. These responses were monitored and regularly compared to what the staff already knew of Nicky's preferences for certain activities. The staff was also instructed to allow Nicky adequate time to indicate his recognition in other ways that were also noted on the procedures page posted on the wall by the display. Through the consistent delivery and monitoring of responses, the classroom staff became aware of Nicky's acceptance of the new environment and object-cue procedures. Eventually, Nicky began to travel independently to various areas throughout his classroom when given the object cues. His anxiety faded as he began to exert more control over his environment through exploration.*

In this way, objects or parts of objects become important to students, especially those for whom transitions or changes in routine are confusing and frustrating, as a way to gain predictable information and to anticipate coming events. In some instances, it may be useful to create a "wild card." If it is known that an unusual event is to occur on a particular day (for example, the taking of school pictures or a visit by an audiologist), you may insert the wild card into that time slot to give the student some advance notice that something different will occur at this time. This advance warning lessens surprise or frustration when the routine is changed.

## TIPS FOR USING CALENDAR BOXES

A calendar box may be made of various materials, such as wood, small plastic tubs secured together side by side, or shoe boxes attached to each other. Whatever the material used, the idea is to have a series of compartments arranged in a row. Specifically, the calendar box should have from three to eight compartments, each large enough to accommodate a representational object of each selected activity.

Calendar boxes are used to help students learn to anticipate activities and form a sequence of the day mentally. The following steps are involved:

● Make a list to match up activities with specific objects. *Always* use the same object to represent a given activity. Use objects that are small enough for the compart-

ments and that represent the activities or are actual parts of the activities, for example, a ball to represent gym.

● At the beginning of each day, place the objects left to right in the box's compartments and adhere to their sequence as the day progresses.

● Either place the box on or close to the student's desk or work area in a particular position or keep it by your desk and place and remove the objects as each of the day's activities occurs.

● At the start of the day, have the student feel each compartment and object left to right and give each an identifying sign (see Module 9). Go through *all* the compartments at the beginning.

● Then have the student remove the first object; perform the activity; and, when finished, put the object in a "finish box" separate from the entire calendar box. Help the student return to the calendar box, feel the empty compartment, and move to the next compartment to the right.

● If you run out of compartments for the activities you have planned for the day, fill the box twice: once for the morning's activities and once for the afternoon's activities.

● Try to avoid unanticipated activities, or, if you know that there will be an unusual event, place an object that represents the event in one of the compartments. ■

Tactile cues, such as the touch and object cues described here, can be a vital part of communication with and by students who are deaf-blind, especially those with additional severe disabilities. These modes of receptive communication can allow the students to develop necessary anticipatory responses and expectations that are critical to further growth in their communication.

# SYSTEMS FOR EXPRESSIVE COMMUNICATION

A variety of systems can be used for expressive communication, and they may be nonelectronic, or low tech, or electronic, or high tech, in nature.

## TANGIBLE SYMBOL SYSTEMS

Nonelectronic (or low-tech) modes of aided expressive communication involve symbolic communication though alternative types of symbol systems. Some of these symbols are tangible. They can represent people, objects, places, activities, and concepts and, unlike gestures, allow a person to refer to entities that are spatially or temporally distant. Symbols can be either abstract or concrete. With abstract symbols, such as spoken, printed, or brailled words and manual signs, there is usually no obvious relationship between the symbols and the physical properties (auditory, visual, tactile, and so on) of the referents. In contrast, concrete symbols are symbols that *do* bear an obvious physical relationship to their referents. Tangible symbols are a type of concrete symbol. They are either three dimensional (objects) or two dimensional (pictures that can be picked up and handed to another person), so they may be physically manipulated by the user. Three-dimensional tangible symbols are tactilely comprehensible (objects), so a person without sight may distinguish among them. Tangible symbols

- have a clear relationship with what they represent and thus make lesser demands on the user's cognitive abilities than do abstract symbols.

- are permanent and only have to be recognized out of a display of symbols; hence they make lesser demands on the user's memory and require a lower level of cognitive skills than do speech and signs. That is, it is not necessary to retrieve the concepts entirely from memory to express meaning.

- may be picked up and handed to someone as a clear indication of the individual's choice or intent or placed next to what they represent to reinforce the relationship between it and the symbols.

- may be selected or indicated through a motor response, such as picking up, touching, or pointing, which places lesser demands on fine motor skills.

## Types of Tangible Symbols

Three-dimensional tangible symbols may be whole objects (as when a cup is used to represent a drink), partial representations (as when the buckle from a roller skate strap is used to represent a roller skate), or artificially imposed symbols (as when a geometric wooden shape is permanently attached to the cafeteria door and the same shape is used as a "schedule" symbol for the cafeteria). As with object cues, use a symbol that already has meaning to the student, and adopt the student's perspective with the design of three-dimensional symbols. If the student who will be using a symbol is totally blind, consider what aspects of the symbol are tactilely meaningful. Although miniature items, such as doll accessories and charms, may seem like ideal items for tangible symbols, they may not be meaningful to blind students, who perceive them only through touch. The examples of Melissa and Bart illustrate what may be meaningful to students.

*Melissa's teacher did not understand why a tiny dollhouse chair was not a good symbol to give Melissa, who is totally blind, to represent her special chair at school. But what do you feel when you sit in a chair? You may pat the broad smooth surface of the seat with your hand before you sit down. Then you experience the familiar sensation of actually sitting. What do these tactile-kinesthetic experiences have in common with the small sharp protrusions that meet your fingers as they examine the miniature dollhouse chair? Would Melissa make a strong connection between the feel of the doll's chair and the sensations of sitting in her own special chair? A better approach would be to tape a distinctively textured piece of material onto the seat of the chair and to use a piece of the same material (perhaps glued to a piece of cardboard) for the "chair" symbol.*

   *Bart was learning to use a cane to enhance his mobility skills. His teacher wanted a tangible symbol for the cane, so Bart could indicate when he needed it. She thought an obvious solution was to use a cane tip as the symbol and was puzzled when Bart did not associate the symbol with the referent. On further reflection, she realized that Bart was unlikely to touch the tip end of his cane; he usually contacted the grip with his hands. When she substituted a rubber golf grip of the same type used on his cane for a symbol, Bart quickly came to understand its meaning.*

▲ *A computer accessory affixed to a door becomes a tangible symbol that tells students the location of the computer room.*

Two-dimensional symbols may be color photographs or black-and-white line drawings. Students who have satisfactory visual discrimination skills and the ability to associate a picture with an object will be able to use them.

## Use of Tangible Symbols

Tangible symbols are used for every aspect of daily life whenever more conventional symbols are used. That is, whenever you would expect a speaking person to use speech or a signing person to sign, you can expect the user of tangible symbols to indicate a symbol or series of symbols. Make certain that a user of tangible symbols has a reliable means of gaining attention and realizes that he or she must gain attention before using the symbols. If the response your student uses is to pick up the symbol and hand it to someone, then that response also gains that person's attention. Individuals who point to or touch, but do not pick up a symbol must have some other means (such as tugging or vocalizing) to gain their partner's attention.

   Who can use tangible symbols? To use tangible symbols effectively for expressive communication, an individual needs to

- be able to perform a specific intentional motor behavior, such as picking up a symbol, pointing, eye pointing, or touching, that can be used to indicate or select a symbol.

- be able to convey some intentional communication, realizing that she or he can control the behavior of another person through some means, generally symbolic gestures, such as pointing, extending objects, tugging, and hand guiding.

- be able to use abstract symbols to communicate. A person who can use a higher, more abstract level of communication with reasonable efficiency should not be asked to use a less advanced level of communication. Tangible symbols also can be used as a supportive system in the event that a more sophisticated system is used but temporarily not available.

## ELECTRONIC SYSTEMS

Some students who are deaf-blind may benefit from electronic systems that support communication. Generally, these tools are designed to enhance the input or output means of another communication system. Electronic devices can be added to aided systems, such as tangible symbols, to allow a communicator easier access to a system and to help communication partners receive the communications.

For some individuals, an electronic adaptation may consist of a system with a limited number (usually 1 to 4) of prerecorded short messages. The most common type, a significant one, is the "calling system," which provides the user with a way to get attention from another person who is not nearby. The communicator operates a microswitch for each message, and the various switches for the messages are distinguished by their positions, tactile covers, or perhaps some symbolic representation fixed to their surfaces. A message may consist of a tone, such as a beep, or be a voiced message, such as a voice recording or synthesized speech.

For an individual who communicates symbolically, a variety of technological options are available. These options may be incorporated with tangible systems, such as three-dimensional symbols, or, if appropriate, two-dimensional symbols, such as photographs or line drawings. Systems that use braille or print words may also have electronic technology. Speech and language specialists are good resources for gaining information about individualized electronic systems that students may use.

### Input and Output: Access to Systems

How does a person using an electronic, high-technology system gain access to the system and use it to interact? *Input* refers to how the communicator gains access to, or puts information into, the system that the system will convert into a form that communicates with someone else. Two methods are generally used for input:

- *direct select*—in which the communicator acts directly on the symbol/word, for example, by pointing to or touching it or typing the correct letters for a word
- *scanning*—in which the communicator follows a light or auditory message, for example, as the system scans all available choices. Through some action, such as activating a switch, the communicator stops the scan when it arrives at the desired message.

With direct-select method devices, communicators with limited motor responses may also use microswitches, joysticks, or other activation devices to identify the desired word or symbol directly. Thus, any purposeful movements a communicator has, such as subtle movement of the hand or arm to depress a switch, turning the head, or blinking an eye, can be used for direct selection.

Each system must also have a form for the communicator's input to be understood by the other partner, which is the *output*. Output can be

- visual, for example, through direct indication of a symbol, by illumination of a symbol with a liquid-crystal display, or by actual print or braille output
- auditory, for instance, through speech output with a whole word or spoken letters to form a word (speech output may be "synthesized," "digitized," or true voice reproduction).

When a communicator is using an auditory system, several factors can influence the system's intelligibility for the listener:

- the pitch (how high or low the sound is)
- the rate of speech
- the gender of the voice
- the age and awareness of the user and the communication partners.

## Identifying Potential Users of Electronic Systems

Who is an appropriate candidate for a technology-assisted communication system? Many individuals have limited ranges of response because of significant physical and sensory impairments. Thus, their options to develop the most basic communication skills may be greatly restricted because they lack detectable, readable signals with which to respond to their social environments. A communication partner of a student with such a disability may not notice feedback that would typically be used to engage in or maintain an interaction. As a result, he or she may not continue attempts to interact with the student. The student, in turn, may feel powerless to control or effect change in this social-communication environment. This sense of control, or "social contingency awareness," is the cornerstone of the further development of communication. Without a sense of control, such development may be impeded.

Students who are deaf-blind can be considered candidates for electronic input-output systems if they appear to have any movements that can be used for input, even infrequent or subtle movements such as occasional changes in the direction of their eye gazes or slight arm movements. Intentional communication skills can be developed using electronic input-output devices. Students who use these devices can also interact with more people in more settings. Electronic input-output devices can be especially useful for deaf-blind students who are symbolic communicators, no matter how restricted their movements may be.

What design factors must be considered? All members of the educational planning team need to consider carefully the student's sensory and motor abilities that will affect his or her input options. If a child uses touch as the primary learning sense, for example, an input system must allow for touch. Other sensory input, such as visual information only, will not be as effective. (See Augmentative Systems and Visual Adaptations and Other Factors in Choosing or Designing Systems later in this module.)

In addition, the appropriate output system supports the possibility that more people will clearly understand the message a student is trying to convey. For example, a three-dimensional system with partial or tactile representations (or both) of objects or events is likely to be understood only by people who are familiar with the system. When these symbols are combined with a voice-output system, signaling with a particular symbol or set of symbols can be translated into a voiced message. Depending on the communicator's residual hearing or vision and the quality of the output, the auditory or visual feedback could help him or her confirm the message he or she has sent. Adding technological adaptations can encourage people to communicate more with the user because interaction is clearer and more easily understood. Systems with auditory output allow a student to gain another's attention even if that person is not close by. They also support other signals that users may give and allow communication partners to listen for communication responses, rather than require constant visual alertness for visible signals. Such factors can be vital in integrated classroom settings, where a student whose communication is not readily understood can be overlooked without technological adaptations.

## Selecting an Electronic System or Device

How do you decide which communication system or device is most appropriate for a student? The team approach that involves the teacher, family, appropriate service providers, and the student is the most effective. Decision making should focus on the quality of the fit among the system, the user, and the social and physical environments to ensure that the student's needs for interaction and development of overall communication are met. Team members should examine

- the sensory, cognitive, and fine motor abilities of the student for whom the system is being considered
- all available information on the student's communication skills and style (see Modules 11 and 12 for additional information on assessment and the selection of communication modes, systems, and devices)
- the individual's motivation and receptiveness for using the system
- systems that may be used—the team's speech and language specialist will be familiar with these options
- how each option meets the current communication needs of the student and the environments in which he or she will interact, including the potential communication partner's abilities and skills (for example, if the student is a young child, can young children understand the output?)
- how well the system can be adapted to the student's future needs
- the costs, if any, of obtaining and maintaining or repairing the system and how the system will be purchased.

A communication system, including those involving a high-technology device, should enhance interactions for the user. It should not restrict interaction with people and the environment. It should be portable, so it can be used in many situations. It is likely that no single system will be satisfactory for all situations or forever. Instead, most individuals who are deaf-blind often use different modes or systems of communication for different purposes, as we all do when we interact with others.

In general, children, including deaf-blind students, can learn to use increasingly abstract symbols over time, when these symbols are paired with the symbols or forms of communication that they already use. Students can learn visual symbols, tactile symbols, signs, and spoken words, for example, if they are exposed to them often and consistently, assuming that their best sensory channels for interaction are being used. It is easier to learn what symbols mean when the interaction occurs in a natural setting and has a natural consequence, such as talking about going to the lunchroom and then going to eat. In the next sections, the visual, physical, and cognitive needs students may have and the adaptations that can be made to support effective communication and learning will be explored. Module 12 contains an in-depth discussion about selecting modes and systems of communication.

# AUGMENTATIVE SYSTEMS AND VISUAL ADAPTATIONS

Augmentative communication systems and devices that use tactile symbols, like objects, or visual symbols, such as pictures, may give many nonspeaking individuals ways to communicate for the first time. For people with disabilities that include visual impairment, the systems may need visual adaptations to be useful. Children who are deaf-blind and have residual vision should be encouraged to use vision for learning and communication.

Systems should be designed with visual adaptations that support good discrimination and the identification of symbols, which will encourage more fluent interaction. Educators and parents who design such systems need to identify students' communication needs while developing Individualized Education Programs (IEPs). However, they sometimes do not consider how visual design can interfere with communication.

For example, an augmentative communication system that uses a "spinner" for the selection of symbols and requires rotary ocular movement (movement of the eyes in a circular fashion, down, around to the side, and up) can be difficult to scan for a child who is deaf-blind and has cerebral palsy with eye-muscle problems. Thus, the communication objective of the system can be lost while the child is trying to perform eye movements that are inappropriate for his or her disability. In programs that emphasize integrating visual goals with other curricular areas, a visual goal may be to increase rotary ocular movement. In such cases, the dial-type system just mentioned can support two goals: communication and integrated vision training. However, if smooth communication is most important, a different device or system should be selected. This section will outline visual factors that influence the design of an effective system for a student who is deaf-blind.

Why make visual adaptations? Adequate visual discrimination depends on many variables, including the reasons for the individual's vision loss and the individual's visual acuity and efficiency in using residual vision. The way that visual information is presented also influences how well an individual can use the information. Visual adaptations affect how visual information is processed and must be considered in the design of an augmentative system or device. Important characteristics of visual information that need to be examined include

- color,
- contrast,
- size,
- distance and angle,
- complexity.

It is not difficult to adapt an augmentative communication system so the visual design supports the objectives of communication. Local experts in vision can help, and members of the IEP and Individualized Family Service Plan (IFSP) teams often know enough about an individual student's visual needs to make optimal adaptations. In designing an augmentative communication system, the technical features (both communication and visual details) need to be changed or expanded until the student responds best.

# BASIC ISSUES IN DESIGNING SYSTEMS

Designers of systems must consider visual layout issues. Depending on a deaf-blind child's functional vision, modifications may be needed in the size, placement, and details of the system's display. Important principles for designing augmentative systems and devices include the following:

- *Avoid visual clutter.* A system that uses many symbols in a single layout may be too cluttered visually for students with certain types of visual impairment and poor visual efficiency who discriminate better when only a few items at a time are displayed.

- *Create a smaller visual array or layout.* A smaller visual array may be necessary for a student with a limited visual field who can miss symbols placed outside that field.

- *Place displays according to a student's visual field.* Some students have visual field losses that are irregular, such as with hemianopsia, and tend to view items using only the side or other parts of their visual fields. These students may "view eccentrically," that is, shift their eyes slightly off center when looking at targets straight ahead (Berg, Jose, & Carter, 1983, p. 290), or change their head positions frequently to view all parts of objects, persons, or symbols. Visual displays for these students may need to be placed where side vision or other peripheral vision (above or below) can be used most effectively.

- *Consider the student's visual field.* Visual disabilities that limit ocular movement may necessitate the placement of visual arrays on only one side of the child. For some children with eye-muscle disabilities, symbols should be presented visually in only one plane, either horizontal or vertical, but not both, and displays that require systematic scanning may also require modification.

- *Accommodate a student's visual tracking abilities.* A system that uses a moving display, such as some computerized or eye-gaze systems, may move too fast for some students to achieve smooth visual tracking. Many students with reduced vision often need to fixate on symbols longer to perceive details before they can process information and begin to communicate. Children with eye-muscle problems may not scan displays as the design of the system requires but instead may use alternate scanning strategies.

- *Accommodate a student's lighting needs.* Some students with visual disabilities have unique lighting needs; they require either more light or less light. Light sensitivity can affect their use of a system, so system designers should adapt light requirements both in the environment and for the system itself. Because lighting and the placement of a visual display can increase glare from the display, which may reduce a student's ability to use a system or device effectively for communication, glare should be monitored.

- *Consider a student's visual prognosis and future needs.* A student whose vision is likely to decrease because of his or her visual disability may need a system that incorporates both visual and tactile symbols. The transition to a new form of communication input is better supported when both forms of sensory information are familiar.

Attention to the considerations just outlined is a significant issue. The successful communication of a deaf-blind student may depend as much on the visual factors of a system's design as on the specific objectives of communication.

## REAL OBJECTS: VISUAL AND TACTILE INFORMATION

Parents and educators use real objects naturally with infants and toddlers to develop concepts and communication skills. For older children who have both visual and communication disabilities, the use of real objects is still an important communication adaptation. For a child who is deaf-blind and has both a severe visual impairment and communication difficulties, designing augmentative communication systems with real objects may be the most practical solution. This can be considered an adaptation of information that would usually be in visual form.

Such children can learn to discriminate both tactile and visual features if they are encouraged to interact repeatedly with everyday objects. Children who are visually impaired especially benefit from the pairing of tactile information of real objects with visual symbols in a system's design. They can learn to interpret both kinds of sensory information and then have two sources of information for communication. This multisensory input supports their later use of the same objects and representations of them as augmentative symbols for communication. Deaf-blind individuals may have definite preferences for tactile, visual, or auditory features in objects while they manipulate or choose from groups of objects. Preferred features can be emphasized in the design of a system. Table 8-3 outlines visual issues and strategies for designing augmentative communication systems that use real objects as symbols.

## VISUAL SYMBOLS

Visual symbols that are used in augmentative communication systems include words or letters and picture-based symbols. This section discusses picture-based symbols, which are often used in such systems for children who are deaf-blind and have other severe disabilities. Each child's response to visual information for communication is affected by both cognitive factors and visual factors.

Photographs are most like real-world visual information, since they are directly produced from real-world images. They are easiest for some students to perceive and interpret because they replicate an actual environment, people, and objects in two-dimensional form. Paintings and drawings are slightly more abstract visually, since they represent the artists' views of the world, but some students use them best for augmentative communication.

Line drawings without color are the most abstract of the three types of picture-based symbols for information processing. Still, some students respond best to line drawings because the visual detail that may conflict with perception and interpretation, such as clutter from colors or background, is reduced.

Picture-based visual symbols can be paired with each other or with print symbols to provide a student with more information or with tactile information to have a second source of sensory input. Visual factors and strategies that must be considered in designing a system with picture-based symbols are described in Tables 8-4, 8-5, and 8-6. As students use specially designed systems, their recognition of symbols can improve through communication and can be enhanced by a design that is adapted for specific visual disabilities.

## HIGH-TECH COMMUNICATION SYSTEMS

Increasingly, augmentative communication systems are designed using high technology to support interaction. Educational computer software

**TABLE 8-3:**
Visual Features for Real Objects

| VISUAL FEATURE | DESIGN STRATEGY/ADAPTATION | REASON FOR ADAPTATION |
|---|---|---|
| COLOR | Use objects and object symbols with bright colors, especially primary and secondary colors, frequently. Also try "neon" or fluorescent colors that are attractive to children. | Red and orange objects are perceived earliest in visual development. Bright, clear, true colors enhance the attraction, perception, and discrimination of objects for children with visual impairments. |
| CONTRAST | Be sure that the contrast is sharp. If an object is dark, make the background light. For example, if calendar shelves or boxes are used with objects, put contrasting colored paper or felt squares under the objects. | If real objects are placed on a background with a strong contrast, visual discrimination of their features may improve. |
| SIZE, DISTANCE, AND ANGLE | Use real objects and object symbols that are large enough for a visually impaired child to see. If small symbolic objects are used, reduce the distance by bringing them closer to the child and add touch for discrimination. Also, reduce distance with object symbols to enhance discrimination. Use a regular-size real objects to enhance discrimination. Use a slanted display, if appropriate, so a child does not need to bend, which can cause back strain. | The size of symbols and objects is important for adequate visual discrimination. Size can be increased simply by moving objects and symbols closer to a person or moving the person closer to objects. Putting materials or communication devices on a slanted desk top or display can reduce fatigue, both visually and physically, while bringing them closer. |
| COMPLEXITY | Using common objects with few complex visual features, especially early in the development of communication skills, can help many children. As a child's skills develop, more visually abstract object symbols can be used. (Miniature objects and partial objects are more complex and abstract than are full-size or complete objects, both visually and tactilely.) | Moving from simple to complex encourages the development of concepts; this fact is especially important with visual information when vision is significantly reduced. |

*NOTE: With real objects, touch and vision can be effectively paired; for children who have significant visual impairment, touch may be used exclusively for augmentative systems.*

**TABLE 8-4:**
Visual Features for Photographs

| VISUAL FEATURE | DESIGN STRATEGY/ADAPTATION | REASON FOR ADAPTATION |
|---|---|---|
| COLOR | When a system's design uses photographs, be sure that the color is as true as possible. | Maximize the clarity of a photograph's colors to match real-world colors for improved discrimination and to support the development of concepts. |
| CONTRAST | Be sure that the contrast is sharp and that the details of objects in photographs are clear. Avoid glare in photographs. Use photographs with a matte finish, if possible, or place clear matte materials over photographs. | Overexposure or underexposure changes a photograph's resemblance to real-world conditions, makes it more abstract, and reduces visual information that is available for discrimination. |
| SIZE, DISTANCE, AND ANGLE | Make sure that objects and people in photographs are large enough to be readily discriminated, especially at first. (Visual information that is seen repeatedly, regardless of quality, *can* be learned and interpreted.) Move photograph symbol displays closer to a child, if necessary. Use a slanted display to reduce visual and physical fatigue. | Photographs replicate real-world settings, people, and objects. If they have good detail and are placed at an appropriate viewing distance, they can support the development of abstract concepts and communication. (Note: Enlarging photographs too much can make details fuzzy and more difficult to discriminate. Instead, "pose" or set up situations to photograph closer, producing a larger image.) |
| COMPLEXITY | Use photographs that show one object or person, as much as possible. Avoid clutter in the background or multiple objects and positioning that is confusing. | Although the real world is visually cluttered, it is also three dimensional and gives more visual information. Reducing clutter in a two-dimensional photograph enhances discrimination. |

NOTE: Add tactile cues or symbols to displays to support visual information of photographs.

**TABLE 8-5:**
Visual Features for Pictures

| VISUAL FEATURE | DESIGN STRATEGY/ADAPTATION | REASON FOR ADAPTATION |
|---|---|---|
| COLOR | Use pictures with bright, true colors. Also try "neon" or fluorescent colors that are attractive to children. (Be sure that colors represent real-world conditions, for example, that trees are not neon pink.) Neon colors can be used for background, too. | True colors enhance the visual attraction, perception, and discrimination of pictures for children with visual impairments. Pictures that closely resemble real-world items and situations support the development of concepts. |
| CONTRAST | Use strong contrast and clearly defined edges. A light background with dark colors or a dark background with light colors will be discriminated most easily. For example, a yellow banana on white construction paper does not contrast well for discrimination, but a yellow banana on black paper does. Use a matte finish and avoid glare from lamination. | Details are easier to discriminate and visual concepts more easily identified with good picture contrast. Fuzzy edges of pictured objects or people make the discrimination of shapes and other defining characteristics more difficult. |
| SIZE, DISTANCE, AND ANGLE | Pictures should be large enough to support discrimination of detail, but not so large that a child loses the "whole-object" concept. Move displays, such as communication books with small pictures, closer, and place displays on slanted trays or desk tops, if necessary, to reduce fatigue from bending to view. | Very small pictures (for example, a one-inch figure of a person held at 15 inches from the eyes) are difficult to discriminate unless the child moves closer; very large pictures may not be seen completely in one look. Typical viewing distances are approximately 12–20 inches for regular print material; children with visual impairments may need to view as close as approximately one inch. Enlarging pictures for the discrimination of details may help, but often displays can be brought closer with the same effect. |
| COMPLEXITY | Avoid cluttered figure-ground picture displays. Individual pictures should appear uncluttered, with important concepts in the foreground, and displays should be uncluttered, with clear separations between pictures. | Visual clutter in pictures and in system displays (as when too many symbols are displayed) interferes with the discrimination and processing of target information. |

*NOTE: Add tactile cues or symbols to support visual information of pictures.*

**TABLE 8-6:**
Visual Features for Line Drawings

| VISUAL FEATURE | DESIGN STRATEGY/ADAPTATION | REASON FOR ADAPTATION |
|---|---|---|
| COLOR | For some students, using color with line drawings is helpful. Colored acetate (yellow) placed over line drawings or a bright "neon"-colored background can be used. | Plain line drawings are abstract and may not have enough visual information and attraction for some children with visual impairments (others use line drawings better because of the reduced visual detail to be processed). Adding color for background enhances the attraction and perception of line drawings for some children, making line drawings more effective for developing concepts and communication skills. |
| CONTRAST | Be sure that the background and the line drawing are adequately contrasted. For example, black lines with white, ivory, or other light-colored backgrounds are appropriate; orange line drawings on a white background with a yellow acetate overlay would not contrast well. | A satisfactory contrast between the background and the foreground enhances discrimination. |
| SIZE, DISTANCE, AND ANGLE | Like pictures, line drawings must be large enough for good detail discrimination and small enough to be seen as "whole concepts." Very small line-drawing displays, like those in communication boards or books, can be brought closer to a visually impaired child. | The discrimination of details is enhanced when a child can see a line drawing clearly. Good visual discrimination promotes the recognition and use of concepts. |
| COMPLEXITY | Be sure that line drawings represent real-world conditions as much as possible. (Some line drawings are "schematic" and appear abstract.) | Line drawings are more abstract than are photographs or pictures; many line drawings are schematic, which reduces their resemblance to real-world objects. Some children with visual impairments need adaptations for typical line drawings to use the visual information for communication effectively. (Others actually use line drawings for communication information best.) |

*NOTE: Add tactile cues or symbols to support visual information of line drawings.*

programs for the development of communication skills are effective for some students. Other technological adaptations for communication involve eye-gaze displays. Table 8-7 explains the visual aspects for designing computer-adapted augmentative communication.

Students who are deaf-blind and have significant communication disabilities can benefit from a variety of augmentative communication devices and systems. Not all visual design factors are important for all students. Therefore, designers of systems should allow students to work with particular systems long enough to see how the students interact with other people and then vary the visual features until the students seem to be using their systems most effectively. System designs that incorporate adaptations for vision problems will enhance the students' abilities to interact with other people.

## OTHER FACTORS IN CHOOSING OR DESIGNING SYSTEMS

In addition to a student's communication needs and abilities and his or her requirements for visual adaptations, a number of other factors need to be considered in selecting or designing a communication system. These factors range from the student's physical needs to environmental and related considerations.

### Physical Considerations

Many people who are deaf-blind also have orthopedic limitations that must be taken into account in choosing or designing a communication system so they can gain access to it reliably and accurately. How does one gain access to the vocabulary of a system? By pointing or touching vocabulary items? By pressing buttons or activating a head switch? What pressure is necessary to do so? Are good fine motor skills, as for sign language or writing, needed? Is flipping the pages of a booklet of pictures involved? Whatever response is required, it must be one the user can produce easily. For some individuals with severe orthopedic impairments, a system may work in one position (such as in a wheelchair with a tray on it), but not in another (such as a side-lying position).

What adaptations are necessary to allow the person to communicate in a different position? In constructing a vocabulary, the number, size, layout, and proximity of the items must be decided. Just as these factors have to be considered in relationship to the user's visu-

**TABLE 8-7:**
Visual Features for Computer Displays

| VISUAL FEATURE | DESIGN STRATEGY/ADAPTATION | REASON FOR ADAPTATION |
|---|---|---|
| COLOR | Use computer displays/software packages that have bright, true colors. | Many children respond well visually to computer displays on color monitors. Using displays with bright, true colors will encourage visual attraction and discrimination. |
| CONTRAST | The contrast on computer displays should be sharp. Use displays that have strong dark/light contrast. Avoid software programs that have picture edges that are not clearly defined. Try negative or positive displays (dark on light or light on dark) as a child's visual needs require. Be sure that the monitor is placed in a way that minimizes glare. | Sharp contrast for computer images also encourages visual attention, perception, and discrimination. "Negative" image displays (reverse, or black background with light foreground or figures) are often used for computer monitors; for some visual conditions, a negative display is preferred. |
| SIZE, DISTANCE, AND ANGLE | Enlarge the image on the monitor, if appropriate. Be sure that the monitor is placed close enough that the student can see the whole picture, but not so close that he or she sees only part of the picture at a time. Using a larger monitor can help, also. | Many computers have enlarging features built into operating software or fonts that can be scaled for larger images. If a computer display is placed too far from a child, visual perception is more difficult. Enlarging the screen image may solve the problem. |
| COMPLEXITY | Some computer software is written for the images to move on the screen. For children with visual disabilities, movement is often too fast and "random" around the screen. Avoid programs with rapidly moving pictures and a cluttered figure/ground, or try to modify the program to slow the movement. | Children are attracted visually by images that move on the computer screen. For many children with visual impairments, their tracking skills are not strong enough to follow rapid-moving computer images. For others, more visual fixation time is needed to perceive and process visual information. Movement of the computer image can interfere with fixation, the discrimination of details, and the interpretation of visual information. |

al abilities, they must also be considered in relationship to his or her motor abilities. The items must be large enough and widely spaced enough for a person with a physical disability to indicate them easily one at a time without excessive movement. They must also be accessible to the user in whatever position he or she is in (sitting, lying on one side, or lying prone), which may be changed during the day. In addition, a person with poor muscle control may require items with raised boundaries that help him or her to stay within a specific box, whereas another person may have more problems with such boundaries because they obstruct his or her movements.

Is there a clear tactile boundary for the entire array of symbols, so the user who is blind easily knows the limits of the array? The more vocabulary that can be made available at one time, the more concepts the person can use, but the number of concepts and words will be affected by the size and layout that the person can use. Often, a person can handle only a limited number of vocabulary items at one time, and different vocabularies must be constructed for each major text or activity. Sometimes a prosthesis is necessary for an individual with fine motor limitations to gain access to symbols clearly. For instance, an adaptive device may be necessary to allow an individual to point clearly. Symbols must be physically accessible for those with physical impairments.

## Cognitive Considerations

Instruction in communication is more effective if the cognitive abilities of the user are addressed in the design of a system or device. Three major cognitive considerations are important.

- Is the individual communicating intentionally? If not, he or she is not ready to communicate through symbols. For instance, the person who does not realize that he or she can hold out an empty cup to someone to request more to drink will not learn to point to a picture of a cup to request a drink.

- For the individual who uses some form of intentional communication, what level of symbolism can he or she comprehend? It takes less cognitive ability to understand that a part of an object (such as a shoelace) represents the whole (a shoe) than it does to comprehend that a picture of a shoe represents a shoe. An abstract representation, such as braille or print, represents something else. When a new system is introduced, start at a level at which success is possible immediately.

- How much can the user remember? The great advantage of aided systems is that they make low demands on the user's memory. Since the entire vocabulary is generally displayed at once, the user only has to recognize the desired vocabulary from the display. With unaided systems like speech, sign language, and written forms, however, the user must remember the entire vocabulary from day to day.

## Environmental Considerations

A communication system must be easily understood by all people who come in contact with the user, or they should be able to be trained quickly to understand it. In addition, potential communication partners must be willing to help ensure that the system is available to the user at all times and hence may need to carry it for the user, check elements like the batteries every day, and modify the system to accommodate the user's changing needs for vocabulary, position, and so forth. Finally, it is helpful if other people enjoy using the device. For example, a voice-output device is sometimes fun for other children and entices them to interact with the user, even though the user has no hearing and does not benefit from that feature of the device.

## Personal Considerations

The preference of the user is critical to his or her success in using a system. It is pointless to provide a system that the user does not want to use or that is more cumbersome to use than another available means. The personal experience of the user is also essential, particularly when it comes to choosing specific symbols for a symbolic system and vocabulary that will be the most meaningful to him or her. Many commercially available two-dimensional symbols will not be meaningful to an inexperienced user, and it is rare that a predetermined set of vocabulary words will meet the needs of all individuals. Therefore, a thorough consideration of the user's preferences and requirements will promote the system's usefulness.

## Specific Systems

A number of other factors to be considered are related to the actual properties of aided systems:

- portability, so the system can be transported to all environments
- durability, especially if the system is to be used by young children

- ease of maintenance, so the system does not have to be recharged frequently
- adequacy of the vocabulary, so the vocabulary can be updated continually.

Addressing these issues in the selection and design of a system will make the system more useful to and effective for the student.

## Use of Multiple Systems

In many cases, a student will use more than one system to communicate. With an aided communication system, the user must also be able to use an unaided system in case the aided system is not on hand or is not working properly. Sometimes two aided systems are used, as when a user has a backup set of pictures in a booklet in case his or her high-tech device breaks down. In any event, it is essential that the user have a means of gaining attention from another person, whether the person is nearby or distant and not attending. Without this ability, the user is restricted to communicating when someone else is already attending to him or her. Many individuals have simple mechanical calling devices (buzzers or clickers) that allow them to attract attention from a distance if they cannot vocalize effectively or approach others.

At the beginning of this module, Table 8-1 listed some questions that may be asked in determining whether a proposed communication system is a good choice for a student. The questions relate to the various factors discussed here. The answers can help point the way to designing effective communication systems for students that contribute to the development of increased communication skills.

# REFERENCES

Berg, R. V., Jose, R. T., & Carter, K. (1983). Distance training techniques. In R. T. Jose (Ed.), *Understanding low vision* (pp. 277–316). New York: American Foundation for the Blind.

Beukelman, D. R., & Mirenda, P. (1992). *Augmentative and alternative communication: Management of severe communication disorders in children and adults.* Baltimore: Paul H. Brookes.

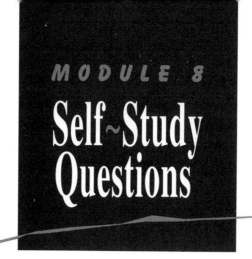

1. Tactile cues (either touch or object) allow the child who is deaf-blind to
   a. develop a beginning form of expressive communication.
   b. clearly understand the communication of others.
   c. begin to develop anticipatory responses to meaningful cues.

2. Two critical factors to remember in implementing a tactile cuing procedure are consistency and
   a. the delivery of cues by anyone interacting with the child.
   b. the expectation of a response from the child.
   c. the posting of procedures.

3. The selection of tactile cues to use for a particular child who is deaf-blind should be determined by
   a. what the child most easily associates with the cues.
   b. what makes the most sense or is the most obvious to the caregivers, so communication is smoother.
   c. what others are using (for example, commercially available lists).

4. When you consider the cognitive abilities of a student in choosing an appropriate communication system, your first priority is to
   a. select a system that will require a higher level of symbolism, so the student's level of communication will grow.
   b. select a system that the student can use now.
   c. select a symbolic system.

5. Of the following considerations for selecting a communication system, which is the least essential?
   a. The system has voice output.
   b. The system enables the student to gain attention.
   c. The system is portable enough to be useful in any context.

6. In developing a calendar box, which of the following is *not* recommended?
   a. Having 13 to 18 compartments.
   b. Matching activities to specific objects.
   c. Using a wild card to represent activities that are not part of the usual routine.

7. Which of the following can be accomplished through touch cues?
   a. Providing directives and information only.
   b. Providing directives and feedback only.
   c. Providing information, directives, and feedback.

8. What are the visual features to consider when selecting pictures, line drawings, and photographs to use with students as an augmentative communication system?
   a. Light and dark, size, clutter.
   b. Color, contrast, size, distance, angle, complexity.
   c. Color, width, height, complexity.

*Answers to self-study questions for this module appear at the end of Unit 2.*

# Manual and Spoken Communication

*JEANNE GLIDDEN PRICKETT*

- *Provide language input for students who are able to use language*

- *Adapt sign language to the student's visual abilities*

- *Understand the importance of name signs*

- *Encourage the use of residual hearing*

- *Learn to use interpreters effectively*

The use of language is the most conventional form of communication, and using language to communicate can be a goal for many students who are deaf-blind. The use of language, spoken or signed, allows interaction and information sharing that is precise and mutually understood by those who are communicating and can support the communicator's participation in the community. This module examines language-based communication as a mode of interaction for students who are deaf-blind.

# ADVANTAGES OF SIGNED AND SPOKEN COMMUNICATION

A major advantage of language-based communication, whether signed or spoken, is that one can interact and share with others who speak or sign the same language. A second advantage is that language uses abstract signed or spoken symbols to express in-depth ideas about the world and situations in the environment and thus allows individuals to refer to items, people, or situations that are not physically present or happening immediately and to express their feelings and other "intangible" ideas.

People who use spoken or signed language well can think abstractly and have a basis for written language, which uses even more abstract symbols than does spoken or signed language (see Module 10). Individuals who can use written language in any medium (for example, braille or print) can find and use the information they need for independent daily living and can interact with many more people in the community and in greater depth than can those who do not read and write well. Their quality of life may be enhanced by this interaction, as may their access to information.

One potential drawback of a single emphasis on signed or spoken language is that so much stress can be placed on developing spoken or signed language that other, more appropriate modes of communication may not be explored for children who do not use language functionally. Students who are deaf-blind and have additional cognitive impairments may not develop language concepts (spoken or signed) because they may not process well information that is abstract and they do not have easy access to adequate sensory information for developing concepts. For these children, other modes of communication with less abstract symbols may be more appropriate. In addition, some educators believe that a potential drawback of communication in sign language is that the general public is usually not familiar with sign language, which may limit the interactions of children who are deaf or deaf-blind. Service providers sometimes cite this disadvantage as a reason for selecting a mode of communication that is not language based, even when a child has adequate cognitive ability to support the development of language. Nevertheless, it is critical to remember that a child who is deaf-blind and is capable of using language (spoken or signed) but does not have language input will not learn language, despite his or her potential, because he or she has no other way to experience and acquire language.

Decisions about communication goals that are made on behalf of deaf-blind students in the development of Individualized Education Programs (IEPs) and Individualized Family Service Plans (IFSPs) can affect a lifetime of interaction. Educational team members who make these decisions need to review students' communication strengths, as well as areas that may need to be developed further. If they have evidence to expect that a deaf-blind student can learn to use signed or spoken language, they should devise goals to support this kind of language development and work together to ensure that necessary services are provided.

# MANUAL MODES

Helen Keller's name evokes an image of her teacher, Anne Sullivan Macy, communicating with her by fingerspelling into her hand. But the tactile spelling of each word is only one of many different language-based ways to communicate with a person who is deaf-blind. In fingerspelling, distinctive hand shapes are used to symbolize letters of the alphabet, which can be read visually or through touch. In sign language, hand and arm movements, natural gestures, and body and facial movements and expressions are used symbolically to constitute a formal language that can also be read visually or through touch. In this module, these and other methods of manual and spoken communication are described.

Communicating tactilely or with near vision is an individual process that depends on the needs and preferences of a person who is deaf-blind. It may require knowledge of several different modes for communicating in various situations. With the advent of modern technology, more communication modes for specific purposes are available. Still, for daily interaction, most people who are deaf-blind and have advanced abilities use a manual form of communication, especially for receptive communication.

A major benefit of communicating in a manual mode is "portability." Hands are always with us, as are voices for those who speak. For people who are deaf or deaf-blind, sign language and other manual forms are analogous to spoken communication for those who hear. The interaction is similar, since no extra devices are needed to communicate in spoken or signed modes. Both modes are used for everyday interactions and to share and gain information immediately.

## SIGN LANGUAGE

Many individuals who are deaf-blind can and do use sign language for both receptive and expressive communication. In most societies with deaf members, there is either a single sign language or several dialects of sign language. All these sign languages use symbols made with the hands, arms, and body language, as well as gestures that are symbolic or are mutually understood by the users.

Like all true languages, sign languages have unique and evolving syntax, grammar, vocabulary, and concepts. As with all true languages, the users mutually understand the meaning of the concepts that are expressed.

Unlike spoken languages, all sign languages have visual-spatial properties, which means that information can be obtained by using vision, that they have characteristics that are identified through vision, and that spatial arrangements or characteristics are used to convey meaning or emphasis. Visual-spatial factors that give signs their meaning include these:

- special hand shapes that are used for the sign-symbol
- hand shapes for the sign-symbol that are located in relation to the body
- a signing area that is typically from one shoulder to the other and from the waist to the top of the head
- movements of hands and arms for the sign-symbol (direction, speed, force of movement)

- facial expressions that accompany the sign-symbol
- body language that emphasizes the meaning.

Users of sign language must have adequate visual-spatial discrimination and interpretation abilities to gain meaning from signed concepts. Sign language can be used with people who are visually impaired, however, with some modifications, which are outlined in Modifications of Sign Language for Use with Visually Impaired Persons.

## Tactile Sign Language

Sign language can be used tactilely, although tactile input is not necessarily processed in the same way as is visual input. Tactile sign language is generally used for receptive communication. An individual who is deaf-blind and receives sign language tactilely usually signs in the air (visibly) for expressive communication, unless communicating with another person who is blind or deaf-blind.

Few have studied tactile processing of signed communication (Griffith, Robinson, & Panagos, 1983). The visual features that give signs meaning for typical users of sign language will not necessarily

**HELP** *at a* **GLANCE**

## *MODIFICATIONS OF SIGN LANGUAGE FOR USE WITH VISUALLY IMPAIRED PERSONS*

- The distance between people who are communicating may have to be changed according to the visual needs of the person with a visual impairment. A person who has lost peripheral vision (for example, from Usher syndrome) may need to be 10 feet or more from a speaker, so enough of the speaker's body is visible that signs can be seen fully, whereas a person with optic atrophy may need to be as close as two or three feet to see enough of the details of signs to understand them (see also Visual and Tactile "Tracking" in this module).

- The speed of sign language may have to be slowed.

- The size of the area in which signs are produced may have to be adapted. For example, an individual with only useful central vision may need to have a speaker use a smaller sign area because of the loss of peripheral vision that leaves only a small tunnel for viewing a sign. With the smaller sign area, the receiver does not lose parts of signs into the missing periphery when the speaker is too close. ■

▲ *To accommodate her student's visual field, this instructor is adjusting both her distance from the student and the way in which she signs.*

have the same meaning for people who receive sign language tactilely. There may be differences between how information is processed when it is received visually and when it is received through touch. However, consistent and repeated interaction helps students who have visual impairments learn to understand information that is signed tactilely. If the iconicity, or the visual associative value, of a sign is high, the sign will also be more recognizable through touch (Griffith et al., 1983). In other words, if a sign "looks like" what it represents, it will probably feel like what it represents, too. For example, the sign for *telephone* resembles the shape, position, and use of a telephone handset so closely that it would be easily understood both tactilely and visually. Also, a sign that has fewer complex visual-spatial features may be more tactilely understandable; the sign for *eat* has a distinct, stable position near the mouth and does not move much in space. Other signs, with more complex visual-spatial features of changes in movement and direction, may be far more complex tactilely. Children who are deaf-blind can and do learn these signs, but they may need more time to do so. Modifications of signs for tactile use should be minimized, because deaf-blind children will

be less able to communicate with typical users of sign language if the signs are greatly altered for them individually.

## Visual and Tactile "Tracking"

Some individuals who are visually impaired do not need to use a sign language that is fully tactile, but they may need tactile clues to follow another person's hand as it moves through space. "Tracking" is a technique that can be used by a person who is visually impaired to follow the speaker's hand or hands through space, especially if the visual impairment involves a reduced visual field, which may prevent the person from seeing parts of signs that go outside the visual field. To understand how parts of a sign can be lost with a reduced visual field, think of a video game in which the character exits the screen in one place and reappears later in another place. Watching sign language can be the same way for a person with a reduced visual field, as is the case with Sally.

> Sally has Usher syndrome, which is accompanied by a significant loss of peripheral vision. She often needs a way to keep track of a speaker's hands in space that vision cannot easily pro-

▲ *In tactile signing, the person receiving information places his or her hand over the hand of the communicator.*

*vide, especially when she sits or stands close to a speaker or an interpreter. So, Sally can use her hand to touch the back of the speaker's hand lightly at the wrist. This touch provides Sally with enough tactile information to follow the movement of the speaker's hand and not lose parts of the information. Still, tracking does not require that Sally cover the speaker's hands fully with her own hands, because she still receives information with her remaining vision as long as she knows precisely where to look.*

## Sign Language: Forms and Instruction

Sign language is not universal. Each country has its own version, just as most countries have their own spoken languages. American Sign Language (ASL) is commonly used in the United States and parts of Canada by individuals who are deaf or deaf-blind (for where to learn sign language, see Module 3). Linguists consider ASL a true language because it is dynamic and has its own syntax and grammar (Fischer & Siple, 1990). And because it has its own syntax and grammatical rules, it is *not* a representation of English signed on the hands. It is structurally different from English and therefore will not make sense in English when translated word for word. There is often confusion about ASL and other forms of sign language because typically not every word that would appear as part of an English sentence is signed.

Most students who are deaf and are in large specialized educational programs have been exposed to ASL, and many use it as a "native" language. Not all languages, including ASL, have written forms (although some researchers are currently working to develop a written form of ASL). So, ASL users must read and write in a language other than ASL.

Newer sign "systems" are also used by some persons who are deaf and have visual impairments. They are usually based on English language syntax and may use ASL signs as base concepts (Moores, 1987; Quigley & Paul, 1984; Vernon & Andrews, 1990). Many systems use signs that make components of English grammar visual, such as word endings like *ing* and *ment*. Some of the most commonly used systems, all of which are "codified [systems] of arbitrary signs and symbols representing English words" (Sauerburger, 1993, p. 8), include Seeing Essential English (SEE I), Signing Exact English (SEE II), Signed English, and Linguistics of Visual English (LOVE).

Some people use Pidgin Signed English (PSE) or Manually Coded English (MCE) as an interface between written/spoken

English and ASL. These forms of manual communication use English order with ASL signs and some ASL features (such as facial expressions and directionality). English-based systems are used in many settings because educators believe that they encourage the development of skills in English that will be useful for reading and writing. (For information on factors used to determine which form of sign language may be appropriate for a child, see Decision Making: ASL or Signed English?)

## DECISION MAKING: ASL OR SIGNED ENGLISH?

Here are some guidelines to consider when determining whether ASL (American Sign Language) or Signed English is more appropriate for a particular child:

● Determine the child's primary learning mode: Is the child a visual learner, an auditory learner, or strictly a tactile learner?

● Collect current information about the child's hearing, vision, and communication skills. If a child has some useful hearing, good initial communication development, and little or no useful vision, an English-based system may be effective, especially if it needs to be modified for tactile use. However, since ASL is based on visual information, you may find that ASL is more effective with a child with almost no hearing but useful vision.

● If the educational team decides that the child may be able to read braille, Signed English may be preferable, since braille is based on English word order.

● If there are deaf people in the school or community who may interact with the deaf-blind student, base your decision on the kind of sign language they use, so the student does not miss out on opportunities to communicate with them.

● Some children who are deaf-blind can benefit from using both forms of sign language for specific interactions. For example, in gym class, the teacher or interpreter may use ASL to describe the movement that a child should try, whereas in language class, the teacher or interpreter may use both ASL and Signed English to convey a concept both ways. When educational team planning occurs, members should look at the child's potential for language development and reading, based on available information, and determine if dual forms might be useful.

● Remember that because each child's learning profile is unique, the decision to use ASL or Signed English should also be unique to that individual, while allowing the child to have opportunities to communicate with as many other people as possible. ■

# Name Signs: A Sense of Oneself

**Samuel J. Supalla**

We use spoken language to name items, events, and people. A name allows a person to establish self-identity and allows others to refer to that person individually. So a name sign, or a special sign that represents a particular individual, is the most personal of all signs, identifying a person to his or her family, friends, and others. A name sign is a vital part of socialization for a person who is deaf or deaf-blind, too.

People who are deaf use specific forms for name signs, just as specific spoken-language names are used. Name signs used by deaf people can also be given to children who are deaf-blind, and they often correlate with spoken names by the use of the handshape of the alphabet letter that begins the name. For a child who is deaf-blind, the name sign becomes tactile, using the same handshapes and basic positions of ordinary name signs. A collection of 525 name signs has been recorded in *The Book of Name Signs: Naming in American Sign Language* (Supalla, 1992). This compilation can be used to help select a name sign for a deaf-blind child, either by families or by service providers working with families.

The one-hand American Manual Alphabet is used to give a person's name sign its basic form. In some cases, initials from both the person's first and last names are used to make the complete sign, especially when two people in a community have the same name sign. For example, a child named Aaron might have an "A" handshape placed at his temple on the right side. That becomes his name, just as the spoken or written form, "Aaron," is also his name. If two people have name signs with the "A" handshape in the temple position, Aaron's family and friends might add the initial of his last name, "Jones," and his name sign will be "AJ" at the temple.

Deaf-blind children, like all children, need to have a way for others to identify them and to establish self-identity. Name signs that are used consistently by everyone who communicates with the child are an effective strategy to accomplish this. ∎

---

A third kind of sign language that may be used by students who are deaf or deaf-blind is "home sign." With home sign, families create signs or visual symbols that are understood at home by the deaf or deaf-blind person and other family members. One type of home sign is name signs, which help a deaf or deaf-blind person identify family members (see Name Signs: A Sense of Oneself). Families usually invent home signs when they have not had access to formal sign language training but still need to communicate effectively with a deaf or deaf-blind member. An individual who only uses home signs because he or she has not had formal education away from home will have difficulty communicating with people who use ASL or other forms of sign language. Most families with a deaf or deaf-blind member do create some home signs, though, since all families want to communicate about unique family experiences for which no formal signs exist.

## FINGERSPELLING

People who are deaf-blind often use other modes of manual communication based on spoken language, primarily fingerspelling. Some persons whose visual impairments occurred early learned to communicate using primarily auditory information and may have to convert to tactile forms of communication, often fingerspelling, when they lose their hearing. Although they use braille or large type for written communications, they may not adapt readily to using sign language that depends on good visual-spatial information not readily accessible to them. Some individuals with significant visual impairments have broad experience only with tactile and movement-based spatial concepts—not with concepts that require an understanding of visual-spatial arrangements.

Since spoken language with an auditory word order is so familiar to most people who are visually impaired and can hear, changing to a manual form that supports an auditory order often is the most practical solution. With this form, the user gets a manual equivalent of auditory information, with exact spoken words, in their spoken order, spelled out letter by letter. With tactile fingerspelling, for example, the exact spoken meaning is retained. With any of the modes that incorporate manual spelling, speakers pause slightly to indicate ends of words and add punctuation if appropriate. Using mutually acceptable shortcuts is appropriate, too.

### Advantages and Disadvantages

People who are deaf-blind may use several types of fingerspelling, according to what is most comfortable and provides the most information to them. A major advantage of fingerspelling, in which each letter of the alphabet is expressed by a different shape of the hand, is that those who are not familiar with it can learn the basic 26 alphabet hand shapes, often in a few hours, whereas sign language vocabulary

FIGURE 9-1:
**The American Manual Alphabet**

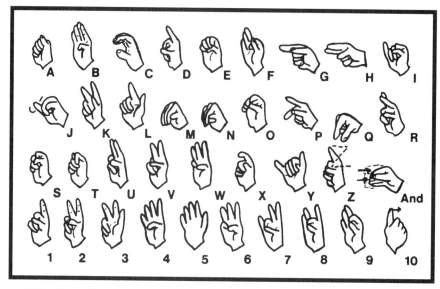

SOURCE: *L. Kates & J. D. Schein,* A Complete Guide to Communication with Deaf-Blind Persons, *Silver Spring, MD: National Association of the Deaf, 1980. Reprinted with permission.*

and usage require more time to learn. In the United States, fingerspelling is done with one hand and is known as the American Manual Alphabet (see Figure 9-1), although it is sometimes done with two hands in other countries. (The Two Hand Manual Alphabet, which is the predominant alphabet used by deaf-blind people in Canada, is a version of the British Manual Alphabet for the Deaf-Blind, commonly used in Great Britain.) A second advantage is the clarity of information that fingerspelling allows; the information available from fingerspelling can be exactly what a speaker has said, word for word.

One drawback, however, is that both the sender and the receiver must be literate, because with fingerspelling, spoken language is spelled out. An occasional problem is fatigue for both the sender and the receiver, depending on their physical positions and the intensity and length of their interaction (see The Fatigue Factor). Nevertheless, the lack of speed of this mode is the most important drawback because it slows down the exchange of information and may cause the receiver to lose some information.

## Tactile Fingerspelling

Fingerspelling, like sign language, can be used as a form of tactile communication. For all types of tactile fingerspelling, the sender usually uses his or her dominant hand, and the receiver usually uses the nondominant hand. If both individuals take turns receiving and speaking with fingerspelling, they may alternate hands, depending on the interaction. Three basic types of tactile fingerspelling are palm-over-palm, palm-in-palm, and birdcage.

**Palm-over-palm.** In palm-over-palm, the palms of both the sender and the receiver face away or down, and the receiver's palm covers the back of the sender's hand. The fingers of both people usually face the same direction (forward). Manual information for letter shapes is read from the back of the sender's hand, so some information given with the finger positions in front may be less clear for the receiver. (This position usually requires both individuals to sit side by side or angled at 45–90 degrees.)

**Palm-in-palm.** In palm-in-palm, both the sender and the receiver face each other or are slightly angled, with their palms facing each other and on the same plane. The receiver's fingers usually curl lightly over the sender's hand. Manual information for letter shapes is read from the palm side of the sender's hand, allowing the receiver precise information on the sender's finger positions.

**Birdcage.** Like palm-in-palm, in birdcage the sender's and the receiver's palms face each other. With this position, however, the sender's palm may be on a plane that is at a 90-degree angle from the receiver's palm. Manual information for letter shapes is read from the palm side of the sender's hand, allowing the receiver precise information on the sender's finger position. Also, letters like *p*, *q*, and *r* may be made in the area between the receiver's thumb and first finger, allowing the receiver to have more information on the shape of the letter. This position can be used face to face or with both individuals seated side by side and with their hands placed forward and down, such as on a knee. The receiver's palm can face up with the back of the hand resting on the knee.

Tactile fingerspelling can be adapted to provide nonverbal information as well. For example, the force and speed of the finger movements can indicate the emotion of a speaker. Words can be emphasized through spelling, just as they can with voice or signs:

"H-O-W *A-R-E* Y-O-U?" (speaker "punches" on ARE) or
"H-O-W A-R-E *Y-O-U*?" (speaker "punches" on YOU).

In both cases, the sender can include additional question marks to show emotion and a period or exclamation point to show emphasis. For clarity, the sender or an interpreter should pause slightly between words and when sentences end. (Interpreters can also indicate emotion by describing the other person's body language, facial expression, and tone of voice. This issue is discussed in more depth later in this module.)

## Other Forms of Manual Communication

With *print-on-palm,* the sender simply prints block letters on the receiver's palm. Individuals who are deaf-blind and have advanced language skills can use this method effectively to participate independently in the community because the general public can communicate with them in stores, libraries, and banks and on buses, among other places.

People who are deaf-blind usually use print-on-palm just for receptive communication—to interact with others who print on their palms. In some cases, those who use it for communication with the general public write notes to respond or simply gesture, if their speech is not understood.

Print-on-palm is most effective when the sender uses block-style capital letters. The receiver will extend a palm and indicate what the sender should do. The sender's index finger can be used as a "pen." Letters should be printed large enough so they are clear to the receiver who is deaf-blind, and the sender should use a moderate pace with slight pauses between words and sentences. If the receiver who is deaf-blind gives the sender a cue, parts of words can be eliminated (for example, a sender may be spelling "IMM . . . " and the receiver may say "immediately" aloud because of the context of the sentence, so the sender can go on to the next word). The most important factor is to make a letter the same way each time it is printed, instead of varying where the letter is started and how the parts are added.

Other forms of manual communication that are used less frequently in the United States include two-handed alphabet systems, finger braille, and Morse code. In Canada, England, and other countries, individuals who are deaf-blind use variations of fingerspelling that are specific to their countries. Most of these manual alphabets use two hands for interaction. They are primarily receptive, but are also expressive when two people who are deaf-blind communicate with each other.

Finger braille uses the braille cell-production format, tapped onto a deaf-blind individual's fingertips or other parts of the body. Braille contractions and short forms may be used, since the sender essentially performs the same activity as when writing in braille.

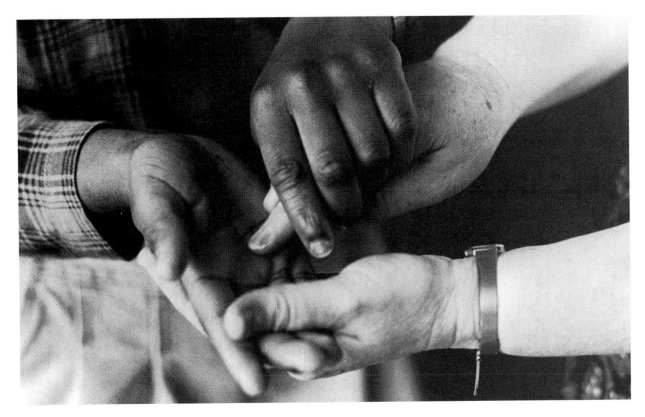

The Morse code is used less frequently by people who are deaf-blind. Because most people are not familiar with it, it is less useful than print-on-palm and fingerspelling. The Morse code can be performed by tapping long and short symbols onto a receiver's hand, arm, or other parts of the body. Also, some persons use electronic tactile receivers that vibrate with pulses sent from other sources, so two people could have sending-receiving units and could signal each other by long and short vibrations using the Morse code alphabetic symbols to spell out words.

▲ *Print-on-palm is a communication method that can be used effectively with strangers who do not know sign language or other specialized methods.*

## SPOKEN MODES

Just like people who are deaf, many deaf-blind people communicate using speech. People who are visually impaired and hard-of-hearing often communicate using strictly auditory information and speech. Some have been taught the "oral" method of communication, which emphasizes the development of speech, speechreading (lipreading), and the use of their remaining hearing with aids or assistive listening devices (see Appendix B on amplification systems). For example, John received oral training long before his gradual loss of vision was detected; he continued to speechread and had oral interpreters (that is, interpreters who mouth what is being said with slightly more lip emphasis but no voice) well into adulthood, although he eventually had to transfer to manual communication. With residual hearing for speech and environmental sounds (such as emergency signals or traffic sounds), people who are deaf-blind can be alerted to unsafe situations and can understand such features of speech as the patterns and length of sentences, the number of syllables in words, and a person's tone of voice or volume. A person who is visually impaired and has residual hearing can use all available sensory information, no matter how reduced or distorted, to gain access to his or her environment and to communicate with the people in it.

Many of the manual communication methods described in this module are paired with speech as an expressive communication mode. For example, people who are deaf-blind and fingerspell or use print-on-palm often use speech to respond to people who communicate with them in the community.

Speech is usually developed with the assistance of a skilled instructor, such as a teacher trained in deafness or a speech-language instructor. However, traditional methods of speech training for students who have hearing losses must be adapted for students who are deaf-blind.

Usually, speech is taught to children who are deaf through visual demonstration, using such devices as mirrors and visual imitation of the lip and tongue positions. Some instructors also use tactile information, so the children feel the vibrations of the various consonant and vowel sounds by touching the teacher's face. Deaf children who are visually impaired need more of this vibrotactile information to imitate the sounds effectively.

Children who have little or no useful vision or hearing are unlikely to communicate through speechreading. Also, speech training for these students may be so difficult and thus take so much time that it may delay or preclude instruction in other essential communication skills for daily living. Teachers and parents who are planning instructional goals should review a deaf-blind child's needs and expected outcomes carefully before they commit resources to intensive training in speech and speechreading. They must consider such important factors as the degrees of the child's vision and hearing losses and how the child uses residual sensory information, as well as the stability of each sensory loss.

## AUDITORY TRAINING

Many children who have visual disabilities and are hard-of-hearing use amplification (for more information, see Appendix B on amplification systems) that enhances their remaining hearing. These children can receive "auditory training" that will help them learn to perceive, recognize, and interpret sounds in their environments.

Some students can hear only gross environmental sounds even with optimal amplification, but they can still make use of these sounds for safety and may learn to discriminate among them. Gross environmental sounds that are especially useful for safety in everyday life are the sounds of various vehicles, fire and police sirens, smoke or fire alarms, timers or buzzers, and doorbells.

Auditory training to discriminate speech is important, even if a child has little residual hearing. Using appropriate amplification or an assistive listening device that is recommended by a qualified audiologist, the child can be taught activities that will help him or her to make sense of sound patterns and to use other features of speech, such as inflection, tone of voice, and patterns of connected speech (spoken phrases or sentences), to gain information about what is being said.

In addition to recommending appropriate amplification or assistive listening devices, an audiologist can work with the communication specialist or teacher of students with hearing disabilities to help the educational team develop instructional activities for auditory training (see How to Find an Audiologist). An orientation and mobility (O&M) instructor can suggest activities related to safe travel and the use of remaining hearing for travel.

For auditory training that supports the discrimination of speech, the communication specialist and the hearing teacher can help develop goals and activities or may instruct the student directly. Usually, instruction in speech and auditory training is given as a unified set of activities. In addition, classroom activities can be used to reinforce these specific speech and auditory activities.

## TADOMA METHOD

A few individuals who are deaf-blind communicate using the Tadoma vibrotactile method. Tadoma is used primarily for receptive communication and requires that the receiver who is deaf-blind place his or her hand or hands on the speaker's face.

## HOW TO FIND AN AUDIOLOGIST

Audiologists are trained non-medical specialists who evaluate hearing and make recommendations for hearing aids or other amplification systems. They may be in private practice or work in college or university training programs or in larger practices and are often affiliated with otolaryngologists, physicians specializing in treating conditions of the ear, nose, and throat. Here are some guidelines for locating an audiologist:

- Check the Yellow Pages under Audiologists.

- Contact local otolaryngologists, most of whom routinely work with one or two local audiologists.

- Contact local colleges or universities to see if they have programs for training audiologists. Those that do can provide names of audiologists who supervise or train their students.

- Be wary of businesses that advertise "free hearing tests," such as those in large chain department stores or stores that only sell hearing aids. The persons testing hearing in such places may not be certified audiologists (since not all states have laws that require hearing aid distributors to be certified audiologists). Certified audiologists have training that is critical for the safe evaluation of hearing and the fitting of hearing aids. ■

- The receiver's fingers are fanned down across the side of the speaker's face, with the little finger (or the last two fingers) touching the throat, to detect vibrations from voiced consonants like *n*, *ng*, *b*, *d*, and *v* (and many other consonants) and vowels, which are all voiced. (When children receive initial instruction in this method, their forefingers may be placed near the speaker's or teacher's nose, to help identify clearly *n*, *m*, and *ng*, which have nasal resonance. More experienced Tadoma users fan all fingers lower on the cheeks and throat.)

- The receiver's thumb is placed on the lips to detect lip movements and some tongue movements, as well as air that is expelled for voiceless consonants, such as *p*, *t*, *th*, and *s*.

The Tadoma method is not taught routinely today, and only a few people actually use it. Those who do use it also use alternative modes or methods for everyday communication. Tadoma is sometimes mentioned in the literature on deaf-blindness, however, because it can support auditory information and give children who are deaf-blind more sensory input for interactions (Reed, Durlach, Braida, & Schultz, 1989). Vibrotactile information can encourage many deaf-blind children to use their residual hearing better for communication.

# INTERPRETING FOR DEAF-BLIND PEOPLE

Interpreters (or transliterators) assist people who are deaf or deaf-blind to gain information from others in large-group meetings, in the community, and even in schools (see Working with an Interpreter for some tips). They usually do not convey spoken messages word for word, but transmit them using a deaf-blind individual's preferred

## HELP at a GLANCE

## WORKING WITH AN INTERPRETER

Here are a few tips for working with an interpreter effectively and for ensuring that the person who is deaf-blind gets all the important information he or she requires:

● Always talk to the deaf-blind person, not the interpreter. Address the person as if the interpreter were not there.

● Remember that the interpreter is a service provider, not a participant, and thus should only facilitate the deaf-blind person's participation.

● Make certain that you or anyone else speaking talks slowly and distinctly enough for the interpreter to keep up.

● Occasionally monitor the interpreter's progress. Slow down if the interpreter continues to convey information long after you stop.

● If the interpreter frequently requests clarification or asks you to slow down, use the next break to find out what the interpreter requires.

● Interpreting, especially tactile interpreting, can be physi-

cally fatiguing for both the interpreter and the person who is deaf-blind, so give frequent breaks.

● Before a presentation, consult with the person and the interpreter to determine the best position for the person to get the information and adjust your setup, if necessary. Give the interpreter any materials you will be handing out. Inform him or her of any technical information that may be conveyed or of tasks that go beyond ordinary interpreting, for example, dealing with a videotape or slide presentation with a script that is concentrated and fast moving. ■

syntax and vocabulary. This form of interpretation is comparable to foreign language interpreting, since the individual's needs direct the interpreting situation. For example, deaf-blind people who grew up using ASL may prefer ASL interpretation, which is not verbatim from spoken language, as was previously mentioned.

People who are deaf-blind and grew up using spoken language may prefer transliteration, which allows them to receive a message in spoken language order, with essentially the exact words the speaker has used. For clarity and because interpreters and transliterators have similar responsibilities in serving people who are deaf-blind, the term *interpreter* will be used throughout this section.

To be certified by the Registry of Interpreters for the Deaf (the national organization of interpreters), interpreters for people who are deaf must meet specific requirements and adhere to the registry's Code of Ethics. The aim of the Code of Ethics is to ensure that confidentiality and respect for the deaf individual and for the interpreter as a service provider can be maintained in all interpreting situations (see Finding an Interpreter for suggestions on where to locate interpreters). Qualifications for the certification of interpreters for people who are deaf-blind have not yet been completely defined, but some general guidelines exist. The unique features of interpreting for deaf-blind people are described in the sections that follow.

## ROLES AND RESPONSIBILITIES OF INTERPRETERS

Like interpreters for people who are deaf, interpreters for people who are deaf-blind must convey messages clearly, using the individual's preferred mode or modes of communication. Thus, they must be fluent in those modes and have enough vocabulary to convey the messages. Tactile interpreting or transliterating for a deaf-blind person may require more time than may interpreting for a person who is deaf, so fluency is essential.

Most interpreters are not skilled in all the possible modes of language-based communication used by deaf-blind people but will know several modes. Therefore, if an interpreter thinks that he or she cannot meet a person's needs, he or she has the responsibility to suggest that another interpreter be found. The most effective way to decide if an individual's needs are being met is simply to ask the person or to judge by the individual's responses to the message that the interpreter gives. If the person asks for many repetitions of concepts

## FINDING AN INTERPRETER

The following are possible sources for locating the services of an interpreter:

• The Yellow Pages under Translators/Interpreters.

• Local colleges and universities that train interpreters.

• Local or state vocational rehabilitation agencies or centers for independent living that may have lists of local interpreters or interpreters on staff.

• Schools with programs for students who are deaf or, in rural areas, itinerant hearing specialists who may know of interpreters.

• Audiologists.

• Organizations for people who are deaf or deaf-blind, their families, or professionals who work with them (see the Resources section of this book).

• Family members of individuals who are deaf or deaf-

blind. Sometimes family members sign well enough to interpret, though they may not have formal certification. If you are familiar with deaf people in your community, or know of a local deaf club, check on availability of interpreters through them.

• Local churches or synagogues that offer interpreted services.

• The Registry of Interpreters for the Deaf—the national organization for interpreters (see Resources). ∎

or seems confused by the information, it may mean that he or she cannot understand the mode in which it is being translated and needs to receive the information in a different form (for example, tactile ASL instead of tactile fingerspelling). An interpreter who is alert will notice this problem and either make adjustments or attempt to locate another interpreter who has the necessary skills.

In addition to the ordinary responsibilities for conveying the content of a speaker's message, an interpreter for a deaf-blind person has other responsibilities, some of which are as follows:

• Conveying important visual information, for example

describing the room or setting (its size and special features) and the people in it (the number of people, their mode of dress, if there are refreshments, and so forth).

describing the extra features of communication, such as who is speaking, the speaker's facial expression, and the audience's response (clapping, frowning). If the speaker is deaf-blind, the audience's reactions to his or her message should be conveyed, for example, laughter at a joke. The interpreter should be close at hand when informing the speaker. Descriptions should convey facts, not the judgments of the interpreter, and should be brief.

telling who is in the room or approaching, especially if the deaf-blind person has expressed an interest in meeting another participant.

- Guiding the deaf-blind person to desired locations (such as a cafeteria) and assisting with tasks (like going through the food line and choosing food) that typically require vision. To do so, the interpreter must know safe and efficient guiding techniques (see Module 17).

- Reading or summarizing information that has been provided only in print or other media that are inaccessible.

- Helping a deaf-blind person obtain transportation, for example, guiding the person to a taxi stand.

Interpreters wear clothing that provides good contrast with their hands and faces (such as dark clothing for light-skinned interpreters) and little or no jewelry or perfume and are careful that their dress and makeup are not distracting. Individuals who are deaf and visually impaired use close-vision interpreting, so visual or olfactory distractions must be avoided. Interpreters who use tactile forms of manual communication should have clean hands and short, neat fingernails for comfort, especially for the person who is deaf-blind.

Occasionally, interpreting for a deaf-blind individual requires special supplies, equipment, or other items used to convey a message (Raistrick, 1988); it is important for both the individual and the interpreter to know who is responsible for furnishing the items before interpreting begins. Module 18 describes how interpreters work with mobility instructors for teaching travel skills.

## THE FATIGUE FACTOR

The process of interpreting can by physically and mentally exhausting for both the interpreter and the deaf-blind person. First, when tactile sign language or fingerspelling is used, almost constant physical contact between the individual who is deaf-blind and the interpreter is needed. That is, both people are seated close enough to permit this physical contact, sometimes touching at the shoulders or knees, which may be awkward, and the deaf-blind person's hands moving on top of the interpreter's may feel heavy. (With close-vision sign language, close proximity is required, but touch may not be needed.)

Second, a great deal of concentration is required. The interpreter must focus on the messages that are being delivered and translate them into sign language or fingerspelling, keeping up with the ideas as they are being conveyed. Similarly, the individual who is deaf-blind must concentrate intensely and remain near the interpreter, often with his or her hands touching the interpreter's hands.

Third, interpreters for deaf-blind individuals must make decisions about what visual information is essential to convey with the spoken message and what is less important. Such decisions require additional focus, so the most essential elements are conveyed. To alleviate fatigue, many individuals who are deaf-blind rotate two interpreters to provide relief approximately every 20 minutes for both the interpreters and themselves.

## RESPONSIBILITIES OF THE DEAF-BLIND PERSON

The individual who is deaf-blind and uses an interpreter must clearly explain his or her needs and preferences and inform the interpreter if the information that is being interpreted is not clear. He or she must also let the interpreter know if mutually agreed-on shortcuts can be used (Raistrick, 1988). Since individuals who are deaf-blind must use the information provided through interpreters, they must make sure that they understand it.

Interpreters and individuals who are deaf-blind should consult briefly before beginning to be sure that the seating arrangements and lighting and background requirements are satisfactory and other needs are met. Signals for relief interpreters and emergencies, alternate modes for interpreting that can be used, and other unique aspects of the interpreting situation should be clear to both of them.

## EDUCATIONAL INTERPRETING

With the increased participation of children who are deaf or deaf-blind in regular classrooms, educational interpreters are needed to interpret for classroom teachers who do not sign fluently enough to use sign language for instruction or to meet students' individual needs, such as for one-to-one tactile interpreting/signing or close-proximity signing. Educational interpreters may be asked to tutor deaf and deaf-blind elementary and secondary students in a variety of subjects and to interpret for such activities as sports in which they never actually participated themselves (Hayes, 1993). An educational interpreter for a student who is deaf-blind may do the following:

- Interpret instructional activities, including lectures and teachers' explanations, and give relevant auditory and visual information.

- Help the student understand the requirements of written work, especially if the directions use unfamiliar language.

- Tutor the student in specific subject areas (this activity should be discussed with the interpreter and clearly specified in the job description before the interpreter is hired).

- Serve on the educational team as a full member.

- Provide in-service training to all school personnel, including classroom teachers, on the use of interpreters in schools.

- Act as liaison between the classroom and other educational team members on the student's behalf, as the one consistent service provider in a student's program with relevant information from a variety of situations within the school.

- Provide assistance to all who work with the student, including the student's parents and other team members, to unify signs used with the student and to promote consistent communication for the student.

Interpreters who are accustomed to working with adults, especially those who are certified by the Registry of Interpreters for the Deaf and must follow its Code of Ethics, may feel uncomfortable with some of these functions. To ensure that the student's interpreting and other needs are met in an instructional setting, the interpreter must be informed of all the duties that are expected of him or her before the person is hired.

## FACILITATED COMMUNICATION

"Facilitated communication" is a communication technique that is relatively new to the United States. It is described as

*a technique for some children and adults with autism or certain neuromotor disabilities who cannot talk—and who do not point independently and reliably. An assistant enables the person to "speak" by physically supporting his or her arm, wrist or hands while the individual hunts and pecks for letters, words or pictures on a keyboard. (Molnar, 1993, p. 18)*

With facilitated communication, words are typed or selected or pictures are chosen, with the help of the facilitator or assistant, that represent what the individual with a disability wants to communicate. Supporters of the technique are facing controversy, especially in regard to the possible influence or interpretive role of the facilitator, but continue to assert that individuals with the disabilities noted above benefit and are communicating for the first time (Molnar, 1993).

Nevertheless, there has been no research to date on the use of the technique specifically with students who are deaf-blind. Therefore, a decision to attempt facilitated communication with a deaf-blind student would require careful consideration, and all the student's needs and abilities would need to be reviewed by the educational team, just as with any other communication development strategy. Evaluating students' individual needs and abilities and developing individualized programs to encourage a student's communication skills are explored in depth later in this unit.

# REFERENCES

Fischer, S. D., & Siple, P. (1990). *Theoretical issues in sign language research.* Chicago: University of Chicago Press.

Griffith, P. L., Robinson, J. H., & Panagos, J. H. (1983). Tactile iconicity: Signs rated for use with deaf-blind children. *Journal of the Association for Persons with Severe Handicaps, 8,* 26–38.

Hayes, L. P. (1993). Clarifying the role of classroom interpreters. *Perspectives in Education and Deafness, 11*(5), 8–10, 24.

Molnar, M. (1993). Whose words are they anyway? *Mainstream,* 18–22.

Moores, D. F. (1987). *Educating the deaf: Psychology, principles, and practices* (3rd ed.). Boston: Houghton Mifflin.

Quigley, S. P., & Paul, P. V. (1984). *Language and deafness.* Boston: College-Hill Press.

Raistrick, K. (1988). *Interpreting and transliterating for persons who are deaf-blind.* Springfield: Illinois Department of Rehabilitation Services, Division of Services for the Hearing Impaired.

Reed, C., Durlach, N., Braida, L., & Schultz, M. (1989). Analytic study of the Tadoma method: Effects of hand position on segmental speech perception. *Journal of Speech and Hearing Research, 32,* 921–929.

Sauerburger, D. (1993). *Independence without sight or sound: Suggestions for practitioners working with deaf-blind adults.* New York: American Foundation for the Blind.

Supalla, S. J. (1992). *The book of name signs: Naming in American Sign Language.* San Diego: Dawn Sign Press.

Vernon, M., & Andrews, J. A. (1990). *The psychology of deafness.* New York: Longman.

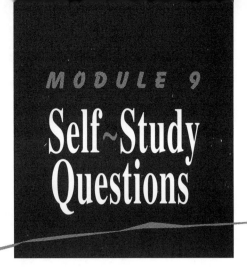

1. Which is not true of ASL?
    a. It is a visual-spatial language.
    b. It can be read tactilely by individuals who are deaf-blind.
    c. It has a written form that is iconic and is widely used.
    d. It has a grammar and syntax different from spoken English.

2. Tactile fingerspelling (select two)
    a. is not useful for receptive communication.
    b. allows a speaker's exact words to be spelled in spoken language order.
    c. can be used by individuals who lost their vision early and became deaf later.
    d. is helpful for deaf-blind people who have minimal language skills.

3. Interpreters for people who are deaf-blind may have primary responsibilities that include
    a. providing guiding service.
    b. conveying visual information and details.
    c. bringing braille paper or other supplies.
    d. assisting with obtaining transportation.
    e. a, b, and c are true.
    f. only a, b, and d are true.

4. The print-on-palm method
    a. does not require advanced literacy skills.
    b. is a written form of spoken language.
    c. is highly portable, since it uses only the hands.
    d. a and c are true.
    e. b and c are true.

*Answers to self-study questions for this module appear at the end of Unit 2.*

# Written Communication: Reading and Writing

JEANNE GLIDDEN PRICKETT

DIANE P. WORMSLEY

CONTRIBUTORS

**ANNE L. CORN**
*Low Vision Devices*

**CAROL CROOK**
*Braille and Students Who Are Deaf-Blind*

- *Appreciate the importance of braille*

- *Explore braille, print, or both as reading options*

- *Become familiar with a range of devices and equipment*

- *Fit available options to the student's current abilities and needs*

People who use spoken or signed language daily usually communicate with written language, too. Although some experiments are being done with written versions of American Sign Language (ASL), it does not have a written form. ASL users read and write in English.

Written languages are established when people agree on the general meanings of the characters they use to represent sounds and combine the characters into meaningful words and phrases. People can then write to exchange ideas and information even over great distances. They can also use written language to communicate with themselves—to write shopping lists, addresses or telephone numbers for later use, and other vital information. People with visual impairments may use a visual (print) form of written language, an auditory form, or a tactile form (braille or tactile converted print, using a device like an Optacon, described later in this module).

## BRAILLE AS A READING AND WRITING MEDIUM

The braille code is a system of various arrangements of raised (embossed) dots that can be felt by fingertips moving across them. The basic unit of braille is a rectangular structure called a cell, which is two dots wide (across) and three dots high (long). Both braille and print represent spoken language, but each braille cell does not necessarily have a one-to-one correspondence with each print symbol (Burns, 1991).

The braille code is actually several different codes. Literary braille, which is used most frequently to transcribe literature or ordinary written material, has three different grades or levels: Grade 1 (consisting of alphabet letters and a few punctuation symbols and numerals), Grade 2 (consisting of Grade 1 plus additional symbols to represent various combinations of words and letters and short forms for a specific group of common words), and Grade 3 (including all the contractions and forms of Grades 1 and 2 with additional shortenings of words). Other codes used are the Nemeth code (for mathematics and science notation), the music braille code, computer braille code (for representing ASCII symbols and computer programs), and foreign language braille. These variations of the basic braille code allow people to read and write in braille for a variety of purposes, just like those who read in print.

Braille is the primary (most often used) reading medium for people who are totally blind or visually impaired and find reading with a tactile medium more efficient than reading print with reduced vision (see Good Candidates for Learning Braille). Some visually impaired people use print and braille interchangeably because they like the flexibility of reading in two media, depending on their immediate needs.

People who learned to read in braille early in life tend to be proficient braille users later in life. Many of today's braille users learned to read in braille as children or young adults. People who are blind or visually impaired often supplement their use of braille with audiotapes, which may not be useful for people with hearing losses.

Braille provides direct access to reading material and allows a person to write and read back to himself or herself. It is also portable. Furthermore, with the sophisticated technology available today, braille can be translated with standard word-processing programs for easy communication with sighted individuals, including teachers who may not know braille.

*T H E O R Y*

*into*

*P R A C T I C E*

## GOOD CANDIDATES FOR LEARNING BRAILLE

A student who is deaf-blind may be a good candidate for learning to read in braille if he or she can:

• Share ideas or converse about simple topics, follow simple directions, and express what he or she wants.

• Think about and communicate not only immediate daily experiences, but nonroutine experiences—what others are doing, his or her family life, and what he or she plans to do in the future.

• Remember sequences.

• Make fine tactile discriminations. For example, Roberto likes to study the teacher's key ring with her home and school keys; he can identify by touch the keys for her car and for the classroom door, and he likes to be allowed to lock the door at night.

• Handle and work with items or materials by touch in an organized fashion, because braille must be followed from left to right and top to bottom.

• Do detailed work and pay attention for prolonged periods. Learning to read requires

Determining if a child will be taught to read and write in braille, in print, or in both has become more difficult in the past two decades for students who are visually impaired. (For students who are totally blind, the decisions are usually clear [Spungin, 1990].) With the advent of synthetic speech output and the enlargement of print on photocopiers, computer screens, and large or small closed-circuit television (CCTV) sets, visually impaired persons can now read in print and thus have access to a wider variety of reading material than is available in braille or on audiotapes (Corn & Ryser, 1989; Jose, 1983).

Some teachers recommend print reading if a child is able to see and perceive, for example, five-inch-high letters on a CCTV. However, they may not consider such factors as portability, fatigue, speed, and the ability to read back handwritten material. The most appropriate reading medium must be carefully considered by members of the educational planning team using extensive background information and support from experts, including the guidance of teachers who understand visual impairments (Caton, 1991; Koenig & Holbrook, 1989, 1991; Mangold & Mangold, 1989).

## SELECTION OF A STUDENT'S READING MEDIA

Several factors should be considered in determining a student's reading media. In addition, periodic evaluation of the appropriateness of the choice of reading and writing media should be performed, because what is most effective for a student may change. Different reading and writing media may also be learned and used for different purposes. Factors to consider include the following:

- the efficiency with which the student gains information overall from the senses
- the student's tactile efficiency
- the student's visual efficiency
- the stability of the student's visual ability
- the stability of the student's auditory ability
- the types of learning media the student uses or can use to perform various tasks
- the student's comprehension using various media
- the student's stamina in using various media

- the student's potential ability to communicate accurately and effectively using various media

- the student's observed preference for exploring the environment

- the portability of reading media as they relate to the performance of various tasks

- the student's potential achievable reading rates using various media

- the student's potential accuracy using various media

- the student's lifelong planning, both personal and vocational (Koenig & Holbrook, 1989, 1993; Mangold & Mangold, 1989).

## BRAILLE AND STUDENTS WHO ARE DEAF-BLIND

Any deaf-blind student who cannot use print and who can acquire the skills of reading and writing should learn to read in braille. How does teaching braille to students who are deaf-blind differ from teaching braille to students who are blind? In general, the major difference is the students' knowledge of language. That is, by the time many children who are blind begin to learn to read, usually in the primary grades, they are fluent in language. They have to learn the skill of reading and the system of braille, but they understand the meaning of the language that they hear and speak. Many students who are deaf-blind may not yet be fluent in language because they have not heard it, and thus they learn language at the same time that they learn reading skills. Eventually, they will be able to learn new language skills through reading.

This difference affects the materials that can be used for teaching. There is no standard beginning reading series, whether transcribed from print to braille or planned especially for teaching reading in braille, that can easily be used with deaf-blind students. The level of language is often too abstract and the children's experiences, on which the development of language, and hence of reading, depends, are often more limited than are those of children who are blind. Therefore, it is preferable for classroom teachers to make their own brailled materials, fitting them to a student's level of language and information, vocabulary, and interests (see Obtaining Educational Materials in Braille for more information).

## OBTAINING EDUCATIONAL MATERIALS IN BRAILLE

Teachers working with deaf-blind students may need to obtain their students' textbooks or other educational materials in braille. Although this is primarily the responsibility of the teacher of visually impaired students who is part of the transdisciplinary team, it is helpful to be aware of the resources that exist for obtaining brailled materials for students. Primary among these are

• Local private agencies that provide services to persons who are blind, which often operate braille presses and provide brailling services to school districts in their communities.

• Local volunteer groups, many of which are affiliated with community organizations like synagogues and churches.

• Several large national brailling services, which accept orders for braille production, as well as small independent businesses producing brailled materials.

It is important to know the amount of time a brailling service requires to fill an order for brailling and to be aware that not all brailling services can handle specialty brailling requests, such as producing music braille, foreign language braille, or braille for advanced science and mathematics. Local state and private agencies for blind persons are likely to maintain resource lists of the individual braille producers in their local communities. In addition, the *Directory of Services for Blind and Visually Impaired Persons*

*in the United States and Canada* (1993) lists local, state, and national producers of braille and other media.

Computer software that converts information from print to braille is relatively inexpensive and readily available. To produce braille using a personal computer, however, it is necessary to have a compatible braille printer. The use of braille conversion software packages enables school district personnel, including school secretaries and teachers' aides, to create simple braille documents in-house. Many large school districts and instructional materials centers (IMCs) are valuable resources for obtaining assistance (see Modules 1 and 5). ■

When reading in braille is taught to a child who is blind and can hear spoken language, the teacher can talk about the dots, their positions in each cell, and the letters each combination represents, with corresponding sounds. For students who are deaf-blind, all these instructional strategies must be altered. Instead, it is more effective to have the children memorize the braille shapes within words they know. For example, Roberto can read the word *egg* because its braille equivalent is recognizable and short, making it easier to read. He knows the sign for "egg" and loves to eat eggs.

So, the word is meaningful for him and he has easily memorized the cell shapes of "e" and "g."

Words written in braille are made up of letters that correspond to sounds and special braille condensed characters that represent parts of words, several letters together, or combinations of sounds. In either case, the signs of ASL or any sign system do not necessarily relate to sound-based written words. Children who fingerspell have an advantage in learning to read, even if they fingerspell only a little. It is easier to teach a word by its letters than by an entire shape (see also How to Teach Reading in Braille).

## PREREADING DEVELOPMENT

With a sighted child, we promote the use of vision every day. "Look here," we say, or "See the helicopter!" We constantly ask the child to look at, recognize, identify, search for, name, and admire objects in

**HELP at a GLANCE**

## HOW TO TEACH READING IN BRAILLE

The following suggestions are useful in teaching braille to students who are deaf-blind:

● Do braille readiness activities. Have the student identify small objects and tactile patterns on paper. The student can place items in rows from left to right. In addition, the student can copy a sequence of fingerspelled letters, followed by the sign, for example, "cat, C-A-T, cat." Some students enjoy describing an experience like a trip to a farm, with what happened

first, second, and so on. This kind of language-experience story also helps children develop the sense of sequence needed for reading.

● Have the student match braille letters and find the same letters in a row or in different rows. This exercise is similar to a standard reading-readiness exercise.

● Label objects in the student's environment, especially when he or she has learned some braille letters and words.

● When you introduce braille, think braille, not print. Easy and difficult letters in braille are different from those in print. For example, *a, b, c, g, k, l,* and *x* are easy to discriminate in braille, but *t, n, y,* and *j* are difficult. Long spaces between words can cause the student to lose his or her place. To understand better what is difficult and what is easy to read, you can practice reading in braille tactilely with your eyes closed. ■

the visual environment. We need to make an even greater effort to involve a child with visual and hearing impairments in his or her environment because the child does not have easy access to the total environment.

Reading is based on language, and language is based on concepts developed from interaction with people and the environment. Part of that interaction is spoken language to share ideas about the environment and to name objects, people, and abstract concepts like feelings. Module 7 and Unit 1 pointed out the importance of fostering and promoting interaction with the environment that will form the basis for the development of language and reading skills, especially for children who do not have complete access to visual and auditory information.

Infants and toddlers who have visual and hearing impairments need to be encouraged to explore the close environment and should be provided with motivating objects to examine. Once a child has found objects he or she needs to learn how to explore them tactilely. Infants and toddlers with visual impairments need help in learning how to touch objects so they get the most and best information about the objects (Barraga, 1986). Several of the skills learned through this process are important for preparing to read and write in braille:

- developing a light touch, while reaching out for as much of the object as possible, so all features can be experienced tactilely

- moving one's hands on an object to perceive all the accessible features tactilely (keeping the hands still will not allow a child to feel what is under them adequately)

- using the fingertips to get the finest details (basic shapes can be sensed through contact with the palms, but the fingertips permit the best discrimination of fine details)

- manipulating the object to make it "do" something, for example, turning a crank to make a jack-in-the-box pop up.

Written forms of communication are learned only after much exposure to the environment and to language (signed or spoken) that explains environmental concepts. Reading and writing also depend on an individual's cognitive ability. Individuals with cognitive impairments may have difficulty reading and writing more than the most basic information, even if they see and hear perfectly. Individuals who are deaf-blind and have cognitive impairments may also not read and write proficiently in braille. Using braille instead of print will not resolve the challenges of instructional design for such children.

A child who has average to above-average cognitive ability and combined visual and hearing impairments still faces significant obstacles to getting environmental information in an understandable form for learning concepts that are the basis for language and reading. To read and write competently, such children should be helped to develop a solid understanding of both concepts and the language that labels those concepts (see Helping a Child to Move Toward Reading and Writing).

## BRAILLE PRODUCTION

### Ways to Read and Write in Braille

**Slate and Stylus.** Of the many instruments that have been developed for writing braille, the most inexpensive and portable is the combination of slate and stylus. Slates come in various sizes, but

*THEORY into PRACTICE*

## HELPING A CHILD TO MOVE TOWARD READING AND WRITING

The following are some basic steps that teachers and parents can take to enable a child who is deaf-blind to move from exploring the environment to reading and writing:

● Help the child to develop an interest in and awareness of the environment.

● Help the child to recognize familiar things in the environment.

● Help the child to learn the names (signed or spoken word) of objects in the environment and then move to actions.

● Provide opportunities for the child to communicate about activities that occur at home and in the community.

● Provide exposure to appropriate written language (in print or in braille, or both).

● Provide story-time activities.

● Provide opportunities to "write" or "draw" in various ways.

● Provide a calendar or time charts that help the child predict sequences of events during the day, week, month, and year.

● Repeat these steps over and over. ■

all slates have two hinged parts. Braille paper is placed between the hinged parts for writing. The top part of the slate has a series of cutout sections, each the size of a braille cell. For each cell cutout, the bottom part of the slate has a corresponding set of six recessed spaces that correspond to the dots in the braille cell. The written braille dots are actually produced on the underside of the paper from right to left and reversed by pushing the stylus into the paper, which goes into the recessed spaces behind it. The writer must take the paper out of the slate and turn it over to read what has been written. The slate and stylus can be compared to the paper and pencil, and their functions are basically the same. Slate-and-stylus notes are immediately useful, and the tools can be used to produce moderate-sized braille documents, including class notes. Skilled slate-and-stylus users can produce brailled notes virtually as quickly as others can produce paper-and-pencil notes.

**Tape Labeler.** Another simple low-tech device for producing braille is the tape labeler, which permits the user to braille on regular plastic labeling tape for labeling items around the home or classroom. Because of the nature of labeling tape and the structure of the label-making tool, this device can be used only for labeling—not for the production of a lengthy braille document.

**Braillewriter.** The braillewriter is another piece of equipment that is frequently used to produce braille. The most well-known and widely used braillewriter, the Perkins Brailler, has been available for over 40 years and is produced by the Howe Press of the Perkins School for the Blind, in Watertown, Massachusetts. The Perkins Brailler is nonelectronic; other producers manufacture both nonelectronic and electronic mechanical braillewriters similar to it. The six main keys on most braillewriters correspond to the dots in the braille cell. Other features for producing braille include a space bar, return key, line advancer, and paper holder, much like on a typewriter. Braille is produced so the dots can be read while the paper is still in the machine, providing immediate feedback for beginning writers.

The many new high-tech braillewriters or notetakers have several common characteristics: They are lightweight and portable and use keyboards similar to the six-key configuration of the Perkins Brailler. These, along with personal computers having the necessary software and add-ons, can store information in various formats and can convert brailled input into several outputs, including hard-copy braille, speech, print, or word-processing files that can be heard using synthetic speech. Standard computer keyboards are assigned keys to coincide with the brailler. A computer print display can be translated into a braille display, and an entire computer file of information can be translated into hard-copy braille using appropriate translation software with a specially designed braille embosser. Learning how to work with each of the various pieces of technology takes time and usually requires a working knowledge of braille.

The type of equipment or device that someone uses to write in braille depends on the intended use of the written material and other situational factors. For example, when Sue wants to label an audiotape, she may use a slate designed specifically for that purpose. When Carlos labels tools or cans of food, he may use a tape labeler, while Stanislaus writes a recipe in braille on a note card using either a braillewriter or a slate and stylus. Bryan writes reports on a portable electronic braille notetaker; however, Akfir uses a personal computer and a specific software program and produces hard copy for himself on a braille embosser that is attached to his computer, as well as hard copy for his teacher in print on a regular printer. The more sophisticated the need, the more likely that high technology will be used.

A sighted child learns to read and then to write by learning the proper way to hold a pencil, the proper position for the paper, and the proper configuration of the letters as he or she has read them. Similarly, a braille reader learns to read in braille and then learns the techniques of writing braille with a variety of basic tools before progressing to the more creative aspects of writing and the use of sophisticated technology.

## Computerized Braille Production

As was already described, word-processing programs can be adapted to either print or braille embossing, allowing individuals who read in braille to prepare and check their work on a standard word-processing system and share it with people who read print. In addition, teachers can prepare students' work on disk with a standard word-processing system and can translate the work into braille easily with translation software and braille-embossing equipment. Adaptive computer equipment may use standard keyboards with touch-typing and word-processing software or adapted keyboard-input devices and software, such as a braille input device. Output devices may also be adaptive or standard. For example, a visually impaired person may use a standard monitor but may use a software conversion package to enlarge the image on the screen or a refreshable braille monitor device that is interfaced with the computer (for more information, see Where to Learn More about Computer Adaptations).

### Refreshable Braille

A refreshable braille display is like a computer monitor display in print in which the display characters change as new information is added. That is, the braille characters appear as words on a computer display do, but only one line at a time instead of many lines. The reader then can press the appropriate control to bring up the next row or the last row of braille cells in the order in which they were written, just as a print reader "scrolls" up or down a computer monitor display.

The computer attachment that produces braille characters does it with rounded "pins" that are raised according to the braille configuration that is represented. Six pins are available for each cell, just like a standard braille cell, and the mechanical portions of the device allow the different combinations to be raised as appropriate, then to be cleared, and new combinations to be raised. A display like this has a multicell configuration, so people who read in braille can read with a natural flow across multiple characters, which makes it easier to process the tactile information. With such a device, the deaf-blind person who reads in braille can receive information from

## HELP at a GLANCE

## WHERE TO LEARN MORE ABOUT COMPUTER ADAPTATIONS

To learn more about computer adaptations that are available, contact your state department of education, which may have vision consultation services; a school for students who are blind or visually impaired; or your state or private vocational rehabilitation network.

Technological adaptations for individuals with visual or auditory disabilities, including deaf-blindness, are evolving rapidly. These resource agencies can help you get the most up-to-date information about the technology your students can use. (See the

*Directory of Services for Blind and Visually Impaired Persons in the United States and Canada* [1993] for listings of these agencies.) ■

**FIGURE 10-1:**

**Examples of Serif and Sans Serif Type**

| TYPE | SIZE | SAMPLE |
|------|------|--------|
| SERIF | 4 | The quick brown fox jumps over the lazy dog. |
| SERIF | 6 | The quick brown fox jumps over the lazy dog. |
| SERIF | 8 | The quick brown fox jumps over the lazy dog. |
| SERIF | 10 | The quick brown fox jumps over the lazy dog. |
| SERIF | 12 | The quick brown fox jumps over the lazy dog. |
| SERIF | 14 | The quick brown fox jumps over the lazy dog. |
| SERIF | 16 | The quick brown fox jumps over the lazy dog. |
| SERIF | 18 | The quick brown fox jumps over the lazy dog. |
| SANS SERIF | 12 | The quick brown fox jumps over the lazy dog. |
| SANS SERIF | 24 | The quick brown fox jumps |

or communicate with people who do not sign or fingerspell well. Systems that use refreshable braille outputs are described later in this module.

# PRINT AND LARGE PRINT

Print is defined by its size and style. Regular print uses many different typefaces (styles) and comes in sizes that enable the normal reader to read about 14 inches away from the page. Large print is generally considered to be from 14 point to 24 point (see Figure 10-1). The two basic type styles are serif (with curls and flourishes on letters) and sans serif—literally "without serifs." Large-print readers often have eye conditions that prevent the use of central vision but allow them to use peripheral vision. Since the loss of central vision blocks out fine visual acuity used for activities such as reading and sewing, for them print letters need to be large enough for the effective use of peripheral vision.

When people think of large print, they often think of huge books that contain large-print material. This is only one way to produce large print for someone to read. Today's technology allows for computer production with scalable fonts (changeable typefaces), specialized software that produces large print on computer displays, high-quality photocopy equipment that allows for various enlargements, CCTVs that magnify regular print and enlarge it for use with a television screen, and many optical devices that magnify regular print. The simplest large-print adaptation is to use a felt-tip marker to hand-print large print for one's own use or for others.

It is important to remember that some individuals who are deaf-blind will read regular print with no adaptations. For example, individuals with Usher syndrome may retain good central vision into adulthood, and although peripheral vision losses may prevent or limit such activities as driving, vision for reading small print may be satisfactory. When regular print can be used functionally for reading, a person who is deaf-blind will not need large-print adaptations, and more materials will be readily accessible. Some students, however, will need to rely on the use of low vision devices, which include eyeglasses, magnifiers, telescopes, CCTVs, and a variety of other aids, for reading print.

# LOW VISION DEVICES

Low vision is a term that in general refers to a vision loss that is severe enough to interfere with the ability to perform everyday tasks or activities and that cannot be corrected to normal by conventional eyeglasses or contact lenses. However, an individual with low vision has enough vision to use this sense as a primary channel for learning. A wide variety of devices are available to help people with low vision make the maximum use of the vision that they have. These devices are prescribed by low vision specialists, who are eye care providers like ophthalmologists or optometrists who have undergone specialized training to help people make the best use of their sight.

**Eyeglasses and Contact Lenses.** Eyeglasses and contact lenses are prescribed to correct refractive errors such as nearsightedness, farsightedness, and astigmatism and to magnify an image for those with visual field problems or other causes of low visual acuity. Prisms may also be added to a prescription for eyeglasses to "expand" a visual field (Jose, 1983).

Some people may not benefit from the use of eyeglasses because their visual disabilities will not be helped by the bending of

light, which is the function of eyeglasses. A child or adult who seems to function at a lower cognitive level than his or her same-age peers may actually have a vision loss and should be evaluated by an eye specialist. Active cooperation is not needed for an appropriate prescription to be given, even to young children and individuals who cannot respond in standard ways for testing. Therefore, students who are multiply disabled and may not yet have a reliable expressive communication system can still be assessed for visual capabilities.

The thickness of eyeglasses does not indicate how well a person can see with them. Since eyeglasses are prescribed from clinical measurements, getting "stronger eyeglasses" will not necessarily improve vision. Information should be obtained on how the eyeglasses will help the person and whether they should be worn for seeing only at near point, only at a distance, or all the time. Because it is sometimes difficult for someone to become accustomed to wearing eyeglasses, preparatory experiences may be needed.

**Optical Devices.** Optical devices or aids use lenses that are not usually found in a standard pair of eyeglasses or contact lenses. These devices are used to magnify, reduce, or otherwise change the shape or location of an image on the retina. They may be held in the hand, rest on a base or stand, or be placed in a pair of eyeglasses. They are made for seeing at near point or, with a combination of lens-

▲ *Closed-circuit televisions enlarge printed material electronically and can be adjusted to change the size of the print and foreground and background contrast.*

es to form a telescope, to enlarge images seen from a distance. At times, reversed telescopes, which make objects appear smaller, are used to "expand" the visual field by bringing additional information into the usable visual field.

Optical devices may also include mirrors, prisms, and electronics. A CCTV, for example, electronically enlarges print, colored pictures, or flat objects onto a television monitor. It can also change polarity, creating a white print on a dark background, or alter the colors of the foreground and background. CCTVs, mirror magnifiers, and some stand magnifiers are used for writing as well as reading and viewing (Corn & Ryser, 1989).

Many individuals with multiple disabilities, especially those who are deaf-blind, may benefit from optical devices. When enlarging objects or bringing objects closer or moving them farther away seems to improve visual functioning, a referral should be made for a low vision clinical evaluation, whose purpose typically is to find ways to optimize the use of someone's remaining vision. Optical devices may also enhance a person's awareness of objects in his or her environment. Follow-up instruction is necessary to help the person learn to use these devices and to do so efficiently.

**Nonoptical Adaptations.** Alone or in conjunction with optical devices, nonoptical devices or aids may be used to enhance visual functioning. The use of colored tape on dials, bold-line paper, enlarged telephone buttons, or additional sources of lighting, for example, can help a person begin to use vision functionally or perform a task more comfortably.

**Light-Absorptive Lenses.** Sometimes specially tinted eyeglasses or contact lenses are given to children or adults who have photophobia (light sensitivity) or impairments related to the retina of the eye. These lenses may appear to be much darker than those purchased in retail stores or contain a special color that enhances contrast. Such eyeglasses may have side and top shields to reduce the amount of light that is coming from above or from the sides of the frames. They can be used both indoors and outdoors, but always in accordance with the recommendation and safety principles outlined by an eye specialist.

Low vision aids and adaptations can be used for a variety of activities. Some are useful for safe and efficient travel, whereas others can help individuals read in regular or large print or perform other activities that require fine visual discrimination, such as sewing. The types of aids and adaptations described here are a few of those that are available; a low vision specialist can help evaluate a student and recommend specific aids and adaptations that the student may need.

# OTHER FORMS OF WRITTEN LANGUAGE

Most people use written information for daily receptive communication and sometimes for expressive communication. Written information includes braille and print that may be displayed in a number of formats. For example, some individuals who are deaf-blind receive information at meetings from an interpreter or speaker who types into a Teletype for the Deaf (TTY) or Telecommunications (or Telephone) Device for the Deaf (TDD) that is attached to an enlarged-print display or a refreshable braille display. These adaptations allow some users fuller participation in community activities and are explained in more depth in the following sections.

## ELECTRONIC ASSISTIVE DEVICES

A TTY/TDD is a specially designed communication system for deaf people that consists either of a separate device with an integrated modem and keyboard into which a telephone handset can be placed or special computer software with a modem that will allow a standard computer to be used for real-time (live) communication by telephone. To use this system, both communicators must have the equipment at their respective telephones and must be able to read and write. As a message is typed on the keyboard, the TTY/TDD produces print with mechanical signals that are translated by the device or special computer program into electronic signals. The electronic signals go directly into the telephone line for transmission to the other person's equipment and get converted into print symbols at the other end.

People who cannot hear voices on the telephone but who can read can communicate by telephone with others using this equipment. TTY/TDD equipment is being used more widely in businesses and public services to accommodate consumers who are deaf and deaf-blind.

## USING A TTY/TDD

**To Answer a TTY/TDD**

**1.** Answer the telephone (with voice) and listen, or proceed to Step 3.

**2.** Decide if it is a TTY/TDD call (it will sound "dead" or beep, similar to a fax machine).

**3.** Place the telephone handset into the "modem" rubber cups of the TTY/TDD with the cord to the left side (most models will show the correct position).

**4.** Turn the power on (the on-off switch is usually on top).

**5.** Type normally and briefly: "Hello. This is _____ (agency or person). May I help you QQ GA" (QQ equals ? and GA equals Go Ahead).

**6.** Let the caller respond. Wait for his or her full response with "GA." If there is no response, you know it was not a TTY/TDD call.

**7.** When the caller types "GA," type your answer to the question, give the information that is requested, or respond appropriately.

**8.** Type "GA" occasionally and let the person take a turn, to check if she or he understands you.

**9.** Proceed as if you are talking back and forth by voice. "Hold" or "Pls hd" both mean that the person talking must do something and the other person should hold on (that is, do not start to type yet).

**10.** After you type "thank you" or a similar closing remark, close with "GA and SK" or just "SK" (SK equals Stop Keying).

**11.** Wait for "GA and SK" or just "SK."

**12.** Add a final "SKSK."

**13.** Hang up, turn off the TTY/TDD, and replace the handset on the telephone.

**To Make a TTY/TDD Call**

**1.** Dial the number. (Listen for an answer.) Place the telephone handset into the "modem" rubber cups of the TTY/TDD with the cord to the left side (most models will show the correct position). You may also begin a call simply by placing the telephone handset into the modem, dialing, and waiting until the person answers.

**2.** When the person answering greets you and types "GA," type your response.

**3.** To let the person talk again, type "GA," so he or she will know to take a turn.

**4.** Proceed as if you are talking back and forth by voice. Always wait for "GA" before you type.

**5.** After you type "thank you" or some similar closing remark, close with "GA and SK" or just "SK."

**6.** Wait for "GA and SK" or just "SK."

**7.** Add a final "SKSK."

**8.** Hang up and turn off the TTY/TDD.

**Tips**

**1.** Be sure the power is adequate; plug in the rechargeable TTY/TDD if necessary, even when you are using it.

*(continued)*

## HELP *at a* GLANCE

### USING A TTY/TDD *(Continued)*

**2.** If you get only numbers and figures (such as "^(7397(6934%$$8"), hit the space bar fast three times, even when the caller is still typing.

**3.** Type "Please repeat; I do not read you."

**4.** Be sure to allow at least 10 rings for the person answering to get to the phone and get set up, especially when you are communicating with a person by TeleBraille.

**5.** Take your turn in short segments. Do not "talk" a long time before giving the other person a "GA," since it is difficult to break in to ask for information or comment.

**6.** If you reach a TTY/TDD answering machine, follow the directions and leave a message. This machine is very similar to a voice-answering machine.

**7.** If all else fails, try to sign off ("SKSK") and just hang up. If you think there is a transmission problem (some line connections are weak, the same as with voice calls), tell the person as quickly as possible, hang up, and call back. ■

The TeleBraille is a device that allows a braille reader to use a typical telephone communication device that deaf individuals use, but with braille output. It incorporates a TTY/TDD and interfaces with it; special hardware and software convert the refreshable print symbols of the TTY/TDD to refreshable braille symbols. A TeleBraille can be used for communication either on the telephone or face to face.

Although the TTY/TDD components are not easily portable, these electronic devices allow a deaf-blind person another option for clear communication in some situations (see Using a TTY/TDD). The most commonly used device of this type is the TeleBraille. Other systems that use similar attachments are more sophisticated typical computer systems with braille output attachments. (For information on these and other devices, see the Resources section.) A full-size computer is less portable than is a TTY/TDD with a TeleBraille attachment or a portable or laptop computer with a braille display.

People with low vision also can use TTY/TDD equipment to receive information, both on the telephone and from another individual face to face. Printed communication on a display for a person who is visually impaired is larger than it is on a regular TTY/TDD display.

The standard typing keyboard is also used for input with this device.

Either a TTY/TDD with a large-print display (for visually impaired people) or a TeleBraille with braille display can be used for everyday communication or in interpreting situations. The speaker or interpreter types, and the person who is deaf-blind reads; when the person who is deaf-blind responds, he or she may choose to speak, sign, or type on the TTY/TDD-TeleBraille.

## OTHER DEVICES

A variety of other devices provide output in various forms that can be "read" tactilely. The Teletouch, for example, is similar to a regular manual typewriter, with a standard keyboard for input. The speaker types each letter while the deaf-blind receiver reads from a single-cell braille output opposite the keyboard. This device is portable. The single-cell output provides only limited information and is "static" (does not allow for movement of the fingertip over several cells of brailled information for smooth tactile processing), so the person who reads in braille does not have a natural reading flow that would be available with multicell displays. Teletouch is used primarily in receptive communication, with some other form of expressive communication like speech. An advantage of Teletouch, like TeleBraille and TTY/TDD devices, is that inexperienced users can communicate with deaf-blind individuals simply by typing on the standard keyboard with print keys.

An alphabet card or device can be formal or informal. It can be prepared by an individual who is deaf-blind or purchased from specialized service agencies. The card or device is usually pocket size and set up in rows of characters: large print, print with braille, or raised print that is both touched and seen. In most cases, the person who is deaf-blind uses such a device to point to the letters for the words he or she wants to say, in English order. The sighted-hearing receiver who reads print can then watch the letters that have been

▲ *Devices like the TeleBraille use technology to enable deaf-blind students to converse with others.*

selected and "assemble" the words mentally. When the sighted-hearing individual responds, he or she can take the deaf-blind person's index finger and guide it to either the appropriate print or braille letters in the same way. This card or device is portable and can support communication in community settings. It can be used receptively or expressively.

The Optacon is a high-tech device that converts optical symbols and characters to tactile forms. It is used to read print tactilely without requiring conversion to braille. Although the availability of devices and computer hardware and software using synthetic speech has reduced the use of the Optacon by many visually impaired persons, it remains an option for people who are unable to use synthetic speech.

▲ *Alphabet cards provide students with another effective means of interacting. This one has a preprinted information card with directions to the reader for using it.*

Print symbols can be scanned using the Optacon's miniature hand-held scanning camera, which transmits the signals into the converter device to be further converted into mechanical information and finally into vibrating tactile information. This final form is produced on small rounded "pins" that are activated according to the symbol that is scanned, vibrating in the symbol's shape. These vibrating symbols can then be read through touch.

The Optacon provides access to a wide range of printed materials, such as ingredients in a box on a supermarket shelf or one's personal mail. An Optacon user can attain more independence for reading without requiring someone to help him or her, waiting for a braille conversion of materials, or waiting for someone to record the material for listening.

This device is relatively compact and portable, making it useful for everyday tasks. Studies suggest, however, that users must have fairly advanced abilities, be highly motivated, and have considerable training and practice to use the Optacon successfully (Barraga, 1986). The privacy factor is a compelling motivator for many individuals. Using the Optacon allows a person who is blind or deaf-blind immediate access to personal mail that would be uncomfortable to share with a reader. Thus, the Optacon can be an important tool for some people who are blind or deaf-blind to get information from print sources rapidly and privately.

Optical character recognition (OCR) systems also employ the principle of scanning material and converting it into forms that are discernible to people with sensory losses. In these systems, a high-tech print scanner interfaces with a computer and uses a camera to scan a page of printed material—even pictures—which is then converted into computer files. (These systems do not convert pictures into spoken or braille output.) Thus, much printed material can be input to a computer quickly, without requiring a person to spend a great deal of time typing in the information. Devices like the original Kurzweil Reading Machine and similar machines have provided blind and deaf-blind individuals access to printed materials for many years, using a scanning mechanism to "read" the print and convert it to voice output. Many OCR systems are similar in purpose, but convert the scanned material for use as computer information and files. They can also be used to scan materials to present large print on CCTVs.

Scanned material that has been converted to computer files can be translated into braille "hard copy"; that is, it can be embossed onto braille paper by a high-speed embosser using the computer file and braille translation software. Also, computer files of scanned material can be read in refreshable braille or with voice-output computer devices.

Using a scanner to read material is similar to using an Optacon in that it affords immediate access to material and privacy for the user, who does not have to rely on another person to read the documents. One drawback of scanning equipment is the high cost, and another is that poor-quality printed materials do not scan perfectly, and the computer files that are generated may have strange characters or combinations that do not look like words. In addition, scanners will not translate pictures or graphic representations. Still, OCR systems provide users who are blind or deaf-blind with one more way to gain access to the same kinds of information that readers without disabilities obtain readily.

Today, through the use of a wide range of devices and equipment, deaf-blind students have a great number of options to help them gain access to information and develop their reading and writing skills. Like the selection of the most appropriate communication methods for a child, the choices regarding effective devices and equipment depend on individual abilities and needs. The two modules that follow focus on how to assess these factors and make decisions regarding how best to help a student develop and learn.

# *REFERENCES*

*Directory of services for blind and visually impaired persons in the United States and Canada* (24th ed.). (1993). New York: American Foundation for the Blind.

Barraga, N. C. (1986). Sensory perceptual development. In G. T. Scholl (Ed.), *Foundations of education for blind and visually handicapped children and youth: Theory and practice* (pp. 83–98). New York: American Foundation for the Blind.

Burns, M. F. (1991). *The Burns braille transcription dictionary*. New York: American Foundation for the Blind.

Caton, H. (Ed.). (1991). *Print and braille literacy*. Louisville, KY: American Printing House for the Blind.

Corn, A., & Ryser, G. (1989). Access to print for students with low vision. *Journal of Visual Impairment & Blindness, 83*, 340–349.

Jose, R. (1983). *Understanding low vision*. New York: American Foundation for the Blind.

Koenig, A. J., & Holbrook, M. C. (1989). Determining the reading medium for students with visual impairments: A diagnostic teaching approach. *Journal of Visual Impairment & Blindness, 83*, 296–302.

Koenig, A. J., & Holbrook, M. C. (1991). Determining the medium for visually impaired students via diagnostic teaching. *Journal of Visual Impairment & Blindness, 85*, 61–68.

Koenig, A. J., & Holbrook, M. C. (1993). *Learning media assessment of students with visual impairments: A resource guide for teachers*. Austin: Texas School for the Blind and Visually Impaired.

Mangold, S., & Mangold, P. (1989). Selecting the most appropriate primary learning medium for students with functional vision. *Journal of Visual Impairment & Blindness, 83*, 294–296.

Spungin, S. J. (1990). *Braille literacy*. New York: American Foundation for the Blind.

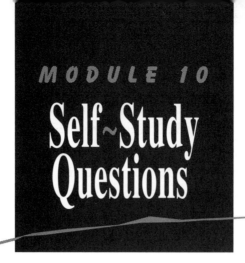

1. Which of the following is *not* a true statement about braille?
   a. It provides direct access to reading material for persons who are deaf-blind.
   b. A braille slate and stylus is comparable to a pad and pencil.
   c. Braille should be taught only if all other options fail.
   d. Braille can be produced by persons who are not familiar with the braille code providing they have access to the necessary computer hardware and software.

2. The major difference between teaching braille to students who are deaf-blind and those who are blind is
   a. the students' knowledge of language.
   b. the students' tactile sensitivity.
   c. the students' motivation.
   d. the students' fine motor skills.

3. Which of the following are optical devices used to enhance visual ability and functioning?
   a. Bold-line paper, felt-tip pens, and adjustable lighting fixtures.
   b. TeleBraille, TTY, and TDD.
   c. Prisms, magnifiers, and closed-circuit televisions.

*Answers to self-study questions for this module appear at the end of Unit 2.*

# Assessment of Communication Skills

HARVEY H. MAR

- *Make assessment an ongoing process*

- *Use an ecological approach*

- *Learn about appropriate assessment tools*

- *Work with input from all team members*

ssessment is at the heart of educating any child. Without comprehensive information on the abilities and needs of a student, how can one plan an educational program that provides maximum benefit? But who should conduct an assessment, and how should the assessment be done? What techniques and tests should be used? How long should an assessment take? These are among the many issues addressed in this module. Although the questions are basic, the answers are not simple, clear, or even the same for all assessments. However, evaluators can be consistent in their approach to the assessment of communication in students who are deaf-blind and can use certain strategies for designing evaluations to ensure that they yield accurate, relevant, and useful information.

This discussion uses the broad definition of communication presented in Module 6 to include a wide range of behaviors, such as facial expressions, vocalizations, physical reactions, touch, and gestures, in addition to signs, speech, and other formal means of receptive and expressive language. Similarly, the concept of assessment that is used here is broad. It includes informal day-to-day observations of students in various settings, periodic and semiformal reviews of students' progress, and formal testing procedures. Such a broad concept reinforces the idea that, in various degrees, any individual who is involved with the learner—parent, teacher, classroom assistant, therapist, or peer—may have direct or indirect roles and responsibilities in assessing his or her communication skills.

This module reviews the major approaches to the assessment of communication of individuals who are deaf-blind and have other severe disabilities, describes the methods of and tools for assessing communication, discusses the decision-making strategies that will help evaluators select the methods and tools of assessment that may be most appropriate for a given student, and offers some guidelines for interpreting and presenting the results of the assessment. It also describes the many important roles that educators may play in assessing communication and considers how information obtained from an evaluation is integrated into the educational plan. One of the more difficult aspects of evaluation is to translate the findings into interventions that are natural, consistent, appropriate, meaningful, and family and community oriented. Throughout the module, the principles and basic concepts outlined in the section that follows will be emphasized as desirable characteristics of assessment.

# BASIC CONCEPTS OF ASSESSMENT

## ASSESSMENTS SHOULD BE INTERDISCIPLINARY

The assessment of communication is a shared responsibility of educators, other service providers, and family members, and input from all these individuals is essential. Traditionally, communication assessments have been conducted by speech and language specialists. However, for persons who are deaf-blind, they must be perceived more broadly as an interdisciplinary task because issues of communication are so often inseparable from physical, cognitive, behavioral, social, emotional, and health issues. When a student's communication behaviors include aggressive or undesired actions, for example, the objectives of training and of psychological intervention are identical: to teach desired behaviors for communication.

Adopting an interdisciplinary perspective also means that the implications of findings from other fields, such as psychology, physical therapy, and medicine, must be considered and that assessments are planned to be clearly meaningful and directly relevant to the various disciplines. The term *transdisciplinary* is often used to describe this kind of exchange. Skills that are typically the focus of other disciplines can be integral to communication. The reports of occupational and physical therapists, for instance, provide insights into the individual's ability to use signs or gestures or to use augmentative communication devices (picture boards or switch-activated objects) to aid communication. The reports of vision and hearing specialists and health care professionals may contain information related to changes in a person's social behaviors or to strategies for enhancing receptive communication. Although the disciplines differ in their perspectives, techniques, and terminology, each contributes to the overall information on the student's communication that the assessment can obtain. The failure to link the goals of assessment directly to the interventions of others can lead to results that have little or no programmatic significance or, worse, to poorly integrated Individualized Education Programs (IEPs) with contradicting recommendations and practices.

Evaluators who have no or few professionals with whom to collaborate may feel overwhelmed and think that they have to perform all the functions of an interdisciplinary team. However, in such situations, they perform the same procedures and have the same goals.

What changes is the degree to which they must coordinate the various parts of the assessment process. Thus, in the absence of an interdisciplinary team, an evaluator may need to perform a number of important tasks, including these: serve as the link between family members and educators; contact all the student's educators and service providers, as well as representatives of local, state, or national agencies that may provide useful information or support; and ensure that paperwork is up to date to support needed services and resources.

## ASSESSMENTS SHOULD BE ONGOING

Assessment is ongoing. It is a continuous endeavor. It not only documents the repertoire of skills that a person has at one point in time, but reviews changes in an individual from one point in time to another and monitors the effectiveness of intervention strategies after they are implemented, as well as other activities in which people engage with a student. The formal collection of data and written reports are simply tools that are used at certain points in the ongoing assessment to review a student's progress.

The view that assessment is a continuous process has two important advantages. First, it emphasizes that the concern at hand is a student's growth from Time A to Time B, not his or her "performance" in relation to some standard or hypothetical curve on a graph. Such information can tell us about the course of a youngster's development that can help us project realistic short- and long-term goals. Second, it suggests a process in which we constantly ask ourselves, "Is the plan working?" It conveys the idea that team members are attentive to the daily opportunities for implementing interventions and that they use the data from the evaluation to modify or fine-tune effective strategies as needed. Thus, the end product of an evaluation should not be perceived as a diagnosis, a report, a team meeting, or a written IEP, but as the starting point for indicating whether interventions are meaningful and maximally effective.

## ASSESSMENTS SHOULD BE DYNAMIC

Assessments are often used to obtain information about the *products* of learning—the knowledge and skills students have acquired—through final examinations, observation scales, and achievement tests. But assessments with a dynamic perspective also focus on the *process* of learning. The evaluator with a dynamic perspective active-ly generates and tests hypotheses about the student's social and communication behaviors. By engaging the student in interaction, exploring ways to convey a message, working with the student on a meaningful task, and joining the student in familiar activities and settings, the teacher begins to identify the conditions that facilitate communication. A dynamic attitude further implies that what is assessed is not just the expressive behavior of the learner, but the give-and-take or the sharing of a communication system among two or more persons (Rowland & Stremel-Campbell, 1987). Communication is as much a receptive ability as it is an expressive ability, and equal attention must be paid to how learners who are deaf-blind respond to or interpret the messages that others convey to them. An evaluator who is not familiar with or fluent in the communication or language system that a student uses should therefore involve others, such as a sign language interpreter, in the assessment or work jointly with another team member. However, while doing so, the evaluator also needs to interact directly with the student because such structured interactions provide a great deal of information on the social aspects of the student's communication skills, which will be discussed later in this module.

A highly detrimental approach to evaluating a deaf-blind student is to attempt to delineate differences that are based on comparisons to students without impairments, because the evaluation will inevitably focus on what the student cannot do in contrast to others. Such an approach does not benefit the student and prevents team members from gaining a greater awareness of the learner's experience in his or her negotiations with the social world. A more productive approach is one in which team members view themselves as "deficient" in communicating with the student to remind themselves that they share responsibility for exploring and learning the means of interacting effectively with the student. Only by learning what these means are can appropriate strategies of intervention begin to be considered.

## *ASSESSMENTS SHOULD BE CONTEXT REFERENCED*

A context-referenced evaluation acknowledges that a person may behave differently in different situations. Since reports of a student's communication skills and competence in various situations may reflect such differences and hence may lead to confusion, disbelief, or disagreements, it is important to assess a student's communication behaviors for all relevant settings. Therefore, team members need to (1) observe or interact with the student in different activities in different domains or routines (home, community, work, leisure); (2) systematically seek information from persons who are familiar with the student in different environments; and (3) take into account observations or interpretations of a learner's communicative competence that may differ, even substantially, from theirs. Within this perspective, family members, friends, interpreters, work supervisors, community members, and others are viewed as potential partners in the assessment process because they often can identify the breadth of cues, signals, approaches, or situations to which a student responds most readily.

## ASSESSMENTS SHOULD BE ECOLOGICALLY VALID

*Ecological validity* means that the approach that best fits the objectives of the assessment is chosen. Rather than try to apply the same assessment model to every student, team members start by taking into account a student's unique skills, needs, and environments and then select the proper tools for the job.

The word *ecology* stresses the need to consider an individual's everyday environments. For the majority of people who are deaf-blind, social integration with persons in community, work, family, school, and recreational settings is the most important goal of communication. An evaluation should lead to the development of instructional strategies that genuinely facilitate learning and social integration.

## GOALS AND OBJECTIVES

Overall, assessments can result in several outcomes. They may provide diagnostic information, such as the nature of a student's learning style, or they may be used to screen students for certain services, document students' status or progress in areas of concern, identify students' strengths and weaknesses, plan or design interventions, or evaluate the effectiveness of current educational programs (Browder, 1987). Although the results of an assessment of communication may be used differently by the various persons who are involved with a student, the evaluator's goals should always be the same: to identify the individual's range of communication skills and behaviors in natural situations and environments and to develop intervention strategies to enhance the social and communication opportunities that a student who is deaf-blind experiences and provides to others.

The focus of the assessment of communication should be to find ways to enhance opportunities, not to remediate deficits; increase expressive behaviors; and promote the use of symbols or signs. Family members, teachers, or peers may sometimes be uncertain about how to respond to the interactive or potentially communicative behaviors of deaf-blind students (Siegel-Causey & Downing, 1987). Therefore, interventions must be designed as much for communication partners as for individuals who are deaf-blind. And on a much larger scale, the objective is to promote the successful integration of learners with and without disabilities in their schools, work environments, and community settings.

Just how many opportunities for communication can there be? After studying videotapes of students in their classrooms, Stillman (1990) estimated that in the course of a typical school day, one individual who is deaf-blind may offer others over 4,000 different opportunities to engage in communication and interaction. Although it is impossible to respond in each potential communication situation, taking advantage of the natural opportunities for communication will have a positive impact—especially for students who are deaf-blind and have cognitive disabilities or behavioral concerns (see Siegel-Causey & Ernst, 1989). These students learn best by applying and generalizing their communication skills in natural environments during meaningful events with a consistent structure.

# APPROACHES TO ASSESSING COMMUNICATION

There are numerous approaches to the assessment of communication that reflect a wide range of orientations. However, since the major approach highlighted in this book is the ecological or functional approach, it is stressed in this module. Other approaches that are discussed are the standardized or test-oriented approach, the developmental approach, and the behavioral approach. Because there are few criteria to indicate when to use or how to integrate particular approaches, techniques, or assessment tools, the first step in designing meaningful assessments is to consider the applicability of each approach to children, adolescents, and young adults with various degrees of visual and hearing disabilities.

## ECOLOGICAL OR FUNCTIONAL APPROACH

An ecological or functional approach to the assessment of communication attempts to provide information that will lead to improved outcomes for the learner by emphasizing communicative behaviors in the context of practical skills (self-care, work, school, and leisure). It also considers how settings and circumstances can influence an individual's communication behaviors. Thus, it is a powerful tool for identifying situational and environmental factors (for example, enjoyable activities, preferred objects and materials, and the presence of certain schoolmates or teachers) that are associated with a student's patterns of communication.

In addition, the ecological approach pays more attention than do other assessment approaches to natural interactions between students. It is closely tied to the major goal of enhancing the student's opportunities for social interaction and communication. It is viewed as an effective approach to evaluating students with severe disabilities whose educational curriculum emphasizes the learning of skills necessary for everyday life (Gaylord-Ross & Browder, 1991) and whose education takes place in integrated school and community environments. Several features are central to the ecological approach:

- The critical communication skills are embedded in important routines of daily living. For example, an evaluator's concerns are the student's communicative behaviors during leisure activities, in work-related activities, or in classes at school.

- Observations and interventions are made in the context of meaningful and natural activities. Assessment and "therapies" are conducted in places where the student usually is during the regular day, not in a designated evaluation area or "pull-out" therapy room.

- The basic units of measurement are sequences of social and communication behavior, as opposed to language concepts and knowledge of words. A sequence can be as simple as the student's basic reaction to someone's greeting or as complex as extended interactions involving give-and-take behaviors.

- The individual's social and physical environments are as important to assess as are his or her communication behaviors. Environmental factors—like the presence of certain classmates or the familiarity of the setting—affect the communication behaviors of the learner and differ markedly in different settings and events.

- Interventions may be directed toward environmental change, as well as toward change in the learner. Therefore, restructuring the social or physical environment to accommodate a student's preferences, strengths, and interests may be a prerequisite for successful intervention.

- The evaluation is community referenced. The objectives are to increase the student's degree of social independence and social access within integrated schools and communities.

The ecological approach embraces context-referenced and dynamic attitudes; a student's communication behaviors are best understood by evaluating his or her patterns and sequences of interaction with others in different circumstances. The social exchanges between students and their schoolmates, family members, educators, and acquaintances are more important than is enhancing the students' specific communication behaviors. Therefore, this approach shifts some of the responsibility of improving communication to the communication partners. Interventions should include strategies for helping others to recognize the opportunities to interact with or respond to the student or to learn the most effective ways to convey a message.


## OTHER APPROACHES

### Standardized Approach

Standardized or formal testing has its roots in the field of psychological measurement. Intelligence tests and achievement measures symbolize this approach, which is defined by the use of specific instruments that have been previously given to a particular population to determine a "normal" range. The following are the main features of the standardized approach:

- The administration of tests usually follows standard procedures, and any significant deviation makes the results suspect or invalid.

- The results of these tests are presented in quantitative form, such as a percentile ranking, grade-level score, age-equivalent score, or standard score. These data are used to determine how an individual deviates from the norm group in some capacity or ability. For example, if a student's score is at the 60th percentile, it means that his or her test score was higher than those of 60 percent of the population on which the test was developed (usually persons in the same age group).

- Some formal tests are "criterion referenced." That is, a student's performance is compared not to a norm group, but to a set of goals or achievements that the learner is expected to master in certain content areas. The focus is on the individual's knowledge and skills in relation to specific competencies (for example, the size of his or her receptive vocabulary or the level of his or her listening or reading comprehension), and skills are often evaluated as being present or not present in the student's repertoire.

Formal tests of communication and language are conducted to assess individuals of all ages with disabilities. However, there are major problems and controversies in this regard:

- The "norm" or the "criteria" of average or expected performance are usually based on the achievements of individuals without sensory impairments. Thus, by using formal tests, we are willing to accept the assumption that learners who are deaf-blind have had qualitatively the same educational experiences and opportunities in acquiring vocabulary, the knowledge of concepts, verbal fluency, comprehension skills, and other communication abilities as has the hearing-sighted population.

- As Rowland (1987) noted, many formal tests require the student to understand verbal directions, follow the sequences of tasks, pay attention and cooperate for extended periods, and respond in a verbal mode. These requirements cannot be met by the majority of students who are deaf-blind, who may then be labeled as untestable by default or "deficient."

- Norm-referenced tests generally sample the knowledge and concepts of formal language as a means of predicting students' strengths and weaknesses in academic instruction. For learners with severe multiple disabilities whose interventions may emphasize such basic skills as the expression of choice, the initiation of a request, the understanding of a tactile cue, or the acknowledgment of another student's greeting, tests assess irrelevant behaviors and skills; they are rarely ecologically valid.

Given all the inherent problems of using formal tests with students who are deaf-blind, are there situations that call for standardized testing? The answer is rarely, if ever. For individuals who are deaf-blind and who do not have cognitive disabilities and whose expressive modalities include formal language, such as American Sign Language, spoken English, or braille, testing may provide limited information that can be used to monitor their progress or to design interventions to increase their fluency in those modes. However, even if tests are used, the scores will be invalid because the basic assumptions of the tests are likely to have been violated and the administration procedures are likely to have been modified.

Unfortunately, the test-oriented approach is still often used with students who have severe multiple disabilities. One reason for their use is that evaluators often are required to administer tests that qualify students for certain school services, yet have no educational significance (Evans, 1991). Another reason is that evaluators who serve a wide range of students may cling to certain assessment models, such as testing, with which they have had the greatest amount of experience and knowledge.

## Developmental Approach

The developmental approach views communication as a sequence or progression of skills that develop through maturation and a child's interactions with the environment. The development of communication proceeds through a series of stages, each of which culminates in the appearance of "milestone" achievements, such as a child's utterance of his or her first word or sentence. The work of Piaget has had a strong influence on this approach (Hatwell, 1985), and several assessment tools are specifically based on his theories of sensorimotor and intellectual development.

The developmental approach has characteristics that are both similar to and different from the standardized approach:

- In contrast to norm-referenced testing, developmental assessment is concerned with qualitative changes, not quantitative differences. The intent is to monitor the time of the appearance, sequence, and progression of specific social and communication behaviors in children. Thus, the quality of a learner's communication skills is judged in relation to the approximate age at which those skills are generally acquired by children without impairments. Attention is given to the hallmarks of the acquisition of language, such as the transition from preintentional to intentional or from presymbolic to symbolic communication.

- The developmental and standardized approaches both focus on the component skills of communication, such as the use of expressive and receptive vocabulary, vocal or gestural imitation, or the ability to use symbols.

- In each approach, the learner's communication skills are often compared to an age level, a stage of development, or a norm-referenced group.

- The developmental approach does have some advantages over the structured approach in that (1) most developmental scales are much less formal than are standardized tests, (2) a learner's accomplishments often can be observed over extended periods and under more casual or natural circumstances, (3) it is easier to monitor the progress of the individual in specific skills, and (4) the characteristics of the individual's communication behavior are more important than is the "correctness" of the learner's response.

The developmental approach is questionable, however, for evaluating the communication behaviors of deaf-blind students. One concern is that our understanding of the development of communication is based mainly on how children without disabilities acquire speech and language. Also, our assessment models and tools often do not regard how early communication is affected by sensory impairments and other disabilities. (An exception is the Callier-Azusa Scale H, which is discussed later.) Thus, when a developmental approach is used, the patterns, sequences, and forms of communication that may be unique to the deaf-blind individual and on which our strategies of intervention can be planned are apt to be missed or minimized.

Another concern with this approach is that there is a tendency to draw parallels between the communication behaviors of deaf-blind students and the language achievements of younger children. Such comparisons can lead to gross misperceptions about the communicative competence of the individual who is deaf-blind whose breadth, depth, and forms of interactive skills may be extensive, yet different from speech and language.

This problem is magnified when measures for infants and developmental scales are applied to adolescents or even young adults who have severe cognitive disabilities in addition to deaf-blindness. Such a practice is never warranted, yet is apparently common (see, for example, Sigafoos, Cole, & McQuarter, 1987). Terms like *presymbolic*, *preverbal*, or *preintentional*, which may accurately describe the stages of development of young children, do a disservice to older, more experienced learners whose 15 or 20 years' worth of social and communication experiences simply cannot be equated with the achievements of toddlerhood. Thus, if the developmental approach is applied to the more experienced learner who is deaf-blind, the planning of interventions, as well as the student's dignity, can be seriously compromised.

The major concern with the developmental approach is that because developmental measures often emphasize vocabulary, imitation, and the matching of symbols to objects, there is a risk of recommending interventions that focus on the training of isolated skills. For example, an IEP may include the goal of increasing a student's receptive vocabulary of tactile signs or extending attention and interest to social stimuli. Such goals may be important, but not if they are literally translated into drill-and-practice exercises that occur during planned teaching periods outside natural and meaningful situations. For learners who have severe disabilities, the more effective approach is to focus on enhancing the communication skills needed for daily activities and environments (see Nietupski & Hamre-Nietupski, 1987), which may also increase the individual's vocabulary or social attention as the natural "by-product" of learning.

## Behavioral Approach

In a traditional sense, a behavioral assessment is conducted when a student has "problem" behaviors that significantly interfere with learning and socializing. The evaluator attempts to understand what factors or antecedents are associated with these problems and to develop specific plans and strategies to remediate them. In the assessment of communication, however, the behavioral approach has been applied only recently in recognition that a broad range of behaviors other than speech and language may have communicative value (for more on this perspective, see Module 6).

The behavioral approach has three primary purposes:

1. To conduct an inventory of a student's repertoire of communicative or potentially communicative behaviors. In the past several years, many new and important tools have been developed to help us recognize the various nonspeech, nonsymbolic communication behaviors of learners with severe disabilities. Most of these tools rely on observations, interviews, and direct interactions with the learner.

2. To design educational approaches to help students substitute appropriate forms of communication for problematic behaviors (Meyer & Evans, 1989). Many students who have multiple severe disabilities in addition to deaf-blindness express themselves in forms that create difficulties for themselves or others. Instead of making a direct request, for example, a student may use self-injurious, aggressive, or repetitive behaviors to signal his or her need. Although our immediate inclination may be to eliminate or decrease the undesired acts, the behavioral approach helps us assess how important a communicative function the behavior may serve. Most assessment tools for this purpose are based on the technology of applied behavior analysis, which is an observational method for systematically identifying the problem behaviors of concern, evaluating their frequency or duration, and implementing interventions that move the student toward more acceptable communication behaviors.

3. To identify positive reinforcers or motivating conditions that can be used to promote specific communication skills. Because these reinforcers must be identified as a prerequisite to teaching or intervention, the behavioral approach ensures that the assessment of communication will be ecologically valid with respect to the learner's educational plan. Numerous reports (see, for example, Goetz, Schuler, & Sailor, 1983) of the use of this approach have indicated that the learner's natural motivation to participate in a desired activity is the critical element used to teach social interaction or the making of direct requests.

326

The behavioral approach has been especially useful for assessing the communication behaviors of students who are deaf-blind and have severe cognitive disabilities who do not use formal language (that is, speech, signs, or written language). The major advantages are readily apparent. Unlike test-oriented and developmental approaches, behavioral assessment focuses entirely on a learner's natural communication behaviors. Comparisons of the individual's communication skills to a normed population or developmental stage are irrelevant. Observation is the primary means of collecting information, which can be done in a variety of contexts and on an ongoing basis. Information obtained through a behavioral assessment also leads directly to interventions for teaching or expanding communication skills.

# METHODS AND TOOLS

The first step in designing and conducting meaningful assessments of communication and interventions is to review the basic approaches to evaluation. With this task accomplished, the next concern can be considered: How to assess the communication abilities of learners who are deaf-blind. The choice of tools for assessment is limited only if assessment is narrowly defined as a formal process conducted by certain personnel that occurs at prescribed intervals. Only a few formal instruments have been developed specifically for use with deaf-blind students. However, the evaluator has many methods and tools from which to choose, including interviews, reviews of records, one-to-one interactions, tests, adaptations of tests, observations, scales, checklists, inventories, behavioral analyses, daily logs, chronologs, anecdotes, and progress notes.

This section describes methods for gathering information about students' communication behaviors and the major forms and functions of assessment tools. The process of assessment differs substantially from one individual to another. The decision to use particular methods and tools will depend on several factors, including the evaluation issues of concern and the learner's characteristics, needs, environments, interests, and communication partners. The primary goal of this discussion is to gain an understanding of the "equipment" for conducting assessments and the powers, functions, and limitations of these various methods and tools, so each assessment is relevant and functional.

## DEFINITIONS

*Methods* are the resources and strategies available to the evaluator for obtaining information. They include the use of historical information, behavioral observations, formal measures, structured interactions, and interviews.

*Tools* are the types or categories of instruments, such as adaptive behavior scales, tests, profiles, behavioral checklists, and interview protocols.

*Instruments* are the specific products and materials that may be used, for example, the Callier-Azusa Scale H and the Scales of Independent Behavior. Each tool and instrument may represent one or more approaches to evaluation (ecological, standardized, developmental, or behavioral), and involve one or more methods, such as interviews, or structured interactions, for obtaining information. For more information on how to conduct assessments, see Assessment Tips for Teachers in Module 5).

## METHODS

### Historical Information

Historical information includes data about the background of the learner: his or her birth history or early development, previous schooling, medical and health background, progress in therapy, social and family history, previous educational objectives, past behavioral concerns, work history, and so on. Evaluations should routinely involve the review of historical information, but in purposeful ways. Assessments resulting in written or oral reports that simply rehash previously recorded facts about the student have little utility. When used strategically, historical data can answer important questions that other methods of assessment cannot address alone. The tools for obtaining historical information are often in the reports of previous evaluations, educational or medical-health records, interviews with persons who are familiar with the student, informal notes kept by parents or teachers, social service records, and so forth.

One of the obligations of the evaluator is to describe the meaningful accomplishments of the learner from the past to the present. Reviews of previous evaluations, reports, and so on are essential because they partially answer the question, "What progress is the student making?" When reviewing this material, the evaluator needs to be guided by several issues with respect to the student being assessed:

- How were the student's breadth and forms of communication behavior described?

- What primary communication concerns were identified?

- What were the educational goals?

- What intervention strategies were used, and how were these strategies carried out?

- What gains were noted?

The rest of the information about the student's progress can be determined only by assessing his or her present communication behaviors in relation to the past descriptions and concerns:

- Has the student achieved those goals?

- Have the intervention strategies been successfully implemented, and have they paid off?

- What specific qualitative gains has the student made in communication and social interaction, and are these gains meaningful?

Comparisons of past and present views of the student's communication skills not only provide information about the student's successes, but they also help in planning because the effectiveness of the interventions are monitored.

A review of the student's medical, health, and psychological histories, including the etiology or cause of his or her deaf-blindness, is especially important when the assessment is to address crucial concerns, including unexpected or sudden changes in the student's communication or social behaviors (and anticipated changes in the student's sensory abilities that will affect his or her expressive or receptive skills). An evaluation of a person whose communication is mostly nonsymbolic or nonintentional may be requested when family members, teachers, peers, or co-workers note changes in his or her social interest, responsiveness, or forms of communication behavior. Such changes occur from time to time in students who have fragile or ongoing health conditions, such as seizures, diabetes, or glaucoma, that require medication. The evaluator must be alert to the possibility that behavioral changes are correlated with these health factors and be careful not to attribute such changes to medical or health conditions when psychological factors (such as known changes in routine) may be involved.

Some causes of deaf-blindness, such as Usher syndrome, are associated with progressive changes in physical or sensory functions. (For more information about Usher syndrome and other causes of deaf-blindness, see Module 3 and Appendix A.) For learners whose visual or hearing disabilities or both may change or increase over time, it is important to evaluate the best media for receptive or expressive communication. Thus, as the student's sensory capability progressively worsens, appropriate intervention strategies for communication will have been considered and implemented, it is hoped, well in advance. Such strategies include introducing the student to tactile signing or braille, helping communication partners modify their behaviors while maintaining social interaction, and considering augmentative communication systems.

## Observations of Behavior

Behavioral observation is the most versatile assessment method. Observations can be made by many individuals who are familiar with the student (family members, teachers, assistant teachers, interpreters, classmates, supervisors, and therapists) and can be made unobtrusively at different times and in various settings. This method does not necessarily require special instruments, although many are available to provide structure to the assessment.

Behavioral observation can be a productive assessment method if some criteria are established to guide observations (Curtis & Donlon, 1985). Since many aspects of communication and social interaction occur simultaneously, the evaluator must be able to define relevant behaviors and skills and recognize their variations among the hundreds of episodes, sequences, and events that occur in an observation period. Therefore, behavioral observations of deaf-blind students should be made according to the following guidelines:

- The purposes of the observations are well defined in advance, so the observations are relevant to particular questions and issues.

- Observations of the student are conducted and analyzed in various natural contexts and situations.

- Observations are made on more than one occasion.

- Observations focus on receptive and expressive communication when the learner has natural opportunities to interact socially.

- Observations are of "whole" behavioral routines, rather than of isolated communication processes or components of skills.

- Observations are made to identify factors in the physical and social environments that may affect communication behaviors.

The evaluator must keep many other considerations in mind. First, although behavioral observation is a less formal method of assessment than is testing, it is not necessarily an informal process. Some tools and procedures may require the extensive collection of data. For example, it may be necessary to record systematically the frequency or duration of problem behaviors over time to determine whether and to what extent an intervention plan is needed. Certain scales of social and communication skills may require the rating of behaviors for their presence, absence, or quality.

Second, even when a specific observational instrument is not used, the recorded information must accurately describe the actual behaviors and interactions that occurred. Although observations are objective, interpretations are subjective. Perceptions that a student is angry, lazy, charming, rejecting, loving, stubborn, or appealing are an evaluator's value judgments that may detract from the functional significance of important behaviors (for example, indications of fatigue, boredom, or social need). Furthermore, different persons tend to view and understand a learner's communication styles, patterns, skills, and behaviors differently. For instance, a behavior that looks like a reflex to one person may look like a response to social stimulation to another. The evaluator must take into account the range of diverse interpretations—not to determine who is right or wrong, but to gain a sense of how various communication partners may identify and respond to the interactive opportunities that the learner provides.

Third, the approaches to assessment that one adopts will be closely tied to the behaviors one observes. For example, in a behavioral approach, observations may focus on the gestures or vocalizations a young woman uses to indicate her desire for a coffee break. In an ecological approach, observations may be directed toward the interaction or communication sequences that occur among the young woman, her co-workers, and her supervisor during a work activity. In test-oriented assessments, observations often occur in particular settings and at set times, such as a few hours in an evaluation room. Developmentally oriented approaches may concentrate on the qualities and progression of particular communication behaviors in infants and young children (such as early turn-taking behaviors, the emergence of the use of symbols, and the transition to intentional communication behaviors).

Finally, some practical aspects of the observation method need to be considered. The most useful observation methods in the assessment of students who are deaf-blind tend to be associated with an ecological or a behavioral approach. For young learners, observation tools that are developmental may also provide useful information, as long as the particular communication and social subskills being observed (for example, picture-to-object matching, association of sounds or touch with certain tasks or activities) are not considered in isolation from functional daily activities. The use of videotapes can be of immense value, since it is impossible to attend to all the aspects and levels of communication behavior at one time. Observations of test-taking skills, however, are only as useful as are the tests for providing valid and meaningful information about competent communication or for reviewing and planning educational interventions. This point is of particular concern with respect to students with severe cognitive disabilities whose communication behaviors may be better observed when there are natural cues in the environment (the smell of food or the touch or smell of a food tray at a fast-food counter or cafeteria) during natural events (mealtimes).

## Formal Measures

Formal measures include the norm-referenced and criterion-referenced tests discussed earlier and thus represent a primary method for collecting data using a standardized testing approach or, to a lesser degree, a developmental approach. Even though there is a general consensus that tests are unsuitable for assessing the communication behaviors of students who are deaf-blind (see Browder, 1987; Evans, 1991), tests are presented here because of their continued popularity among evaluators and because their use is often required to prescribe special services, such as speech and language therapy, on IEPs.

There are many measures of picture vocabulary, auditory discrimination and comprehension, reading and writing for print and braille skills, expressive vocabulary, knowledge of concepts, syntax, speech production, and so on. The appeal of using formal measures is that they are perceived to carry a certain authority. They are the predominant assessment tools in general education, are used to make absolute "pass-fail" types of decisions, have been validated, and relate to the concepts and skills of language with which people are most familiar. In addition, data from them can be presented neatly and concretely, the reporting of results can be cut and dried, and there are a clear beginning and end to the process.

To extend the use of formal tests to assess learners who are deaf-blind, adaptations and modifications of test materials and procedures are frequently designed. Some of these modifications include enlarging print, allowing extra time to respond, using braille or a sign language interpreter to convey instructions, presenting materials with optical aids, omitting test items, increasing the contrast between test stimuli and their backgrounds, providing more practice or sample items, accepting alternate responses (pointing, nodding), substituting test materials, and using different scoring procedures. However, it is important to remember that modifications do not make formal measures more relevant. They merely help the examiner administer the tests and facilitate the learner's perception of stimuli after it has been determined that the skills being measured are the critical skills to assess for educational planning.

## Structured Interactions

Structured interactions include a host of informal assessment methods in which the evaluator engages directly with the individual being evaluated. Such interactions may include working on one-to-one activities with the learner, providing direct instruction or assistance, or participating in events in which the learner takes part. The general objective is to gain firsthand experience of the unique styles, patterns, sequences, and forms of social exchange that occur between the learner and his or her communication partners. Much of this information cannot be observed from a distance, captured through interviews, or assessed with formal measures.

The forms of structured interaction are infinite. The evaluator and student may engage in a leisure activity, work on a problem together, perform a daily routine, participate in a group activity, explore or examine objects, go from one location to another, or simply exchange greetings. Each activity provides opportunities to test hypotheses about how the student best understands and conveys information in a variety of contexts and activities.

From an assessment point of view, the exact forms of structured interactions in which the evaluator and student engage are less critical than are the opportunities for communication that these situations

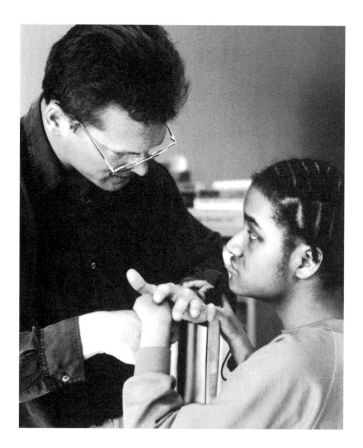

▲ *Engaging directly with a student offers firsthand experience of the unique ways in which he or she communicates with others.*

provide. Nevertheless, the evaluator should consider several criteria when using structured interactions:

- Interactions occur in the context of meaningful activities in the student's regular environments.

- The evaluator assumes an active role as the communication partner in these situations by teaching, assisting, instructing, cuing, or guiding the learner and by responding directly to the learner's cues and reciprocal behaviors.

- Many structured interactions are planned so the evaluator can directly communicate with the learner during different events. More important, the evaluator can experience how increased familiarity between communication partners can play a significant role in the learner's styles and patterns of interaction and how barriers to communication, forms, approaches, sequences, and preferences can be better understood over time and with increased opportunity.

- Materials and activities for structured interactions should be consistent with the learner's interests, experience, and age.

What information should the evaluator seek through structured interactions? What purposes do these interactions serve? The primary importance of this method is that the interactions are real-life events in which the full complexity of a student's communication behaviors can be assessed. The evaluator can directly determine the ways in which the learner initiates interactions; the learner's responses to the evaluator's efforts to communicate; the range, quality, and complexity of the learner's expressions, symbols, and gestures; the means of conveying directions or instructions; and the extent of the learner's interest and ability to engage in give-and-take activities.

The unique advantage of structured interactions is that they provide opportunities to test hypotheses on the spot about specific communication interventions. They permit the evaluator to analyze the differences in a student's communication behaviors with subtle or discrete changes in strategies of intervention and to note, for example, the degree to which hand-over-hand guidance may be required, how close or far away the communication partner should be from the learner, how tactile cues or signs must be presented, what tactile symbols are most easily recognized, how much prompting may be required to gain a student's attention, and so forth. Although information obtained from other methods of assessment (such as behavioral observations or formal measures) can lead to recommendations of appropriate intervention strategies, none of the other methods will yield information that is precise enough to suggest the most promising techniques for delivering those interventions.

Ultimately, it should be recognized that this method is essentially no different from teaching. Teachers, teaching assistants, and other classroom-based service providers are constantly engaged with their students. Therefore, they are often in the best positions to use structured interactions for assessment on an ongoing basis.

## Interviews

No assessment is complete unless those persons who are most familiar with the learner, including family members, teachers, teaching assistants, therapists, providers of related services, work supervisors, and peers, are interviewed. The evaluator should strive to conduct more than one interview, since the social and interactive behaviors of a student will vary, depending on the communication partner, as will the perspectives and observations of the person being interviewed.

Interviews can be formal or informal. Formal interviews follow specific protocols, such as assessment instruments that are designed to be administered to providers of care or educators. However, formal interviews need not be published instruments, since many evaluators design their own interview protocols. The main advantage of using formal interviews is that they ensure that a wide range of issues will be covered in an organized fashion. Most formal instruments, however, focus exclusively on the individual being evaluated and thus communication behavior. In contrast, informal interviews tend to be more individualized or personal, allowing the evaluator and person being interviewed to discuss the unique behaviors and concerns of the learner who is deaf-blind.

The content of an interview will vary from one evaluation to another, depending on the persons being interviewed, communication issues, and the availability of data from other methods of assessment. However, several categories of basic questions should be addressed in any interview, formal or informal (see Basic Questions to Ask in an Interview).

## TOOLS AND INSTRUMENTS

Tools and instruments for the assessment of communication should be perceived as vehicles to help organize information, not to dictate what information should be gathered. However, because preconceived ideas about what assessments are may prevail, or because an educational agency may impose certain criteria for conducting eval-

**HELP**
*at a*
**GLANCE**

## BASIC QUESTIONS TO ASK IN AN INTERVIEW

The following are basic questions that can serve as a starting point for more detailed queries about a student:

● What means does the student use to indicate his or her needs, interests, desires, and preferences? Is the student consistent and consistently understood in using these indicators? If not, what happens?

● Which communication goals and specific interventions are being used for different situations? Are they applied? Who applies them?

Do they work? What makes them work or not work?

● What gains and achievements has the student made? What has most helped the student to achieve these gains?

● Which persons are most significant to the student? How does the student recognize, request, and respond to each person? How do interactions differ among them? How effectively do other people communicate with and understand the student?

● What are the various forms (gestures, vocalizations, body movements, signs, tactile signals, print, braille, spoken language) of the student's expressive and receptive communication skills?

● What opportunities does the student have for social interaction with peers in his or her community?

● What are the long-term plans and goals to facilitate the student's opportunities for social interaction and to improve his or her communication? ■

uations, an evaluator's first reaction may be to think about what tests, scales, forms, checklists, and other such devices be can used. Although this is a necessary step, it is not the first step.

The critical issues that need to be evaluated must be identified before tools and instruments are selected. Assessments are relevant and meaningful primarily when the tools and the issues of evaluation are matched.

A good fit between the identified issues and the methods and tools of assessment can be found in several ways. First, the evaluator should seek to gain some consensus among members of the educational team about the central concerns that should be addressed. Second, the evaluator should become familiar with the student by reviewing historical information, observations, interviews, and direct interactions. Third, the evaluator should review the purposes, strengths, and limitations of the assessment tools and instruments.

The assessment tools that are reviewed here are organized according to their purpose. They include

- communication profiles
- developmental scales and inventories
- behavioral records, checklists, and rating scales
- tests of language and communication.

Specific instruments are described for each type of tool. However, it is not possible (or desirable) to include an exhaustive list of instruments that may be applicable to a learner who is deaf-blind, and several compilations of assessment instruments are already available. Furthermore, the instruments that are described here are not necessarily the tools of choice. Rather, they are examples to illustrate the purposes of tools and the extent to which they can be utilized to address issues of evaluation. (Information on obtaining these and other instruments is found in Appendix C.)

## Communication Profiles

Communication profiles are frameworks for analyzing levels of communicative competence that characterize the social and communication behaviors of individuals with severe multiple disabilities. Because they regard the entire range of reflexive, reactive, nonintentional, and nonsymbolic behaviors as being directly or potentially valuable for communication, they are considered state-of-the-art tools for assessing learners who are deaf-blind and have other disabilities.

Most of these profiles apply to individuals of all ages; they do not ascribe age levels to the qualities or complexity of communication behaviors. However, an individual's communication or social skills are generally described along a continuum or hierarchy of competence (Level I, Level II, and so on), from basic reactive behaviors at one extreme to the sophisticated and formal use of language systems at the other. It should be noted, however, that because the communication behaviors of students who are deaf-blind are heterogeneous, they often cannot fit neatly within the levels and profiles that are described.

These tools emphasize the assessment of functional communication behaviors in natural environments and thus reflect the values of the behavioral and ecological approaches. They can be used to assess learners in a variety of home, school, community, and work settings, using various sources of information: behavioral observations; interviews; structured interactions; and, to some degree, educational records. Several of these instruments, which can be used by educators and providers of related services and whose use can involve the participation of family members, were designed to lead directly to the planning of interventions. For the most part, these tools incorporate all the "attitudes" of evaluation described earlier. The following are some examples.

*The Communication Matrix* (Rowland, 1990) is a thorough, organized instrument that describes seven levels of competent communication. It was designed to evaluate students with severe sensory, cognitive, and physical disabilities. Communication is assessed by rating whether and to what extent an individual uses behaviors or symbols (for example, facial expressions, head movements, vocalization, words, signs, and object cues) to express a wide range of internal states, needs, and interests—hunger, protest, request, attention, and so forth. The learner's behaviors are scored as present if a cue is given, spontaneously produced, or generalized. Different parts of the instrument focus on learners whose communication behaviors differ in degrees of intentionality. This instrument helps the evaluator make direct links to relevant intervention issues. A similar instrument was described by Rowland and Stremel-Campbell (1987).

*The Assessment of Social Competence (ASC): A Scale of Social Competence Functions* (Meyer et al., 1985) was designed and validated (Meyer, Cole, McQuarter, & Reichle, 1990) for use with children, adolescents, and adults with severe disabilities. Its orientation is ecological in that communication is of interest only in the context of the important social functions that occur in the individual's daily interactions in the community, at work, at home, or in school. Critical behaviors can be directly observed or reported by others. The ASC defines 11 subscales of social competence in which communication is integral, including the initiation of interaction, following rules, obtaining cues, offering assistance, and indicating preferences. On each subscale, behaviors can be scored according to their level of competence, ranging from 1 (basic skills) to 8 (mastery). The validation study reports good test-retest reliability and good parent-teacher reliability.

*Profiles of Expressive Communication and Social Interaction* (Mar & Sall, 1991) was designed as a research tool to describe the breadth, uniqueness, and complexity of the communication behaviors of persons aged 3 to 21 with severe multiple disabilities, and a large sample of students who are deaf-blind was included in the research. During observations or structured interactions, the evaluator rates the learner's behavior on seven dimensions (intentionality, the use of symbols, complexity, relevance to the context, social give-and-take, initiation, and the conventionality of expressive forms) in natural situations (rather than emphasizing the hierarchical progression of communication levels) and assembles an overall profile of the breadth of communication behaviors. Each rating for each dimension is associated with a set of desired goals or outcomes, which enables the evaluator to consider appropriate intervention strategies.

*Nonverbal Prelinguistic Communication: A Guide to Communication Levels in Prelinguistic Handicapped Children* (Otos, 1983) is arranged by nonspeech communication modes: tactile (such as touch cues, tactile gestures, and tactile signs), objects (including cues and pictures in the environment), and gestures (for example, coactive movement and imitation). (For more information, see Modules 7 and 8.) A learner's expressive and receptive communication behaviors can be considered for a variety of modes, which is especially helpful for the deaf-blind student. The nine levels of communication development used reflect increasingly complex and abstract skills. Some features, such as its emphasis on the sequences of skills and the association of age ranges with each of the nine levels of communication, relate this instrument to the developmental approach.

## Developmental Scales and Inventories

Some scales and inventories represent a developmental approach to assessment, although they may be considered behavioral and ecological approaches as well. They are distinguished from communication profiles, however, because of their intended use with young children. In addition, unlike communication profiles, which rely primarily on analyzing behaviors in natural activities, many developmental scales are composed of specific "items" or "situations" in which the evaluator deliberately attempts to elicit a particular behavior from the learner, such as having the child imitate a vocalization or response to a one-step command. Since their main purposes are to assess the acquisition, processes, and sequences of the development of skills, many of these scales and inventories are organized by language and the "domains" or categories of social skills, such as vocal imitation, gestural imitation, symbolic development, and comprehension. The major methods of obtaining information for them are behavioral observations, interviews, and structured interactions that are often planned to elicit particular behaviors. The limitations are that the sequential nature of the development of language does not typify the development of communication in children who are deaf-blind and the communication behaviors of older students.

The majority of developmental scales and inventories use age levels or age ranges as points of reference. That is, a child's accomplishments are judged in relation to the age at which those achievements are usually made by children without disabilities or, in some instances, with particular disabilities. Developmental scales and inventories may be used to assess the qualities of specific communication behaviors that deaf-blind infants and toddlers typically display for interactive situations (for example, responding to a social greeting, expressing rejection or disinterest, or indicating the desire for "more") and that can be taught in the context of natural activities. The following are some examples.

*The Callier-Azusa Scale H* (Stillman & Battle, 1985) was developed specifically for use with children who are deaf-blind. It extensively identifies specific situations to observe or assess, yet is flexible enough to consider a range of responses that a student may offer in each situation. The scale is divided into four components that focus on representational and symbolic development, receptive communication, intentional communication, and reciprocity. Its developmental orientation is reflected in the ordering of items according to normal developmental progression, but the assignment of age levels or age ranges to performance is deemphasized. Assessments rely on observations of the learner in familiar environments, especially in the classroom.

This instrument reflects the desirable attitudes of evaluation. It acknowledges the importance of context and communication partners, and it is suggested that the assessment be conducted over an extended period. A related instrument, the Callier-Azusa Scale G (Stillman, 1978), is used to assess the general skills of deaf-blind children.

*The Reynell-Zinkin Scales: Developmental Scales for Young Visually Handicapped Children* (Reynell, 1979) focuses on cognitive and language development and include subscales for vocalization, expressive language, general communication, social adaptation, sensorimotor skills, exploration, and response to sound. Designed for children up to age 5, the instrument offers age levels of performance, based on the development of children with blindness, visual impairments, or multiple disabilities. Data are collected through observations or structured interactions.

*The Carolina Curriculum for Preschoolers with Special Needs* (Johnson-Martin, Attermeier, & Hacker, 1990), an assessment-intervention package, favors the use of structured interactions for everyday assessments. It is designed for young children with disabilities, although not specifically for deaf-blind children. However, the sections on gestural imitation and communication and social skills may suggest interventions and significant responses to monitor. The curricular contents were selected from norm-referenced tests of development and ordinal scales, so the approach is essentially developmental. Many behaviors are elicited through structured interactions, but many can also be observed in the context of natural activities. A similar guide for infants and toddlers is also available.

## Behavioral Records, Checklists, and Scales

Behavioral checklists and rating scales are designed to provide extensive information about the characteristics, forms, and qualities of social and communication skills. When the evaluator is not familiar with a student, these tools can help determine the various modalities of reception and expression and evaluate how effectively the student is able to convey and receive messages. Some of these instruments can be used directly for planning interventions when an individual has problematic behaviors that serve communicative functions. Most behavioral checklists are not concerned with age-level descriptions of the students who are evaluated or of comparisons between them and others. Information for these instruments is usually obtained from interviews, structured interactions, or observations. The following are some examples.

*The Assessment of Individuals with Severe Disabilities* (Browder, 1991) describes an applied behavioral analysis approach to assessing the life skills of students with severe disabilities. In book form, it contains sections on communication skills and social behaviors that provide many examples of how data from assessments can be translated into appropriate interventions. Several forms and charts are presented as tools for assessments. Case studies help to integrate the various aspects of assessment presented in this book. Because of its emphasis on applied behavioral analysis, it views assessment as an ongoing process.

*The Observational Evaluation of Severely Multi-Handicapped Children* (Curtis & Donlon, 1985) contains detailed descriptions and procedures for evaluating learners through observation. These procedures cover many situations that are relevant to evaluating students who are deaf-blind, including observing excess behaviors (such as light gazing), olfactory skills, and mobility problems. The extensive section on communication behaviors addresses observations of interactions, responses to sounds, play, tactile communication, and visual communication. Suggestions for videotaping an individual's behaviors are also presented. A book that is mostly behavioral in its orientation, it contains many features of an ecological approach. It cannot be easily adopted as an instrument, but its approach to observation is sensitive to the communication behaviors and concerns of children with severe multiple disabilities.

*The Behavior Rating Instrument for Autistic and Other Atypical Children* (Ruttenberg, Wenar, & Wolf-Schein, 1977), originally a behavioral observation tool to evaluate children with autism, has been applied to children who are deaf-blind (Kates, Schein, & Wolf, 1981). It focuses on the social reactions and interactions of children and has scales of auditory reception, relationship to others, receptive-gestural language, and expressive-gestural language, among others. Students' levels of behavior and performance can be rated on a 10-point scale, and the reliability of the rating scale is judged to be good. Ratings are based on observations of the student.

*The Motivation Assessment Scale* (Durand & Crimmins, 1992) is a questionnaire that identifies situations in which a student's specific behaviors are elicited. It is not designed as a tool for assessing communication, but through its use, many challenging behaviors can be identified as having communicative value. By rating the frequency of a behavior in the 16 specific situations and contexts that are presented, one can consider whether the behavior is motivated primarily by the need for sensory stimulation, escape from a situation, attention, or a tangible object or reward, the last three of which have significant communicative components. Interventions are designed, in part, by considering the motivation of the problematic behavior.

*The Communication Profile for Severe Expressive Impairment* (Shane, 1987) was designed as a clinical tool to identify and describe the communication behaviors of individuals with severe disabilities. It is organized by communicative functions (requesting behavior, negations, declarations, expression of needs, and so on), the activity and location of the communication behavior, the uniqueness of the behavioral form, and the frequency of occurrence. This interview and observational instrument also examines the student's preferences; spontaneous gestures, symbols, and behaviors; and responses to prompts. No age levels or scores can be obtained. The value of this instrument is its ease of use, the comprehensiveness of the questions, its organization, and the practical nature of the questions.

*INCH: The INteraction CHecklist for Augmentative Communication* (Bolton & Dashiell, 1984) describes features of the dynamic interactions of learners who use augmentative communication systems and communication partners. Because its goal is to assess the efficiency of communication, information obtained from it can be easily related to specific interventions. The instrument acknowledges the variations in an individual's behaviors by recognizing that observations should be made in both familiar and unfamiliar contexts. It is not specific to any type of augmentative system and may be applicable to many students of any age who use informal or formal communication systems. However, it is best applied to learners with intentional and symbolic communication behaviors.

## Formal Tests

Few formal instruments (norm referenced with standard administration procedures) can be used to assess the communication behaviors and skills of learners who are deaf-blind. Some formal measures may be partially applied when the student has functional vision and is able to follow the demands of tasks given through oral, gestural, signed, or written instruction. Tests usually focus on specific aspects of communication, such as receptive vocabulary, expressive vocabulary, written language, symbol or picture recognition, or the ability to learn tactile symbols. They may be used to sample a student's knowledge or skills in these areas, but scores and age levels are likely to be invalid. Some examples follow.

*The Nonspeech Test for Receptive/Expressive Language* (Huer, 1988), a standardized instrument, was designed to assess communication skills of nonspeaking children, adolescents, and adults whose language skills are presumed to be equivalent to the birth to 48-month range. Test items consist of specific skills ("Identifies one body part," "Smiles as examiner speaks," "Imitates new behaviors") in regard to which the individual either passes or fails. A total raw score can be derived, which can be translated to an age equivalent. Students with multiple disabilities were part of the norm group. The evaluator directly administers the test to the student.

*The Expressive One-Word Picture Vocabulary Test—Revised* (Gardner, 1990a) and its companion, the *Receptive One-Word Picture Vocabulary Test* (Gardner, 1990b), are formal measures of single-word vocabulary, designed for children aged 2 to 12. The expressive version requires the student to name pictures of objects, whereas the receptive version requires the learner to indicate the correct picture when the examiner names an object. Both tests are formally administered and yield age equivalents, standard scores, and percentile ranks.

# *DECISION MAKING IN ASSESSMENT*

Attitudes, approaches, methods, tools, and instruments: How do we juggle all these factors in designing an assessment strategy? How do we decide what to use for which student to address what issues? For learners who are deaf-blind and have other severe disabilities, no one formula can be applied. Each assessment design must be guided by unique educational and social issues, as well as the learner's skills, competencies, resources, environments, and needs. In fact, decision making should be conceptualized not as one definitive process that leads to an evaluation plan, but as a sequence of considerations and options that evolve only as the evaluator becomes increasingly familiar with the student. This section reviews these considerations and describes a process for designing an evaluation.

In selecting assessment strategies and procedures, a few obvious truths should be recognized. First, no two evaluators would conduct an assessment of the same student under the same circumstances with exactly the same approach. However, the differences between two plans matter only if they lead to substantially different outcomes in regard to the relevance and meaningfulness of interventions and teaching strategies. Thus, rather than creating a "decision tree" or "flowchart" to direct the evaluator toward selecting particular methods, tools, and instruments, this section considers how the evaluator's decisions will affect the outcomes for the student.

Second, the picture of assessment that is portrayed here is, admittedly, idealized. It has been suggested that good assessments yield extensive data about the learner's breadth of communication behaviors and skills, progress, contexts of interaction, preferences, natural environments, and so on (on which plans for interventions can be based). Yet, assessments are often needed for specific purposes, such as screening an individual to determine his or her eligibility for services, determining whether IEP goals have been met, or checking the layout of an augmentative communication system. Since practical issues and circumstances often influence an assessment's design, the concept of the entire educational team (rather than any particular individual) as "the evaluator" will be discussed. This concept requires the broader view of assessment as an ongoing process that was discussed in Module 5. When the functions of evaluation are distributed among teachers, teaching assistants, speech and language specialists, parents, and providers of related services, standards of assessment need not be compromised by any requirement or constraint.

Third, when several team members are involved in the assessment process, they must decide what information is needed, who will collect the information, whether to seek the assistance of outside consultants, how and when family members should be involved, and how information will be gathered. The decisions that the evaluation team must consider are discussed here, as are the many important functions of evaluation and the critical roles that educators can take in the process.

## THE "CONSUMER'S TEST" OF OUTCOMES

The true worth of an assessment can be judged only from the perspective of the consumer—the individual who is deaf-blind. Therefore, decisions about what approaches, methods, and tools to use for assessment should be made with respect to the likely outcomes for the learner and whether those outcomes will be meaningful.

To make decisions as concrete as possible, one can raise the questions that a consumer may ask—a "consumer's test" of sorts. Each consumer may have a different set of unique concerns, but as for any other "product" (for example, an automobile), a consumer may use certain indicators of quality to judge how well the plan will meet each of his or her particular concerns and needs. The consumer may ask the following:

- "Will the evaluator be able to describe sufficiently my competencies and the ways that I can best communicate?" *Indicators of quality:* use of methods to identify all forms of expression and reception that the learner uses, including non-intentional, interpretable, or potentially communicative behaviors; structured interactions; interviews; communication profiles or behavioral observation tools; and measures of specific competencies used only when the basic competencies are in the learner's repertoire of communication skills.

- "Can I learn what progress I have made?" *Indicators of quality:* reference to previous evaluations (review of history), plans for periodic observations with documentation (informal notes), interviews with familiar communication partners, the "ongoing" attitude reflected in the assessment's design, and use of developmental scales for young children only to evaluate changes in their natural behaviors or structured interactions.

- "Will the assessment be used to help me express my needs, desires, choices, and interests better in everyday situations and settings?" *Indicators of quality:* observations in natural contexts, inventory of communication behaviors in functional routines, interviews with teachers and teaching assistants, interviews with family members, and the use of the behavioral or ecological approaches.

- "Will the assessment help my family, teachers, and schoolmates to communicate with me better and me with them?" *Indicators of quality:* involvement of family members in the assessment process, natural observations of interactions among students, observations using behavioral profiles to identify the opportunities for initiating and responding to a learner's communication behaviors, and an assessment of the social environment.

- "Will the assessment lead to interventions that make sense to me?" *Indicators of quality:* a plan to monitor the effectiveness of current interventions; context-referenced observations to identify natural motivators and preferences that increase social and communication behaviors; structured interactions in ordinary contexts to test hypotheses about effective approaches to communication training; a "dynamic" attitude reflected in the design, which focuses on engaging the learner in interaction to identify conditions that facilitate communication and examines the process of learning; and an age-appropriate assessment approach, materials, and recommendations.

- "Will the assessment identify the services and help I really need?" *Indicators of quality:* team planning of assessment issues and needs; interviews with family members, interpreters, and providers of related services; a review of the person's history in receiving educational services; and an emphasis on services and interventions, not on placements.

- "Will the assessment help other people who work with me?" *Indicators of quality:* team planning; an interdisciplinary attitude reflected in the design; identified communication issues that can be directly related to therapies, medical or health concerns, and vocational training; and interviews with personnel.

- "What can I know about the long-term plan?" *Indicators of quality:* interviews with family members to determine long-term interests, acknowledgment of the larger goals toward which specific interventions are directed, a review of educational records to monitor the achievement of goals, and a plan to monitor the effectiveness of current interventions, reflecting the attitude that assessment is an ongoing process.

## TEAMWORK IN DECISION MAKING

The evaluator must comply with certain conditions that will affect the design of an assessment. In some programs, for example, assessments may be narrowly defined as a three-hour process resulting in placement decisions or recommendations for categories of educational services. Elsewhere, individuals who are officially responsible for conducting assessments may view the process differently from what has been described here. In some clinical settings, such assessments may involve "screenings" of specific aspects of behavior.

When the entire educational team, rather than one identified specialist, is perceived as the evaluator, the educational functions of assessment do not need to be compromised. For example, a requirement for one member of the team to report the use of standardized measures when they are not appropriate can be acknowledged while that evaluator and other team members focus on the more relevant issues for the learner. Time-limited assessments can be seen as fulfilling certain requirements to determine a student's general communication needs, with the understanding that educators or other service providers will continue to plan and conduct ongoing assessments that are more functional and relevant to the student's social experiences in school and at home. The evaluator must make many such practical decisions. When the entire educational team is involved in the decision-making process, judgments can be more readily made about which assessment strategies, approaches, and tools will serve the best interests of the student and of how to deal most effectively with the constraints on or the impediments to assessment.

If the educational team is considered to be the evaluator, the process of assessment should be viewed as compiling an ongoing database of information to be used for the primary purpose of developing and monitoring effective interventions for the student. Each member of the team, including the family members, has responsibilities to enter information about a student's communication and social behaviors into this database. Not unlike users of a computerized database, users (members of the evaluation team) may gain access to specific clusters of information to address particular concerns as they arise. Thus, certain members of the educational team may apply information from the database in specific ways at specific times (for example, a triennial evaluation, a quarterly progress report, the monitoring of specific intervention strategies, and a review of an augmentative communication system), but the essential purposes and the educational applications of the larger database remain virtually unchanged. The following case illustrates how an evaluation team identified specific concerns about a student's communication.

*Joan, age 17, was born profoundly deaf, and her visual impairment is becoming increasingly severe. Her acuity is poor and her vision has worsened over the past 12 months, but she is able to read books by bringing them within an inch or two of her eyes or by using text magnifiers. Joan's primary means of* expressive language is American Sign Language (ASL). Joan's guardian and her high school teachers have been concerned about how her progressive loss of vision may affect her reception of communication, as well as her social interactions. (Currently, Joan stands or sits to the right of and close to the person who is signing to her or shifts her head position, so she can more readily perceive the signs.) Therefore, they requested that the evaluation team conduct an assessment to determine which alternative or supportive means Joan could learn for the reception of language. In the assessment, the team, which consisted of some of Joan's teachers, her guardian, a speech and language specialist with sign language skills, and a psychologist, used the assessment tool, the Communication Profile for Severe Expressive Impairment, and a number of methods (observation, structured one-on-one intervention, a review of Joan's history, and interviews with teachers and teacher's aides) to explore these alternative or supportive means.

When the communication specialist explored tactile signing and fingerspelling with Joan, she found that Joan could readily identify all the letters and could decode words that were spelled into her hand; she thought that Joan could also learn to identify whole words signed into her hand, which would be less time consuming and laborious, since ASL was her primary language. One of the teachers on the team, who examined Joan's potential for using tactile resources (such as tactile maps), thought that Joan could quickly learn to associate tactile symbols and their meanings.

Joan's visual impairment obviously imposed some difficulties in group activities, both in and outside the classroom. Teachers on the team noted that Joan frequently participated in ongoing discussions in class, but often could not detect when her classmates, other than those who were seated directly next to her, were signing. Furthermore, even if Joan sat next to an interpreter, she was still unable to participate fully without some special considerations, including materials in larger print and extra time for the interpreter to repeat others' comments. As a result of her limited reception of information, Joan often made remarks that were out of context or "tuned out."

The evaluation team thought that Joan needed some preparation in using different modalities for receptive communica-

*tion and recommended that two forms of reception should be introduced while Joan still could benefit from visual cues. First, Joan could be helped to improve her braille skills, which she was taught several years ago, by resuming braille lessons with her itinerant vision teacher. Second, interpreters in her classroom or other instructors could introduce Joan informally to tactile signing, so it would become a supplement for her primary and natural means of receiving sign language, to be used when needed. In addition, Joan's guardian suggested that Joan's participation in classroom discussions could be enhanced by the use of small-group formats for appropriate classroom activities and by allowing sufficient time for an interpreter to convey others' comments to Joan. By working together and pooling their input, Joan's evaluation team focused on using appropriate assessment approaches to generate an effective set of interventions to meet Joan's needs.*

## TEAM ROLES

Because of their daily involvement with students, teachers, teaching assistants and aides, and classroom-based therapists have many of the most important roles and responsibilities of assessment (see Major Assessment Responsibilities of Teachers and Classroom-based Specialists). They are usually the keepers of the database of information on each student in whatever form or forms it may take—files of written reports and educational plans, informal notebook records, videotapes, mental notes, computerized records, and various other formats of information in different locations. They are also responsible for carrying out interventions during the school day and must constantly evaluate the effectiveness of the intervention plans. Although they may or may not be responsible for conducting formal assessments that are required for administrative purposes, such as an annual review, they can conduct assessments or contribute to the process in many ways.

To contribute effectively to the assessment process, all the evaluators on the team must coordinate their activities to fulfill several needs by doing the following:

- Arranging meetings periodically to share information about the learner's range of behaviors, to generate agreed-on goals and objectives of the assessment, to relate the interventions to

# MAJOR ASSESSMENT RESPONSIBILITIES OF TEACHERS AND CLASSROOM-BASED SPECIALISTS

In the school, teachers or classroom-based speech and language specialists often assume the primary coordinating role for the educational team. In addition, teachers and teaching assistants can and should assume many specific roles in the assessment process. Here is a brief review of the major responsibilities, each of which requires some form of documentation, formal or informal:

• Conducting observations in natural settings to identify the intentional and nonintentional opportunities that a learner provides for interacting with others and the breadth and range of behaviors that have communicative potential or meaning.

• Testing hypotheses about effective approaches to social interaction, receptive communication, and expressive communication in the contexts of the student's various school routines.

• Monitoring the effectiveness of particular methods and techniques of intervention and interaction and the consistency with which they are applied, through regular contact with members of the educational team, and suggesting how to fine-tune them.

• Observing the student's interrelationships with schoolmates and how schoolmates initiate interaction and seek to involve, ignore, assist, or otherwise show interest in the student.

• Completing communication profiles or behavioral checklists or adding to these documents periodically, noting the qualities of behavior that change over time.

• Working with family members to identify shared concerns and the goals of communication, to develop strategies for implementing interventions, to learn about the student's competence in familiar settings, and to review long-term plans.

• Observing the communicative functions and antecedents of problem behaviors and considering educational approaches to teaching the student alternative forms of expression.

• Keeping informal "progress notes" or documenting the student's new skills and competencies, extensions of communication behaviors, changes in the quality of social interaction, and contexts in which these changes are observed.

• Identifying the variables and approaches to social interaction (for example, favorite activities, preferred lighting conditions, the presence of peers, and approaches to greeting the student) that maximize the student's motivation for and interest in communicating.

• Periodically interviewing others who work with the student (interpreter, work supervisor, recreation therapist, vision teacher, orientation and mobility [O&M] instructor, audiologist) to update knowledge of the student's skills, behaviors, progress, and concerns and to consider future needs. ■

all the various contexts in which the team members may interact with the learner, to review the learner's progress, and to note special concerns as they arise.

- Helping establish the specific roles and responsibilities of each member of the educational team, including members of the family.

- Considering and implementing methods to keep the database on the learner's communication skills, behaviors, needs, interventions, and goals up to date, accessible, and functional.

In some situations, outside consultants or "experts" may be hired to assist with the evaluation. The roles and responsibilities of consultants also vary and must be defined by the educational team before the consultants are involved. In general, outside consultants will not be as comprehensive or effective as family-educator teams in assessing all aspects of communication for a deaf-blind learner. Furthermore, they are often not in a position to monitor closely the ongoing effectiveness of interventions or recommendations that may be suggested as evaluation outcomes. However, they can serve as resources to help organize the evaluation team, teach specific strategies of assessment to team members, provide in-service training on practical issues, help the team establish effective monitoring programs, design realistic data collection procedures, and help identify resources for the student in the school and community and at home.

# PRESENTATION OF ASSESSMENT RESULTS

Although the assessment process should be an ongoing one, there are times when closure is necessary. These occasions are often marked by scheduled events: the deadline for a written report, the updating of intervention plans, a family conference, or the student's graduation from school.

For these occasions, the learner's communication database must be summarized or interpreted and the information translated into goals, general strategies of intervention, specific intervention techniques, and blueprints for the future. These summaries are of great significance, educationally and emotionally. For the student and his or her family, they can highlight the important accomplishments made over time or the objectives that were not fulfilled. They can place emphasis on the natural opportunities for social interaction or the behaviors that interfere with learning. They can help establish positive, realistic expectations or reinforce the limitations that are related to deaf-blindness and other severe disabilities. This section discusses the interpretation and presentation of the findings of assessments in three contexts: the assessment report, the instructional design, and plans for the future.

## ASSESSMENT REPORTS

The assessment report is the primary vehicle for summarizing information about a learner's communication skills and behaviors. It is often a permanent record, following the student throughout his or her educational life. It may give other educators or evaluators certain preconceptions about the student and is often the basis for designing intervention plans.

The assessment report, delivered in written or oral form, is a reflection of the assessment process itself. As with an assessment, there are no specific guidelines for presenting information in a report, standard formats for summarizing the data by sections or domains, or required length. However, in whatever format it is presented, the report is a central document because communication is infused in virtually all activities in which the learner engages in all settings. It can have a great impact, positive or negative, on how others approach the learner, perceive opportunities to respond or interact, or directly intervene.

The same desirable characteristics that were outlined at the beginning of this module and applied to designing assessments are applicable to constructing the report. That is, when the summaries are assembled, the results and issues should be presented so they are clear to other members of the team, including the family members (for a summary of issues, see Assessment Reports: Do's and Don'ts), and the following characteristics should be reflected: interdisciplinary, ongoing, dynamic, context referenced, and ecologically valid.

- The concept of interdisciplinary is reflected in the report when technical language is avoided and descriptions of specific competencies and skills (for example, the use of gestures and the use of functional vision for picture symbols) are relevant to the issues with which other team members are concerned.

- The concept of ongoing is reflected when the student's progress since the last report is reviewed and descriptions are

H E L P
at a
G L A N C E

## ASSESSMENT REPORTS: DO'S AND DON'TS

**Do's**

• Avoid technical language.

• Choose terms that accurately depict a specific behavior or quality.

• Describe specific competencies and skills.

• Indicate the student's progress (changes in behavior and accomplishments) since the last report.

• Emphasize the functionality of communication behaviors in various contexts.

• Describe the student's interactive and social behaviors in different settings and with various people.

• Suggest opportunities for greater response and interaction and ways to help the student understand messages better.

**Don'ts**

• Do not use disability conditions as adjectives.

• Avoid subjective interpretations.

• Do not present quantitative data, including standard scores and percentile rankings.

• Do not reference descriptions of children to age levels or to age equivalents of children without disabilities.

• Do not use general terms or terms that are not reality based. ∎

included of his or her behaviors and accomplishments that will enable others to note specific areas of progress in the future.

• The concept of dynamic is apparent when the report includes descriptions of interactions with the student, the ways to greet or approach the student, suggestions for helping the student understand others' messages better, and indications of the opportunities for response and interaction.

• The concept of context referenced is reflected by descriptions of the student's interactive and social behaviors in different settings with various people and by an emphasis on the functionality of the communication behaviors in those contexts.

• The concept of ecological validity is reflected in how useful the reported information will be for planning direct interventions. (Note that the student, educators, and family members can also evaluate the utility of written summaries by applying the "consumer's test" described earlier.)

Terminology and language are important. Reports should refrain from using a disability condition as an adjective; it is preferable to refer to a student simply as a student. Certain words are often misused, and the report writer must be careful to choose those that accurately describe a specific behavior or quality. For example, terms like *preintentional* and *presymbolic* are appropriate if there is an expected transition to *intentional* or *symbolic* qualities of communication. Otherwise, the prefix *non-* may be a more accurate descriptor. However, even *non-* must be used with caution, since many learners with severe disabilities whose communication behaviors tend to be nonintentional or nonsymbolic may exhibit a few intentional or symbolic behaviors in certain situations or contexts. Some terms and concepts have no counterparts in reality (for example, "the student's inner language") or are too general to be useful (for instance, "a nonverbal child"). Objective and precise descriptions of communication behavior (such as "the learner pushed away the materials") are preferable over possibly erroneous subjective interpretations (for example, "the learner seemed bored").

The use of quantitative data, including age levels, age equivalents, standard scores, and percentile rankings is usually inappropriate and irrelevant in describing the communication skills of deaf-blind students. If such data are presented, the report should clarify precisely how their use can directly benefit the learner. However, descriptions of older children, adolescents, and adults who are deaf-blind should never be referenced to age levels of children or adults without disabilities (for example, "This 14-year-old student is functioning on a _____-year-old level").

## INSTRUCTIONAL DESIGN

The primary outcomes of assessment are interventions and teaching strategies to enhance the student's communication and social interactions. However, the translation of information from the assessment into instructional methods is not easy. For each student, there are probably dozens of educational objectives that are relevant, hundreds of natural and planned learning activities that can address those objectives, and perhaps thousands of daily opportunities to interact or intervene.

The members of the team must therefore plan interventions in several critical steps. They should (1) identify the goals and objectives that have priority, (2) design interventions that can be integrated into activities that are functional and meaningful, (3) delineate the opportunities to intervene in natural contexts, and (4) specify the forms and techniques of intervention that will complement the student's expressive and receptive communication behaviors.

Each step can be broken down into smaller steps, much like the process of task analysis. For example, identifying the opportunities to intervene in natural contexts requires a review of the learner's various daily routines at school, at home, and in the community and an understanding of the sequence of steps involved in each routine, so specific opportunities for interaction can be anticipated. It also requires knowledge of how the learner tends to initiate or respond to interaction during each routine (for example, making a request, following an instruction, responding to a cue or signal, or taking a turn). Strategies must then be considered to promote the expansion, generalization, accuracy, consistency, and quality of the student's communication behaviors at each opportune moment in these contexts.

Siegel-Causey and Ernst (1989) described several guidelines for enhancing interactions of students with severe disabilities whose communication behaviors are mostly nonsymbolic. They emphasized that interventions should be provided in the forms of natural interaction during functional tasks with age-appropriate methods. They also suggested that interventions should do the following:

- provide a supportive and caring atmosphere
- enhance sensitivity (to be aware of and receptive to the cues of others)
- sequence experiences (to organize activities in predictable formats)
- increase opportunities (to provide favorable climates in which the learner can participate)
- utilize movement.

In addition, under each of these five general guidelines, they presented specific suggestions that can be incorporated into intervention techniques.

Many of the same general goals may apply to different students, but the forms and techniques of intervention will be individualized according to the learner's unique communication behaviors, interests, needs, and experience. For example, such general goals as "to increase a student's accuracy in expressing choices and preferences," "to extend the learner's social interaction with peers," "to increase the learner's use of functional and conventional symbols," and "to extend the learner's request for assistance or social attention to other environments" are broad in scope. In accordance with the guidelines offered by Siegel-Causey and Ernst, the task of the educational team is to specify the environments and activities in which these goals are relevant, identify as many opportunities as possible in which interventions can be applied, and describe the exact sequences and procedures that will facilitate the learner's communication and social interaction skills. The team should be concerned with two potential problems. First, a "cookbook" approach should be avoided in specifying goals and interventions so they do not become trivialized. For example, "The student will respond to a peer's greeting 7 out of 10 times" takes away from the genuine concern, which is the quality of interaction and the extension of social interest. Second, there must be some method to ensure that when an intervention is actually applied, it is not interpreted too broadly and that it resembles what the team had in mind. The following example illustrates how information from an assessment can be used to individualize goals, objectives, and interventions.

*Eduardo, age 5, has multiple disabilities, including a moderate-to-severe hearing impairment, a severe visual impairment (able to detect light and perhaps shadows of people and objects under certain conditions), significant developmental delays, and spastic quadriplegia. He also has a seizure disorder. Eduardo's parents and teachers have been reviewing his progress and considering appropriate communication goals and interventions.*

*The educational team, consisting of Eduardo's classroom teacher, his parents, an occupational therapist, an orientation and mobility (O&M) instructor, a physical therapist, and a psychological evaluator, conducted an assessment using the communication profile, Profiles of Expressive Communication and Social Interaction (Mar & Sall, 1991). The evaluators engaged Eduardo in structured interactions and observed him during his daily routines, both at school and at home. In addition, Eduardo's parents provided detailed information about his interests and activities at home.*

*Eduardo's communication behaviors were mainly reactive. He expressed himself by crying or vocalizing to signify distress or discomfort, pushing away or turning his head to indicate rejection, becoming more active to denote excitement, becoming quiet or pausing to reflect interest, and turning his head or shifting his body to orient himself socially to others. Although Eduardo required total or near-total assistance to meet his daily needs (eating, dressing, and toileting), he was partially able to participate in various routines by relaxing his body, orienting toward the provider of care, feeding himself certain foods, and so forth. Various members of the evaluation team noted that Eduardo had acquired skills that are important for social and communication behaviors, including the ability to orient to others when given tactile and some auditory cues, to recognize familiar persons, to discriminate between preferred and nonpreferred toys and objects, and to indicate that he anticipates certain events by smiling and extending his arms outward, for example, in response to being greeted by other children.*

*After reviewing Eduardo's skills and progress, the team formulated several general and specific goals and described some activities that could promote the achievement of these goals. One general goal was to increase Eduardo's awareness that by producing certain behaviors, he could communicate his interests and needs and get the attention of or responses from other people. It was suggested that in a tickling game, his teacher's aide should first observe his anticipatory reactions and then reinforce them with the stimulation he enjoys. Similarly, during snack time, the person who fed him could wait until he actively searched for his favorite foods before placing them on the tray. Likewise, for activities such as making music during music time, a change in Eduardo's body position or muscle tension during a pause could be rewarded by a resumption of the activity.*

*Another goal was to help Eduardo associate tactile or auditory cues or both with different familiar routines to increase his anticipatory behaviors. It was thought that, over time, Eduardo would learn to associate these cues (such as feeling the spoon before being fed or having water rubbed on his hands or legs just before swimming) with the actual events and would acquire some preparatory behaviors (for example, relaxing his body, opening his mouth, or extending his hand to search for the spoon).*

# PLANS FOR THE FUTURE

A communication assessment must deal with a student's current educational and social issues, but it must not lose sight of long-term plans and goals. Therefore, it is necessary to give some thought to planning for the future. Planning refers not to predicting what skills and behaviors a learner will acquire by a certain age, but to the systematic and routine review of the learner's needs in future contexts, environments, and vocations. Some of the more critical long-term issues pertain to the learner's primary forms of communication, to transitions, and to providing support to the learner and his or her family.

## Primary Forms of Communication

As the student acquires more extensive communication skills, it will in all likelihood be necessary to decide which receptive and expressive forms will best serve his or her future needs. Many factors, including the family's interests, possible changes in the student's functional vision or hearing over time, and the student's motivation and ability to use different forms of communication (tactile sign language, visible sign language, tangible symbols, gestures) will affect these decisions. The "survival skills" of communication—the basic functional social skills that will prepare the student for involvement in work and community environments—must be identified and targeted for instruction. The evaluator must also consider a variety of questions about whether and how assistive and augmentative devices (for example, magnifiers, speech synthesizers, communication boards) may benefit the person in the future (Reichle, 1991).

## Transition Planning

Communication issues in transition planning are discussed in greater detail in Module 14 and so are only summarized here. The major concerns have to do with preparing the individual who is deaf-blind, as well as his or her communication partners (household members, co-workers, companions, and people in the community), for meaningful interaction. Goals must be directed to helping the person acquire expressive and receptive vocabularies that are increasingly functional and that give him or her greater access to and greater independence in the community. They should also be directed to teaching communication partners to provide social support, understand messages and signals, and identify opportunities to respond to the person. For many deaf-blind people, assessments of communication will also need to address the use of assistive devices or applications of technology to enable them to perform certain jobs or to increase access to telecommunication.

Graduation from school or a family's move to a different community may be exciting, but it is also confusing when the student faces new environments and communication partners. The evaluator should therefore consider several measures in advance to facilitate the change with the least amount of disruption. Such measures may include contacting members of the student's new educational team, ensuring the continuity of intervention strategies, or even helping the student become familiar in the new environment.

## Provision of Support

Finally, the assessment of communication must help guide and support the student and his or her family to make decisions that will create positive long-term outcomes. The evaluator's supportive role is critical at many stages and levels. It begins with involving the parent or provider of care directly in the assessment process by discussing the family's concerns and obtaining information from those who are closest to the learner. As a partner to the family, the evaluator can provide useful information about enhancing the student's competencies and various forms of intervention or services, incorporate the effective communication methods used at home into the school, objectively review the learner's progress and needs, provide information about resources and materials, and present issues that the family must think about to prepare for significant life changes. Thus, the family plans for the future, but the evaluator must be sensitive and responsive to the family's goals for the learner.

A comment by Shriner, Ysseldyke, and Christenson (1989, p. 160) illustrates many of these ideas: "When all is said and done, the only valid reason for assessing a student is to make a positive difference. . . ." This is no small charge. The positive difference is a step toward greater social integration among the learner, family members, educators, and friends.

Assessment provides team members with vital information about the abilities and skills that a student has developed and about the skills that the student needs to develop in the future. This information guides team members in the actual selection and design of specific communication modes, devices, and features of a system, as well as instructional strategies that are suited to the student's assessed needs. Module 12 discusses how assessment information is applied as service providers proceed systematically to implement a communication development program for each student.

# *REFERENCES*

Bolton, S., & Dashiell, S. (1984). *INCH: INteraction CHecklist for augmentative communication*. Wauconda, IL: Don Johnston, Inc.

Browder, D. M. (1987). *Assessment of individuals with severe disabilities*. Baltimore: Paul H. Brookes.

Browder, D. M. (1991). *Assessment of individuals with severe disabilities* (2nd ed.). Baltimore: Paul H. Brookes.

Curtis, W. S., & Donlon, E. T. (1985). *Observational evaluation of severely multihandicapped children*. Berwyn, PA: Swets North America.

Durand, V. M., & Crimmins, D. B. (1992). *Motivation assessment scale*. Glenview, IL: Monaco & Associates.

Evans, I. M. (1991). Testing and diagnosis: A review and evaluation. In L. H. Meyer, C. A. Peck, & L. Brown (Eds.), *Critical issues in the lives of people with severe disabilities* (pp. 25–44). Baltimore: Paul H. Brookes.

Gardner, M. F. (1990a). *Expressive one-word picture vocabulary test—Revised*. Austin, TX: PRO-ED.

Gardner, M. F. (1990b). *Receptive one-word picture vocabulary test*. Austin, TX: PRO-ED.

Gaylord-Ross, R., & Browder, D. (1991). Functional assessment: Dynamic and domain properties. In L. H. Meyer, C. A. Peck, & L. Brown (Eds.), *Critical issues in the lives of people with severe disabilities* (pp. 45–66). Baltimore: Paul H. Brookes.

Goetz, L., Schuler, A., & Sailor, W. (1983). Motivational considerations in teaching language to severely handicapped students. In M. Hersen, V. Van Hasselt, & J. Matson (Eds.), *Behavior therapy for the developmentally and physically disabled* (pp. 57–77). New York: Academic Press.

Hatwell, Y. (1985). *Piagetian reasoning and the blind*. New York: American Foundation for the Blind.

Huer, M. B. (1988). *Nonspeech test for receptive/expressive language*. Wauconda, IL: Don Johnston, Inc.

Johnson-Martin, N. M., Attermeier, S. M., & Hacker, B. J. (1990). *Carolina curriculum for preschoolers with special needs*. Baltimore: Paul H. Brookes.

Kates, L., Schein, J. D., & Wolf, E. G. (1981). Assessment of deaf-blind children: A study of the use of the behavior rating instrument for autistic and other atypical children. *Viewpoints in Teaching & Learning, 57,* 54–63.

Mar, H. H., & Sall, N. (1991). *Profiles of expressive communication and social interaction.* New York: Developmental Disabilities Center, St. Luke's-Roosevelt Hospital Center.

Meyer, L. H., Cole, D. A., McQuarter, R., & Reichle, J. (1990). Validation of the *Assessment of Social Competence* (ASC) for children and young adults with developmental disabilities. *Journal of the Association for Persons with Severe Handicaps, 15,* 57–68.

Meyer, L. H., & Evans, I. M. (1989). *Nonaversive intervention for behavior problems: A manual for home and community.* Baltimore: Paul H. Brookes.

Meyer, L. H., Reichle, J., McQuarter, R., Cole, D., Vandercook, T., Evans, I., Neel, R., & Kishi, G. (1985). *Assessment of social competence (ASC): A scale of social competence functions* (rev. ed.). Syracuse, NY: Inclusive Education, Syracuse University.

Nietupski, J. A., & Hamre-Nietupski, S. M. (1987). An ecological approach to curriculum development. In L. Goetz, D. Guess, & K. Stremel-Campbell (Eds.), *Innovative program design for individuals with dual sensory impairments* (pp. 225–253). Baltimore: Paul H. Brookes.

Otos, M. (1983). *Nonverbal prelinguistic communication: A guide to communication levels in prelinguistic handicapped children.* Salem: Oregon Department of Education.

Reichle, J. (1991). Defining the decisions involved in designing and implementing augmentative and alternative communication systems. In J. Reichle, J. York, & J. Sigafoos (Eds.), *Implementing augmentative and alternative communication* (pp. 39–60). Baltimore: Paul H. Brookes.

Reynell, J. (1979). *Reynell-Zinkin scales: Developmental scales for young visually handicapped children.* Wood Dale, IL: Stoelting Co.

Rowland, C. (1987). Perspectives on communication assessment. In M. Bullis (Ed.), *Communication development in young children with deaf-blindness: Literature review III* (pp. 1–22). Monmouth: Oregon State System of Higher Education.

Rowland, C. (1990). *Communication matrix.* Portland, OR: Portland Projects, Washington State University.

Rowland C., & Stremel-Campbell, K. (1987). Share and share alike: Conventional gestures to emergent language for learners with sensory impairments. In L. Goetz, D. Guess, & K. Stremel-Campbell (Eds.), *Innovative program design for individuals with dual sensory impairments* (pp. 49–75). Baltimore: Paul H. Brookes.

Ruttenburg, B. A., Wenar, C., & Wolf-Schein, E. G. (1977). *Behavior rating instrument for autistic and other atypical children (BRIAAC)* (2nd ed.). Wood Dale, IL: Stoelting Co.

Shane, H. C. (1987). *Communication profile for severe expressive impairment.* Boston: Communication Enhancement Center, Children's Hospital.

Shriner, J. G., Ysseldyke, J. E., & Christenson, S. L. (1989). Assessment procedures for use in heterogeneous classrooms. In S. Stainback, W. Stainback, & M. Forest (Eds.), *Educating all students in the mainstream of regular education* (pp. 159–181). Baltimore: Paul H. Brookes.

Siegel-Causey, E., & Downing, J. (1987). Nonsymbolic communication development: Theoretical concepts and educational strategies. In L. Goetz, D. Guess, & K. Stremel-Campbell (Eds.), *Innovative program design for individuals with dual sensory impairments (pp. 15–48). Baltimore: Paul H. Brookes.*

Siegel-Causey, E., & Ernst, B. (1989). Theoretical orientation and research in nonsymbolic development. In Siegel-Causey, E., & Guess, D. (Eds.), *Enhancing nonsymbolic communication interactions among learners with severe disabilities.* (pp. 15–51). Baltimore: Paul H. Brookes.

Sigafoos, J., Cole, D. A., & McQuarter, R. J. (1987). Current practices in the assessment of students with severe handicaps. *Journal of the Association for Persons with Severe Handicaps, 12,* 264–273.

Stillman, R. (1978). *Callier-Azusa scale G.* Dallas: Callier Center for Communication Disorders, University of Texas at Dallas.

Stillman, R. (1990). *Procedures for evaluating and enhancing information exchange between service providers and persons with deaf-blindness: Final report.* Dallas: University of Texas at Dallas.

Stillman, R., & Battle, C. (1985). *Callier-Azusa scale H: Scales for the assessment of communicative abilities.* Dallas: Callier Center for Communication Disorders, University of Texas at Dallas.

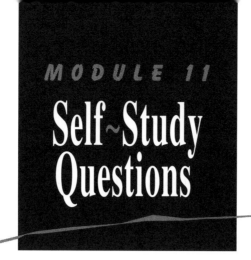

1. The primary objectives of the assessment of communication for a student who is deaf-blind are to
   a. identify the student's range of communication skills and behaviors in different environments and develop interventions to enhance his or her opportunities for communication and interaction.
   b. determine the student's level of functioning and facilitate the use of symbolic communication.
   c. test hypotheses about the student's expressive and receptive communication and assess his or her progress from the past to the present.

2. To assess the communication abilities of an adolescent who is deaf-blind and has severe multiple disabilities, it is best to use an assessment approach that
   a. involves developmental methods so the student's competencies can be closely matched to the tasks of the assessment.
   b. emphasizes communication in the context of practical skills and natural social environments.
   c. involves applied behavioral analysis to identify motivational factors that increase spontaneous communication.

3. When evaluating a learner who is unable to perform formal test activities, one should
   a. not use tests.
   b. adapt the tests.
   c. use developmental age ranges instead of test scores.

4. Observations of students' communication and social behaviors should be conducted
   a. at different times and in different environments.
   b. during structured interactions that can be task analyzed.
   c. to validate information obtained through interviews.

5. Profiles of communication and social interaction behavior help to determine
   a. strengths and weaknesses across language and communication measures.
   b. students' preferences for activities and social interaction partners.
   c. the breadth and range of behaviors that are communicative or have communicative potential.

6. Which of the following is not likely to be an effective practice in making decisions for assessments of communication?
   a. The entire educational team is viewed as the "evaluator."
   b. Educators assume multiple, "transdisciplinary" roles and responsibilities.
   c. The distinction between evaluation procedures and effective instruction is kept clear.

7. Reports of assessments should strive primarily to
   a. emphasize the strengths of the student and deemphasize the areas of difficulty.
   b. be objective and sensitive to the needs and concerns of students, their families, and team members.
   c. document the current database as completely as possible.

8. Generally, interventions and instructional activities should be designed to be
   a. as replicable as possible from one context or environment to another.
   b. provided during functional tasks and natural interactions.
   c. interpreted as broadly as possible to promote generalization.

*Answers to self-study questions for this module appear at the end of Unit 2.*

# Choosing Systems and Modes of Communication

ELLIN SIEGEL-CAUSEY

- *Identify the student's communication strengths and needs*

- *Consider the demands of the student's environment*

- *Assess current communication forms and functions*

- *Increase the student's skills by expanding on current forms*

- *Monitor the system's effectiveness*

Since students who are deaf-blind have varying degrees of sensory loss, varying skills and abilities, and hence varying needs, the selection of modes for communication and systems or devices to support communication requires careful consideration. Such decisions affect an individual's ability to interact effectively with others every day. This module is designed to help members of the educational team to choose the appropriate modes and systems for deaf-blind students, including those with multiple disabilities, through the following systematic steps:

1. identifying how the individual communicates
2. defining the demands of the individual's environment
3. specifying effective communication modes, systems, and devices that are appropriate to the needs of the individual and the requirements of the environment.

These procedures are only part of the overall process of enhancing the communication of students who are deaf-blind. The assessment of communication skills and an explanation of the types of assessment approaches, methods, and tools that may be used have already been discussed in Module 11.

Communication can be both simple and complex, and it is especially important to consider this principle when selecting modes, systems, and devices that support communication for deaf-blind students that is as effective and advanced as possible. Because the student must have effective ways or modes of making his or her needs and desires known to others, and others must have effective ways or modes of conveying information to the student, the educational team should first identify (1) the student's communication strengths and needs, and (2) the ways that others communicate with him or her (see Beukelman & Mirenda, 1992; Cook & Coleman, 1988; Hagood & Watkins, 1991; Rowland & Stremel-Campbell, 1987; Siegel-Causey & Guess, 1989).

# MODES OF COMMUNICATION

As was discussed in Module 8, modes of communication can be aided or unaided. Unaided communication (saying or signing an idea or gesturing or making a specific sound to indicate it) does not require equipment or an item to convey a message; the student uses his or her own body or voice. In contrast, aided communication requires additional equipment; for example, a student may write a note using a pencil and paper or a braille slate and stylus or use a communication picture booklet or high-technology equipment with pictures to convey ideas.

It is common for people to use more than one mode of communication and several forms within that mode and to choose the mode and form that best suit a given circumstance. Forms of communication include speech, body movements, and the use of external objects, such as tangible symbols. Three basic communication modes (unaided modes, both vocal and nonvocal, and aided modes) are presented in Table 12-1 and are examined in detail in this section. In this module, vocal and nonvocal modes are considered separately, although both are unaided modes. The distinction between vocal and nonvocal modes is important for students who are deaf-blind, since

**TABLE 12-1:**
**Modes and Forms of Communication**

| MODES | FORMS | | | | | |
|---|---|---|---|---|---|---|
| **VOCAL (UNAIDED)** | Sounds | Babbling | Speech | | | |
| **NONVOCAL (UNAIDED)** | Alertness (behavioral state) | Facial expression and affect | Body movement | Visual forms (eye gaze, eye-blink codes) | Gestural forms (gestures, pantomime, yes/no headshakes) | Sign language (signs, finger-spelling) |
| **AIDED** | Objects (real objects, parts of objects, miniature objects) | Texture | Photographs (color and black and white) | Graphic symbol sets (color drawings, black-and-white drawings, commercial black-and-white symbols, alphabet) | | |

typically used modes and forms may be inaccessible to them because of their sensory losses. Planning for instruction in communication and selecting a student's communication system should begin with a focus on the student's needs and current modes and forms of communication (Beukelman & Mirenda, 1992; Bullis & Fielding, 1988; Musselwhite & St. Louis, 1988).

It is important to note that in their daily interactions all individuals, including persons who are deaf-blind, frequently communicate using different forms within the three communication modes discussed here. Some individuals may use one mode to express ideas and information to others but understand a different mode in receiving ideas and information from others.

## UNAIDED COMMUNICATION: VOCAL MODE

The vocal mode is unaided because no special external devices are used; the individual uses only his or her voice to communicate. This mode consists of sounds, including vocalizing, babbling, and speech. It is familiar, since most people speak and use sounds to convey messages to others. Infants make sounds (vocalize), such as cries, giggles, whimpers, screams, or sighs, to communicate long before they can talk. Parents become sensitive to the sounds their infants make and the messages that are conveyed, and the infants gradually learn that their sounds can influence the people in their environments. Before they develop actual speech, infants start to babble by repeating basic sounds (da–da, ma–ma, ba–ba) that are the building blocks of words and use these sounds to interact with those around them (Chen, 1990).

Speech develops first with single words, then with increasingly complex combinations of words arranged in sentences that express full and complete thoughts. Some deaf-blind students may use vocal communication, including a combination of forms (for example, babbling and a few words or vocalizations). Many students who are deaf-blind, however, do not use the vocal mode effectively because they have little, if any, remaining hearing with which to monitor vocalizations.

## UNAIDED COMMUNICATION: NONVOCAL MODE

The nonvocal mode involves the use of the individual's face or body to communicate and does not require external aids or devices, so it is also unaided. People use nonvocal forms to convey messages to others around them every day. For example, in a crowded room in which

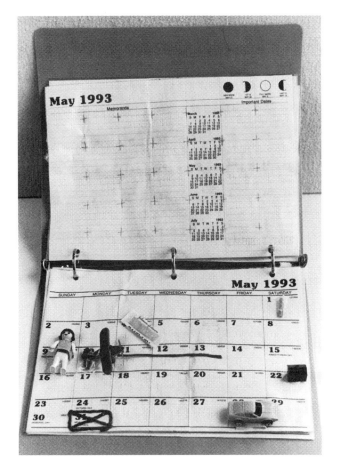

▲ *Symbols displayed on a page, board, or other surface can be used effectively as part of an aided communication system.*

a meeting has started, a latecomer may see others point to an empty chair, rather than speak out loud. People wave at others from great distances when shouting would not be as effective or appropriate. Basketball and football players signal their teammates with gestures during games. These forms of communication are commonplace and are defined by most cultures. Nonvocal communication behaviors that are appropriate in Eastern cultures may be different from those that are acceptable in Western cultures, for example.

The nonvocal mode includes level of alertness, facial expressions or affect, body movements, visual direction and gaze, gestures, and sign language. For example, a student may motion to a teacher when a wind–up toy stops moving to request that the toy be started again, grimace when the toy stops moving, or sign the word "stop." Most deaf-blind students use many nonvocal forms.

## AIDED MODE

Aided communication involves the use of systems and devices that are external to oneself or a combination of several modes and devices that are incorporated into a person's overall communication system to give the person many options (see Module 8). Communication aids are designed to help the individual convey messages by using symbols, such as objects, textures, and photographs, or the alphabet. These symbols can be displayed separately on a page or board or through an electronic device. For example, rather than speaking to order a cheeseburger at a restaurant, a person may order by presenting a photograph of the item or pointing to a line drawing on a board or to an item pictured on the menu. Why are such systems and devices needed? Some people communicate more effectively with the support of these aids because their use of both vocal and nonvocal communication modes is less effective than it might be, usually because of their disabilities.

## STEPS IN CHOOSING A COMMUNICATION SYSTEM

The selection of a communication system must be based on the student's skills in vocal, nonvocal, and aided communication. An effective and appropriate system uses the student's present array of skills and helps the student move to a more complex level of communication (Reichle, 1991). Whatever system the student's teachers and family and the rest of the educational team choose will probably involve the use of all three modes of communication.

The five primary steps involved in selecting a communication system (gathering basic information in an assessment, selecting the mode or system, designing the mode or system, implementing the mode or system, and reevaluating the mode or system) are outlined in Figure 12-1. This module focuses on the first three steps in particular; additional information on the last two steps is presented in Module 13. The use of sequential steps is important to support the educational team's careful consideration of the student's strengths and areas that should be developed further, which, in turn, supports the student's overall development of communication.

As Figure 12-1 suggests, the selection of a communication system or mode is an ongoing process. After an instructional plan for a system is designed and implemented, it is evaluated by routinely assessing the student's needs and the effectiveness of the system (Cress, Mathy-Laikko, & Angelo, 1989). Thorough assessments should be conducted at least twice a year, and the system should be

**FIGURE 12-1:**

Steps in Selecting Communication Systems

---

## STEP 1: GATHER BASIC INFORMATION IN AN ASSESSMENT

| ASSESS THE STUDENT'S SKILLS AND NEEDS | ASSESS HOW THE STUDENT COMMUNICATES | ASSESS THE FUNCTIONS OF THE STUDENT'S COMMUNICATION BEHAVIORS | ASSESS THE DEMANDS OF THE ENVIRONMENT |
|---|---|---|---|
| Determine what skills and needs the student currently has. | Define the forms and modes with which the student currently communicates and how others communicate with the student. | Determine for what purposes (functions) the student communicates and for what purposes others communicate with the student. | Determine what reasons there are to communicate, who the communication partners are, and the settings in which communication takes place. |

---

## STEP 2: SELECT THE COMMUNICATION MODE OR SYSTEM

| MATCH THE STUDENT'S COMMUNICATION | MATCH THE SERVICE PROVIDER'S COMMUNICATION | CONSIDER OTHER FACTORS |
|---|---|---|
| Match the modes and functions used by the student to the student's skills and needs. | Match the modes and functions used by the service provider to the student's skills and needs. | 1. Use team decision making.<br>2. Include the family as part of the team.<br>3. Focus on age-appropriate skills.<br>4. Emphasize functional tasks and materials.<br>5. Use natural settings for training. |

---

## STEP 3: DESIGN THE COMMUNICATION SYSTEM

## STEP 4: START USING THE SYSTEM

## STEP 5: REEVALUATE THE SYSTEM

---

redesigned or modified on the basis of the new information that is obtained, to ensure that it fits the changing needs of the student as he or she develops new skills and needs.

# STEP 1: GATHER INFORMATION

An assessment should provide members of the educational team with four types of information: (1) how the student communicates, (2) how others communicate with the student, (3) the functions of the student's communication behaviors, and (4) the demands of the environment. This information is obtained in a number of substeps that are outlined in the form of an exercise for readers.

**Determine the various modes of communication that a student uses and that others use with the student (Substeps 1 and 2).** In performing these substeps, it is helpful to list the modes on a set of forms after you use an assessment strategy (discussed in Module 11). Examples of filled-out forms relating to one student, Christopher, are presented in Figures 12-2–12-13 at the end of this module; blank forms that you may fill out are in Appendix C. Figure 12-2 presents examples of the vocal mode and forms—sounds, babbling, and speech (actual words)—that Christopher uses. Figures 12-3 and 12-4 list the nonvocal and aided modes, respectively.

Figures 12-5–12-7 are copies of the three forms that list examples of the forms of communication that the adult, Suzanne, uses with the student Christopher. When you fill out copies of these forms (in Appendix C), it may be helpful to videotape some interactions that you usually have with the student and then to list the words to which you expect the student to respond, especially directions, such as "sit," "find," and "show," and the names of objects and people.

After you have completed the forms, consider the following questions:

- Do these lists describe what you think the student expresses?
- Has the student had opportunities to learn to express himself or herself with the modes that were left blank?
- Do you tend to use one mode more than the others and to use certain forms with one mode?
- Does your communication match the student's and what the educational planning team has identified as the student's communication needs?

**Assess the functions of the student's communication behaviors (Substep 3).** The function of a communication behavior refers to the purpose of the behavior. This module emphasizes three basic purposes or functions of communication (Siegel-Causey & Wetherby, 1993):

1. *behavioral regulation:* communicating to get others to do something (requesting an action) or to stop doing something (protesting an action)

2. *social interaction:* communicating to get others to look at or notice you, in order to request a social routine, permission, or comfort; to greet; to call; or to show off

3. *joint attention:* communicating to get others to look at an object or event, to comment on an action, or to request information.

Examples of filled-in forms for this substep are presented in Figures 12-8–12-10 for Christopher and Figures 12-11–12-13 for Suzanne (for examples of the functions of communication in each mode, see Tables 12-2, 12-3, and 12-4 at the end of this module). To complete this substep, list the functions of the student's communication on one set of forms and the functions of your communication with the student on another set. Complete these figures using the forms of communication that you listed, as in the examples in Figures 12-2–12-7. For instance, in filling out the form as in Figure 12-8, list any of the sounds from Figure 12-2 that the student uses to fulfill any of these functions. Be as specific as possible in identifying the student's behaviors.

It should be noted that many people use one form of communication for more than one function. For example, smiling (a nonvocal form) may be used for all three functions: behavioral regulation, social interaction, and joint attention. Furthermore, in determining the functions of your communication, it is again helpful to see if you use specific functions more than others.

**Evaluate the demands of the environment (Substep 4).** Most people adapt their communications to the places where interactions are occurring and to the various persons with whom they are interacting. All the environments in which a student who is deaf-blind participates influence his or her communications, too (see Noonan & Siegel-Causey, 1990). Therefore, in assessing demands of the environment, it is helpful to consider the following three questions:

1. What reasons are there to communicate?

2. With whom is the student communicating?

3. In what settings does the communication take place?

The environment and the people within it define the opportunities for students to understand that their functions and forms of communication are recognized and answered. For example, students will use gestures when they realize that others notice the gestures (respond to them) and that the gestures affect others (regulate others' behavior). Thus, in selecting the modes, systems, and devices of communication, it is important to determine how your mutual environment (usually a school) affects the use or nonuse of specific forms and functions. In this regard, it is helpful to consider the following questions:

- Do you provide opportunities for the student to understand that his or her communication behaviors (forms) are important and recognized and that these forms can affect you and the environment?

- Do you respond to the student's forms of communication consistently and appropriately in relation to their apparent purposes?

Similarly, it is helpful to know who the student's other communication partners are and to determine

- whether some partners are more significant than others
- how the partners communicate with the student
- whether some modes, systems, or devices are especially effective in supporting the communication partners' interactions with the student
- whether training is available to help the partners interact more effectively with the student (see Module 13 for instructional strategies to help service providers and parents become aware of the communication behaviors of students who are deaf-blind).

The specific elements of the student's various environments must be considered, since each student performs everyday activities in different settings. Often, one or two settings take priority for defining the appropriate forms and functions of communication and for selecting vocabularies. In choosing specific goals, modes, systems, and devices for instruction in communication, it is important to determine those that can be useful for the student in many or all environments in which he or she participates daily. A form or function that can be used in several ways and in several settings and with many communication partners should be emphasized in instruction because it will allow the student more opportunities to interact.

## STEP 2: SELECT THE MODE OR SYSTEM

In this step, you identify and describe the modes, systems, and devices of communication that the student and you and his or her other communication partners are using, based on the information gathered in Step 1, including the areas in which the student needs instruction, the appropriate instructional techniques, and the appropriate forms and functions of communication (instructional strategies are discussed in Module 13). The modes, systems, devices, and goals of communication (the communication development program) that you choose will build on the student's current skills and help the student develop new skills in all areas of intervention. This program will allow the student to express himself or herself and demonstrate what he or she understands with modes and forms that he or she already uses skillfully. Successful interaction promotes the desire to interact more, and using successful modes and forms with appropriate responses from others motivates the student to continue to communicate.

It bears repeating that the educational team should select additional communication modes, forms, systems, and devices on the basis of what the student already responds to best. For example, if the student has useful vision, responds to gestures, and uses gestures frequently with others, he or she may benefit from sign language. If a student does not seem to respond to language input from either voice or signs, the team may decide that it is important to pair tangible symbols with speech and sign language, giving the student all three symbolic options. Often, the team members' choices will be educated guesses; despite solid assessment information, it may be difficult to determine if one mode, form, system, or device will be most effective for the student. Therefore, the team will probably have to combine several kinds of communication input over weeks, months, or even years to determine what works best.

## Respond to and Expand the Student's Modes and Functions

In interactions and instruction with students who are deaf-blind, all the communication partners should incorporate the modes and forms that the students currently use and should notice, acknowledge, and answer them appropriately. If a student is being taught to indicate what she wants from two options for several activities (such as meals, leisure-time activities, or choosing a partner to sit near), then you should look for and respond to the modes and forms of communication that she is likely to use. If she can choose between a cookie and a banana at snack time, indicating by touching or grasping the one she wants, then her partners should respond by giving her the chosen item.

Once you and others understand and are responding consistently to the modes that the student uses, the next step is to expand these modes and forms of communication, as appropriate. Table 12-1, Figure 12-1 and Tables 12-2–12-4 suggest ways to expand communication.

Expanding the modes may involve vocal, nonvocal, and aided communication. It probably will not be useful to either the student or to others in the student's various environments to expand on a mode or form that requires the student to use sensory information that is inaccessible because of his or her hearing or visual impairment. Thus, if a student currently uses nonvocal forms, such as reaching for an object or person close by, it may be appropriate to expand these forms by teaching body movement (moving toward the person) or gestures (reaching to take a person's hand and pulling or tugging on it to indicate a request) that will expand the reaching behavior. It is important to maintain any current communication that the student has (vocal, nonvocal, or aided) and to encourage its use while adding other modes and forms.

It is also important to remember that your expressive modes become the student's receptive modes. That is, the information you give, in the forms you give it, become what the student receives and the forms in which he or she receives it. Ultimately, if the student has a good receptive grasp of the expressive modes you are using, he or she may give them back to you expressively. So, if you do not use a form with a student, you cannot expect the student to give it back, since it is not fully in the student's communication experience with you. If you want to expand the student's use of pictures as tangible symbols, you will need to use pictures for all interactions. By pairing the tangible symbols you use with speech and sign language for a student who is deaf-blind, you will provide the student with maximum multimodal input.

Do not be dismayed if a student does not automatically respond or appear to comprehend receptively what you are giving expressively. Some students, such as those who have additional motor disabilities, may not be able to use the same forms expressively that they use receptively. Students who can benefit from sign language receptively may be prevented by motor impairments from signing expressively but may understand what is signed to them and need that input. These students can benefit from having an expressive form that involves tangible symbols or some other form instead of more conventional signs or speech.

## Expand the Functions of Communication

In Step 1, you identified the functions of the student's communication. In this step, you attempt to expand them. For example, you may want to help a student who uses behavioral regulation functions (request and protest) to add the social interaction functions of requesting routines or comfort using established modes.

As you enhance the student's functions, the final step is to expand the forms the student uses for specific functions. Thus, if a student communicates for behavioral regulation only through the vocal mode (for example, screaming when she does not want food), you can help her use more vocal forms (for example, to babble "nnnn" with a strong inflection to approximate "no" when she does not want food) to convey these functions. Also, you can teach the student to use additional nonvocal or aided modes and to expand the forms, for instance, using body movements, such as turning the head or pushing away the plate, to reject food. You should define the modes and forms to be expanded by reviewing your assessment of the student's current modes and forms. Remember, the goal is to teach the student that he or she can use many forms for the same function. People receiving messages are more likely to understand what the student intends if he or she communicates with clear and commonly used modes and forms.

Typically, deaf-blind students use behavioral regulation and social interaction before they demonstrate joint attention functions. Within the social interaction functions, requesting social routine and comfort (the first two) are usually evident before the remaining four (greet, call, show off, and request permission). Students need to understand reciprocity and know that others and the environment can be influenced before they will convey social interaction functions and joint attention functions. It is important that forms and functions that are new to the student be expanded in the context of an overall individualized instructional program.

## Match the Student's and Your Communication

You can use the information you collected in Step 1 (as in Figures 12-2–12-7) to determine how well matched the student's and your forms of communication are. It is important to recall that what students understand is linked to the forms they use. Generally, students comprehend forms that are at just a slightly higher level than the expressions they use. Thus, if the student communicates primarily in the nonvocal mode with alertness and gestures, and others mainly use speech, the student is unlikely to receive messages clearly. If the student does not hear spoken responses, he or she may not understand that his or her communications have been received. When the student's and others' communications do not match, the student cannot have a strong influence over the environment and others in it.

Matching the student's and your communication also requires a consideration of the functions of communication, which you identified in Step 1. In addition to being aware of which functions you use with the student, you may have to work on expanding the forms you use for certain functions, as in the following example.

> *Sherry has shown Mr. Riley, her teacher, that she understands and effectively uses the tactile gestures that he uses for communication functions. Mr. Riley suspects that Sherry may even be able to use more symbolic communication, like sign language, because she has interacted so effectively with the current form (gestures). He has defined communication behaviors and forms that he and Sherry use and has identified possible ways to expand them, so he can use her current form (gestures) and expand it by providing a model of the next higher level of forms (signs for the same concepts that the gestures express). He realizes that it is important to continue to use the original form (gestures that express specific concepts that they both understand) with Sherry but also to use the new form (signs for the same objects, people, or ideas).*

Sometimes, identifying forms for expansion may mean that you must have additional training to learn new skills, such as sign language, or the use of a specific system or device for communication. Now you can help your student use his or her current interaction modes (vocal, nonvocal, and aided) to increase communication with others. Try to expand your model of new communication functions for the student using his or her preferred mode or modes. Review Tables 12-2–12-4 for the typical communication functions you may show the student during ordinary daily interactions. Modeling both behavioral regulation and social interaction functions simultaneously is preferable to modeling one at a time, since communication generally serves more than one purpose. And also keep in mind that all this instruction occurs as part of the student's overall educational program (Siegel-Causey & Guess, 1989; Siegel-Causey & Wetherby, 1993).

## Consider Other Factors

Although the student and the teacher are the primary actors in the process just described, other factors are essential to make a program successful:

- using team decision making
- including the family as part of the team
- focusing on age-appropriate skills
- emphasizing functional tasks and materials
- using natural settings for training (Beukelman & Mirenda, 1992; Noonan & Siegel-Causey, 1990; Siegel-Causey & Guess, 1989).

All the decisions about which communication mode, system, or device and which intervention you choose need to be made by a team of people who work and interact regularly with the student who is deaf-blind. Information that you and the other team members gather is shared with the entire team to develop the most useful program for the student (see Module 5 for more information about team planning and the value of family participation). The family's needs and desires must be a priority, and definitions of a student's communication needs must include the contexts of home and community. Furthermore, a student who is deaf-blind, like all students, needs to know behaviors and activities that are suited to his or her age and stage of life. The behaviors and activities you teach should also be functional, motivating, and important for the individual who is deaf-blind; otherwise, instructional time lacks purpose. Finally, the student should be taught in the natural settings of his or her home, school, and community, rather than in isolated places, such as therapy rooms.

## STEP 3: DESIGN THE SYSTEM

### Put the Pieces Together

Deaf-blind students have individual, diverse learning styles and thus may not follow a typical progression or learning sequence that you expect because of differences in hearing and visual impairments, cognitive and physical impairments, experience, and many other factors. Therefore, you need to build on the modes and forms of communication that students are currently using and continue to expand them as the students use more new forms (Lombardino & Langley, 1991; Rogow, 1977; Rowland & Stremel-Campbell, 1987).

Some students may proceed suddenly to a new communication form or new mode or may use some functions and not others, even though you use them with the students. They may skip around from form to form and may not progress smoothly through them in order. Students who are deaf-blind are just like other students—they do not always do what we expect. Following two essential principles will be helpful:

1. Plan to build on how a student is communicating, and accept his or her current forms and functions of communication.

2. Do not impose a system that does not incorporate the skills the student already has. (For example, do not try to teach speech first to a student who has profound hearing and vision losses when he or she uses only a few nonvocal forms, such as gestures.)

The figures presented in this module offer a format for considering the modes, forms, and functions of a student's communication. After incorporating assessment information, defining the student's needs and how he or she communicates, identifying the demands of the environment, and matching the student's communication with that of the student's communication partners, members of the student's educational planning team need to study the information that has been gathered through the process to determine which modes and forms are to be developed on the basis of the student's skills and needs (Cress, Mathy-Laikko, & Angelo, 1989). If unaided modes of communication (vocal and nonvocal) seem to be the most promising for the student, it is important to document how the currently used forms within those modes will be expanded and how each team member will interact to support the expansion. If the aided mode seems to be the most beneficial, there are additional issues to be considered.

Before aided (especially augmentative) systems and devices are selected, all the team members must know which systems and devices are available through brochures, catalogs, and other sources of commercially made products, as well as those that other team members have produced for a student. They will need to study that information, discuss it, and decide as a team how specific systems or devices meet the particular student's defined needs for communication, both current and expanded (Baumgart, Johnson, & Helmstetter, 1990; Beukelman & Mirenda, 1992). Thus, they must review the characteristics of the system or device, its layout, and the specific techniques and other requirements for using it and determine if the student's characteristics, current communication behaviors, and needs will be well served by the particular system or device (see Module 8 for types). Then, they must document how the selected mode and design of the system will be implemented, so that everyone in the student's environment can use it consistently. (For a summary of this process, see Tips on Moving from Assessment to Implementation.)

## Monitor Performance

Finally, it is vital to monitor and record how the student responds to and uses the new, expanded mode, system, or device for interaction. If the student is not learning to communicate and is not responding well to using the new mode, system, or device after a reasonable period (for some students, it may be many weeks or even months), further review and modifications will be needed.

Here are some measures that can be taken: Start again with the basic steps outlined in this module, and go back to the information gathered when the communication program was first modified. Make some comparisons. Does the student still use the same communication modes, forms, and functions that he or she did before the new system or device was implemented? (If not, why not?) Has the student lost additional hearing or vision or had other experiences that may affect his or her use of the system? (If so, what adaptations to the current modes and systems may help?) Can another new mode or device be tried to give the student more opportunities for communication? Answer these questions and redesign the communication program. The members of the student's educational team may need to try out a new system or device, since not all modes, devices, and systems work with all students who are deaf-blind. In some cases, you may need to continue to modify the system until the student begins to respond consistently. (For more detailed information on implementing and reevaluating communication systems, see Module 13.)

# TIPS ON MOVING FROM ASSESSMENT TO IMPLEMENTATION

• Assess to determine what a student currently uses or responds to in routine interactions.

• Meet with the team to decide how to expand those modes and forms.

• Determine if new modes, forms, systems, and devices should be added for specific communication purposes and with specific communication partners.

• Design instruction to include expanded or new modes, forms, systems, or devices for communication.

• Implement the new forms or modes or use of devices or systems.

• Give consistent, constant input, so the student can establish receptive comprehension for the new communication modes, forms, systems, or devices over time. Remember to continue to pair earlier communication modes and forms with the new modes and forms for expansion.

• Watch for signs of receptive comprehension. Alertness, appropriate responses to what you are trying to communicate, and even spontaneous expressive use may be signals that the new modes or forms are meaningful to the student.

• Continue to assess and expand if you feel you are observing appropriate responses and the student appears to comprehend.

• Document responses to compare for consistency in the student's responses. Be especially aware of emerging expressive uses of newly expanded modes or forms and whether the student uses any new systems or devices or simply uses speech or signs. Also be aware that the student may use one form expressively, such as bringing you a tangible symbol from a vocabulary shelf to request an activity, but may use your speech, signs, and the symbol receptively for the same concept.

• As you continue to modify a communication program, you may wish to discontinue modes or forms that do not seem to be working; be sure that you have much documentation before any communication instructional component is discontinued. Also, evaluate if the mode or form should be continued because it is effective in another of the student's environments. For example, the student may use sign language with you, but communicate more effectively with pictures at the grocery store.

• Continue these steps, always keeping in mind that everyone changes communication styles over time and in different situations. Your student should have enough communication options to be flexible in how and with whom he or she communicates. ■

Overall, the basic concepts to follow in selecting a system and device for aided communication are these:

- *Adapt everything that is needed and appropriate to support effective communication, but do not adapt more than is necessary.* For a teenager who is deaf-blind who wants to shop in the community and communicate with store personnel, a simple note card with both braille and print alphabet letters that he or she can point to may be a more effective and portable aid for communication than may a high-tech TeleBraille, which weighs far more, requires several minutes to set up, and is less portable for everyday use. A child who has a moderate vision loss may use small pictures viewed closely for a communication board as effectively as greatly enlarged pictures, so having smaller pictures on his or her board will allow for a larger communication vocabulary.

- *Use as many modes, systems, and forms as the student needs for effective communication.* If a student has significant hearing and vision losses, some elements of the vocal, nonvocal, and aided communication modes may be inaccessible. Still, any accessible sensory information can support effective communication. A student may not hear speech but may hear a person's tone of voice, which helps him or her understand the person's mood. A personal amplification system used with a teacher's spoken words and signs would combine all three modes. Such a combination increases the information that the student receives and his or her potential for understanding.

- *Modify as often as seems necessary.* With ongoing monitoring, you should have enough current information to know if the student is learning to communicate and if his or her communication skills are increasing. If progress is not apparent, use the information you have to change or add to the current system.

# SUMMARY

In all likelihood, your use of the selection process described in this module has taught you what you already knew: that students who are deaf-blind communicate in a variety of ways and that you convey important information to them. Selecting a communication mode, system, or device is not a onetime activity. It is an ongoing process and must be expanded each time a student's communication needs change. You can track the student's progress with the steps outlined in this module and redesign the program as needed. Helping the student achieve the most sophisticated level of communication possible is important, and it can be done by combining and expanding communication modes, systems, and devices as appropriate. The goal is to select and develop communication modes, systems, or devices that will support effective communication with others for the student who is deaf-blind and refine them as the student becomes more and more successful with communication.

*The author acknowledges the work of Christine Mayhall in conceptualizing and writing this module.*

# REFERENCES

Baumgart, D., Johnson, J., & Helmstetter, E. (1990). *Augmentative and alternative communication systems for persons with moderate and severe disabilities.* Baltimore: Paul H. Brookes.

Beukelman, D. R., & Mirenda, P. (1992). *Augmentative and alternative communication: Management of severe communication disorders in children and adults.* Baltimore: Paul H. Brookes.

Bullis, M., & Fielding, G. (Eds.). (1988). *Communication development in young children with deaf-blindness: Literature review.* Monmouth: Teaching Research Division, Western Oregon State College.

Chen, D. (1990). *Assessing infant communication.* In D. Chen, C. Friedman, & G. Calvello (Eds.), *Parents and visually impaired infants.* Louisville, KY: American Printing House for the Blind.

Cook, A., & Coleman, C. (1988). Selection of augmentative communication systems by matching client skills and needs to system characteristics. *Seminars in Speech and Language, 8,* 153–167.

Cress, C., Mathy-Laikko, P., & Angelo, J. (1989). *Augmentative communication for children with deaf-blindness: Guidelines for decision-making.* Monmouth: Teaching Research Division, Western Oregon State College.

Hagood, L., & Watkins, M. (1991). *Assessing communication skills in severely handicapped children.* Paper presented at the National Conference of the American Speech, Language and Hearing Association, Atlanta, GA.

Lombardino, L., & Langley, M. B. (1991). Augmenting the communication of children with severe cognitive, sensory, and motor dysfunction. In M. B. Langley & L. Lombardino (Eds.), *Neurodevelopmental strategies for managing communication disorders in children with severe motor dysfunction* (pp. 159–198). Austin, TX: PRO-ED.

Musselwhite, C. R., & St. Louis, K. W. (1988). *Communication programming for persons with severe handicaps*. Boston: College-Hill Press.

Noonan, M., & Siegel-Causey, E. (1990). Special needs of students with severe handicaps. In L. McCormick & L. Schiefelbusch (Eds.), *Early language intervention: An introduction*. Columbus, OH: Charles E. Merrill.

Reichle, J. (1991). Defining the decisions involved in designing and implementing augmentative and alternative communication systems. In J. Reichle, J. York, & J. Sigafoos (Eds.), *Implementing augmentative and alternative communication strategies for learners with severe disabilities* (pp. 39–60). Baltimore: Paul H. Brookes.

Rogow, S. (1977). A communication curriculum for blind multiply handicapped children. In S. Mangold (Ed.), *A teacher's guide to the special educational needs of blind and visually handicapped children* (pp. 20–27). New York: American Foundation for the Blind.

Rowland, C., & Stremel-Campbell, K. (1987). Share and share alike: Conventional gestures to emergent language for learners with sensory impairments. In L. Goetz, D. Guess, & K. Stremel-Campbell (Eds.), *Innovative program design for individuals with dual sensory impairments* (pp. 49–75). Baltimore: Paul H. Brookes.

Siegel–Causey, E., & Guess, D. (1989). *Enhancing nonsymbolic communication interactions among learners with severe disabilities*. Baltimore: Paul H. Brookes.

Siegel–Causey, E., & Wetherby, A. (1993). Nonsymbolic communication. In M. Snell (Ed.), *Systematic instruction of persons with severe handicaps* (4th ed.)(pp. 290–318). Blacklick, OH: Glencoe.

TABLE 12-2:
Examples of the Vocal Mode

|  | | FORMS | |
|---|---|---|---|
| FUNCTIONS | SOUNDS | BABBLING | SPEECH |
| **BEHAVIORAL REGULATION** Request an action or object | The student giggles when her favorite stuffed animal is out of her reach. | The student produces consonant and vowellike sounds (babababa) when her mother stops rubbing her back to request that the backrub continue. | The student says "more" when her brother stops pushing her on the swing. |
| Protest an action or object | The student vocalizes loudly when lunch is removed. | The student repetitively vocalizes loud "ahs" (ahahahahaha) when her tangled hair is being combed. | The student says "no" when his mother puts more vegetables on his plate. |
| **SOCIAL INTERACTION** Request a social routine | The student makes a sound when his mother pretends to tickle him. | The student vocalizes "bababa" when he wants to play a ball-rolling game with a peer. | The student says "go" when it is time for her daily walk to the park. |
| Request comfort | The student whimpers after her knee is scraped. | The student vocalizes "mamama" while he is ill with a cold. | The student says "bear" to request his stuffed animal to hug during nap time. |
| Greet | The student vocalizes the gleeful sound "eeeee" when his good friend appears. | The student vocalizes "dadadada" when his friend walks in the door. | The student says "hi" when her friend walks toward her. |

*(continued)*

**TABLE 12-2:**
Continued

| | | FORMS | |
| --- | --- | --- | --- |
| **FUNCTIONS** | **SOUNDS** | **BABBLING** | **SPEECH** |
| Call | The student looks at his peer across the room and vocalizes "uuuhhh" at the swing set. | The student vocalizes "ahahaha" when a cat walks past her. | The student calls "ma" when his mother is in the next room and he needs her assistance. |
| Show off | The student vocalizes "eeeee" when she is finished making a Play-Doh shape. | The student hides under a cloth and babbles and laughs until others notice. | The student says "look" after she makes a finger painting. |
| Request permission | The student vocalizes to the teacher with a rising intonation when he wants a cookie. | The student vocalizes "gagagaga" to ask to sit on the teacher's lap. | The student says "water" to request permission to go to the drinking fountain. |
| **JOINT ATTENTION** Comment on an action or object | The student looks at the teacher and laughs while watching his friend blow bubbles. | The student babbles gleefully as she is rocked and held in a rocking chair. | The student says "cookie" when a snack is given to her. |
| Request information | The student vocalizes "mmm" to the baby-sitter as her parents leave to go out. | The student babbles with a rising tone (questioning) as he smells lunch being prepared to find out if the food is for him. | The student says "dada" when he hears the garage door open. |

**TABLE 12-3:**
Examples of the Nonvocal Mode

| FUNCTIONS | | FORMS | | | | | |
|---|---|---|---|---|---|---|---|
| | ALERTNESS | FACIAL EXPRESSION, AFFECT | BODY MOVEMENT | VISUAL FORMS | GESTURAL FORMS | SIGN LANGUAGE |
| **BEHAVIORAL REGULATION** Request an action or object | The student becomes active as a toy is brought closer to her. | The student raises his eyebrows and his eyes brighten when a wind-up toy stops moving. | The student tilts her head toward books when she wants to be read to. | The student looks at an object that is out of reach. | The student nods "yes" to the teacher when asked if he wants a toy. | The student signs "milk" when she wants more milk. |
| Protest an action or object | The student becomes agitated and cries when put to bed. | The student grimaces when she is fed food she dislikes. | The student turns his head away when his father wipes his nose. | The student averts his gaze when his face is being washed. | The student shakes her head "no" when she wants to stop being pushed on the swing. | The student signs "stop" when she wishes to end an activity. |
| **SOCIAL INTERACTION** Request a social routine | The student moves from a drowsy to an alert state as the teacher starts a peek-a-boo game. | The student smiles and blinks his eyes to ask to look at a picture book. | The student moves her head up and down to get an adult to push her on the swing. | The student closes his eyes to request the bedtime game "open-shut them." | The student pantomimes the movement of holding up a blanket to play peek-a-boo. | The student signs "play" to request a game with a peer. |
| Request comfort | The student displays a stereotype when he cannot find his jacket. | The student displays a wrinkled brow and sad face after he falls down. | The student wiggles in a chair to get someone to adjust her position. | The student looks down at his scraped knee to request comfort. | The student holds out her arms to be picked up. | The student signs "sad" when he wants comfort. |

(continued)

**TABLE 12-3:**
Continued

| FUNCTIONS | ALERTNESS | FACIAL EXPRESSION, AFFECT | BODY MOVEMENT | VISUAL FORMS | GESTURAL FORMS | SIGN LANGUAGE |
|---|---|---|---|---|---|---|
| | | | FORMS | | | |
| Greet | The student becomes active when a peer says "hello." | The student smiles at her friend. | The student lifts up his hand when a peer enters the room. | The student looks toward a person who enters the room. | The student waves "hello." | The student fingerspells "hi." |
| Call | The student looks up for an adult when he wants to be taken off the toilet. | Not applicable. | The student leans to the side in his seat when he wants someone to help him out of it. | The student gazes at her teacher to get her attention. | The student tugs on the teacher's pant leg to get him to notice her. | The student signs "me" to indicate it is her turn. |
| Show off | The student moves her limbs when the teacher compliments her on her new dress. | The student grins when he finishes a task. | The student lifts her arm up and down to show her new watch. | The student looks around the table at everyone after he cleans up his work space. | The student claps her hands when her name is sung in a song to her. | The student signs "look" when he has finished a project. |
| Request permission | The student looks at the door to ask to go outside. | The student displays a sad face as her classmates go outside. | The student rocks when he is near the swingset to ask to go on the swing. | The student uses a code (blinks twice) to request a snack. | The student asks to go outside by pantomiming pushing a door open. | The student signs "please" when he wants to do an activity. |

*(continued)*

**TABLE 12-3:**
Continued

| | | | FORMS | | | |
|---|---|---|---|---|---|---|
| **FUNCTIONS** | **ALERTNESS** | **FACIAL EXPRESSION, AFFECT** | **BODY MOVEMENT** | **VISUAL FORMS** | **GESTURAL FORMS** | **SIGN LANGUAGE** |
| **JOINT ATTENTION** Comment on an action or object | The student becomes active when he finds a new toy he likes that a peer is holding. | The student looks and smiles at her peer and the new toy she is showing. | The student shakes his head from side to side when offered a cup. | The student looks out the window at two squirrels playing in a tree and at his friend who is watching them. | The student shows a toy to get others to look at it. | The student signs "look" to the teacher to focus her attention. |
| Request information | The student cries and becomes agitated when his best friend is not available during playtime. | The student knits her brow and frowns to request information. | The student leans toward a strange object and looks at his peer who is showing it. | The student raises her eyebrows and looks questioningly at a new person in the classroom. | The student gets his mother's attention and points at food on his plate that he has never seen before. | The student signs "what?" to request information about what is in a box. |

**TABLE 12-4:**
Examples of the Aided Mode

| FUNCTIONS | | FORMS | | | |
|---|---|---|---|---|---|
| | | OBJECTS | TEXTURE | PHOTOGRAPHS | GRAPHIC SYMBOL SETS |
| **BEHAVIORAL REGULATION** Request an action or object | | The student presents a cup to indicate he wants a snack. | The student touches a soft knitted square attached to her lap tray to indicate she wants juice. | The student presents a photograph of a hamburger at a restaurant to order. | The student presents a card with a line drawing of a house to indicate that it is time to go home. |
| Protest an action or object | | The student pushes away a glass during a meal to refuse a drink. | After a peer guides the student's hand to feel the soft knitted material, the student pulls her hand away and grimaces to indicate that she does not want juice. | The student hands a photograph of himself turned away from the camera to indicate that he does not want to go outside. | The student displays a symbol for "water" when she is given a cup of milk to express her preference. |
| **SOCIAL INTERACTION** Request a social routine | | The student taps a rocking chair to get an adult to hold and rock her. | The student touches a wood square to ask to be rocked in a rocking chair. | The student shows a photograph of a computer to a peer to indicate that he wants to play computer games together. | The student displays a color drawing of a restaurant to ask to go out for dinner. |
| Request comfort | | The student pulls on a person's sweater to ask to be comforted. | The student touches blanket material to ask to be comforted. | The student presents a photograph of people hugging to get comfort. | The student displays a picture symbol of a frowning face with an adhesive bandage on the forehead to request comfort. |

*(continued)*

**TABLE 12-4:**
Continued

| | FORMS | | | |
|---|---|---|---|---|
| FUNCTIONS | OBJECTS | TEXTURE | PHOTOGRAPHS | GRAPHIC SYMBOL SETS |
| Greet | The student activates a buzzer as she enters the room to say "hello." | Not applicable. | The student hands a photograph of himself with a message on the back when his mother's friend says "hello." | The student uses the card "hi" when a friend greets him. |
| Call | The student hits a button on a tape recorder with the message "Please help" while looking at his cup that fell on the floor. | Not applicable. | Not applicable. | Not applicable. |
| Show off | The student pushes a wind-up toy toward the teacher when it is his turn to share. | Not applicable. | The student shows photographs of her birthday party to peers. | The student displays a picture symbol of "big" and points to his muscle to show off his strength. |
| Request permission | The student touches a miniature replica of a cookie to ask for another cookie. | The student touches a metal square to request permission to take a break. | The student touches a photograph of a bus to request permission to get ready to go home. | The student displays a picture symbol "?" and looks toward the door to request permission to go out. |

*(continued)*

TABLE 12-4:
Continued

| FUNCTIONS | FORMS | | | |
| --- | --- | --- | --- | --- |
| | OBJECTS | TEXTURE | PHOTOGRAPHS | GRAPHIC SYMBOL SETS |
| *JOINT ATTENTION* Comment on an action or object | The student taps on a blender to direct her peer's attention to bubbles that form while making pudding. | Not applicable. | The student points to a photograph of his mother when an adult says it is time to go home. | The student shows a drawing of milk when deciding what is needed to make a malted. |
| Request information | The student presents a miniature plate and cup to see if it is time for lunch. | Not applicable. | The student points to a photograph of the teacher when he cannot see her in the room. | The student displays picture symbols of "where?" and "cat" to ask where the cat is. |

**FIGURE 12-2:**

**Vocal Mode: Forms of Communication of Student**

Student ___Christopher___          Date completed ___4/3/95___

*List all the forms of communication that the student uses with others.*

| SOUNDS | BABBLING | SPEECH |
|---|---|---|
| giggles | ahahah | None observed |
| cries | babababa | |
| humming sound | | |

**FIGURE 12-3:**
Nonvocal Mode: Forms of Communication of Student

Student __Christopher__                    Date completed __4/3/95__

List all the forms of communication that the student uses with others.

| ALERTNESS | FACIAL EXPRESSION | BODY MOVEMENT | VISUAL FORMS* | GESTURAL FORMS* | SIGN LANGUAGE* |
|---|---|---|---|---|---|
| active | smile | clenches fists | | | |
| "shutdown," withdrawn | grimace | pulls away | | | |
| agitated | | rocks | | | |
| | | waves arms | | | |
| | | | | | |
| | | | | | |
| | | | | | |
| | | | | | |
| | | | | | |

* Examples of visual forms include eye gaze; examples of gestural forms include gestures; examples of sign language include manual signs.

**FIGURE 12-4:**

**Aided Mode: Forms of Communication of Student**

Student _Christopher_          Date completed _4/3/95_

List all the forms of communication that the student uses with others.

| OBJECTS* | TEXTURE | PHOTOGRAPHS* | GRAPHIC SYMBOL SETS* |
|---|---|---|---|
| None currently used | None currently used | None currently used | None currently used |
| | | | |
| | | | |
| | | | |
| | | | |
| | | | |
| | | | |

* Objects include real objects, parts of objects, miniature objects; photographs include color and black and white; graphic symbol sets include color drawings, black-and-white drawings, commercial black-and-white symbols.

**FIGURE 12-5:**
**Vocal Mode: Forms of Communication of Adult**

Adult ___Suzanne___     Date completed ___4/3/95___

*List all the forms of communication that the adult uses with the student.*

| SOUNDS | BABBLING | SPEECH |
|---|---|---|
| mmm | mimics "ahahah"  w-eeee | Hi, Christopher Up/Down Time to eat Diaper time Calm down, it's OK. What a good boy! |

**FIGURE 12-6:**
Nonvocal Mode: Forms of Communication of Adult

Adult  Suzanne

Date completed  4/3/95

List all the forms of communication that the adult uses with the student.

| ALERTNESS | FACIAL EXPRESSION | BODY MOVEMENT | VISUAL FORMS* | GESTURAL FORMS* | SIGN LANGUAGE* |
|---|---|---|---|---|---|
| "upbeat" | smiles | cuddles | | pats | |
| "calm" | frowns | sways/rocks | | | |
| | | rocks | | | |
| | | bounces | | | |
| | | | | | |
| | | | | | |
| | | | | | |
| | | | | | |
| | | | | | |

* Examples of visual form include eye gaze; examples of gestural form include gestures; examples of sign language include manual signs.

**FIGURE 12-7:**
**Aided Mode: Forms of Communication of Adult**

Adult: Suzanne                                    Date completed  4/3/95

List all the forms of communication that the adult uses with the student.

| OBJECTS* | TEXTURE | PHOTOGRAPHS* | GRAPHIC SYMBOL SETS* |
|---|---|---|---|
| Touches diaper to hand | | | |
| | | | |
| | | | |
| | | | |
| | | | |
| | | | |
| | | | |
| | | | |
| | | | |

* Objects include real objects, parts of objects, miniature objects; photographs include color and black and white; graphic symbol sets include color drawings, black-and-white drawings, commercial black-and-white symbols.

## FIGURE 12-8:
## Vocal Mode: Functions of Communication Behavior of Student

Student __Christopher__     Date completed __4/3/95__

List all the forms and their functions that the student uses with others.

| FUNCTIONS | FORMS | | |
| --- | --- | --- | --- |
| | SOUNDS | BABBLING | SPEECH |
| **BEHAVIORAL REGULATION** | | | |
| Request an action or object | | bababa | |
| Protest an action or object | cries | | |
| **SOCIAL INTERACTION** | | | |
| Request a social routine | humming sounds | | |
| Request comfort | cries | | |
| Greet | | ahaha | |
| Call | | bababa | |
| Show off | | | |
| Request permission | | | |
| **JOINT ATTENTION** | | | |
| Comment on an action or object | giggles | ahaha | |
| Request information | | | |

**FIGURE 12-9:**
Nonvocal Mode: Functions of Communication Behavior of Student

Student __Christopher__     Date completed __4/3/95__

*List all the forms and their functions that the student uses with others.*

| FUNCTIONS | FORMS | | | | | |
|---|---|---|---|---|---|---|
| | ALERTNESS | FACIAL EXPRESSION, AFFECT | BODY MOVEMENT | VISUAL FORMS | GESTURAL FORMS | SIGN LANGUAGE |
| **BEHAVIORAL REGULATION** | | | | | | |
| Request an action or object | | | waves arms | | | |
| Protest an action or object | "shuts down" | grimace | | | | |
| **SOCIAL INTERACTION** | | | | | | |
| Request a social routine | active | smile | | | | |
| Request comfort | agitated | | rocks | | | |
| Greet | | | | | | |
| Call | | | | | | |
| Show off | | | | | | |
| Request permission | | | | | | |
| **JOINT ATTENTION** | | | | | | |
| Comment on an action or object | | | waves arms | | | |
| Request information | | | | | | |

**FIGURE 12-10:**

**Aided Mode: Functions of Communication Behavior of Student**

Student Christopher Date completed 4/3/95

*List all the forms and their functions that the student uses with others.*

| FUNCTIONS | FORMS | | | |
|---|---|---|---|---|
| | OBJECTS | TEXTURE | PHOTOGRAPHS | GRAPHIC SYMBOL SETS |
| **BEHAVIORAL REGULATION** Request an action or object | None currently used | | | |
| Protest an action or object | | | | |
| **SOCIAL INTERACTION** Request a social routine | | | | |
| Request comfort | | | | |
| Greet | | | | |
| Call | | | | |
| Show off | | | | |
| Request permission | | | | |
| **JOINT ATTENTION** Comment on an action or object | | | | |
| Request information | | | | |

FIGURE 12-11:
Vocal Mode: Functions of Communication Behavior of Adult

Adult ___Suzanne___          Date completed ___4/3/95___

*List all the forms and their functions that others use with the student.*

| FUNCTIONS | FORMS | | |
| --- | --- | --- | --- |
| | SOUNDS | BABBLING | SPEECH |
| **BEHAVIORAL REGULATION** | | | |
| Request an action or object | | | Calm down |
| Protest an action or object | | | |
| **SOCIAL INTERACTION** | | | |
| Request a social routine | | | |
| Request comfort | | | |
| Greet | | | Hi, Christopher |
| Call | | | |
| Show off | | | |
| Request permission | | | |
| **JOINT ATTENTION** | | | |
| Comment on an action or object | mmmm | Weee/ahahah | |
| Request information | | | Up/Down, Time to eat |

*FIGURE 12-12:*
**Nonvocal Mode: Functions of Communication Behavior of Adult**

Adult Suzanne     Date completed 4/3/95

*List all the forms and their functions that others use with the student.*

| FUNCTIONS | ALERTNESS | FACIAL EXPRESSION, AFFECT | BODY MOVEMENT | VISUAL FORMS | GESTURAL FORMS | SIGN LANGUAGE |
|---|---|---|---|---|---|---|
| **BEHAVIORAL REGULATION** | | | | | | |
| Request an action or object | | | | | touches | |
| Protest an action or object | | frown | | | | |
| **SOCIAL INTERACTION** | | | | | | |
| Request a social routine | upbeat | | swings, bounces | | touches | |
| Request comfort | | | cuddles | | | |
| Greet | | smile | | | | |
| Call | | | | | | |
| Show off | | | | | | |
| Request permission | | | | | | |
| **JOINT ATTENTION** | | | | | | |
| Comment on an action or object | | | | | | |
| Request information | | | | | | |

FORMS

**FIGURE 12-13:**

Aided Mode: Functions of Communication Behavior of Adult

Adult __Suzanne__    Date completed __4/3/95__

*List all the forms and their functions that others use with the student.*

| FUNCTIONS | FORMS | | | | |
|---|---|---|---|---|---|
| | OBJECTS | TEXTURE | PHOTOGRAPHS | GRAPHIC SYMBOL SETS | |
| **BEHAVIORAL REGULATION** | | | | | |
| Request an action or object | | | | | |
| Protest an action or object | | | | | |
| **SOCIAL INTERACTION** | | | | | |
| Request a social routine | | | | | |
| Request comfort | | | | | |
| Greet | | | | | |
| Call | | | | | |
| Show off | | | | | |
| Request permission | | | | | |
| **JOINT ATTENTION** | | | | | |
| Comment on an action or object | Touches diaper to hand | | | | |
| Request information | | | | | |

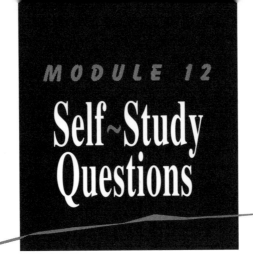

1. With regard to the modes of communication, which statement is correct?
   a. It is important to narrow down a single mode that the student uses to communicate.
   b. If a student typically expresses herself using aided modes, then she will only understand others who communicate with her using aided modes.
   c. It is important to know the modes a student can understand when selecting a communication system.
   d. Students who are deaf-blind do not use modes of communication.

2. Examples of vocal communication include all but which one of the following?
   a. A student uses an angry intonation when lunch is removed.
   b. A student hides under her coat and babbles and laughs until her teacher notices her.
   c. A student starts to rock his body when his brother stops pushing him on the swing.
   d. A student says "more" when her sister stops pushing her on the swing.

3. A student who uses an aided communication system will
   a. grimace when he is fed food he does not like.
   b. present a picture of an empty dish drainer to her teacher when she finishes putting the dishes away.
   c. whimper to be held after he skins his knee.
   d. sign "milk" when she wants more to drink.

4. Which one of the following is not an example of the use of nonvocal communication?
   a. A student who signs "hi" when her favorite friend enters the room.
   b. A student who squeals "eeee" when it is his turn to pick the computer game to play.
   c. A student who points to the cassette player to request her choice of a leisure activity.
   d. A student who tugs on his teacher's leg when he needs attention.

5. In selecting a communication system, you consider all but which one of these issues?
   a. The ways in which the student currently uses the vocal, nonvocal, and aided modes.
   b. Repeated evaluations and redesigns of the system.
   c. The goal of designing a high-quality system that the student can use the rest of his or her life.
   d. Moving the student to a higher level of communication.

6. Assessing how students communicate involves all but which one of these considerations?
   a. Determining the modes they use.
   b. Defining a single mode for them to use to facilitate communication for them and their families.
   c. Providing information that can be translated into functional skills.
   d. Determining the modes that service providers use with them.

7. The functions of communication are characterized by all but which one of the following?
   a. They are not relevant until the student uses the vocal or aided mode.
   b. They are the purposes served by the behavior.
   c. They are assessed as part of the demands of the student's environment.
   d. They include behavioral regulation, social interaction, and joint attention.

8. All but which one of the following are true of the communicative environment?
   a. It affects the input students receive and influences their understanding.
   b. It includes opportunities for students to respond to communication.
   c. It is unaffected by the interactional styles of the communication partners.
   d. It includes opportunities for students to initiate communication.

9. In designing a communication system, members of the educational team match the student's modes and functions to
   a. the modes of communication the service provider is most skilled in teaching.
   b. the student's skills and needs, on the basis of information from the assessment.
   c. the most common modes and functions used by the student's peers.

10. In designing a communication system, the service provider and other team members should
    a. begin by teaching the student the highest level of communication hoped for.
    b. eliminate spoken interaction with the student who is deaf-blind at the beginning of the intervention.
    c. match the service providers' modes and functions to the student's skills and needs.
    d. plan to teach joint-attention functions immediately to the student who is deaf-blind.

11. In designing the communication system, members of the educational team should do all but which of the following?
    a. Build a system for all students starting with gestures, then moving to objects, then to sets of graphic symbols.
    b. Model modes, forms, and functions at a level just above where the student currently functions.
    c. Be aware that some students do not progress smoothly through sequences of communication and can skip around through the modes, forms, and functions they learn.
    d. Build on what the student is currently capable of and expand from there.

*Answers to self-study questions for this module appear at the end of Unit 2.*

# Strategies for Classroom and Community

**KATHLEEN STREMEL**

**STEVE PERREAULT**

**THERESE RAFALOWSKI WELCH**

## CONTRIBUTORS

**NANCY JOHNSON-DORN**
*Fostering Communication among Students*

- *Make communication instruction integral to all activities*

- *Encourage social interaction and friendship*

- *Use activities the student enjoys to expand forms of communication*

- *Teach all potential communication partners how to communicate with the student*

Opportunities for interaction with others are important for developing communication and other skills. The instruction of children who are deaf-blind needs to be based on the premise that long-term participation in the community, including the development of social and community relationships, is a critical educational objective. This module examines how this central value can be applied to teaching deaf-blind children communication skills to be used in the classroom and community. It is not sufficient for instruction relating to communication and social participation to occur only part of the time, with an occasional field trip or school party. Communication instruction needs to be an integral part of the student's daily program and should include activities to help the student develop friendships and participate in the world beyond the classroom.

This module also stresses the concept that teaching skills to expand the capacities of students who are deaf-blind to communicate and to be independent should be centered in the activities that the students enjoy. Instructional activities should take place with people with whom students want to communicate and interact and in the students' homes, schools, and communities. The process that is described includes gathering information, developing a program, and using methods that facilitate learning in classroom and community environments.

# INTERACTIONS AND THE PHYSICAL ENVIRONMENT

The availability of interactions for deaf-blind students depends on the environments in which the students live and learn. Some students interact only in their homes and classrooms, whereas others interact in many different environments, including the homes of relatives and friends, school, and various work and community settings. Students' interactions and ways of communicating may differ from setting to setting. This section examines how to make the most of the physical environment to enhance communication skills. Although this module emphasizes enhancing students' communication skills, it is important for teachers to remember that students are learning to move and explore at the same time that they are learning to communicate. Therefore, teachers should be aware of the value of physical environments for developing both communication and mobility skills and refer to Module 18 for details on how physical environments are used for orientation and mobility (O&M) instruction.

## PHYSICAL ENVIRONMENTS AND EXPANSION OF ACTIVITIES

The first step is to determine the specific physical environments to which the student has access. The family and other members of the educational team are the best sources of information to determine where the student spends his or her time.

In addition to identifying the number of environments, assessing the teaching possibilities in each setting is essential. Whether there are two or 20 environments, every environment has opportunities for learning. It is important to make the most of each setting. If only a few environments are available to the student, the teaching activities and interactions should be expanded within them. If the student has access to numerous environments, the quality of active teaching and social interactions in them should be assessed. These activities are important because although a student may be "exposed" to many different environments, little active teaching or learning may result from that exposure unless planning is done to ensure it.

In considering the environments that are available to a student and expanding the activities that promote communication, it is helpful to focus on four domains: daily life, community, work, and recreation-leisure. The following guidelines can be used to expand teaching activities (this approach should also be used to build a student's O&M skills):

- Consult with the student's family to identify the family's priorities for activities and developing skills, the student's preferences, and the student's current skills.

- Conduct an inventory of the recreational and vocational options that are available in the student's community to determine which activities can be used to expand the student's skills.

- Determine the level of participation that is required for a particular activity and the adaptations that may be necessary.

- Select activities that are functional and important to the family and are appropriate to the student's age.

In reviewing the environments in which opportunities for students to communicate may exist and be expanded, the following possibilities may be kept in mind: the student's home, backyard, and neighborhood, as well as the homes of neighbors, relatives, and friends; school facilities, including classrooms, cafeteria, playground, hallways, bathrooms, and study hall; retail stores and shopping malls; family leisure activities; house of worship; day care center; and work settings.

## ENGAGING ENVIRONMENTS

It is important that the environments in which the student who is deaf-blind spends the most time are engaging environments, that is, environments that are *predictable*, *responsive*, and *organized*. In such environments, changes should occur, but they should be carefully planned. Although engaging environments should also be stimulating, activities should lead to direct outcomes for the student, not just provide stimulation. Engaging environments are arranged to invite active participation, teaching and learning, social interactions, and a minimum of confusion and downtime.

It is easy to determine if an environment is engaging by observing it for a short time. You have probably walked into a classroom in which few materials were available and there was no apparent schedule or organization. It may have been difficult to determine what was being taught, but it was obvious from the students' lack of engagement in meaningful activities that it was not a facilitative educational situation. In these environments, if students are not actively engaged in meaningful activities, if teaching is not occurring, and if positive feedback is not provided, the students may withdraw or engage in inappropriate behaviors to be active and to get some attention (see The Communicative Purposes of Behavior, Module 6). The teaching staff are then engaged in addressing problems and maintaining basic caregiving activities and have less time available for active teaching.

One of the major features of a predictable environment is *consistency*. That is, each person involved uses the same specific tactile and object cues each time to announce, for example, "I'm taking you out of your wheelchair" or "We're going to eat." Another key feature is *temporal regularity*. That is, activities occur at the same time each day for the same amount of time. If there are changes in the routine, they are announced to the student, and there is a system for the student to know his or her daily schedule or to help determine his or her schedule.

Teachers can assess the predictability of environments in the community to select the most engaging environments for interaction. For example, one fast-food restaurant may have a high turnover of employees and clientele, whereas another may have a steady staff and a consistent clientele that comes in at specific times. If the same person waits on a student each time he or she comes in to order a meal, that person will become familiar with the student more rapidly than if many different employees do so at various times. (Such factors play a part in the instructional strategies that are selected for teaching. Effective instructional strategies do not only involve the student who is deaf-blind. They also involve potential social partners to facilitate social interactions.)

An engaging environment should also be well organized and reflect a schedule that indicates who teaches or interacts with a specific student at a specific time for a specific activity or skill. The physical organization of the major environments involved is important, too. The student should have spaces in all the environments that are clearly his or hers, and there should be specific areas for specific activities and for quiet time. Materials should be organized, so the student knows where they are and can get them (or request them).

The age of the student must be considered in developing an organized environment. For an older student, the entire school may be considered the major environment. If the student is learning O&M skills, adaptations may be used in the hallways and rooms to facilitate skills acquisition (see Module 18). The school staff should also be aware that unpredictable barriers should not be placed in the routes he or she uses.

Establishing a schedule that varies fast-paced activities, slow-paced activities, and preferred and nonpreferred activities is also important in organizing the learning environment. Too often, all fast-paced and preferred activities take place in the morning, and one may wonder why the student even attends the educational program after lunch.

The specific phases of activities—the preparation-planning phase, active participation phase, and termination-closure phase—must be considered as well. In some preschool settings, a child and his or her teacher may spend 20 minutes a day putting blocks in a container, and afterward the teacher throws the trash away for the child and puts objects away in their appropriate containers when the child could be helping and, in doing so, continuing to develop skills. By analyzing each phase of an activity, teachers can target additional functional skills and expand the activity so that more interaction occurs and opportunities for teaching functional skills are not missed.

# INTERACTIONS AND THE SOCIAL ENVIRONMENT

Social interactions with key persons in a variety of environments form the basis for instruction in communication. It is important to remember that communication will also serve as the basis for teaching many other skills and activities that the individual who is deaf-blind will learn. Teaching communication through meaningful social interactions requires careful assessment to determine how the student communicates with important others, including family members, teachers, peers, neighborhood friends, and members of the educational team, in various activities and places (see Modules 11–12).

## PERSONAL FUTURES PLANNING

One method of gathering information that is essential for working on the development of communication skills is Personal Futures Planning (PFP). PFP is a process that "helps groups of people focus on opportunities for people with disabilities to develop personal relationships, have positive roles in community life, increase the control of their own lives, and develop skills and abilities to achieve these goals" (Mount & Zwernick, 1989; see also Mount & Zwernick, 1990). It involves gathering information and mapping an individual's environment pictorially to provide information for creative short- and long-term planning. This process outlines (1) who interacts with the student; (2) the environments in which interactions occur; (3) the types of activities in which the student engages; (4) the student's likes, dislikes, and strengths; and (5) other personal facts about the student.

The best sources of information for these pictorial maps are the people who interact with the student most often (parents, relatives, friends). The PFP maps in Figures 13-1 to 13-4 were created by Randy's family and friends and compiled by his mother. They are

**FIGURE 13-1:**
Map of Randy's Relationships

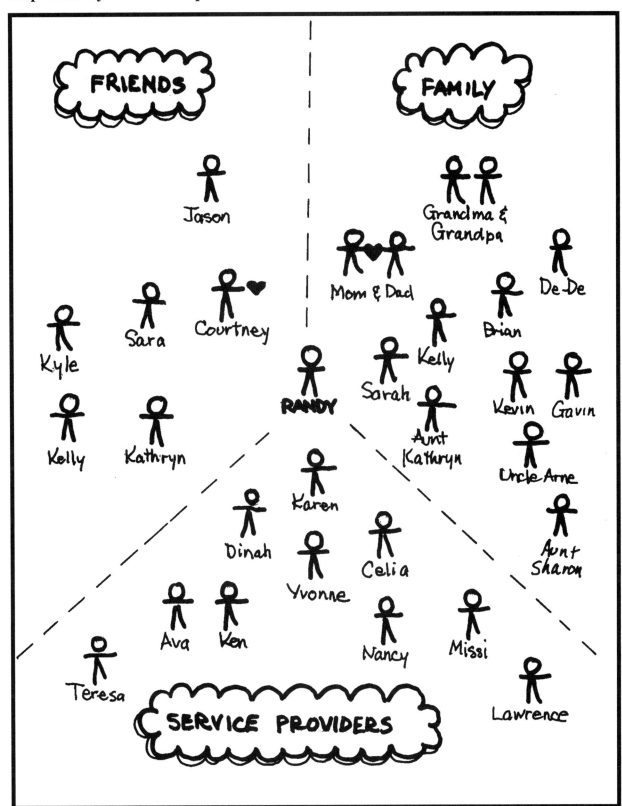

**FIGURE 13-2:**
**Map of Randy's Favorite Places**

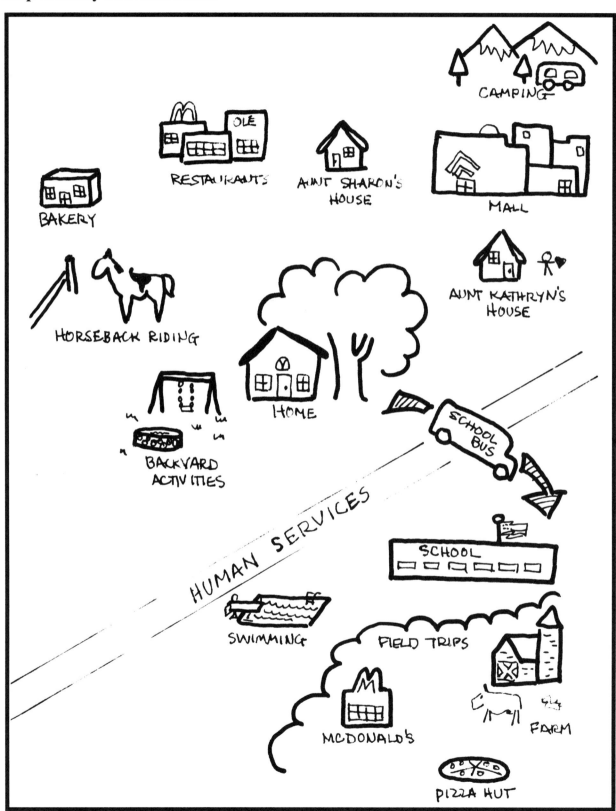

**FIGURE 13-3:**

**Map of Randy's Preferences**

| THINGS THAT WORK<br>*(create vitality, interest, energy, motivation)* | THINGS THAT DO NOT WORK<br>*(cause frustration, boredom, depression, upset)* |
|---|---|
| Gross motor activities: running, jumping, swinging, bouncing, teeter-tottering, rocking | Fine motor activities: those that result in little consequence or meaning |
| Games: silly teasing that allows for spontaneous interaction | Meaningless activities, such as puzzles by shape, and a puzzle box |
| Foods that are sweet and easy to chew and can be handled, such as sweet rolls, individual candy, breads, crackers | Meats, raw vegetables, slippery foods, NutraSweet |
| Familiar routines with anticipated outcomes, including bathtime, the morning routine, lunch, and a calendar box | Confining physical manipulation |
| Familiar areas with boundaries and supports, for example, the bedroom, classroom, physical therapy room, and family room | Activities in large areas without supports or boundaries, such as being alone in a backyard or playing with balls in a bin |
| Communication centered on objects, tactile cues, people, events, the calendar box | Meaningless communication that is not related to objects or events, for example, "Find the toothbrush" |
| Familiar pleasant smells that give cues to the environment, people, or places, such as the bedroom air freshener, Mom's perfume, and Aunt Kathryn's house and perfume | Unpleasant smells, for instance, disinfectants that irritate the eyes and cause headaches |
| Warm water: bathtime; playing in the sink; wading pool, or a hot tub; swimming with adequate heat protection (wet suit) | Cold things: water, drinks with ice, ice cream, hands in the snow, cold railings |
| Learning activities with food, for instance, thermoforms, lunchtime, snack time | Activities without a motivator, including hearing testing, and blocks in a can |
| Minimal amounts of clothing in a sandbox, footbath of beans, and water play, for example | Clothes that confine or reduce input: hats, mittens, socks and shoes, life jackets |
| Activities involving turn-taking with others, such as on a teeter-totter and in games, dancing, and jumping | Being left alone |
| Opportunities to make choices and have independence: thermoforms, object cues, rest time, unstructured playtime | Forced situations, in which Randy is told what to do and has no choice or power over the environment |

**FIGURE 13-4:**
**Map of Randy's Interactions**

| TYPES OF COMMUNICATION INITIATED BY RANDY | | TYPES OF COMMUNICATION INITIATED BY OTHERS | |
|---|---|---|---|
| • Gestures<br>• Signs: hungry, eat, drink, swing, jump, more<br>• Body language<br>• Emotions<br>• Withdrawal<br>• Behavior<br>• Intuition | | • Signs/verbal<br>• Object cues<br>• Touch body<br>• Calendar box<br>• Thermoform figures<br>• Gestures<br>• Intuition<br>• Firm movements | |

| WHO INTERACTS WITH RANDY | METHODS OF COMMUNICATION | |
|---|---|---|
| | USED BY RANDY | USED BY OTHERS |
| Mom and Dad | • Using signs and gestures<br>• Pulling on wrist to go<br>• Moving to continue activity<br>• Touching<br>• Making happy sounds<br>• Low energy, sadness, withdrawal | • Using signs or speech<br>• Touching<br>• Using object cues<br>• Hugging and kissing<br>• Teasing and tickling<br>• Using firm movements for displeasure |
| Courtney (age 6) | • Touching<br>• Smiling, making happy sounds<br>• Using gestures<br>• Intuition (as reported by Randy's mother) | • Touching<br>• Talking and laughing<br>• Hugging<br>• Intuition |
| Karen (interpreter) and Celia (teacher) | • Using signs and gestures<br>• Using thermoform figures and objects for choices<br>• Behavior<br>• Moving to continue activity<br>• Low energy, sadness, withdrawal | • Using signs, speech, and gestures<br>• Taking action on objects<br>• Using a calendar box<br>• Using thermoform figures<br>• Hugging and patting |
| Aunt Kathryn and Aunt Sharon | • Using gestures and signs<br>• Behavior<br>• Touching<br>• Making happy sounds<br>• Using body language | • Touching<br>• Using speech<br>• Using environmental cues, such as a railing, chair, air freshener, and special toys<br>• Hugging and patting<br>• Asking Courtney |
| Bakery attendant | • Smiling<br>• Behavior: impatient, fussy<br>• Using body language: extension | • Patting and touching |

only some of the key maps that are part of the PFP process (additional examples are shown in the photographs in this module).

When this information was gathered, Randy was 8 years old, in a special class in a public school, accompanied by an aide-interpreter throughout the school day, and just learning some basic signs. The goal in drawing the maps was to address Randy's long-term life goals, including participation in the community, and to examine how Randy's educational plan would contribute to their achievement. As the maps show, some of Randy's most effective interactions were with the people and activities that he preferred. In each situation, it was important to examine both how Randy expressed himself and how he received responses.

The figures provided a wealth of information that was used as the basis for designing a program to expand Randy's involvement with friends and community activities. The educational team asked the following important questions when they examined these maps: What kinds of activities does Randy like? How does he communicate his enjoyment? How does he communicate in different environments? Is his communication different at home, at school, and with friends?

The team used this information to complete a communication-interaction map and selected a sample of preferred people, environments, and activities from the earlier maps. This new map presented a picture of some of Randy's best communication skills, ones that he used when he was the most motivated and involved with people and activities of his choice. In each situation, it was important to examine both how Randy expressed himself and how he received responses (see Figure 13-4 for a partial summary of this information; a blank form appears at the end of this module to assist readers who wish to adapt it for their own use).

## Variety of Communication Methods

A teacher often works to establish a single communication method in a classroom and then assumes that, as a result of the educational process, a student will later learn to apply it in other environments. The map of Randy's interactions (Figure 13-4) shows that Randy is developing formal and informal communication skills that he uses effectively in different situations. Communication behaviors, such as gesturing, touching, vocalizing, and smiling, seem to be most effective for Randy when he communicates with a friend (Courtney) and with the attendant at his favorite bakery. Formal communication

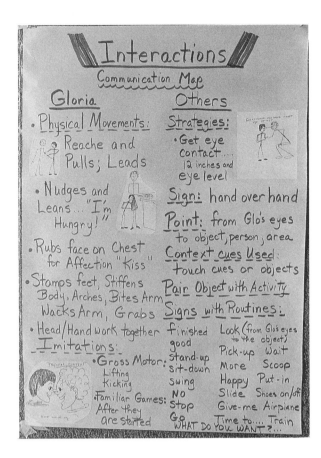

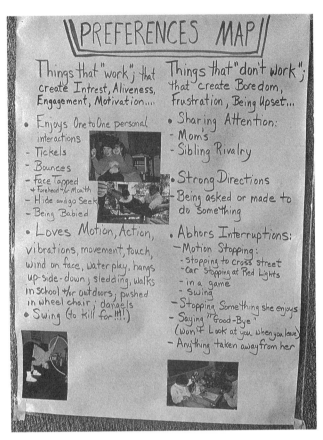

▲ *Mapping a student's environment pictorially provides essential information about preferences, activities, and communication methods that can form the foundation for planning and for further expanding skills.*

modes, such as the tangible symbols and sign language that Randy uses in school and with his parents, may later be used in other community settings and social situations.

For example, Randy may be learning the sign for "more" in school settings like the cafeteria and practicing it at home. Then, it will be important to see how the sign can be used in interactions with a friend or in a restaurant. Instruction in communication, including the development of a vocabulary of signs or the use of augmentative communication devices, can be designed for activities like a trip to the bakery. Signs of or pictures for "bakery" and "cookie," for example, can be taught during the visit to the bakery, and "cookie" can also be used at home, with a friend, and in the cafeteria.

## Interaction in the Community

Communication supports Randy's involvement in a variety of relationships and community environments. Randy's personality and what he likes play significant roles in his interaction with others and in places that he enjoys. In those situations, he smiles and shows excitement, and others respond positively to him and want to interact, so everyone benefits.

Often, those working with a child focus only on a method of communication and identify the child's success by measuring the increased number of signs, gestures, or vocalizations that the child uses. However, when success is measured in relation to a long-term goal of expanded relationships and participation in the community, activities that support the growth of skills that are useful in communities, such as smiling and appropriate touching, are included.

## DEVELOPING A PROGRAM

Information from the PFP process helped Randy's educational team maintain a holistic view of their student and consider more than just his interactions in school or at home. It also helped the team focus on long-term goals and think of Randy's future options. Each of Randy's key maps assisted them in making specific program decisions.

- The Map of Randy's Relationships (Figure 13-1) identified Randy's current communication partners—those with whom he can practice, develop, and enhance his skills. After evaluating the breadth of Randy's social circle and the types of relationships he had, the team determined that a major goal was to help Randy develop friendships with peers.

- The Map of Randy's Favorite Places (Figure 13-2) identified the environments that Randy frequents. The team members agreed that Randy already had access to a number of settings in the community that are important to his family. Therefore, they decided that the educational program would focus on improving the quality of interactions in these settings, rather than on expanding the number of environments.

- The Map of Randy's Preferences (Figure 13-3) identified Randy's likes and dislikes. The team used this information to determine the best means to engage Randy in activities and which ones should be avoided. Their decision was to change some of the current teaching environments and strategies used, to ensure more successful instruction.

- The Map of Randy's Interactions (Figure 13-4) identified the means by which Randy communicates with others and how others communicate with him, information that the team used to consider the variety of communication options available. A major goal was to teach some of Randy's communication partners key signs.

## GUIDELINES FOR DESIGNING A COMMUNICATION PROGRAM

A student's educational team may find the PFP process helpful in designing a program that enhances the student's interactions with others and involvement in his or her community. Regardless of the methods or tools they use, there are a number of guidelines to keep in mind:

- Make sure the preferences of the student's family are given priority. The student's involvement in the community is generally built on his or her family's activities.

- Remember that the student will use a variety of means to communicate with others in his or her community. The type of communication option used will depend on the skills and preferences of both the student and his or her communication partner, the demands of the situation (such as lighting, time available for interaction, and type of information to be exchanged), and the features of the communication option (such as portability, ease of use, and flexibility). Do not limit the student by limiting the communication options taught.

- Provide training for the individuals who may interact with the student to help them become familiar and comfortable with the ways in which the student communicates. Public awareness training in some of the settings the student frequents may also be needed. Make sure the student's school peers have learned how to communicate with him or her. (Information on fostering communication between deaf-blind students and other students appears later in this module.)

- Make sure that everyone who interacts with the student truly interacts as a partner. Do not let interactions be only one sided and directive, implying, "I'll tell you what to do, and you do it without questioning." Be especially careful to help peers develop relationships with the student as "peer buddies."

- Help the student and his or her communication partners to interact as directly as possible. Sometimes, when it is important to have others function as intermediaries, it is best to use an interpreter. However, when interaction is frequent, the student and others can learn appropriate ways of communicating, including the use of augmentative aids.

- Remember that since communication is a dynamic process, so are all aspects of program planning to enhance interactions in the student's community. Because environments, partners, skills, and interests may all change, program plans need to be responsive to change and may even have to instigate changes in some cases.

It may also be helpful for members of the student's educational team to review the general teaching strategies outlined in Unit 1. Many of those simple, commonsense strategies should be incorporated routinely in the student's program in every learning environment.

# INSTRUCTIONAL STRATEGIES TO INCREASE COMMUNICATION

Strategies to increase communication between the student who is deaf-blind and his or her social partners should be used in a social context in which frequent exchanges occur. Promoting the development of communication is more than providing a cue or prompt for a specific response from a student and then supplying feedback. And teaching communication requires more than interacting with the student and hoping that his or her communication skills will increase as the result of the interaction. Both general and specific instructional strategies need to be considered in individualized instruction for a student. The following are four features that should be considered to achieve effective teaching interactions:

1. Communication should occur with many different people (including peers).

2. Communication exchanges should occur frequently.

3. All communication partners should know or be taught the student's forms of receptive and expressive communication.

4. During interactions, systematic procedures should be used to expand the student's communication system.

It is important for deaf-blind students to develop relationships with their peers, and effective communication skills go a long way to foster such relationships. Many students form peer relationships primarily in the classroom, and various techniques can be used to promote these relationships.

# FOSTERING COMMUNICATION AMONG STUDENTS

For students who are deaf-blind to be successful in general education settings, they and their classmates must learn a common mode of communication and how to interact with each other. Such communication and interaction among students can be encouraged in a number of ways, depending on the characteristics of the student who is deaf-blind, the characteristics of the teacher or teachers, the needs of the other students in the classroom, and the way in which the classroom operates. The key to success is to be flexible in developing what works for all students in the classroom. The following are some suggestions for fostering communication:

- Model "peerlike" interactions with students who are deaf-blind. Often the other students in the classroom will imitate the types of interactions they observe in others. If they see a teacher using gestures or a communication object board with a deaf-blind student, then they are more likely to use the same type of interaction with the student. The same is true of interaction styles. The teacher who models "peerlike" interactions with a student who is deaf-blind is more likely to see peerlike or friendly interactions among the students. Often classmates want to be friendly or to interact with a deaf-blind student but do not know how to act.

- Teach classmates how to use a student's communication system or mode of communication in a variety of ways, from informal demonstrations with the student to the establishment of specific times for teaching the student's communication system. For example, one teacher used 15 minutes each day to teach specific signs to the class. Her student, who was deaf and had some functional vision, participated by demonstrating some of the signs he used, so his classmates could practice with him. After the lessons, the use of sign language between the student and his classmates increased.

- Teach classmates to recognize and interpret a student's communication. Some nonsymbolic communication may be difficult for the student's classmates to recognize. Therefore, the teacher should help the classmates (1) recognize when the student is communicating, (2) interpret the student's message, and (3) learn how to respond to the student's message. All these steps are imperative if a truly communicative relationship is to be established among the students.

- Teach students who are deaf-blind to recognize their classmates as "communicators." Since deaf-blind students are often taught to initiate contact with and respond only to adults, they may need to learn that their classmates can also communicate and respond to them. Teachers frequently find that once the communicative relationship is established, students who are deaf-blind are much more motivated to communicate with their classmates than with adults.

- Teach deaf-blind students how to take turns communicating and interacting with classmates. Turn-taking is an essential component of communication.

- Teach classmates about a student's degree of vision and hearing. If they understand what the student can and cannot perceive, they can learn to communicate with the student better.

- Encourage classmates to discover ways to communicate with students who are deaf-blind. Ask them how they may "tell" a student something or interpret when the student is communicating something to them. For example, ask, "What do you think Ethan means when he holds out his hands like that?" Everyone may not have understood that Ethan was trying to communicate with them, and you may need to help them interpret Ethan's message. Encouraging classmates to solve communication problems can be much more powerful than simply providing a solution. When they have helped with a potential solution or strategy to overcome an obstacle, they believe that they have a personal investment and are more likely to remember and use a strategy that they have devised.

Many schools have developed various kinds of peer-support programs to increase the involvement and interaction of students with and without disabilities. The following is a brief description of some of the most common programs:

- *Peer tutors* act under the guidance of a teacher and help students who are deaf-blind to acquire new skills or to practice skills that already have been learned.

- *Peer buddies* volunteer to provide social support to students with disabilities, such as by accompanying a student to the cafeteria, helping a student open and find things in his or her school locker, hanging out together, and assisting a student on and off the school bus (Villa & Thousand, 1992).

- *Peer advocates* serve a number of functions in Individualized Education Program (IEP) planning teams and in other types of planning sessions for students who are deaf-blind. For example, they act as the voice of students who cannot speak for themselves and offer them "moral support" and assistance with self-advocacy, particularly when the students differ with their parents or professional educators on the focus of their education or the content of their IEPs (Villa & Thousand, 1992).

- *Natural support networks* are reciprocal relationships in which classmates and schoolmates assist and support one another as peers, friends, or colleagues (Stainback, Stainback, & Jackson, 1992). When a student needs help preparing for or carrying out an activity, another student, rather than an adult, helps.

- *Peer-support networks* are groups of students who meet to discuss the social interactions that students who are deaf-blind had with their friends throughout the week and formulate plans to increase the students' inclusion in various school activities (Block & Haring, 1992).

To achieve genuine inclusive schooling for students who are deaf-blind, teachers and classmates must be able to communicate and interact with them. However, many deaf-blind students may use unconventional modes of communication, such as gestures, sounds, and body movements, rather than speech or written language, to express themselves. Their classmates may not understand or recognize these modes of communication and may think that the students are misbehaving or are peculiar. This lack of common communication or interaction styles can impede the relationships of individuals who are deaf-blind and their family members, teachers, and potential friends. Another complication is that intervention usually focuses on the individual who communicates in an alternative way. Since communication involves the efforts of at least two people, intervention should concentrate on the interactive process, rather than solely on remediation of the limited repertoire of an individual (Siegel-Causey & Downing, 1987). Thus, all people in an interaction, including the classmates of a deaf-blind student, need to be taught how to communicate with each other.

## STRATEGIES FOR INTERACTION

Whether in the classroom, the community, the home, or any other environment, special considerations and adaptations must often be used to interact with an individual who is deaf-blind. At times, everyone on the educational team will have his or her own idea about how to interact with the student. For example, the student's parent may suggest the best way to respond to the student, the physical therapist may indicate the most appropriate ways to position and handle the student if he or she has motor impairments, and the teacher or the communication specialist may teach everyone else who interacts with the student to implement certain general skills. (See Suggestions for Interaction for the specific steps to use.)

The suggestions for interaction outlined in this module will not necessarily "teach" the student new forms and functions of communication. They will, however, provide the student with exposure to (1) cues, so he or she can begin to anticipate what will happen; (2) information to learn new concepts; (3) opportunities to engage in more meaningful interaction; and (4) opportunities to increase the frequency of his or her current forms and functions of communication. These interactions should also give service providers information about more specific strategies that should be implemented to expand the student's level of communication.

In the two descriptions that follow, the students differ in age, vision, hearing, and cognitive and motor skills. Such differences must be considered in order to individualize the strategies to be used during interactions with a particular student. After you read each description, read the age-appropriate activities that are provided for each student and think about the questions that are asked regarding each. In so doing, picture yourself interacting with each student using the strategies just listed.

> *Maria is a 5 year old who has a severe hearing impairment and wears hearing aids, which she leaves on unless she is angry or does not understand what is happening. Both her retinas have been detached since birth, so she has no useful vision. Maria can walk and run. She has been in early intervention programs since birth. Her records show that her behavior was never tactilely defensive, that she interacted with people and toys at an early age, that she took her first steps at age 17 months, and that she smiles when she enjoys a person*

## SUGGESTIONS FOR INTERACTION

The following are recommended strategies for interaction to be used in all routines and activities with a student:

• Get the student's attention (through touch, gestures, or oral cues).

• Wait for a response from the student.

• Identify yourself (for example, through auditory, visual, or tactile object cues).

• Prepare the student for the specific activity (individualized for each student).

• Announce what is about to happen (specific to the student).

• Provide correct positioning, handling, or orientation and mobility (O&M) techniques.

• Involve the student in gathering and setting up materials that are needed for the activity.

• Position the materials to be used in the activity in the best location, depending on the student's visual and motor skills.

• Communicate any changes in the activity before starting.

• Be responsive to any behaviors that the student may exhibit that may communicate his or her dislikes, preferences, or choices.

• Provide multiple opportunities for the student to communicate.

• Use adaptations as necessary to facilitate active participation in the activity.

• Allow the student to participate in the activity.

• Provide consistent prompts and cues.

• Wait for responses from the student.

• Provide appropriate feedback.

• Encourage the interactions of the student and others (such as siblings, peers, other staff).

• Announce the termination of the activity (in fact, the student can assist in ending the activity).

• Involve the student in cleaning up or returning the materials used. ■

or an activity. She can also express herself by throwing tantrums when she does not want to do something or when she cannot anticipate what is about to happen.

Picture yourself taking Maria outside in the playground during recess with the regular kindergarten class and interacting with her.

• Did you tell Maria your name and let her feel your hair or ring for identification?

- Did you make sure that Maria had her hearing aids turned on or help her to do so?

- Did you say or sign "outside/play" and let her process this cue?

- Were you responsive to Maria when she threw a tantrum because you forgot to let her get her coat, and did you and she go back for it?

- Did you give Maria an object cue, such as a chain, to represent the swing?

- While you were pushing Maria on the swing, did you give her opportunities to request "more," or did you push her with no discussion?

- Did you communicate to Maria when it was another child's chance to swing?

- Did you provide consistent cues? For example, did you rub Maria's arm and sign or say, "Good girl," when she got off the swing without throwing a tantrum?

- Did you give Maria a chance to play on the seesaw with a peer?

- Did you do anything to encourage other people to interact with Maria?

*Carlos is an 18 year old who is profoundly deaf, blind in his left eye, and has low vision in his right eye. He did not attend any type of educational program until he was 12 years old. Carlos uses a wheelchair and can use his hands. He attends to people and seems to enjoy social interactions, communicating primarily through facial expressions or by looking toward something. He enjoys pounding on the organ and going out in the community.*

Now, picture yourself going with Carlos to a community center where more people know him than know you.

- Did you stand to Carlos's right side, so he could see you? Did you move closer and smile at him, and wait for him to notice you and smile back? Did you say or sign "hello" to him?

- Did you make sure that Carlos had his tray on his wheelchair and was correctly positioned in his chair?

- Did you show Carlos a picture of the community center and let him help get his own membership card?

- Were you responsive to Carlos when he was looking at his peer buddy and not you as you started to push his wheelchair? (Did you let his peer buddy push the wheelchair?)

- Did Carlos have choices about which games to play? Did you provide Carlos with the help he needed when he communicated to you?

- Did you let Carlos know when something new was about to happen? Did Carlos have an opportunity to interact with people?

- Did you provide consistent cues? Did you give Carlos time to respond to your questions before repeating the same question again and again?

- Did you smile at Carlos and shake your head "yes" or sign "yes" when he completed tasks or accomplished goals?

- Did you do anything to encourage other people to interact with Carlos?

How would you rate yourself for your imagined interactions with Maria and Carlos? Consider these factors: Did you provide sufficient and appropriate cues? Did you give them enough opportunities to interact? Were you responsive to their attempts to interact? Did you remember Maria's hearing aids? Did you let Maria and Carlos know what was about to happen? Did you think Maria might have been trying to communicate when she started to have a tantrum?

You may also ask yourself whether there are other forms of communication that Maria and Carlos can use. They both seem to enjoy social interactions and anticipate events. And you may have noticed that Maria either used body movements to indicate "more" or threw tantrums when things were not going right, and Carlos only looked at something to indicate that he noticed it or to request more of something, a choice, or his protest or dislike. Yet both students have enough use of their hands that they could extend objects, gesture, and use yes-no gestures and sign language. Carlos has enough vision in his right eye so that he can point to a picture if he understands the meaning of the picture. Now you have some information about both students. You also have more questions to ask. What instructional procedures should be used with each to expand their specific communication systems and to increase the number of social partners with whom they communicate?

# EXPANDING A STUDENT'S COMMUNICATION SYSTEM

It is possible to observe a student who is deaf-blind in a natural environment and see little or no communication. Should you assume that the student cannot communicate or has extremely limited communication skills? Too frequently, we observe students during specific activities and assume that the communication forms they use are their only forms of communication.

## Identifying the Current System

To develop systematic instructional strategies, it is important to determine the student's current forms of communication. Service providers who are responsible for the development and implementation of communication skills should ask the family how the student communicates, observe the student interacting with others, and interact with the student during a number of different activities to determine his or her highest form of communication (see Modules 11 and 12). Here are some useful strategies:

- Begin an interaction by providing something "free" (without discussion); let the student know that you are available for interaction.

- After you establish a sequence of a few free preferred objects or activities (bites of food, pushes on a swing, or minutes of listening to a favorite song), interrupt the pattern.

- Be patient. Notice how the student communicates "want more." Be responsive to his or her form of communication and help expand the response.

- Encourage further interaction. For example, if a student leans forward to get another sip of a drink and can move his or her hands, provide a touch cue for "more" and place your hand close, so he or she can touch it. If the student has sufficient motor skills and some vision, encourage him or her to reach for the cup. You may point to the picture of the correct object if his or her vision is not severely impaired, or you may expand the communication by providing a tactile or visible sign as a model and wait to see if the student will imitate it.

- Provide opportunities for the student to reject an object or activity or show his or her dislike for it, to get your attention, to make choices, to offer, and to comment.

- Communicate your choices (likes and dislikes) to the student.

- Engage as much as possible in turn-taking activities to provide opportunities for different communication functions.

- Note the conditions under which the student communicated at his or her highest level. For example, what did you do before the student responded? Did you extend your hand before the student extended his or her cup for more? Did the student sign "more" only after you gave assistance, imitate your model, or sign "more" when you said or signed "more"? The conditions under which the student is successful will depend on his or her visual skills, auditory skills (usually with hearing aids or other amplification), cognitive ability, motor skills, previous instruction, and personal motivation. The student's age will play a part in how you interact and what you communicate about.

Many students who are deaf-blind do not initiate communication even with more cues; they are dependent on prompts to make responses. Therefore, before the educational team decides to expand the student's communication, you may need to do the following:

- Increase the frequency of consistent overall communication responses.

- Increase the persons, environments, and activities with which the student interacts, so he or she has the opportunity to generalize his or her current communication to different persons, places, and things. For example, you may want Sam to learn that he can sign "more" for more time on the swings in the playground with his teacher's aide, a peer, or his teacher, since he already can sign "more" in the cafeteria or in the gym. You need to make sure that Sam knows what "more" means, so he knows when "more" is not appropriate. O&M activities, in which students explore their neighborhoods and communities, present other opportunities for expanded interactions in such places as local shops, restaurants, or nearby post offices.

- Increase the student's initiation of the communication form, so he or she can respond to cues in order to initiate the same communication form with more natural cues (such as using the gesture or sign for eat when he smells food, not just when you ask, "What do you want?" at lunchtime).

Some specific instructional strategies to accomplish these activities are the following:

- Use the receptive communication forms that the student understands to teach expressive forms. For example, if a student uses objects in a calendar box (see Module 8) as symbols to order the activities of the day, help him or her to use them and other objects to make requests.

- Interrupt patterns of routine interactions or the chain of the activity. For instance, if you are playing a game with a student, stop the activity and do not resume playing until the student indicates to you (for example, by nudging you, signing, or handing you the materials) that he or she wants the game to continue.

- Delay longer before you provide the level of assistance that the student is used to receiving. Thus, if the student is having difficulty opening an object, such as a milk carton, wait a while before you intervene. The student may attempt to get your attention and communicate a request for help.

- Use expansions. When a student extends a cup, for example, sign "juice" or "You want juice?" if sign language is a possible mode of communication.

## Interacting to Provide Structural Support

Once you have determined the different forms and functions that the student uses to communicate, know which communication forms and functions he or she responds to, and have increased the opportunities for interaction and for communication, then you are ready to teach new communication forms or to decrease your structured support. However, you still need to provide enough support (or adaptations) so that the student is successful and your interactions are successful, although the student does not have to comply with your directives or respond to your physical prompts all the time.

In general, you need to individualize specific procedures based on the student's skills and needs. The specific prompts that you use and the times that you use them will depend on the form being targeted or taught and the student's responses and initiations for different social interactions. In addition, the student will not use just one form or one function of communication to communicate different things. He or she may extend some objects (such as money to buy things), extend a hand (to receive change) in response to a gesture prompt, shake his or her head "no" when asked a question, and need physical assistance to use new signs that are being taught. Service providers need to make thoughtful decisions about when to expand different forms and different functions during a specific interaction.

In any interaction, you need to be responsive to whatever communication the student initiates. Furthermore, you need to request more from the student to achieve a higher communicative response and provide only the support the student needs. In addition, you need to engage in appropriate social interactions and to be aware that your social interactions with your students who are deaf-blind are "teachable moments" and that you can systematically provide support as you interact. You also need to model the new forms of communication that you want the student to follow. Doing all these things takes skill and practice. It may help to think about your teaching in this way as you interact:

- I predict that Carlos will make specific communicative responses during this specific activity and interaction; I know that Carlos understands certain cues (touch and object) when I communicate with him.

- I predict that Carlos will demonstrate his specific responses under specific conditions.

- On the basis of past experiences with Carlos, I predict that he is most likely to respond again if certain events follow when he makes the response.

- I predict that if I expect just a little more from Carlos, without letting him fail, wait for that response without frustrating him, and give him even more attention for making that response, he is more likely to make that response again.

For example, Carlos will look at an object if he wants it. His educational team decided to expand his expressive communication system by first teaching him to extend objects and to use gestures. The IEP objectives for him include demonstrating skills to order and eat a meal in a restaurant, to select and purchase items in a grocery store, and to go to a movie with a peer buddy. (See Module 18 for an explanation of how this communication strategy is integrated with

O&M skills, which the student needs to learn simultaneously with communication techniques.) You need to analyze the skills being taught in those activities to determine how you can best teach extending objects and gestures in each activity. The following is an example of the training procedures:

Use an array of object representations in "preparing to go to the restaurant," and place a photograph of each object behind the object. When Carlos indicates which object he wants by looking at it, point to that object. Wait four to five seconds for Carlos to point to each photograph. If he does not imitate your pointing response, provide only the physical assistance necessary to get him to point.

Carlos will then take the photographs he has selected to the fast-food restaurant. When he extends the photographs (of a hamburger and a soft drink) to the clerk, he may still not understand what they mean, but he is learning that they will get him something. After the clerk hands Carlos his food items, gesture for Carlos to give the money to the clerk. When Carlos does so without a physical prompt, give him an "OK" gesture or sign "OK" as feedback.

You could also order before Carlos does and hand money to the clerk as a model or take a peer along to model these behaviors. As you pass by the straws and napkins, point to them and then to Carlos, indicating, "Do you want one?" When he smiles, shake your head "yes." Later, pass by the straws and napkins and wait for Carlos to point to them, so you interrupt your usual pattern to get him to initiate the action.

Use as little physical assistance as necessary and as many "natural" cues and prompts as possible. Prompt Carlos at a slightly higher level after he is familiar with the task, and wait for a higher-level response or a response to a less supportive prompt. Through your interactions with Carlos, you will know the level of support that you will need to give him for him to be successful. Your observations will confirm if you are giving him too much or too little support. For learners with no vision, the visual modeling prompts will not be effective. Therefore, you will have to consider each learner's visual, auditory, cognitive, and motor skills and needs to determine the level and kinds of supporting prompts that are necessary.

## Facilitating Generalization

You will not have time to teach every response, under every possible condition, with every possible social partner, in every possible activity. However, you can use a number of active teaching strategies to help the student generalize his or her use of forms and functions for new persons, settings, and activities. The active generalization strategies that you can incorporate into instruction include these:

- Use objects and actions and persons who are the most common for the different activities and environments. Remember that the persons who spend the most time with the student are the most important for developing communication skills.
- Use many different persons (parents, adults, siblings, peers, and team members) to help with teaching.
- Use numerous different objects, activities, and settings for teaching.
- Use natural consequences for teaching and maximize feedback when generalization occurs. That is, praise the student for using a specific communication response appropriately in a new situation; the effects of using the response appropriately will also be positive and reinforcing.
- Use various cues and prompts to avoid the student's dependence on a specific prompt.

It is important to note that these strategies are useful in both communication and O&M programs.

## Teaching Other Social Partners

It is also necessary to teach other persons, including family members, school staff, therapists, O&M instructors, and others who interact with the student regularly, to use specific prompts consistently and correctly. The numerous possible "teaching-to-teach" or "teaching-to-interact" strategies include the following:

- Demonstrate the correct strategies to the other person while interacting with the student.
- Describe the specific prompts and strategies, so the other person will know the critical skills.
- Give a videotape of the interaction procedures to the other person.
- Actively coach the other person during interactions with the student by providing positive feedback and additional modeling, if necessary.

- Use videotaped samples of the other person and the student to help analyze the strategies that were used effectively and to modify those that were not.

## EVALUATING EFFECTIVENESS

How do you know if your instructional strategies are effective? How do you know if the student is ready to learn a new skill? How do you know if you have to change the interactions or the prompts you are using? You can determine the effectiveness of your teaching and interactions only by observing, recording, and analyzing information. The data can consist of a simple tally of the number of opportunities the student was given under what conditions (see Figure 13-5) and how the student responded.

As instruction progresses (in a few days, weeks, or months, depending on the particular student), you should eventually expect to see more responses made to a gesture (for example, the student naturally extending his or her hand to receive an object) and fewer responses to the model or the need for full physical assistance. You should also observe multiple communication forms, functions, content, levels and kinds of prompts, and communication with peers. These observations will indicate if the student is demonstrating the targeted forms or higher forms and if the person interacting with him

**FIGURE 13-5:**
**Sample Communication Form: Extending Objects and Using Gestures**

| STUDENT _____ DATE _____ | | | |
|---|---|---|---|
| ACTIVITY | WITH GESTURES | WITH THE MODEL | ASSISTED |
| ACTIVITY 1 | // | //// | / |
| ACTIVITY 2 | /// | // | / |
| ACTIVITY 3 | /// | / | |
| TOTAL | 8 | 7 | 2 |

or her is using active instructional strategies. A probe (a sample observation) can be taken for 10 minutes of an interaction, or an interaction can be videotaped and data can be collected at another time. One of the roles of the speech-language specialist may be to collect and chart the data as he or she observes the interactions.

The educational team may discuss modifications or decide to move ahead in the teaching process on the basis of these data. You may need to ask more specific questions and collect data about additional behaviors or prompts to make decisions. For example, perhaps you observe that Maria is now using some signs and some gestures and is touching objects or people to communicate. You may want to know if she is using the correct sign to refer to the object she is requesting and the types of errors she is making. You may also want to know the meaning of her gestures and touching, so you can select new signs to convey what she is currently communicating about. If she does not indicate in some way that she wants a cracker, there is little reason to teach that sign even if she eats a cracker when it is given to her.

By changing your role or the role of another person in the interaction, you can expand the content and functions of communication and perhaps increase the frequency of opportunities to communicate or the frequency of initiations. Gradually increase the complexity of the activity, so the student completes the activity more independently and cooperatively or uses more communication to finish it.

All the student's social partners should respond to his or her communication, communicate with the student, and provide opportunities for the student to communicate from the moment the student awakens until he or she goes to sleep. The service providers who work with the student are responsible for using systematic instructional procedures to ensure that he or she has access to the most effective and efficient systems of communication, so the student can communicate with various partners and has a shared system of communication that persons unfamiliar with him or her can understand. The specific communication systems—the forms, functions, content, and context of communication—will depend on characteristics of the individual student. Decisions will be made by members of the educational team. A concentrated focus on enhancing the student's skills can lead to an increase in self-esteem and independence, and the educational team can then plan additional interventions that may lead to the student's further skill development. An accompanying goal, as a student approaches secondary school, is to plan for the student's transition to postsecondary activities. Such transitions are discussed in the module that follows.

# *REFERENCES*

Block, J. H., & Haring, T. G. (1992). On swamps, bogs, alligators, and special educational reform. In R. A. Villa, J. S. Thousand, W. Stainback, & S. Stainback (Eds.), *Restructuring for caring and effective education* (pp. 7–24). Baltimore: Paul H. Brookes.

Mount, B., & Zwernick, K. (1989). *It's never too early, it's never too late: A booklet about personal futures planning*. St. Paul: Minnesota Governor's Planning Council on Developmental Disabilities.

Mount, B., & Zwernick, K. (1990). *Making futures happen: A manual for facilitators of personal futures planning*. St. Paul: Minnesota Governor's Planning Council on Developmental Disabilities.

Siegel-Causey, E., & Downing, J. (1987). Nonsymbolic communication development: Theoretical concepts and educational strategies. In L. Goetz, D. Guess, & K. Stremel-Campbell (Eds.), *Innovative program design for individuals with dual sensory impairments* (pp. 15–48). Baltimore: Paul H. Brookes.

Stainback, S., Stainback, W., & Jackson, H. J. (1992). Toward inclusive classrooms. In S. Stainback & W. Stainback (Eds.), *Curriculum considerations in inclusive classrooms: Facilitating learning for all students* (pp. 3–17). Baltimore: Paul H. Brookes.

Villa, R. A., & Thousand, J. S. (1992). Student collaboration: An essential for curriculum in the 21st century. In S. Stainback & W. Stainback (Eds.), *Curriculum considerations in inclusive classrooms: Facilitating learning for all students* (pp. 117–142). Baltimore: Paul H. Brookes.

| MAP OF STUDENT'S INTERACTIONS | |
|---|---|
| **TYPES OF COMMUNICATION INITIATED BY STUDENT** | **TYPES OF COMMUNICATION INITIATED BY OTHERS** |
| | |

| **WHO INTERACTS WITH STUDENT** | **METHODS OF COMMUNICATION** | |
|---|---|---|
| | **USED BY STUDENT** | **USED BY OTHERS** |
| | | |

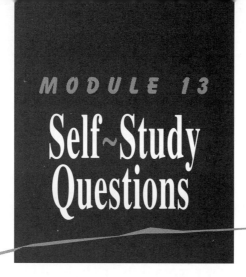

MODULE 13

# Self-Study Questions

1. Instructional activities should be selected on the basis of
   a. the developmental skills of the student.
   b. the cognitive age of the student.
   c. what works best for the teacher and the school.
   d. the activities selected by the family and appropriateness for a student's needs.

2. *Engaging environments* are those that
   a. primarily offer stimulation for the student.
   b. are predictable and organized.
   c. are those immediately around the school.
   d. are those to which the family has access.

3. Instructional environments should be selected on the basis of
   a. those that are available in the student's community.
   b. those in which typical peers would be included.
   c. those that will be important in the student's future.
   d. All the above.
   e. None of the above.

4. You are feeding Sara, who is blind and profoundly deaf. When she wants another bite, she opens her mouth. You interpret this gesture as "want more." Each time Sara opens her mouth, you give her a bite. The team has decided that Sara could touch a person or an object to communicate with a higher, more intentional form of communication. What instructional strategy would you use to get Sara to use touch to communicate "more eat"?
   a. Take her hand and touch the spoon or your hand before she opens her mouth to indicate "more."
   b. When she indicates she wants "more" by opening her mouth, provide a touch cue for "more" so she knows you are available; place your hand about a half-inch from yours so she feels the warmth of your hand; wait four to seven seconds; and if she has not touched your hand in that time, touch your hand to hers.
   c. When Sara opens her mouth, say, "Touch my hand." If she does not reach out and touch your hand, do not give her a bite. Repeat this procedure until she responds appropriately.

5.  Tom has no peripheral vision and can see objects when they are within 18 inches of his face. He has a severe, bilateral hearing loss and uses hearing aids. Tom currently communicates by using gestures, by vocalizing, and by coming to get you to show you what he wants. His parents want him to learn sign language to communicate. You are teaching Tom some cooking skills and interacting cooperatively with him. What strategies and prompts would you use to get Tom to sign?

    a.  Sign every word to him until he gets the idea.

    b.  Use the signs in context that you will be teaching before you ask him to use them, so you know that he understands them receptively and he begins to understand their meaning and use. When he gestures or vocalizes, respond to his form of communication and then say the word and model the sign.

    c.  Physically assist Tom to make the signs before he can use his gestures, so the higher level of communication is reinforced.

    d.  Model the signs for Tom. If he does not imitate the signs, continue to model and respond to him only when he signs.

6.  You observe a peer buddy interacting with Jody, who has no usable vision or hearing. The buddy signs, "Get up." When Jody does not respond, the buddy helps her to her feet. You are responsible for teaching the peer buddy more appropriate ways of communicating and interacting with Jody. What "teaching-to-teach" strategies would you use?

    a.  Tell the buddy that Jody cannot see, so he or she does not need to sign.

    b.  Tell the buddy not to jerk on Jody.

    c.  Show the buddy how to use touch cues to communicate with Jody and to wait. Then if Jody does not get up, the buddy should gently guide her. Also, the buddy should indicate to Jody where they may go, so she will be motivated to stand up.

    d.  Explain to the buddy that Jody will get up when she is ready and that he or she should just wait for her to initiate standing up before they go somewhere to interact.

*Answers to self-study questions for this module appear at the end of Unit 2.*

# Transition to Adult Life

CAROLE R. GOTHELF

DANIEL B. CRIMMINS

SARA B. WOOLF

JEANNE GLIDDEN PRICKETT

- *Begin transition planning early*

- *Build training programs on the student's preferences*

- *Consider present and future environments in developing skills*

- *Focus on independent living, community participation, and employment*

- *Provide opportunities for the student to communicate choices*

- *Promote the student's self-determination skills*

*T*ransitions occur frequently in life, and they start early for students who are deaf-blind. These students and their families undergo transitions as early as during infancy, when babies who are born with intensive medical needs and spend long periods in hospitals just after birth go home and must adjust to family life and a different environment. Although not all children who are deaf-blind undergo this sort of transition, most receive early intervention services and make transitions from home instruction to preschool programs and then to primary school programs, middle school or junior high school programs, and high school programs.

Each transition during the school years requires preparation; students, their family members, and the service providers who work with them must learn and adjust to the new aspects of each environment. At the end of the school years, a critical transition occurs: from school to adult life in one's own community. That transition, and the communication skills that need to be developed as a part of it, are the subjects of this module.

The successful transition from the classroom to vocational and community settings is an important goal for students who are deaf-blind. For many students, the ability to make the transition depends on their classroom experiences and effective transition planning. Because the most fundamental skill necessary for participation in the workplace and the community is the ability to communicate, it is critical to identify generalized communicative competence as a goal of intervention and a focus of instruction during the transition planning process. Educational experiences must promote communication skills that are directly relevant to students' daily lives and are appropriate for the environments in which the students are to participate. (The ability to move independently, another skill essential to workplace and community participation, and its role in regard to transition, is explored in Module 20. That module is intended to be companion reading to the present one.)

## THE TRANSITION PROCESS

The transition from being a student in school to being an adult in the community can be difficult for young people, especially those who are deaf-blind. Choosing a job and preparing for an adult lifestyle

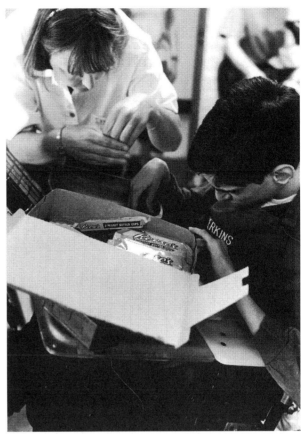

present students, families, and service providers with a series of complex decisions. Therefore, the process of planning for this transition needs to begin long before the student leaves school.

▲ *Preparing for adult life means preparing for a job whenever possible. Here a young woman learns data entry and a young man learns tasks related to cafeteria work as part of their transition programs.*

## TRANSITION PLANNING

The goal of transition planning is to broaden the options available to young people when they leave school (see Postsecondary Options for Students Who Are Deaf-Blind). Transition planning and services for young adults (aged 14–21) who are deaf-blind are an essential part of the educational process, now mandated under the Individuals with Disabilities Education Act (IDEA—P.L. 101-476).

According to Section 602(a) of IDEA, transition services must

- be coordinated
- be outcome based
- move a student between school and postsecondary experiences that are appropriate for the student, including

    postsecondary education

    vocational training

## POSTSECONDARY OPTIONS FOR STUDENTS WHO ARE DEAF-BLIND

Students who are deaf-blind have a range of options after they complete their secondary education. If they pursue additional vocational training or education in a two-year college or technical school or a four-year college, they may do so in a specialized program, especially for students who are deaf, or in an ordinary program with supports, such as an interpreting service and braille and transcription services. There is no single program or special college just for deaf-blind students. Nevertheless, because of new technologies and devices, students who are deaf-blind can study for a variety of careers, including computer programming, just as nondisabled students do, according to their interests and aptitudes.

Students who choose to work directly after they leave high school may have the required job skills as a result of their transition planning and instruction or may need support from a state or local vocational rehabilitation agency, a center for independent living, or another social service agency. (Some college-educated deaf-blind students also need these services.)

These agencies offer a variety of services. One primary service is the assistance of a job coach, who goes to the work site with a student, learns the necessary tasks, teaches them to the student, and often periodically monitors the student's progress. Other services include orientation and mobility (O&M) instruction for getting to and around the workplace, assistance with interpreting when needed, and additional job training as new tasks are added. ■

integrated employment (including supported employment)

continuing and adult education

adult services

independent living

community participation

- be based on the student's identified needs
- consider the student's preferences and needs
- include instruction
- include community experiences
- include the development of employment skills
- include the development of postschool adult living objectives

- include acquisition of daily living skills
- include functional vocational evaluation.

This is a significant mandate for members of educational teams because these issues and factors must be addressed annually in each Individualized Education Program (IEP) by the time students who are deaf-blind are 16 years old. IEP decisions for students of high school age should be based on evaluations of students' current living situations, preferences for activities, and styles of interaction, as well as on the goals for their adult lives (for more on IEPs, see Module 5). Consideration of these factors often requires a change in the manner in which educational programs are designed.

In the transition planning process, an Individualized Transition Program (ITP) is developed by a transdisciplinary team with the student's and family's participation (see Getting a Transition Team Started for tips on beginning the process). The purpose of the ITP is to establish specific transition goals for the individual student, to assign responsibility to members of the team for ensuring that the goals are achieved, and to identify instructional objectives for the IEP that support the student's postschool goals. Community living and integrated employment are emphasized as goals for the student.

The ITP should reflect the student's preferences, involve appropriate community agencies, and be coordinated with both formal and informal systems of support. In the following case example of Elliot, aged 16, who is deaf-blind and has multiple disabilities (expanded from O'Neill, Gothelf, Cohen, Lehman, & Woolf, 1990, which contains detailed information on transition planning), the initial phase of the transition planning process included gathering information about Elliot's style of communication and preferences and interests and identifying possible adult-living objectives and priorities for instruction. Elliot's transition plan is referred to throughout parts of this module to illustrate the design of instructional methods and strategies that support the development of an effective system of communication.

## ELLIOT'S TRANSITION

At the transition planning meeting, Elliot's mother and his teacher completed an assessment-and-planning package (see Figures 14-1, 14-2, 14-3, and 14-4 at the end of this module; these forms also

## GETTING A TRANSITION TEAM STARTED

As a student reaches transition, it is vital for the educational team to incorporate service providers who will facilitate the move from school to postsecondary activities. In most cases, the transition team consists of the student and his or her parents, as well as those members of the educational team from the student's elementary and early secondary years who have worked with the student: teachers, paraprofessionals and other service providers, such as occupational and physical therapists, speech and language specialists, orientation and mobility (O&M) specialists, audiologists, low vision specialists, and rehabilitation counselors. Information from peers can also be helpful in transition planning, although peers' attendance at Individualized Education Program (IEP) meetings should be considered carefully, so it does not diminish the role of the student.

For the first IEP meeting where transition goals will be generated for a student, you can invite the following service providers to become part of the team:

• A specialist, counselor, or case manager from the local or state department of rehabilitation.

• Providers of adult services, if appropriate.

• A representative of a postsecondary program, if available. If a postsecondary program that the student wants to attend is local, this person may be available to guide the development of goals for the student on the basis of entrance expectations or requirements for the program.

• An advocate from the community who is deaf-blind.

• The student's guidance counselor, if appropriate.

The purpose of transition goals and activities is to prepare students to move smoothly from school to postschool life. Therefore, it is important for the student to be involved in setting the goals. To facilitate the student's participation, an interpreter or another individual should assist the student with communication. Parents and service providers who are members of the team should not have this responsibility because it can interfere with their participation.

At each meeting, the entire transition team should address the student's progress and goals that will promote a smooth transition. In addition to considering the student's communication and O&M goals, as well as other life skills, the team now focuses on specific tasks that will help the student gain independence as a young adult leaving school. ■

appear as blank forms in Appendix C for the use of readers) to identify the goals they considered important for his life at home and for his future. This is the profile of Elliot that they developed:

*Elliot enjoys interacting with his peers and family members when he is invited to do so, but he rarely initiates an interaction. Elliot's mother gives him many opportunities to learn domestic skills at home; he especially enjoys helping in the kitchen. He has satisfactory self-care skills.*

*Elliot's favorite recreational activities are using his brother's weights and playing modified card and board games. He has a significant visual impairment, but he is able to use his vision in conjunction with tactile cues for mobility and to locate and identify objects. He also has a moderate hearing loss and wears binaural (bilateral) hearing aids; he responds to loud, simple oral cues paired with signs. Elliot has a vocabulary of approximately 20 signs and uses a picture communication book containing simple black-line drawings on a yellow background. He communicates spontaneously when he is comfortable and when he wants something.*

When Elliot finishes school, his mother would like him to be able to walk to the neighborhood store to purchase food and walk home safely, as well as to take the bus to her brother's nearby restaurant. She would also like him to be able to fix a snack for himself when he is hungry, to interact more with friends and family members, to initiate communications that reflect his needs and desires, and to develop a larger repertoire of recreational activities that he enjoys. (See Figures 14-1, 14-2, 14-3, and 14-4 for details.)

This information immediately influenced the kinds of goals the educational team began to think were appropriate for Elliot. Prompted by input from Elliot's mother, the team identified orientation and mobility (O&M) instruction as a service to be added to Elliot's IEP through the appropriate procedure and the development of recreational and leisure activities as appropriate goals. The classroom teacher took note that Elliot's mother reported his enjoyment of lifting weights with his brother. Since Elliot did not seem to be enjoying his current physical education program in school, the teacher revised his program to include weight lifting with a partner. Team members agreed that this was an activity Elliot could continue after he left high school. Domestic goals were revised to focus on food preparation, and vocational experiences in food services were designed, starting with activities in the school cafeteria.

A member of the team also began to look for community sites for vocational and leisure experiences. These new activities were analyzed to develop a detailed picture of the communicative demands and opportunities that they presented. This information then served as a guide for identifying the types of communication skills that were important for Elliot to develop to be more independent in recreation, work, travel, shopping, and food preparation.

On Elliot's behalf, his mother contacted her brother, who owned a restaurant, to explore possible employment opportunities. Elliot's uncle indicated that he was willing to hire Elliot when Elliot completed school, provided that he could perform meaningful work at the restaurant.

When Elliot leaves school (at age 21), it is likely that he will need some of the support services typically provided by vocational rehabilitation and developmental disabilities service agencies. For instance, he may need direct job support and supervision during his initial on-the-job training, perhaps in the form of the modification or restructuring of tasks. Over time, the rehabilitation agency may work with Elliot and his employer to shift the job-coach function gradually from a paid rehabilitation specialist to a co-worker; this shift would give Elliot the opportunity to rely on natural supports at his workplace. Job support and coaching from the adult service agency could continue, for example, on an intermittent basis as needed, if problems were encountered, or if Elliot's job changed. Beyond vocational support services, he may need to apply for his state's independent living services, including housing support services, recreational services, and social services.

The effective coordination of services and case advocacy are necessary for the smooth transition from school to gainful employment. State or local agencies for vocational rehabilitation and developmental disabilities are responsible for planning (and implementing) needed services immediately after an individual's graduation. Therefore, rehabilitation counselors must be included as part of the transition planning process early to allow ample time to arrange for a smooth transfer of services, including identifying the appropriate service provider.

## COMMUNICATION NEEDS

The development of a system of communication is critical to ensuring an individual's participation in society (O'Neill et al., 1990). The task of teachers and other educational team members is to help students learn how to communicate their desires effectively and appropriately in a variety of settings. Moreover, team members should make sure that students of transition age are being taught the skills they will need as adults by evaluating whether the strategies already being used help the students function in community environments. Families, teachers, service providers, and other members of the team should focus a student's transition plan on programs that promote independent living, participation in the community, and productive employment. Students who are deaf-blind benefit from being taught functional skills in community settings, and learning situations that are relevant to their daily lives promote the development of important communication skills. These and several other points that are essential to the development of communication skills should be considered in designing appropriate school programs for deaf-blind students (Gothelf & Crimmins, 1991). The following principles are helpful guidelines for the transition process.

*Curricula for adolescents should be built on their preferences and interests.* Some teachers have students participate in activities that are "functional" but are often unrelated to the students' needs or preferences. However, students are more motivated to learn when instruction is directly connected to their preferences and interests. When they do not value activities, they may develop behavioral problems and have difficulty acquiring skills. Therefore, team members should work together to identify the activities that a student prefers.

> *Elliot's transition planning meeting centered on identifying activities that Elliot enjoyed; these activities were incorporated into the plans for his curriculum. Since lifting weights was a functional and age-appropriate activity that Elliot enjoyed, it was incorporated into his physical education program, replacing other activities that were age appropriate and functional, but that he did not enjoy. In addition, since Elliot liked participating in domestic chores, opportunities were sought that could support and expand his preference by developing a vocational option based on it.*

*The successful acquisition of skills and their generalization to other natural settings and routines is most likely to occur in the context of preferred activities in natural settings.* Students who are deaf-blind can have significant problems generalizing what they learn in school to everyday and new situations. Through training in community settings, they become familiar with natural cues in the environment that a classroom cannot offer and that prompt, support, direct, and reinforce appropriate behavior. Furthermore, activities the student prefers motivate the student and reinforce his or her efforts.

*The team identified Elliot's enjoyment of domestic chores in the kitchen as a preferred activity that could be developed into a vocational option but realized that his interest needed to be developed for it to become a viable job skill. At first, Elliot worked in the school cafeteria; this work gave him an immediate opportunity in a familiar setting to perform real work and begin to transform his domestic interests into work skills, in addition to providing him with the chance to learn other related skills appropriate to an actual work environment.*

*Language is embedded in daily life activities and is not effectively acquired in meaningless contexts.* Opportunities to communicate and reasons to do so are abundant in one's daily routines and in natural everyday situations (Siegel-Causey & Ernst, 1989). To be effective, instruction that facilitates the development of communicative competence needs to be presented during these times.

*Elliot's weight-lifting program gave him the opportunity to learn new words and new applications of words he already knew. For example, he had to respond to such questions from his partner as, "Is this too heavy?" "Are you tired?" "Can you handle this?" and "Are you up for another set?" He also needed to learn how to indicate when he wanted assistance and how to select the daily workout routine.*

*Communication that enables students to control different aspects of their environments is the most meaningful and motivating and therefore reinforces the continued development of communication skills.* Students who are deaf-blind and have additional disabilities often have few opportunities to exercise control over their lives because their caregivers and teachers frequently anticipate their needs and wishes. As a result, the students often do not perceive the need to assert control over their immediate environments through appropriate communication. When students are encouraged to exercise control and are made aware of the impact of their communicative behaviors on their environments, they are strongly motivated to increase their attempts to communicate (Siegel-Causey & Ernst, 1989).

*At home, Elliot relies on others to prepare food for him at mealtimes or whenever his mother offers him a snack. Teaching Elliot to ask for a snack when he is hungry, both at home and at school, will strengthen his ability to communicate an important need. Moreover, to support his independence, Elliot will be taught to prepare his own snacks. Many activities have both communicative and skill-building components, and it is important that both types of components be addressed.*

# THE ECOLOGICAL MODEL

The ecological model (see Module 11) emphasizes the kind of preparation and support that enables students to participate more fully in their daily lives and the need to teach appropriate functional skills in the settings in which they are actually performed (Brown, Evans, Weed, & Owen, 1987; Helmstetter, 1989; Nietupski & Hamre-Nietupski, 1987). It is best implemented through assessment of the student's preferences for activities and of the demands and opportunities presented in the environments in which the student is expected to function. A "discrepancy analysis" reveals how the student's skills compare to the skills required to participate in designated activities (and relevant environments) and the individualized adaptations needed to augment his or her performance of the skills, as in the following example:

*The teacher visited the restaurant of Elliot's uncle to determine what job possibilities there were for Elliot. A possible job was washing and preparing vegetables to be used by the cook. The teacher then completed a task analysis of this job after she observed a kitchen worker performing it. She knew that Elliot would need training and support in a number of areas. Next, she and Elliot went to the restaurant and performed the activities for the first time. The teacher noted the discrepancies between Elliot's ability and the skills necessary to do the job on an Ecological Inventory form (see Figure 14-5 at the end of this module). She then identified relevant teaching objectives along with the necessary adaptations for Elliot.*

## THE ECOLOGICAL MODEL AND TRANSITION PLANNING

When the ecological model is used in transition planning, as described in the previous section, members of the educational team consider the present and future environments in which a student is likely to participate and assess the student's potential responses to and preferences for activities in these environments. In the sections that follow, team efforts in planning for Elliot's future are described.

> *The team members recognized Elliot's pleasure in helping in the kitchen, which led to plans for vocational experiences in the area of food services. As Elliot's mother explored employment opportunities for Elliot with her brother, an informal system of support began to develop. Elliot's recreational program was changed to reflect activities in which he wanted to participate. O&M instruction was added to Elliot's IEP to prepare him for greater independence in the community, as well as for work. In addition, the communication goals that were critical for Elliot's participation in integrated environments were identified.*

Transition planning emphasized the following skills that Elliot needed and the supports that would be required:

- ability to function in an integrated work environment
- ability to participate with others in enjoyable and meaningful recreational and leisure activities
- ability to maintain himself in his home
- ability to use such local community services as transportation, stores, and restaurants.

Once the student's abilities, needs, and preferences have been identified and environmental requirements assessed, necessary strategies for promoting communicative competence can be implemented. Team efforts need to take a variety of factors into account.

## THE ECOLOGICAL MODEL AND ASPECTS OF COMMUNICATION

The ecological model helps expand the process of analyzing tasks by including the teaching objectives and adaptations necessary for the student to perform a specific task and by identifying the steps that focus on the development of communicative behavior. It ensures a fit between the skills needed for the activities that a student is expected to perform and the relevant communication objectives that must be targeted for intervention. Considering the communicative demands and opportunities of different activities allows teachers and other team members to target for instruction the communication skills that enable the student to participate in those activities in various community settings. The activity and its relevant environment are analyzed to determine

- important communicative functions (requesting, rejecting, offering information) and vocabulary necessary for the student to respond appropriately and effectively
- the natural cues and consequences that serve as signals to alert and guide students to appropriate communicative actions and responses in a setting
- the mode or modes of communication (for example, speech, sign language, object cues; see Modules 8, 9, and 12) that the student is most likely to use independently (Sigafoos & York, 1991).

## Spontaneous and Generalized Communication

The ecological model supports the development of communicative behaviors in natural environments by engaging students in meaningful activities in typical community settings. The ITP goals should focus on the development of communicative competence in meaningful functional activities by focusing instruction on the use of situational cues for establishing spontaneous and generalized communication (Calculator, 1988; Reichle & Sigafoos, 1991). *Spontaneity* refers to communication that is initiated without prompting (for example, the student appropriately communicates "I need help" and does not passively wait or act disruptively to attract attention). *Generalization* refers to communication that occurs in a variety of settings (for example, the student communicates that he or she needs help whether at home, at school, or in the community). Spontaneity and generalization are features of communication that enable students to become more independent. Instruction in preferred activities in their natural settings creates numerous opportunities to support the emergence of spontaneous communication. Varying the activities in which the student participates, where they take place, and with whom they are performed promotes the generalization of communicative interactions.

Some skills are likely to be needed in a variety of situations. Therefore, it is important to identify the situational cues (cues related to physical arrangements, materials, and consequences) that define the activity as it usually occurs and, through a series of rehearsals that include deviations from the usual sequence of activities, to support the student's identification of cues that lead him or her to complete the activity independently or to ask for help.

> *Elliot may need to know how to request assistance in a gym, in making a snack, at work in a restaurant, while traveling on a city bus, or when purchasing food in a store. At his uncle's restaurant, when the vegetables are not in their usual location (see Figure 14-5), Elliot will be taught to go to the supervisor and indicate that he needs help by pointing to a picture in his communication book. When making a snack, if he cannot open a package of bologna, he will be able to let his mother or brother know that he needs assistance by signing "Help."*

## Communicative Demands and Opportunities

The ecological model provides a detailed picture of the communicative demands and the opportunities for communication and its instruction that a preferred activity and its relevant environment provide (Sigafoos & York, 1991). The nature of the opportunities for communication must be evaluated in light of a specific situation. In some situations, communication is obvious and essential, whereas in others, it may depend on specific situational cues. Other communicative demands of activities may be more subtle and may depend on recognizing and responding to a specific situation.

> *Elliot's request for assistance in opening a package of bologna reflects a communicative demand that may be necessary when preparing a snack in the kitchen, but only if he actually requires help (for example, if the package is difficult to open). Ordering a sandwich in a restaurant embodies a more obvious communicative demand.*

## Communicative Functions

In addition to revealing opportunities for the student to engage in communicative behavior, the ecological model provides information on the specific vocabulary that will prove useful in the identified setting. Mealtime is typically targeted as an area of instructional priority for transition-age students who are deaf-blind and have multiple disabilities. Having a meal is a single activity that provides opportunities for learning many skills necessary for performing activities of daily living, as well as for enhancing opportunities for communication in a social setting. It gives students the chance to interact with others through the expression of choices and participation in conversations. Effective communication during meals results in natural consequences that are generally self-reinforcing because communication obtains the desired outcome (foods that are preferred) and contributes to creating and maintaining a pleasant and congenial social atmosphere.

> *On the basis of the request of Elliot's mother at the transition planning meeting, the team targeted communication during meals for intervention. Elliot usually eats lunch with his peers at school and dinner with his family at home. In the past, he was served his food and given few choices about his meals. Now, his IEP identifies his need to request specific items of food during meals and snack times, which provides him with the opportunity to accept or reject food when it is offered and engages him in conversation during mealtimes.*

## Instructional Cues

As part of the ecological inventory, natural cues that bring about and maintain communicative behavior are identified, and strategies for prompting and then gradually reducing instructional prompts are developed. Prompting may begin with a teacher's directives that set up instructional opportunities in natural environments.

> *After Elliot washed half the vegetables (see Figure 14-5, Step 6), the job coach asked if he wanted to take a break or if he wanted to continue working. By asking this question, the coach engaged Elliot in a communicative interchange that was both instructional and functional. The job coach taught Elliot that the halfway point of Step 6 is the appropriate time for Elliot to communicate that he wants to take his available break. The coach used the appropriate vocabulary and set up the vegetables in two equal portions in two bins, so when one bin was empty, it was the halfway point of the task. The coach's strategy was to fade the direct-sign and verbal prompts, so that Elliot would communicate that he wanted a break in response to emp-*

*tying one of the two bins. To support the generalized sponta-*
*neous communicative behavior of expressing, "I want a break,"*
*Elliot's teacher set up numerous opportunities throughout the*
*day for Elliot to ask for a break. Then the teacher worked with*
*Elliot's mother to set up situations at home in which Elliot*
*could ask for a break while doing his chores.*

## Expression of Choices

In developing students' communication skills, it is important for teachers and caregivers to build opportunities for students to communicate their choices throughout the day, rather than giving them directives that require only motor responses or anticipating their needs and desires. This communication of choices gives students a sense of control over different aspects of their environments. Interventions that support students' exercise of their initiatives and choice making require the systematic teaching of how to make choices and the means of communicating the choices, as well as the provision of opportunities to practice choosing (Gothelf, Crimmins, Mercer, & Finocchiaro, 1994; Newton, Horner, & Lund, 1991). Increased opportunities for effective communication can be provided in a variety of ways (Brown, 1991), such as through the selection of preferred foods, objects, and activities from available alternatives and the rejection of items or activities. It is essential to state that communication is the goal—not the enforcement of decisions previously made by service providers or parents.

*Opportunities were created for Elliot to express his desires and*
*preferences throughout the day. When selecting a soda from*
*the vending machine, he would be asked, "Do you want a*
*Coke or a ginger ale?" He would have to communicate his*
*choice before putting money in the machine and making his*
*selection. At snack time, he would be given the choice of*
*preparing either a peanut butter and jelly sandwich or a*
*bologna sandwich. And in the gym, he would be given the*
*choice of selecting which exercises he preferred or not partic-*
*ipating at all. Elliot's team worked together to prepare these*
*opportunities for Elliot to communicate his choices, acknowl-*
*edged his decision not to participate as a valid choice, and*
*presented him with other options that might bring about his*
*participation.*

## Mode of Communication

By the time students reach high school, they should have developed systems of communication that enable them to express their needs and preferences. As the mode of communication that is most effective for a student is determined, team members need to keep focusing on the student's abilities, as well as on the communication demands and opportunities that they expect to arise in the natural environment (see Modules 11 and 12).

Remember that it is helpful for students to learn to use more than one mode of communication, so they have more flexibility in different situations, as noted in Module 12. For example, students may be taught to use picture cues in the workplace but encouraged to use sign language in the classroom and at home. Access to different modes of communication will help them respond in an alternative way when something is misunderstood during interchanges or attempts to communicate (Calculator, 1988; Sigafoos & York, 1991).

> *Elliot's instructional program includes weekly food shopping at the grocery store near the school, where Elliot and his teacher have been practicing three modes of communication. On one such shopping trip, Elliot, the teacher, and a classmate divided the shopping list. Using total communication (spoken, signed, and graphic modes), the teacher asked the students who would like to get each of the various items to be purchased. Elliot indicated that he would like to get the milk by pointing to a picture cue of a carton of milk. The teacher gave him the picture, and he walked to the appropriate aisle. Elliot could not locate the item because it was not in its usual location, so he looked for a store clerk (as he had been taught to do in the event of a problem). Elliot signed "milk" to the clerk. As it happened, this particular clerk was a new employee and, unlike the other clerks who had gotten to know Elliot and his classmates, did not understand Elliot's signing; Elliot repeated the sign. The clerk shook his head and shrugged his shoulders. Elliot finally responded by showing the picture cue. The clerk immediately smiled in recognition and took Elliot to the new milk section.*

## Functional Communication Training

In helping students move toward greater independence, teachers may find that some youngsters behave in ways that place themselves or

▲ *Learning activities of daily living like how to shop are important in getting ready for independent life.*

others at risk or that interfere with their progress in attaining goals or being accepted and integrated in the community. Functional communication training (Bird, Dores, Moniz, & Robinson, 1989; Carr & Durand, 1985; Durand, 1990) is an approach that is based on the view that maladaptive behaviors (tantrums, aggression, self-injury) are a form of communication—a way of giving a message, such as, "Pay attention to me," "I want food now," "Leave me alone," or "I don't want to do it." The behaviors cannot be ignored and may serve as the students' most effective means of communication.

The goal of training in functional communication is to develop an appropriate replacement communication that achieves the same purpose as does the problematic behavior. (It is important to remember that labeling something as "problem behavior" or "acting out" is a matter of someone's implicit judgment of the appropriateness of a behavior for a specific situation. For a student, a behavior is not a problem if it gets the desired response.) Once it has been determined what communicative functions a behavior serves, a satisfactory replacement communication can be taught that serves the same function (Durand & Crimmins, 1991). At the same time, the undesirable behavior can be responded to in ways that make it nonfunctional or not effective for the student in obtaining the desired outcome (Durand, 1990). (For a more detailed discussion, see The Communicative Purposes of Behavior in Module 6 and Points for Focus in this module.)

*Elliot occasionally responds to situations he does not like by pushing objects or people away and then walking away. This behavior interferes with his integration at work, in the community, and at home. By teaching Elliot a more acceptable, functionally equivalent replacement communication, his teacher utilized a positive communicative approach to address his challenging behavior.*

The principles of planning for transition outlined in this module are important for all students' programs. However, it is essential to individualize planning efforts by taking students' strengths and needs into particular account. This holds true for students with advanced skills as well as for those whose skills are not as advanced.

# STUDENTS WITH ADVANCED SKILLS

Some students who are deaf-blind have specific transition needs because of their advanced abilities and educational levels. Many of the principles of transition programming just described in relation to the example of Elliot also apply to advanced-level students, but often with a slightly different focus. There may be more input from the students. And their transition goals, like the goals of other students, need to reflect the students' interests and preferences, their current levels of skills, and the demands of the present and future environments in which they are likely to participate.

For example, most students who have Usher syndrome begin to experience more significant visual effects during their transition

## THEORY into PRACTICE

### POINTS FOR FOCUS

• The development of suitable communication skills for students of transition age who are deaf-blind should be optimized.

• Communicative competence enables students to achieve independence as adults by becoming active participants in integrated home, community, and work environments.

• All programming efforts should be based on the assessment of a student's communication style, preferences, and interests and the goals considered important for life at home and for the future.

• Programming efforts must be evaluated on the extent to which the student achieves

independent living, participation in the community, productive employment, and self-satisfaction.

• Teams can design programs that support the development of effective systems of communication that enable individuals to participate in activities of their choice. ■

years (see Module 3 for more information on Usher syndrome). These students often have advanced abilities and need extra training in the development of new skills, as well as counseling for social and emotional issues that can accompany progressive vision loss, to prepare them for some aspects of that vision loss that will gradually continue through adulthood. As a group, they therefore point out the importance of focusing on the individual's needs and circumstances and adopting an ecological approach to providing transition services. Thinking of future needs is vital for most teenagers with Usher syndrome, who in all likelihood will need to find ways to compensate for additional losses of visual information. Each new "milestone" of visual change may require further adjustments, the giving up of certain activities, or the learning of new skills. Talking about how to manage peers' comments and teasing, how to make important decisions about driving, how to let others know what visual adaptations are needed, and many other issues related to Usher syndrome will help young people remain full participants in educational and social settings. In addition, developing the skills outlined in the remainder of this module will be important for students with Usher syndrome. Overall, the transition goals of students who have Usher syndrome revolve around developing an array of strong communication skills that can, if needed, be adapted with gradual vision loss.

In general, well-developed communication skills will probably be expected and required of most students with advanced skills, not only those with Usher syndrome, as they proceed to postsecondary opportunities that can include vocational-technical training, independent living in their communities, college work, and similar pursuits. The following sections suggest communication areas that must be addressed for these students during the transition years, and Module 20 provides information on O&M needs for this critical life stage.

## SELF-DETERMINATION AND ADVOCACY

Students who are deaf-blind and have done competitive academic work or somewhat modified academic work in high school may still not have all the communication skills they will need for more independence when they leave high school for postsecondary experiences. Educational planning teams must ensure that transition goals cover the vital communication skills related to the basic domains of life, although the specific skills to be developed may differ from those just described as needed by Elliot.

During the transition process, the first and most vital skill that must be addressed in setting goals is the ability to undertake self-determination and advocacy. It is important to remember that students with limited or basic abilities and skills also need instruction to advocate for themselves and to solve problems; for students with advanced abilities and skills such instruction is imperative, and the form it takes will differ. This is often a difficult goal for service providers and families to establish because it means encouraging the student to speak for himself or herself, which may require relinquishing control to the student. Students can and should participate in goal setting, IEP meetings, and all decision making concerning their futures. During this process, the other team members should actively elicit their preferences and interests and incorporate them into the transition goals as much as possible. A student who is involved in goal setting and supports the goals because he or she has had input into them is more likely to acknowledge responsibility for achieving those goals.

What are some ways a student who is deaf-blind and has advanced skills can advocate for himself or herself? There is no "optimal" age for a student to begin self-advocacy, but team members can decide when and how it is appropriate for such a student to begin to assume responsibilities that others have been performing on his or her behalf. For example, a student who is in typical high school classes may be instructed in how to order textbook materials in braille or large type and then be expected to order them in senior year. Or a student who has an interpreter-tutor (see Module 9 for information on educational interpreting) may have a conflict with a classroom teacher that was previously handled by the interpreter-tutor and a consulting teacher of students with hearing impairments. This student can be shown how to communicate directly with the classroom teacher by exchanging notes, typing face to face on a TeleBraille, or using the interpreter-tutor strictly to interpret. The student may need to role-play an interaction before it really occurs, so he or she knows how to organize the ideas to be shared with the classroom teacher, and the classroom teacher may need a brief explanation of how to use a TeleBraille or an interpreter-tutor in this way. Both these examples stress interactional-interpersonal communication skills that build self-determination and advocacy using modes of communication that are important for independence in adult life.

## PROBLEM SOLVING AND RESOURCE IDENTIFICATION

A second general transition goal for each advanced student who is deaf-blind addresses the student's ability to solve problems and identify the necessary communication skills and resources to perform some activity of daily living. Most people require outside assistance in their daily activities; even such simple resources as telephone directory assistance are helpful at some time. Deaf-blind students may not know that such resources exist for them to access or lack skills to use the resources unless they are specifically guided through the process of determining when a resource is needed and how to obtain it. This process, too, is a vital communication-building component for eventual independence in adulthood.

In addition, the development of skills in several areas is vital for students who are deaf-blind and have advanced abilities. The environments in which communication skills will be the most necessary are the home, workplace, leisure activity settings, and the community. Specific examples that teams should address in transition planning are outlined in the next sections. Note that communication skills that relate to utilizing transportation are included in the section concerning the community but apply equally to work and leisure settings.

## HOME

Communication skills that adults must exercise in their own homes are diverse and often involve interaction that extends to the community. For example, in maintaining one's financial affairs, it may be necessary to call a bank to get an account balance, which involves aspects of the development of both home- and community-related skills. The following list of important skills is not exhaustive but suggests areas to address in regard to home daily living activities:

- communicating with family members who may not sign or read braille, especially if the student is living semi-independently at home and communicating with others, for example, leaving important notes for housemates
- having strategies for communicating with oneself, for example, keeping notes to remind oneself about appointments and maintaining a systematic record of important telephone numbers, whether in braille, large print, or another medium

- finding ways to gain access to and use directions on foods and performing other self-maintenance activities (such as reading labels or finding assistance to have them read and following directions to prepare foods or wash clothing)

- using a telephone for emergencies and daily business, whether by relay systems set up by state or regional telephone companies; with TeleBraille, Teletype for the Deaf (TTY), or Telecommunications (or Telephone) Device for the Deaf (TDD); or by telephoning with an interpreter (see Module 10)

- communicating appropriately with service people, such as repair persons, meter readers, or delivery persons

- identifying and obtaining adaptive devices for the home and instruction in their use

- communicating with neighbors, both for social purposes and to establish an immediate support network

- reading or having access to resources to obtain information from one's mail (such as obtaining reading services from a volunteer or paid reader) and responding as needed.

All these suggested areas may involve just a few skills or a series of skills that must be developed, depending on a student's previous experience and anticipated needs. At a minimum, every student who is deaf-blind and is anticipating semi- or fully independent living must have communication skills for handling a variety of home emergencies. Many of the areas just noted as important at home are equally important in other daily environments.

## WORK

How a deaf-blind person communicates in the workplace is likely to have a direct bearing on his or her job performance, just as it does for persons who are not deaf-blind. During the transition years, a student who is deaf-blind and has advanced skills may be learning such skills as these:

- how to apply vocabulary needed to complete a job application and a systematic way of keeping track of information that may be requested for every job application, such as signifcant dates and references

- how to use a reader to help complete a job application, so it is clear that the applicant who is deaf-blind is ultimately responsible for the information on the application and that the other person merely assisted by reading the application

• how to communicate during an employment interview, including how to ask the interviewer questions and how to answer questions appropriately (skills in this area encompass developing an awareness of nonverbal communication skills, such as smiling or facing the person for "eye contact," that influence another person; using an interpreter to interview; and understanding the terms used for benefits offered)

• how and when to use a TTY/TDD, TeleBraille, or other equipment for work-related telephone calls (for example, when having to call in to work when ill) or for face-to-face communication with co-workers and supervisors

• how to use an interpreter in the workplace to help clarify the tasks and responsibilities of a job or such work-related matters as benefits, how to get clarification when an interpreter cannot be present, and how and when to request help

• how to help a supervisor understand the best ways to communicate information to the employee who is deaf-blind

• how to obtain or implement training for supervisors and co-workers on dealing with a deaf-blind colleague in a work-related emergency situation

• how to function and communicate in a work-related emergency situation

• how to obtain training and necessary adaptive devices, if appropriate, for job advancement

• how to advocate for oneself and pursue a complaint or grievance appropriately.

Again, these areas should be considered in light of a student's identified preferences and abilities, and work-related communication skills should be specifically selected for that student. Within these areas, several subskills may be important, such as learning several modes of communication with a supervisor that are based on the length and nature of the interaction. For example, a personnel evaluation may require an interpreter's assistance, but communication about a change in schedule for a specific day may require that the supervisor use print-on-palm or tactile fingerspelling for a short conversation. The student in transition can learn both methods of communicating with a supervisor who is not deaf-blind and how to decide which one is the most effective and efficient for the purpose.

## LEISURE ACTIVITIES

Leisure activities may be divided into those that are done individually and those that are done interactively. It may be difficult for students to develop communication skills in this area because of time constraints in their already-full schedules or the lack of access to appropriate leisure opportunities or to the adaptations necessary to make a leisure activity meaningful; still, it is important.

Students who are deaf-blind and have advanced communication and academic skills have more opportunities for participating in leisure activities and communicating with peers because of their greater access to technology and to adaptive aids than ever before. Although the cost of such equipment as a TeleBraille or large-print TTY/TDD, which allows students to communicate with peers, is higher than that of standard equipment, the advantages of this equipment for both leisure and business activities are substantial.

### Individual Leisure Activities

Activities that people who are not deaf-blind enjoy are also enjoyed by people who are deaf-blind. Some do not require extensive communication, and some may. With every activity, though, a certain level of communication skill is required to learn or understand how to perform its steps or procedures. Here are examples of individual leisure activities and the communication skills that students may need to learn to pursue them, which could be a part of transition programming:

- Knitting, sewing, woodworking, making crafts, and gardening require such communication skills as reading and understanding a series of directions or a pattern; knowing how to obtain the materials to complete the activity, including an awareness of sources for assistive devices like a braille ruler; and knowing how to request assistance when a difficult step is encountered (note that these activities may or may not require vision, and hearing is not imperative for any of them).

- Exercise-workout programs require communication skills for obtaining assistance and understanding a program that is developed for one's physical needs; knowing how to identify, locate, and obtain desired equipment or exercise devices; and communicating to obtain transportation to a gym or pool (swimming, although an individual activity, may be interactive in the sense that people go to a pool together or even do joint activities in a pool or other bodies of water).

- Gourmet cooking requires such communication skills as reading and following directions for prepared food mixes or recipes and knowing where to find exotic foods or ingredients and how to obtain them.

- Leisure reading requires, in addition to the reading skills for enjoying the material, skills for identifying, locating, and obtaining brailled, large-print, or audiotaped books, newspapers, and magazines or technological equipment to read regular print, such as a reading machine or enlarger.

- Watching television or videotapes of films requires reading skills for those who use captions and the ability to identify and obtain resources for either brailled telecaptions or enlarged telecaptions (or audiodescription for people who can hear adequately but cannot see the action on the screen). (Telecaptioned programs allow access to sports, news, and virtually every other kind of television programs that are captioned. Since 1993, all television sets with screens of more than 13 inches that are sold in the United States must have built-in telecaption capability, according to federal legislation. Neither braille telecaptions nor enlargement capabilities are mandated; therefore, equipment for brailled telecaptions must be obtained separately, or larger television screens with proportionately larger captions be used).

- Computer network communications and on-line leisure computer activities, including reading newsmagazines and communicating with others on subjects of interest, require advanced language and computer expertise and equipment.

## Interactive Leisure Activities

Individuals who are deaf-blind may spend much time alone and hence may feel isolated. Therefore, it is crucial that they develop skills and are given opportunities to participate in interactive activities. The following are examples of activities and the skills required.

**Games**. Some popular board games in adapted formats with brailled and enlarged game components are on the market, so students will need to know how to identify sources for games and how to obtain games. In addition, they will need to know the rules and procedures for playing the games, which may involve reading directions for clarification and following sequences.

**Telephone Socializing**. Social telephone calls require not only knowledge of how telecommunications equipment is operated and how to place a call, but social communication skills and understanding, for example, when to call, how to begin and end conversations, and various other social niceties, such as asking if it is a good time to talk. Although it is possible to make social calls through a relay system, such calls are more awkward than is direct communication between two people with the proper equipment (two TTY/TDDs, including those with enlarged displays; a TTY/TDD and a TeleBraille; or two TeleBrailles).

**Participation in Social Events**. Deaf-blind students can participate in social events, including religious services, plays, and lectures, but they often need a one-to-one communication assistant or interpreter to do so. Participation skills include finding out the communication parameters for an event; identifying and obtaining necessary assistance from a friend, family member, or paid interpreter; obtaining transportation to the event; and developing strategies for self-determination that ensure full participation by, for example, role-playing or other forms of instruction to learn to recognize one's own responsibility for successful participation. If the communication access for an event is not satisfactory, the student needs to recognize it and use strategies, such as giving other participants tips on how to help, that will ensure a more satisfactory experience.

**Contact with Peers Who Are Deaf-Blind**. Teachers of deaf-blind students are often concerned that their students do not have contact with other individuals who are deaf-blind, especially when these students are the only deaf-blind youngsters in their classes or schools. Some students have the language skills to converse with other deaf-blind students either face to face or through correspondence or the use of a TTY/TDD or telephone relay system. If the communication modes of students who may want to communicate with one another do not "match" (for example, one student

▲ *Socializing is a key part of peoples' lives. Deaf-blind students should be encouraged to participate socially with each other as well as with people who are not deaf-blind.*

may use tactile signing and the other may use speech and amplifiers), an interpreter or special equipment may be necessary. Students who have limited communication and cognitive skills may have problems with mismatched communication modes, as well as general difficulties in receiving and conveying information, and may benefit from deaf-blind peer or adult tutors who have strong communication skills and can both work with these students and serve as role models.

It is especially important for students with advanced skills and self-awareness to learn more about deaf-blind culture. These students can contact the regional offices of the Helen Keller National Center to learn if there are any deaf-blind consumer groups in their areas and the American Association of the Deaf-Blind for information about national meetings and activities. (See Resources for information on contacting both organizations.)

## COMMUNITY

Most people interact in community situations routinely to conduct their personal business and participate in community activities. People who are deaf-blind do the same, although they may need to go about their community participation differently. Several general areas are vital to community participation.

**Communication about Transportation**. To participate in a community, an individual must be able to travel within it. Students who are deaf-blind and will live independently must learn how to identify, locate, and obtain access to transportation, which may include volunteer services, local paratransit services, or standard public transportation. They also must learn how to communicate with transportation personnel, both for routine travel and for emergency situations. (More information on this subject is included in Unit 3, which focuses on O&M skills and further explores communication that is required for successful travel.)

**Communication to Conduct Business**. To be truly independent, a deaf-blind student will have to learn skills to communicate with the general public in the community to shop, to conduct banking and legal business, and to obtain medical care. The student must understand the communication issues of each business situation and how to get full information from business personnel, whether directly (through print-on-palm, writing notes, using a braille-print alphabet card, and so forth) or through an interpreter. The vocabulary and concepts of each of these four basic business activities (shopping, banking, conducting legal business, and obtaining medical care) are vital goals of transition programming.

The minimum community-related skills a student must have when leaving secondary education are included in the general areas outlined here, but some students may need or want communication skills for community participation that go far beyond them. Team members can work with the student to delineate what is necessary for community participation, what is desired, and what is practical, given the constraints of a typical school day.

For students who are deaf-blind and have advanced abilities, the focus of team members needs to be students' completion of secondary education having learned strategies to communicate and advocate for themselves that will enable them to obtain and make use of all the information they need for daily living and decision making. For students who are deaf-blind of whatever level of skills, the purpose of all communication-related goals for transition planning needs to be the student's eventual independent participation as an adult at home, at work, in leisure activities, and in the community.

# REFERENCES

Bird, F., Dores, P., Moniz, D., & Robinson, F. (1989). Reducing severe aggression and self-injurious behavior with functional communication training: Direct collateral and generalized results. *American Journal of Mental Retardation, 94*, 37–48.

Brown, F. (1991). *Teaching service providers to increase choice opportunities within the daily routine.* Paper presented at the meeting of the Association for Persons with Severe Handicaps, Washington, DC.

Brown, F., Evans, I. M., Weed, K. A., & Owen, V. (1987). Delineating functional competencies: A component model. *Journal of the Association for Persons with Severe Handicaps. 12*, 117–124.

Calculator, S. N. (1988). Promoting the acquisition and generalization of conversational skills by individuals with severe disabilities. *Augmentative and Alternative Communication, 4*, 94–103.

Carr, E., & Durand, V. M. (1985). Reducing behavior problems through functional communication training. *Journal of Applied Behavior Analysis, 18*, 111–126.

Durand, V. M. (1990). *Severe behavior problems: A functional communication training approach.* New York: Guilford Press.

Durand, V. M., & Crimmins, D. B. (1991). Teaching functionally equivalent responses as an intervention for challenging behavior. In B. Remington (Ed.), *The challenge of severe mental handicap* (pp. 71–95). New York: John Wiley & Sons.

Gothelf, C. R., & Crimmins, D. B. (1991). *Transition-aged students with dual sensory impairments: A technical assistance model.* Paper presented at the meeting of the Association for Persons with Severe Handicaps, Washington, DC.

Gothelf, C. R., Crimmins, D. B., Mercer, C. A., & Finocchiaro, P. A. (1994). Teaching choice making skills to students with dual sensory impairments. *Teaching Exceptional Children, 26,* 13–15.

Helmstetter, E. (1989). Curriculum for school aged students: The ecological model. In F. Brown & D. H. Lehr (Eds.), *Persons with profound disabilities: Issues and practices* (pp. 239–264). Baltimore: Paul H. Brookes.

Newton, J. S., Horner, R. H., & Lund, L. (1991). Honoring activity preferences in individualized plan development: A descriptive analysis. *Journal of the Association for Persons with Severe Handicaps, 16,* 207–212.

Nietupski, J., & Hamre-Nietupski, S. M. (1987). An ecological approach to curriculum development. In L. Goetz, D. Guess, & K. Stremel-Campbell (Eds.), *Innovative program design for individuals with dual sensory impairments* (pp. 225–253). Baltimore: Paul H. Brookes.

O'Neill, J., Gothelf, C. R., Cohen, S., Lehman, L., & Woolf, S. B. (1990). *A curricular approach to support the transition to adulthood of adolescents with visual or dual sensory impairments.* Albany: New York State Department of Education, Office of the Education of Children with Handicapping Conditions. (ERIC Document Reproduction Service No. ED 333-693).

Reichle, J., & Sigafoos, J. (1991). Establishing spontaneity and generalization. In J. Reichle, J. York, & J. Sigafoos (Eds.), *Implementing augmentative and alternative communication strategies for learners with severe disabilities* (pp. 193–214). Baltimore: Paul H. Brookes.

Siegel-Causey, E., & Ernst, B. (1989). Theoretical orientation and research in nonsymbolic development. In E. Siegel-Causey & D. Guess (Eds.), *Enhancing nonsymbolic communication interactions among learners with severe disabilities* (pp. 17–51). Baltimore: Paul H. Brookes.

Sigafoos, J., & York, J. (1991). Using ecological inventories to promote functional communication. In J. Reichle, J. York, & J. Sigafoos (Eds.), *Implementing augmentative and alternative communication strategies for learners with severe disabilities* (pp. 61–70). Baltimore: Paul H. Brookes.

## FIGURE 14-1:
## Communication Style Assessment

Individual's name  Elliot                                   Age  16

Completed by  Mrs. M.                                       Date  1/17/95

1. How does the individual generally make himself or herself understood (e.g., vocalizing, gestures, graphic, object cues)?

   He signs and points to pictures in his communication book when I give it to him.

2. How do you communicate with the individual?

   I sign and I talk in a loud voice to him. Sometimes I use his communication book with him.

3. What kinds of information does the individual communicate spontaneously?

   When he is very familiar with something and wants something he likes very much, he may sign. He mostly only answers questions that I ask him.

4. How does the individual gain your attention when you are not paying attention to him or her?

   He finds me or his brother and stands very close to me or follows us around. Then when we ask him what he wants, he will show us.

5. How does the individual ask questions for information, personal needs, and directions?

   He really does not. I take care of everything for him.

6. When the individual likes something, how does he or she communicate it (gestures, smiles, takes, vocalizes)?

   He smiles and grabs the thing he likes and brings it close to his face or holds it.

7. When the individual dislikes something, how does he or she communicate it (gestures, tantrums, looks away, cries)?

   He may push things or people away, or he may get up and leave the room.

8. Under what circumstances does the individual interact with others (play games with others, have a conversation)?

   He loves to play Uno and Othello and to lift weights with his brother.

9. How does the individual communicate choices or indicate preferences?

   He just takes what he wants.

## FIGURE 14-2:
**Preference and Interest Assessment**

Individual's name  Elliot                                    Age  16

Completed by  Mrs. M.                                        Date  1/17/95

1. What are the individual's three favorite activities?

   Spending time with his brother, either playing games (such as Uno or Othello) or lifting weights and helping me, especially in the kitchen.

2. What are the three activities the individual likes least?

   Going to the eye doctor, cleaning his room alone, and waiting while I prepare his food.

3. Does the individual begin activities on his or her own? If yes, describe.

   No, not really, except he will bug his brother to do things with him, like watch TV, use his weights, or go to a store.

4. Does the individual seek out people with whom to do things? If yes, describe.

   Yes, my older son and myself. He gets my older son to use weights with him, or one of us takes him to the store.

5. How does the individual respond to new situations and settings (explores, withdraws)? Describe what he or she actually does.

   He is quiet and stays very close to me, holding my arm until I show him around a few times.

6. What does the individual do in his or her free time at school or day program or at home?

   At home, most of the time he just sits. But if you bring him a game that he likes, he enjoys playing it, or like I said, he gets my other son to use weights with him.

7. Has the individual ever indicated anything that he or she would like to do as an adult?

   No, not really, but he really does enjoy doing different little jobs for me in the kitchen. He is always happy in the kitchen.

## FIGURE 14-3:
## Activity Planning Checklist for Adolescents and Adults

Individual's name ___Elliot___                     Age ___16___

Completed by ___Mrs. M.___                     Date ___1/17/95___

For each of the activities listed, indicate whether (a) the individual does the activity independently, (b) the individual does the activity with help, (c) the individual does not do the activity at all, (d) the individual enjoys or might enjoy doing this or a related activity, (e) the individual clearly dislikes doing this or a related activity, and (f) indicate which activities are most important to ensure success in the home, work, and community (instructional priorities).

| WORK-RELATED ACTIVITIES | IND. | WITH HELP | NOT AT ALL | ENJOYS DOING | CLEARLY DISLIKES | INSTRUCTIONAL PRIORITY |
|---|---|---|---|---|---|---|
| Neighborhood jobs | | | | | | |
| School jobs | | | ✓ | ✓ | | ✓ |
| Household jobs | | ✓ | | ✓ | | ✓ |
| Community-based work experience | | | ✓ | ✓ | | ✓ |
| Other: | | | | | | |
| **RECREATIONAL ACTIVITIES** | | | | | | |
| Activities to do alone (TV, music, games, hobbies) | | ✓ | | ✓ | | ✓ |
| Activities to do with family & friends (cards, board games) | | ✓ | | ✓ | | ✓ |
| Participating in sports/exercise | | ✓ | | ✓ | | |
| Attending a neighborhood recreational facility (park or gym) | | | ✓ | ✓ | | ✓ |
| Going to a movie or concert | | ✓ | | | ✓ | |
| Other: | | | | | | |
| **NEIGHBORHOOD ACTIVITIES** | | | | | | |
| Using local public transportation | | ✓ | | ✓ | | ✓ |
| Using neighborhood services (barber, post office) | | ✓ | | ✓ | | |
| Grocery shopping | | ✓ | | ✓ | | ✓ |
| General shopping (drugstore, stationery) | | ✓ | | ✓ | | |
| Selecting clothes to be purchased | | ✓ | | ✓ | | |
| Eating in a restaurant | | ✓ | | ✓ | | |
| Using public bathrooms | ✓ | | | | | |
| Other: | | | | | | |

*(continued)*

**FIGURE 14-3:**
Continued

| HOUSEHOLD ACTIVITIES | IND. | WITH HELP | NOT AT ALL | ENJOYS DOING | CLEARLY DISLIKES | INSTRUCTIONAL PRIORITY |
|---|---|---|---|---|---|---|
| Selecting foods for meal or snack | | ✓ | | ✓ | | ✓ |
| Preparing food | | ✓ | | ✓ | | ✓ |
| Eating a meal or snack | ✓ | | | | | |
| Setting the table and cleaning up | | ✓ | | ✓ | | |
| Selecting clothes to wear | | ✓ | | ✓ | | |
| Dressing and undressing | ✓ | | | | | |
| Housecleaning | | ✓ | | ✓ | | |
| Bedmaking | | ✓ | | ✓ | | |
| Doing laundry | | | ✓ | | | |
| Caring for plants and pets | | | ✓ | | | |
| Outdoor maintenance | | | ✓ | | | |
| Using the telephone/TDD | | | ✓ | | | |
| Other: | | | | | | |
| | | | | | | |
| **PERSONAL HYGIENE** | | | | | | |
| Bathing | ✓ | | | ✓ | | |
| Caring for hair and nails | | ✓ | | | | |
| Using bathroom | ✓ | | | | | |
| Shaving | | | ✓ | | | ✓ |
| First aid | | | ✓ | | | |
| Using makeup | | | | | | |
| Managing menstrual needs | | | | | | |
| Other: | | | | | | |
| | | | | | | |
| **FAMILY LIFE AND RELATIONSHIPS** | | | | | | |
| Takes part in family events | | ✓ | | ✓ | | ✓ |
| Joins in activities with peers | | | ✓ | ✓ | | ✓ |
| Has special friendships (e.g., preferred peer to eat lunch with) | | | ✓ | | | |
| Takes an interest in the needs of others | | | ✓ | | | |
| Is helpful to others | | ✓ | | ✓ | | ✓ |
| Other: | | | | | | |
| | | | | | | |

## FIGURE 14-4:
## Identifying Adult Living Objectives

Individual's name ___Elliot___                    Age ___16___

Completed by ___Mrs. M.___                    Date ___1/17/95___

Identify two or three activities in each specific area that are reflective of the individual's preferences and that you would like him or her to learn in preparation for a more independent life.

1. Work-related activities:

My brother owns a restaurant. He has seen Elliot helping me in the kitchen and told me that if Elliot could do real work, he would give him a job.

2. Recreational activities:

I want him to learn to play more than two "real" games, so he can interact more with people. I don't want to have to always tell him to do things. Even if he could put on the TV by himself, this would be great.

3. Neighborhood activities:

If he could learn to go to the store for me, that would be wonderful for him as well as for me. Also I'd like him to be able to travel on public buses. Is it possible for the school to teach him how to get around at the local YMCA, so he could use their weight room?

4. Household activities:

Prepare snack when desired, clean his room without getting upset, join in mealtime conversations with my other son and me.

5. Personal hygiene:

He has very good hygiene skills. He takes pride in his appearance. He doesn't have much facial hair at this time, but soon he will need to learn to shave.

6. Family life and relationships:

I would like for him to talk with us, at mealtimes and when my family visits. I want him to have people to do things with other than me or my other son. It's a lot of pressure, and besides, my other son will not always be living with me.

FIGURE 14-5:
**Ecological Inventory**

| Individual's name | Elliot | | Age | 16 |
| Completed by | Ms. J. | | Date | 2/3/95 |
| Activity | Wash vegetables at uncle's restaurant. | | | |

| TARGET ACTIVITY AND RELATED SKILLS | PRESENT SKILLS | DISCREPANCY ANALYSIS | TEACHING OBJECTIVES OR ADAPTATIONS |
| --- | --- | --- | --- |
| 1. Greet his uncle and co-workers, hang his coat in the locker, put on the smock and hat. | Not present | Communication Mobility Activities of daily living (ADL) | Sign a greeting. Learn the route from the locker. Manipulate the lock. |
| 2. Wash his hands. | Present | | |
| 3. Check the daily menu ingredients posted on the wall by the refrigerator. | Not present | Cannot read the listing. | Adapt the list to a pictorial presentation. |
| 4. Obtain the vegetables listed. | Not present | If the vegetables are not in their usual spot, he cannot locate them. | Position the vegetables consistently; teach to request assistance. |
| 5. Bring the vegetables to the workstation. | Not present | Mobility | Learn the route to the workstation. |
| 6. Wash and drain the vegetables. | Present | | |
| 7. Place the cleaned vegetables in separate storage bins. | Not present | He separates the vegetables without visually discriminating them. Ask the supervisor to check his work. | Learn to look at vegetables and match them to pictures on each bin. Learn to request assistance. |
| 8. Return the vegetables to the refrigerator. | Not present | Mobility | Learn the route to and from the refrigerator. |
| 9. Clean the workstation. | Present | | |
| 10. Discard smock and hat and retrieve coat. | Not present | Mobility ADL | Learn the route to the locker. Manipulate the lock. |

SOURCE: *Adapted from L. Backus, D. Crimmins & S. Woolf,* Assessment and Educational Planning for Students with Severe Disabilities, *Albany: New York State Education Department, 1991.*

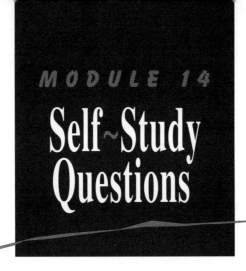

MODULE 14

# Self~Study Questions

1. According to IDEA (P.L. 101-476), the goal of transition planning is to broaden the options available to young people when they leave school. This goal is best accomplished by which of the following?
   a. A transdisciplinary team that includes the student's family during the last year of school.
   b. Taking into account the student's preferences and interests and including community experiences.
   c. A 30-day evaluation of the student's vocational potential.

2. What assessments are central to the transition planning process?
   a. Health, speech and language, psychosocial, psychological, and educational evaluations.
   b. A preference-and-interest inventory, a vocational evaluation, a psychosocial evaluation, and a speech-and-language assessment.
   c. Evaluations of the student's communication, preferences and interests, and possible adult living options.

3. When evaluating the effectiveness of instructional strategies and transition planning, you should focus on which of the following?
   a. Placement in a day program following graduation, with no gap in services.
   b. Independent living, participation in the community, and productive employment.
   c. Placement in a community residence that resembles a domestic setting within a year of graduation.

4. What is the best way to teach communication skills?
   a. Provide speech and language therapy five times per week, in half-hour sessions.
   b. Teach total communication (the use of spoken, signed, and aided modes).
   c. Identify the communicative demands and opportunities in everyday situations.

5. What does the ecological model emphasize?
   a. Teaching students to function in domestic settings and community environments through the use of classroom instruction in simulated functional environments.
   b. Teaching students to participate more fully in their daily lives through the use of volunteer trainers.
   c. Teaching students functional skills in the settings in which the skills are actually performed.

6. The development of spontaneous and generalized communication is best supported through which of the following?
   a. Instruction in various preferred activities in their natural settings.
   b. Instruction by the same teachers of a functional activity in the setting in which it will occur.
   c. Instruction in a preferred activity by the same teachers in a functional simulated classroom environment.

7. Which is the best way to encourage or stimulate students to perform tasks or activities in community settings?
   a. Train communicative responses through repeated trials in functional simulated situations.
   b. Identify the natural cues that bring about and maintain communication, and devise strategies to promote interaction.
   c. Initially direct the student's attention to the activities with partial physical contact and fade to either signed or spoken directions.

8. What advice would you give a teacher in considering which mode of communication is likely to be effective for an adolescent student?
   a. Encourage the student's family to learn sign language.
   b. Use aided augmentative communication devices if the family has a safe place to keep the equipment.
   c. Focus on the characteristics of the conversational partners and the environment in which communication takes place.

9. The most vital skills to be addressed by students in setting goals for transition relate to
   a. orientation and mobility.
   b. computer literacy.
   c. food preparation.
   d. self-determination/self-advocacy.

*Answers to self-study questions for this module appear in the section that follows.*

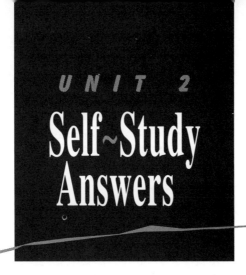

UNIT 2
Self~Study
Answers

# MODULE 6

**1. (a):** You are conveying information to your student, so this is an example of receptive communication from the student's perspective and expressive communication from yours. It is symbolic, since both the picture and the signed words are used as symbols.

**2. (c):** An abstract symbol is something (such as a sound, a written code, or a hand configuration) that is used to stand for something else (a referent). It does not physically resemble the item it represents.

**3. (b):** One of the first strategies you use to move a child from a preintentional form of communication to an intentional form is to respond to specific preintentional behaviors as if they were intentional. For instance, you may say "Hi" and respond to a child whenever he bats his or her arms. This batting movement may become an intentional means of gaining attention as the child learns that you will pay attention every time he or she makes that movement.

**4. (b):** Central to functional communication training is the belief that behavior does not persist in the absence of rewards. Therefore, the behavior is a functional way for the individual to convey a message. Functional communication training focuses on teaching the student an appropriate means of expressing that message.

**5. (c):** All the evaluations mentioned yield information that may be useful. However, the kind of information gained from the functional analysis is essential for determining the communicative functions of behavior. This assessment process leads to the design of effective intervention strategies that focus on the development of appropriate responses.

**6. (c):** This strategy teaches Luke to request help in an appropriate way. It gives him the opportunity to exert control over the activity he finds difficult and unpleasant by using a mode of communication that is effective for him. In addition, Luke can choose which activity he wants to participate in. Building in opportunities for Luke to communicate throughout the day will make him aware of the impact that his communicative behavior (pointing to pictures) can have on his environment and will motivate him and increase his desire to communicate and exercise control over his life.

**7. (b):** These interventions will teach Justine to participate in domestic life with less supervision and to request a leisure activity that provides her with sensory input comparable to her rocking, but that does not interfere with her family's life.

## MODULE 7

**1. (b):** The attachment behaviors of infants (smiling, vocalizing, looking, and clinging) are important for maintaining physical closeness and for keeping in contact with the caregiver. In turn, these behaviors attract and reinforce the caregiver's attention and evoke feelings of affection for the baby.

**2. (c):** A responsive environment can be adapted to an infant's specific needs, preferences, and abilities and enables an infant to develop a sense of trust and mastery.

**3. (a):** Infants have individual personalities and preferences. By recognizing these characteristics, caregivers can provide daily routines and expectations that build on the infants' abilities and support their individual needs.

**4. (c):** Infants vary in their abilities to make sense of sensory stimulation, and those who are deaf-blind may be extremely sensitive to certain kinds of stimulation. Fussing and pulling away are signs of stress that indicate an infant's need to take a break.

**5. (c):** Contingent responses involve careful observations and interpretations of the infant's behaviors and thus meet the infant's interests and focus of attention. Infants learn to participate in early conversations through familiar turn-taking activities that involve give-and-take.

**6. (b):** Research indicates that infants pay attention to "motherese" speech. The nonverbal features of motherese are more meaningful to infants than are the actual words.

**7. (c):** Through repetitive routines, infants develop a sense of predictability, an understanding of words that are linked to actions, and a knowledge of how to take turns.

**8. (b):** Contact with different caregivers and program staff may be confusing for an infant who is deaf-blind. The use of such tangible cues as name signals or signs can help an infant become familiar and more comfortable with significant people; this recognition may enable the infant to learn these persons' characteristics and the relationships to the roles they play in the infant's life.

**9. (a):** The focus of and activities in preschool programs vary according to the programs' theoretical perspectives. The participation of a child who is deaf-blind is more likely to be successful if the structure and expectations of the program match the child's interests and needs.

**10. (a):** Rather than use a "disabilities" approach that focuses on what the child cannot do, use an "abilities" approach that identifies what the child likes to do, and develop activities that build on these strengths to promote learning in other areas.

**11. (b):** Listing what children do in the preschool identifies the program's expectations and allows you to plan an individualized instructional program that is functional and chronologically age appropriate for the preschooler who is deaf-blind.

# MODULE 8

**1. (c):** Although the use of tactile cues may eventually help some children who are deaf-blind to use a similar form expressively (such as three-dimensional objects as expressive signals) or to begin to understand the communication of others, the initial focus is on the child's development of anticipation and the expectation of a specific response from the environment.

**2. (b):** The expectation of a response from the child is equally important. Therefore, the communication partner must allow adequate time for the child to respond and observe the child for this response.

**3. (a):** The selection of tactile cues should be governed, when possible, by what is relevant to the individual child.

**4. (b):** When you introduce a new communication system, your first priority is to encourage the frequent use of the system. Therefore, you should generally choose a system that a student can use right away. Once a student is using the system easily and frequently, then you may focus on introducing symbols or using more abstract symbols.

**5. (b):** It is more important for students to gain attention when necessary and to communicate in any context than to have a particular means of communication that seems conventional.

**6. (a):** Generally, a calendar box should have at least three and no more than eight compartments to accommodate representational objects for the student's daily activities.

**7. (c):** Touch cues can be used to direct a student effectively, give the student information, and relate both positive and negative reinforcement or feedback.

**8. (b):** The characteristics of color, contrast, and size, including distance and angle, and complexity are all critical features to consider. Students will respond differently to bright, dull, and, neon colors. Some students need to view things eccentrically; therefore, angle is critical. Some students have significantly reduced fields of vision, so the smaller the picture, the better. Uncluttered and simple drawings, pictures, or photographs may promote discrimination and processing skills.

# MODULE 9

**1. (c):** ASL currently does not have a widely used written form, although research is in progress to develop one. ASL is a visual-spatial language, based on visible features produced by a person's arms, hands, body, and face. It can be read tactilely, even though it is primarily visible. Its syntax is different from spoken (auditory) languages.

**2. (b and c):** Tactile fingerspelling, like all communication, is an expressive (sending) and receptive (receiving) form of communication. It requires that the sender's (speaker's) exact words be fingerspelled in the order presented. It can be used regardless of the time of onset of the deafness or blindness. It does require that the receiver and the individual presenting the fingerspelling have a command of the spelling of words and structure of language.

**3. (f):** An interpreter should be able to guide a person who is deaf-blind safely and comfortably. An interpreter should also convey visual information about the environment and other visual information that may be requested or is relevant to the situation. An interpreter may be required to summarize information that is in an inaccessible medium and also be requested to assist with such activities as obtaining transportation to and from a location.

**4. (e):** Print on palm (POP) is a highly portable form of manual communication because one does not need any devices or aids to use it. Only the receiver and sender are necessary. It is also a written form of communication. The written language is duplicated in print on the palm of the hand, letter by letter. Because it is a replication of the language, spelling and language skills are required.


# MODULE 10

**1. (c):** Braille is a communication method that provides access to reading material and allows people who are deaf-blind to communicate with themselves and others who are blind or others who know braille. It should be considered an option for deaf-blind students who have language abilities for reading.

**2. (a):** The major difference is the students' knowledge of language. Blind students are often more advanced in their language development in the primary grades because most children who are deaf-blind have not heard language and often learn it simultaneously with reading skills.

**3. (c):** Although all the items listed may be used by individuals who are deaf-blind, the optical aids are prisms, magnifiers, and closed-circuit televisions because they incorporate optics and actually modify the way the eye perceives the image.

# MODULE 11

**1. (a):** Learners who are deaf-blind may use forms of communication that are difficult to recognize, yet serve as the bases for natural interactions and social experience. Developing strategies to enhance these opportunities should be the primary goal of assessment. Testing hypotheses, assessing progress, and promoting specific skills are also important aspects of assessment that contribute to the achievement of the overall goals.

**2. (b):** An ecological approach is most relevant for evaluating students with severe disabilities whose educational curriculum focuses on basic life skills. A developmental approach is not appropriate for assessing adolescents, and applied behavioral analysis, although useful, is often concerned with specific communication or social behaviors.

**3. (a):** Most likely, for students who are difficult to test, the critical concerns will be the enhancement of social interaction and communication abilities in school, home, and community activities. Tests would not provide ecologically valid information about the student's competence in communication. Ecological validity will not be improved by adapting tests or using age ranges to describe the student's performance on the test.

**4. (a):** Because every individual's communication skills and behaviors vary from one moment to the next and from one environment to another, the evaluator should conduct observations in many situations to get a more complete picture of a learner's patterns, styles, and skills. Identifying the cues and opportunities that facilitate communication in different settings is a key step in the development of strategies of intervention.

**5. (c):** Profiles are useful to characterize the range of communication behaviors that a student may have, even if the behaviors are not symbolic or intentional. They incorporate the idea that communication can consist of unique behaviors in vocal, tactile, gestural, and other forms and may not be easily assessed in traditional ways.

**6. (c):** Important information about a student's communication and social skills can be obtained from day-to-day instructional and interactive events. Family members, teachers, and teaching assistants are often in the best position to note a student's interests, preferences, and expressive and receptive behaviors over time and across situations. These observations and the monitoring of intervention methods often lead to better descriptions of a student's skills than do formal procedures conducted by specialists.

**7. (b):** To be meaningful, the written report must be relevant to the concerns of teachers, teaching assistants, family members, and others who are involved with the student. Information must be included that can be understood and translated into intervention strategies and approaches.

**8. (b):** Interventions and opportunities for social interaction conducted in meaningful and functional activities will promote the acquisition of natural social skills and give the student a range of experiences that will be required for generalization. Interventions must necessarily differ from one context or environment to another because the social and communicative circumstances are likely to be different.

## MODULE 12

**1. (c):** All people display and respond to a variety of communication modes. In selecting a communication system, you should consider all the modes a student uses. For each student, it is important to identify the modes he or she uses to communicate and those that he or she understands.

**2. (c):** Students who use body movements, such as rocking, are using a nonvocal mode. Intonation, babbling, and speech are examples of vocal communication.

**3. (b):** An example of the aided mode is the use of a picture to communicate. Grimacing and signing are examples of nonvocal communication, and whimpering is an example of vocal communication.

**4. (b):** Giggling and squealing are examples of the vocal mode, and signing, pointing, tugging, and pulling are examples of the nonvocal mode.

**5. (c):** A communication system cannot meet a person's needs for a lifetime. The goal is to choose a system that changes over time as the student develops new skills and has new needs. Selecting a system involves a consideration of the ways the student currently uses vocal, aided, and nonvocal modes; repeated evaluations and redesigns of the system; and moving the student to a higher level of communication.

**6. (b):** Selecting a single mode of communication does not create an individual system that will meet a person's unique strengths and needs. It is important to define all the modes a student uses and to make use of them to the greatest extent possible. Assessing communication involves determining the modes the student uses, providing information that can be translated into functional skills, and determining the modes that others use with the student.

**7. (a):** Functions of communication exist within all modes and are relevant for every student. The functions of communication are the purposes served by the behavior; are assessed as part of the demands of the student's environment; and include behavioral regulation, social interaction, and joint attention.

**8. (c):** The interactional styles of communication partners are primary influences in the environment and affect what the student receives and learns to understand. The communicative environment includes opportunities both to respond to communication and to initiate communication.

**9. (b):** The design of the communication system is driven by the information gathered by team members in all phases of the assessment. The system should be tailored to each student's current skills and needs.

**10. (c):** First, the team members gather information on the student's skills and needs and then define what modes and functions of communication the student is using. The service providers also match their modes and functions to support and enhance the student's current communication.

**11. (a):** All students should have communication systems that are individually designed to meet their needs and incorporate their skills, not a standard system applied to everyone. The team members should build on the student's current capabilities and be aware that development may not be smooth. Modeling communication just above where the student currently functions is a sound method for facilitating development.

## MODULE 13

**1. (d):** Instructional activities should be functional activities that are based on the choices of the family and, if possible, the person who is deaf-blind.

**2. (b):** Engaging environments should be predictable, responsive, and organized. Changes should occur, but they should be planned and announced. Although engaging environments should also be stimulating, the activities should lead to direct outcomes for the student, and not just provide overall stimulation.

**3. (d):** Instructional environments should be selected according to the student's current and future needs in the domains of daily life, recreation, work, and community. To the extent possible, these environments should include persons without disabilities.

**4. (b):** Use as little physical assistance as necessary to decrease Sara's dependence on prompts, and use teaching strategies in which the student is successful. This strategy uses shaping and a time delay.

**5. (b):** By using the signs receptively in the context of the activity or when the student initiates a communicative intent, you are providing meaning, so the new form (sign) is paired with the context of its meaning and the student's intent. Signing each sign without the student's having a one-to-one correspondence may be confusing for a student who is deaf-blind.

**6. (c):** Peers should be taught the student's receptive and expressive communication system. They may also be "coached" to *wait* for a response and to use other cues-prompts if a successful interaction does not occur.

# MODULE 14

**1. (b):** Transition planning should transform the student's preferences and interests into vocational and community experiences that will serve as possible options for adulthood.

**2. (c):** Any of the evaluations mentioned will yield information pertinent to program planning and development. However, the information gained from an assessment of the student's communication style, preferences and interests, and possible adult living options is the most beneficial for establishing priorities for educational experiences and effective transition planning.

**3. (b):** The transdisciplinary team must focus on enabling the student to achieve a satisfying adult lifestyle. These plans are evaluated according to the extent to which the student achieves the outcomes of independent living, participation in the community, and productive employment.

**4. (c):** Opportunities and reasons to communicate are abundant in one's daily routines. Therefore, to be effective, instruction in communication needs to be structured and presented in the context of naturally occurring, everyday situations.

**5. (c):** An ecological approach to instruction focuses on the demands presented to students in natural settings. An analysis of these demands in the context of ongoing routines reveals the skills or adaptations that the student may require to succeed in that environment. This approach may lead to the successful acquisition of skills and enduring behavioral change.

**6. (a):** Varying the activities in which the student participates, where the activities take place, and with whom they are performed promotes the generalization of communicative interactions. Instruction in preferred activities in their natural settings creates opportunities to support the emergence of spontaneous communication.

**7. (b):** Instructional procedures that direct the student's attention to cues in the natural setting promote self-prompting, and teaching students to ask for help when no prompts are forthcoming supports their independent performance.

**8. (c):** A student's mode of communication should enable the student to express his or her needs and preferences effectively, as well as to respond to his or her conversational partner. In addition, establishing alternate modes of communication gives the student flexibility in different situations.

**9. (d):** The most vital skills needed for setting goals related to transition concern self-determination and self-advocacy. Students need to learn to solve problems, represent themselves, be assertive in expressing their needs and desires, and participate in goal setting and decisions that will affect their future.

# Motor Development

*SANDRA ROSEN*

*ELGA JOFFEE*

- *Motivate students to move*

- *Plan activities to strengthen muscle tone*

- *Help families structure motor activities*

- *Introduce basic O&M techniques early*

Communication and physical movement are among the basic components of most of life's activities. They also help form the building blocks for the development of the individual.

The importance of communication as the basis for learning all other skills was described earlier in this volume, as was the essential interrelationship between communication and movement. This module and those that follow explore the importance of movement for individual development, the effects of sensory impairment on the skills related to movement, and the various ways in which these skills can be encouraged in students who are deaf-blind.

As children develop motor skills—the ability to execute and control the body movements used for going from one place to another—they develop purposeful movement, or self-directed movement whose goal is to fulfill one's needs (see Module 4). This module discusses the motor development of children who are deaf-blind, how these children acquire skills for purposeful movement, how the skills facilitate learning, and how teachers can help deaf-blind children benefit from the motor development process.

# IMPORTANCE OF MOVEMENT

Children's experiences with movement during infancy and early childhood are the basic building blocks for the development of skills. The sequences of their motor development can be regarded as a series of naturally occurring "lesson plans" that provide the structure for learning motor skills and related cognitive, communication, emotional, and social life skills.

## INFLUENCE OF EARLY MOVEMENT

The first movements made by all newborns open doors to discovering the existence of themselves, other people, places, and things. They help infants to perceive what their bodies are like. Early movements of the head, arms, and legs, for example, provide information about the weight of the limbs; the feel of skin when it rubs against other surfaces; and the body's sensations of pressure, temperature, and texture.

The earliest movements also create the foundation for discovering that other people and objects also exist. For example, the reflexive extensions of their arms and legs cause infants to touch nearby people or objects accidentally and are their first experiences of reaching out and finding something beyond themselves.

As infants mature, early movements that are often regulated by primitive involuntary reflexes are integrated into higher levels of movement that come under the voluntary control of the central nervous system. Voluntary movement implies intent and control—that is, children are able to identify what they wish to do or where they wish to go and are able to achieve their desired objectives. In this process of development, many opportunities for growth occur, especially in children's sensory systems, awareness of position and movement, sense of balance, development of muscle tone and coordination, and sensorimotor integration.

In addition, voluntary movement also fosters the emergence of self-determination, curiosity, and the urge and confidence to explore the world as babies learn that they can actively influence their interactions with the environment. Furthermore, movement and exploration help infants define the capabilities of their bodies in relation to space. Thus, infants begin to feel the positions of their body parts and the muscle power needed to perform certain movements, learn how to use movement to achieve a desired objective, and develop self-esteem through these accomplishments. When a baby reaches for a toy suspended in a crib, for example, repeated attempts to grasp the toy initially result only in the infant grazing the toy, but never having it firmly in hand. The infant then moves to a different position, and persistent efforts to reach the toy finally enable him or her to grasp it. During this movement and play activity, the baby "discovers" just how far the arms reach, how to move the body to a new position, how to adjust the direction of the reach, and how strong the grasp is.

Effective motor ability is also directly related to social, language, and emotional development. Moving about the environment enables young children to encounter and interact with other people and objects. Through these interactions, they learn who and what are out there, what these people and objects do, and how to link words and concepts with objects, people, and experiences.

Similarly, motor development facilitates emotional growth. The delicate balance between children's close emotional attachments to their parents and other caregivers and their ability to separate from those significant adults is affected by their ability to move independently during early childhood. Children develop emotional security as they learn how to move physically away from and toward others and to control their ability to be physically close to or distant from others at will.

## EFFECTS ON LIFE SKILLS

The acquisition of skills for movement is important for developing the life skills used to perform the routines of daily activities, such as grooming, dressing, and toileting. The early motor activities that lead infants and toddlers to learn about their environments and to form concepts are critical for performing these skills. For example, when a young child leaves his or her seat in a preschool classroom to use the toilet, movement skills are at the foundation of learning the entire process. The skills start with the child's initial exploration of the classroom and end with the actual performance of the tasks associated with traveling to and using the toilet.

Learning about and participating in community life are also tied to the development of motor skills. As typical children acquire motor

**H E L P**
*at a*
**GLANCE**

## DEVELOPMENT: A SUMMARY

• Development occurs sequentially over time, with each newly developed skill based on previously acquired ones.

• Development proceeds from the head downward to the toes (in a cephalocaudal direction).

• Development proceeds from the midtorso to the fingers (in a proximodistal direction).

• Increased sensorimotor maturation results in a shift of movement patterns from those that involve the total body to those that involve finer and more selective movements.

• Developmental steps typically overlap as already-demonstrated skills are mastered and are refined while newer ones are developed.

• Each individual's developmental schedule is unique.

• Opportunities for practice, encouragement, and instruction play a key role in sensorimotor development.

• Opportunities for broad exposure to the environment and for learning a wide variety of motor skills are vital. ■

skills, they move away from the familiar circles of home and school. At first accompanied by others and later independently, they explore their neighborhoods and participate in community activities, such as going to corner mailboxes or playing in local parks. This module and Module 16 explain how motor development can be affected when children do not see and hear and the things that educators can do to help children who are deaf-blind enjoy the benefits of full motor development.

# HOW PEOPLE MOVE

Like the development of communication, the development of movement is the result of the complicated interplay of internal and external factors. The sensorimotor system plays a role in determining the way in which this development proceeds.

## SENSORIMOTOR SYSTEM AND SENSORIMOTOR DEVELOPMENT

The sensorimotor system is the vast and complex network of sensory organs, muscles, and nerves that control the movements of the body and the actions of the limbs. Sensorimotor development—an integral part of human development—is the increasing ability to control the body's movements through space (see Development: A Summary for a list of the primary characteristics of human sensorimotor development). This development is the result of the interplay of the sensory input systems (vision, hearing, taste, smell, sense of position, and touch) and the motor output systems (muscles and "efferent," or motor, nerves). Simply put, children learn to move about by combining motor action with what they see, hear, smell, taste, and feel. Efficient sensorimotor development requires sensory awareness, the optimal functioning of all the sensory systems, and experience in interacting with the environment. Table 15-1 presents the stages of human sensorimotor development for each area of sensorimotor functioning and the principal characteristics of that development. The building blocks of sensorimotor development—sensory awareness, primitive neurological reflexes, and mature neurological reactions—and the elements of efficient sensorimotor functioning—muscle tone and coordination—are discussed in the next sections.

**TABLE 15-1:**

Stages of Sensorimotor Development

| AREA OF FUNCTIONING | PRINCIPAL CHARACTERISTICS |
|---|---|
| **CONTROL OF THE HEAD** | Lifts the head from a prone position.<br>Lifts the head and shoulders from a prone position; supports weight on forearms.<br>Lifts the head, shoulders, and trunk from a prone position; supports weight on hands.<br>Holds the head steady when pulled to a sitting position from a supine position. |
| **LOCOMOTION** | Rolls from the back to the stomach.<br>Rolls from the stomach to the back.<br>Crawls with the stomach on the ground.<br>Creeps on all fours.<br>Creeps reciprocally (using opposing arms and legs). |
| **BALANCE WHILE SITTING** | Has equilibrium (balance) reactions—sitting position.<br>Begins sitting; leans forward on the hands.<br>Balances while sitting.<br>Goes from sitting to a prone position.<br>Goes from sitting to standing—assisted or unassisted. |
| **BALANCE WHILE STANDING** | Bounces; bears weight with the feet and legs.<br>Pulls to the feet with assistance from a sitting position.<br>Stands momentarily.<br>Goes from standing to sitting.<br>Stands without assistance. |
| **WALKING** | Walks while two hands are held.<br>Cruises along objects or furniture<br>Walks while holding another person's hand.<br>Walks alone. |

## Sensory Systems and Sensory Awareness

Sensory systems receive information from the environment and transmit this information to the brain. Sensation and sensory awareness refer to the ability to perceive the information that is transmitted through the organs of the sensory system. Children who do not see or whose eyes sense the presence of light but whose brains do not perceive the light do not experience visual sensation. Similarly, children who do not hear or whose ears receive sound that is not perceived by the brain do not sense sound. For children to use sensory information, they must have sensory awareness. The sensory systems that receive information that is needed for movement are the proprioceptive-kinesthetic system, the tactile system, the auditory system, the visual system, and the vestibular system.

**The Proprioceptive-Kinesthetic System.** Proprioception provides information about the body's position at a given instant through proprioceptive sensory endings that are located in the muscles, joints, and skin. Kinesis is the cumulative effect of a succession of pieces of proprioceptive information that produces an awareness of movement and is the foundation for many aspects of balance and coordination.

**The Tactile System.** The tactile sense provides information about sensations received through the skin, including the awareness of touch, the discrimination of textures and surface features of objects, pain, and temperature.

**The Auditory System.** The auditory sense provides information about sounds, including pitch, timbre, loudness, and the position of sources of sounds with respect to the listener.

**The Visual System.** The visual sense provides information about stimuli received by the eyes, including the perception of color, light and dark, contrast, size, shape, movement, and depth.

**The Vestibular System.** The vestibular system (in the inner ear) provides information about the position of one's head in space and about movement of the head with respect to gravity.

**The Olfactory System.** The olfactory sense provides information about scents and aromas and is not directly related to motor functioning.

**The Gustatory System.** The gustatory sense provides information conveyed by the tongue about taste, texture, consistency, and temperature and is not directly related to motor functioning.

Among the senses, vision and hearing are the distance senses. These senses play critical roles in sensorimotor development, with vision being primary. They facilitate major portions of children's early interactions with their surroundings. Vision motivates, guides, and verifies this interaction by providing quick and continual feedback about the location of objects and people and of the body's relationship to them.

Hearing also provides information about distant things, but only when objects or people produce or reflect sound. The other senses (except smell) play lesser, but still significant roles in sensorimotor development by providing information about features of the environments with which children come in direct contact and that children integrate with their movement experiences.

It is the constant stream of information provided by vision, integrated with other sensory information and movement, that is essential for sensorimotor development. Ensuring the effective sensorimotor development of children who are deaf-blind depends on the development of strategies to provide adequate sensory information about things that are "distant." Intervention strategies presented later in this module can help teachers and other educational team members develop activities for the classroom and home to facilitate this process (see also Modules 18 and 19).

## Primitive Neurological Reflexes

Primitive neurological reflexes, or involuntary responses that strongly influence infants' first active movements, are observable as rigid movement patterns. As children mature, these primitive neurological reflexes fade and give way to mature neurological reactions that facilitate coordinated voluntary movement. Problems occur when these reflexes do not fade or do not become integrated into more complex movements.

The asymmetrical tonic neck reflex (ATNR) is an example of a primitive reflex that can affect the movement of children who are deaf-blind. The ATNR can be seen when a child's head is turned toward one side and his or her arm and leg on that side extend (straighten) while the arm and leg on the opposite side flex (bend). Teachers have observed the action of the ATNR when some deaf-blind students begin using the long mobility cane or perform activities that require placing the hand or arm at the body's midline. In these instances, a student pulls one shoulder backward, turning his or her head to one side while extending one arm forward. This reflex interferes with the ability to begin moving and to maintain a straight direction of travel. Strategies for breaking the hold of primitive reflexes, such as the ATNR, include working with therapists to help children integrate the reflexes early in their development and using modified orientation and mobility (O&M) techniques (see Modules 17 and 18 for more information).

Primitive reflexes, such as the startle, tonic labyrinthine, and grasp reactions (see the definitions of these reflexes in Effects of Neurological and Physical Impairments in this module), are most noted as contributors to movement difficulties in children who are deaf-blind and have cerebral palsy or another injury to the motor centers of the brain. Primitive reflexes can also be unconsciously called into play when a person is under physical or emotional stress. For many deaf-blind children, moving about can impose an underlying level of stress that is related to the physical demands of movement and to the high level of concentration that travel entails. Children who have neurological impairments may experience other primitive reflexes, such as the tonic labyrinthine reflex, as well. Teachers work closely with occupational and physical therapists, as well as O&M instructors, to devise modified mobility techniques or to create muscle positioning that minimizes the effects of primitive reflexes on the children's performance.

## Mature Neurological Reactions

Mature neurological reactions, or voluntary motor responses that develop as the primitive reflexes fade, facilitate voluntary activities, such as lifting and turning the head, rolling over, rotating the trunk, maintaining balance while walking, and moving one part of the body without moving other parts (isolating the motions of individual body parts). Unlike primitive reflexes, children can call mature reactions into play or actively inhibit them at will. For example, a child can use the righting reaction to roll or can inhibit it to rotate the trunk and pelvis in isolation to walk comfortably. As maturation takes place, mature neurological reactions and later voluntary movements are further integrated with sensory information.

In planning educational activities, it is important to understand how reflexes and reactions are related to sensorimotor development. Although a description of the complex details of these reflexes and reactions is beyond the scope of this work, many texts cover the basic principles of human sensorimotor development (see, for example, Gallahue, 1985). The following list highlights the human reflexes and reactions that most notably affect the performance of motor skills by children who are deaf-blind:

### Reflexes

- *ATNR.* When the child's head is turned toward one side, the arm and leg on that side straighten (extend) and reach toward that side; the arm and leg on the opposite side bend (flex).

- *Symmetrical tonic neck reflex (STNR).* When the child's neck extends, the arms extend and the legs flex; when the neck flexes, the arms flex and the legs extend.

### Reactions

- *Neck righting.* In the supine position, when the child turns his or her head to one side, the upper trunk rotates in that direction to maintain a forward alignment with the head.

- *Body-on-body righting.* In the supine position, when the upper trunk rotates to one side, the pelvis rotates in that direction to maintain a forward alignment with the shoulders.

- *Labyrinthine righting.* When the head is passively tilted away from the vertical position, it tilts in the opposite direction to regain its vertical alignment.

- *Landau.* When the child is supported under the trunk (arms and legs unsupported) while lying on his or her stomach, the extensor tone of the muscles of the back, arms, and legs increases; the back arches and the arms and legs rise.

- *Protective extension.* In response to a sudden tip or loss of balance, the arms or legs or both straighten and stiffen in the direction of the fall in an effort to break the fall.

- *Equilibrium.* Equilibrium involves the use of balance reactions to maintain balance in the lying, sitting, quadruped (on all fours), kneeling, and standing positions. Mature gait patterns depend heavily on equilibrium reactions to maintain overall stability as balance is momentarily lost and regained with each step.

## Sensorimotor Functioning

Sensorimotor functioning is the fine-tuned combination of the senses working in concert with the body's muscles to accomplish movement. It is the consequence of sensorimotor development—the process by which children learn to integrate information received by the senses with the actions of the motor system to achieve coordinated movement.

**Muscle Tone**. Muscle tone, the state of firmness or tension of the body's muscles, can be viewed as motoric "readiness for movement." Muscles must be ready and able to move for movement to occur. The muscle tone of many children with visual impairments, as well as of many children who are deaf-blind, is characteristically low. This condition is known as hypotonia, or low tone. A teacher can recognize low muscle tone when children's limbs and muscles look or feel "soft" or the children look "floppy" as they move about or are moved and positioned (Ferrell, 1985). The various theories about why children with visual impairments and children who are deaf-blind have low muscle tone all suggest that the disruption or absence of vision in infants limits early movement experiences, the development of a sense of position, and the muscle strength that comes with the repeated activity associated with early exploration (Dodson-Burk & Hill, 1989).

Several postural and gross motor consequences can result in the absence of sufficient muscle tone to support efficient movement. They include difficulty holding the head erect, reduced strength in the shoulder girdle and abdomen, and the lack of rotation in the trunk or hips. To compensate for the difficulties associated with low muscle tone, children who are deaf-blind often naturally begin to use "postural fixes" to maintain a position or to support movement. Examples of these fixes include elevating the shoulders to stabilize the neck and rotating the pelvis forward to lock the hips in place to maintain an erect posture. These positions, in turn, interfere with such motor activities as moving the head for visual and auditory scanning; using the arms for reaching; developing posture, gait, and balance; and maintaining a straight line of travel during movement. Early intervention activities that address the needs of infants who are deaf-blind to "get moving" and "keep moving" are the best-known strategies for minimizing the risks of low muscle tone (see Module 16 and also Modules 18 and 19 for techniques for teaching O&M). Older children can benefit from overall body-strengthening activities, including calisthenics, brisk walking, swimming, or running. Teachers and families, in consultation with the children's health care professionals, can develop movement activities to enhance the children's muscle tone.

**Coordination**. Coordination, the harmonious relationship and actions of the sensory and motor systems in achieving movement, develops through the interplay of muscle tone, awareness of the position of the body and limbs (proprioceptive awareness), and the integration of neurological reflexes and reactions. Gross motor coordination involves coordination of the trunk and limbs, whereas fine motor coordination involves coordination of the fingers and hands.

As was mentioned earlier, mature voluntary reactions provide the foundation for coordinated movement, and children who are deaf-blind often experience primitive reflexes that fail to be integrated into mature reactions or are called into play under stress. These primitive reflexes can compete with voluntary movement, so the children are bound to a pattern of movement and have difficulty moving one part of their bodies without moving the other parts. The key to coordinating the performance of movement skills is to release the "hold" of primitive reflexes. Teachers can facilitate this process by working closely with therapists on the educational team who provide motor development activities to help children integrate the primitive reflexes during infancy and by using modified O&M techniques that limit the effect of primitive reflex patterns (see Module 18 for suggestions for individualizing and modifying O&M techniques). In working to help students develop and integrate motor skills, it may be useful to keep in mind the strategies presented in Tips to Enhance Motor Skills and the following overview of the motor development of deaf-blind children:

- Primitive neurological reflexes may not always fade completely. They can persist to affect motor development and the ability to move.

- Sensorimotor integration may not be completely refined, primarily because of the impairment of sight and secondarily because of the impairment of hearing.

- Low muscle tone, or hypotonia, a characteristic of many children who are deaf-blind, is believed to be a consequence of limited movement experience in the environment. It restricts

**HELP at a GLANCE**

## TIPS TO ENHANCE MOTOR SKILLS

Following these strategies can encourage the motor development of children who are deaf-blind:

- Provide exercises, positioning, and activities recommended by occupational and physical therapists, as well as O&M instructors.

- Provide activities to stimulate the senses and engage students in movement.

- Individualize exercise and movement programs by considering students' interests and physical and neuromotor capacities. ∎

further interaction with the environment because it limits the efficient use of motor skills.

- The effects on sensorimotor development of other related and nonrelated neurological and other physical impairments are individual.

## EFFECTS OF NEUROLOGICAL AND PHYSICAL IMPAIRMENTS

Neurological and physical impairments (related or not related to deaf-blindness) are additional factors that influence a child's sensorimotor development. Just as there may be a unique character to the motor development of deaf-blind children because of impairments of the distance senses, so, too, cerebral palsy and many other physical impairments can have a significant impact on the course and outcomes of motor development. Children who are both neurologically or physically impaired and deaf-blind, for example, experience the milestones of motor growth in ways that reflect the effects of these conditions on motor function. This situation is highly individual and can be evaluated only according to individual circumstances. Teachers should be aware that many students who are deaf-blind have cerebral palsy or other physical impairments for the same reasons that caused deaf-blindness, such as prematurity (see Modules 2 and 3 and Appendix A).

The following are neurological reflexes and reactions that can affect the efficiency of movement of children who are deaf-blind and have cerebral palsy:

- *Startle*: Sudden movement or a loud noise causes the child to experience a quick succession of body flexion, extension, and flexion again. The child appears to jump as if startled.

- *Tonic labyrinthine*: A child in the prone position (lying on the stomach) experiences increased tension in muscles that move joints in a flexor pattern (bending joints or moving them forward or away from the midline); in the supine position (lying on the back), the child experiences increased tension in muscles that move joints in the extensor pattern (straightening joints and moving limbs backward or toward the midline).

- *Grasp*: Contact of the palm with an object causes the fingers to close around the object until it is removed. The child may not have sufficient control to release this grasp voluntarily.

In educational programs, many service providers address the sensorimotor development needs of deaf-blind children. Two key team members are the physical therapist and the occupational therapist. The physical therapist provides therapy to facilitate normal gross motor development and sensory integration. The occupational therapist provides therapy to facilitate fine motor development and sensory integration. Occupational therapists apply clinical treatment to instruction in daily living skills for people with physical impairments. In a team structure, occupational and physical therapists collaborate with specialists in visual disabilities when serving individuals who have visual and physical impairments.

# PATTERNS OF SENSORIMOTOR DEVELOPMENT

Because children who are deaf-blind have limited access to sight and sound, the strength of the naturally occurring motivators and reinforcers that support the emergence of fine and gross motor skills may be compromised. The loss or limitation of sensory information that motivates and guides movement may delay the development of gross and fine motor skills in deaf-blind children who are not exposed to early intervention. These delays, in turn, can have continuing long-term effects on the eventual level of motor skills that is developed; consequently, it is important for those who live and work with deaf-blind children to be aware of these possible accumulating effects.

## DEVELOPMENT OF FINE AND GROSS MOTOR SKILLS

The development of gross and fine motor skills is inextricably linked. The stage for the development of fine motor skills is set when an infant uses early gross motor skills to lift the head, raise the torso, and lean on the hands. Then, as an infant bears the weight of the upper body on the palms, he or she develops the muscle tone, proprioceptive awareness, and strength in the fingers and hands that contribute to the development of fine motor skills and the further development of gross motor skills. This tone and strength are important for carrying out fine motor tasks, such as grasping objects, and gross motor activities, such as pushing to roll over or sit.

The development of fine motor skills also occurs when infants move their hands in front of their faces, manipulate and poke at objects, play with their fingers and toes, and carefully watch what they are doing and integrate the results. Vision is a fundamental element in this process. It has been noted that some children who are visually impaired or deaf-blind may often spontaneously initiate and then stop this activity and thus their progress in developing fine motor skills may be slowed (Warren, 1984).

Therefore, the relationship between the development of fine and gross motor skills is a two-way street. Limitations in the early development of gross motor skills affect the subsequent development of fine motor skills. In turn, limitations in the development of fine motor skills may ultimately affect the overall emergence of gross motor skills. For example, without the fine motor skills to examine objects in the environment, children's motivation to move and explore the environment can be diminished. Early intervention activities (see Module 16) facilitate the refinement of gross motor skills and the emergence of fine motor skills and stimulate children's curiosity and motivation to move about and explore. Thus, when teachers of children who are deaf-blind provide instruction to facilitate the development of gross motor skills, they must also include activities that address the development of fine motor skills, and vice versa.

## Neck and Head Control

Spontaneous head and neck movement among children who are deaf-blind is often limited, primarily because of the weakness or absence of visual or auditory stimuli that would motivate them to lift their heads, prop themselves up on their hands and arms, and look about. Therefore, these children require activities to help them develop the strength and coordination necessary to control their necks and heads.

The previous discussion of the early development of gross and fine motor skills explained that there can be reverberating consequences for overall motor development when these motor skills are delayed. Similarly, children who are deaf-blind experience a "ripple effect" from weak neck and head control that may influence their ability to creep, stand, and walk efficiently and, in turn, their motivation and capacity to explore.

Restricted motivation and opportunities for babies who are deaf-blind to bear weight on their arms while lifting their heads limit the emerging strength in their necks, arms, shoulder girdles, and trunk muscles. Deaf-blind infants may feel as if their bodies are top heavy and may not have sufficient strength and control to hold up their heads and turn them at will. They also experience limited opportunities to turn their heads repeatedly in response to interesting sights and sounds. Their failure to turn their heads repeatedly affects the ease with which they learn to rotate their bodies, along with their abilities to creep and walk efficiently, since rotation of the trunk, pelvis, and hips is integral to creeping and walking.

▲ *Using toys as motivators for movement can help young children strengthen their bodies by improving their muscle tone and neck and head control.*

## Ability to Creep and Walk

The dynamic combination of these unique sensorimotor patterns makes it difficult for deaf-blind toddlers to scoot about, creep on all fours, and walk upright readily and comfortably. Observational studies of the patterns of development of gross motor skills in blind children have reported a "stop-start" pattern of motor development (Adelson & Fraiberg, 1974). Babies who are blind learn to assume the positions necessary for dynamic gross motor activities but do not immediately take off and move about in these positions. Those who assume the creeping position are slow to creep forward and, in the absence of an imitative model, may never do so. Toddlers who learn to stand spend a long time in this stage before they begin to cruise along furniture and walk unassisted. Families and teachers have observed that babies who are blind or deaf-blind often do not creep about, but begin their locomotor activity when they walk. (Module 18 describes a helpful approach for encouraging young children who are deaf-blind to creep.) The following sections on the development of coordination, balance, posture, and gait patterns also consider the ripple effect, in which one aspect of motor development affects the emergence of other skills.

## REFINEMENT OF GROSS MOTOR SKILLS

Sensory awareness, muscle tone, and coordination are the building blocks of the development of motor skills. Coordinated movement, mature gait patterns, and good posture are vital for the ultimate development of effective motor skills and purposeful movement. These refinements of motor skills allow children to use their sensorimotor skills to maximum effectiveness in performing daily activities. Children who are deaf-blind have unique patterns for developing balance, posture, and gait. Understanding the factors that contribute to these unique patterns is important for planning early intervention strategies and activities.

## Balance

There are two kinds of balance—static and dynamic. Static balance is used to maintain a posture or position when one sits or stands still. Dynamic balance is used to maintain stability when one is in motion. It has been observed that children who are visually impaired or deaf-blind often exhibit poor (unstable) static and dynamic balance, which is associated primarily with hypotonia (low muscle tone)(Leonard, 1969) and the early limitations on their development of the sense of position in space (proprioception). Balance can also be a problem if children have a hearing impairment that involves damage to the inner ear and the vestibular system or an astigmatism that needs refractive correction.

## Posture

Posture is the alignment of the body parts—the feet, legs, pelvis, trunk, arms, and head—with the center of gravity of each part directly balanced over the center of gravity of the part below. In good posture, a vertical line suspended from the ceiling would pass through the ear lobe, tip of the shoulder, immediately behind the top of the hip bone (the greater trochanter of the hip), immediately behind the kneecap, and immediately in front of the ankle bone.

Characteristic postural patterns have been observed by teachers and O&M instructors who work with students who are deaf-blind. It is believed, but has not been documented, that the students' visual impairments are the primary reasons for these observed patterns, which most likely result from limited opportunities for visual imitation of other people, low muscle tone, poor static balance, and decreased proprioception (Rosen, 1990).

The typical characteristics of posture observed among children and youths who were born with visual impairments include excessive neck flexion (when the head hangs downward), rounded shoulders, scoliosis (an abnormal lateral curvature of the spine), lordosis (a swayback), excessive knee flexion, a backward lean of the trunk, and flat feet (Rosen, 1986). Although these are typical patterns, individual students will exhibit variations that are related to their individual experiences and characteristics. Teachers and families can work cooperatively with children to facilitate good posture by providing opportunities to model or copy others, to develop an awareness of body parts and their positions (see Module 18), and to strengthen their overall muscle tone so they can maintain the alignment of their body parts.

## Gait

Gait is the manner of walking. Characteristic gait patterns have been observed among deaf-blind students. As with other motor functions, it is believed that students' visual impairments are the primary contributing factors to these patterns, which result from limited opportunities for visual imitation of other people, low muscle tone, limited trunk rotation, poor dynamic balance (balance while moving), and decreased proprioception and kinesthesia (the ability to sense the position and movement of the body and its parts).

The gait of a child with visual impairments is often characterized by the absence of reciprocal arm swing, limited trunk and pelvic rotation, toeing out, shortened lengths of steps, excessive flexion of the knees, and a wide base of support at the feet (Rosen, 1986). It is important for teachers to remember that these are typical patterns for these students and that individual students will exhibit variations that are related to their individual experiences and characteristics. Throughout the children's growing years, teachers and families can work together to develop activities that include movements to facilitate the emergence of effective gait patterns. It is essential to give students opportunities to experience different aspects of gait by manipulating their limbs (for reciprocal arm swinging), allowing them to feel others' limbs in motion, or introducing games and exercises that require arm swinging or encourage students to use an even, rhythmic gait (by walking to a beat played on a drum or on the students' bodies). Body-strengthening activities, such as vigorous walking, swimming, and calisthenics, can enhance students' sense of security and enable students to narrow a wide toed-out base of support.

# *MEETING UNIQUE NEEDS*

In planning intervention activities on the basis of information about sensorimotor patterns and those of children who are deaf-blind, it is useful to group the implications of deaf-blindness for motor development into short- and long-range consequences and issues. This perspective is important because long-range implications are extensions of short-range effects.

Organizing intervention activities to address interrelated short- and long-range factors and concerns will help provide opportunities for deaf-blind children to acquire motor skills, ensure their personal safety, and make the most of the benefits that motor activities offer them. It is important that a program include activities whose purpose is to address short- and long-term considerations regarding sensorimotor development. Activities that address short-term effects of deaf-blindness need to focus on the following immediate areas:

- isolated movement of body parts
- trunk and pelvic rotation
- development of muscle tone
- awareness of body parts and movement
- development of gross and fine motor skills
- posture and gait patterns.

Accompanying ongoing planning needs to address the following long-term concerns:

- cognitive development: object, positional, and directional concepts and spatial awareness
- acquisition of expressive and receptive language skills (especially related to movement and the concepts discussed earlier)
- social and environmental awareness
- emotional development, self-esteem, and self-determination
- decision-making behaviors
- ability to protect personal safety.

## ATTENDING TO THE ROLE OF FAMILIES

A teacher's first consideration in addressing a student's motor development needs and planning interventions is to view the student in the context of his or her family. Families are at the center of their children's lives and education. Educational teams and service providers who work with students who are deaf-blind need to involve the students' families in helping the students acquire sensorimotor skills. A preponderance of a child's early life is spent at home. Since most opportunities for moving and learning sensorimotor skills occur in the context of family life, teachers and families need to be at ease with each other and to share information freely. In an ideal partnership, parents share their unique understanding of and insights into their children's likes, dislikes, motor needs, and skills, and teachers guide families in how to structure ongoing opportunities for children to learn and use their bodies effectively and show them techniques for encouraging safe movement and exploration. Families often need information about what to do and how to do it, and Modules 16–19 offer concrete information on O&M techniques that can be shared with them.

## ENHANCING THE DEVELOPMENT OF SENSORIMOTOR SKILLS

Enhancing the development of sensorimotor skills means addressing the short-term effects of deaf-blindness by providing students with the motor skills they need to move about freely. In this way, long-term, accumulating effects of limited motor skills can be avoided. Programs to enhance the development of these skills include activities that motivate students to explore and move about, therapeutic activities, and instruction in the use of O&M skills and techniques.

### Motivation of Students to Move and Explore

Ensuring that students are motivated to move about is basic to all efforts to enhance their sensorimotor development. As was mentioned earlier, students develop this motivation when they become aware of and interested in the environment beyond their bodies and realize that movement allows them to have access to their surroundings. Early intervention programs, beginning in infancy, introduce activities that teach children to use meaningful substitutes for visual and auditory stimuli or, when possible, to enhance their use of visual and auditory information. Children are taught to use their hands, mouths, feet, and entire bodies to explore and learn about objects and other people. Close cuddling and other appropriate forms of handling by families is recommended to support this exploration.

Teaching students to appreciate their environment is an ongoing process. As students mature, they are encouraged to expand their explorations and to learn behaviors for touching and exploring that are appropriate for their ages and consistent with the social customs of their communities (see Modules 18 and 19 for specific techniques).

## Therapeutic Activities

Physical therapists and occupational therapists, who work in cooperation with transdisciplinary educational teams, have devised many useful strategies for developing sensorimotor skills. The aim of these strategies is to ensure that students benefit from the motor activities associated with each step in the sequence of development. Team members who design and select sensorimotor activities should keep the following principles in mind:

- Teach motor skills using a team approach to integrate skills in functional activities in all settings.
- Facilitate the development of normal muscle tone.
- Facilitate the development of all the senses.
- Facilitate the integration of primitive reflexes and the fine-tuning of mature neurological reactions.
- Provide experiences for steps in the sensorimotor-development sequence.

**Facilitating Muscle Tone**. To facilitate muscle tone, which is the firmness and readiness of muscles to move, transdisciplinary teams work with occupational and physical therapists who develop service plans for fine and gross motor functioning. Teachers and families participate in this process by incorporating fine and gross motor activities at home and in school that support the therapists' objectives.

Activities that families and teachers can do with young children to facilitate the development of muscle tone include encouraging active exercises, especially those in which the muscles are used against opposing forces. Young children may enjoy such activities to develop muscles used for fine motor skills as finger painting, playing with modeling clay, striking keys on toy pianos and activity boxes, or sorting small objects. School-aged students may benefit from such activities as brailling, knitting, sewing, setting the table, kneading dough, or other activities that require the repeated use of their fingers and hands. Older students can work at similar tasks that require fin-

▲ *Members of educational teams can use planned activities like calisthenics and climbing to work with children on improving their motor functioning.*

ger and hand movements that are functional and appropriate for their ages and individual interests.

Activities that require students to use their bodies and limbs to resist motion or to engage in general body exercises, such as calisthenics, are effective in strengthening muscle tone for gross motor functioning. Push-pull activities like tug-of-war, exercises in which students bear weight on their arms and legs, swimming, climbing, pulling wagons loaded with toys or other objects, and pushing carts are examples of such activities.

Structuring learning environments that are conducive to movement, exploration, and discovery will encourage students to use their gross motor skills to venture forth to see what they can find (see Module 18). Incorporating daily living routines that involve movement at home, at school, and in the community also creates natural opportunities for students to exercise their fine and gross motor skills, as does encouraging them to participate in chores around the house, such as setting or clearing the table, washing clothes, and throwing away the garbage.

When structuring opportunities to develop muscle tone and sensorimotor skills, activities should be selected that are appropriate for both a student's age and individual interests. For example, students who hear and enjoy music and sounds may benefit from fine and gross motor activities that include moving to sound or music, such as marching to an audiotape of drumbeats. Other students will enjoy jumping on trampolines or walking on treadmills. Activities that young children enjoy, such as pushing doll carriages and toy trucks or working with Play-Doh, are not suitable for teenagers, even though teenagers may continue to require intensive attention to developing muscle tone. Pushing a food or newspaper delivery cart at a work site and kneading dough in a class on home and career skills, for example, are more appropriate.

**Facilitating the Development of the Senses**. Sensorimotor development is facilitated when children learn how to use the information they receive through all their senses. This principle is especially important for students who have residual vision or hearing. Commercial sensory-stimulation kits are available, although such kits can also be made individually. It is important to note that most commercial kits are designed for young children and are not appropriate for teenagers and young adults. The important elements of sensory-stimulation kits include objects that produce a variety of sensory experiences, especially different sounds, textures, temperatures, and colors.

An effective strategy for teaching infants, toddlers, and preschool children to use sensory information is to present a variety of sensory experiences as the children assume the body positions associated with the various stages of motor development. Children typically progress through the following developmental steps: lifting their heads, pushing up on their hands and arms to raise their torsos, rolling over, sitting, creeping, standing, and walking. Thus, for example, students who are learning to lift and turn their heads need to be provided opportunities to experience how their environment looks, feels, and sounds when they are lying on their stomachs and when they raise and turn their heads from side to side. Sensory stimuli can be presented singly or in combination, depending on students' individual needs. As children progress through the stages of the developmental sequence, learning to sit, creep, stand, and walk, they should be taught to use sensory information.

Older students also benefit from being systematically exposed to sensory stimulation. Teachers can provide sensory training for them using a variety of common items associated with daily living activities, including clothing, construction materials (bricks, wood, or metal), radios, television sets, and so on. Calisthenics and mat exercises that are performed in conjunction with sights, sounds, and tactile experiences will enable students to experience sensory stimulation from a range of body positions.

Because the population of students who are deaf-blind is extremely diverse, teachers should be alert to individual differences that can affect how their students respond to specific instructional strategies. For example, teachers have observed that some students are not comfortable and do not learn well when they receive stimulation from multiple sources at one time. These students seem to learn best when their exposure to sensory stimuli is carefully structured to allow them to process one stimulus at a time and to increase their tolerance for processing multiple stimuli gradually.

**Facilitating the Integration of Reflexes and the Fine-tuning of Neurological Reactions.** Physical therapists and occupational therapists have the primary responsibility for facilitating the integration of primitive reflexes and the fine-tuning of mature neurological reactions. Working in close cooperation with other members of the educational team, they develop objectives and activities to suit the needs of individual students. They recommend daily living activities that teachers and families use to reinforce the integration of the primitive reflexes and help them devise comfortable and natural extensions of therapeutic exercises.

For example, students who are working to integrate the ATNR will benefit from practicing and using activities in other environments that require them to use both hands at the midline. Such activities include clapping hands, grasping two handfuls of silverware at the midline to set a table, and using two hands to crumple paper to throw it away. Students who are working on coordinated motor skills can benefit from rockerboard games, walking, hiking, climbing, rolling, swimming, or skiing.

**Providing Experiences for Steps in the Sensorimotor-Development Sequence**. Programs that address sensorimotor development should make every effort to ensure that children have the opportunity to experience each of the necessary developmental steps. Doing so results in a higher quality of motor performance at later stages in development. For example, students who creep before they walk develop trunk and pelvic rotation more easily than if they had skipped the creeping stage and thus walk more efficiently and comfortably.

There are critical decision points, however, for educational teams to consider. Occasionally, despite conscientious early intervention activities, some children do not complete a stage of motor development before they go on to the next. When it becomes apparent that students are skipping or have skipped a developmental stage, teams may decide to move on with the student. To provide students with the opportunity to benefit from the learning associated with a skipped stage, teams can plan activities and experiences similar to those in the missed stage. Students who skipped creeping may be guided to jungle gyms or ladders that require the same trunk and pelvic rotation and reciprocal movement they would have had from creeping. Similarly, if it appears that older students lack the skills they could have acquired at one of the stages of sensorimotor development, teams can plan activities that provide the appropriate movement experiences.

## Instruction in O&M Skills

Students who are deaf-blind develop motor skills in a way that is unique to their individual characteristics, including deaf-blindness. Transdisciplinary educational teams plan programs in sensorimotor development to enable them to reap the benefits of full motor development and ultimately to travel with maximum comfort, safety, and independence.

These programs are integrated with natural environments and support the students' total educational experiences at home, at school, in their communities, and at work. Students learn to use O&M techniques and skills to determine where they are located in their environments, to plan their paths of travel to specific destinations, and to travel to the destinations safely. O&M instruction often involves teaching students to use special travel tools, such as long mobility canes. The effective use of O&M skills and techniques gives students the freedom of movement they need to conduct their daily lives as independently as possible. The modules that follow will explore these skills and techniques.

# REFERENCES

Adelson, E., & Fraiberg, S. (1974). Gross motor development in infants blind from birth. *Child Development, 45*, 114–126.

Dodson-Burk, B., & Hill, E. W. (1989). *An orientation and mobility primer for families and young children.* New York: American Foundation for the Blind.

Ferrell, K. A. (1985). *Reach out and teach: Materials for parents of visually handicapped and multihandicapped young children—Parent handbook.* New York: American Foundation for the Blind.

Gallahue, D. (1985). *Understanding motor development in children.* New York: Macmillan.

Leonard, J. A. (1969). Static and mobile balancing performance of blind adolescent grammar school children. *New Outlook for the Blind, 63*, 65–72.

Rosen, S. (1986). Assessment of selected spatial gait patterns of congenitally blind children. (Doctoral dissertation, Vanderbilt University, 1986). *Dissertation Abstracts International, 47*, 3000A.

Rosen, S. (1990). *Posture and spatial gait patterns in congenitally visually impaired people.* Paper presented before the California Association of Orientation & Mobility Specialists, Ventura, CA.

Warren, D. H. (1984). *Blindness and early childhood development* (2nd ed.). New York: American Foundation for the Blind.

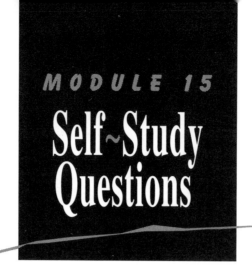

**MODULE 15**

# Self~Study Questions

1. The development of motor skills is important for the following reasons:
   a. It enhances cognitive and language development.
   b. It encourages emotional development and the development of daily living skills.
   c. Parents empathize more readily with physically athletic children.
   d. Young children love to run around.
   e. a and b.

2. Emotional growth is linked to motor development because
   a. children may feel more secure about themselves when they can come and go as they wish.
   b. toddlers like to be physically active.
   c. families overprotect children who do not seem strong.
   d. parents are proud of children who are early walkers.

3. Primitive neurological reflexes
   a. are always observed in primates but seldom in humans.
   b. are present at birth in every human being.
   c. fade away completely for everyone.
   d. are the cause of muscle tension and fatigue.

4. The term *muscle tone* refers to
   a. the coloration of muscle tissue.
   b. the firmness and tension of the body's muscles.
   c. "floppy" arms and legs.
   d. the way young children support their necks and heads.

5. In general, the motor development patterns of children who are deaf-blind can be affected by
   a. primitive neurological reflexes that do not fade completely.
   b. low muscle tone.
   c. the combined affects of vision and hearing loss.
   d. all the above.

6. To facilitate the development of gross motor skills, teachers should
   a. provide activities for the development of fine and gross motor skills.
   b. give children abundant opportunities for free play.
   c. do calisthenic exercises with their students two times a day.
   d. assure parents that there are ways to protect students from injury associated with movement.

7. Babies who are deaf-blind sometimes skip the creeping stage of development because
   a. they have limited incentives to move about and explore.
   b. creeping is unsafe for babies who are deaf-blind.
   c. it is better to walk than to creep.
   d. creeping makes babies tired.

8. The posture and gait of students who are deaf-blind typically include all the following except:
   a. a wide base of support.
   b. the head held down.
   c. limited rotation of the trunk and pelvis.
   d. reciprocal arm swing.

9. The short-range effects of deaf-blindness on sensorimotor development include which of the following areas?
   a. Social awareness.
   b. Muscle tone.
   c. Posture and gait patterns.
   d. b and c.
   e. a, b, and c.

10. Why are families important to the success of a sensorimotor development program?
    a. Young children spend the preponderance of their time at home.
    b. Families know their children's medical history.
    c. Teachers will never understand how to work with students without communicating with families.
    d. Families must sign consent slips for all mobility and motor development activities.

11. To help students who are deaf-blind learn to use their senses effectively, teachers should
    a. be sure students have body massages each day.
    b. provide systematic experiences with a variety of sensory stimuli.
    c. advise families to leave radios on at all times.
    d. use "smelly stickers" as rewards for good work.

*Answers to self-study questions for this module appear at the end of Unit 3.*

# Movement and Early Childhood

**THOMAS JAMES LANGHAM**

- *Teach movement as a natural part of daily life*

- *Use consistent daily structures and routines*

- *Encourage infants to reach*

- *Encourage toddlers to walk*

- *Use games to teach body parts*

- *Withdraw hands-on assistance gradually*

Motor skills are the basis of an individual's ability to explore, move about in, and interact with the surrounding environment. For this reason, they are integral to a child's continuing development and later capacity to travel safely and independently. This module presents specific strategies for teaching the basic motor development activities and techniques that young children who are deaf-blind need to build a foundation for travel skills. The modules that follow outline the basic concepts of orientation and mobility (O&M) and the instructional techniques with which these skills are taught in O&M programs that are designed to meet the needs of deaf-blind children.

# STRUCTURES AND ROUTINES FOR MOVEMENT

To make learning movement skills a natural outgrowth of daily activities, transdisciplinary educational teams should incorporate the development of gross motor skills into everyday activities and routines.

## ENCOURAGING GROSS MOTOR ACTIVITIES

The types of movement skills that are typically part of a young child's learning experiences include reaching, creeping, crawling, walking, running, jumping, carrying, climbing, lifting, hanging, and throwing. These movements, called gross motor activities, are carried out by the large muscle groups of the body to produce efficient total body movement. Although most children have the potential to carry out these activities, practice and instruction are necessary to develop efficient and mature movement patterns, especially for children who are deaf-blind and may also have gross motor difficulties and inefficient movement patterns. Children with such difficulties may appear unable or clumsy when attempting activities that require balance or the coordination of the large muscle groups. Starting at birth, children who are deaf-blind require specific assistance to develop and refine the skills they need for self-initiated movement and exploration of the environment. As they grow, they also need to learn to communicate with others and to integrate their emerging communication and movement skills.

## Activities

Activities of daily living are naturally occurring opportunities for young children who are deaf-blind to develop and refine movement skills. For these activities to benefit young children, however, they should be predictable and consistent. That is, they should be established and used at the same time, in the same order, and in the same way each day, to enable the children to anticipate the activities and to eliminate the disorientation and fright that may result when the children are picked up, carried about, or guided without any idea of where they are going, with whom, or why.

To help young children anticipate upcoming activities, the adults who guide them in these activities should identify naturally occurring cues (objects or experiences associated with specific activities) and use them to signal the children about upcoming events. Examples of such cues are a diaper for diaper-changing time or toileting, a plastic spoon for eating, and a washcloth for cleaning up.

Thus, allowing young children to feel their bottles before feeding or tug on their soiled diapers before going to the changing table or potty will provide them with ways to anticipate the upcoming movements and activities associated with feeding and changing.

To set a pattern for teaching O&M skills that will carry a young student through the growing years, use the following steps:

- *Break down learning experiences into small units and introduce activities one step at a time in the context of daily living routines.* For example, when teaching a toddler to travel purposefully in the home, begin with a walk from the bedroom to the bathroom after naptime. Introduce this route using a modified sighted guide technique combined with trailing—O&M techniques that are explained in the modules that follow. Integrating the child's individualized communication system, hold the child's hand, and position the child's other hand to trail the wall lightly, consistently following the route you have selected for this trip each time you travel from the bedroom to the bathroom.

- *Provide abundant amounts of concrete hands-on assistance and repetition until a child begins to demonstrate that he or she understands the task at hand.* Withdraw assistance gradually as the child performs movements with increasing independence. Good observation skills are critical when working with children who are deaf-blind because these children communicate in a variety of ways that may not be readily observed or understood. For instance, a young child who stiffens when feeding time is signaled with a bottle may be communicating a message about food, about movement, or about being interrupted during another activity.

- *Be patient.* Go slowly when introducing young children to new activities, places, mobility tasks, toys, people, or skills.

- *Allow children time to react and respond.* Often, adult caregivers are quick to assist deaf-blind children with movement activities before the children have had a chance to do what they can on their own out of fear for the children's safety or because of a desire to help the children complete an activity.

- *Communicate ample positive feedback and praise in a way that is meaningful and rewarding.* Some children may not be able to see facial expressions or hear spoken praise as others respond to them. To ensure that they receive messages, interact and pair responses with the individualized communication systems or modes that the children understand.

A final point to consider is the amount of assistance, or handling, that should be provided during activities for teaching movement skills. The term *handling* refers to the way a person helps another person move or assume various body positions or, in the case of very young children who are deaf-blind, how they are lifted and carried. The most common method is to direct a child's body movements physically or to provide touch cues for movement (see Modules 8 and 18 for more information on touch cues).

Sometimes a student may need to be guided physically to help him or her assume the correct position for performing an O&M technique such as trailing, for aligning body parts so all the parts face in the same direction, or for providing hand-over-hand support. If you need to guide a toddler who is learning to walk, place your hands on the child's hips, shoulders, upper arms, or upper trunk (do not raise the child's arms above his or her head), and walk along with the child ahead of you.

The range or amount of physical assistance provided to a child can be extensive or minimal. Maximal assistance is physically putting a child through an activity without expecting any effort by the child. Moderate assistance involves helping a child while the child is attempting to perform an activity. Minimal assistance means prompting or guiding the child in the activity while the child takes the initiative and usually involves only a light touch prompt that keeps the activity on course.

Family members and teachers need to monitor children's activities for safety and correctness. Where you position yourself and how often and in what manner you intervene depend on a child's individual needs and circumstances. Important considerations include the child's skills in performing activities independently; balance and motor control; and ability to respond to obstacles, to remain oriented, and to get back on track after being corrected. The occupational or physical therapist on a child's educational team should work closely with everyone involved in the mobility program and provide suggestions about the specific types of physical assistance and monitoring that should be used to meet the child's individual needs.

▲ *Providing hands-on assistance as appropriate and monitoring a child's position for safety and correctness are important parts of movement activities.*

## Toys

Toys that help young children who are deaf-blind develop mobility skills include a wide range of common objects and toys, including quilts with various colors, textures, and sounds; rattles; brightly colored mobiles that create sounds; shape sorters; building blocks; push toys; dolls; and climbing and riding toys. Special switch toys for communication and mobility development and balance and coordination devices are also available.

It is important to consider children's visual, auditory, and tactile skills, as well as their preferences, when choosing toys. Regardless of the nature of their auditory or visual skills, most children enjoy playing with toys that have a range of colors, shapes, textures, and sounds. However, children with visual impairments may prefer brightly colored toys with contrasting colors, whereas children who are totally blind may like toys that vibrate, have certain textures, or make sounds. Some children may prefer certain textures and dislike others.

Individual differences that are unrelated to a visual or auditory disability affect children's preferences for toys as well. For example, children who enjoy using their hands may want to play with toys that have pull strings, knobs to turn, or parts to manipulate, whereas others may be happier with simple toys, such as blocks or balls, or like toys for gross motor fun, such as climbing, jumping, and running.

The same caution about the safety of toys should be taken for children who are deaf-blind as for any child. Pay special attention to the fact that many young children who are deaf-blind, as well as those who have neuromotor impairments that interfere with their upper-body fine and gross motor skills, explore objects with their mouths. Therefore, these children need toys that are too large to be swallowed, do not break apart into small pieces, can be cleaned easily, feel pleasant to the tongue, and can generally withstand the treatment they receive.

Everyday household objects, including plastic spoons and cups, boxes, and paper wrappings (not plastic wraps of any kind), which have amused and educated children for generations, can be used safely by deaf-blind children. When opportunities are provided for young children who are deaf-blind to identify, explore, and play with common household items, the children have a chance to develop their fine and gross motor skills, to have fun, and to stay in the mainstream of family activities.

It is important to bear in mind that young deaf-blind children need specifically directed activities to help them understand the functional and play uses of household objects. Repeated and consistent experiences with directed play and participation in daily activities, as well as clear and consistent communication about when "to play" and when "not to play," help them make this distinction. For example, you can help a preschooler who enjoys playing with a dishpan understand the function of a dishpan by introducing him or her to it when a family member is washing dishes or by letting the child carry silverware to the dishpan in the sink. Guide the toddler to fill the pan, add the detergent, wash the dishes, and place them on a towel to dry. Providing opportunities for young children to assist with daily routines is a practical way to teach them about movement and household objects. It also increases their knowledge of functional daily activities and builds skills for eventual independence in performing them.

## STRUCTURING MOVEMENT EXPERIENCES

When planning daily activities for a young child who is deaf-blind, it is important to structure the home or classroom environment so it is conducive to free and safe movement and stimulates the child to explore and travel (see Module 18 for further information). Consider the movement associated with every daily living task at home or at school to be a mobility experience. Every time children who are deaf-blind move, they have the opportunity to learn either that there is order and reason to what they are experiencing—that they can learn to move about at will—or that there is no order or reason—and hence that they will experience the confusion of being in one place and then another and of having no sense of where they are, how they got there, or how they can control what happens to them. Under the latter circumstance, children often "tune out" movement experiences or resist them.

Making the most out of early movement experiences is not intended to turn family life into one long, tedious, unspontaneous, planned educational program. Rather, its purpose is to emphasize that with planning and organization, teaching purposeful movement skills and O&M can be a natural part of the daily life of a young child who is deaf-blind.

Young deaf-blind children learn to travel effectively when their daily movement experiences are highly structured to include communication about where they are going, who they are going with, and how they will be going (carried, walked, pushed in a stroller, and so on) and when they can follow the same routes to destinations, use O&M techniques consistently, and experience predictable routines of daily activities. For example, a consistent daily routine can be planned that includes time for eating, bathing, playing, napping, and outings and a time when the family is together. The use of individualized communication systems and the predictability of the routines will help young children anticipate upcoming activities. It is also important to devise ways to signal young children about breaks in their routines and plan to use "wild-card" cues for youngsters who use augmentative communication systems (see Modules 8–11).

Here is an example of how predictability fosters the development of purposeful movement skills. Typically, young children nap at specific times each day. When a child wakes from a nap and it is time to change his or her diaper, this fact can be signaled by patting the child's diaper before lifting the child from the crib or bed. The person changing the child's diaper should identify himself or herself and guide or carry the child from the bed to the changing table, following the same route and communicating consistent meaningful information about the event. Landmarks along the way should be pointed out and the purpose of the trip and the destination identified. As the child grows and learns to travel on his or her own using trailing techniques, the same routine should be continued. Eventually, the child will learn to anticipate the walk from the bed to the toilet when he or she feels the pat (on the diaper). Similar strategies can be easily incorporated into all day-to-day routines.

## PROVIDING NATURAL OPPORTUNITIES TO LEARN

Playtime, bath time, and leisure time are particularly good times for young children to use natural daily activities to learn basic reaching and movement skills, environmental and object concepts, position and distance concepts, and indoor and outdoor environmental awareness. The following are some activities that will facilitate this growth.

### Encouraging Children to Reach

Placing an infant on a blanket on his or her stomach and then on his or her back for a few short periods at the same time each day encourages the development of reaching skills. Structure the environment, so initially the infant is on a blanket surrounded by a few familiar toys within reach. Toys, bells, or rings suspended over the crib also help keep the infant's attention focused on the outside world. Toys should be close enough so they can be encountered as a result of any random movements the infant makes.

Select toys because they vibrate or move on contact, are brightly colored, have high contrast, feel pleasant to the touch, or in some way engage the infant's attention. An O&M instructor can work with a communication specialist to adapt switch toys or use the musical apparatus of musical greeting cards, so they chime or vibrate when they are touched or manipulated. Children can feel a sense of control and have fun when they operate the switches, which can motivate them to move and eventually to initiate movement on their own. It is important to coordinate all switch-toy activities with the child's educational team because these toys may be reserved for other applications.

A switch toy is usually a simple, battery-operated device that the child can control by pushing a button or by rocking it back and forth on a surface to control different kinds of stimulation. For example, one button may be attached to a fan and another to a vibrator; when the child activates a button, he or she receives the immediate reward of that particular stimulation. By letting the child choose which button to push, you give the child the opportunity to demonstrate his or her preferences and initiate movement to control the environment. Switch toys may be obtained from local toy stores or can be ordered from catalogs that carry toys for special children. (Teachers may be able to obtain these catalogs by contacting the director of special education in their school district or their state's special education resource center.) Many toys that are available commercially can serve as switch toys. Examples of toys in this category can be found in the *Guide to Toys for Children Who Are Blind or Visually Impaired* (1994).

Using toys that engage children tactilely, visually, or aurally can stimulate them to continue to reach and explore, especially when positive feedback from caregivers or teachers accompanies their exploration. Changing positions from prone to supine regularly (beginning on the stomach and ending on the back) during each play period will provide children with opportunities to reach from different positions and will lay the foundations for the development of body awareness and movement skills.

To encourage an infant to execute body movements together with reaching motions, gradually add new toys to the play blanket or the area around it and shift the toys just beyond the infant's immediate reach. It is also important to create similar reaching sequences to encourage the infant to learn to roll over, sit, stand, cruise along furniture, and walk about.

## Encouraging Children to Move

Module 15 explored how limited visual and auditory stimulation affect young infants' head-lifting and turning movements. The challenge to educators and families is to stimulate and encourage infants who are deaf-blind to lift their heads and raise themselves onto their elbows and thereby to develop neck and upper-body strength, rotation, and muscle control. Often, the introduction of outside stimuli, such as engaging toys with interesting textures (during blanket play) or vibrations or gentle strokes under the chin (while the babies are being held vertically) will encourage them to do so. Caregivers and teachers need to be consistent in their efforts to encourage infants to lift and turn their heads and to continue these efforts as the children grow.

Infants learn to turn over by wiggling, squirming, and thrusting with their feet (Raynor & Drouillard, 1975). Therefore, it is important to determine that they are comfortable with the textures and consistency of the surface upon which they are lying. Some infants and young children who are deaf-blind may be averse to touching some textures, such as woolen blankets, perhaps because they cannot predict what a surface will feel like until they encounter it, or to being touched because they simply dislike it. Children who have averse reactions to certain types of tactile contact (sometimes referred to as "tactile defensiveness") may lie still and not experiment with movement on surfaces they find unpleasant, although they may be content to wiggle and squirm around on surfaces they find pleasant.

A surface that includes a variety of pleasant textures and sensations can have a motivating effect. Teachers and families may sew simple patchwork quilts with four to six contrasting fabric textures or stitch squeaky toys securely inside the patchwork boxes (for children who can hear sounds) to provide stimulation for movement.

Another strategy for encouraging deaf-blind children to move about is to place interesting toys in their paths. Leaving favorite objects in playpens, along the walls in corridors, on the floor where they are playing, or along the edges of furniture will stimulate children to examine what they have found and seek to learn what else is out there. Do not provide so many toys, however, that the child cannot appreciate each one and is simply motivated to move from one to another. Remember that even though play and exploration are children's work, they should also be fun for the children, as well as for their family members and teachers. Devote a lot of time to play.

Frequently changing infants' body positions and helping them to use reaching movements to discover nearby objects, favorite toys, or textures will motivate them to move and explore. This kind of assistance may also be helpful to older children. When providing hand-over-hand assistance, be sure to give a child ample opportunity to respond to and to repeat the movements. Children will need experience with a variety of positions to be ready for later motor patterns, and touching and communicating will prepare them for future exploration.

Encouraging children to use their favorite toys and replacing ones that they avoid will encourage them to explore and move because they will have a sense that they can exercise control over their environments by selecting what they like and eliminating what they do not. However, since young children with little or no sight and hearing are not always aware of objects or textures that may be located only inches away, it is important to create predictable, consistent, and uncluttered learning environments.

Many families of young children who are deaf-blind are concerned about their children's progress in learning to creep or walk (see Module 15 for the issues involved in achieving milestones in motor development). It is therefore important for teachers to be able both to talk knowledgeably with families about motor development and to work with physical and occupational therapists to plan programs that teach creeping and walking skills. Remember that no one discipline is paramount in this area with a child who is deaf-blind and that it is truly a time for transdisciplinary activity. Without structured learning environments; visual, tactile, or auditory stimulation; and sensorimotor exercises, activities to facilitate creeping and walking will not be successful. On the other hand, neither structuring environments nor teaching environmental awareness, concept development, and body awareness is sufficient without transdisciplinary cooperation.

## INTRODUCING CONCEPTS

### Objects and Object Concepts

Young deaf-blind children have no way of knowing that objects beyond their bodies exist without useful sensory information about these objects. Therefore, early experiences in the crib, playpen, and around the home should be structured to introduce them to objects (such as beds, sheets, towels, doors, bathroom facilities and fittings, and cooking and eating utensils) that are used daily and to teach them how the objects are used (the functional approach). The family and the teacher should work together to inventory the objects that a child may use daily and develop consistent and meaningful systems for communicating about and using these objects. For example, they can identify and name the water faucet in the kitchen and help the child examine it, so the child knows what it is, how it is used, how it can be located, and so on. This level of learning about objects is important because when children are not aware that objects exist or that a specific object they may wish to avoid or want is present, their motivation to move and explore may be constrained.

The concept of object permanence is the basic understanding that objects exist even if they cannot be seen, heard, or otherwise perceived. Children who are deaf-blind require structured intervention to learn this concept because it fosters the growth of purposeful movement skills, as well as other forms of cognitive development.

## Body Awareness and Spatial Orientation

Throughout the growing years, all children learn to recognize and control their own body parts. Deaf-blind children require specific intervention to learn to identify the parts of their bodies, understand movement, and learn what the bodies of other people are like. Activities to support the development of this awareness should begin in early infancy. Blanket and bath games are excellent vehicles for teaching body awareness to infants, as are such games as "Angels in the Snow," "Simon Says," "Giant Step," and "Follow-the-Leader" when adapted to the needs of preschoolers who are deaf-blind (Leary & von Schneden, 1982; Zegers ten Horn, 1988). These games should be developed in cooperation with the communication program, so children learn communication and awareness of body image together, and should complement the objectives of occupational and physical therapy.

Closely associated with body awareness is the range of concepts related to the position, movement, and directionality of the body, such as up-down, top-bottom, bent-straight, in-out, on-under, near-far, fast-slow, forward-backward, front-back, and right-left. By understanding these concepts, children define their relationship to their world. Teachers of O&M have developed checklists of these concepts (Dodson-Burke & Hill, 1989).

A consistent physical environment is also critical for laying the groundwork for developing concepts and motivating children to move and explore. Consistency helps them learn how the environment is organized and how they fit into it. Every time children who are deaf-blind move about, their relationship to the environment changes. They need to reorient themselves to their surroundings—to know where they are and what surrounds them. For example, if they turn around, what was in front of them is now behind them. When the environment also varies, as when furniture and toys are rearranged, the reorienting process that children must do every time they move about may be unnecessarily complicated. In a consistent environment, in which landmarks and other objects are fixed, each movement does not require a child to relearn the environment. A student can find the objects with which he or she is familiar and use them as landmarks for reorienting to the surroundings.

The following are suggestions for structuring the home environment to facilitate a young child's understanding of position, movement, and directionality (see Module 18 for further information):

- Household furniture can be placed in an uncluttered arrangement.

- Toy boxes can be placed in each room the child uses.

- Toy boxes can be organized in a similar fashion at home and at school.

- Toys can be set out in consistent patterns at playtime in the crib, in the playpen, or on the floor.

- Outdoor toys can be placed consistently near closets where outdoor clothing is stored.

## Environmental Awareness

Young children who are deaf-blind learn about the people, places, and things in their environment through structured learning experiences; spontaneous exploration; and opportunities to participate fully in daily activities at home, at school, and in the community. Thus, they should be included in such family and class outings as trips to stores or playgrounds or "petting" zoos; encouraged to walk if they are ambulatory, instead of being pushed in strollers; and allowed to do such things as push traffic-control or elevator buttons. (For more on encouraging awareness of the environment, see Environmental Awareness in Preschoolers: Tips for Parents and Teachers in this module.)

## *MEASURING PROGRESS*

Comparing children is unproductive because each child develops at a different pace. However, in teaching young deaf-blind children, it is helpful to be aware of the range of movement activities and skills that children learn, in order to give deaf-blind students the opportunity to learn as much as possible. The following list of developmental milestones that children may typically demonstrate during early development may be useful in planning activities:

- lifts head slightly from prone position

- lifts head more fully from prone position

- puts weight on forearms in prone position

- lifts head 90 degrees and turns head

# Environmental Awareness in Preschoolers: Tips for Parents and Teachers

Rona L. Pogrund

Awareness of the environment is the first factor in motivating young children who are deaf-blind to move. It also helps them make sense of what can often be a confusing world and leads to their eventual development of orientation skills. The following guidelines will help parents and teachers facilitate this awareness at home, at school, and in the community:

• Provide opportunities for the child to explore various parts of the house in a systematic manner to piece together the environment in a meaningful way.

• Provide descriptions of the household environment in the child's own primary mode of communication, while the child is exploring it tactilely. Give the child additional information about his or her relationship to the environment. Also start the process of "landmarking," which helps develop an important orientation skill by which the child designates certain objects as landmarks.

• Make sure that the child is not familiar just with one or two rooms of the house but has explored the whole house to promote the child's understanding of the concept of "house."

• Note textural differences (carpeted, tiled, or wooden floors) and auditory cues (toilets flushing, garbage disposals grinding, radios playing, and wind chimes ringing) if the child has enough functional hearing and visual cues (such as the shape of objects, the color of walls and floors, and contrasts) if the child has enough functional vision. These cues heighten the child's sensory awareness—which serves as a foundation for future orientation skills.

The child's awareness of the school should not be limited to the routes from the bus to the entrance to his or her classroom and to the bathroom and play area and back, but should include the entire school environment, so his or her conceptual knowledge increases and "gestalts" (overall concepts) of the world are built. Many children who are deaf-blind or cognitively delayed or children with spatial orientation problems may be taught rote travel to learn the necessary functional routes. However, they should also have opportunities to explore environments in more generalized ways even if they cannot transfer orientation strategies and concepts to larger environments. An orientation and mobility (O&M) specialist should initially teach awareness of the school environment, so children can learn correct orientation strategies, but other service providers should reinforce this awareness regularly during functional daily routines.

Deaf-blind children do not have the many incidental opportunities that sighted-hearing children have (such as observing businesses and stores in the community or watching television and movies) to take in the world visually and auditorially and to expand their understanding of concepts. They are aware only of the places and activities in the community to which someone has exposed them and carefully interpreted what is happening. Tactile, auditory (if possible), olfactory, and visual (if pos-

*(continued)*

sible) exploration, accompanied by meaningful verbal (signed or spoken) or nonverbal descriptions, is the only way deaf-blind children can begin to make sense of the world around them.

Outings in the community should be an important component of environmental awareness and O&M programs for young children who are deaf-blind. Parents and service providers can create opportunities for children to visit pet stores, grocery stores, airports, restaurants, gas stations, post offices, taxis, buses, office buildings with elevators and escalators, and bowling alleys, for example. Each new experience in the community, especially at an early age, adds another piece to the conceptual puzzle.

For deaf-blind children with little or no receptive or expressive language, nonverbal methods of communicating about the environment may be useful. Lots of hand-over-hand touching and exploring, along with physical prompts that are paired with descriptions, are necessary to bridge the communication gap.

In summary, awareness of environmental concepts can begin at an early age, as parents and service providers expose children to the outside world and take the time to explain complex environments carefully. ■

- extends arms and raises chest from prone position
- lifts legs high in an extension from prone position
- rolls part of the way to one side from prone position
- rolls to one side independently
- rolls over intentionally from stomach to back
- rolls over from back to stomach
- begins to reach for items on a blanket
- assists when pulled to a sitting position
- bobs head erect when sitting
- lifts head when sitting
- maintains head control when pulled to a sitting position
- assumes a symmetrical posture when sitting
- holds head steady when sitting.

As members of the educational team determine which activities are priorities, their goal is to assist children to perform appropriate activities that are developed in a generalized sequential order and that are realistic for particular students. Some teachers recommend beginning at a level that is comfortable for the child and using this level as the groundwork for introducing the next stage. For example, a young child who requires intervention to learn to begin activities for sitting may be most successful starting out with games that include rolling and being pulled to the sitting position.

Families can help their infants who are deaf-blind learn these activities by positioning and guiding them through the movements associated with each milestone and making these activities pleasurable for them. Babies may or may not learn all the motor skills (holding up the head, sitting, reaching, grasping, creeping, and walking) spontaneously, but may, depending on their sensorimotor skills, do so in time and with practice.

# SUGGESTIONS FOR GETTING STARTED

## WORKING WITH INFANTS

The first activity is simple. The infant should be held in the arms and his or her position should be changed frequently. An infant 3 months or older can be placed prone on a blanket for a few short periods each day to encourage him or her to lift the head and possibly raise up onto the elbows (check with a physician or physical therapist; extensive periods in the prone position can trigger spasticity in some children). Common baby toys, placed in a consistent pattern around the crib or blanket, can motivate the infant to continue to move and to reach. While reaching, the baby can also learn to turn over by wiggling, squirming, and thrusting with his or her feet and soon turn, first from back to front and then from front to back. If the baby does not learn by himself or herself, provide just enough assistance at the hip and shoulder to help. Again, the baby's physical and occupational therapists should be asked for assistance.

Introducing infants to nursery rhymes and songs that involve physical contact and body movement, such as "This Little Piggy Went to Market" and "Pat a Cake," is also important. (These games are especially appropriate for infants with some residual hearing.) To stimulate crawling, cruising around furniture, and trailing, put strips of material with different textures on the floor or furniture and on toys that make noises or vibrate on contact.

## Movement Exercises

Movement exercises can help an infant learn to move his or her arms and legs together in preparation for more advanced movement patterns. Here are some suggested exercises; they should be discussed with the family physician or physical therapist before they are used to ensure that they are medically appropriate for the baby.

- Place the infant on his or her back with the legs and knees straight (relaxed, not stiff). Kneel above the baby and move the infant through these positions: Raise the infant's arms from the sides to touch his or her ears and back again; then move the infant's legs apart, and back together. This exercise should look like "Angels in the Snow" or "Jumping Jacks" while lying on the floor. Next, hold the infant's ankle and wrist on one side of his or her body and then simultaneously move his or her leg out slowly and gently, until resistance is felt, while moving the baby's arm so it touches his or her ear.

- Before an infant can learn to creep, he or she must learn to move the arms and legs alternately. Place the baby on his or her back, with elbows and knees straight, and kneel beside the baby and put him or her through the following movements: Gently raise the infant's arms one at a time. Then lift one leg and then the other gently and return them to their original positions. Continue to alternate lifting the baby's legs and arms. Do not continue these exercises too long because the infant will tire of them if they are not fun.

- Alternate these leg and arm exercises with water play. Fill a small plastic tub half full and add some plastic cups and spoons, sponges, and bath toys the child likes. Let the baby play in the tub, moving and splashing as he or she pleases. For older infants and toddlers, you can play "Roll the Ball" by sitting on the floor a foot or two from the baby, showing the baby the ball, and helping him or her catch it as you roll it. Start with a left-to-right roll, so the baby can stay in contact with the ball. Do not expect to play a game like "catch" with a child this young, however, especially one with a significant visual impairment. Soft balls that produce auditory stimulation may be purchased from stores or specialty catalogs. For children who cannot hear the auditory tones or see brightly colored objects, select balls with interesting, pleasing, and varied textures for this activity.

For children who have receptive language skills or can hear, signed or spoken cues, such as "Here's the ball" (when playing with a ball) or "Up we go" (when moving through positions), can be used. Parents and teachers should work closely with the communication specialist to develop appropriate touch or object cues for an infant who has a profound hearing loss.

## Further Considerations

Infants will progress at their own speed. Remember to let them try these exercises by themselves periodically, give the assistance they need, and never rush through activities. Add some early experiences on a hard floor, too, like softly bouncing the infant on his or her feet or letting the infant creep along. Such experiences will encourage the baby to become accustomed to hard surfaces, so he or she will not fear the harder floors later or become uneasy moving from one ground surface to another as travel expands from indoor to outdoor environments.

As the infant's skills improve, provide less assistance with an activity and go to the next one (see the list of early development milestones). Additional activities can also be devised for the following sequence of skills:

- lifts head from sitting position
- sits erect momentarily
- leans on hands briefly when sitting
- sits briefly
- bears large part of weight in the sitting position
- sits steadily
- pivots
- gets on hands and knees
- leans forward and rights himself or herself while creeping
- creeps
- stands holding rail or wall or chair
- stands briefly while his or her hands are held

- pulls himself or herself to feet, raises himself or herself from a sitting position
- lowers himself or herself to the floor from a standing position
- holding a support, stands and lifts one foot briefly
- steps when supported
- walks when hand is held.

The skills on this list overlap those on the previous one because each child will develop skills and abilities at a different pace.

## WORKING WITH TODDLERS

### Indoor Activities to Encourage Walking

Once children are creeping (see Helping Children Learn to Creep in this module) or beginning to walk (either by themselves or by holding onto someone's hand or a piece of furniture), encourage them to explore and locate objects. During explorations, place the children in contact with walls or sturdy pieces of furniture; never leave them alone in open spaces because they may feel uneasy or disoriented by the openness. Being consistently in well-defined, familiar places will help them build the security necessary to take the next few steps of development. In addition, continue to provide opportunities to experience a range of ground and floor surfaces. Allow children to walk barefoot indoors through safe parts of the house with an adult, so they can feel changes in the flooring, from carpeting to wood to tile, while the differences in flooring are explained to them using their individual communication systems.

Playing games will help children learn to identify their body parts and those of other people. For example, place a child's hand on your head and see if the child can then touch his or her own head and identify it. Play the game with large body parts first (such as the head, trunk, legs, and hands) and then move on to smaller parts (such as elbows, ankles, cheeks, earlobes, and shoulders). Indicate the different functions of body parts, and explain or demonstrate what each part does in a way the child will understand. If speech or signs are not useful, work with the communication teacher to adapt these activities to meet the child's communication needs.

Other important skills related to using body awareness for effective movement and walking include understanding how far body

## HELPING CHILDREN LEARN TO CREEP

Babies who are deaf-blind may often display a "stop-start" pattern of motor development. They sometimes learn to assume the positions necessary for dynamic gross motor activities but do not immediately take off and move about in these positions. Creeping is typical of this phenomenon. Many babies may assume the creeping position (up on all fours) but may be slow to crawl and creep. Some never creep forward, but go directly to walking.

Creeping is important for babies who are deaf-blind for many reasons (see Module 15). In creeping, children have raised their bodies off the floor, and their hands and knees are bearing the body's weight. In crawling, the body from the knees to the shoulders or chest is still mainly in contact with the ground, and the arms are used for forward movement, to pull the body along. Crawling precedes creeping, and it is important to guide children's development from crawling to creeping, which is significant in turn for development of such elements as isolated movement, rotation, strength, and coordination. Teachers have found the following innovative approach helpful for developing skills for creeping in deaf-blind infants, who may not have the external motivation that is offered by visual and auditory stimulation.

Fold a large terry-cloth towel to create a long rectangular sling. With the baby on all fours (in a creeping position), place the towel beneath the baby's abdomen, draw the ends of the towel together, and hold them. A gentle upward and forward movement of the towel positions the baby to lift the abdomen, bear weight on the palms and knees, and move forward. A favorite toy within the baby's reach is a good reward for moving forward and serves as a motivator for future movement (be sure the baby knows where the toy is). Another person can touch the baby to help him or her move forward and continue to prompt the baby from in front.

During this activity, you may need to reach down to position the baby's hands to bear weight on his or her palms. If the baby's fists are clenched, gently stroke the back of the baby's hands from the wrist to the fingers, so the baby will open the palms for weight bearing. It may also be helpful to work with another person who can help position the baby's limbs while you hold the towel. Consult with the infant's occupational therapist or physical therapist to integrate this approach into the baby's activities. ■

parts can reach and bend and knowing where the body fits as movement takes place. One activity for teaching these skills that is fun for a child is to adapt a large empty appliance carton as a special place the child can crawl in and out of. Cut "doorways" and "windows," cover the inside with wallpaper and carpet remnants, and put objects in it for the child to find and play with. A bolster can also be made by cutting a large fabric tube (available at fabric stores) into a two-foot piece and covering it with a heavy, padded, washable fabric. The child can roll the bolster around or prop it under his or her arms when lying on the stomach to keep the hands free and head up. Bolsters can also be purchased through catalogs for special toys.

Infants and toddlers may not be independent at this stage of their development, but they are able to use their movement experiences to gain an understanding of what is around them and how they fit into their surroundings. By moving them through the patterns of walking and giving them the assistance they need, parents and teachers can facilitate their development of more formal mobility skills and techniques. For example, you can introduce trailing to infants and toddlers long before they walk independently. (By placing their toys near a wall and allowing them to follow along the wall as they creep, you will build concepts related to shorelining, or following a border or edge, that they will use well into their adult lives.) (See Module 17 for definitions of concepts and techniques like trailing and shorelining.)

Once children can walk alone, they need more and more practice to become independent. When practical, encourage toddlers to go from place to place on their own. Although carrying young children to destinations may be quicker and easier, it does not teach them to move independently.

## Indoor Activities: Stair Climbing

A young child can be helped to learn how to climb stairs by having him or her grasp the handrail with one hand while facing straight up the stairs (do not let the child use two hands and pull himself or herself up the steps). Have the child place one foot on the first step, then bring the second foot up to the first step. Repeat until the child reaches the top of the staircase. The child should learn from the beginning that a person climbs all the way to the top or bottom and does not stop in the middle. Teach the child to go down stairs using the same procedure. Remember that this takes time and practice.

## Other Indoor Activities

Scooter boards on which children can ride while sitting and pushing with their legs or using their hands and feet while lying prone are fun and beneficial for developing motor skills and mobility concepts. Children can explore freely and cover quite a bit of territory on these toys while gaining time-distance, motion, and environmental awareness. Do not let children stand on scooters and be sure that all staircases are protected with secure guard gates. Standing on stools or boxes to reach things on countertops helps children begin to learn about heights, but establish clear rules about what the children may *not* use for climbing. Children will also enjoy pulling or pushing toys like wagons or doll carriages.

## Outdoor Activities

Walking outdoors can be scary for any young child, and children with hearing and visual impairments are no exception. Therefore, young children need constant encouragement and reassurance while being guided outdoors. One activity that can stimulate them to explore the environment is a "nature walk" in the yard or local park. Spend time at each "discovery" to allow the children to "landmark" the area. For example, place toys near one of the landmarks or near the edges of the yard, so the children can find them. Encouraging children to use trailing techniques will be useful here (see Module 17).

Another activity that is effective and appropriate is "Ring-Around-the-Rosy." Children love to hold your hands and spin around with you. Be sure to start slowly, and do not go so fast that the children lose control. Other children may join in the fun with adequate supervision. Still another activity is "Copy Cat," in which you and a child sit on the floor and the child copies what you are doing, or you copy what the child does. Start with simple activities like clapping or touching the top of your head and give hand-over-hand assistance until the child begins to initiate the activity. This game can be expanded to "Follow-the-Leader" when the child's skills increase, but to adapt the game for children who have no usable vision, you need to plan strategies for communicating information in the child's preferred communication mode.

Outdoors, encourage children to initiate the following playground activities: playing in the sandbox, swinging, climbing, sliding, balancing and crawling, hanging, riding the merry-go-round, or jumping rope.

## Safety

Parents need to safeguard against accidents in the home, and the following principles should always be kept in mind:

- Keep windows locked or open them from the top; do not trust a window screen to support a child's weight.
- Use window safety guards for windows on upper floors.

- Insist that all doors be kept completely open or closed.
- Put gates at the top of staircases to ensure that the child does not tumble down the stairs.
- Check with the local Red Cross chapter for more information about how to child-proof an area.

## Teaching O&M Skills and Techniques

Structuring the environment to provide consistency, introducing gross motor movements through exercises, and carrying out all the other activities described in this module are the foundation of a formal O&M program. Such programs and the basic O&M skills on which they focus are described in Modules 17 and 18.

Children need to be assisted to perform specific movements in order to understand O&M techniques and concepts. For toddlers and preschoolers, these techniques may include trailing; squaring off; and using toys, little canes, or other mobility devices as probes. Parents should introduce these techniques in conjunction with their children's teachers, O&M instructors, occupational therapists, and physical therapists (Pogrund, Fazzi, & Lampert, 1992).

Families and other educational team members need to consider individual needs when selecting travel tools for young children who are deaf-blind. Regardless of whether a child is visually impaired or has both a visual and a hearing loss, he or she still requires supervision when given objects to use as tools, such as canes, that may be used inappropriately. A cane can and should be introduced early in a child's program if it has been determined to be a necessary travel tool; however, the child's family needs to monitor its daily use (see Advantages of Using Canes with Preschoolers in this module).

Push toys with a secure base of support are an alternative to canes for children who do not have access to regular O&M instruc-

▲ *Push toys like this one can be used as mobility aids to probe the environment and act as safety bumpers.*

# Advantages of Using Canes with Preschoolers

Rona L. Pogrund

A qualified orientation and mobility (O&M) instructor, with input from other school personnel and parents, is the person to determine if a long cane is the most appropriate mobility device for a young deaf-blind child. The instructor also identifies appropriate instructional methods. It should not be assumed that because a child is of preschool age and is deaf-blind that a long cane is not an appropriate mobility tool. Many of the traditional arguments against the early introduction of long canes, such as young children's lack of motor coordination, maturity, and need, are not supported by actual work with young children. The early introduction of the long cane may significantly improve the motor, cognitive, and social development of young children who

are deaf-blind. The potential advantages of introducing the long cane to a child as early as age 2 or 3 include these:

- increased freedom of movement
- increased ability to explore the environment, which results in increased knowledge of the environment
- development of a more secure, natural gait and a more appropriate and relaxed posture
- increased stimulation of the vestibular system, which may result in a decreased need for self-stimulation
- potential for increased self-confidence and autonomy as the child appears more competent to others and is thereby treated more respectfully
- early acceptance of the long cane by the child, family, peers, and others. ■

tion or are not able to manage the safety requirements of canes. Other options for travel tools can be considered, including adapted travel tools, often called precanes or noncane devices. These tools, as well as push toys, probe the environment, provide information about the ground surface ahead, and serve as bumpers. (See Module 18 for additional information about canes and the other devices mentioned here.)

For an older child, sliding a hula hoop in front as a probe can be a useful technique. Part of the hoop touches the ground in front of the child, and since the hoop is generally wider than the child, it clears a safe path. Hula hoops have been modified and adapted by using polyvinyl chloride (PVC) piping material that can be purchased from hardware stores and can be fabricated by O&M instructors to meet individual needs. When adapted in this manner, they serve as precane devices.

By paying attention to the individual needs and characteristics of a child, parents, teachers, and other members of the child's educational team can help the child build a strong foundation from which to continue to develop O&M skills and the ability to move purposefully and more confidently in his or her environment. The following modules detail how these skills can be further encouraged.

# *REFERENCES*

Dodson-Burke, B., & Hill, E. W. (1989). *Preschool orientation and mobility screening.* Nashville, TN: George Peabody College of Vanderbilt University.

*Guide to toys for children who are blind or visually impaired.* (1994). New York: Toy Manufacturers of America and American Foundation for the Blind.

Leary, B., & von Schneden, M. (1982). *"Simon Says" is not the only game.* New York: American Foundation for the Blind.

Pogrund, R. L., Fazzi, D. L., & Lampert, J. S. (Eds.). (1992). *Early focus: Working with young blind and visually impaired children and their families.* New York: American Foundation for the Blind.

Raynor, S., & Drouillard, R. (1975). *Get a wiggle on: A guide for helping visually impaired children grow.* Mason, MI: Ingham Intermediate School District.

Zegers ten Horn, Henriette. (1988). *Touch toys and how to make them: Especially designed for the visually handicapped but also safe and suitable for all.* Rockville, MD: Touch Toys Inc.

**MODULE 16**

# Self~Study Questions

1. Young children who are deaf-blind benefit from daily routines and structures because
   a. they are easier for families and teachers.
   b. they help children anticipate upcoming activities.
   c. the children enjoy repetition.
   d. the children will otherwise be exposed to unsafe conditions.

2. When selecting a toy for a child who is deaf-blind, it is most important to consider
   a. the toy's size and color.
   b. the toy's cost.
   c. the child's visual, auditory, and tactile skills.
   d. the toy's texture.

3. All the following are examples of daily living activities that teach mobility skills and concepts except
   a. bathing.
   b. napping.
   c. accompanying families on shopping trips.
   d. playing.

4. Why is it important for children to have the opportunity to learn concepts about objects, their bodies, and the environment?
   a. These concepts are essential for learning mobility techniques.
   b. These concepts help children become motivated to move and explore.
   c. Without conceptual understanding, children will not be able to learn how common objects are used.
   d. Conceptual understanding reduces the chances that children who are deaf-blind will get lost or injured.

5. Movement exercises for young infants who are deaf-blind
   a. are valuable only as part of a physical therapy session.
   b. should be integrated into children's daily living routines.
   c. should be avoided at home because they can disrupt family life.
   d. may be too taxing for children with sensorimotor impairments.

6. The primary focus of movement experiences for toddlers is to
   a. encourage them to move purposefully and explore their surroundings.
   b. build strong muscles.
   c. teach them to walk on a variety of surfaces indoors and out.
   d. help them learn body-image concepts.

7. When youngsters who are deaf-blind are ready to walk up stairs, they should
   a. be restricted from doing so because it can be dangerous.
   b. use a sighted guide at all times.
   c. be taught to face straight ahead and hold the handrail with one hand only.
   d. practice stair climbing often each day.

8. Little canes, precane devices, and hula hoops
   a. are important mobility tools for every toddler who is deaf-blind.
   b. are dangerous for children under age 4.
   c. can be valuable tools to encourage free movement and exploration.
   d. are prescribed to improve the posture and gait of children who are deaf-blind.

*Answers to self-study questions for this module appear at the end of Unit 3.*

# Orientation and Mobility: Basic Concepts and Techniques

KATHLEEN MARY HUEBNER

- *Observe and assess the student's use of sensory information*

- *Develop a sensory training program*

- *Encourage body and environmental awareness*

- *Learn the sighted guide technique*

- *Become familiar with O&M procedures*

- *Reinforce the student's O&M skills*

The importance for a child's development and independence of the ability to move about purposefully has already been discussed in earlier modules. Just as the ability to communicate is vital for all of us, including people who are deaf-blind, so too is the ability to move about. Being oriented to the environment and able to move as independently as possible within it is a primary goal for students who are deaf-blind. This module provides basic information about orientation and mobility (O&M) that should enable anyone who works with deaf-blind students to help them develop O&M skills and participate in O&M programs.

# FUNDAMENTALS OF O&M INSTRUCTION

Can we move about without being familiar with our environments? Of course we can. The act of moving, or mobility, is not dependent on knowing where we are or where we are going. Are we at a greater risk of having accidents when we travel in unfamiliar areas? Probably so, because we are less likely to anticipate potential hazards.

If we are familiar with the areas in which we are moving, then we are oriented to the environment. If we notice things about unfamiliar environments (such as the location of the bathroom in relation to the entrance of a building) as we move through them, then we are orienting ourselves to the environment. If we notice other details in the environment and remember and use the information to assist us the next time we go to specific locations, then we have become oriented to the environment. Although we can move about without being oriented, our movement will be more purposeful, comfortable, independent, and safe if we know where we are, where we are going, and what we may expect on the way.

Families and teachers tell children to "stop, look both ways, and listen" before they cross streets. This set of actions constitutes a special procedure or mobility technique that is used to enhance children's safety. An entire body of procedures exists that, once taught, enables persons who are blind or visually impaired to get around the environment safely and efficiently. These procedures form the basis of O&M instruction. When taught formally, this involves sensory, concept, and motor development and the formation of O&M skills. Students who are deaf-blind need to learn various special techniques if they are to travel independently. Later sections of this module describe some of these techniques, and the modules that follow contain additional information on various aspects of O&M instruction for deaf-blind students.

In addition to the O&M techniques outlined in this module, people who are deaf-blind use a number of mobility tools to increase their independence and safety, such as canes, dog guides (dogs that are specifically trained to lead people who are blind or deaf-blind), and electronic devices (used alone or with a cane or a dog guide—see Electronic Travel Aids in Module 18). Each tool is used as an extension of the body to protect it and to provide information to the senses. Other mobility tools that may enhance the physical needs of some students include orthopedic canes and walkers, to support body weight, and wheelchairs.

# KEY COMPONENTS OF ORIENTATION SKILLS

Some of the key components of teaching students how to orient themselves in the environment are sensory training and training in the following areas: awareness of body image; conceptual, spatial, and environmental awareness; mental mapping; and rote and route travel. The following are definitions of some of the basic concepts involved in teaching orientation skills:

- *Awareness of body image*: knowledge of one's and others' body parts and their placement, functions, and relation to oneself, others, and a particular environment.

- *Clue*: an object or stimulus (a sound, odor, temperature change, or visual or tactile stimulus) that is not permanent in the environment but is useful for determining one's location and for establishing a line of travel. An example of a clue is the aroma of hot dogs from a roving street vendor's cart.

- *Conceptual awareness*: knowledge of the sizes, shapes, functions, positions, spatial relationships, and directions of objects in relation to oneself and the environment.

- *Cue*: an object or stimulus (a sound, odor, temperature change, or visual or tactile stimulus) that is permanently or predictably present in the natural environment and is used to determine one's position relative to other elements in the environment, to a line of travel, or to a specific location. An example of a cue is a stone wall at the entrance to a park.

- *Environmental awareness*: knowledge of predictable patterns, structures, and textures in indoor and outdoor environments and how they relate to each other.

- *Guideline-shoreline*: the border or edge of a sidewalk, grassline, or wall; the edge that marks the difference between one travel surface or another that is tactilely or visually discernible, such as the edge between the sidewalk and grass or the floor and the hallway wall.

- *Landmark*: any object, odor, sound, temperature, or visual or tactile cue that is recognized and is a permanent object in a certain location in the environment, for example, a bed, refrigerator, door frame, toy box, water fountain, or telephone booth.

- *Mobility*: the act of moving from place to place.

- *Mobility techniques*: a set of specific skills and strategies, developed for individuals who are visually impaired, deaf-blind, or have additional disabilities, that afford an individual safety while traveling.

- *Mobility tools*: canes, electronic and other devices, and dog guides that serve as extensions of one's senses to help one determine obstacles and changes in the terrain of the path of travel.

- *Orientation*: the process of becoming familiar with, establishing, and maintaining one's position and relationship to significant objects in the environment.

- *Sensory training*: a course of study in which one learns to be more receptive to sensory stimulation and to interpret and apply sensory information while carrying out daily activities.

## SENSORY TRAINING

Contrary to popular belief, individuals who are blind, deaf, or deaf-blind are not automatically more receptive to stimulation provided through their intact sensory systems, nor are they automatically better able to interpret subtle nuances of, the reasons for, or the meaning of sensory stimuli. For example, as a 6-year-old girl who is deaf-blind walks along a concrete sidewalk in a small seashore business district shopping for souvenirs with her father, she may not notice changes in the texture of the sidewalk's surface as she crosses narrow patches of asphalt. Although she may notice that every so often a cool sea breeze blows from the right, she may not understand why there are intermittent breezes or associate them with the concurrent changes in the sidewalk's surface. The change in the surface texture from concrete to asphalt and changes in the temperature and flow of air are cues that there may be an alley or a narrow, intersecting street. The meaning of sensory input that is perceived, and whether it indicates information that is helpful for orientation or potential danger to be avoided, needs to be recognized and interpreted, so appropriate O&M techniques can be applied to ensure safe travel.

To be useful, sensory cues—whether auditory (hearing), visual (seeing), olfactory (smelling), gustatory (tasting), or tactile-kinesthetic-thermal (feeling)—must be recognized, identified, interpreted, and applied (see Module 15 for related information). The primary senses that a deaf-blind person uses for purposeful movement in both familiar and unfamiliar environments are the tactile-kinesthetic-thermal. The sense of taste is the only sense that is not generally applied for purposeful movement. The other senses, including usable hearing and vision, should be applied as much as possible. Even the sense of smell can be helpful for orientation, for example, to identify stores, such as bakeries or shoe repair shops, while walking through a shopping mall. The use of all possible senses adds to one's awareness of the environment, which increases one's pleasure and ability to interact with it.

Travelers who are deaf-blind usually need to combine several sensory cues to learn about new environments or to maintain orientation in familiar areas. For example, a deaf-blind student may first use the tactile sense to notice a change in the surface texture of a floor at the recessed entrance of a shoe store in a business district. He may then use the thermal sense to feel warm air coming from the store, and as he turns and locates the door, to recognize the long entrance-way that is common to shoe stores. On entering the store, he may use the olfactory sense to smell the leather and rubber, verifying that the place is indeed the shoe store. The student needs to be receptive to sensory cues of all types, identify them, interpret their meanings, and use them to move purposefully.

Teaching students who are deaf-blind how to maximize the use of their senses involves the provision of individualized instructional programs in sensory training. Such programs can be team taught by all the student's teachers, as well as family members, but they must be coordinated. The first step in setting up such a program is a thorough assessment of how each of a student's senses functions. In addition to obtaining and interpreting clinical measures and information, evaluating a student's use of sensory cues in many different environments is essential. Table 17–1 presents a sensory training list that identifies the major sensory skills that are generally taught by O&M instructors, along with other special education teachers and other members of the transdisciplinary team. Along with the information presented in the Functional Sensory Assessment in this module, this sensory training list can be used as a guide to observe and determine a student's sensory abilities. A basic principle to follow is the importance of observing a student's receptivity to different sensory cues as the student interacts in a number of settings and while he or she is performing various tasks and engaging in play activities.

Observe the student to determine the sensory information he or she is receiving, how the student is responding, and the sensory information the student is not using but needs to use. The reception, interpretation, and use of some types of sensory information (such as the recognition of temperature changes) that are important cues to a deaf-blind traveler may be difficult to observe. Strategies to ensure a thorough assessment include interviews with the student, family members, and teachers; a review of clinical assessments and the results of criterion-referenced assessments (see Module 11); and observations conducted in a variety of settings.

The use of one or two strategies will not be sufficient. For example, although a clinical ophthalmological or optometric report may indicate that the student has light perception, the student's family may report that he or she performs some activities that suggest more than light perception. Therefore, additional interviews, observations at home and in school, and criterion-referenced assessments should be conducted to determine the student's potential functional vision (Barraga, 1976, 1980; Corn, 1989; Roessing, 1982).

Following a thorough assessment, the next step is to develop an individualized program of sensory training instruction and include it in the student's Individualized Education Program (IEP)(see the other modules in this unit for tips on sensory training

**TABLE 17-1:**

List of Sensory Training Behaviors and Skills

| | |
|---|---|
| **STUDENT'S USE OF THE TACTILE-KINESTHETIC-THERMAL SENSES** | 1. Identifies shape and form.<br>2. Identifies texture.<br>3. Estimates size.<br>4. Estimates weight.<br>5. Identifies temperature changes.<br>6. Identifies indoor travel surfaces.<br>7. Identifies outdoor travel surfaces.<br>8. Identifies gradient changes.<br>9. Makes accurate turns.<br>10. Recognizes acceleration.<br>11. Recognizes deceleration.<br>12. Estimates distances while walking.<br>13. Estimates time.<br>14. Estimates time-distance while riding in vehicles. |
| **STUDENT'S USE OF THE CHEMICAL SENSES (OLFACTORY AND GUSTATORY)** | 1. Identifies familiar odors.<br>2. Locates source or direction of odors.<br>3. Identifies dangerous odors, such as natural gas and spoiled foods.<br>4. Identifies familiar tastes. |
| **STUDENT'S USE OF THE AUDITORY SENSE** | **DIRECT SOUNDS (INDOORS AND OUTDOORS)**<br>Direct sounds are sound waves that come directly and unaltered to an individual's ear without intervening doors, buildings, or large objects. A sound is direct when there is nothing between the produced sound and the listener.<br>1. Recognizes the presence of stationary sounds.<br>2. Identifies familiar stationary sounds.<br>3. Localizes stationary sounds.<br>4. Locates dropped objects.<br>5. Selects a direct sound from a group of unlike sounds.<br>6. Selects a direct sound from a group of like sounds (such as a familiar voice from many voices).<br>7. Estimates the distance to stationary sounds.<br>8. Identifies moving sounds.<br>9. Tracks moving sounds.<br>10. Analyzes intersections.<br><br>**INDIRECT SOUNDS (INDOORS AND OUTDOORS)**<br>Indirect sounds are sound waves that come to an individual's ear after they have been modified by intervening obstacles, such as closed doors and large buildings. They are sounds that move around or through objects before they are heard by the listener.<br><br>*(continued)* |

**TABLE 17-1:**
Continued

| | |
|---|---|
| | 1. Identifies an indirect sound.<br>2. Localizes an indirect sound.<br>3. Selects an indirect sound from a group of unlike sounds.<br>4. Selects an indirect sound from a group of like sounds (such as a familiar voice).<br>5. Estimates the distance to indirect sounds.<br><br>**REFLECTED SOUNDS (INDOORS AND OUTDOORS)**<br>Reflected sounds are sound waves that come to a listener's ear after they have contacted an object and bounced back to the listener. These sounds have an echolike quality.<br>1. Identifies changes between open and closed areas.<br>2. Localizes open and closed areas.<br>3. Estimates the depth of open areas.<br>4. Estimates the size of rooms. |
| **STUDENT'S USE OF THE VISUAL SENSE** | 1. Visually attends to a stimulus.<br>2. Identifies familiar stationary objects at near distance.<br>3. Describes stationary objects at near distance.<br>4. Describes details of stationary objects at near distance.<br>5. Tracks moving objects at near distance.<br>6. Discriminates among a set of stimuli.<br>7. Identifies familiar stationary objects at far distance.<br>8. Describes stationary objects at far distance.<br>9. Describes details of stationary objects at far distance.<br>10. Tracks moving vehicles at far distance. |

SOURCE: *Adapted from J.A. Kimbrough, K.M. Huebner, & L.J. Lowry,* Sensory Training: A Curriculum Guide, *Bridgeville, PA: Greater Pittsburgh Guild for the Blind, 1976; and Leon County School System,* A Resource Manual for the Development and Evaluation of Special Programs for Exceptional Children: Volume V–H, Part 1, *Tallahassee: State of Florida Department of Education, 1985.*

in motor development and early childhood and in classroom and community programs). Because sensory information is used in all activities of daily life, all members of the transdisciplinary educational team will be involved in providing sensory training. Therefore, it is necessary to indicate which member of the team will be responsible for providing instruction in specific sensory skills and to establish an effective system for communicating the student's progress to other team members.

# Functional Sensory Assessment

George J. Zimmerman

Not all children who are deaf-blind are totally deaf and totally blind. Therefore, for teaching orientation and mobility (O&M) skills and techniques, it is important to conduct an ecologically sound *functional assessment* of a student's sensory abilities. This assessment will help the team develop appropriate instructional strategies to enhance the student's use of residual sensory input. The important areas to assess are the student's daily environments and his or her use of visual, auditory, and tactile skills. The following are general guidelines for conducting sensory assessments, and they are followed by guidelines for specific areas:

● Conduct assessments in the natural context of daily routines.

● View sensory functioning as a total picture, not just as a collection of individual skills.

● Assess sensory skills by watching how the student uses and responds to sensory information as he or she moves through the environment.

## Assessing the Daily Environment

● Determine if the environment is simple and organized or cluttered.

● Note the lighting conditions. Are they bright or dim? Do they contain shadows or glare? Do they change significantly over the course of the day?

● Note the presence and location of obstacles, protrusions, and steps.

● Note the presence and source of ordinary ambient sounds and special sounds (such as a fire alarm). Also note sounds that may interfere with the student's ability to hear at certain locations, such as the noise of a ventilating fan in the ceiling above a work table.

● Note the characteristic textures of objects and places in the environment, for example, the floor of the exercise room is carpeted, the toys are furry, and the classroom floor is smooth.

## Assessing Visual Skills

● Imagine the environment from the perspective of the student's height and position relative to it.

● Observe visual functioning while the student is stationary, when the student is in motion, and when objects are moving toward or away from the student.

● Observe the student's visual performance in areas that are both familiar and unfamiliar to the student.

● Observe the student's visual performance under a variety of lighting conditions and when the student moves from one lighting condition (such as a brightly illuminated area) to another (such as a dim or dark area).

● Observe the student's visual performance in cluttered, unstructured settings and in structured settings.

● Observe the student's skills in judging distances and depth, including the ability to locate landmarks or avoid obstacles; reach for objects; and negotiate stairs, curbs, and cracks in the floor or sidewalk.

● Observe whether the student exhibits a con-

*(continued)*

sistent pattern of visual performance, that is, whether the student consistently makes contact with obstacles on a particular side of the body, experiences problems with obstacles underfoot, performs well in bright or dim light, and so forth.

### Assessing Auditory Skills

• Observe the student's auditory skills in quiet places, as well as in environments with ordinary noise and unusual amounts of noise.

• Observe the student's auditory functioning while the student is stationary, when the student is in motion, and when sound sources are moving toward or away from the student.

• Observe the student's performance in areas that are both familiar and unfamiliar to the student.

• Observe the manner in which the student uses visual input to support his or her auditory performance.

• Observe the student's skills in recognizing common sounds, such as a door closing, a car horn blaring, or water running.

• Observe the student's skills in localizing the source of a sound, in judging distance from sound cues, in walking toward a sound, and in following a moving source of sound.

### Assessing Tactile Skills

• Observe the student's skills in recognizing and identifying common textures (rough, smooth, slippery, and the like).

• Observe the student's skills in associating textures with common daily objects and places (for example, a toy is silky, the floor is cool tile, and the brick wall outside the school is rough).

• Observe the student's skills in using tactile cues as landmarks in travel (for instance, the bench is located at the end of the grassy lawn). ■

## AWARENESS OF BODY IMAGE

The first thing that infants explore, touch, and feel is their own bodies; while lying in their cribs, infants play with their hands and toes, grasp them, try to put them in their mouths, and sometimes succeed. In addition, their parents play such games with them as "this is a nose: touch your nose, and then mommy's nose" and "Simon Says" that teach babies about their body parts (where they are, how they work, what they can and cannot do, and how they are the same or different from other people's).

Knowledge of one's body is central to learning about other things. As babies learn about their bodies, family members, friends, and teachers build on that knowledge to teach additional concepts about movement, direction, measurement, spatial relationships, and environments (Swallow & Huebner, 1987). An instructional program in awareness of body image should include the identification of parts of the body and their location; planes; movements; position in relation to the child, others, and the environment; direction; laterality; directionality; and movement through space.

## CONCEPTUAL, SPATIAL, AND ENVIRONMENTAL AWARENESS

A concept is a mental representation, image, or idea of concrete objects (houses, airplanes, fires, and human beings), as well as intangible ideas (feelings, attitudes, movement, and space). The three basic stages in the development of concepts are concrete, functional, and abstract.

▲ *Helping young children become aware of parts of their bodies through the use of tactile stimulation contributes to the development of movement.*

When children who are deaf-blind are taught and understand concepts, they can discriminate between the similarities and differences of objects and intangible ideas and start to categorize information. A child fully understands and incorporates a concept when he or she uses it in many daily living activities, whether or not the child knows how to describe it.

Deaf-blind students are taught to use a variety of spatial, environmental, and community concepts to organize information about the environments and their positions in them. These concepts include above, below, over, under, side, back, right, left, inside, outside, inch, foot, yard, wall, floor, ceiling, curb, ramp, driveway, alley, street, intersections with stop signs or traffic lights, four-point or plus-shaped intersections, city block, small business district, mall, shopping center, playground, park, and highway (Swallow & Huebner, 1987). Students may understand these concepts without having full language facility.

It is possible to move purposefully without a complete understanding of environmental concepts. For example, if children desire something in the environment, they may move toward it and reach their goal. They do not need to understand right, left, behind, chair, carpet, and so on to get to where they wish to go. However, such concepts are needed to understand and follow directions, plan routes and alternate routes, and understand when to apply travel techniques to ensure safe and independent travel.

## MENTAL MAPPING

Have you ever had the following experience? A friend says, "I'll meet you at the theater," and you respond, "I have no idea how to get there." Then your friend says, "But we've been there dozens of times," and you answer, "But I didn't drive, and when I don't drive, I don't pay attention to where I'm going." This scenario is common. When drivers are behind the wheel, they pay close attention to potential dangers, landmarks, route numbers, the number of blocks they must travel before a turn, and so forth. When people are not driving, they are often so busy chatting that they do not pay attention to routes. The same phenomenon takes place among students who are deaf-blind. When they travel with others who are guiding them, they may not pay attention to where they are going, but when they travel independently, they must pay attention to identify and sequence landmarks and cues.

Deaf-blind students do not, however, count the steps in every route and objective. No one could remember this kind of information. Not only can students not remember how many steps there are in all the routes they travel (some students may not fully grasp concepts of number), but even if they could, they could not count every step and still be attentive to other clues. Students who are deaf-blind need to be taught to make and practice using mental maps of how to get to their objectives. They need to be taught to review the direction in which they wish to go and what they will pass on the routes and in which order. As they travel to their objective, they also need to learn to review the route mentally, anticipate and then recognize landmarks, mentally check off the ones they have passed, and continue to anticipate those that are still to come. This mental mapping requires them to use their knowledge of environmental concepts and concentration.

## ROTE AND ROUTE TRAVEL

Most of us are route travelers, that is, we can travel one way to an objective, but feel comfortable taking a different route or varying the route, if necessary, when we travel again to that location. Even in foreign countries, we can vary our routes; if a fire truck is blocking the entrance to the street on which our hotel is located, for example, we know we can go around the block and enter the hotel from the back. We can reverse routes and develop alternate routes because we understand the basic concepts of developed environments: the structure of city blocks and their relationships to each other, the relationships between parallel and perpendicular streets, the shapes of T and Y intersections and cross streets, and so forth.

Children who are deaf-blind need to learn the concepts involved in traveling, as well as mobility techniques, before they can reverse routes and develop and use alternate routes. While they are learning spatial and environmental concepts, they are often rote travelers, that is, the only routes they know to objectives are the ones they have specifically learned. Some children, particularly those who are cognitively impaired, are stymied when they come across barriers on learned routes, as was the case with Jenny.

> Jenny, a teenager who is deaf-blind and cognitively impaired, learned to walk to a convenience store and purchase small items. This activity gave her great pleasure because she recognized her responsibility and contribution to the family and was proud of her accomplishment. When she left her home, she would turn left onto the sidewalk and proceed to the market, crossing an alley on the way.
>
> One day her grandmother asked her to go to the store to buy a pound of butter. It had snowed that morning, and when Jenny got to the first alley, there was a pile of snow, 6 inches wide and 12 inches high, which the snow plow had left when it plowed the alley before it turned onto the street. Jenny located the barrier of snow with her cane and repeatedly explored its width, height, and length. However, she could not solve the problem of how to get around it, nor was she able to conclude that she could step over it and continue on her way. After trying to work out the problem for some time, she turned around and went home.
>
> Jenny needed to understand that she could climb over or around the mound of snow and then continue walking. She also needed to know the environment beyond her learned route; for example, whether the alley intersected the other side

*of the parallel street. Jenny had many alternatives but had not learned another route.*

Children become route travelers, rather than rote travelers, when they are taught concepts needed to plan alternative routes. Paying attention to alternatives also helps them learn to solve problems and increase their potential for independence.

# TECHNIQUES FOR INDOOR TRAVEL

Several mobility techniques can be used to provide the student who is deaf-blind with a means of safe travel indoors; among them are the sighted guide technique (often used outdoors as well), self-protective techniques (sometimes referred to as hand and forearm techniques), and the diagonal cane technique. The touch technique, described in the next section on techniques for outdoor travel, is used in both unfamiliar indoor areas and outdoors. (You may find it helpful to go through the motions of these procedures as you read this section and to refer to the module that follows for more information on how the procedures can be adapted and performed.)

## SIGHTED GUIDE TECHNIQUE

The sighted guide technique facilitates fast and efficient travel. This technique requires the participation of a sighted person, who serves as the guide to the deaf-blind person and therefore is always in the forward position. The procedure is as follows:

1. The sighted person approaches the student who is deaf-blind, makes contact with the student, and identifies himself or herself in the student's primary communication mode, using the signal or sign that identifies him or her.

2. The student acknowledges the presence of the sighted guide.

3. The two communicate about where they are going and the route they will follow. The sighted guide may use a gentle physical cue (such as a tap on the back of the student's hand), together with the spoken or signed communication "take my arm" or "come with me," to indicate to the student that movement is to begin.

4. The student puts his or her hand in a C position (the thumb to the outside and the four fingers to the inside of the guide's arm), and grasps the guide's arm just above the elbow (or the wrist if the student is small). The student keeps his or her grasping arm tucked beside the body, with the elbow bent at a 90-degree angle to maintain a distance of a one-half step behind the guide.

5. The guide keeps his or her guiding arm tucked close to the body, so the shoulder of the student's gripping arm is directly behind the shoulder of the guide's arm.

6. The student's grip should be firm enough to maintain contact and be comfortable for the guide and the student.

▲ *The sighted guide position enables students to travel fast and efficiently by following the movements of the guide.*

7. Before the sighted guide leaves the student, he or she should let the student know their location and place the student's hand on a recognizable object, wall, chair, or other concrete feature.

The student learns to follow a guide's movement by walking along with the guide and feeling the movement. As the guide starts and stops, changes pace, steps up or down at curbs and stairs, walks through narrow or congested areas, passes through doorways, or shows the student a seat, the student feels the guide's activity and follows. The guide hesitates briefly to indicate significant changes in the pace, direction, or terrain of travel, such as ramps, curbs, and stairs. The pause, which can be paired with a simple message or other signal, allows the student to anticipate the change in movement and to react accordingly. Procedures for switching sides, for traveling through narrow passageways and doorways and on stairs, and for seating follow.

## Switching Sides

When a sighted guide and a student who is deaf-blind are walking, it is sometimes advantageous for the student to be on the opposite side of the guide when, for example, the only railing for the stairway is on the guide's side. In such situations, the guide should communicate with the student to transfer sides. If the student is on the right side of the guide, the procedure is as follows: Starting from the basic position (holding onto the guide's right arm with his or her left hand), the student takes his or her right hand and grasps the guide's right arm, for a moment, in both hands. The student then steps behind the guide and grasps the guide's left arm first with the left hand and then with the right hand. Next, the student releases his or her left hand and resumes the normal sighted guide position, but on the opposite side of the guide's body. This procedure assures physical contact between the guide and the student. (The guide may then direct the student's hand to the start of the railing, rather than stop to communicate by signing again or using another type of signal.)

## Narrow Passageways

When the sighted guide is approaching an area that is too narrow or crowded for the student and guide to move through side by side, the guide sharply moves the guiding arm back behind his or her body and rests the back of the knuckles in the small of his or her back. At this point, the student moves his or her grasping hand to the guide's wrist without losing contact. The student also straightens the arm and adjusts it toward the center of the body, so he or she is a full step and directly behind the sighted guide. After they pass through the narrow passageway, the guide returns the guiding arm to the normal position, and the student does the same, while sliding the grasping hand from the guides' wrist to his or her upper arm, taking care not to lose contact with the guide.

## Doors

When preparing to pass through a doorway, the student is positioned on the side of the doorway to which the door is hinged because this position facilitates smooth movement and safety while approaching the door. The guide pauses and communicates to the student that they are about to go through a door and tells the student if the door opens on the right or left and whether it is a push or a pull door. This information permits the student to prepare to transfer sides, if necessary, and provides a cue about whether to hold the door open before (pull door) or after (push door) moving through it. As they move through the door, the student moves his or her free arm to hold the door open while passing through and then removes the arm from the door to avoid getting fingers caught in the space between the door frame and the door. (The sighted guide may wish to help the student monitor this action also.)

## Stairways

When approaching ascending or descending stairs, the guide approaches them as directly as possible, with the student on the side closest to the railing, and pauses. The student then locates the railing, feels the edge of the stairs with his or her feet, and places the free hand on the railing. The student waits to proceed until after the guide has taken the first step, so the student is one step behind the guide. On reaching the landing, the guide takes one step forward and pauses to signal the student that he or she is at the end of the stairs and to provide room for the student to stand on the landing next to him or her before proceeding forward. It is not necessary to count and communicate the number of stairs.

## Seating

The guide approaches a chair and communicates with the student that they are at a chair—and at the front, side, or back of the seat. The guide then places his or her guiding arm on the chair so the student can release his or her grip and follow along the guide's arm to contact the chair. If the guide brings a student to the front of a seat, the student is positioned so his or her legs are in contact with the seat. The student uses the back of the hand to determine that the seat is clear. If the seat is approached from the rear or the side, the guide places the student's hand on the furniture, and the student follows its structure to the seat. This procedure gives the student the opportunity to become familiar with the type of chair before he or she actually sits in it. The student then checks that the seat is clear of objects before sitting down.

▲ *When ascending or descending stairs with a sighted guide, students position themselves near the stair railing and one step behind the guide for maximum safety.*

## SELF-PROTECTIVE TECHNIQUES

### Upper Hand and Forearm Technique

The upper hand and forearm technique is sometimes used for protection while traveling in familiar indoor environments. It is meant to protect the upper body from objects that would contact the body from the waist up, such as a wall-mounted pay telephone. In this technique, one forearm is extended in front of the body at shoulder height, held horizontally across the body, with the elbow bent at an obtuse angle, the palm turned outward, and the fingertips in line with the opposite shoulder.

### Lower Hand and Forearm Technique

The lower hand and forearm technique is used when the traveler anticipates obstacles that would contact the body at the waist and below, such as a floor-based water cooler. In this technique, the arm is used to protect the lower body (groin area). To protect the lower body, one arm is extended diagonally down across and away from the body, with the inside of the upper arm maintaining contact with the side of the chest and the palm of the hand turned toward the body.

## TRAILING

Trailing affords protection and aids orientation. It helps the student recognize where he or she is, locate specific objects, and maintain a line of direction because when one trails, one stays in direct contact with objects in the environment. Trailing is generally done with one arm while the other arm is in either the upper or lower hand and forearm technique.

The student gets into a trailing position by standing a comfortable distance away from the trailing surface, with the shoulder a few inches from the surface—generally a wall, but it can be the edge of any surface, such as a table or a kitchen counter. The student then extends the trailing arm forward at hip level, keeping the inside of the upper arm against the side of the chest area, and makes contact with the surface to be trailed with the back of the hand that is closer to the surface. The fingers of the trailing arm are kept slightly curled inward, so they are not jammed into objects projecting from the wall. The student walks

▲ *Trailing can be done while using a cane. This little girl is maintaining contact with the wall for protection and orientation.*

along, maintaining contact with the surface area and noting objects and clues in the environment. Modified trailing techniques are often used by students who are deaf-blind and use wheelchairs (see Module 18).

## ALIGNMENT

Alignment is a procedure by which students position themselves laterally to an object or a sound. For example, they may follow a wall with one hand, aligning or positioning themselves with the wall to one side, so when they come to an intersecting hallway in front of them, they have established a line of direction. Alignment enhances their ability to continue forward across the open area, in a straight line, without the wall at one side, and to contact the other side of the intersecting hallway. Therefore, it reduces the probability that students may veer to one side or the other and the extent to which they do. Students who have the ability to discriminate fine auditory differences can use the sound of parallel traffic to align themselves for straight street crossings when they use this technique outdoors.

## SQUARING OFF

Squaring off is used to establish a line of direction, usually perpendicular to an object. In this technique, students position their bodies squarely against the object. For example, by placing his or her back against the front left-hand side of the teacher's desk, a student can be positioned directly in front of his or her work station. As the student steps away from the teacher's desk, having squared off with it, the student can independently locate his or her work station while moving forward.

## SYSTEMATIC SEARCH PATTERNS

The use of systematic search patterns is an approach to locating or determining the position of an object or a landmark. For example, if a student drops a hairbrush, he or she squats and then kneels down and makes larger and larger concentric circles on the floor with the hand. If the brush is not located, the student makes another series of circles, overlapping the first series, and continues to do so until the brush is found.

Systematic search patterns can also be used to orient oneself to larger environments, such as a room, a school, a house, a community center, a mall, or an entire community. The student determines a starting or focal point that can be easily identified, such as a doorway or entrance to a room. He or she then travels around the perimeter of the room, familiarizes himself or herself with the central parts of the room, and determines their relationships to the focal point or perimeter, using newly learned landmarks.

## SELF-FAMILIARIZATION

Self-familiarization is the ability to become acquainted with a new or unfamiliar environment in an organized way. For instance, a student may become familiar with the bathroom of a friend's house by trailing the bathroom wall in an organized fashion, locating the toilet, toilet paper, sink, soap dish, and towel rack. Although the bathroom may have other fixtures, the student may not need to use them, so the degree of self-familiarization will depend on those parts of the bathroom that the student needs to use.

## DIAGONAL CANE TECHNIQUE

The diagonal cane technique was designed to be used in familiar indoor areas. In this technique, the student holds the cane in one hand with the arm extended and the inside of the upper arm touching the side of the chest. The cane is positioned diagonally across the body, and the tip of the cane slides across the floor in front of the student. When traveling on carpeted areas, the student holds the tip of the cane up slightly from the surface so the tip will not catch on the carpeting; in this position, the cane serves solely as a bumper. When the cane tip comes into contact with something, such as a door that has been left ajar, the student is protected from bumping into it. When the cane tip is on the travel surface, it will slide off the edge of a descending flight of stairs and alert the student that there is a drop-off. In trailing with a cane, the student keeps the tip of the cane against the wall baseboard, thus maintaining orientation by maintaining contact with the wall.

# TECHNIQUES FOR OUTDOOR TRAVEL

Because of safety and liability issues, teaching individuals who are deaf-blind strategies for safe travel in outdoor areas should be left to the O&M instructor. However, the educational team is involved in assessments, decisions about the program, and reinforcement activities.

Individuals who are deaf-blind use sighted guides, canes, electronic travel aids (ETAs), and dog guides for outdoor travel. Sighted guide techniques are the same for indoor and outdoor areas. The cane technique used for outdoor travel or while traveling in unfamiliar indoor areas is called the touch technique. In this technique, the individual extends his or her preferred arm, which is holding the cane, away from the body and with the wrist centered in relation to the body. By moving the wrist, the person alternately moves the cane from side to side, slightly above the travel surface, touching down to the surface a few inches beyond the width of his or her shoulder. The tip of the cane is slightly elevated, and it moves across in front of the body and touches to the right and left side. The cane serves as a bumper to obstacles, protecting the user from the waist down, and alerts the user to tactile and gradient changes in travel surfaces. The major shortcoming of the cane is that it does not protect the user from the waist up; this is why self-protective techniques are important.

A variety of ETAs are available. Some are used with the cane, some are mounted on the cane, and others are used alone by individuals with visual impairments or deaf-blindness (see Electronic Travel Aids in the next module). Some travelers who are deaf-blind use dog guides after being trained at one of several dog guide training schools. These schools have specific entry requirements; one is that the dog guide user must be sufficiently mature to maintain a working relationship with and care for a dog.

These basic O&M techniques are taught by specially trained and certified service providers. The roles of these individuals are critical for teaching safe outdoor travel techniques.

# O&M SERVICES

## PROVISION OF SERVICES

O&M instructors generally teach one person who is deaf-blind at a time. Because the O&M profession was originally developed to teach people who are blind, O&M instructors are hired primarily to work in programs for individuals who are blind or visually impaired (see How to Find an O&M Instructor in Module 4 for more information). Therefore, they are usually employed as full-time faculty by residential schools for blind children, by large public day schools or school districts in which children with visual impairments have been identified, and by agencies that mainly serve blind adults. In a geographic area in which few children need O&M services, school districts frequently collaborate and employ an O&M instructor who teaches all the children in the area who need O&M instruction. Some O&M instructors work as private consultants.

The O&M instructor frequently provides services through an itinerant model. After a thorough assessment of the student's needs, he or she develops short- and long-range goals and provides instruction based on the needs identified. For example, the instructor may provide instruction every day to some students or three times a week or even less frequently to others, depending on the students' individual needs.

In some situations, O&M instructors spend a greater percentage of their time instructing other teachers, family members, O&M assistants (OMAs), or other service providers than students who are deafblind. This service delivery model may be used for a variety of reasons, such as students' needs or the absence of O&M services. For example, in remote rural Alaska, an O&M instructor may have to travel hundreds of miles by plane to visit a student and stay in the student's home village for a week or more, but may do so only for three or four times during the academic year. In this situation, he or she may, following an assessment of the student, spend more time teaching other teachers and family members how to teach the student a specific set of skills and may videotape the lessons with all involved so they can be reviewed in his or her absence. Between visits, the O&M instructor maintains contact with other members of the educational team via telephone and the mail.

## SERVICE ROLES

### The O&M Instructor

The O&M instructor is responsible for assessing a student's short- and long-range mobility needs; developing a plan of instruction; providing instruction; evaluating the student's performance in O&M; and communicating with the student, the student's parents, and teachers and other service providers. The vast majority of O&M instructors have master's degrees in O&M; others have bachelor's degrees or have been trained at agencies that serve blind or visually impaired persons (Uslan, Hill, & Peck, 1989). Since certification as an O&M instructor is not mandatory for professional practice in most states, few states offer state certification in O&M. However, most public schools require O&M teachers to meet other types of state certification requirements for teachers (Huebner & Strumwasser, 1987). Therefore, the majority of O&M instructors are certified in such areas as special education, rehabilitation teaching, or elementary or secondary education. Many are certified both as teachers of children who are blind or visually impaired and as O&M instructors. Professional certification as an O&M instructor is available through the Association for Education and Rehabilitation of the Blind and Visually Impaired (AER), an international organization of service providers (see Resources).

O&M instructors may be referred to as O&M specialists, O&M teachers, or peripatologists—the terms are interchangeable. There are over 160 competencies that O&M instructors are expected to have, which fall under several goal areas: concept development, O&M skills and techniques, assessment, instructional methods and strategies, sensory-motor development, psychosocial aspects, human growth and development, systems of O&M, history, philosophy of O&M, program development, supervision, and professional information (Uslan et al., 1989).

## The Orientation and Mobility Assistant (OMA)

The OMA is a paid employee who receives training from an O&M instructor and provides selected O&M services under the direction and supervision of an O&M instructor. The role of the OMA is to monitor a student's practice of indoor mobility skills. The use of an OMA helps ensure shorter intervals between practice sessions for the student and increases the frequency of skill-reinforcing sessions. The O&M Division of AER offers a training program for OMAs. It recommends that OMAs have a minimum of a high school diploma, although an associate's degree and experience with persons with disabilities are preferred (Wiener & Hill, 1991).

## Families and Caregivers

Parents, family members, and other caregivers are essential to the development of mobility among children who are deaf-blind. These are the individuals who spend the most time with the children and share thousands of experiences and opportunities for growth. Families and caregivers need to encourage exploration and reinforce the formal mobility strategies and techniques.

## The Transdisciplinary Team

The members of the transdisciplinary educational team are also vital to the development of mobility. They need to know what the student is learning, what the student knows and does not know, what they should and should not expect at any time regarding the student's independent mobility, and the mobility techniques the student is using and practicing. The entire educational team should be involved in all aspects of the student's O&M program and encourage the student to use newly acquired independent skills. Through the coordinated efforts of team members and those who live and work with the student, enhanced O&M skills and greater independence and self-assurance for the student can result.

# *REFERENCES*

Barraga, N. C. (1976). *Visual handicaps and learning: A developmental approach.* Belmont, CA.: Wadsworth.

Barraga, N. C. (1980). *Program to develop efficiency in visual function.* Louisville, KY: American Printing House for the Blind.

Corn, A. (1989). Instruction in the use of vision for children and adults with low vision: A proposed program model. *RE:View, 21* (1), 26–38.

Huebner, K. M., & Strumwasser, K. P. (1987). State certification of teachers of blind and visually impaired students: Report of a national study. *Journal of Visual Impairment & Blindness, 81,* 244–250.

Roessing, L. J. (1982). Functional vision: Criterion-referenced checklists. In S. S. Mangold (Ed.), *A teachers' guide to the special educational needs of blind and visually handicapped children* (pp. 35–52). New York: American Foundation for the Blind.

Swallow, R. M., & Huebner, K. M. (Eds.). (1987). *How to thrive, not just survive: A guide to developing independent life skills for blind and visually impaired children and youths.* New York: American Foundation for the Blind.

Uslan, M. M., Hill, E. W., & Peck, A. F. (1989). *The profession of orientation and mobility in the 1980s: The AFB competency study.* New York: American Foundation for the Blind.

Wiener, W., & Hill, E. W. (1991). *Orientation and mobility assistant curriculum manual.* Alexandria, VA: Association for Education and Rehabilitation of the Blind and Visually Impaired.

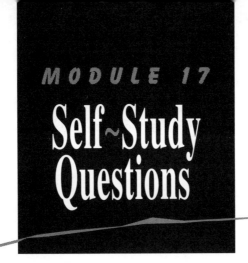

# Self~Study Questions

1. Objects that are relatively permanent and can be used as cues and landmarks that facilitate the recognition of where one is in the environment include
   a. chair, couch, and lawn mower.
   b. chair, couch, and stove.
   c. sink, chair, and stove.
   d. sink, toilet, and stove.

2. Which of the following strategies should be used when assessing the sensory abilities of students who are deaf-blind?
   a. Observation and interviews.
   b. Formal clinical measures.
   c. Criterion-referenced tests.
   d. a, b, and c.

3. To be a route traveler, you need to
   a. count all your steps.
   b. understand basic concepts of developed environments.
   c. memorize street names as they relate to compass directions.
   d. b and c.

4. When guiding a student who is deaf-blind, the sighted person should
   a. be in front of the student.
   b. walk slowly.
   c. be to the left of the student.
   d. a and b.

5. Using the back of a hand to trail surfaces is done to
   a. follow a specified route without getting lost.
   b. recognize places in the environment, maintain a line of direction, remain in physical contact with the environment, and protect the body.
   c. prevent one from falling down stairs.
   d. all the above.

6. When a student places his or her back against a wall to establish a line of direction before crossing the room to the computer station, the technique he or she is using is called
   a. diagonal.
   b. trailing.
   c. squaring off.
   d. orientation.

7. Which mobility tools are most often used by elementary-aged students who are deaf-blind?
   a. Canes.
   b. Dog guides.
   c. Electronic travel aids.
   d. a and b.


*Answers to self-study questions for this module appear at the end of Unit 3.*

# Approaches to Teaching Orientation and Mobility

*ELGA JOFFEE*

- *Rely on team collaboration to plan the student's O&M program*

- *Base instruction on thorough assessment*

- *Use the student's communication modes in all O&M instruction*

- *Adapt travel techniques and tools to individual needs*

To be effective and successful, the instruction of students who are deaf-blind in moving about on their own as safely and independently as possible should be based on the students' individual needs. In addition, effective teamwork that incorporates a family-centered approach to learning orientation and mobility (O&M) is essential. Following a number of principles that are explained in this module will help ensure success:

- Team collaboration is necessary for conducting O&M assessments, formulating goals, implementing programs, and delivering services.

- The transdisciplinary educational team develops the systems and modes of communication used in teaching O&M and in conveying information about movement with the individual student in mind, and all members of the team use these modes and systems consistently when working with the student.

- Specific training in O&M skills and techniques takes place in enabling (structured) learning environments that have been especially chosen or created to motivate students and to facilitate their learning.

- O&M instruction is provided in natural environments as students participate in their daily routines.

- Students are taught O&M techniques using the individual communication systems that they use and techniques and mobility devices that are modified to meet their individual needs.

- Students' safety is the primary consideration in O&M instruction at all times.

## PHASES OF TEAM COLLABORATION

The collaboration of team members is fundamental to addressing the unique and complex educational needs of students who are deaf-blind and for planning and implementing O&M programs. The following sections describe the purpose and composition of teams and the roles that team members play during the various phases of planning and implementation.

## ASSEMBLING THE TEAM

The first step in planning an O&M program for a deaf-blind student is to assemble the transdisciplinary educational team. This team may consist of the student, the student's parents and other family members, a communication specialist, a deaf-blind specialist, a teacher of students with visual impairments, an audiologist or hearing specialist, an O&M instructor, the primary classroom teacher (for example, an early childhood teacher, a special education teacher, a teacher of students with severe and profound handicaps, or a general education teacher), an occupational or physical therapist (or both), and a classroom aide (teaching assistant). The team should also include or solicit input from any other individual who has a significant role in how the student uses movement skills in daily activities. (See Unit 1 and Module 9 for more information on how to contact such team members as O&M instructors and audiologists.)

The next step is to ensure that all the team members know what O&M is and appreciate its importance in the overall educational program. The team members must also be familiar with the basic O&M techniques to help the student use them consistently in all daily activities. As is the case with communication skills development, consistency is critical for O&M to become a truly embedded life skill.

In ideal circumstances, the O&M instructor on the team will present an in-service workshop on basic O&M techniques. However, many schools and programs do not have access to an O&M instructor. In such a situation, a teacher of students with visual impairments or of deaf-blind children may be able to teach the members basic indoor O&M skills. If this is the first time the team is developing an O&M program, visiting a facility that provides O&M services or inviting an instructor from the facility is helpful in getting started.

During this initial phase, all the team members should learn about the individual communication system and modes that the student uses. The communication specialist is the ideal person to present this information and to stress the importance of communicating consistently with the student. (An appreciation of how essential consistent communication is for mobility can be felt if one imagines that one is learning a new movement skill, such as downhill skiing, and is receiving instruction from five or six teachers—each of whom speaks a language one does not understand.)

In the second phase, the team members begin to plan the O&M program by starting the assessment process. Because the goal of

O&M programs is to teach students the skills that they need for every aspect of their lives, assessment must be broad based and examine mobility needs for all daily living activities.

## CONDUCTING ASSESSMENTS

All the members of a student's educational team need to work together to identify the student's needs, interests, capabilities, and learning style. Each team member has special skills and information to contribute and brings unique perspectives to the process.

The information about assessments (the assessment process, methods of conducting assessments, and applications of assessment findings) included in Module 11 is applicable to conducting O&M assessments. Of particular importance is the material on teaming and assessments, systematic observation and recording of the student's activities, caution about using assessment instruments derived from normative developmental scales, the preparation and presentation of assessment reports, and the use of quantitative data when referring to a student's skills. It is also important to remember that although assessments may be conducted to comply with the requirements of the Individualized Education Program (IEP) or other administrative regulations, the outcomes of assessments should be instructional designs that fulfill the student's needs.

Although standardized formal O&M assessment instruments are not available for use with students who are deaf-blind, service providers know that it is important to evaluate certain aspects of a student's behavior and functioning, including the student's communication skills, motor development, level of concept development, body and environmental awareness, and means of ambulation. (Additional information on assessment can be found in Appendix C.) Team members also need to assess how the student obtains and uses information about the environment, identify the factors that motivate the student to move, learn how the student expresses his or her interest or displeasure in moving, and determine the exact movement tasks that the student performs during daily activities in natural settings—at home, at school, and in the community. The team gathers information about all these factors through observations of the student's behavior during all these daily activities.

It is essential that team members assess how the student obtains and uses information from the environment through his or her senses. Some students learn primarily by using visual information, some by using tactile information, some by using auditory information, and some by using a combination of sensory information. Students with multiple sensory impairments may require a combination of sensory information to learn. For example, a student who is deaf-blind and has some useful vision may be a tactile and visual learner, using both objects and pictures to learn. Functional vision and hearing assessments should be conducted to learn how the student uses visual and auditory information (see Module 17). Team members with expertise in vision and hearing impairments can help the other members to select, use, and interpret these assessments.

This approach to assessment, in which all aspects of a student's skills and needs are examined in all areas of his or her life (school, social-recreational, family, and vocational activities) is called the *ecological assessment model* (Nietupski & Hamre-Nietupski, 1987). (For more on the ecological approach, see Modules 11 and 14.) For example, in the social-recreational domain, the team members would assess the student's mobility behavior in such environments as shopping malls, movie theaters, and restaurants. Some school systems may categorize the domains and environments used for ecological assessment differently. Regardless of how the domains and environments are broken down, however, all must encompass the student's real-life situations and needs for a comprehensive O&M program to be developed.

Team members will find it helpful to create or adapt existing assessment checklists to use during the early phase of assessment, when structured observations take place, so their observations are recorded in a uniform and organized manner. The sample Orientation and Mobility Assessment Fact Sheet (Figure 18-1) was created by combining and adapting assessment materials from a communication department, an O&M program, a travel training program, and a physical therapy program. (A blank copy of this form appears in Appendix C for the use of readers.)

After the structured observation phase of assessment, the team members need to get together to pool their observations and plan the O&M program. The team coordinator guides the process of setting goals; selecting the instructional content, teaching strategies, and learning environments; and establishing each member's role in the program.

**FIGURE 18-1:**

## Orientation and Mobility Assessment Fact Sheet

Date _September 12, 1994_

Completed by _Nancy Silverstone_

Student's name _Toni Graham_

Date of birth _September 22, 1989_

School _Sweet Valley Elementary School_

Placement _Mainstream setting with related services_

---

### BACKGROUND INFORMATION
**Information from the Student's Eye Report**

Visual condition _Congenital cataracts with cortical blindness_

Acuity: OD (right eye) _20/400_   OS (left eye) _20/400_   OU (both) _20/400_

Visual fields _Normal visual fields_

Uses low vision aids   ☑ No   ☐ Yes

Specify _____

Primary eye care physician _Jane Milner, M.D._

Address _23 Greenhill Road_

_Sweet Valley_

Telephone _702-5300_

**Information from the Student's Audiological Record**

Cause of hearing loss _Prematurity_

Measure of hearing loss in decibels (average):

  Left ear unaided _NR_ dB   aided _100_ dB

  Right ear unaided _NR_ dB   aided _90_ dB

  Speech reception threshold (both ears) _NR_ dB

**Information from the Student's Health Record**

Medical diagnosis or diagnoses _Prematurity. Student has a mild seizure disorder (petit mal seizures)._

Medications _None_

Health alerts _Seizure disorder_

*(continued)*

_NR = No response._

**FIGURE 18-1:**
**Continued**

Physical impairments   None _____

_____

Orthopedic or mobility devices   None _____

_____

Primary care physician   David Johnson, M. D. _____

_____

Address   403 White Birch Avenue _____

        Sweet Valley _____

_____

Telephone   702-3612 _____

**Information from the Student's School Record**

Previous O&M service    ☑ No      ☐ Yes

Where? _____

_____

Duration of service _____

Related services currently included on the IEP _____

_____

_____

**COMMUNICATION SYSTEMS, MODES, AND DEVICES**

**Receptive language** (indicate all systems and modes, and include relevant comments):

Speech _____

ASL _____

Signed English _____

Tangibile symbols (object cues) __✓__ Recognizes common objects & toys. _____

Touch cues ____✓__ Recognizes anticipation touch cues. _____

Picture symbols __✓__ Recognizes simple black & white drawings. _____

Natural gestures __✓__ Uses many nonverbal gestures to convey feelings. _____

Other _____

**Expressive language** (indicate all systems and modes, and include relevant comments):

Speech _____

ASL _____

*(continued)*

*FIGURE 18-1:*
**Continued**

*Expressive Language (continued)*

Signed English _____

Tangible symbols (object cues) ✓ *Uses objects to express choice.*

Picture symbols ✓ *Points to pictures to express choice.*

Natural gestures ✓ *Responds to exaggerated gestures.*

Other *Tries to get others' attention by touching them.*

## BEHAVIOR

Describe your observations briefly:

Behaviors that may affect movement *Gazes into lights.*

Responses to tactile stimuli *Appears uncomfortable when touching unfamiliar objects.*

Responses to auditory stimuli *None*

Responses to visual stimuli *Reaches for brightly colored toys.*

Behaviors used to express pleasure *Smiles.*

Behaviors used to express displeasure *Muscle tone is tense, and she cries out in a high-pitched voice.*

## MOTOR DEVELOPMENT

Describe your observations briefly:

Muscle tone *Normal to low tone in upper body and extremities.*

Head control *Student has strength for head control, but holds head down.*

Balance *Appears to be normal.*

Coordination *Appears to be normal.*

Posture *Head down, shoulders rounded, with broad-based toed-out stance.*

Gait *Slow uneven gait with toeing out. Stiff legs and limited rotation in hips. Arm swing OK.*

Fine/gross motor skills *Student can grasp objects and control hand movement for trailing.*

*(continued)*

**FIGURE 18-1:**
**Continued**

**AUDITORY SKILLS**

Describe your observations briefly:

Responds to a discrete sound stimulus ___No_____

Localizes a sound stimulus ___No_____

Follows a sound stimulus with head movements ___No_____

Moves toward a sound stimulus ___No_____

**BODY IMAGE AND COGNITIVE SKILLS**

Describe your observations briefly:

Identifies large body parts ___Yes_____

Identifies parts of the face ___Knows mouth and nose only._____

Identifies parts of the arm and hand ___No_____

Executes movements associated with concepts of position on request:

Stand up ___Yes_____          Sit down ___No_____

Walk forward ___No_____       Turn around ___No_____

Stop ___No_____               Put your hands up ___No_____

Put your hands down ___No_____  Turn to the right or left ___No_____

**ENVIRONMENTAL AWARENESS**

Describe your observations briefly:

Recognizes the following indoor elements:

| | | |
|---|---|---|
| Wall ___Yes___ | Table ___Yes___ | Doors ___Yes___ |
| Chair ___Yes___ | Handrail ___No___ | Water fountain ___No___ |
| Stairs ___Yes___ | Toilet ___Yes___ | Windows ___No___ |
| Sink ___No___ | Desk ___No___ | Elevator ___No___ |

Recognizes the following rooms/areas:

| | | |
|---|---|---|
| Classroom ___No___ | Gymnasium ___No___ | Lunchroom ___No___ |
| Auditorium ___No___ | Bathroom ___Yes___ | Job site ___N.a.___ |

*(continued)*

*NA = Not applicable.*

*FIGURE 18-1:*
**Continued**

Recognizes the following outdoor elements:

Sidewalks _Yes_       Trees _No_       Curbs _Yes_

Poles, signs, parking meters _No_       Corners _No_

Buses, trains, automobiles, vans _No_       Driveways _No_

## SOCIAL SKILLS

Describe your observations briefly:

Responds to his or her name when addressed _Yes_

Responds to familiar voices _No_

Responds when someone enters a room _No_

Acknowledges an introduction with a greeting _Yes_

Is aware of a person departing _No_

Interacts with peers _No_

## TRAVEL SKILLS

Describe your observations briefly:

☑ No apparent travel system in use

☐ Uses a sighted guide

Travel environments _____

☐ Uses trailing

Travel environments _____

☐ Uses self-protective techniques

Travel environments _____

☐ Uses techniques for squaring off and aligning

Travel environments _____

☐ Uses indoor cane techniques

Travel environments _____

☐ Uses outdoor cane techniques

Travel environments _____

## SETTING GOALS AND DEVELOPING THE PROGRAM

In formulating O&M goals and developing and implementing O&M programs, team members need to make a detailed list of all the movement activities that the student engages in each day in each domain or setting that are covered in the ecological assessment. They then identify how the student accomplishes these activities and decide which movement tasks should be targeted for instruction, and at what level. Next, they need to identify the O&M skills and techniques to be taught, along with the communication and instructional strategies that will be used. Each team member's role in relation to the student and the other members is also determined. Figure 18-2 is a sample worksheet that can be used to plan an O&M program (a full-length version of this worksheet that readers can use appears at the end of this module).

The following example illustrates how a rural school district used a team to plan a mobility program for a young child who is deaf-blind:

> *The school district has decided that Toni, who is 5 years old and deaf-blind, should begin an O&M program. The decision was made after Toni's parents met with her classroom teacher, requesting that Toni's IEP address her mobility needs. (Toni's parents made this request after they attended a national confer-*

### FIGURE 18-2:
**Sample Mobility Planning Worksheet**

Student's name _____

School _____

Date of planning meeting _____

Completed by _____

| STARTING POINT | DESTINATION | PRESENT METHOD OF TRAVEL | MOBILITY GOAL |
| --- | --- | --- | --- |
| _____ | _____ | _____ | _____ |
| _____ | _____ | _____ | _____ |
| _____ | _____ | _____ | _____ |
| _____ | _____ | _____ | _____ |
| _____ | _____ | _____ | _____ |

*ence sponsored by a parents' organization at which they heard a speech about O&M instruction and met O&M instructors.)*

*Toni's classroom teacher called a meeting of the educational team (all staff who were working with Toni and her family) to address Toni's mobility needs. Toni's parents invited an O&M instructor they had met at the conference to attend this meeting. The instructor gave the team a general rationale for O&M instruction and demonstrated several O&M techniques to the members and to the director of special education. Toni's school could arrange for monthly consultation services from the O&M instructor if such services were appropriate for Toni. During this meeting, the O&M instructor distributed O&M assessment fact sheets to the team members and asked them to complete the forms for the next team meeting and to think about how their specific disciplines could contribute to teaching O&M skills to Toni.*

*One month after the first meeting, the team met again to continue planning Toni's O&M program. Toni's parents, classroom teacher, communication specialist (speech and language teacher), teacher of visually impaired students, occupational therapist, physical therapist, classroom aide, and mobility instructor returned with their completed assessments. At the suggestion of Toni's family, the O&M instructor coordinated the team's efforts to use the assessment information that was gathered to develop Toni's mobility program. It was clear to all the members that Toni was eligible for and could benefit from instruction. The team chose to begin working out the details of Toni's program by focusing on activities in the school domain. They made a list of Toni's mobility tasks in school and identified starting points for movement, destinations, and how Toni actually got from one place to the next during the school day. As the team members completed the worksheet, they formulated O&M goals for each mobility task. Figure 18-3 shows how Toni's educational team completed the O&M planning worksheet.*

*At the team meeting, the communication specialist suggested how Toni's communication systems and needs could be integrated into her mobility program. The occupational and physical therapists developed sensorimotor activities to facilitate Toni's use of O&M techniques. The classroom teacher and aide developed ways for Toni to use O&M skills and techniques through-*

**FIGURE 18-3:**
## Completed Mobility Planning Worksheet

Student's name ___Toni Graham___

School ___Sweet Valley Elementary School___

Date of planning meeting ___September 21, 1994___

Completed by ___Nancy Silverstone___

| STARTING POINT | DESTINATION | PRESENT METHOD OF TRAVEL | MOBILITY GOAL |
|---|---|---|---|
| Bus area | Cafeteria | Goes with aide | Use sighted guide technique with aide |
| Cafeteria | Classroom | Goes with aide | Use sighted guide technique with aide |
| Classroom | Bathroom | Goes with aide | Learn route, trailing, and direction-taking techniques |
| Bathroom | Classroom | Goes with aide | Learn route, trailing, and direction-taking techniques |
| Classroom | Gym | Goes with aide | Learn route, trailing, and direction-taking techniques |
| Gym | Bathroom | Goes with aide | Use sighted guide technique with aide |
| Bathroom | Cafeteria | Goes with aide | Use sighted guide technique with aide |
| Cafeteria | Classroom | Goes with aide | Learn sighted guide travel with peer |
| Classroom | Playground | Goes with aide | Learn route, trailing, and direction-taking techniques |
| Playground | Bathroom | Goes with aide | Use sighted guide technique with aide |
| Bathroom | Classroom | Goes with aide | Learn route, trailing, and direction-taking techniques |
| Classroom | Bus | Goes with aide | Learn sighted guide travel with peer |

*out the school day and began to examine how they would incorporate concepts for orientation, environmental awareness, and safety into the instructional activities of the general classroom. The teacher for students with visual impairments developed a program for teaching Toni the basic concepts related to awareness of body image, position, movement, and the school environment and developed strategies to teach her to use her limited vision effectively in school. Toni's family was eager to work with the O&M instructor and classroom teacher to plan opportunities for Toni to use O&M skills at home.*

*The team decided to begin Toni's O&M program immediately. The O&M instructor taught an introductory lesson on the sighted guide and trailing techniques and reviewed these techniques with the team members. The team decided to meet again in one month to review Toni's progress and to plan to extend Toni's O&M activities into the family domain.*

*To ensure that the implementation of Toni's O&M program would go smoothly, the team members developed a way of communicating with each other. They decided that Toni's classroom teacher would coordinate the implementation of Toni's O&M program at school and would be responsible for communicating with Toni's family and the O&M instructor. They identified the teacher of students with visual impairments, who visited the school three times a week, as the team member who would monitor Toni's indoor O&M techniques and would address specific questions that arose related to indoor skills and Toni's visual and hearing impairments. The communication specialist accepted responsibility for helping each team member become comfortable using the correct communication techniques.*

*The team developed a schedule for teaching Toni that allowed them time to observe and communicate with each other. They decided to contact each other weekly for an informal update and to prepare a progress report to bring to the next team meeting.*

# INDIVIDUALIZING COMMUNICATION

Communication systems, modes, and devices need to be individualized for teaching O&M and for conveying information about movement. These systems should be used consistently by all team members whenever a student moves about his or her home, school, community, and work environments (see Modules 6, 8, and 9 for an overview of symbolic and nonsymbolic communication and for a description of communication systems, modes, and devices).

An example of accommodating to individual needs can be seen when a teacher (or another team member) who does not know sign language is called on to teach O&M to a student who is deaf-blind and uses sign language. In such a case, the teacher may use an interpreter for communicating. During an O&M lesson, the teacher would communicate directly with the student, speaking in a natural tone of voice to convey the content of the lesson, and the student would respond by using sign language. The interpreter's job is to interpret what the teacher and the student are saying to each other by converting the teacher's speech into sign language and translating the student's signs into speech. The interpreter does not help the teacher conduct the lesson or provide explanations to the student that alter what the teacher has said. The teacher reviews the O&M lesson with the interpreter just before the session, so the interpreter is aware of the route that will be followed and knows where to stand in relation to the student as the lesson progresses and how the teacher plans to handle emergencies (see Working with Interpreters in this module and Module 9 for further information on working with interpreters).

Students who are deaf-blind have a wide range of visual, auditory, and communication skills and rely on various individualized communication systems, modes, and devices. When teams plan and implement O&M programs for deaf-blind students, they require information about the students' levels of communication skills and the individual systems, modes, and devices that the students use. Therefore, they need to get input from communication specialists to develop communication strategies that are effective for teaching O&M and appropriate for an individual student. The following example illustrates how a specific communication system using object and touch cues (see Module 8 for more information) is integrated into the teaching of O&M and shows how Toni's O&M program was developed to accommodate and integrate her individual communication needs.

*At Toni's team meeting, the communication specialist's assessment report revealed that Toni's skills were at the nonsymbolic level for receptive and expressive communication and that her*

# Working with Interpreters

**David Miller**

An interpreter is critical for teaching orientation and mobility (O&M) for numerous reasons, including the following:

• Clear and convenient communication is essential for establishing rapport. In turn, building rapport is basic to establishing a sense of trust and confidence for the student who is learning O&M skills.

• The aim of O&M instruction is safe and independent movement, and maintaining safety depends on the accurate communication of information.

• Students who are receiving O&M instruction may have a variety of questions and concerns. It is difficult to address their concerns or to be confidential when communication is impaired.

How do teachers, O&M instructors, and others work with interpreters during O&M instruction?

• They all work as a team.

• The O&M instructor needs to prepare the interpreter by teaching him or her O&M concepts and techniques, including sighted guide and basic cane techniques.

• The O&M instructor retains his or her teaching role; the interpreter works to make things clear; and the two consult with each other frequently. The O&M instructor checks the interpreter's sighted guide techniques and interpretation and provides the student who is deaf-blind with tactile experiences as often as possible.

• Goals and methods need to be modified during instruction as all members of the team refine their methods of communication and see how the student is progressing.

• Because working with an interpreter may be a slow process, patience is essential.

• Success depends largely on the student and the rapport and quality of communication between the student and the professionals with whom the student is working. ◼

*hearing was not functional. Therefore, she recommended that Toni use a system for learning O&M that included touch cues to convey information about body position and movement and specific object cues to identify landmarks and destinations. Because the vision teacher reported that Toni had sufficient vision to recognize common objects and pictures visually, the communication specialist suggested that Toni should also begin to learn to relate simple signs and pictures to her touch and object cues. The communication specialist and the vision teacher set aside time to develop this aspect of Toni's program.*

*The communication specialist then created specific touch cues for asking Toni to stand, sit, turn left, turn right, begin walking, stop, and turn about face. She also selected object cues for Toni to identify the classroom, the cafeteria, the bathroom, the gym, the playground, and the bus area. Before she selected these cues, she consulted with the other team members to determine Toni's interests and preferences. Toni's touch and object cues were as follows:*

| *Touch cues* | *Meaning* |
|---|---|
| *Stand* | *A gentle upward tug under the armpits* |
| *Sit* | *A gentle pat on the small of the back* |
| *Start walking* | *A gentle nudge to the nape of the neck* |
| *Stop moving* | *A gentle tap above the sternum* |
| *Turn right* | *A gentle tap of the right shoulder* |
| *Turn left* | *A gentle tap on the left shoulder* |
| *Turn about face* | *A gentle tap on both shoulders* |

| *Object Cues* | *Meaning* |
|---|---|
| *Book* | *Classroom* |
| *Spoon* | *Lunchroom* |
| *Soap dish* | *Bathroom* |
| *Rubber ball* | *Playground* |
| *Beanbag* | *Gymnasium* |
| *Backpack* | *Bus area* |

*The O&M instructor, vision teacher, classroom teacher, and classroom aide obtained the object cues Toni needed, selected a place in Toni's classroom to store them, and began to structure a physical learning environment in the classroom and school that would motivate Toni and be conducive to teaching her to use O&M skills and techniques. To help the team members be consistent, the teachers created a bulletin board that contained an attractive display of Toni's touch and object cues.*

As students refine their O&M skills and learn to travel, they may learn that the particular communication systems they use at home and at school are not appropriate for travel in their communities. For example, students who use sign language or object cues at home and at school may find that these systems are not effective at work or for purchasing items in stores. Thus, they may learn to use pictures, notes, gestures, prewritten messages on cards, or other communication systems at work and in their communities. They may also learn how to inform people in their communities how to respond to them in a way that is useful for travel and to organize the materials they need to take with them for communicating with the public (see Modules 19 and 20 for more information on how travelers who are deaf-blind communicate with the public).

# ENVIRONMENTS THAT FACILITATE LEARNING

The environments within which O&M instruction takes place can make learning easier or more difficult for the student. Well-organized, well-ordered environments in which sources of confusion and distraction have been eliminated are critical, and natural environments help ensure success by making instruction especially meaningful and useful to students.

## STRUCTURED ENVIRONMENTS

Structured environments are created to motivate students and to facilitate the instruction and use of O&M skills and techniques. These kinds of environments are called enabling learning environments. In schools, they consist of simple uncluttered classrooms and hallways that contain stimulating and useful things for students to see and do. These environments include clear and direct pathways for moving from place to place that stimulate students to move about and are free of obstacles that block movement or are safety hazards. Once structured environments are developed and students are familiar with them, every attempt is made to keep them the same or to inform the students of any changes that are made.

Classrooms that are structured to encourage movement contain clearly identified activity areas, where students can participate in exciting learning experiences (see Module 19 for specific examples of how classrooms are structured). In these classrooms, the teachers make certain that the students go to different activity centers several times a day as part of the required routines, rather than sit in the same seats all day. (Families can create similar environments at home to encourage their children to move about freely and keep themselves busy.) In structuring enabling learning environments, teachers consider students' interests and visual and auditory needs. Although most students with visual impairments benefit from environments with full illumination that do not create glare or shadows and cues that make use of bright contrasting colors, some students with specific visual disorders (for example, albinism or other conditions accompanied by sensitivity to light) benefit from more dimly lit environments. Teams need to work with teachers of students with visual impairments and O&M instructors to structure visual environments that are suitable for their students and are conducive to the students' effective use of their remaining vision.

Students who can hear sounds require learning environments in which they can use their remaining hearing. Thus, environments with extraneous ambient noises (from a ventilating fan, for example) should be avoided as much as possible when students are listening to auditory information as they learn. Team members should work with O&M instructors and hearing specialists to create enabling learning environments in which these students are taught to use sounds in the environment to develop their awareness of the environment and their sense of orientation.

Teachers often have classrooms that contain many types of specialized equipment, including wheelchairs, walkers, prone boards, and feeding tables, and equipment that is stored in open spaces in the classroom or along walls in the hallways when not in use. Every effort must be made to store specialized equipment in other, safer places.

A student who is deaf-blind should be assigned to a permanent seat that is located in a direct line of travel to the important areas in the classroom, such as the door, the place where object cues are stored, and the bookshelf, or in a spot that requires as simple a route as possible from the student's seat to these areas. The student's seat should be marked clearly with an appropriate cue, such as a bright or uniquely textured cloth, a favorite toy or object, or a card with the student's name written in print or braille, that the student easily recognizes and understands.

All the other rooms that the student uses regularly should be marked, so the student can easily recognize them as he or she travels from place to place. The markers that teachers use to label landmarks in the school can be the actual object cues the student uses to identify specific locations. For example, a student who uses a spoon as an object cue to represent the cafeteria recognizes the cafeteria by finding a spoon on the doorjamb beside the cafeteria. Object cues can be posted using Velcro fasteners, so they can be removed for cleaning or be replaced or eliminated when the student no longer needs them.

It may not be necessary to create a highly structured environment or mark landmarks for every student. However, the team should consider the degree of structuring that may be required when planning a student's individualized O&M program.

## UNSTRUCTURED ENVIRONMENTS

Students develop their skills, environmental awareness, conceptual abilities, and self-confidence when their O&M instruction begins in structured environments. To prepare students to manage the day-to-day travel that is part of adult living, however, O&M instruction should be provided in both structured and unstructured learning environments.

Unstructured environments generally consist of the student's home, school, community, and workplace, which contain few modifications or adaptations. Instruction in these environments is introduced to build the student's awareness of real-life environments and to teach the student the O&M skills he or she needs to travel in unstructured situations. A student's awareness of unstructured environments begins early, when he or she accompanies family members and friends to social events in the community. Teachers also build community and environmental awareness into classroom activities and trips in the community (see Module 19 for examples of how teachers can incorporate such awareness into regular classroom activities).

As students master O&M skills and develop confidence in their ability to travel during lessons in structured learning situations, they are gradually taught to use their skills to travel in unstructured community environments that expose them to unanticipated obstacles and situations. Because it is impossible to predict what will occur in unstructured situations, teachers initially need to assist students through these environments and explain what is taking place. For example, students may find their routes blocked or disrupted by construction, noise from a jackhammer, showers from lawn sprinklers, interruptions by strangers, and disrupting comments from passersby. They and their teachers need to spend a great deal of time experiencing the reality of the day-to-day world and interpreting what these experiences mean. Through this process, the students learn to manage unanticipated obstacles, drop-offs, changes in their planned routes of travel, individuals who offer inappropriate assistance, and others' reactions and comments to them about them and individuals with disabilities in general. Activities that are described in Module 19 build students' problem-solving skills and confidence and increase their safety in unstructured environments.

## NATURAL ENVIRONMENTS AND CONTEXTS

O&M instruction for students who are deaf-blind is provided during daily living activities in natural environments because many deaf-blind students, especially those who also have cognitive impairments, find it difficult to transfer O&M techniques that are taught in contrived instructional situations to real-life situations. In addition, instruction in natural environments creates a built-in motivational structure for the students and means that all movement is actually an O&M learning experience (Gee, Harrell, & Rosenberg, 1987).

Teachers should look for natural opportunities to teach and reinforce O&M techniques. Again, the case of Toni can be used to illustrate this point.

> Toni's team developed a mobility program that included teaching her to use the sighted guide, trailing, and direction-taking techniques for travel in the school building. The team members identified natural opportunities for teaching these techniques as they completed the O&M Planning Worksheet at the team meeting. They determined that Toni would learn to travel to the bus area and cafeteria using the sighted guide technique and would learn to travel to the bathroom and playground using trailing and direction-taking techniques.
>
> Toni's O&M instructor introduced these techniques to Toni and her teachers during the course of the school day as Toni traveled from her classroom to the specific destinations identified by the team. Then, each day as Toni engaged in her daily activities at school, the teacher and classroom aide continued to help her use the techniques correctly.

Individual differences among students mean that teachers work with a range of students who have different abilities and needs for travel and hence may use O&M techniques that are different from the ones Toni used. Because the aim is for students to integrate O&M techniques into their lives, teachers need to help families embed O&M skills and techniques in daily living activities at home.

Teaching travel skills within the context of naturally occurring daily activities means that students who are deaf-blind learn the O&M techniques required to travel in specific situations, rather than follow a predetermined order for learning O&M skills and techniques, as has traditionally been used for building O&M skills. This is called the "functional approach" to teaching O&M because the emphasis is on teaching students to function in daily environments, rather than on building skills sequentially that will be applied after all skills are acquired. O&M instructors who are familiar with these functional approaches can provide valuable assistance to educational teams in selecting the O&M skills and techniques for students to learn (Joffee & Rikhye, 1991).

# TEACHING APPROACHES

It is essential to adopt certain approaches to teaching O&M skills and techniques when working with students who are deaf-blind. Paying special attention to the individual learning styles of students, empha-

## O&M with Deaf-Blind Students: Some Suggestions

### David Miller

• When following a student, it is best to stay within arms' reach and watch him or her closely in case you have to warn the student about some obstacle or other danger.

• Fanny packs and shoulder bags are helpful for storing travel tools and other items and allow the student's hands to remain free.

• Use an interpreter effectively, take time to become acquainted with him or her, and enjoy the interaction.

• Make mobility fun by giving the student who is deaf-blind the opportunity to visit new places and learn about his or her community.

• Get as much exposure as possible to the deaf-blind culture.

• Consider learning sign language and encourage a reciprocal relationship for learning.

• Be flexible and respect the student's input and participation, work cooperatively, and allow the student to make choices.

• Understand what deaf-blindness means for each student.

• Let the student define for himself or herself what it means to be independent. ■

sizing careful physical positioning, using specific routes as teaching tools, and noting appropriate levels of mastery of techniques are crucial aspects of O&M instruction for these students (for a summary of tips, see O&M with Deaf-Blind Students: Some Suggestions).

## INDIVIDUAL LEARNING STYLES

When working with a student, the teacher considers the student's interests, needs, and learning styles that the transdisciplinary team identified during the assessment phase when planning which O&M skills and techniques to teach. For example, students who enjoy movement may learn best during lessons that are structured around long walks, whereas those who are sedentary may benefit from short repeated sessions of mobility activities. Furthermore, some students enjoy close physical contact, whereas others do not care to be touched. In this regard, the team should consider and respect the family's cultural preferences, particularly regarding physical contact between males and females, when devising an O&M program for a student.

## PHYSICAL POSITIONING

In general, students who are deaf-blind learn mobility techniques effectively by being physically positioned and helped to perform them. This approach may make use of coactive movement (see Module 7), in which the teacher and student move together while the teacher explains the techniques using the student's individual communication systems and imitation.

The following is an effective procedure for introducing all O&M techniques to students:

1. Using the student's individual communication systems, the teacher indicates that it is time to travel to a new activity or place (or the student may have communicated his or her need or desire to move about).

2. Then, standing behind the student, the teacher positions the student to perform the specified technique and physically assists (or prompts) the student to travel using the technique.

3. As the student continues to use the O&M technique consistently in daily activities, he or she learns correct forms of the technique and the appropriate times to use them.

4. When the student is secure in moving about with the O&M technique, the teacher gradually withdraws the physical positioning and prompting, and the student assumes increasing responsibility for his or her own travel.

For example, to initiate the sighted guide technique, the teacher informs the student that he or she will be traveling from one location to another and then helps the student grasp the guide's wrist or arm just above the elbow (see Module 17 for more information). The teacher establishes and monitors the student's and guide's body positions until the student gets the feel of what is being done. Gradually, responsibility for using the correct technique shifts from the teacher to the student, who learns to signal his or her intention to move or responds to a request to travel to a new location by initiating and correctly using the sighted guide technique.

A similar process can be used with trailing. The teacher informs the student that he or she will be traveling to a new location. The teacher then physically prompts the student to trail by getting behind the student and assisting him or her to reach out to the guideline in the correct trailing position. Remaining in position behind the student, the teacher may extend his or her arm out behind the student's arm and begin moving forward with the student to trail. This is literally hand-over-hand assistance. As the student responds to the physical prompt to trail, the teacher withdraws the close physical support and encourages the student to assume increasing responsibility for using the correct form of the technique.

▲ *By standing behind her student and positioning him physically, this teacher is providing effective instruction in how to use a mobility aid.*

## THE ROUTE AS A TEACHING TOOL

A route is a specific path of travel from one place to another that has clearly identified beginning and end points. Students learn O&M techniques by traveling routes from designated starting points to specific destinations. Team members collaborate to determine the routes selected for teaching O&M skills at home, at school, and in the community and for vocational needs.

Several important factors are considered when selecting routes for O&M lessons. One factor is the complexity of the route. At first, simple direct routes are preferred, but the routes gradually become more complex and involve one or more changes in direction (see Module 19 for concrete examples of how teachers use increasingly complex routes to teach travel skills). Another important factor is the environment the route traverses. Initially, the student learns to travel along routes in highly structured and protected environments where events and physical dangers are controlled. Instruction in such environments gives the student the opportunity to master the techniques without confusion and interruptions during practice and to develop confidence in the techniques and in himself or herself as a traveler. As the student becomes accustomed to traveling along these routes, the teacher selects routes through dynamic indoor and outdoor environments, where unanticipated obstacles are found and unanticipated situations occur, to expose the student to the realities of daily travel.

In addition, students who are deaf-blind develop orientation skills when they learn travel skills by following specific routes. Instruction in route travel teaches students that movement is not random, that all travel begins at a specific point, that a path of travel is predictable, and that following a selected travel path will lead to a specific destination. It also teaches them that they can be aware of where they are at all times and can exercise control over where they wish to go.

While developing orientation skills during O&M lessons, a student also gains a sense of where objects and people are located. This sense allows the student to create a functional mental map of his or her daily environments and to discover how he or she fits into the world.

Because routes are such a valuable teaching tool for deaf-blind students, consistent repetitive travel along them is essential for learning O&M skills. Therefore, teachers should encourage and assist students to use their mobility routes each time they travel, regardless of when and with whom they travel. Teachers also should convey information about route travel to the students' families, so the families can work with them to plan routes for travel at home and in their communities. In addition, the members of the student's educational teams should review the students' routes regularly and be consistent when traveling with the students.

Students who are deaf-blind and do not use signed or spoken language or have severe cognitive impairments rely on a unique system for learning route travel that incorporates object and touch cues (Joffee, 1989). This system is used when students do not have the communication skills needed to receive or process specific information about the starting points and destinations of routes.

Object cues serve two purposes: to inform students about where they will be going and to label and identify destinations. Object cues that are used to provide information about intended destinations (such as a spoon to indicate the lunchroom) are called *anticipation cues*. Object cues that are used to label and identify destinations (such as a spoon placed at the doorway of the lunchroom) are called *destination markers* (Joffee & Rikhye, 1991). (For more about object cues, see Module 8.)

Teachers use anticipation cues and destination markers in the following manner to teach O&M using route travel: At the beginning of a route, the student takes his or her anticipation cue and, using the appropriate O&M techniques and carrying the anticipation cue (some students use small packs or pouches that are clipped around their waists), follows the route until he or she arrives at the destination. The student recognizes that the destination has been reached when he or she locates the destination marker, matches it to the anticipation cue, and deposits the anticipation cue in a closure box that is placed at the destination.

A student with severe cognitive impairments learns to return to the starting point of a route by treating the return trip as an entirely new route. That is, he or she uses a new anticipation cue (sometimes a "home base" cue) for the route back to the starting point, travels the route, and identifies the destination.

## FUNCTIONAL LEVEL OF MASTERY

O&M techniques are selected on the basis of the needs and preferences of individual students. One issue to consider is whether a student has achieved a level of functional mastery of the techniques that suits his or her individual situations and needs. If a student moves about safely to accomplish what needs to be done, he or she has reached this level.

Another issue to consider is the relative nature of independence. Students who are able to use the sighted guide technique effectively have achieved independence when they choose to travel using this technique. Personal preferences, environmental conditions, individual levels of skills, and a host of other personal factors may lead students to make this choice. However, when others require a student to use a specific technique or restrict the range of techniques from which a student may choose, the student is not functioning at the maximum level of independence. Thus, teachers need to present options for maximum independence when teaching O&M, but also need to recognize that not all students may be comfortable with or can master all the O&M skills and techniques.

# SPECIFIC TECHNIQUES

Some students who are deaf-blind may find it difficult to use conventional O&M techniques that require the unrestricted use of the hands and arms, balance, and coordination. However, these students can travel in purposeful ways using O&M techniques when both the techniques and mobility tools are modified and adapted.

## USE OF LONG MOBILITY CANES

Deaf-blind students, including young children, who can walk without support canes or orthopedic mobility aids can learn to use long mobility canes if transdisciplinary teams and O&M instructors determine that these devices are appropriate for their needs (see Principles of Cane Use for Preschoolers). Long mobility canes are prescribed by O&M instructors, who are also responsible for teaching students adapted and modified skills and techniques for cane travel.

Long canes can be modified for students who are ambulatory but have physical impairments of the hands and arms. Occupational therapists, working with O&M instructors, can fabricate lightweight molded grips (made of the malleable material used in splints) that fit and support students' hands as they grip their canes.

The students' arm and hand positions when holding and swinging long canes can also be adapted. Students who have difficulty holding their hands at midline when they swing canes can secure a hand in the correct position by using the other hand to grasp and support the cane arm. Students who cannot use this modification can be taught to swing wide arcs to ensure that a cane covers the side of the body opposite the cane hand. These students may need slightly longer canes or may need to be taught to walk at a slower pace.

# Principles of Cane Use for Preschoolers

Rona L. Pogrund

The following are basic principles related to the use of the long cane by preschool children:

• The development of cane skills in young children is slower than in adults. Instruction involves shaping the skills and giving children enough time to acquire them. It is also important to make learning to use a cane a fun, positive, and relevant experience.

• It is not necessary for children to master many of the concepts, cognitive abilities, and motor skills that have been considered prerequisites for introducing the long cane. For a child who is deaf-blind and has no other physical impairments, two motor abilities are key to success with the long cane: (1) the ability to hold the cane in some fashion and (2) the ability to walk independently with adequate balance so the child does not have to use high- or medium-guard positions (in which the arms are bent up at 90 degree or 60 degree angles, respectively, for balance) or to get help from a person or balance device. If a child who is deaf-blind has additional physical impairments that preclude his or her holding a cane or maintaining an acceptable gait pattern while using the cane, the orientation and mobility (O&M) specialist can consult the physical therapist for suggestions.

• Some children who are deaf-blind may never master all the concepts that were considered prerequisites to cane instruction. They may become rote travelers, but they can still learn to move safely with canes along those routes. To continue to work on concepts and basic skills before the cane is introduced may take far longer than is beneficial for the children.

• Expressive language abilities are not necessary for receiving instruction in cane travel. Modeling, nonverbal communication, physical prompting, and receptive touching (for example, interpreting a touch on the shoulder as a message to stop) are effective instructional tools for children who have limited receptive language abilities. Children who are deaf-blind may initially need to be physically assisted with cane techniques until sensory integration occurs, especially if their language development is delayed.

• Only limited awareness of objects in the immediate environment is necessary for receiving instruction in the long cane. An understanding of object permanence, cause-and-effect relationships, and the function of a cane as a bumper can be gained from cane instruction and movement activities, as can spatial concepts and environmental awareness. • Children who are deaf-blind do not have to identify or locate specific body parts to use long canes; they only need to be able to use some of those body parts functionally.

• Methods of holding the cane while accompanied by a sighted guide should be taught because a young child will frequently use this skill as he or she goes to and from lessons and travels with friends, parents, and teachers.

*(continued)*

• Cane skills can and should be integrated into instruction in basic skills and the development of concepts, language skills, and body awareness, rather than be treated as an isolated instructional activity.

• Use of the cane should be incorporated into daily activities as soon as possible to provide many natural opportunities for practice and to help a child learn that the long cane is a useful tool in his or her life, not just during O&M lessons.

• Family members, other children, and related professionals should receive in-service training before a young child who is deaf-blind uses the cane in a specific setting.

• The young child should have an assigned place to store the cane when it is not in use. Folding canes are usually best kept with the child's personal belongings to foster the child's sense of autonomy and responsibility. ■

Electronic travel aids (ETAs) can be used in conjunction with long canes to enhance travel, but these devices may not be simple to use. The laser cane provides advance warning of obstacles above waist height—the area for which the long cane does not offer protection—as well as warning of mid-height and of low-lying obstacles and drop-offs. Other ETAs that are handheld or chest mounted use sonar signals to detect obstacles as well (see Electronic Travel Aids in this module).

## USE OF WHEELCHAIRS

Students who use wheelchairs have a range of options for purposeful travel. For example, every time a student is moved in a wheelchair, he or she is actually using a modified sighted guide technique in which the person pushing the wheelchair, the guide, is behind, rather than ahead of, the student. In this modification, the guide makes a point of providing the student with the information about the surroundings that otherwise would have been conveyed through body movements.

Using students' individual communication systems, modes, or devices to convey information, guides orient students to where they

## ELECTRONIC TRAVEL AIDS

Electronic travel aids (ETAs) are portable electronic devices that emit sonar or laser signals that are reflected back to the devices and are converted into information via tactile (vibrations) or auditory stimuli (beeps or tones). The devices signal travelers who are blind or deaf-blind about the objects in their path of travel. The feedback of ETAs supplements the information available from long canes, guide dogs, or the use of vision. For example, an ETA can provide information about objects beyond the reach of a cane's tip or about obstacles, such as tree branches, that overhang the travel path.

Orientation and mobility (O&M) students learn to interpret the signals from ETAs as part of their O&M instructional programs. Sometimes referred to as secondary mobility aids, ETAs are prescribed by O&M instructors and sold commercially as hand-held, chest-mounted, head-borne, wheelchair, or cane-mounted devices (see Resources for a list of vendors and sources for locating O&M instructors who are qualified to teach ETA travel).

ETAs vary in their complexity. Some, such as the Russell Pathsounder, the Mowat Sensor, the Polaron, and the laser cane, signal a traveler about objects that are present within a specified field surrounding the device and their distance from him or her. These devices make use of range settings. For example, a device set at a four-foot range creates a tactile or auditory stimulus when it identifies the first obstacle within four feet of the traveler, the stimulus changing (the vibrations intensify or the pitch changes) as the traveler approaches the object. By positioning ETAs strategically and using them to scan travel paths, travelers can determine approximate locations and sizes of objects and estimate distance to locate landmarks or to avoid obstacles.

Other ETAs, such as the Sonic Guide and the Sensory 6, display detailed auditory information that allows travelers to localize objects; determine sizes; and, in the case of the Sonic Guide, gather information about some physical properties, as well as determine configurations of objects within the ranges of these devices.

ETAs for travelers who use wheelchairs can be either chest mounted or installed on the vertical supports of the chairs' armrests. Chest-mounted ETAs provide advance information about objects in travel paths. ETAs that are installed on wheelchairs probe the environment for obstacles at or above chest height, for drop-offs, and for low-lying obstacles. Sonar probes can be fitted to allow travelers to trail walls or guidelines. ETA technology for wheelchair travel is limited at this time to applications in familiar indoor or campus environments.

ETAs are costly, currently ranging from approximately $500 for a hand-held device to $5,000 for a wheelchair installation. Because of their high costs and the dearth of funding sources for purchasing them, an ETA-certified O&M instructor working with the educational team should conduct a thorough evaluation before an ETA is recommended. Some O&M instructors even recommend borrowing an ETA from the vendor or manufacturer to test its potential use by a student.

Teachers and families who are interested in purchasing an
*(continued)*

## ELECTRONIC TRAVEL AIDS *(Continued)*

ETA for a student may find it helpful to review financing options with the manufacturer or distributor, who sometimes can suggest charitable foundations that may provide funds for its purchase. Occasionally, school districts or state rehabilitation agencies have purchased ETAs because they have been recommended in Individualized Education Programs (IEPs) or Individualized Written Rehabilitation Plans (IWRPs). Also, some health insurance policies may provide coverage for ETAs as "durable medical equipment" if a prescription is written by a physician. ■

are, where they are going, and how they will get there. Students who are able to extend their arms to trail may follow along the guidelines using trailing techniques as they travel routes with their guides. By doing so, they can stay alert, oriented, and involved in travel. Students who are not able to trail using their hands and arms can receive information about the guidelines they are following when automobile "curb feelers" are attached to the wheel rims used to propel the wheelchairs on each side. Curb feelers, available in auto-parts stores, are long wire springs that extend to surfaces and scrape along them in bouncing motions (Welsh & Blasch, 1980).

When students trail surfaces using curb feelers, they receive auditory and tactile information about the guidelines they are following. Some students with severe auditory impairments or those who use heavy wheelchairs or orthopedic wedges to support their bodies may not benefit from the feedback provided by curb feelers and must rely on other appropriate communication from their guides to stay oriented. Students who are visually impaired can be taught to use their vision effectively to stay oriented by following along guidelines and identifying cues and landmarks, such as doorways and special-purpose rooms.

When students who are deaf-blind use wheelchairs to travel in familiar protected areas without assistance from guides, they can use a combination of trailing and cane techniques. They trail guidelines (this is easier for students who use electric wheelchairs because one hand is free for trailing) by extending a hand at regular intervals to trail and extend the folding cane to explore obstacles and drop-offs in

▲ *Students in wheel-chairs who are able to use their arms can use trailing as an orientation and safety technique. Those with useful vision can distinguish and utilize visual landmarks.*

paths of travel. They can also use ETAs, which provide information about obstacles, landmarks, and drop-offs in familiar environments (see Electronic Travel Aids) (Warren, Horn, & Hill, 1987).

Deaf-blind students who travel independently in wheelchairs must be thoroughly familiarized with the routes they use. In the rush and activity of home and school life, it is easy to overlook the need to communicate with students when they are moved about in wheelchairs. However, teachers and family members will discover that the benefits students get from receiving information about where they are, where they are going, and how they are getting there are well worth the effort.

## USE OF SUPPORT CANES OR CRUTCHES

Students who use support canes or crutches require specialized O&M modifications that are usually developed collaboratively by O&M instructors and physical and occupational therapists. Such modifications include placing an ETA at a strategic place on a student, such as in a hand or on the chest; adapting a support cane to serve as a probe and a support tool; or combining the use of a support cane and a long cane for travel applications. Physical therapists and O&M

instructors develop safe travel strategies for encountering and responding to obstacles and drop-offs in travel paths, and physical and occupational therapists provide clinical treatment to maximize students' gross and fine motor functioning for travel.

## USE OF WALKERS

Students who use walkers cannot use long canes in conjunction with this equipment. Therefore, they cannot protect themselves against obstacles and drop-offs; their hands are not free to trail guidelines without stopping to extend their hands to trail and explore.

ETAs with sonar probes that are mounted on the students' chests or clamped to walkers can provide advance information about upcoming obstacles, but they do not provide advance warning of drop-offs and steps (Welsh & Blasch, 1980). Furthermore, as with other ETA solutions, they are costly and require sophisticated technical assistance from O&M instructors and the companies that supply them. Therefore, transdisciplinary teams should carefully consider whether ETAs are appropriate travel solutions for students who use walkers. When teams plan such adaptations for students with physical impairments, they must be sure that the modifications provide forward protection from obstacles and drop-offs and enable students to gather the information they need for orientation and wayfinding.

## USE OF ADAPTED CANES AND PRECANES

A growing number of O&M instructors have come to consider instruction in mobility devices a vital component of O&M training for young children with visual disabilities. Young children can learn to use several kinds of mobility devices: modified long canes, called "kiddie canes"; adapted canes; and a host of precane, or noncane, devices that do not physically resemble long white canes but serve as travel tools. (Precanes and noncanes are usually used as interchangeable terms; another common term used is alternate canes. Although the term "precane" may imply that the device is always used in preparation for the use of a long cane, this is not the case. A precane may be the mobility device that best meets the needs of students who may not go on to use a long cane.) Unlike conventional long canes and kiddie canes, adapted canes and precanes (except for one or two devices that look like modified walkers) are not available commercially. Generally, these devices are fabricated by O&M instructors for individual students.

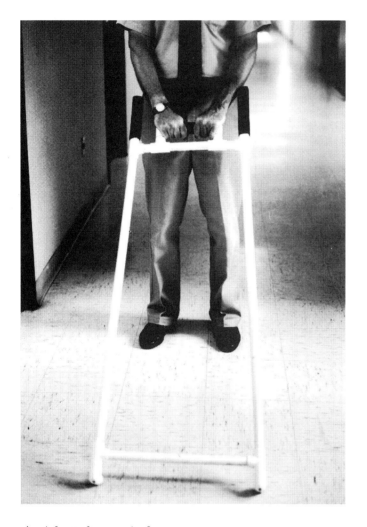

▲ *Adapted canes in forms such as push probes like this one are made by orientation and mobility instructors to meet the individual needs of students.*

There are several categories of adapted canes: T-bar-handle canes with conventional tips, T-bar-handle canes with wheels, and T-bar-base push probes that are fitted with wheels. Precanes include modified hula hoops or push frames that are fabricated from polyvinyl chloride (PVC) piping, frame walker-type devices, and children's push toys (Pogrund et al., 1993). Some precanes have glides at the floor on either side of them that look like sled runners, some have rollers fitted to a bottom crossbar, and others have a bottom crossbar to which wheels have been attached. Whether a student should use an adapted cane or a precane, which device is the most appropriate, and how the device is to be fabricated should be determined by a qualified O&M instructor with input from the student's family and school personnel.

Students use adapted canes or precanes to probe the environment and gather information about obstacles and details (such as drop-offs or changes in texture) that are underfoot along the path of travel. These devices provide protection as travelers push them in a forward line of travel while walking. Devices that are shaped like frames or modified walkers provide protection across the full width of the traveler's body; other devices provide less coverage, depending on their width. Each device has its own relative advantages and disadvantages for individual students.

In general, O&M instructors think of using adapted canes or precanes when students have difficulty grasping the grip of the conventional long cane, swinging an arc with the long cane, or interpreting feedback from the long cane (Morse, 1980).

## SAFETY ISSUES

O&M techniques have been designed to provide protection against physical obstacles and danger and information about the environment that is necessary for maintaining orientation and making judgments during travel. Under the best circumstances, all travel, including travel using O&M techniques, involves certain normal risks as well as benefits. Families, teachers, and students weigh these risks in deciding when and how specific skills and techniques will be used. Free and ongoing communication between the home and the school helps ensure that appropriate decisions will be made. Teachers and families work together with O&M instructors and students to learn as much as possible about O&M skills and techniques, not only to feel confident about using them, but to appreciate their strengths and limitations.

Overprotection may be just as harmful as the potential physical dangers of travel. Students whose travel is unduly restricted have limited opportunities to learn about their environment; to develop concepts about movement, time, and position; and to achieve the autonomy and self-esteem that come with being able to move about at will and performing life skills. Many adult travelers who are deaf-blind have asked that they be permitted to have the "dignity of risk." Teachers and families of deaf-blind students need to consider that the goal of O&M instruction is to provide students with a safe, effective system for negotiating the environment—not to protect them from experiencing their environment and the ordinary risks that all people face in their daily lives.

The following O&M instructional techniques and strategies are used to teach students to understand danger and to protect themselves in various situations:

- Teachers and classroom aides monitor dangerous situations. They can help students who are about to bump into obstacles by placing the palms of their hands between the students and the obstacles and by allowing the students to bump with buffers so students learn from their experience while avoiding injury.

- To protect themselves against the dangers of traveling with unsuitable guides, students learn strategies for assessing the fitness of individuals who offer to assist them—to recognize guides who behave carelessly, touch them in inappropriate ways, use incorrect guiding techniques, or take them where they do not wish to go.

- Teachers and O&M instructors involve students in classroom activities and role-play situations that increase the students' awareness and judgment (see Module 19).

- Students learn to use cards with preprinted messages to obtain help from sighted guides to minimize the risks of being guided to the wrong places and to learn ways to reorient themselves when they are lost (see Module 20 for further information).

- Students learn to separate physically from guides when it is necessary to disengage themselves from someone who is leading them unsafely. To overcome feelings of discomfort or reluctance about resisting a stranger's assistance, role-play during O&M lessons can help students and teachers work out safe and satisfactory solutions.

By working to ensure students' safety while traveling, teachers and other team members can make substantial contributions to the students' well-being, independence, and continued progress in developing O&M skills.

# REFERENCES

Gee, K., Harrell, R., & Rosenberg, R. (1987). Teaching orientation and mobility skills within and across natural opportunities for travel: A model designed for learners with multiple severe disabilities. In L. Goetz, D. Guess, & K. Stremel-Campbell (Eds.), *Innovative program design for individuals with dual sensory impairments* (pp. 127–157). Baltimore: Paul H. Brookes.

Joffee, E. (1989). Developing O&M services for severely and profoundly retarded students in the New York City public schools. *Long Cane News, 8* (1), 3–4.

Joffee, E., & Rikhye, C. H. (1991). Orientation and mobility for students with severe visual and multiple impairments: A new perspective. *Journal of Visual Impairment & Blindness, 85,* 211-216.

Morse, K. A. (1980). Modifications of the long cane for use by a multiply impaired child. *Journal of Visual Impairment & Blindness, 74,* 15–18.

Nietupski, J. A., & Hamre-Nietupski, S. M. (1987). An ecological approach to curriculum development. In L. Goetz, D. Guess, & K. Stremel-Campbell (Eds.), *Innovative program design for individuals with dual sensory impairments* (pp. 225–253). Baltimore: Paul H. Brookes.

Pogrund, R., Healy, G., Jones, K., Levack, N., Martin-Curry, S., Martinez, C., Marz, J., Roberson-Smith, B., & Vrba, A. (1993). *Teaching age-appropriate purposeful skills: An orientation and mobility curriculum for students with visual impairments.* Austin: Texas School for the Blind and Visually Impaired.

Warren, S. F., Horn, E. H., & Hill, E. W. (1987). Applications of advanced technologies. In L. Goetz, D. Guess, & K. Stremel-Campbell (Eds.), *Innovative program design for individuals with dual sensory impairments* (pp. 283–309). Baltimore: Paul H. Brookes.

Welsh, R., & Blasch, B. (Eds.) (1980). *Foundations of orientation and mobility*. New York: American Foundation for the Blind.

# MOBILITY PLANNING WORKSHEET

Student's name _____

School _____

Date of planning meeting _____

Completed by _____

| STARTING POINT | DESTINATION | PRESENT METHOD OF TRAVEL | MOBILITY GOAL |
|---|---|---|---|
| _____ | _____ | _____ | _____ |
| _____ | _____ | _____ | _____ |
| _____ | _____ | _____ | _____ |
| _____ | _____ | _____ | _____ |
| _____ | _____ | _____ | _____ |
| _____ | _____ | _____ | _____ |
| _____ | _____ | _____ | _____ |
| _____ | _____ | _____ | _____ |
| _____ | _____ | _____ | _____ |
| _____ | _____ | _____ | _____ |
| _____ | _____ | _____ | _____ |
| _____ | _____ | _____ | _____ |
| _____ | _____ | _____ | _____ |
| _____ | _____ | _____ | _____ |
| _____ | _____ | _____ | _____ |
| _____ | _____ | _____ | _____ |
| _____ | _____ | _____ | _____ |
| _____ | _____ | _____ | _____ |
| _____ | _____ | _____ | _____ |
| _____ | _____ | _____ | _____ |
| _____ | _____ | _____ | _____ |
| _____ | _____ | _____ | _____ |
| _____ | _____ | _____ | _____ |
| _____ | _____ | _____ | _____ |

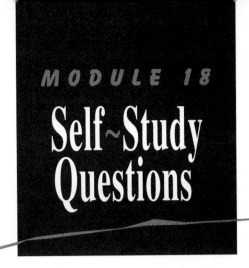

# MODULE 18
# Self~Study Questions

1. Which of the following is *not* important for teaching O&M to students who are deaf-blind?
   a. Working with transdisciplinary teams and using consistent communication.
   b. Structuring learning environments.
   c. Teaching in natural environments and protecting the student's safety.
   d. Teaching O&M techniques.
   e. Determining that students understand basic concepts as a requirement for instruction.

2. When teaching O&M techniques to students who are deaf-blind, teachers consider which of the following factors?
   a. Students' learning styles and preferences.
   b. Modifying techniques and mobility devices for students with physical impairments.
   c. How fast students learn techniques.
   d. Safety.
   e. Mastery of a sequence of prerequisite skills and concepts.

3. Individualized communication systems, modes, and devices used by students who are deaf-blind
   a. are the most important part of the O&M program.
   b. are used only by communication teachers who understand them.
   c. must be understood and used consistently by all members of the transdisciplinary team.
   d. are created by the specialists in communication.

4. O&M instruction in natural environments
   a. should be avoided because it is dangerous to take students who are deaf-blind to places where there is traffic.
   b. should be avoided because it disrupts the class routine.
   c. is the preferred way to teach O&M skills and techniques to students who are deaf-blind.
   d. is possible only at home.

5. Touch cues used in O&M programs
   a. help students overcome "tactile defensiveness."
   b. provide information about body positions.
   c. include complex systems of prompts and signals.
   d. should be different, depending on where the student is and whom the student is with.

6. Structured learning environments in O&M programs for deaf-blind students
   a. are used to ensure that students never get hurt or lost.
   b. can be detrimental because students never have the opportunity to learn about real-life situations.
   c. are difficult to create because of clutter in classrooms.
   d. help students learn O&M techniques and develop confidence.

7. Which two of the following statements are the most true of unstructured environments?
   a. Unanticipated events occur.
   b. The physical environment is not predictable.
   c. The lighting is poor and causes shadows and glare.
   d. There is a lot of clutter.

8. Teachers introduce students to travel in unstructured environments for which two of the following reasons?
   a. Students who are deaf-blind become aware of real-life situations.
   b. Students lose interest when traveling only in structured environments.
   c. Students learn O&M techniques for negotiating complex environments.
   d. It is easier for teachers to take advantage of natural unstructured environments than to create structured learning environments.

9. Students who are deaf-blind learn O&M skills in natural environments because
   a. there are not enough O&M instructors to take students out of class for lessons.
   b. students learn how and why O&M skills are used best when they learn as they go about their daily activities.
   c. students are frightened when they are removed from class for O&M lessons.
   d. none of the above.

10. Routes are used to teach O&M skills to students who are deaf-blind for which two of the following reasons?
   a. Students learn orientation skills in this manner.
   b. Students who are deaf-blind enjoy routines.
   c. Routes can be varied for instruction in protected or complex environments.
   d. Teachers find it easy to plan lessons using routes.

*Answers to self-study questions for this module appear at the end of Unit 3.*

# Strategies
# for Classroom
# and Community

DENNIS LOLLI

ELGA JOFFEE

- *Provide opportunities to use O&M skills during the school day*

- *Organize classrooms to encourage movement*

- *Familiarize the student with the classroom and the school*

- *Use field trips to teach environmental awareness*

- *Conduct O&M lessons and activities in the community*

Effective orientation and mobility (O&M) instruction for students who are deaf-blind affects all aspects of the students' daily routines and involves all people with whom the students interact regularly. Incorporating opportunities to use travel skills in the daily lives of these students constantly reinforces those skills.

One approach that offers many opportunities for deaf-blind students to become as mobile as possible at home, at school, and in the community is to link the transdisciplinary school curriculum to the student's home life and to teach specific mobility skills in actual settings in which the skills are needed. This approach provides natural continuity between school-based O&M instruction and the student's real-life needs and interests and gives students the opportunity to learn mobility skills that address their specific daily living needs. The active participation of all members of the transdisciplinary team in the student's O&M program gives the program a distinctly broad-based family and community flavor.

## ASSESSING AND PLANNING FOR O&M NEEDS

As the educational team gathers information about a student's needs, interests, and skills at home, at school, and in the community for a wide variety of activities and develops an O&M program on the basis of what they learn, the classroom teacher is in an excellent position to contribute valuable information to the team and to the O&M instructor. Through informal observation of daily classroom activities, much can be learned about all the factors related to students' collective "life situations" in school: their cognitive, social, and communication skills; skills for interacting with peers and adults; preferences for specific activities; motivational factors; relationship to home and family; and self-image.

Teachers can also provide insights into how students function during the school day relative to their individual visual and auditory skills. Do students use their visual or auditory skills for all tasks, for only some tasks, or not at all? Do they use tactile strategies to gather information and, if so, which ones and under what circumstances? Do various social or environmental situations (crowded, quiet, noisy, or brightly or dimly lit areas) interfere with their abilities to participate in social, mobility, or academic tasks? Teachers and other team members should observe students' posture, gait, facial expressions, and body language to see if these or any other observable behaviors change when the students are in unfamiliar settings, familiar settings, or varied environmental conditions. They should then ask what mobility tasks the students are willing or capable of initiating in the classroom, school, or community, and what tasks they need to learn (see Figures 18-1, 18-2, and 18-3 in Module 18).

All students benefit from moving purposefully, regardless of the travel tools they may use or whether they are guided or use wheelchairs. The role of the classroom teacher—to determine how to maximize students' ability to move about purposefully—is a critical role in helping students achieve this benefit.

Some students who are deaf-blind may be unable to express themselves in ways that are easy to understand. These students may be mobile, but uneasy about moving. Some may be unaware of the reasons for their anxieties or of the importance of learning to travel safely. The following behaviors are often clues that a student needs O&M instruction:

- tripping on curbs or steps
- bumping into the sides of doorways
- stopping when the situation does not warrant it
- overreaching or underreaching for objects
- confusion in new settings
- bruises on the shins or knees
- veering (walking at an angle)
- vertigo.

Students who use wheelchairs will also need O&M instruction pertaining to wheelchair travel when they exhibit behaviors similar to those just mentioned.

Classroom teachers are in a good position to share information effectively with the educational team to determine if and in what manner students can benefit from learning to use O&M techniques. They are often responsible for developing annual goals for the students' Individualized Education Programs (IEPs). IEP goals for learning O&M skills and techniques may be developed by the O&M instructor in collaboration with other team members. However, when an O&M

instructor is not available, team members should work with the teacher of students who are visually impaired to write O&M goals that reflect the outcomes of planning and address students' fundamental O&M needs, while efforts are made to obtain the services of an O&M instructor (see How to Find an O&M Instructor in Module 4).

Often, classroom teachers, teachers of students who are visually impaired, and family members view O&M instructors as "the experts" and, therefore, are reluctant to become involved in O&M programs. Although cane-travel skills and advanced outdoor travel techniques need to be taught by O&M instructors, you can, and should plan to, address basic indoor travel needs and plan educational activities to teach students spatial orientation, body image awareness and related mobility concepts, environmental and community awareness, safety, communication skills, and sighted guide travel for school-based travel and activities in the community.

# IMPLEMENTING O&M PROGRAMS

To facilitate the safe and independent mobility and teaching of O&M to students who are deaf-blind, special classroom layouts and class activities are important. Simple accommodations that complement general classroom management (and benefit all students) can be accomplished with or without the presence of an O&M instructor. Classroom teachers can make these arrangements on their own, but there are people who are available to help. Assistance and information can be obtained from a school district that employs an O&M instructor, a university program that prepares O&M instructors, or the state department of education (for sources of information and help, see Resources).

This section presents some suggestions for specific classroom layouts and activities. In the field of O&M, progress "from the simple to the complex" is a sound principle to follow. Teachers can apply it to the classroom and encourage parents to apply it at home as they work together with families to link the school and the home.

## ORGANIZING THE CLASSROOM

In organizing the classroom to make it a maximal environment for deaf-blind students, there are a number of simple steps to take. To begin, teachers can focus on creating well-defined work areas, effective lighting and illumination, helpful combinations of color and contrast, and organized materials storage.

## Creating Work Areas

Keep the classroom layout simple and uncluttered, and add any details or new items gradually. Divide the room according to subject areas, such as those for music, work, or snacks. Next, create a work space for each student who is deaf-blind and help each student learn to recognize the work space and the entrance to it and feel comfortable in it. One way to make the area recognizable is to cover the floor of the area with a bright-color carpet (secured to prevent tripping). The carpet will provide tactile feedback for children with no vision and visual feedback for children with functional vision. Solid-color carpets are generally preferred to carpets with patterns because they are less visually distracting, and it is easier to locate objects that are dropped. However, not every student will benefit from this solution, so it is important to individualize the classroom structure according to the students' needs and interests (see Module 18 for suggestions on structuring learning environments).

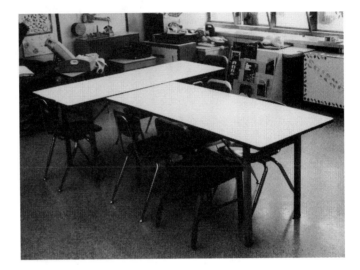

▲ *Creating well-defined work areas with simple, well-organized layouts encourages movement and creates an optimal learning environment for students who are deaf-blind. In this classroom, students can sit in various locations according to their need for illumination and mobility experiences.*

Some students who are deaf-blind can be easily distracted by visual and auditory stimulation. These students usually benefit when teachers design simple work spaces in quiet areas that are free from extraneous sights and sounds.

## Using Lighting and Illumination

Be aware of the levels and sources of incandescent, florescent, and natural lighting in the classroom, check for the occurrence of glare, and be sure that work areas are positioned so that light comes from behind the students and is directed onto their desks. Seating students with their backs to classroom windows is usually an effective way to control glare and focus light. If possible, create a classroom setup in which the amount and source of light can be controlled. Rheostat switches and window shades or blinds are useful for controlling general room illumination, and gooseneck lamps are useful for controlling illumination on individual work desks.

## Using Color and Contrast

Highlighting color and contrast in the classroom and school makes it easier for visually impaired students to distinguish items. Although black with white provides the greatest contrast, other combinations of colors and hues also provide useful contrasts. Before the colors or hues are selected, experiment with a variety of contrasts to determine which combinations the students respond to best. The following suggestions may be helpful in creating an environment with contrast:

- Use a contrasting band of molding to differentiate walls and floors.
- Use a band of color on the top and bottom edges of stairs that contrasts with the stairs, and paint the handrail of the staircase a color that contrasts with the wall of the stairwell.
- Highlight light switches with switchplates that contrast with the wall.
- Select bright colors for everyday classroom furniture and supplies, including chairs, tables, clothes hooks, building blocks, chalkboard erasers, and daily living supplies (such as toothbrushes).
- Use contrasting materials and lettering on bulletin boards.

Because some students who are deaf-blind and have cortical blindness find it difficult to tolerate excessive visual stimulation, it is preferable not to create too much exciting visual stimulation in their work areas. These students may fare better away from visually complex areas and in places with simple highlighting contrasts.

## Storing Materials

Designate specific areas for storing work materials, books, and toys and be consistent about storing and returning materials to their defined areas. Place the storage areas where the students can reach them easily from their seats, and keep individual students' storage areas distinct by marking them clearly with visual or tactile indicators, so the students can find their belongings by themselves.

## FAMILIARIZING STUDENTS WITH THE CLASSROOM

Students who are deaf-blind, both those who are ambulatory and those who are in wheelchairs, need to learn their classroom layout and to move about the classroom. Classroom familiarization includes teaching students the locations of their work spaces and of other significant classroom elements, such as a clothing closet, classmates' desks, play areas, group activity spaces, and storage spaces. The goal is to enable students to move about their classrooms as freely, safely, and independently as possible using O&M skills that are taught within the context of natural daily school routines.

Start by selecting travel destinations and simple routes to be performed using basic mobility techniques, preferably the sighted guide technique combined with trailing (for information on how to modify these techniques for students in wheelchairs, see Module 18). As the students master these routes, introduce more complex travel routes using more complex mobility techniques, such as trailing and the diagonal-cane technique, in any combination that is appropriate for the students. For example, a classroom teacher may decide to introduce increasingly complex routes (one, two, or three turns along a route), using the sighted guide technique, or to teach a student to focus on one simple route but use increasingly complex mobility techniques, such as trailing and direction taking without the sighted guide technique.

To teach students the locations of their work spaces and other areas from either their work spaces or the classroom door, you may find the forms shown in Figures 18-2 and 18-3 useful for selecting the students' travel objectives and techniques. The most logical choice for the first route (among those the students use each day) is the way from the classroom door to the students' work spaces (see Teaching the First Route).

Although students may learn or already know how to get from the classroom door to their work spaces without any instruction, the routes they use and the ways in which they travel and protect themselves may be inefficient and unsafe for other more complex environments. Thus, they will lose the opportunity to develop good orientation, travel, and self-protection skills if basic classroom familiarization activities are not part of the educational program.

When students demonstrate mastery of the first route (sometimes by anticipating or leading the way), add new routes and destinations, decrease the amount of tactile assistance you provide, and increase the complexity of the mobility techniques. It is important to add these new routes in systematic ways:

- Select a point of orientation to serve as a "home base" for travel about the classroom. Initially, all travel should begin

## TEACHING THE FIRST ROUTE

In teaching students their first route—from the classroom door to their work spaces—use the sighted guide and trailing techniques, so students can maintain contact with the objects they pass as you guide them along.

• Position yourself on the student's free (or nontrailing) side and have the student grasp your arm with one hand and use the other hand to trail.

• With your free hand, guide the student's trailing hand, so it maintains contact with the surface of the wall or other objects that you may pass.

• It is important to integrate all applicable communication systems in this activity, so the student is aware of who he or she is with, the starting point, the desired destination and how he or she is getting there, and when he or she has arrived at the destination.

• Modify this procedure to accommodate students who use wheelchairs by working with the occupational therapist to devise strategies for arm and hand trailing or, if such trailing is not possible, by attaching curb feelers to the rims of the wheels on the wheelchairs.

Try to avoid interruptions while teaching this route, so the student experiences the full route he or she is learning. After repeated practice, students will develop "muscle memory" of specific routes that is supported, in part, by information from their large muscles and their kinesthetic-proprioceptive systems and a tactile sense of specific routes that is based on the information they perceive with their trailing hand. ■

and end at the home base (the classroom door or a student's work space).

• Because it is difficult for a student who is deaf-blind to figure out the way back from a destination to a starting point, teach the return route separately within the context of regular travel routines.

• As students become more familiar with the classroom and increasingly adept at using O&M skills, they can learn to travel between destinations without returning to their home base.

• It is also useful to point out characteristics (such as the presence of many windows or a sink) that distinguish one side of the classroom from another. Some teachers find it helpful to name classroom walls by their characteristics (such as the

**622**

"window wall") and to use these names when they orient their students or give them directions to destinations.

To help students learn relationships between discrete locations, devise games or errands that require them to travel between various classroom "stations." Treasure hunts and the "mail delivery" of toys to a classmate at a specified location are suitable games for younger students, and activities like putting away or distributing classroom materials are suitable for older students. As the students become familiar with the classroom, also look for opportunities to fade the amount of sighted guide assistance and the amount of hand-over-hand assistance provided when they are trailing. As part of this process, teachers may (working with the O&M instructor or a teacher of students who are visually impaired) help the students establish their lines of travel using appropriate techniques, such as squaring off and aligning. An O&M instructor working with a physical therapist can devise direction-taking strategies for students who use wheelchairs.

It may be helpful to mark the places along the students' routes where it is necessary to square off using systems that are consistent with the students' individual communication systems. It is also important to use a student's communication system, together with body positioning, to present the techniques being used in connection with a trip. Teachers can consult with a communication specialist to be sure that they are communicating this body position information appropriately and that everyone on the team is being consistent. Some students who are totally blind tend to veer (walk on diagonals) when they move across large open areas. If a student is doing so, review this situation with an O&M instructor to learn body image and motor control exercises that the student may do to alleviate veering.

## FAMILIARIZING STUDENTS WITH THE SCHOOL BUILDING AND GROUNDS

Students should be comfortable with the physical environment of the school building and its surrounding walks and recreational areas. The same principles for classroom familiarization apply to teaching students to travel about their school and its grounds:

- Using the Mobility Planning Worksheet in Module 18, work with the educational team to select relevant destinations, travel routes, mobility techniques, and points of orientation to introduce to the students (see Figure 18-3 for a sample).

- Consider whether the students need to know all the landmarks in the complete school structure at first. For example, if students follow a departmental schedule or leave the classroom for related services, consider how many new routes they can become familiar with initially and the order in which to introduce them.

- In selecting the initial destinations, be guided by the students' individual interests and needs. For instance, choose the gymnasium and playground for students who enjoy physical activity and the music room for those who enjoy music.

- In cases where the school is a multistory or large building, defer familiarization to areas that the students rarely use until they are comfortable in the sections they use daily.

▲ *Familiarizing students with the school building and grounds and teaching them routes for safe travel reinforces skills and allows them to build further on what they already know.*

Ultimately, students' repertoires of destinations and routes will grow until the students are familiar and mobile in all areas of the school.

As in the case of classroom familiarization, introduce simple routes using basic techniques and gradually increase both the number and complexity of the routes and the O&M techniques. The front door of the school, students' point of entry into the school, or homeroom classrooms are points of orientation for the entire building and grounds. Start with a sighted guide experience of the school's interior before introducing exterior environments and unassisted or independent travel. Use the modifications discussed earlier for students who use wheelchairs.

Once students are familiar with the classroom and the general layout of the school, it may be necessary to conduct detailed room familiarizations of several other rooms within the school building. Work with other members of the educational team to decide which rooms to introduce, in what order, and in how much detail. As students become experienced travelers, they learn to explore areas on their own and familiarize themselves with new indoor environments.

Supervised games and appropriate errands to specific locations are among the activities that can help students learn to do so.

## INTRODUCING RELATED SKILLS

Familiarization lessons can be used to lay the groundwork for teaching basic skills—map reading skills, social and communication skills, responsibility, and personal safety skills—that students can use to travel in environments beyond the classroom and the school. These skills are useful for all students, including those who use wheelchairs.

### Visual and Tactile Maps and Models

Tactile and large-print maps, as well as models of school classrooms, buildings, and grounds, are effective instructional materials (see Edman, 1992, for further information on how to make maps and Designing and Constructing Maps and Models in this module for guidelines). Using them depends on the students' levels of cognitive, tactile, and visual skills, as well as a host of individual learning styles, preferences, and needs. Teachers who believe that their students may benefit from using maps and models should work closely with their students' O&M instructors or consultants to select and design these materials.

Before students are taught to use maps and models, the classroom teacher, the O&M instructor, and the communication specialist should develop effective communication strategies and modes that are consistent with the students' individualized communication systems and are used by all members of the educational team. Begin map reading lessons by providing the students with a gradual progression of learning experiences. Start by using maps that portray basic information, perhaps about a corridor that is depicted by a thick darkened line or a raised straight line. Then take the student (using the sighted guide technique and trailing, as for classroom and school familiarization) for a short walk along a straight familiar corridor to give him or her a concrete mobility experience that corresponds to the information portrayed on the map. Modify the sighted guide technique for students who use wheelchairs.

Next, present the student with a tactile or visual representation of the same straight line, but add symbols at the beginning and endpoints of the line to correspond to landmarks in the corridor. Guide the student

# DESIGNING AND CONSTRUCTING MAPS AND MODELS

The following are guidelines for designing and constructing mobility maps and models:

**Size and scale.** Construct large-print or tactile maps so they are large enough to allow visually impaired students to read them and to discriminate the tactile details with their fingers. Avoid constructing maps and models that are so large that landmarks are too far apart to be perceived in relation to each other and that are too heavy or awkward for students to carry during lessons and travel. Maintain a relatively accurate scale for the size of objects and the distances between objects.

**Materials.** Use materials that are easy to obtain, inexpensive, sturdy, lightweight, pleasant to touch or view, and easy to clean.

**Symbols.** Label all important details with symbols that are simple and clearly understood and include a key to interpreting the symbols. Be consistent in your use of symbols from one map or model to another. If you decide to use a triangle to represent a doorway on one map or model, for example, use the same symbol in the same way on subsequent maps or models.

**Textures.** When you incorporate various textures into a map or model, try to have them correspond to the surfaces they represent (for instance, a smooth and wavy material to represent water and a coarse material to represent dirt or gravel) and do not use textures that students do not like. Add a key for interpreting the meanings of the textures.

**Organization.** Maps and models need logical orientation points to be read effectively.

Either establish a starting point or home base on the map itself or create a reference system, such as an indicator of compass points (north, south, east, and west).

**Color.** Use bright, contrasting, attractive colors on matte or nonglare surfaces for students who are visually impaired. However, keep color combinations to a minimum for simplicity and ease of reading.

**Simplicity.** Maps and models are most effective when they are clear and simple and contain only the details that are necessary to serve their purposes. For example, a map of a school that is used to show the locations of classrooms and special-function rooms need not portray the locations of windows, vents, and the like. ∎

to read the map either visually or tactilely. Again, using the sighted guide technique, bring the student to the start of the route in the corridor that is depicted on the map. Guide the student to reread or retrace the map with his or her fingers and then travel the route with the student, noting the landmarks at the beginning and end of the corridor, both on the map and in the actual environment. This process will teach

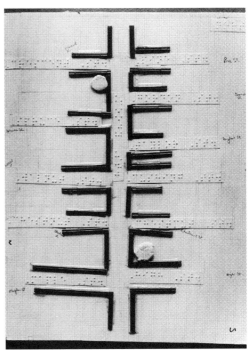

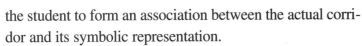

the student to form an association between the actual corridor and its symbolic representation.

Gradually increase the complexity of the maps by adding turns to the straight-line route and by increasing the number of landmarks that are included. Eventually, the student can learn to use maps to study familiar and unfamiliar areas or to plan routes in complex environments.

*▲ Tactile models and maps like these are effective instructional tools that lay the groundwork for teaching basic routes and techniques.*

The student may also find it educational and fun to help plan and construct a simple model of the school that highlights various locations of interest. This experience gives the student the opportunity to explore the environment, identify relationships, plan how to portray what is important in a useful manner, and check the work against reality. By the time the student has completed this project, he or she will have learned a large range of mobility skills and concepts. The technology instructors or art teachers in the school can suggest materials to use, such as papier-mâché, modeling clay, and wood composition board, and give advice on how to construct the map or model.

## Social and Communication Skills, Responsibility, and Personal Safety Skills

By embedding mobility assignments in the natural course of the school day, teachers can use travel tasks to enhance students' social and communication skills, as well as their responsibility and safety skills. Assignments such as asking students to deliver important messages to the school principal require the students to travel to the school office from the classroom, know how to attract the attention of the school secretary, communicate the purpose of the mission, and do so in a timely and socially appropriate way.

Mobility assignments can also teach students how to deal with the simple things that can go wrong along a route, situations of potential danger, and situations that require them to make judgments about requesting and accepting assistance or calling for help in an emergency. These learning opportunities do not always need to be contrived because they tend to arise naturally when students who are deaf-blind participate in daily school activities. Furthermore, these experiences can be incorporated into classroom discussions about how to handle emergencies, and how to ask for and accept assistance. They can also be the basis for language instruction on the meaning of words, such as *safety*, *danger*, and *help*.

Although classroom teachers can help their students learn basic O&M skills without the direct ongoing assistance of O&M instructors, when an O&M instructor is available to provide regular services, students have the opportunity to learn O&M techniques that go beyond basic indoor skills. The O&M instructor can involve all members of the educational team, including the family, by inviting them to observe selected O&M lessons (with the consent of the student), focusing on the content, methods, and strategies used during the lesson. After the observations, the team members (including the students if they wish to participate) can meet to address questions, fill in gaps, and exchange information. During these discussions, the O&M instructor can elicit suggestions from the team members for enhancing the O&M lessons and for extending O&M beyond the lessons.

## BRANCHING OUT

It is important for students who are deaf-blind to learn O&M and communication skills and techniques during the school years that take them far beyond their school buildings and their school yards. These skills and techniques need to be as diverse as the population of deaf-blind students and are individualized for each student.

O&M instructors teach outdoor travel skills. The other team members support this instruction by providing natural opportunities during the day for students to use their travel skills and by involving them in activities that enhance the students' environmental awareness, conceptual development, body image awareness, and judgment and their social, personal safety, and communication skills.

## EMPHASIZING SAFETY

It may be difficult to think about students who are deaf-blind in conjunction with travel in environments in and beyond the school without considering their physical and personal safety. All schools address safety issues primarily in classroom discussions about crossing streets, not associating with strangers, and etiquette on school buses and public transportation. However, school-based programs that address the safety of deaf-blind students need to go beyond discussions of these common safety concerns because of the complex and unique needs of the students.

Students who are deaf-blind are taught to develop a habitual awareness of safety issues gradually by constant exposure to procedures for safe travel in every aspect of their lives and by receiving ongoing feedback about their performance. They, as do all growing children, learn to understand what safety means as they mature and are provided with opportunities to assume increasing responsibility for their own safety. Their habitual awareness increases as you teach mobility techniques and their applications; communicate clearly and consistently the importance of using the techniques correctly; help students develop strategies for requesting, accepting, and declining assistance; and explain the meaning of safety and danger in relation to the environments in which the students move.

Do not assume that because students are engaging in behaviors associated with safety that they are intentionally acting to protect their safety. For example, when students walk on the right in the hallways in school, they may not intentionally be keeping to the right to avoid contact with people walking in the opposite direction. Students need to be taught deliberately always to use the right side of walkways or halls, and the reasons for doing so need to be communicated during O&M and general class activities so they will understand these safety principles and develop safety habits.

Because stairways are potentially dangerous elements, a student's ability to use them correctly needs to be developed. Consistency, correct technique, and communication are the keys. When guiding a student at a flight of stairs, it is important always to come to a full stop at the top or bottom approach, so the student has the time to familiarize himself or herself with the stairs and to prepare to ascend or descend them. At first, a student may need to be taught to move to the right side of a stairway and to place one hand in contact with the railing, but once the student is familiar with traveling on stairs, he or she will probably reach for the stair rail without assistance. The student should also be taught to follow both the direction of the stair railing and the movement of the guide's elbow, so the student develops the habit of maintaining attention while negotiating stairs. To increase the student's skills and confidence, provide the student with consistent and repeated experiences of traveling correctly on stairs and communicate clearly why the procedures are safe. Fire drills provide excellent opportunities to assess a student's safety skills in this regard.

In teaching the judgment skills for protecting personal safety during mobility experiences and classroom discussions, it is important to focus on three critical areas: observing, comparing, and deciding. Students are taught to be keen observers of their environments, to compare their observations to objective guidelines, and to decide how they will respond. It is only as a result of repeated experiences with travel environments, ongoing feedback, and discussions about personal safety in these situations that they will develop effective skills in these areas.

Another important safety skill to emphasize is the judgment of when and how to accept or decline assistance while traveling. Many deaf-blind students may be trusting, especially of adults who present themselves as caregivers.

Role-play activities are a good way to teach students how to judge whom they can trust and how to protect their personal safety during travel. To conduct these activities, enlist the help of a fellow teacher, classroom assistant, or O&M assistant whom the students do not recognize to serve as a "stranger" who approaches. Have the "stranger" approach a student and offer to take him or her to another classroom in a manner that is consistent with the safety guidelines already worked out with the student. Then arrange a contrasting activity with a "stranger" who stops the student, pushes the student forward, and takes the student off without indicating who he or she is or where they are going. Review these two experiences with the student.

As students acquire O&M skills for travel in a variety of environments in their communities, O&M instructors can work with classroom teachers to plan a regularly scheduled series of role-play experiences and classroom discussions. Topics of particular value may include interacting with the public at street crossings and asking for help in stores, on public transportation, and in shopping malls.

# TEACHING SKILLS FOR HOME AND COMMUNITY LIVING

## Involving the Home and Family

During the school years, the amount of time that students who are deaf-blind spend at home and in their communities is significantly greater than the time they spend at school. This factor underscores the importance of linking the home and the community to school-based O&M instruction—both specific O&M instruction for outdoor travel conducted by O&M instructors and O&M exposure to the community provided by classroom teachers.

Teachers can help families structure their home environments and family activities to encourage deaf-blind children to move about as freely and as safely as possible. Ongoing open communication between the school and the home, as well as the involvement of the family in the development of O&M goals and activities, is essential for this process to work effectively.

One important way that O&M instructors can facilitate the family's involvement in the school's mobility program is to plan lessons in playgrounds, shopping areas, and stores near students' homes whenever possible. Scheduling O&M lessons in neighborhoods where the students' friends or relatives live or work also creates a link among the school, family, and community. This solution may not be practical for all school O&M programs because some students live too far from school. In such cases, the O&M instructor should take the time to learn firsthand and from the students and their families about the students' homes, neighborhoods, and communities and teach the students the skills they will need to travel in those environments. By involving families and students in planning O&M lessons and choosing lesson sites, the O&M instructor shows families that everyone is truly involved in the process.

## Teaching about the Community

Children begin to learn about their communities at an early age while they accompany their families on errands and recreational activities. Teachers and families of young children who are deaf-blind need to rely on specific strategies to be sure that the children learn community and environmental awareness. The O&M instructor teaches students the specific O&M skills and techniques they need to travel in their communities and works closely with the communication specialist to integrate effective communication strategies and modes for travel.

During the school years, educational programs continue to include activities that enable students to learn about their neighborhoods and communities. Classroom units and trips into communities to explore the rich variety of features associated with neighborhoods and communities are the most beneficial when they lay the groundwork for community-based O&M instruction and support the students' work during their O&M lessons.

General class trips to local libraries, firehouses, bakeries, factories, farms, and the like, which are a part of the experiences of all children, are effective ways to enhance deaf-blind students' understanding of the world in which they live. During these trips, classroom assistants or mobility assistants accompany the students who are deaf-blind, to ensure that the students participate fully in the trips and develop their skills. Before any trips, it is necessary to plan how the students will travel, assign the classroom assistant or O&M assistant to monitor the students' travel, and prepare communication materials that the students will need to interact with their classmates and people in the community.

Begin neighborhood lessons by planning community trips in a small quiet area that is free of confusing details and distractions, such as a short walk to a neighborhood bakery that includes a visit with the baker and an opportunity to make a purchase. Be wary of including too much. Rather, gradually build the students' exposure to the neighborhoods in their communities until they have acquired a working sense of where they live.

During these trips, direct students' attention to outdoor environmental features, such as traffic signals, mailboxes, doorways, and driveways, and give them opportunities to experience these environmental elements when it is possible (see Environmental Awareness in Preschoolers in Module 16). The following is a list of some concepts to explore:

| | |
|---|---|
| house | duplex |
| apartment building | driveway |
| parking lot | sidewalk |
| yard | curb |
| street | corner |
| block | front and side walkways |
| grassline | fence |
| hedges | walls |

| | |
|---|---|
| telephone poles | hydrants |
| street signs | traffic signs |
| curb cut | crosswalks |
| mailboxes | parking spaces |

Plan various classroom activities to teach the students these concepts, so they understand what they encountered during the trips. For example, students can build a neighborhood model that includes the environmental features and outdoor concepts that they located on their walks.

During community trips, students will encounter various people at work in stores or performing other tasks (mail carriers, police, sanitation workers, and salespeople, for example). If their attention is directed to these people and they are taught the roles these individuals play in their communities, they will develop an accurate and fuller understanding of the world around them. For example, a neighborhood walk can be planned when the local mail carrier is delivering the mail and students can be given the opportunity to learn what the mail carrier does. On subsequent walks, assign the students to play the role of mail carrier by delivering items about school activities to local stores.

## Dealing with Business Districts

Teachers, families, and O&M instructors work together to develop school-based programs and activities to teach students who are deaf-blind how to function in their communities' business districts. In a school without an O&M instructor, the teacher can use such trips to develop the students' environmental awareness; social, safety, and judgment skills; communication skills; and general poise and confidence.

As with other community trips, ways in which the classroom teacher, the classroom assistant, or an O&M assistant will direct the student's attention to the relevant features of the environment should be included. Pay special attention to sidewalks, corners, intersections, traffic controls, traffic patterns (one-way streets, two-way streets, and so on), buildings, and shops and the relationships of these elements to one another and to the students. Also note the types of objects the students are likely to encounter along the sidewalk, including street lights, telephone poles, trash cans, newspaper dispensers, signs, portable store racks, mailboxes, and parking meters. Be prepared to provide opportunities for the students to experience the differences in pedestrian and vehicular traffic at different places in the business district and, over time, do so at various times of the day. These experiences will help the students attach functional meaning to such terms as *crowds*, *crowded*, *rush hour*, *lunchtime*, and *off-peak hours*.

Class activities that take place in business areas expand the students' understanding of safety concepts, and increase their ability to make judgments about their personal safety outdoors. Critical areas include appropriate communication with the general public; requesting, accepting, or declining assistance; crossing streets safely with a peer guide; and any other issues that may pertain to particular students. If an O&M instructor is available, efforts should be coordinated for maximum effectiveness. If an O&M instructor is not available, safety topics for deaf-blind students can still be addressed.

## Introducing Students to Public Transportation

It is important that educational programs that introduce students to public transportation systems are coordinated with the O&M instructor and reflect realistic goals and expectations. Instruction in the actual travel skills that students who are deaf-blind use to negotiate public transportation systems is the responsibility of the O&M instructor. However, teachers and families can and do play important roles.

Educational activities can support O&M instruction, especially in areas related to students' social, money management, personal safety, and communication skills. The following topics are typically covered in O&M public transportation programs:

- cane or other travel techniques for using trains or buses
- communication skills
- route planning
- use of schedules and timetables; how to call for transit information
- map reading
- money management
- boarding and disembarking
- maintaining appropriate attention and orientation during travel
- judgment of time and distance
- recovery from errors and other coping methods.

Communication during public travel is an essential topic for consideration. Communication Aids for Using Public Transportation

## COMMUNICATION AIDS FOR USING PUBLIC TRANSPORTATION

Students can use a number of aids and methods to communicate with others when using public transportation:

• Handwritten notes created by students themselves during travel that are written with a felt-tipped pen on a paper with ample room left for a written response.

• Prewritten notes prepared by the classroom teacher, family member, orientation and mobility (O&M) instructor, or O&M assistant.

• Picture books containing combinations of words with symbols or pictures for referring to destinations or specific items.

• An alphabet card (see Module 10).

• Print-on-palm (see Module 9).

• Oral communication that is clear and intelligible to the public (see Module 20 for more information on communicating with the public). ■

presents some ways of communicating that students can be taught to use. (Additional methods are explored in Module 20.)

It is also valuable for teachers to integrate lessons and community trips related to public transportation in instruction on community awareness. The goal is to acquaint students with the characteristics of public transportation and to help them understand how people use public transportation to travel about their communities.

The availability and nature of the transportation system in the community will determine how students' public transportation programs are developed. If only public buses are available, exposure to bus travel will be the priority. However, at appropriate times students need to have opportunities to learn about other modes of travel.

If the community is served by a variety of public transportation modes, your plan should be guided by the students' families' preferred modes of travel because they often must travel together on public buses or trains for social, health care, or other activities (see Integrating O&M Goals at Home). If the families express no need or preference, expose the students to bus travel before other modes of transportation (see Public Transportation: Buses; additional information related to public transportation appears in Module 20).

# Integrating O&M Goals at Home

**Brent R. Bailey**

The student's home is a place to teach techniques because purposeful movement at home is both functional and meaningful, and numerous occasions for travel-related opportunities occur throughout the day. Applying orientation and mobility (O&M) skills within a student's daily routine is the best way to ensure that the student has sufficient time to practice and to recognize the purpose and value of skills that increase independent functioning.

As in all environments, O&M skills that are taught at home should be appropriate for individual students' skills and needs and be integrated with the natural context of activities and tasks performed at home. Typical opportunities to teach O&M include dressing, personal hygiene activities, and preparing food. Learning O&M occurs through participation in actual domestic activities and is different from learning in an artificial environment (and then transferring skills to new situations).

The transdisciplinary educational team needs to evaluate a student's performance in relation to specific O&M skills that are required to carry out actual household tasks by conducting a task analysis of the components of daily activities to identify the student's travel and movement needs at each step of the tasks. The steps that the student cannot accomplish are identified and targeted for intervention to allow the student to move toward participating more fully in the activity. Instruction is then designed to teach the rele-vant skills that the student needs for daily functioning. Situational instruction that may have no relevance to the student's daily needs or future is avoided.

For example, teaching a student to empty a dishwasher and put away dishes is divided into necessary and meaningful instructional components. The student is first taught to trail along a wall in the kitchen to find the sink and then to search for the dishwasher next to the sink, open the door of the dishwasher, locate the top shelf, remove all the clean plates and place them on the countertop, and finish by closing the dishwasher. Next, the student will learn to take a stack of clean plates and square off against the counter to cross an open space to a cupboard. At the cupboard, the student will learn to put the plates on the counter, locate the handle, open the door, pick up the plates, and place the dishes on an empty shelf. Squaring off again to return to the countertop by the dishwasher, the student will repeat the tasks until all the plates are put away. Upon finishing, the student will trail back to the doorway and leave the kitchen. The same basic squaring-off and crossing procedure could be used for transporting folded towels from the laundry room to a storage space across the hallway or for traveling back and forth between the house and the backyard.

Students can both practice mobility techniques and learn meaningful orientation clues while participating in typical daily routines.

*(continued)*

# Integrating O&M Goals at Home
## Continued

Another example can be seen when, at the end of a day, a student trails from the living room to the bedroom, opens the door, enters the bedroom, and crosses the open space to the dresser with arm and hand extended in a lower-protective technique. At the dresser, the student removes clean pajamas, closes the drawer, places his or her back against the dresser to square off, and crosses to the bed on the far wall. After changing into his or her pajamas, the student gathers up the dirty clothes, trails around the bed and wall to find the door, exits, and trails down the hallway to deposit the clothes in a hamper in the closet next to the bathroom. From the closet, he or she enters the bathroom, completes the night-time routines (such as brushing teeth), and then returns to the bedroom to go to sleep.

These examples illustrate that students practice O&M skills while performing daily activities. It is activities, not discrete skills, that are important for persons with severe sensory impairments. This focus on life-enhancing intervention encourages students to practice behaviors they need to lead active lives. ∎

Community instruction that includes travel on public transportation also provides students with opportunities to develop and refine their social skills. Because such travel may be a new experience for the students, you may wish to provide opportunities for them to ride with you or a classroom assistant at first, then gradually introduce them to sitting with classmates, and later with the general public. Build skills on a series of nonthreatening and positive experiences.

Students respond to each other and to the general public differently when they are in the company of their teachers or other adults than when they are with their peers. After community experiences, class discussions in which the students review their feelings and reactions to riding on public transportation will help them evaluate their social skills, strengths, and weaknesses.

The following section describes how O&M instructors teach their students some of the basic skills that are related to using O&M techniques in public transportation systems. If students are working on skills for O&M public transportation, it is necessary to develop class activities that support the O&M program.

# Public Transportation: Buses

### D. Jay Gense and Marilyn Gense

For many students who are deaf-blind, bus transportation is the primary means of travel. Therefore, components of O&M instruction need to include education not only for the person who is deaf-blind, but for bus-system employees and members of the community.

Instruction on bus travel for persons who are deaf-blind follows the basic curriculum for students who are blind. The following additional considerations are supplemental to this curriculum:

• Provide orientation to the bus and bus system. Generally, transit systems that operate buses will allow access to an out-of-service bus for instructional purposes. Orientation to the bus should include entrance and exit doors, the handrail, the driver's seat, the coin box, seating, and other passengers.

• Develop and teach the student to use a portable communication system specific to bus travel for communicating basic needs and soliciting assistance and information when necessary. Some examples of communication systems include handwritten messages, printed cards, interpreters, print-on-palm, and print-braille cards. Whatever system is chosen must be usable by the traveler who is deaf-blind, the bus driver, and the other passengers. An effective portable print or print-braille card should include three pieces of information in the following order (Sauerburger & Jones, 1992):

1. Request: "Please help me find bus number __."

2. Statement of disability: "I am deaf and blind."

3. Method of communication: "Tap my shoulder if you can help."

• Develop a method that can be used for contacting the bus company to plan the route, determine the location of bus stops, learn the schedule, and get additional help. Many systems are now available for people who are deaf-blind to communicate with the public, including print and large-print TTYs/TDDs (Teletype for the Deaf/Telecommunication [or Telephone] Device for the Deaf), TeleBraille, local phone "relay" systems for deaf persons (see Module 14), and the use of interpreters and friends or relatives.

• Provide appropriate equipment and materials. For example, a card printed with the student's destination and handed to the bus driver serves as a good reminder to the driver to let the student who is deaf-blind know when the bus arrives at the destination.

When problems, such as getting off at the wrong bus stop, missing the bus, encountering altered schedules, and not being able to obtain the necessary assistance, arise, they will be more manageable if practical solutions are taught as part of O&M instruction or class discussions, and possible solutions are practiced in functional settings.

During in-service training, the O&M instructor should provide bus personnel with general information about persons who are

*(continued)*

# Public Transportation
## Continued

deaf-blind, including basic guided travel techniques, communication systems, appropriate seating on the bus (the best seat is behind and across the aisle from the driver to allow the driver visual contact with the student), emergency procedures (who, where, and how to call in case of an emergency and how to let the deaf-blind person know of the emergency), and the proper use of "destination" cards (including how to indicate to the deaf-blind person that the destination has been reached).

To help educate the community, general informational brochures about deaf-blindness, either commercially available or specifically prepared, can be distributed through local service organizations such as the Lions and Elks clubs, local restaurants, and neighborhood associations. Involving local high school students and members of youth organizations in service projects will help them understand deaf-blindness and its implications for travel. In addition, community support can be fostered through local public service announcements on television and radio stations and letters to the editor or general "informational announcements" in local newspapers. ■

**Methods of Handling Money.** Many students who are blind or deaf-blind may find it difficult to handle paper money or to count change. If a student does not have a working understanding of money and its value, the O&M instructor can place the fare in an envelope marked with the student's destination and teach the student to present the envelope to the driver when boarding or disembarking from a vehicle if the transit system's fare collection policy allows for this procedure.

When a student uses this approach to travel by taxi or a paratransit service (special van service), the O&M instructor works with the student to determine the fare and tip in advance of the student's trip.

A student who understands money management learns strategies for folding paper money and storing it in a wallet according to a specific system (20s, 10s, 5s, and 1s in separate places) and sizes of coins. Students learn to identify or sort coins by feeling the milled or smooth edges of the coins (nickels and pennies have smooth edges, and dimes and quarters have milled edges). Some students find it helpful to use coin-sorter purses with compartments for each coin denomination, whereas others prefer to use conventional coin purses or keep loose change in their pockets.

Teachers can also provide students with emergency identification cards to which a quarter (or the appropriate exact change) is affixed, so students can telephone for help if problems arise during travel. Such cards contain the student's name, school, the phone number to call and the person to ask for, a brief message ("Can someone come for me?"), the student's location (supplied by the caller), and a thank-you message. The message on the card must be consistent with the school's policy for protecting students' safety and privacy.

**Use of Maps and Route Planning.** Students who have the skills to work with the abstract information contained in maps of public transportation systems can use large-print or tactile maps to learn to plan trips. Board games with raised magnetic plastic strips can also be effective for teaching students how to follow routes to specified locations or stops within a transit system. The games make use of plastic markers that can symbolize a traveler. A student moves the "traveler" marker through the "transit system" according to a roll of dice that determines how many stops a player will advance. You can create similar games that are individualized for your students and include the outdoor environments served by the local transit system.

**Time-Distance Judgments and Attention-span Activities.** Activities that help students appreciate time-distance relationships are useful in developing the skills students use to stay oriented while traveling. Teachers help their students learn to make time-distance judgments by providing them with concrete experiences. For example, they may tell their students that they are leaving and will return in one minute to teach the students to anticipate when they will return. Teachers may begin with brief units of time to allow for frequent reinforcement and successful experiences and to help their students gradually build this understanding. Encouraging students to make use of external references, such as a timer, while they wait, may be useful.

**Use of Schedules.** Teachers can develop activities that simulate following a transit schedule. To grasp this concept, a student should understand time and know how to tell time. If a student does not know how to tell time, the teacher should work with the rest of the team to teach the student how to do so and use strategies that link transit schedules with concrete activities in the student's day. For example, students can be taught to take the train to a work site after they have breakfast and to take the bus home after they finish their day's work. Simplicity is the key to the success of these activities.

**Safety.** Students' personal and physical safety on public transportation is everyone's concern. By the time a student who is deaf-blind is ready to learn to travel on public transportation, it is expected that many safety habits have become natural routines. Nevertheless, teachers need to present specific strategies to protect students' safety in transit environments. For example, students should be taught to carry identification cards that include their names, addresses, phone numbers and, if possible, a photograph. They should also be taught to carry and use request-for-assistance cards, which are useful for dealing with frightening and dangerous situations.

When teaching skills for personal safety outside transit systems, O&M instructors need to respect school policies about how students are to obtain help outdoors. These policies may require the establishment of predetermined locations to serve as home bases, points of return if the students are separated from a class during community instruction, or code words that students must recognize to accept assistance or a ride home or to school. Identification cards may also be used.

Team members should also teach students about the messages their posture and gait convey. Recently, they have been emphasizing the need for students to have sure strides, even at uncertain moments, to avoid looking like potential victims; for girls to wear their handbags diagonally across their bodies; and for boys to keep their cash or wallets well concealed.

# *DOG GUIDES DURING THE SCHOOL YEARS*

Travel with dog guides offers deaf-blind students an option that is different from cane travel. The use of dog guides for travel is taught at special dog guide training schools that are separate from the general educational system. Students who learn to use dog guides usually arrange to attend a training program during their summer vacation because the training lasts four weeks. When a student returns to his or her school with the dog, the O&M instructor, teacher of visually impaired students, and the student provide information to other students and school personnel about the proper way to relate to a student who uses a dog guide.

A student who is deaf-blind and wishes to use a dog needs to be evaluated by an O&M instructor and personnel at a dog guide training program to determine his or her ability to care for and travel with a dog. Because the admission considerations of dog guide schools vary substantially, training programs need to be contacted individually to determine their requirements regarding age, physical stamina, and sensory abilities. (A listing of schools appears in the *Directory of Services for Blind and Visually Impaired Persons in the United States and Canada* [1993].)

To travel with and care for a dog guide, a student needs specific management, orientation, and travel skills. These skills include feeding, grooming, and toileting the dog; maintaining the dog's health; planning and following routes; recognizing travel destinations; and correcting the dog's behavior, if necessary. For these reasons, youngsters less than 13 years old will generally not be viewed as candidates for training to work with a dog.

Working on O&M skills in the community as well as the classroom prepares students for travel on their own beyond school. As the transition years approach, O&M skills become more important than ever. In the next module, transition and O&M needs are explored.

# *REFERENCES*

*Directory of services for blind and visually impaired persons in the United States and Canada* (24th ed.) (1993). New York: American Foundation for the Blind.

Edman, P. (1992). *Tactile graphics*. New York: American Foundation for the Blind.

Sauerburger, D., & Jones, S. (1992). *Corner to corner: Effective ways to solicit aid by deaf-blind people*. Unpublished manuscript.

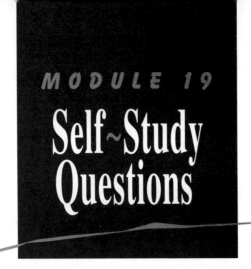

MODULE 19

# Self~Study Questions

1. Of the following, which is *not* an indicator that your student may need O&M instruction?
   a. Tripping.
   b. Constant veering.
   c. Stopping for no apparent reason.
   d. Reluctance to engage in group activities.

2. If an O&M instructor is not available for the students, O&M activities should still be included in the annual IEP goals. Who would be the primary resource in this process?
   a. School principal.
   b. Curriculum coordinator.
   c. Teacher of students who are visually impaired.
   d. The educational team.

3. If the students are receiving instruction from an O&M teacher, the role of the classroom teacher in this area will be
   a. minimal.
   b. to teach O&M skills that the O&M instructor has not yet covered.
   c. to ensure that classroom activities and programs support O&M skills.

4. It is likely that students who use wheelchairs
   a. will not need O&M instruction because they are not ambulatory.
   b. can benefit from O&M instruction that is individualized to address the specific situation of wheelchair travel.
   c. can learn to travel only indoors.
   d. will need curb feelers on their wheelchair rims.

5. In the classroom, furniture should be
   a. rearranged approximately twice a month.
   b. never moved from its position.
   c. moved occasionally, but never when teaching classroom familiarization.
   d. set up to encourage the students to move about.

6. Which environmental adaptation is likely to result in more confusion than assistance?
   a. Installing solid-colored carpets in work spaces.
   b. Using different floor textures in different areas of the classroom.
   c. Highlighting light switches and handrails in contrasting tones.
   d. Providing maximum exposure to auditory and visual stimuli in work spaces.

7. If an O&M instructor is not available, teaching classroom familiarization should be
   a. deferred until an O&M instructor can be hired.
   b. conducted only by the teacher of students who are visually impaired.
   c. integrated into the students' educational program.
   d. eliminated.

8. Students who use wheelchairs
   a. cannot benefit from familiarization to classrooms and buildings because they may not be able to travel unaccompanied.
   b. should be taught classroom and building familiarization.
   c. need to exercise caution in schoolyards.
   d. must have electronic travel aids to travel in the school building.

9. Of the following, which are important for teachers to understand when teaching room familiarization?
   a. Selecting a home base.
   b. Teaching and practicing skills as part of natural class routines.
   c. Using models, when appropriate.
   d. Teaching a return route as a separate skill.
   e. All the above.

10. Teaching safety skills to students who are deaf-blind
    a. is accomplished when a classroom safety curriculum is made accessible in braille or large print.
    b. is a lifelong process beginning with the first O&M lesson.
    c. is the responsibility of the O&M instructor and the students' families.
    d. is usually not successful enough to permit students who are deaf-blind to travel on their own.

11. When an O&M instructor is not part of the educational team, the classroom teacher can teach students who are deaf-blind all the following except
    a. concepts of neighborhoods and communities.
    b. information about business districts.
    c. techniques for accepting or declining assistance.
    d. long cane techniques and their applications.

*Answers to self-study questions for this module appear at the end of Unit 3.*

# Transition: Travel Skills for Adult Living

DONA SAUERBURGER

GEORGE J. ZIMMERMAN

## KEY CONCEPTS

- *Use O&M experiences to prepare students for transition*

- *Include O&M training in transition-to-work programs*

- *Teach skills for interacting with the community during travel*

- *Provide many and varied community experiences during the transition years*

oving from childhood to adulthood is an individual journey, during which a child must learn to navigate his or her way successfully in the world beyond his or her family and school. The transition years, in which students move from school to the workplace, are a time when most youngsters face many new challenges. Students who are deaf-blind need to make the same journey—from the relatively protected environment of school to the wider sphere of the outside world—as do other students, and their educational programs can do much to help them do so.

By combining vocational activities with educational programs during the transition years and providing a continuum of services that lay the groundwork, the transdisciplinary educational team can help students to develop the skills they need to be successful in their work and careers. Students with severe disabilities, especially those who are deaf-blind, need specific training in career education and in the basic skills (such as choosing and deciding about careers, activities of daily living, orientation and mobility [O&M], and communication strategies) that are necessary to obtain integrated and meaningful employment in their communities. To ensure that the transition from school to work is successful, this preparation needs to begin early and continue throughout the educational program. (See Module 14 for more information on preparing for transition. This module is a companion to Module 14 and should be read in conjunction with it.)

This module explores the importance of O&M skills for students who are involved in the transition process. It also describes specific O&M instructional activities for teachers and families that facilitate independence during the school years, support an effective transition from school to work, and prepare students for other aspects of adult living, including integration into competitive employment, communicating with others to carry out activities of daily living, and traveling using O&M skills and techniques.

## PREPARING FOR TRANSITION

To ensure that students who are deaf-blind develop travel skills that support their participation in transition-to-work programs, O&M instruction should begin in early childhood (see Modules 15 and 16);

continue throughout the school years (see Module 19) and into the transition years; and carry on into the workplace, if required. Many aspects of O&M instruction build skills that are necessary for work, including skills for traveling indoors and outdoors and for adjusting to moving about in unfamiliar places. During each phase of the educational process, O&M instruction enhances the student's readiness for the transition from school to work or higher education programs.

## EARLY YEARS

The O&M instructor, working in cooperation with other members of the transdisciplinary educational team, should develop a training program in motor skills during the preschool years (see Module 16). The emphasis here is on the child's acquisition of gross and fine motor abilities that are fundamental to the development of proper posture and gait, as well as hand and finger dexterity, all of which are important for learning O&M travel skills. For example, teaching preschoolers climbing activities during playtime can facilitate later stair travel, and encouraging crawling behaviors early can help children develop fluid arm and leg gait patterns. Although these motor activities are not unique to O&M, they promote natural movement patterns that are essential for later complex O&M instruction (and ultimately for the skills used to move safely and purposefully in the community and the workplace).

Early O&M instruction in the proper use of the sighted guide technique, trailing, squaring off, and aligning, as well as the use of travel tools, such as the long cane or precane devices, promotes the development of specific O&M skills and techniques that are used for travel in adult life. Furthermore, O&M instruction can increase students' ease and comfort, and hence their poise and confidence. Students who use wheelchairs benefit from early instruction in O&M in that they learn orientation skills and how to use guided assistance in a manner that fosters their independence.

## ELEMENTARY SCHOOL YEARS

The transition from preschool to elementary school presents students who are deaf-blind with an early opportunity to learn orientation and travel skills that are necessary for adjusting to moving about in new and unfamiliar settings. Teachers, O&M instructors, and families, working with other members of the educational team, need to determine the skills a student should acquire to travel in a new environment and plan an instructional program to build these skills. These may include exploration and self-familiarization skills, as well as a knowledge of how to request assistance and utilize the basic O&M techniques that are needed to move about. The planning process the team uses should be repeated when the student makes subsequent educational transitions—for example, to middle school or high school—so he or she is taught how to make transitions as well as how to use O&M skills and techniques for travel in a variety of settings.

To prepare a student to move from a preschool to an elementary school, the preschool team can invite the elementary school teacher or principal and relevant support staff to attend the preschool team meetings, to observe the student's activities at home or in the preschool, and to see the student travel in a familiar environment. In addition, the family and other members of the preschool team can visit the elementary school well in advance of the new school year to see the classroom and school environments.

At this point, the O&M instructor needs to begin to assess various aspects of the new environment that relate to building purposeful, independent, and safe travel skills. In addition to suggesting possible modifications of the indoor environment, the O&M instructor and other team members should talk with the student's future teachers to determine where in the school the student will need to travel, to plan routes, and to determine the skills and techniques that the student will have to use to travel safely and efficiently. Considerations include techniques the student will need to travel from the school entrance to the classroom and to other similar important locations in the building (see Modules 17 and 18).

As students progress through elementary school, O&M skills should be emphasized and developed that will prepare them for the transition to middle school and to the community. As they master travel in primary routes in school (from their classrooms to the cafeteria, for example), additional routes within the school, home and school neighborhoods, and the community should be learned. Teachers should continue to reinforce the use of vision and hearing; sighted guide, protective, trailing, and cane techniques; and other techniques that students in wheelchairs may use to achieve purposeful movement (see Modules 18 and 19). An integral part of the O&M program is the development of effective communication and social skills, so students can identify themselves to others, request assistance if lost, participate in classroom projects and other school activities, and interact with people in their community. Students should be encouraged to use O&M skills to perform classroom jobs, such as taking the attendance list to the principal's office each day. These experiences foster a positive attitude about travel, build skills, and contribute to the development of a sense of responsibility, all of which are necessary for the successful transition from school to work.

## SECONDARY SCHOOL YEARS

Throughout their middle and high school years, students should continue to develop vocational skills through O&M programs and activities, including

- participating in classroom- and school-related jobs (such as picking up mail from the mailroom)

- building O&M skills that increase safety and independence at school, at home, in their neighborhoods, and in the community

- planning for and traveling to various destinations in their communities, including shops, the post office, the public library, a community center, and the like

- improving communication skills to obtain assistance appropriately from the public

- participating in career development activities, such as field trips and career fairs, that provide opportunities to learn about different occupations and the tasks involved in various jobs (see Jobs that People Who Are Deaf-Blind Do in this module)

- learning mobility skills for future employment by participating in work programs in community-based settings.

O&M instruction that is carried out in the community is an integral part of a transition program. As in the earlier school years, it gives students the opportunity not only to learn and use O&M skills for traveling to and from a job, but to develop the related communication and social skills that are necessary for looking for and keeping a job. To accommodate training sessions in the community, teachers need to work with O&M instructors to modify students' classroom schedules, so the students have long-enough periods during the school day for learning to travel to distant sites.

# *JOBS THAT PEOPLE WHO ARE DEAF-BLIND DO*

People who are deaf-blind can do the same kinds of jobs that many people without disabilities can do. According to the Helen Keller National Center for Deaf-Blind Youths and Adults (Earle, 1994), people who are deaf-blind are working as

- administrators
- bakers
- book binders
- braille proofreaders
- carpenters
- child care workers

- clinical psychologists
- computer programmers
- disc jockeys
- drill press operators
- duplicating clerks
- editors
- electronic assemblers
- food service workers
- guidance counselors
- housekeepers
- laundry workers
- librarians
- mail clerks
- teachers
- upholsterers
- writers.

These are a few of the careers pursued by individuals who are deaf-blind. With the availability of more adaptive devices and technology to perform tasks and to communicate with others and with legislation such as the Americans with Disabilities Act supporting full participation in the workplace, a student who is deaf-blind can prepare for a variety of satisfying jobs. ∎

Transdisciplinary educational teams plan for students' future vocational needs in the preschool and school years when they think of transition to work as a long-range educational goal. This kind of thinking ahead helps teams to address skills that are the basis for future vocational success and to target these skills for instruction at each stage along the way.

## *ROLE OF THE EDUCATIONAL TEAM*

Preparing for transition requires the cooperative efforts of all members of an educational team who are responsible for providing the services that have been identified in the student's individual written transition plan (for more on Individualized Transition Programs [ITPs], see Module 14). The composition of the team is related to the needs of the individual student. Although the members of the team for an infant or toddler who is deaf-blind are different from those for a high school student, throughout the student's educational career, family members, the administrator of the program, and educational specialists—the O&M instructor, vision specialist, hearing specialist, communication specialist, and, as needed, the occupational therapist, physical therapist, and related assistants—should consistently be members of the team. Each member brings his or her expertise to the team to enhance transitional efforts. For example, the O&M instructor is responsible for both direct service and for training key staff and team members, and the communication specialist works to ensure that all members of the team use the student's preferred system of communication.

As the student's needs change, so should the makeup of the team, particularly when the student is going from middle school to high school. Any new team members should be invited to attend team meetings well in advance of the formally scheduled transition meeting to become familiar with the anticipated needs of the student and with the current team.

It is important to include a representative of the adult service agency (for example, the state or local rehabilitation agency that will be providing services to the student) during transition to offer the rest of the team insights into the types of adult services available to the student, as well as to give the representative information related to the student's transition needs. Toward the end of the high school years, adult services become increasingly important because the student's vocational goals and choices may become clearer, and the team's emphasis should shift from education to future employment.

As the student's employment possibilities become more focused, a job coach may be invited to join the team. The job coach analyzes the job skills needed for a particular job, teaches the student the job skills, works daily with him or her at the work site, and assures the employer that regardless of the initial transition effort, the student will be able to perform the job.

At graduation, the composition of the team changes again, and the team's focus shifts to helping the student use the communication, O&M, and social skills acquired during the school years to adjust to the demands of living and working in the community. Although the team has worked to help the student who is deaf-blind acquire these skills from the beginning, at the actual time of the transition, support may be necessary to make the adjustment work smoothly. For example, the O&M instructor may continue to work directly with the job coach to assess the specific workplace environment or college or vocational training campus.

Because the success of the student's transition is heavily dependent on the employment needs of businesses in the community, team members should develop aggressive plans for involving local business representatives in the middle school and high school transitional programs. This can include involving business leaders in school career days; giving presentations and demonstrations about the capabilities of deaf-blind students at civic organization meetings; and discussing the possibility of using community-based training sites during the regular school year and summer vacations. The coordination of efforts between schools and the local business community is important; the best-laid transition plans can quickly become unusable without the participation of employers in the community.

# METHODS OF TRAVEL

Just as communication skills are essential to students' ability to interact with others and therefore to obtain and perform jobs, O&M skills play an important role. Because students' travel skills can be critical in deciding the kind of work a student is able to do or the feasibility of selecting a specific job site, the role of the O&M instructor during transition planning is especially important.

When considering the transitional process and the employment options of students who are deaf-blind, the O&M instructor evaluates the safety of the range of travel options that are available for traveling to and from a work site, the safety of the proposed work environment, and ways of traveling within it to determine the extent to which the student possesses the skills to manage a potential placement. This section discusses issues that the O&M instructor, working with the other members of the transdisciplinary team, considers when choosing the safest and most effective means for the student to travel to, from, and within a work site.

## GETTING TO AND FROM WORK

One of the first issues that the O&M instructor and team need to address is which mode of transportation the student will use to travel to and from work. (For more information on introducing students to public transportation, see Module 19 and Michaud, 1990).

## Foot and Wheelchair Travel

For some students who are deaf-blind who live near their workplaces, walking familiar routes to and from work or traveling in their neighborhoods in wheelchairs is the preferred method of travel, since they have already experienced the reality of outdoor travel during community-based instruction throughout the school years. However, during the transition period, the O&M instructor should continue to be alert to any elements in the environment (such as street crossings) that require the student to develop additional skills. For example, if the student experiences difficulty using residual vision or hearing to monitor traffic to execute safe street crossings, the O&M instructor will have to teach the appropriate orientation and communication skills for soliciting assistance and using the sighted guide technique. The O&M instructor will also need to work with the student to assess various routes to and from the work site and enable the student to choose routes that best suit his or her needs and abilities. To ensure that the transition goes smoothly, the O&M instructor should familiarize the student with the route before the student starts a new job and, if necessary, continue to provide support once the student is working.

## Public Transportation

For a variety of reasons, public transportation may be an individual's best or only choice for traveling to work. When teaching a student who is deaf-blind to use public transportation (see Module 19), the transition team, working with the O&M instructor, should consider the following questions:

- What public transportation systems (buses, taxis, subways) are available and useful?
- Do these systems have stops near the student's home and workplace?
- Is the transportation schedule consistent with the student's work and social schedules? (Schedules may change on weekends.)
- Is the student able to use the available transportation systems?
- What sensory landmarks are available at the pickup and destination points to help the student locate and distinguish transit stops?
- Is the system accessible to a student who uses a wheelchair?

Public transportation encompasses a variety of modes, including buses, subways, special-access vans, and taxis; and these modes are often used in combination for travel. To use public transportation, students also make use of their community travel skills, especially for traveling to and locating a transit stop. In most environments, this travel requires specific cane technique applications for locating stops, boarding and exiting vehicles at desired locations, and finding seats on the vehicles. Effective communication systems for using public transportation are important for requesting schedules, verifying the arrival of desired transit vehicles, identifying the correct stop, obtaining tokens and paying fares, crossing streets, and maintaining orientation. Travel on buses and trains requires a well-developed set of O&M and communication skills. Travel on special-access vans and taxis may be less demanding of specific O&M skills; however, effective communication strategies are equally essential for using taxis and special-access vans because the student must be able to contact the transportation office or taxi company to schedule a pickup, indicate a destination point, and communicate with the driver. (See Module 14 for additional information on telephone relay services and other communication options.)

Many local transit systems provide door-to-door transportation services, called paratransit services, usually in the form of special-access vans, for persons who are unable to travel to regular transit stops or use regular transportation services. In general, paratransit services are available within a radius of three-quarters of a mile of a community's regular transit routes and usually require determinations of eligibility, advance reservations, and payment of fares that are often higher than those for regular services. Students who are deaf-blind may be eligible for services for some or all of their non-school-related travel. Since paratransit services differ from community to community, it is necessary to contact the local transit system for details on the individual system's operations and to complete a paratransit eligibility application.

## Additional Considerations

In addition to the methods of travel, the student and the O&M instructor, together with other team members, should consider various other factors when developing and implementing travel instruction during the transition years. For example, adverse weather conditions and the effect they have on the student's chosen methods of travel, motivation to travel in bad weather, and ability to remain safe in changing weather conditions need to be taken into account. Also, whether the job requires the student to work at night, after dark during winter, or in areas with poor illumination will influence decisions about the student's O&M program needs. For a student who uses residual vision for travel, traveling by foot or wheelchair in dim lighting or at night may require the use of different O&M techniques from those used in daylight. If so, the O&M instructor should plan to teach night-travel techniques. For instance, the student who uses residual vision for day travel may benefit from learning to use a long cane, in conjunction with a bright flashlight, at night or in areas where the lighting is poor. Light-colored reflective clothing is usually recommended for travel outdoors when it is dark, and such issues should be discussed with the student. Students who use wheelchairs may need to use special-access vans for traveling at night, and arrangements for vans and other relevant services should not be overlooked.

The final decision regarding which mode of travel to use should be made by the entire team, including the student who is deaf-blind. Weighing the transportation options and matching them with the student's travel skills and needs require a complete and thorough analysis of the risks and hazards of traveling to, from, and within the workplace.

## TRAVELING AT THE WORK SITE

Before the student begins to work at a job site, the O&M instructor and appropriate team members (such as the employment specialist) need to conduct a thorough analysis of the physical environment at the site. At this time, the team learns what the student's duties and responsibilities will be and determines the level of familiarization to the facility and grounds needed. They also identify the places in the work site to which the student will need to travel; note the safest and most efficient routes, as well as alternate routes; and develop emergency evacuation plans.

Using the sighted guide technique, the student works systematically with the O&M instructor and other team members to become familiar with the setting. It is helpful to select logical starting points (such as the entrance doorway and the specific work station), which serve to establish orientation to the various routes the student will use. For example, the routes to the work station and to the time clock may originate at the entrance doorway, whereas the routes to the rest room or the supervisor's office may originate from the individual's work station, the cafeteria, or the fitness facility. In addition, the teaching of routes should be sequenced to provide the individual with the skills necessary to be as independent and productive as possible (see Modules 17 and 19 for details).

With regard to emergency evacuation procedures, the O&M instructor should work with the student and team to assess whether the student with residual vision or hearing has sufficient and dependable sensory skills to hear or see an emergency alarm and whether he or she can get to designated emergency exits quickly and safely from anywhere in the building when an alarm is sounded. If it does not appear that the student has dependable sensory skills or can learn to travel multiple routes in the work setting, then the team should consider alternative plans for emergency evacuation that are developed before the student's first day at work and shared with all relevant individuals. (Alternative vibrating warning devices can be obtained for use in work settings; see Resources for some examples.)

When a student enters a new work site, the O&M instructor and O&M assistant should present a brief in-service training program to demonstrate basic O&M skills to the management and employees. The use of blindfolds and low vision simulation devices for this training will increase the other employees' awareness of mobility issues and highlight the danger of constantly rearranging furniture and leaving movable obstacles, such as trash cans, in hallways or other undesignated locations. The team members should encourage the managerial personnel and other employees at the job site to be sure that aisles and hallways are kept clear of clutter and inform the student when furniture or other objects are moved. Travel in a work environment that is predictable and safe is the desired objective.

## COMMUNICATION AND TRAVEL

The ability of students who are deaf-blind to communicate expressively and receptively is crucial to the transition process and to their successful and safe travel. The team must address the issues of expressive and receptive communication related to travel early in the student's educational program. The O&M instructor and communication specialist should begin to target the most appropriate communication methods for a variety of travel situations by the time the student reaches secondary school. The choice of a communication method or methods needs to be contingent on the student's familiarity with the methods and the settings in which the methods are used (see Selecting Communication Systems for Travel in this module). Giving secondary school students opportunities to apply these methods in the environments in which they will live and work can greatly increase their chances for successful transition to work.

Some of the common communication strategies that students who are deaf-blind use during travel are the continuous loop tape, prewritten cards, Teletouch, print-on-palm, and picture communication books (Michaud, 1990; Sauerburger, 1993). Students need to learn to use these systems to meet their specific travel needs as they master O&M in the community and the workplace.

The continuous loop tape is used on any type of tape recorder that has playback features. A message for assistance is recorded on tape that repeats itself until a pedestrian makes contact with the student who is deaf-blind. These tapes are particularly useful for soliciting assistance for street crossings. Because the student must carry the tape recorder while traveling, it is preferable for the tape recorder to be small, lightweight, and water resistant.

## SELECTING COMMUNICATION SYSTEMS FOR TRAVEL

Orientation and mobility (O&M) instructors and other members of the transdisciplinary team should consider the following factors when selecting expressive and receptive communication systems for a student who is deaf-blind to use while traveling in the community:

• The suitability of the methods for the particular student.

• The usefulness of the methods for conveying information to and obtaining information from the general public.

• The applicability of the methods to most travel situations.

• The usefulness of methods only for specific trips (methods that are "route specific").

• The usefulness of the methods for coping with disorientation and emergencies. ■

Prewritten cards are small (no more than 4 inches by 8 inches), usually laminated, and contain brief typed notes that are useful on short routes that are traveled frequently. The user displays the card to a pedestrian or service provider to ask for help in traveling (crossing the street or using public transportation) or obtaining service, such as in a store. For example, while riding on a bus, the student may display a prewritten card to another passenger that asks the passenger to tap him or her when they reach the desired stop. Although it is feasible to join multiple cards for one route, the fewer cards the individual has, the less confusion there will be. If a number of cards are used for a trip, the cards should be color coded or braille coded and placed in order of their use on a card ring or in a credit-card holder or a similar device, so they are easily accessible.

▲ *Prewritten cards like this one can have a variety of messages for use in many different travel situations.*

Similar to a typewriter, the Teletouch is a mechanical device that translates print letters into braille symbols. The machine can be used by a student who is deaf-blind and another person at the same time. For example, a pedestrian would use the letter keyboard to type out a message that the student would read simultaneously. Unlike the user of prewritten cards and the continuous loop tape, the user of the Teletouch can generate tailored messages to suit his or her specific travel needs, but he or she must be able to read braille.

Print-on-palm (POP) allows another traveler to print block letters or numbers on the palm of the deaf-blind student. It is particularly useful in travel situations when the student needs only brief information. Another means of making contact with others (such as a prewritten card) is necessary to attract the attention of others before POP can be used. A prewritten card may also be used to describe to pedestrians how to use POP (see Module 9). This method is useful only for students who understand print letters and numbers.

Picture communication books or cards have one or a few words and corresponding pictures that express the individual's specific travel needs. They are frequently laminated but can be handmade. Depending on the individual's speech skills, these cards may be an effective form of expressive communication for O&M purposes.

A student's unique form of deaf-blindness and individual sensory skills will influence how he or she ultimately chooses to communicate with the public during travel and the extent to which the student will need to communicate with others to get around safely. During the transition process, students and their instructors need to work out and practice strategies for communication and mobility in the community and at the work site. Individual differences that influence those decisions may include the following:

- the extent of the student's visual and auditory impairments
- the nature of any residual sensory capacity that is useful for communication, both indoors and outdoors
- the extent of the student's visual or auditory skills or both for localizing sounds and objects and for following movement.

For example, a student who has some residual vision and some experience in written communication or the use of gestures may find it easier to obtain information from the public than may a student who is totally deaf-blind from birth. And a student who is visually impaired may find a telescopic optical device helpful when reading signs, locating pedestrians, or locating landmarks in the distance. For students who have limited communication skills and no residual vision or hearing, the use of a continuous loop tape recorder, picture cards, or object cues may be the most appropriate communication strategies. With thoughtful planning and training that is appropriate to his or her individual needs, a student can be prepared to move successfully from the classroom to the world beyond the school.

# INTERACTION WITH THE PUBLIC

## WHAT IS INDEPENDENT TRAVEL?

Not many years ago, it was unusual for deaf-blind people to travel alone. Today, because of self-determined people who are deaf-blind, innovative programs, resourceful instructors, supportive families, a more informed public, and legislative efforts, countless people with both hearing and visual impairments, as well as those with additional disabilities, commute to work, shop, run errands, go to the doctor or barber or beauty salon, and visit friends and relatives independently. They do so on foot, in wheelchairs, or using various forms of mass transportation or special-access vans (Michaud, 1990; Sauerburger, 1993).

To prepare deaf-blind students to become adult travelers, members of the educational team need to keep the following skills and abilities in mind because these skills should be developed throughout childhood:

- awareness of the environment
- mobility skills
- communication skills
- orientation skills
- skills for participating in activities
- skills for handling unexpected situations or emergencies.

But traveling independently does not always mean traveling alone or without the help of others. Somewhere, sometime, everyone needs some form of assistance to travel on his or her own. People who drive depend on car mechanics and gas station attendants to maintain their vehicles and sometimes to give them directions, and those who use mass transportation depend on drivers and conductors to take them where they want to go and sometimes to tell them when they have reached their destinations.

In the same sense, people who are deaf-blind can go when and where they choose and arrange to get assistance, when necessary, in such ways as being guided across streets or getting directions or other information along routes, as well as receiving services from salespersons or other personnel. A critical element in the ability to travel independently is the ability to communicate with others when assistance is needed.

## COMMUNICATION METHODS

When sighted travelers are lost, they ask others where they are and get directions. At stores, they communicate with salespersons either verbally or by bringing their purchase to the counter and handing the cashier the money. Travelers who are deaf-blind have the same needs to communicate, but they may also have to communicate for additional reasons, such as to obtain help to cross streets, to get on the right bus, to get off at the right stop, and to make appropriate selections in stores of all kinds. However, many communication methods

▲ *This deaf-blind young man holds up a card requesting information. When tapped, he asks for assistance to find a nearby store and is guided to his destination. His card has also explained how to print on his palm.*

Please **HELP ME** get some
# INFORMATION
so I can find where I am going.
**TAP ME** if you can help because I am
## DEAF and BLIND.
You can print letters on my palm with
your finger. THANK YOU.

---

Please **HELP ME** find a
# SALESPERSON.
**TAP ME** if you can help because
I am both **DEAF** and **BLIND.**

You can **print letters in my palm**

with your **fingertip.** Thank you.

---

Please help me to
# CROSS STREET.
**TAP ME** if you can help because
I am **DEAF** and **BLIND.**

Thank you.

▲ *Some examples of cards requesting assistance from the public.*

that are useful to deaf-blind students for interacting with family members, teachers, and friends may not be useful for interacting with strangers. Therefore, students who interact with the public need to use communication methods that most people can understand. Because communication can be a basic part of independent travel for a student who is deaf-blind, attention needs to be paid to various aspects of communication, such as what method to use, how to plan for communicating effectively, and how to understand others.

## Choosing Communication Methods

The student who is deaf-blind who uses sign language at home and school may use notes or gestures to inform strangers how they should communicate back to him or her; these notes can be written at the time they are needed, or if the person's English or handwriting skills are not good, they may be prepared with help or typed ahead of time. The student who understands conversation well only in quiet areas may carry an assistive listening device when traveling in public and ask others to speak into the microphone. The student who asks family members for milk by pointing to a cup may hand a store clerk a prewritten note that asks for milk or bring a communication book and point to the word *milk* that is written or pictured next to the tactile or braille symbol that he or she can feel and recognize.

Some travelers who are deaf-blind feel frustrated when they have to use communication methods that seem awkward to them to obtain assistance from others. However, they may find that the effort required to communicate with the public is lessened if they have been taught and have used communication skills throughout the school years, so that these skills are now a regular routine of daily living. For these reasons, teachers' emphasis on helping their students develop and practice communication skills from early childhood on is vital.

## Understanding the Behaviors of Others

Skilled travelers who are deaf-blind know that most people they encounter do not realize that they are deaf as well as blind—even if they are wearing a button or holding up a card that says "I am deaf and blind" or if they tell others that they are deaf. Often, when people do realize that a traveler is deaf-blind, they are too surprised to pay attention to what the traveler is explaining to them.

Therefore, the deaf-blind traveler needs to understand that when others behave strangely, it may be the first time they have met a person who is deaf-blind and they are unsure about how to interact. Thus, deaf-blind travelers usually must initiate communication and put other people at ease. Frequently, they must patiently explain to bewildered strangers how to communicate with them and must repeat the explanations in various ways (notes or cards, gestures, voice) until others understand (see Modules 17 and 19).

## Initiating Communication

Occasionally, people will approach and contact the traveler who is deaf-blind who needs assistance, but generally the traveler must first get another person's attention and establish communication. The public is more likely to interact or offer assistance if deaf-blind travelers first convey their specific needs, then explain how others can communicate back to them, and finally disclose their visual and hearing impairments. Often, if travelers first indicate that they cannot hear and see well, people are too dumbfounded or perplexed to pay attention to the rest of the message. However, if travelers first let others know exactly what they need (such as help to cross the street or to buy something), people are more willing to stay and find out how they can help. Travelers can communicate with the public in several ways:

- Display or hand others notes or cards with prewritten messages.
- Use voice or play prerecorded messages.
- Use gestures that most people will understand, such as pantomiming crossing a street or demonstrating how others can print on the traveler's palm with their fingers.

Early during the communication, it is critical that the traveler tell others exactly how to communicate back to him or her, so they do not become bewildered or leave. The following methods can be used by the general public to respond to deaf-blind travelers, and each traveler needs to convey a method that he or she finds helpful:

- Members of the public can tap the traveler to indicate their presence, their willingness to help, or their understanding of what is requested.

- They can print letters on the traveler's palm, write a note on paper that the traveler has given them with a marker thick enough for the traveler to read, type into the traveler's Teletouch machine, or touch letters that have been printed on an alphabet card that the traveler has memorized and carries.

- They can speak to the traveler after the traveler has given them specific directions, such as to speak in a normal voice close to the traveler's ear; to speak into the traveler's microphone; or to talk in good lighting, so the traveler can speechread (lipread).

- They can signal "yes" or "no" by, for example, tapping once for "yes," twice for "no," and three times for "I don't know" or "maybe" or nodding their heads "yes" or "no," depending on the traveler's written or spoken instructions.

- They can point to or touch symbols, maps, or pictures that the traveler has provided and explained how to use.

## Preparing for Interaction

To communicate effectively with the public, it is usually essential for the traveler who is deaf-blind to organize and have readily at hand whatever equipment or notes he or she needs. Some people who use many cards keep them organized on a ring or in a folding credit-card holder in the order that they will use them during a trip. The cards are marked (by holes, clips, or braille, for example), so the traveler can identify them and knows which way to hold them. Before starting a trip, the traveler can type or write notes, such as shopping lists or directions for a taxi or bus driver, or have someone else do so if his or her English skills are not sufficient (see Sauerburger, 1993).

Students who are deaf-blind may need to practice their preferred methods until they are comfortable with them. For example, before they can use print-on-palm, they should practice understanding what others are printing. (Such practice is especially important for braille readers who do not use print.) Similarly, they should role-play to prepare for some of the possible responses of salespeople when they point to pictures or show empty containers of the products they want to buy.

# MOBILITY SKILLS

Most mobility techniques and tools that are used by deaf-blind travelers, such as the sighted guide technique, dog guides, or long canes, are identical to those used by blind travelers who hear. Two areas— street crossings and public transportation—require different techniques, which are taught throughout the educational program.

Capable deaf-blind travelers know how to use canes, the sighted guide technique, dog guides, or their remaining vision to avoid tripping over or bumping into obstacles and to keep from falling off curbs and steps. (Some of these skills were explained in Module 17.) Those who also have precarious balance or other physical impairments have learned how to adjust their gait or to use a support cane, walker, or wheelchair, so they can move safely. While doing so, they use whatever necessary devices (a cane or electronic travel aid [ETA], for example) to detect obstacles.

## SKILLS FOR CROSSING STREETS

Travelers who are deaf-blind may use unique strategies for crossing streets independently or for requesting help, several of which are described here.

### Deciding How to Cross

When a traveler cannot see or hear traffic at all or well enough, decisions about where to cross alone and where to get assistance can be complex. Some travelers who are profoundly deaf-blind consider it safe to cross their neighbors' driveways alone, but not busy streets. They need to determine whether it is safe to traverse such crossings as specific driveways of businesses, entrances to parking lots, alleys, quiet dead-end streets, and isolated residential streets.

To make these decisions, deaf-blind travelers must know as much as possible about particular streets or driveways, such as how busy such intersections are at certain times of the day, whether the drivers normally slow down or stop there, and how visible they would be to drivers. They should not assume that their canes will be able to halt dangerous traffic, since many drivers will not stop even when they clearly see white or long mobility canes. These skills and judgments are outgrowths of the mobility experiences that students have during their school years and are especially related to their instruction in and use of safety and responsibility skills. The following example illustrates how one man who was deaf-blind made these decisions.

*Juan, who is deaf-blind, must cross seven streets and entrances on his way to the store. Two of them are short, quiet dead-end streets, two are entrances to the parking lot of a school, and one is an alley that goes behind the store. Because each intersection has a stop sign and almost no traffic, he decided that they are not too dangerous, and he usually crosses them himself (although occasionally he avoids the crossing by walking to the end of the street or into the parking lot and coming back on the other side). Before he crosses these intersections, he warns any driver who may pull in front of him by holding his cane out while he stands at the curb, then lowering the cane and walking across.*

*One of the two intersections that Juan considers too dangerous to cross alone is a quiet residential street with no stop sign, and he does not want to rely on drivers to stop for him. Therefore, he walks to the end of the street (a long block) where there is a stop sign and crosses there.*

*The other dangerous intersection is at the entrance to the high school, but it crosses a busy street where there is a traffic light. Pedestrians pass by only once in a great while, so Juan may have to wait some time before he can get assistance. He decided it was not feasible for him to go into the entrance and cross at the parking lot because the lot was sometimes filled with teenage drivers. Although he investigated the possibility of getting a traffic-signal button (that he could feel vibrating when the light is green), he rejected this option because he was concerned that when he crossed the intersection, drivers turning in front of him might not realize that he is deaf-blind and thus he might walk into a car or be hit. Instead, he decided to get assistance from the drivers themselves. He now approaches the curb and holds up an 8½-inch by 11-inch sign that says "Please help me cross the street" and is easy for them to see. Usually, he waits about five minutes for a driver to pull over and get out of the car to guide him across.*

## Obtaining Assistance to Cross

To get help in crossing streets, a traveler who is deaf-blind must first get another person's attention and let the person know exactly what assistance he or she needs. The traveler can do so by holding up a card, calling out, playing a tape-recorded message, or gesturing effectively. The best place for the traveler to stand while asking for help is at the curb, facing the street he or she wants to cross, so passersby will not have to ask which street he or she wants to cross.

While being guided across, a traveler should hold the guide's arm, in the manner described in Module 17, so he or she remains in control and cannot be abandoned halfway across or can break free if the guide does not want to stop guiding when they reach the other side. If someone does grab the deaf-blind person's arm, he or she can use a technique called the Hines break to remove the person's hand politely (but firmly) and then take the guide's arm instead.

▲ *Standing at the curb and holding up a card requesting assistance is one effective way of soliciting aid for crossing the street safely.*

Some people who are deaf-blind live or work where there are many pedestrians, so it is easy for them to get assistance to cross; others arrange to get help from neighbors or shopkeepers. To get to her subway station, one traveler may use a telephone relay system (see Module 14 for more information on such systems) to call the store that is across from a busy street on her route that has few pedestrians; the store manager may have someone meet her and help her and her dog guide across. Another blind woman who has a hearing impairment may need to cross a street to get from the bus to the beauty salon, and she may call the salon and ask for someone to watch for her. When she gets there, the shampoo woman can come out to guide her across, and she can include an extra tip for the woman. Also, as was mentioned before, drivers may be willing to help deaf-blind people cross if they can safely pull their cars over and get out.

Travelers who are deaf-blind avoid crossing difficult streets where they cannot get assistance by planning alternate routes or by using taxis or public or paratransit systems. If a traveler must cross such a street to get to or from a bus, he or she may choose to ride the bus to the end of the line and back so it passes on the right side of the street.

## PUBLIC AND PRIVATE TRANSPORTATION

People who are deaf-blind travel independently in car pools, paratransit systems, taxis, buses, subways and other trains, and airplanes. In each instance, they decide how much assistance they will need for routes and how to get it. To use any of these systems, they must have good communication skills, be confident in using them, and know the routes or sequences of travel and how to use the transportation systems.

Every traveler will work out his or her preferred ways of managing each particular transportation system. However, the following sections present some general tips that have been helpful to travelers who are deaf-blind:

### Buses

After getting to a bus stop, a traveler needs to know when the bus arrives. Those who cannot hear or see buses approaching can hold up signs that inform drivers or other passengers which bus they are waiting for. Such a sign can ask others to tap the traveler when the bus arrives and guide him or her to the door and inform people how to communicate.

The traveler may also use a small (about the size of a cigarette pack) ETA, such as a Mowat Sensor or Polaron, that vibrates when it detects something in front of it. The traveler can aim the aid where the bus will arrive and, when the aid detects a vehicle, confirm its size (for further information on ETAs, see Module 18 and Michaud, 1990).

To make sure it is the right bus, a traveler can use the communication methods discussed earlier to ask the driver or passengers. A traveler who needs help to know when he or she has arrived at the correct stop can hand the driver a note that reads, "Please return this card to me when we arrive at the intersection of __ and __. I am deaf-blind; you can print letters in my palm with your finger." This type of note helps the driver remember which stop is requested and reminds the driver that the traveler cannot hear spoken announcements.

## Subways

Although some travelers think that subways are frightening, others prefer them because once they are familiar with their routes, little communication is needed. Mobility skills are important, however. Those who normally can see well may be practically blind in a subway's poor lighting, and all travelers must have reliable mobility skills to avoid falling from platforms (see Michaud, 1990).

If they know how to find other people or station attendants, travelers can get help to maneuver through unfamiliar stations. If they know how many stations must be passed before theirs is reached, they can sit near a door to count how many times the door opens (sometimes trains stop between stations, but the doors do not open).

## Taxis and Paratransit Systems

Travelers need to learn about available paratransit and taxi services and arrange for pickups. They should tell dispatchers how they should be informed that a driver has arrived ("I will be standing outside with my white cane; tell the driver to tap me on my shoulder" or "Tell the driver to knock on the door very hard; I will be standing on the other side with my hand on the door to feel it vibrate" or "Tell the driver to have you call me when he is waiting outside").

When the driver arrives, the traveler should have the directions or name of the destination already typed or written and inform the driver how to communicate with him or her. As always, the traveler must be aware that drivers may not grasp the explanation or even realize that the traveler is deaf-blind the first few times it is explained to them. Often, a taxi driver will guide the deaf-blind traveler to the door of the destination; he or she can be tipped for this service.

# ORIENTATION SKILLS

In addition to knowing effective communication and mobility skills, independent travelers who are deaf-blind need to know how to orient themselves and how to solve problems to contend with challenges they encounter during travel.

## ORIENTATION TECHNIQUES

Deaf-blind people use a variety of orientation skills to travel independently. They pay attention to landmarks, the sun, and their own sense of distance and turns, as well as any visual or auditory information they can use. The following example illustrates how JoAnn remains oriented on her route to the bus stop.

> To get to her bus stop, JoAnn goes out of her house to the sidewalk, turns left, crosses three driveways, and walks uphill. At the driveways, she recognizes when she is veering toward the street by the slope. If she veers in a driveway to the grass on the other side, she knows to attend to her direction while searching along the grass for the sidewalk. When she is past the last driveway, her arm brushes against a row of overhanging bushes; then she reaches the curb of a short dead-end street. After she crosses the street, the sidewalk is level; then it begins to slope downhill. When she reaches the next corner, she gets help to cross the street. After crossing, she turns left and walks along the curb until she finds the third pole, which is her bus stop.
>
> JoAnn stays oriented by knowing the route and verifying it by contacting landmarks, such as bushes, driveways, and curbs. She has developed her kinesthetic sense to know how far she has walked, how much she has turned, and whether she is walking on level ground or on a slope. If the sun is out, she may notice it and verify in which direction she is headed. If a block that she expected to be short seems much longer, or if she notices she is going uphill when she should be going downhill, that the street that should be on the right is now on the left, or that the landmarks are different from what she expects them to be, she may suspect that she is not going the right way.
>
> Once she recognizes that there is a problem, JoAnn copes with it in various ways. For example, if she does not brush against the bushes after three driveways, she will reach over to see if they have been trimmed. If the bushes are not there, she knows either that they have been removed or that she is not where she should be. She then checks for other landmarks to verify where she is or retraces her steps to see if she went the wrong way.

These orientation techniques are used by any traveler who is blind, whether hearing or deaf. Although most people who are deaf-blind cannot use sounds to orient themselves, these other cues are more than adequate for experienced, competent travelers.

Some deaf-blind travelers go to new places by themselves. They may find out how to get there from others or by calling their destinations or the bus company for directions. They may have enough vision to use city maps and plan their own routes. Or they may go where they know their destinations generally are and get more detailed directions or guidance from passersby. For example, if a person knows that the dry cleaner is somewhere on the same block as the drug store, he or she can go to that block and hold up a card or verbally ask for help to find it.

Other people travel only in familiar places. They follow specific routes that they have practiced until they have memorized the directions and the landmarks. Again, if they somehow miss turns or make mistakes and the landmarks suddenly are different, they try to retrace their steps or get assistance.

## COPING SKILLS FOR UNEXPECTED PROBLEMS

Like everyone else, people who are deaf-blind must be able to recognize when something is wrong and when they must take action. Everything cannot always go perfectly, with no detours, construction, distractions, or mistakes. Unexpected predicaments cannot be avoided, and deaf-blind students need to practice being in situations in which something is wrong.

The ability to recognize when something is wrong (or different) along a route and to cope successfully should be emphasized starting in childhood. The child who is faced with an obstacle needs to learn how to get around it and to continue as before, so he or she can do so as an adult traveler (see Modules 14 and 19). When strategies fail, travelers need to know how to cope without endangering themselves. Since they often need assistance, they must be experienced in methods of communicating with the public or others they may contact for help.

### Problem-Solving Strategies

To get out of a predicament, the first step is to realize that you are in one. The second step is to recognize that you must do something about it yourself. The third step is to stay calm and try to get yourself out of the situation. Learning how to accomplish these steps requires lots of practice and an understanding of many concepts.

The following are some coping strategies that travelers who are deaf-blind can use:

- If lost, go back until the route becomes familiar and try again.

- If left at the wrong bus stop or train station, get information and assistance from the other passengers who may be standing there, or wait for the next bus or train to get help. If the correct bus stop or station was passed, find out where to get the bus or train going back.

- Find a place of business or a home and hand the salesperson or homeowner a note or prepared card that requests assistance.

- Ask passersby for assistance by holding up a note or a prepared sign or card, playing a recorded message, or using speech or gestures.

## Applications and Examples

The ability to handle unexpected situations can be developed through repeated experience. At each stage of development, from the child's first movement until the adult is a competent traveler, a person must be allowed to make mistakes and figure out how to correct them. In teaching students to travel, it is important to teach them how to do things correctly to avoid difficulties and then allow them to make mistakes and get into difficulties, so they can practice solving them, as Sarah did.

*Sarah, a young woman who is blind, hard of hearing, and learning disabled, was learning her way around a shopping center. Between the stores, there is a walkway that leads to a parking lot. The teacher showed her the walkway entrance and explained that she must cross it, rather than follow the wall into the parking lot. As Sarah practiced walking along the stores by herself, she repeatedly followed the wall into the walkway. The first few times, the teacher reminded her that it was the wrong way. The next time, she let Sarah walk into the opening, to give her the opportunity to recognize the problem. Sarah walked about 100 yards along the wall behind the stores before she realized there was a problem.*

*Sarah thought for quite a while, and the teacher watched to see how she would solve the problem. She had several options, one of which was to get assistance from people who passed her. She chose instead to retrace her steps until she got back to the entrance, where she was able to reorient herself and cross the opening.*

The specific assistance that is requested depends on the individual. The traveler who does not have many coping skills, such as Peter in the next example, may simply request that the other person call a specific number or the police to get someone to come and pick him or her up. Skilled travelers with good communication skills, such as Ray in the subsequent example, may request that the other person let them know where they are and how they can proceed to their destinations.

*Peter has Usher syndrome (he was born profoundly deaf and now has poor peripheral vision) and is learning disabled. He was learning how to take the bus to and from his day program and was doing exceptionally well. The teacher then gave him a laminated card with a quarter taped to it and, using sign language, explained that he must carry it in his wallet to use when he was lost. The card said: "I am lost or need help. Please call one of these numbers and tell them where I am. My name is Peter O'Neill. I am deaf and can't see well. Please dial my family at __. If no one answers, please call the police and tell them I am lost or need assistance. Thank you very much."*

*The teacher and another staff person from Peter's day program worked together to teach Peter how to use the card. They took turns serving as role models to show him how to find a stranger or salesperson to whom he could give the card and the quarter to make the telephone call. On his trial run, Peter went into a store and gave the card to a salesperson, who made the phone call for him. However, Peter left before anyone could have come for him.*

*The experience was repeated in a variety of places; one staff person would leave Peter "stranded" and return to the agency to wait by the phone, while the other would stay with Peter and help him cope. After about seven more trials, Peter finally understood what to do. While on a shopping trip, the teacher signed to Peter that they needed to get home. She signed: "Our ride—GONE! What to do!? What to do!?" Peter calmly went by himself to a store, reached into his wallet for the card and the emergency quarter, gave them to a salesperson, and waited alone in the store for about 20 minutes until help arrived. Peter now takes the bus to and from his day program by himself and knows what to do if he is lost or stranded.*

*Ray is profoundly deaf and totally blind. He had learned to travel competently in his community and how to get to several stores within a few blocks of his home. To practice being lost and finding new places, the teacher drove around the community, dropped Ray off without telling him where he was, and told him to meet her at the florist, on Adams Road, about halfway between Carronade Way and Glenn Street, where he had not been before.*

*Because his neurological disorder sometimes makes it difficult for him to unravel complex problems, Ray decided he would get assistance to orient himself. After the teacher drove off, he held up a card that said, "Please give me some information so I can find where I am going. Tap me if you can help. I am deaf and blind; you can print letters on my palm."*

*After about five minutes, a man approached Ray and touched him while asking if he needed help. Ray explained that he wanted to know where Adams Road is and told the man how to print in his palm. As often happens, the man did not realize that Ray is deaf and did not understand that he should print on Ray's palm. However, he did guide Ray to Adams Road, talking to him the whole way. Once there, Ray recognized the unusual surface of the sidewalk on Adams Road and patiently asked the man several times to print the name of the other street in his palm. Finally, the man understood and printed "Southwood Avenue." Ray pointed to the next corner and asked him to print the name of that street, and the man printed "Carronade Way."*

*Ray then knew where he had to go. He thanked the man, walked to Carronade Way, and got assistance to cross. He walked about halfway to Glenn Street and again held up his card asking for information. This time, a young man stopped and printed "What do you want?" on Ray's palm. Ray explained that he wanted to find the florist. The man looked around, saw the florist shop, and guided Ray to it.*

With preparation and training that address both their needs and abilities, students like Sarah, Peter, and Ray who are deaf-blind can live and work independently to the utmost of their potential. Education for all students is aimed at precisely this goal—to help each child develop his or her abilities to the maximum extent possible. Through thoughtful planning, coordination of effort, work with members of the educational team, and attention to the individuality of each child, teachers and others who work with deaf-blind children can play a role that is nothing less than critical in helping them reach this maximum point.

# REFERENCES

Earle, S. (1994). [What we think deaf-blind people do for a living]. Unpublished material, Helen Keller National Center for Deaf-Blind Youths and Adults.

Michaud, M. M. (1990). Making the difference for deaf-blind travelers in mass transit. In M. M. Uslan, A. F. Peck, W. R. Wiener, & A. Stern (Eds.), *Access to mass transit for blind and visually impaired travelers* (pp. 136–152). New York: American Foundation for the Blind.

Sauerburger, D. (1993). *Independence without sight or sound: Suggestions for practitioners working with deaf-blind adults.* New York: American Foundation for the Blind.

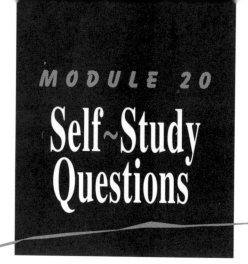

# MODULE 20
# Self~Study Questions

1. An important skill that students who are deaf-blind can learn during early childhood O&M experiences and that is especially relevant in preparing for transition is
   a. the cane technique.
   b. adjusting to new environments and people.
   c. the sighted guide technique.
   d. requesting and declining assistance.

2. During the transition process, team members should
   a. focus all attention on the current phase of the process.
   b. continue to evaluate the success of the previous phase of the process.
   c. think ahead and plan for the next phase of the process.

3. The use of public transportation by students who are deaf-blind
   a. is recommended only when traveling by special-access vans is not feasible.
   b. is one of many methods of travel for students who are deaf-blind.
   c. is the method of choice for students who are deaf-blind.

4. Before a student who is deaf-blind begins to work in an integrated, competitive employment setting, the appropriate team members should
   a. analyze the indoor environment and suggest necessary environmental modifications to the employer.
   b. make sure that the employer and employees receive in-service training in basic O&M techniques and emergency evacuation procedures.
   c. analyze and become familiar with all the routes that the student will need to travel.
   d. all the above.

5. Students who are deaf-blind and use wheelchairs
   a. are viable candidates for vocational placement because they have techniques they can use to travel on their own.
   b. may travel to work using special-access vans or lift-equipped (accessible) buses.
   c. require sighted guide assistance for all travel.
   d. a and b.

6. When an individual who is deaf-blind needs to cross a street at an intersection, he or she may
    a. hold the white cane vertically in the air.
    b. stop at the corner and reach out to contact pedestrians.
    c. use a continuous loop tape or prewritten braille-print card to ask for help.

7. Being able to communicate one's desired route effectively and to solicit assistance from the public at any time during travel
    a. is mandatory to complete O&M training.
    b. is essential for remaining safe and oriented in space.
    c. is useful only during bus travel.

8. Prewritten braille-print cards are most useful
    a. when a student needs to communicate with the public and needs to receive clear information back.
    b. only in stores when requesting assistance.
    c. at intersections when asking for help to cross a street.
    d. when used in sequence with other cards.

9. Which is the best communication method for a deaf-blind person to use when interacting with the public?
    a. The method with which the person is most proficient.
    b. The method that most strangers can understand.
    c. The method that can be used most quickly and efficiently.

10. When deaf-blind travelers ask for assistance, they should first inform others
    a. that they are deaf and blind.
    b. what assistance they need.
    c. how to communicate with them.

11. To communicate with the public, the person who is deaf-blind must
    a. understand English.
    b. be able to write legibly.
    c. use prewritten cards, recorded messages, or other signals that the general public can understand.

12. When a person who is deaf-blind gets help to cross the street, he or she should
    a. stand wherever most people pass by.
    b. be sure to take the guide's arm.
    c. use the cane to let drivers know he or she is blind.

13. Use of public transportation by a deaf-blind person requires
    a. a companion or guide.
    b. good communication skills with the public.
    c. enough vision or hearing to be able to tell when the bus or train arrives.

14. Which of the following is true?
    a. It is not usually feasible for people who are deaf-blind to travel alone on airplanes or subways.
    b. If there are no pedestrians at an intersection, travelers who are deaf-blind can get assistance to cross from passing drivers.
    c. Neither of the above.

15. When deaf-blind people go independently to new places, they should do the following:
    a. Practice the routes with assistance or supervision.
    b. Get directions ahead of time, but ask passersby for assistance if they need more information.
    c. Get directions from someone who can give them specific landmarks so they will not get lost.

16. Children and adults who are deaf-blind should
    a. be allowed to make mistakes, so if they find themselves in difficult situations, they can learn from their mistakes.
    b. be prevented from making mistakes, so they can develop self-confidence and improve their skills.
    c. not be informed about the unpleasant or problematic things that may be happening around them.

17. The basic indoor orientation techniques that children who are deaf-blind learn
    a. are not applicable to outdoor situations.
    b. must be adapted as they grow older.
    c. are used effectively indoors and outside when they are adults.

*Answers to self-study questions for this module appear in the section that follows.*

## MODULE 15

**1. (e):** The development of motor skills is a dynamic process that results in the efficient use of the body for all movement activities. It plays a role in children's cognitive, language, and emotional development, as well as in their acquisition of daily living skills. Movement and exploration help children understand and use their environments.

**2. (a):** Emotional growth is linked to motor development because children feel secure when they know they can seek and obtain what they wish to have and remove themselves from unpleasant situations. Self-esteem also develops as children learn that they can exercise control over their environments by moving about at will or requesting assistance, rather than being dependent on others to help them at all times.

**3. (b):** Primitive neurological reflexes are present at birth in every human being. They gradually fade as they are replaced by mature neurological reactions. For example, newborns reflexively grasp any item placed in their palms, but later voluntarily hold or drop such objects.

**4. (b):** The term *muscle tone* refers to the firmness and tension in the body's muscles. Muscle tone is described as being normal, high, or low. Normal muscle tone, or optimum firmness and tension, generally connotes a readiness and ability to move with efficiency. High muscle tone refers to extremely tense muscles, whereas low muscle tone describes "floppy" muscles. Children who are severely visually impaired or deaf-blind often exhibit low muscle tone, and children who have some forms of cerebral palsy and some forms of spinal cord injury can have high muscle tone.

**5. (d):** The combined effects of vision and hearing loss often contribute to primitive neurological reflexes that do not fade completely, as well as to low muscle tone. These factors, combined with children's individual attributes, affect the motor development patterns of children who are deaf-blind.

**6. (a):** To facilitate the development of gross motor skills, teachers should provide activities for both fine and gross motor development that are embedded in the context of daily activities throughout the school day. This strategy allows children to have opportunities to use the skills they learn during therapy sessions, exercise periods, and the like. Teachers should encourage families to provide similar activities at home and to understand that a child who is deaf-blind can expect to experience a "normal" amount of "accidents," just as can any other growing child.

**7. (a):** Babies who are deaf-blind sometimes skip the creeping stage of development because they have limited imitative models and incentives to move about and explore and their muscle tone is not well developed. Babies who are deaf-blind may set out to creep when objects beyond their bodies attract their attention. If they are unaware that objects they desire are within their reach, they have little reason to move in pursuit of these objects.

**8. (d):** The posture and gait of students who are deaf-blind typically include wide bases of support, heads held down, limited rotations of trunks and pelvises, and the absence of reciprocal arm swing. These are the most characteristic aspects of posture and gait patterns, although other common postural positions are also observed. It is important to remember that every student is an individual and may not exhibit what is considered to be a "typical" pattern.

**9. (d):** The short-range effects of deaf-blindness on sensorimotor development are those that have an immediate impact on the child's development; long-range effects are the consequences of living with the short-range effects. Therefore, low muscle tone and characteristic posture and gait patterns are considered to be short-range effects of deaf-blindness, and social awareness is considered to be a long-range effect. Students' social experiences can be related to their freedom of movement and the posture and gait patterns they exhibit.

**10. (a):** Working with families and transdisciplinary educational teams is fundamental to all aspects of teaching students who are deaf-blind. Sensorimotor development is an essential part of the early educational program and consequently depends on team collaboration. Young children spend the preponderance of their time at home with their families, who know their children best of all the team members. Therefore, teachers cannot fully understand how to work with their students without communicating with families to learn about the students' and families' needs.

**11. (b):** Teachers need to provide systematic experiences with a variety of sensory stimulation in a manner that is consistent with students' individual needs, preferences, and learning styles. Answers a, c, and d are examples of the kinds of stimulation that may be useful in certain instances, but would not be appropriate unless they were included in a planned systematic program for sensory stimulation.

## MODULE 16

**1. (b):** Structures and routines help children who are deaf-blind anticipate upcoming activities. They lend a sense of orientation and security to the day, minimizing the chance that children will be confused about where they are, what they are doing, where they are going, and how they are getting there.

**2. (c):** It is most important to consider the visual, auditory, and tactile skills of children who are deaf-blind when selecting toys that are suitable for them. Teachers and families should consider the characteristics (size, color, texture, and cost) of the toys in relation to individual skills and interests.

**3. (b):** Children learn mobility skills as they participate in naturally occurring routines of daily living that involve movement. Bathing and playing are opportunities to learn reaching and to refine gross motor skills. Accompanying families on shopping trips provides many opportunities for learning about the environment and for moving about. Napping is the one daily activity that provides few, if any, opportunities for learning movement skills.

**4. (b):** It is important for children who are deaf-blind to learn concepts about objects, their bodies, and the environment so they will have a sense of a world beyond their bodies and be motivated to move and explore. However, children should not be restricted from moving and exploring before they have fully learned concepts. They can develop increased conceptual appreciation as they move about, since conceptual development can come about as children use mobility skills to explore the world around them.

**5. (b):** Movement exercises for very young infants who are deaf-blind should be integrated into children's daily living routines. Integration of this kind is especially important because it provides children with the benefits of the real life experiences that are the natural consequences of movement. At the same time, it creates the opportunity to enhance body strength, balance, coordination, muscle tone, and environmental and body image awareness. Planning to make movement activities introduced during a physical therapy session an integral part of daily activities will not disrupt family living, but can enhance it.

**6. (a):** The primary focus of movement experiences for toddlers is to encourage them to move purposefully and explore their surroundings. Early purposeful exploration provides the foundation for later development of orientation and mobility (O&M) skills and contributes to the development of muscle strength, familiarity with a wide range of surface textures in indoor and outdoor environments, and the learning of body image concepts.

**7. (c):** When youngsters who are deaf-blind are ready to climb stairs, they should be taught to face straight ahead and hold the handrail with one hand only. This instruction is important in developing orientation and safety skills for stair travel. With the correct use of O&M techniques, there is no need to restrict the use of stairs or require sighted guide assistance for travel on stairs. However, families and preschool staff are advised to take precautions for protecting staircases with toddler gates, as appropriate.

**8. (c):** Little canes, noncane devices, and hula hoops can be valuable tools to encourage free movement and exploration because they serve as environmental probes and bumpers. Using these tools helps young children gather information about their environment and feel safe as they move about and explore. Little canes and noncane devices are prescribed by O&M instructors to meet the unique needs of their students but are not necessarily an appropriate travel tool for all children who are deaf-blind. It has been observed that when young O&M students move about freely and explore using little canes or noncanes, there is often an improvement in their posture and gait patterns. Young O&M students are taught appropriate safety procedures for little canes and noncane devices, but they need to be supervised for safety by their families and teachers when they travel using these devices.

## MODULE 17

**1. (d):** It is unlikely that the placement of a sink, toilet, or stove will change. All these items are potential landmarks that may be tactilely or visually recognized and can give an individual information about where he or she is in the environment.

**2. (d):** Students will demonstrate sensory abilities differently in various settings and while performing various tasks. All available information should be gathered and analyzed to determine the students' sensory capabilities.

**3. (b):** To modify and use alternate routes, it is critical to understand the concepts involved in developed environments, such as the structure of buildings and city blocks and the shapes of rooms and intersections. A person who does not understand such concepts is likely to be a rote traveler who knows only one way to get somewhere and is unable to reverse or modify routes.

**4. (a):** The sighted guide is always in the forward position; however, the pace can vary with the situation. It does not matter which side the guide is on; the side should be determined by what is most advantageous for the student, for example, the student should be on the side closer to the railing while on a flight of stairs.

**5. (b):** Trailing is used to maintain contact with the environment and to assist in locating objectives and maintaining a line of direction. As one trails, one is also protecting the body from bumping into things that may be projecting from the wall at arms' height. Many other strategies and techniques are used to maintain orientation or to prevent one from getting lost or falling down stairs. Trailing with the back of the hand does not forewarn someone of stairs, unless the hand contacts a railing and gives the person some advance warning.

**6. (c):** Squaring off is used to establish a line of direction to help ensure a straight line of travel. It is a specific type of alignment. Students may place their back, sides, or other parts of the body against a straight surface in their environment to enhance their ability to establish a straight line of travel.

**7. (a):** Most elementary school-age children who are deaf-blind use the sighted guide, hand-and-forearm, and cane techniques to move about in their environments. They are unlikely to use dog guides or electronic travel aids. Therefore, of the tools listed in this question, the cane is the most often used.

# MODULE 18

**1. (e):** The important principle in teaching O&M to students who are deaf-blind is that the program is a multifaceted effort that is carried out by the entire team. O&M programs include communication systems, modes, and devices that are developed to meet individual travel needs, structured learning environments, and specialized techniques for travel. O&M is taught in the environments where the actual skills are needed. The safety of students is always a primary concern when planning and implementing O&M programs.

**2. (a):** Teachers consider students' learning styles and preferences, including the rate at which students are able to learn techniques, when they plan and carry out O&M programs for students who are deaf-blind. Modifying techniques and mobility devices is appropriate for students who have physical impairments in addition to deaf-blindness, but is not necessarily appropriate for all students. In the functional approach to teaching mobility, a sequential curriculum based on the mastery of prerequisite skills is not used.

**3. (c):** Individualized communication systems, modes, and devices are most useful when they are created collaboratively by the team and are applied consistently by all team members. Although communication is a critical component of O&M programs, the synthesis of many elements, including communication, is the key to teaching O&M to students who are deaf-blind.

**4. (c):** The preferred way to teach O&M to students who are deaf-blind is to introduce and reinforce skills and techniques in the natural environments in which students need to use them—at home, at school, in the community, and in the workplace. Careful planning avoids the disruption of ongoing activities. Students who participate in O&M lessons in outdoor environments learn techniques for safe travel at intersections, on public transportation, and so forth. O&M instructors are trained to protect their students' safety during these lessons.

**5. (b):** Touch cues are a valuable means of communication when teaching students about body position and movement and are most effective when they are simple and distinct from one another and are used consistently. Although students who exhibit discomfort when being touched (sometimes ungraciously referred to as being "tactually defensive") become less uncomfortable as they learn to respond to simple touch signals, the primary purpose of using touch cues in an O&M program is not to address how students respond to tactile stimulation.

**6. (d):** Structured learning environments help deaf-blind students learn O&M techniques and develop confidence and enable them to have the experiences they require to explore, learn techniques, and become increasingly independent. Although these environments may be difficult to create and maintain because of clutter in classrooms and hallways, the benefits to students far outweigh any organizational problems that may result for teachers or families at home. Safety is a primary concern for all O&M programs and mobility activities, and all efforts are made to protect students from injury. However, the normal incidents of childhood are an integral part of growing up and may occur even in the most carefully structured environments. Teachers sometimes structure lessons so that students become lost (under supervision); the purpose of these lessons is to teach students the judgment, poise, and skills to deal with becoming disoriented during travel.

**7. (a and b):** In unstructured environments, students learn to deal with unanticipated events and unpredictable physical elements. These situations may include traveling from a familiar area to a new destination, traveling along a route that is familiar but is undergoing construction, or unexpectedly encountering members of the general public during travel.

**8. (a and c):** Teachers introduce students to travel in unstructured environments to expose them to real-life situations and help them learn the O&M techniques necessary for negotiating complex environments.

**9. (b):** O&M is taught to students who are deaf-blind in natural environments because this is an effective strategy to help students grasp the relevance of O&M techniques in their daily lives. For example, when students learn to protect themselves from protruding obstacles, such as a door left ajar, using the diagonal cane technique during routine trips through school, the relevance of the technique is immediately apparent. The relevance of this technique would be much less apparent if students learned to detect obstacles by following an obstacle course in a gym.

**10. (a and c):** Routes are a key teaching tool in an O&M program. Working to travel along routes during lessons helps students learn orientation skills and enables teachers to vary the travel experiences that students have to include specific work in protected or complex environments.

## MODULE 19

**1. (d):** A reluctance to engage in group activities is generally associated with social, rather than O&M, concerns.

**2. (c):** The teacher of students who are visually impaired is familiar with the content of O&M programs and can guide the educational team in planning and implementing programs and locating resources related to O&M.

**3. (c):** A working relationship between the classroom teacher and the O&M instructor is vital for a student's program to be beneficial. Approaches a and b will not fulfill a student's actual needs.

**4. (b):** Students who are deaf-blind can learn to travel using strategies and techniques that are devised for wheelchair travel (see Module 18). Each student's needs should be individually assessed and each program should be developed to satisfy those needs. It is a misconception that students who are deaf-blind and use wheelchairs will not benefit from O&M instruction or will be limited in what they may learn to handle.

**5. (d):** An uncluttered room in which the placement of furniture is clear encourages students to move about throughout the day. Rearranging furniture can be confusing and disruptive to students who are deaf-blind. If you must rearrange the furniture, be sure that the rearrangement is conducive to safe and free movement and the students are immediately familiarized with the changes.

**6. (d):** The excessive use of bright colors and sound stimuli may cause overstimulation, which can distract students. Items a, b, and c are useful adaptations for students who are visually impaired.

**7. (c):** Students must know where they are and how to get what they need to benefit from learning in school. Familiarization to the classroom is essential and can be done by the classroom teacher. To wait for an O&M instructor or to eliminate this goal is to deprive students of a vital educational benefit.

**8. (b):** All students, including those who use wheelchairs, should be systematically taught the layout of their classrooms, the location of their seats, and strategies for moving about the classroom and school. Individualized modifications of mobility techniques make it possible for students who use wheelchairs to learn these layouts, even if they need to use sighted guides for some or all travel tasks.

**9. (e):** All the concepts listed are critical to keep in mind when teaching students how to move about the classroom. Another critical concept is to be consistent and to use students' particular communication systems and modes throughout the familiarization process.

**10. (b):** When a student who is deaf-blind learns about safety from the moment he or she begins to travel, it becomes an ingrained habit. The entire educational team works to support the student's safety, and the student learns to protect himself or herself to travel independently.

**11. (d):** Classroom teachers can teach students who are deaf-blind a great deal of the environmental and social information that is necessary for O&M even if an O&M instructor is not available.

## MODULE 20

**1. (b):** An important transition skill that is introduced during early O&M instruction is adjusting to new environments and people. This skill is taught when students learn the O&M skills and techniques that are necessary for moving about in elementary school after they complete preschool. Cane techniques, requesting and declining assistance, and the sighted guide technique are among the many O&M skills that students may use in this regard; they apply to but are less specific to transition skills.

**2. (c):** To ensure a smooth and successful transition from one phase to the next, it is essential that every member of the team begin planning well in advance for the next phase of the process.

**3. (b):** Students who are deaf-blind use public transportation when it is appropriate for them to do so. Public transportation is one of the many methods of travel available to students who are deaf-blind. It is chosen when the student has the skills to use the particular public transportation system, and the transit route and schedule are consistent with the student's needs.

**4. (d):** When a student who is deaf-blind begins to work in an integrated competitive employment setting, members of the transdisciplinary team should analyze the employment environment and suggest modifications to enhance the student's ease of movement and safety, provide in-service instruction to the staff in basic O&M techniques and emergency evacuation procedures, and prepare in advance the routes that the student will need to use to travel in that environment.

**5. (d):** Students who are deaf-blind and use wheelchairs can and do learn to travel successfully to and within employment settings using techniques that meet their individual needs. For traveling to and from work, they often use lift-equipped buses or special-access vans that accommodate their wheelchairs.

**6. (c):** The use of a continuous loop tape or card has been shown to be an effective means for students who are deaf-blind to solicit assistance from the sighted public.

**7. (b):** If the student who is deaf-blind becomes disoriented, he or she must be able to communicate effectively with the public to become reoriented and to remain safe.

**8. (c):** Prewritten braille-print cards are most useful when the individual who is deaf-blind is requesting assistance that is straightforward and does not require discussion to carry out. For example, these cards are useful for requesting assistance in crossing a specific street, but may not be useful for asking about the location of the nearest public library.

**9. (b):** Although the ideal method is one with which the person who is deaf-blind is proficient and that can be used quickly and efficiently, it will not be useful if strangers cannot understand it.

**10. (b):** Strangers respond better when they are first informed about what the person who is deaf-blind is asking for.

**11. (c):** Although the ability to understand English and write legible notes makes communication with the public easier, some methods, such as the use of prewritten cards, recorded messages, or signals, can be used effectively without these skills.

**12. (b):** If the person does not take the guide's arm, the guide may leave him or her before they reach the other side or may try to keep helping after they do. By taking the guide's arm, the deaf-blind person has more control of the situation. To get help to cross, he or she should stand at the curb facing the street. Although carrying a cane can be helpful, the deaf-blind person should know that many drivers do not respect it.

**13. (b):** The traveler who is deaf-blind usually must communicate with the driver and other passengers to find the right bus and know when to get off. Many travelers can use public transportation without a companion or guide, even if they have little or no vision or hearing.

**14. (b):** By holding up a small sign, a traveler who is deaf-blind can get help to cross from drivers at intersections where the drivers can see the sign and can safely pull over. Many people who are deaf-blind travel on airplanes and subways.

**15. (b):** Although traveling is always easier on familiar routes or with specific directions, people who are deaf-blind are not limited to such travel. Those who learn effective communication techniques with the public can get assistance to find unfamiliar destinations or to reorient themselves when they are lost, even if they have specific and clear directions.

**16. (a):** Teachers must not always prevent their students who are deaf-blind from making mistakes or getting into difficult situations. Most people learn to solve problems by getting out of predicaments; children and adults who are deaf-blind must be given the same opportunities to learn. Teachers should also strive to let them know what happens around them, both pleasant and unpleasant.

**17. (c):** Orientation techniques (such as squaring off and trailing, developing a cognitive map, and developing the use of all the senses, including the kinesthetic sense) are all applicable at any age, both indoors and outdoors.

The mission of the American Foundation for the Blind (AFB) is to enable persons who are blind or visually impaired to achieve equality of access and opportunity that will ensure freedom of choice in their lives.